CW00793958

# THE
# LETTERS
## OF
# PIER PAOLO
# PASOLINI

## VOLUME I
### 1940-1954

Other works by Pier Paolo Pasolini
published by Quartet Books

*A Dream of Something*
*Theorem*

# THE
# LETTERS
## OF
# PIER PAOLO
# PASOLINI

## VOLUME I
### 1940–1954

Edited by Nico Naldini
Translated by Stuart Hood

Quartet Books

First published in Great Britain by Quartet Books Limited 1992
A member of the Namara Group
27/29 Goodge Street
London W1P 1FD

A catalogue record of this book is available from the British Library

ISBN 0 7043 2748 1

Typeset by Contour Typesetters, Southall, London
Printed and bound in Great Britain
Bookcraft Ltd., Midsomer Norton, Avon.

# INTRODUCTION

## 1921

On 21 December 1921 Carlo Alberto Pasolini, lieutenant in the Artillery, married Susanna Colussi, an elementary schoolteacher. Their engagement had begun before the First World War when Pasolini had recently embarked on his military career with the rank of sergeant and was posted to Casarsa della Delizia in the province of Udine. A first son, born secretly during the long engagement, had lived only a few months and his death cancelled the scandalous event from the memory of the children born later. The marriage was celebrated in the Colussi house in Casarsa and was attended by many guests, including village children orphaned by the war, all the bride's relations and Carlo Alberto's mother, Giulia Drudi, widow of Argobasto.

Of the old Pasolini, whom an ancient heraldic squabble had recognized as a descendant of a branch of the Counts Pasolini dall'Onda, there remained – over and above the ideas about his 'noble Ravenna blood' projected by his ancestors – the memory of a patrimony of 'lands and palaces' (which became run down during the adolescence of Carlo Alberto) and, later, of a guardian who, after Pasolini's death, administered what was left on behalf of the son. The rare and modest sums which in these years continued to be remitted to him were spent with great generosity on gifts for Susanna of flowers and jewels; but the jewels, thirty years later, turned out to be a heap of imitations.

Other Pasolini relatives – sisters and nephews – lived in Bologna but relations were intermittent to the point of indifference. But Susanna's relatives were numerous and closely knit. The Colus – a family name Italianized as Colussi – were a peasant family whose antiquity dated back to 1499. In that year the terror of the last Turkish invasion had been exorcized by the Christian faith and, as a sign of gratitude for deliverance from danger, Zuane Coluso and Matia de Montico built the little church of San Rocco, in which a tablet bore witness to their vow.

In 1921 the head of the family was Domenico (Meni) Colussi. From being a peasant he had turned himself into a smalltime agricultural industrialist; he had studied oenology in Piedmont and in Casarsa had become proprietor of a *grappa* distillery and of the first mechanical threshing-machines. He married Giulia Zacco, a young woman from Casale Monferrato [in Piedmont] *

---

* Translator's interpolations appear in bold brackets throughout.

with a passion for opera, whom he met in the entrance to a theatre. Giulia had been living in Casarsa for more than thirty years, and dressed like a village woman with apron and black leather slippers; she had learned the two dialects spoken there: the Venetian of the petty bourgeoisie of the village and the Friulano of the right bank of the Tagliamento river, with which she addressed the customers at the distillery and the peasants who bargained over the threshing of the wheat. From her native Piedmont she remembered lullabies and recipes for a few dishes with which she varied the peasant menu of Casarsa.

She had two sons and four daughters. The first-born, who died very young, was given the name of a forefather, Vincenzo (Centin), whose memory was still alive in the family. Having gone to Russia with Napoleon's army, he had met in the suburbs of Warsaw during the famous retreat a Jewish girl called Susanna, who had followed him to Casarsa, where they had got married. This latest Vincenzo, son of Domenico and Giulia 'Batiston' (a nickname which distinguished their lineage within the great Colus clan), led an adventurous life. After a restless adolescence he emigrated to the United States at the age of nineteen and died there mysteriously a few months after his arrival.

Family figures such as Vincenzo Centin formed the humble epos of which Pasolini's mother was the passionate narrator and inspired the epic–lyrical section of *La meglio gioventú* ['The finest youth'], entitled 'I Colus' ['The Colussi'].

Susanna was the second child in the family; she was thirty when she married – a year older than her husband. A schoolteacher, for some years before the war she taught in elementary schools in the district round Casarsa. The third child, Chiarina, was drawn to a more restless life and spent frequent sojourns in the Italian colonies in Africa; Enrichetta, the third daughter, married Antonio Naldini, a young man from Ferrara brought to Friuli by the war, along with Carlo Pasolini. Gino and Giannina completed the family.

After the wedding-party Susanna and Carlo left for Bologna and there settled down in the flat of the old Pasolini widow, an aggressive lady and great drinker of Chianti; she too disappeared leaving few traces of memory.

## 1922–6

In Bologna, on 5 March 1922, Pier Paolo was born. For Carlo Alberto, who had been promoted to captain, a career with frequent postings now began. In 1923 they were in Parma, in 1924 in Conegliano, in 1925 at Belluno.

Pier Paolo's memories of childhood were very precocious. Of Bologna he remembers the gloomy courtyard and his grandmother's bedroom with an enormous bed shut away in a wooden alcove. Of Parma, a guinea-pig 'of which I remember only the name'. More coherent images belong to the house of the fourth posting – to Belluno:

> Of the kitchen I remember the table on which I began to measure my height and a big fireplace full of the broken pieces of my toys. I remember my parents' bedroom. I slept in a little bed at the foot of their big double bed.
>
> (*Quaderni rossi* of 1946)[1]

At Belluno, on 4 October 1925, the second child, Guidalberto, was born:

THE TIGHTROPE-WALKER. I remember an immense crowd in the streets and above all in a square of which I have no other memories. (But I had already been told that a little brother was going to be born for me. Now I am walking held by the hand by an aunt who had come to visit us. It was she who plunged me into painful disquiet – which is like a veil over this whole episode – by telling me that children come from heaven.) Above the square – I don't know how – a rope was suspended; after a little a tightrope-walker began to walk on it.

On the morning when Guido was born I was first up, ran into the kitchen and saw him in a cradle. I flew into my mother's room to tell her the news. For long I gloried at having been the first to see him.

A few days later here are my mother and father in the kitchen looking happy. Here is the table – there near the fireplace Guido's cradle. 'Mamma,' I ask, 'how are babies born?' She looks at me and laughs and says: 'From their mother's stomach.' My father is smiling too. I hear the sentence as if it were a joke, something absurd and inconceivable; I hotly defend my self-respect. 'It's not true,' I cry, 'they come from heaven.' They quickly end up by saying I am right. But I am overwhelmed (if one can use that word of a child of three) at this contact with an order of things so contradictory.

In these months I experienced the feeling, if not of dying, then certainly of not waking up again, of plunging into an infinite darkness. The cause of this was a slight ailment of the eyes which meant that in the morning, the moment I woke up, I found myself with my eyelids sealed and was not able to lift them. The sense of abandonment, of death, I had early on, when I kept my ailment hidden from my parents.

It was at Belluno. I was not much more than three. What struck me more than anything else about the boys who played in the public gardens in front of the house was their legs – particularly the convex part of the inside of the knee where the muscles, bending as they run, stretch with an elegant and violent gesture. I saw in the sudden movement of these muscles a

3

symbol of the life to which I had still to attain; I imagined *being big* through that gesture of the running boys. Now I know that it was an intensely sensual feeling. If I experience it once again I feel accurately in my guts the tenderness, the anguish and the violence of desire. It was the sense of the unattainable, of the carnal – a sense for which a name has not yet been invented. I invented it then and it was *teta veleta*, something like a tickle, a seduction, a humiliation. One day secretly I left my house and made for the house where two brothers lived – two adolescents who, more than the others, made me experience that tender feeling with their bodies, which were so distant from mine, so much a part of the interior of that world at the threshold of which I stood. I went to see them expressly to feel *teta veleta*. I still remember how I felt that it was a wrong thing to do and how I was trembling all over as I climbed the stairs, knocked on the door. I do not remember what happened after the door was opened to me; I remember only the first second when it was opening.

*( Quaderno rossi* of 1946 )

Susanna was a Catholic but not practising; in fact she was obviously impatient of religious unctuousness and maintained in herself a religious feeling that was poetical and natural, the Christian virtues of peasant humility; she preferred to illuminate the lay virtues with the loyalty, the altruism, the sense of duty, which her modest culture had led her to embrace. She had an aversion, too, to political rhetoric which made her relationship with her husband more difficult. She was faithful to him, loved him, but as a duty, just like a peasant wife. During the years of their engagement she had had a crush on a young clerk in Casarsa, but now perhaps she had forgotten him. She defended herself from her husband's obsessive attentions by her reserved and independent nature, which was sometimes capricious. She took extraordinary care of herself, of her dresses, of her make-up, accentuating her fragile elegance which, however, was sinewed by peasant strength. An ironical gaiety accompanied her natural shyness. And behind it, concealed by her fragility and elegance, the strength of a character which was to reveal itself on many occasions in defence of her sons.

Carlo was strong and thick-set. Bushy eyebrows – the left one gripped his monocle tight – impeccable uniforms, the etiquette that goes with a haughty demeanour, made of him a distant imitator of von Stroheim.

When he was young he spoke little. Not so in old age when he became known among his son's friends as 'the colonel who bores the pants off you' – a description coined by an enraged Carlo Emilio Gadda.[2] His sense of dignity prevented him from talking very much with his new relations; he concealed behind his arrogance an extraordinary naïvety and lived in a world where first place is accorded to personal and national honour, to deep respect for forms, to contempt for weaknesses. These were not mere poses because he was truly a brave man. He saved three people from drowning in the lake at Mantua and was awarded a civilian medal for courage. An adherent of Fascism from its first hour, he demonstrated his loyalty in an obscure episode of complicity. Giving evidence at the trial of Anteo Zambini,[3] he declared that he was present at the attempt on Mussolini's life. Since this attempt probably never took place but was invented by the regime, Carlo Pasolini collaborated in it with his own piece of invention. His Fascism was not without its menacing side – even within the family circle – since at this precise time he stated his intention of denouncing his brother-in-law's brother, a Communist baker from Ferrara, for subversive activities.

Within his family he won only formal respect, shot through with recurrent clashes, while Susanna, entirely taken up with her delicate balancing act of forebearance, poured out on her elder son – who at four began to draw with great ability and at seven to write his first poetry – the love she denied her husband. The family scenes were an extension of those which began in the early days of wedlock and which were made still more desperate and aggressive with the passage of the years by Carlo's passion-inspired tyranny. Susanna tried to locate her share of guilt but fended off the deeper causes, among which there was perhaps the violence suffered so many years before when her first son was conceived. During a holiday at Riccione in the summer of 1930 she wrote to her husband:

I don't know what this insomnia is. Some nights I am so excited that I almost feel like throwing myself from the window. Good luck or bad luck if I had this urge? The difficult judgement is Yours. This excitement comes over me specially when I think if you, about what you will do, how you will behave, if you really dislike me as much as you show sometimes, about my inability to find responses to deal with your disgust.

In the discord between the parents Pier Paolo was no exception to the rule about children lovingly taking the mother's side – in his case the love was excessive and 'also monstrous' – while he felt that the reasons for the conflict with his 'overbearing, selfish, egocentric, tyrannical' father had been transferred to himself.

But in the course of the years the fixed image of this conflict underwent a radical change. After thinking for so long that his erotic and emotional life was the result of excessive love for his mother, Pasolini was writing his verse-drama *Affabuazione* [*Affabulation* – inspired by the relationship between a father and his son] when he discovered in his own childhood roots not of hate but of love for his father, a love no less important than that for his mother in determining his emotional future. This realization came about some years after his father's death.

Other childhood memories run through the pages of the *Quaderni rossi*:

> I had very many toys because I was an incredibly spoilt child (so they tell me), so much so that I got to the point of demanding one from my father every day. The only toy that lasted was a little red car with pedals in which I drove about in the nearby gardens. I was envied by the other boys and even by the bigger ones who pushed me. But what pleased me about the gardens were the games of the bigger boys – I'm not sure whether they were still under the age of puberty or adolescents; as I have said their actions, particularly the way they bent their legs, seen from behind when they suddenly stopped running or bent down, upset and excited me.

## 1927

By October 1927 the Pasolinis had moved to Conegliano. Before he was six Pier Paolo was enrolled in the first class of elementary school. He writes in the *Quaderni rossi* of 1946:

> I recall many days and many things from that peaceful period. I was not yet aware of the discord between my father and my mother and lived with them in a state of blissful comfort. I remember the rooms of our flat, the windows . . . One Sunday evening I, my mother and my father had just come back from the cinema. (I had seen a film in which I remember an interminable chase involving a horseman, a dog and I don't know what other animals which pursued each other in a kind of mad round-dance, always ending up in the water of a pond.) While waiting for supper I was looking at some leaflets which had been given out by the cinema as advertisements. I remember one solitary illustration but remember it with a precision that still disturbs me. How much I looked at it! What uneasiness, what voluptuous feelings it gave me! I devoured it with my eyes and all my senses were aroused in order to taste it to the full. I felt the same spasm which now grips my heart when faced with an image or a thought which I do not feel capable of expressing. The picture showed a man face down between the paws of a tiger. Of his body one saw only the head and back; the rest – or so I imagined – disappeared under the wild beast's muzzle. But I thought the rest of the body had been swallowed just like a mouse in the maw of a cat . . . The young adventurer seemed to be still alive and conscious of being half-devoured by the stupendous tiger. He lay with his head on the ground, in a posture that was almost that of a woman, unarmed, naked. Meanwhile the animal was swallowing him

fiercely. Confronted with this figure I was overcome by a feeling like that I felt when I saw the boys in Belluno two years before but it was more disturbing, lasted longer. I felt a shudder within me like a moment of abandon. Meanwhile I began to desire to be myself the explorer being devoured alive by the wild beast. From then on, before falling asleep, I often imagined I was in the midst of a forest and being attacked by the tiger. I let myself be devoured by it . . . and then naturally – although it was absurd – I thought out how to manage to free myself and kill it.

A similar fantasy I had some years later but before puberty. There rose up before me, I believe, as I saw or imagined it, an effigy of Christ crucified. That naked body, barely covered by a strange piece of cloth over the thighs (which I took to be a discreet convention) awoke in me thoughts which were not openly illicit and although I very often looked on that silken band as a veil spread over a disquieting abyss (this was the absolute gratuitousness of childhood), yet I quickly turned these feelings of mine into piety and prayer. Then in my fantasies there insistently flowered the desire to imitate Jesus in this sacrifice for others, to be condemned and killed although innocent. I saw myself hanging on the cross, nailed to it. My thighs were scantily draped with that light strip of cloth and an immense crowd was looking at me. This public martyrdom of mine ended up by becoming a voluptuous image and gradually I was nailed there with my body entirely naked. High above the heads of those present, who were rapt in veneration, with their eyes fixed upon me, I felt myself [blank] in front of an immense turquoise sky. With my arms open, with my hands and feet nailed, I was perfectly defenceless, lost . . . Sometimes [illegible] embracing with wide-open arms a gate or a tree to imitate the Crucified Christ; but I could not endure the overwhelming audacity of that position.

## 1928–9

One day – my father was away – I learned from my mother that at home we were penniless by some chance or other. I suggested to her to dress me in rags and give me a little bag: I would go begging.

(*Quaderni rossi* of 1946)

In the winter of 1928–9 the intense cold had preserved intact the snow that had fallen back in the autumn. In the courtyard of the house in Casarsa a little igloo was constructed by the bigger boys with a slide of frozen snow where Pier Paolo and his cousins Annie and Franca went every day to play, propelling themselves down it with wooden clogs which had two thin iron blades; sometimes their mothers joined in the game.

Carlo Pasolini was under arrest for gambling debts. The furniture in the house in Conegliano had been hurriedly moved to the barn of the one in Casarsa and Susanna had gone back to teaching to deal with the difficult situation. Each day she cycled eighteen kilometres to the school at Sesto al Reghena. For the first time Pier Paolo spent a whole year at Casarsa in his mother's house with relations who were wont to express themselves in a merry and disorderly atmosphere with great use of 'the family lexicon', compiled line by line around the various incidents of their communal life. Linguistic ambiguities, expressive witticisms, ironical darts hurled at any number of targets in village life: these were sources of inexhaustible mirth in the intervals between displays of bad temper and recurrent squabbles. Pier Paolo went up into the second class of elementary school with his cousin Franca, a dark and very beautiful girl with whom he described himself as being in love.

> Sometimes when it rained we were forced, I and my cousin, to stay shut up in the house in an immensely strong smell of damp . . . Oustide an orchestra of moss and oleanders beat on the gutters in bitter intervals: a drop falling irregularly on a tin can pierced the confused roar of the drain while a thousand arrows harped cruelly on the irises. In a dark corner of the kitchen, drunk with the savage incense of the dampness, I and my girl companions played at making coral necklaces. The tiny pearls punctuated with icy mineral lights the neutral atmosphere in which our unhappiness sank. Little by little we became bad-tempered; I remember the nasty things we did to each other – at which, alas, I did not excel – lulled by the muffled rhythms of the storm.

In 1928 old Colussi died, an event which left no mark on Pasolini's memory. The following year the Pasolini family was reunited in Sacile, the last little Friulian town at the gates of Venice. Pier Paolo was now in the third elementary class and wrote in a notebook, illustrating them with drawings, his first poems on nature and his love for his mother in *stilus sublimus*; he began to fill a chest with childish manuscripts. He said to his mother: 'Mamma, when I am big I want to be the captain of a ship and a poet', and his father regarded him with pride, remembering that in his family there had been another Pier Paolo who was a poet. The notebook, preserved for many years, was lost during all the wartime postings.

## 1930–2

Because of his father's nomadic lifestyle, in 1939 they found themselves in Idria, beyond the northern frontier of Friuli. On 4 October Pier Paolo was enrolled in the fourth elementary class. The following year they were back in Sacile.

> I lived through adventures which took my breath away; only a tiny difference separated fantasy from reality and I always deluded myself that it would have required only an equally tiny effort (a shrug of the shoulders, a furious shout) to enter the tremendous world of Adventure. All this filled me with a sorrow, an agitation, which was tinged with pain.
>
> (*Quaderni rossi* of 1946)

At a cinema run by the priests, he saw the last of the silent films and his first sound film, a war story. At his examination for admission to the middle school he was failed in Italian because his essay was 'not up to standard'. His father, who was furious with the teachers, took him to Udine to resit the examination.

The first class in the *ginnasio* was at Congeliano and Pier Paolo travelled there every day from Sacile on the fast local train from Udine to Venice:

> These were dark cold mornings, immense ones, from Pian Cavallo to the sea. The wind blew on the mud and on the ugly little sleeping houses of the town . . . There were days when I was the only person in the big, dark carriage that jolted along; in a corner, next to the window which was bitter with smoke, not properly shut; and I watched the sun rise.

'Not tall, small but strong', he lived through 'the heroic period of life' – a model son, an ideal scholar, the consolation of his parents, admired by the whole family. His poetry notebooks were enriched by new compositions illustrated with drawings and he considered the vocation of poet to be a duty. When they went to the sea on holiday for the first time, at Riccione, Susanna wrote to her husband:

> Round about, one sees nothing but happy laughing people who want only to amuse themselves and laugh. How down-at-the-mouth our usual life is! . . . Amid all this joyfulness I am like a duck out of water. But the children at once got used to it and are having a wonderful time. As I write to you they are on a swing in the middle of the water.

And Pier Paolo in the same letter to his father:

I am just going to have a bathe so I'm only writing you a few lines and in these few lines I express all my joy . . . Guido certainly won't be here to write to you but in any case I kiss and greet you for him.

# 1933–5

The Pasolinis were living in Cremona in a house in via XX Settembre. 'Cremona slowly made me its citizen in the way a breath of air, a ray of light, can be a citizen: masked by the wisdom of a twelve-year-old.' In addition to going to school he took a course in fencing; his reading had changed – no longer the 'incomparable' choices of Salgari[4] but the Homeric poems, *The Lusiads* [the epic by the Portuguese poet Camoens] and all Carducci.[5] His literary imitations were becoming more coherent, continuous; and epic poems – dramas in verse – expanded with perfect metrical skill on his passion for the Italy of Carducci, at once rural and barbarous. His passion for drawing also makes progress:

> Once I had entered puberty, drawing acquired a new meaning; the 'average' aspirations inspired by my family upbringing and by my teachers, mingling with those ardently fantastic ones drawn from the reading of Homer and Verne, gave me a whole world, another world, which I desperately sought to set down in the horrid pages of my drawing-album. Here the discourse should focus on the shield of Achilles; how much that tremendous shield made me suffer would take too long and be too difficult to tell. It was then that I experienced my first anguish when confronted with the relationship between two extensions – so different, one from the other, as are reality and its representation. I had really had bad luck with that canto of the *Iliad* in which representation and reality owe to the so-called ingenuousness of the epic a fusion designed to reduce the naïve person I was to despair. These reciprocal borrowings between the real oxen, judges and girls (which were, of course, of Homer's time) and the imaginary ones were in the nature of a continual hesitation that turned my perplexity into an obsession.
>
> I remember that I subdivided the page into ten or so segments and drew in them the creation of the world; I had just turned thirteen and we were living in Cremona. The kitchen was the theatre for my wild adventures. I saw myself bending over that page, constantly urged on by the pure problem of the relationship between the real and the imaginary. At that time the fact of representation seemed to me to be something terrible and primordial, precisely because it was in a state of purity: the equivalent had to be definitive. Faced by the problem of reproducing a maddening meadow, the question for me was this: did I have to draw each blade of

grass? I did not know at that time that by filling in a whole area with green pastel I would have achieved the movement of the meadow and that this would have been sufficient excuse to neglect the blades of grass. Such hypocrisies were still very remote from me and it was with real suffering that I submitted to colouring in a green background which was supposed to be the meadow on which God breathed life into Adam.

My favourite subject was battles: probably Morandi's[6] famous recidivism as a painter of bottles is trifling compared with my childish predilection for a certain horse covered, head and back, by some sort of medieval mantle and with its forelegs stretched out, straight. My battles always began with a profile of that galloping horse that had by now become mechanical; it was followed by the rider with a helmet like Guerrin Meschino's,[7] and his lance in repose. Around this central figure the battle piled up, but I only rarely brought the undertaking to a conclusion, being discouraged by the difficulty of composition! I can remember only too well the first moment of doubt – it was the sudden way in which what I was aspiring to lost its fascination – a poisonous sting as a result of which I began to smell the pastels. Indeed it was precisely because of that sudden spleen – that first step towards ill-temper before I was seventeen that – as happens to everybody – the idea of suicide came to me so often, that I remember the intensely cruel smell of the colours.

(*Quaderni rossi* of 1946)

Summer, after the holiday at the seaside, brought them – as every year – to Casarsa. Out of the house the two brothers were attracted by different things, and had different friendships. Guido was a 'normal boy' and formed his own circle of friends with whom he went hunting in the fields, firing off his first shot-gun. His friend Renato had a carpenter's workshop where they built sailing ships and launched them in a little ditch that ran round the house before plunging into the drain. Pier Paolo had progressed from a little bicycle to a bigger one with which he crossed the domestic frontier for his first explorations of the *lucus* [grove] of Friuli, of the countryside and the banks of the Tagliamento. 'I know Friuli as the first place in my life and the mystery of its reality is clear to me by birthright.'

## 1936–7
They moved to Scandiano; the *ginnasio* he attended was in Reggio Emilia, to which he again travelled by train:

It was much more comfortable than the amazing and marvellous local train at Sacile. I left when it was already light and shortly arrived at my destination – Reggio's station in twentieth-century Fascist style. Also it was always full . . . I was now a youth at a period when youths in northern Italy are ugly and shy. I was in the fourth class of the *ginnasio*. I was still writing poetry but at my desk now; with a little library hanging on the wall.

After school he took a course of violin lessons, and absorbed new poets: Pascoli[8] and D'Annunzio[9] to crown his first literary education.

Up to fifteen I believed in God with the obstinacy of children; adolescence increased the rigidity and seriousness of my false faith. Characteristic was my devotion to the Madonna. I provoked in myself effusions of religious feeling (so much so that on several occasions I convinced myself that I saw the images of the Madonna move and smile) and in brief discussions on religion I was decidedly committed. Greater religious anxiety and the first sins coincided. At R.E. [Reggio Emilia] I felt the violence of the first desires, committed my first lewd acts (I was a schoolboy of fourteen); I obeyed my inclinations without judging them and without everyone [space] me. At night before sleeping I did penance for sins which today I would be ashamed to confess to; I recited hundreds of Avemarias.
   It is odd that I do not remember how this faith faded. It is perhaps the only internal event in my life which has vanished without leaving a trace.
                                                                                   (*Quaderni rossi* of 1946)

At the *ginnasio* he met the first friend of his youth, Luciano Serra, whom he was to encounter again at the Galvani *liceo* in Bologna. A lay school after the detested priests' schools.

## 1937–8
At Bologna, the last of their postings for some years, the Pasolinis settled into a flat in via Nosadella.

In B. [Bologna] at fifteen and a half I took communion for the last time because pushed into it by my cousin; but it was already an act that seemed pointless to me. From then on I could not even conceive of the possibility of believing in God.
                                                                                   (*Quaderni rossi* of 1946)

Pier Paolo's literary horizons changed too – Shakespeare and Dostoevsky – and for a couple of years he stopped writing poetry.
   At the Galvani *liceo*, according to Serra, he found other friends: Ermes Parini called 'Pariah', his 'dearest companion', Franco Farolfi, Agostino

Bignardi, Sergio Telmon, Carlo Manzoni, Elio Melli. He frequented the military club, 'La Casa del Soldato', played football, first as centre-half and then as a forward. His scholastic career continued with results which were always excellent, while his literary journeys took him deep into modern poetry. In the second year of the *liceo*, during the scholastic year 1938-9, a temporary teacher of the history of art, the poet Antonio Rinaldi, read Rimbaud's *Bateau ivre* in class. This reading – it was somewhat legendary in recollection – was both a literary and a political baptism which at once swept away academic and provincial culture, Fascist conformism, and put in crisis the very social identity of the adolescent poet.

## 1939-40

At the end of the school year his marks allowed him to jump ahead a year and in the autumn of 1939, together with his comrade, Elio Melli, he matriculated in classical studies.

The summer, as always after the holiday at Riccione, was passed at Casarsa, with swimming in the Tagliamento and games of football on the sports field, but with a little less freedom than in previous years because of his academic commitment. In preparation for his next examination, Pier Paolo read for a few hours every day in the shade of a little wood of acacias at the edge of the wide river-bed.

During a juvenile football tournament between the villages of the right bank of the Tagliamento he formed a friendship with a comrade from the team, Cesare Bortotto, and subsequently discovered that he too secretly wrote verses. In their discussions they began to formulate their first vague notions about the anti-Fascist activities which the Spanish conflict had everywhere set in train. 'He told me above all who the "opponents" of Franco's supporters were, who had come from all over the world,' Bortotto recalls.[10] Together they took nocturnal rambles in the countryside of Casarsa and a very lively picture of that period remained in the mind of his friend.

With his Bolognese friends, too, Farolfi, Parini, Serra, he played football and went on bicycle rides – 'happy students from the *liceo* on holiday'.

He entered university at seventeen and enrolled in the Faculty of Letters. 'The university represented two or three things for Pasolini. It represented Longhi [the distinguished art historian and critic] and Arcangeli, whose friend Pasolini became' (L. Serra).[11]

His literary efforts, which had up to now been influenced by solitary reading and by dreams elaborated in provincial circles, were now confronted by an urban culture dominated by outstanding figures and by the presence of contemporaries who were also maturing and sharing the same experiences: modern poetry and painting, retrospectives of cinema classics, Freud.

Because of the contradiction inherent in authoritarian regimes, which cannot hold the clock back, this change of direction took place right inside the Fascist institutions and the final goals, even if confused, seemed easily attainable.

Pier Paolo read 'a book and a half a day' – after the Provençal poets (the examination in Romance philology was one of the first he took), all the Italian hermetic school from Ungaretti[12] on. In Bologna there was only one original interpreter of hermeticism, the poet Alfonso Gatto,[13] who soon became a friend of this circle of friends. 'I did not live through that experience merely as an apprentice but rather as an initiate,' remembered Pier Paolo.

Projects only vaguely dreamt of at that time were to re-emerge later on – in some cases, many years later: a production of *Toda la vida es sueño* by Calderón de la Barca, a monograph on modern Italian painting (his private library was becoming packed with monographs on art), the script of a 'mad, d'Annunzian, barbaric, sensual' film for the competition mounted by the film section of the Guf [the Fascist student organization], essays on literary critcism. He frequently attended a ciné club where he saw all René Clair, his first Renoir film, some films by Chaplin; 'there my great love for the cinema began'.

And then sport, 'the purest, continual, spontaneous consolation'; he was captain of the football team of the Faculty of Letters, played basketball, went on bicycle rides with 'Pariah' to meet Farolfi who had moved to Parma. With other friends he went camping in summer; in winter he went skiing.

> . . . but in our heads we had poetry and literature. In Cappelli's bookshop, helped by the chief assistant, Otello Masetti, a very dear friend who died recently, we sought out the books of Ungaretti, Montale, Cardarelli, Luzi, Gatto, Sereni, Sinisgalli, Betocchi, Bertolucci, Penna, Fallacara, de Libero, or went there to transcribe them with immense dedication.
> . . . And the Bologna evenings stretched out in animated discussions . . .
> (L. Serra)[14]

The change in the family's summer-holiday arrangements – San Vito di Cadore instead of Riccione – meant that afterwards Casarsa was a bicycle-ride of 130 kilometres away.

The Provençal poets and the first encounter with Romance philology gave a new resonance to places in Friuli which charged the peasant speech with historical echoes and brought out in it the ancient Ladin purity peculiar to this 'solid and grey' countryside.

The summer in Casarsa followed its usual pattern of adventures – the Tagliamento, the evening bicycle rides through the villages situated along the line of springs with streams that had the freshness of the mountains and were already taking the colour of marine skies.

Pier Paolo knew Friulano from having learned it among the peasants but still did not habitually speak it; it was merely a means of communication with the boys he met by the Tagliamento or round the wooden platforms of the village dances. At home, with his relatives, he spoke a bit of Italian, a bit of Venetian. He spoke Venetian too with his companions in the football team because they were lower-middle-class boys.

The peasant boys, on the other hand, never had time to get to the playing fields; but in the evening players and boys from the fields found themselves together washing in a pond called 'Le fonde' [The Deeps]. In a few minutes the peasant boys gave vent to the enthusiasm of the evening holiday, then went back home, some of them to sixteenth-century houses with big doorways and on the keystone of the arch the coat-of-arms of the Colussi. For Pier Paolo there thus began the taste for research into the past, for the mystery of the peasant and the nostalgia 'of the present time'.

The nineteen letters written in this period were all sent to his friend Farolfi; in one, dated presumably from Bologna in the autumn, is the poem 'Il Flauto magico' ['The magic flute']: 'formally very naïve but so charged that its meaning produces a dazzling effect'.

On 1 December he enrolled as a volunteer and was admitted to the first preliminary course for officer cadets of the reserve at the headquarters of the autonomous university detachment of the MVSN [Volunteer Militia for the Defence of National Security – i.e. the Blackshirts] of Bologna.


## 1941

In these letters there is the boy growing up in a poor confined Italy with its pre-Littorals,[15] which are kept alive while the country is lazily, stupidly, going to war. Pier Paolo reads what he can, discovers for himself Freud and Hölderlin and the Greeks of Quasimodo,[16] existentialism, *Quai des Brumes*[17] and *Our Town* [by Thornton Wilder]. It is touching this difficult apprenticeship spent between Bologna and Casarsa. But it is at Casarsa, even if in Bologna there are teachers and companions of great value, that Pasolini finds and reveals himself. It is a Casarsa splendid with meadows, harvests, canals, girls and boys and children, an intact province of the neo-Latin atlas, between a de Bartholomaeis[18] whose voice still echoed, spelling out Le bon Roy Charles, within the walls of via Zamboni and a Pound probably not yet known. Thus our great friend and poet lived through his difficult twenties; and these letters which help us to understand his first uncertain, but very soon dazzling beginnings, seem to us not unuseful to be read today . . .

(A. Bertolucci)[19]

*Introduction*

Back in Bologna with regrets at the end of another summer and the grape harvest in which he was not able to join, he started attending the university again along with Luciano Serra and made friends with two other students of his own age, Francesco Leonetti and Roberto Roversi. A few months later the four youths were already 'hatching' their passionately held idea for a literary review which would be all theirs.

Thus I come to the memory which I have always kept alive through the years. We are in the Margherita Gardens, sitting on a newly cut stretch of grass; amid the splendid yellow of the sun and the grass there rises a compact scent – very typical of the Po valley – of mown hay drying in heaps. Not many people – only the vivid presence of women and girls walking to and fro. We three (Leonetti, Pasolini and I) are sitting talking about a review to be put together, which we want to put together, which we must put together. The name, already proposed, is *Eredi* [Heirs]. We are talking with the lightheartedness that spells happiness because of a decision of ours which we will have to realize by committing ourselves. We feel excited. That scent and that feeling leave a mark on my body, are engraved on my memory. A man on a bicycle passes. He is in civilian clothes. Slowly he moves his head, searching. Does he need to speak to someone? He sees us, looks at us, comes up, does not stop, says in a low voice: 'Hitler has invaded Russia.' It is 22 June 1941 and at that moment of our youth we were out of this world.

(R. Roversi)[20]

Infinite discussions condensed into a poetic programme 'which we intended to represent the continuity of classical poetry filtered through the modern poetry of Ungaretti, Montale, Sereni' (L. Serra), while Pasolini defined their poetic aim as archaism, as inheritance.

Although the review could not come out at once because of ministerial restrictions on the use of paper, the four poets threw themselves into the undertaking to publish very soon a small book of poetry dividing the costs of printing by four.

At the university the lectures on the history of medieval and modern art had been given since 1934 by Roberto Longhi; his courses which 'arouse a wave of enthusiasm and form the first school of followers of Longhi' (G. Contini) are this year on 'The phenomena of Masolino and Masaccio'; they demand Pier Paolo's 'feverishly excited' attendance.

Besides art, Longhi loved the cinema and travelled to Paris specially to see Renoir's *La Grande Illusion* and Chaplin's *Great Dictator*. In Bologna he frequently attended the showings at the Cinema Imperiale, where Pasolini also went 'with immense enthusiasm' and in the stalls recognized his teacher, 'the first and perhaps the only great man whom he [Pasolini] had met and to whom he remained faithful; which was reciprocated'.[21] So said Contini who, in the course of time, was to be the second 'great man' (with equal reciprocal loyalty) in the poetic life of Pasolini.[22]

With Longhi as teacher, Fascism also became more clearly defined and, by a natural evolution, Pasolini cut his last, naïve links with it, without renouncing those institutions in which modern culture had a minimal circulation – such as the cultural Littorials where he took part in the first round for literary criticism and was awarded first place.

Favourite meeting places for the friends of *Eredi* were the Capelli bookshop in via Farini and the Pasolini house in via Nosadella.

> . . . And there, along with another of his classmates, Manzoni, we put on plays, acted. The Irish – Synge above all: *Riders to the Sea* and *The Playboy of the Western World*; we read and learned them in Linati's good translation. In turns we would get up on a bench or chair, against a wall at the end of a short corridor; I do not ever remember the young brother being with us . . .
>
> (R. Roversi)

The Faculty of Letters football team – with Serra as halfback and Pasolini as forward – won the inter-faculty championship. They trained in the deserted suburbs out towards Borgo Panigale, at the Virtus gym, at branches of the Gil [Fascist youth organization] and the Guf [Fascist student organization], which organized winter camps where Pier Paolo went skiing.

Before the summer holidays, his father, Carlo Alberto, who had been promoted major and awarded the colonial Order of the Star of Italy, left for the war in East Africa, his destination Gondar [the last remaining Italian stronghold in Abyssinia].

Since they had come to live in Bologna, the boys had grown up and the conjugal life of Susanna and Carlo had settled down into habit and mute agreement over their reciprocal difficulties. A certain economic well-being ensured the good running of the household, while pride at the success of his sons blunted the most obsessive points in the father's character. Guido got good results at school too – especially in science subjects – but it was on Pier Paolo that the father continued to place his stakes. 'He had guessed at, poor man, but had not foreseen the humiliations that went with the satisfactions. He thought he could reconcile the life of a writer son with his own conformism, which had become deformed and had progressed to the point of being definitive.'

From Bologna Pier Paolo wrote to Farolfi with the transports of a prolonged adolescent friendship and to Parini, who in the spring had joined up as a volunteer; for the three friends this break represented the end of adolescence. The letters Pier Paolo sent Parini in his barracks in Padua and later at the Russian front have all been lost.

From Casarsa, where he arrived in the middle of July, he wrote to the three friends of *Eredi*, addressing the letters to Serra on the understanding that they would be read by everyone. The happiness of the summer of 1941 was found between dream and reality in 'the mysterious mornings of Casarsa'. Pier Paolo slept and worked in a big room, climbed up to by a wooden staircase and an external balcony, above the old storeroom for the grape-pressings from the grandfather's distillery. He wrote poems and collected them in a file he called his Rough Notebook; among a large number in Italian some in Friulano suddenly made their appearance. He also drew, on cellophane paper with green ink or with a tube of ochre from among the oil colours.

Into this rustic *bohème*, from the houses round about, came the voices of the peasants, cutting into the silences of the mornings, inspiring the musings of the young poet, depicting with perfect accuracy the surrounding reality in a language both virginal and ancient.

The Friulano spoken in Casarsa is a frontier variety, 'sweetly mingled with Venetian dialect, which is spoken on the right bank of the Tagliamento'. It was not spoken in the Pasolini family where Italian was obligatory – nor in the Colussi family who passed from Venetian to Italian in their relations with the Pasolinis and from Venetian to Friulano only on rare occasions. What spoke Friulano was the whole world around them, which was still authentically peasant. Pier Paolo, who had heard it since he was a child, when he first began to write it, was conscious of carrying out 'a sort of mystical act of love', thus mastering that uncontaminated and absolute language which was the myth he had pursued in his reading of the hermetic poets.

Every day he met his friend, Bortotto:

He talked to me for the first time about his linguistic discovery of the spoken language of Casarsa. At various times, almost in secret, he read me his poetic experiments – the ones that the next year made up the nucleus of *Poesie a Casarsa* ['Poems to Casarsa']. There seemed to me to be something ridiculous in the clash between the Friulano of the centre [of the province] and the Friulano of Casarsa, so poor and crude. Then the conjunction of the little dialectical world of Casarsa and Pier Paolo, whose culture was totally Italian, was odd.

(C. Bortotto)

For the Friulano of the centre, spoken in Udine, there existed an artistic tradition, philological studies and poetic ambitions, but Pier Paolo had not yet opened Pirona's[23] dictionary of Friulano nor did he know the dialect poets of the region.

After Bologna, Friuli was the second site of his development, 'although it was somehow artificial, since I had chosen it as a sort of ideal place for poetry and my aestheticizing, mystical imaginings'. That is how he was to put it thirty years later in a rapid synthesis of his poetical autobiography, to which however he restored a more articulate sense of the time and the experience because, in reality, the peasant world of his mother and its language were from the start less artificial than they were congenial – those, in fact, of his own people. Here no gap separated the student from Bologna from the young peasants and an identical history stemmed from their past; and his absolute language, too, if ever there was such a thing, was soon to be poetically pervaded by the sense of reality, thus arriving at – in accordance with Jimenez's[24] appeal – the exact name of things.

Once I had come into contact with dialect, that inevitably produced its effects, although initially I had adopted it for purely literary reasons. The moment I began to use it, I realized that I had touched something living and real, something that acted like a bomerang. It was through Friulano that I came to understand a little of the real peasant world.

One evening in the cinema at San Vito al Tagliamento he met a young painter, Federico (Rico) De Rocco, a pupil of Saetti's[25] Venetian school. They went painting together and Pier Paolo was introduced to the pictorial techniques he wished to use. He painted landscapes 'a bit like De Pisis',[26] feeling that he had arrived at a palette of his own and a manner of his own.

No sooner were the pictures finished, and that summer there were more than a dozen, than they went to cover the walls of 'the big room'. Pictures and poems were born against the same Friulian backcloths.

The line of springs which separates and links Upper and Lower Friuli and which determined the ancient foundation of Casarsa cause an infinite number of freshets to gush out; they form the irrigation canals of Casarsa which flow down to the sea. One of the first poems written in the summer of 1941 was in praise of their freshness. It is called 'Acque di Casarsa' ['Waters of Casarsa'] and was enclosed in a letter of July to Serra:

> Fountain of water of my village.
> No water is fresher than in my village.
> Fountain of rustic love.

Translated a few days later into Friulano, it was to open his imminent collection of verses.

The first poem written directly in Friulano in the second half of July was inspired by the word *rosada* (hoar-frost), an 'experimental' poem which has disappeared from his collected verse. The second Friulano poem, written next day, was 'Il nini muàrt' ['The dead child'] composed in two stages, as emerges from the letters to Serra, along with the request to Serra to translate it himself into the dialect of Reggio Emilia.

> . . . he had an extraordinary tranquillity and speed when writing that never ceased to astonish me; and he began to dominate those of us who were feeling our way by the extraordinary invention of coloured dialect (so it seemed to me) – that is to say, of a language driven to the limits in terms of feeling but with so much restrained modesty (a language sufficiently celestial in the true sense of the word) as to make it new and different, that is to say true and original . . .
>
> (R. Roversi)

All summer he wrote one or more poems a day; many were in Italian, some in dialect. Of some of the Italian ones there would at once be a translation/reworking in Friulano. Others in Italian, on which a second reading cast doubts, would render up something of themselves – an image, a name – to a new dialect poem before being rejected.

Having declared a 'very vague' aversion to modern lyric poetry, he developed his Italian poems in accordance with the programme of 'hereditary archaism', with epigraphs which were of great value as evidence. These verses, which speak of the humble people of Casarsa – 'friendly people, I am one of you' – place the poet on a grandiose confessional plane and the humble world that surrounds him in a mythical perspective with powerful foreshortenings of real events and symbologies. The poems in Friulano, on the other hand, were born with immediacy; they almost wrote themselves. Both were written on the same days.

In a letter to Silvana Mauri[27] of 19 February 1950 he was to confess to having had in this period a crisis resolved by a 'not very serious neurosis', with an obsessive thought of suicide 'and then by recovery'. Perhaps it was a question of that secret mechanism of healing which for the first time wove the homosexual visions he suffered into 'the peasant mystery', thus giving shape to the originals – the silhouettes – of the dialect poems without the need for any further literary scenarios.

The Italian poems were to have been collected under the title *I confini del giorno* ['The frontiers of the day'] or simply *Confini* ['Frontiers'] – one of the four little books planned by the Bolognese friends. But Pier Paolo did not seem to foresee – although he said he was at a most pleasant turning point in his life – that his book was to become something quite different: not a volume of high literary archaism, overflowing with the 'tragic' sense of life, but of humble dialect speech; and that that 'hypersensitive and sick adolescent', whom he would like to have killed in order to prevent him polluting his life as a man, would be the subject of his poetry.

Thus the poems in Friulano began to appear somewhat casually, like flowers that had fallen into the thick weft of the literary theory of 'the Heirs'. The language was that of Casarsa but some features were taken over from the *koiné*[28] of Udine, the only one which had up to then had a written tradition.

At the end of the summer he announced that he had a 'whole collection of lyrics dedicated to Casarsa', but it must be assumed that it was composed only of Italian poems. The other poems, those in Friulano which were to form the first slim volume, were to come to maturity only in the following months when, in Bologna, he suffered so from home-sickness for the peasant world.

To poetry he dedicated the morning hours, with the sun blazing on the wooden balcony. The afternoons were for the Tagliamento and poetic reflections under the bushes on the banks between swims; but since these afternoons were eternal, they continued in the sports-field behind the railway station where the Casarsa team trained; Pier Paolo played on the left wing and was admired more for his speed in running than for his aim at the goal.

Painting pictures won for itself a little of the time dedicated to poetry, a little from that by the Tagliamento. In the evening there were the meetings with his friends in Casarsa.

Bortotto remembers:

The evenings we spent at Savorgnano and at San Vito, in the hamlet of Fabria, where we met more or less 'steady' girls, and others, in a group. At the centre of these memories there is the little orchestra of Tunin Cancellier and of Paolo Carta (the first on the drums, the second on the violin) which travelled about on an ice-cream tricycle with a sign written on its side 'Jaz Band' [*sic*]. Pier Paolo went round among the cluster of spectators with the saucer to collect the pennies.

His brother Guido, who was equally absorbed into the world of Casarsa, led a life which rarely crossed that of Pier Paolo. He had different friends – the closest was Renato Lena, with his passion for hunting and woodwork. They made wonderful things – revolvers and increasingly complicated sailing-ships. They shot past the house on roller skates and at the end of summer came home at night with trophies of clusters of grapes stolen in the fields.

Susanna was somewhat worried about her husband, away fighting in Africa. His absence had had the effect of tightening the emotional ties with all the family, even if Carlo Alberto was the one who had always believed – and still did – in the victory of Fascism. Word arrived that he had been decorated in the field – he would in time receive a Silver Medal – before being taken prisoner by the English.

The letters written during the summer to his friends in Bologna (each letter contained his latest poems, while those he received gradually contained those of the three correspondents) continued the discussion around the project of the review *Eredi*, with many undertakings and duties spelt out; others were implicit and across them there sometimes fell the shadow of jealousy and suspicion. As when Pasolini, in a outburst of bad temper, reproved his friends for being under the influence of Antonio Meluschi. Poor Meluschi, who led an obscure, persecuted existence in Bologna with his wife Renata Viganò (also mysteriously despised by Pasolini), had just emerged from a trial before the Fascist Special Tribunal and in order to survive was working as a journalist on the *Corriere Padano*.

The holiday at Casarsa extended to the middle of September when Pier Paolo was forced to go back to Bologna for his impending exams.

## 1942

'Healthy as a fish and sound as a tree' in March 1942 Pasolini was twenty. He continued to go to the Guf and the Gil where he met other friends, very young literary people, philosophers and budding painters: Fabio Mauri, Fabio Luca Cavazza, Achille Ardigo, Luigi Vecchi, Mario Ricci and the prodigious girl, Giovanna Bemporad, who at fourteen had already published a translation of some cantos of *The Odyssey*.

Fabio Mauri, just after he met him, took him to his parents' house and introduced him to his sister, Silvana:

My brother, Fabio, sixteen years old and so four years younger than Pier Paolo and myself, brought him home, having met him at the editorial office of a youth review *Il Setaccio* ['The Sieve'] in Bologna where – and it is one of the strange coincidences in our fates – the Pasolini family and my own had settled provisionally and basically by chance. These first memories are confused for me by the fine gold dust of youth, amid that 'incandescence' that blurs the outlines. Like meetings in a dream. He seemed very beautiful to me with his face where Slav, Romagnolo, Jewish traits had composed unique lines, an unrepeatable mask. His body almost too expressive, like a Mantegna or even a poor man from the Middle Ages, so strong and virile that if he seized your wrists to show affection he squeezed them between two pincers. From his timid attitude – one of reserve and northern sobriety, so different from my overflowing extraversion of a girl from Central and Southern Italy – there emerged slow, hesitant talk with that harsh, bare, oily, bitter accent of the Venetians of Friuli.

(Silvana Mauri)

The *Eredi* project, postponed as far as the publication of the review was concerned, became concrete with the imminent publication of the little volumes of poetry, one for each of the friends (*Sopra una perduta estate* ['On a lost summer'] by Leonetti, *Poesie* ['Poems'] by Roversi, *Poesie a Casarsa* ['Poems to Casarsa'] by Pasolini, *Canto di memorie* ['Song of memories'] by Serra), and at the same time came to an end.

More easy to bring into being was the review for the Bolognese Gil *Il Setaccio*, around which discussions and programmes immediately began.

At the beginning of July Pier Paolo was at the military camp of Porretta Terme for three weeks to take a course for officer cadets of the reserve. He had just come back from two large gatherings of Fascist youth – the first in Florence, the second in Weimar in Germany, where he had met young people from every part of Europe in the grip of Nazi Fascism. The extensive propaganda deployed for the occasion struck him as deeply anti-cultural (he was shortly to describe it in an article), while in conversation with foreigners of his own age he formed for the first time a picture of the Nazi dictatorship receiving at the same time, the reverse of the coin, cultural news of the Europe in which the names of poets and painters hostile to Fascism were circulating.

During the camp at Porretta Terme he corrected the proofs of his little volume in Friulano which came out at the end of July in three hundred numbered copies. It contained the poems written during the previous summer at Casarsa, others written during the winter in Bologna and the last in Casarsa again, where, breaking with the family habit, he had gone to pass a period from April into May. He was 'very, very pleased' too with the pictures painted in the spring at Casarsa.

Carlo Alberto had been a prisoner in Kenya for some months and there received his son's slim volume, written in that dialect he so much despised. 'In spite of the absurdity of the language used, it was dedicated to him and this consoled him, made him exult.'

At the beginning of August Susanna and her two sons left for Casarsa for the usual holidays but this time with plans for a definitive move until the end of the war, to be carried out in the course of the year.

. . . he takes refuge with his mother in Casarsa which is his too by now, because of the poems written in the praise of and in lyrical mimesis of the city. Casarsa, from that moment, entered the poetic geography of Europe, rather like the Soria of Antonio Machado[29] whom Pasolini always loved greatly.

(Bertolucci)[30]

Before leaving Bologna he received this note from Gianfranco Contini: 'Dear Pasolini, yesterday I received your *Poesie a Casarsa*. I liked it so much that I at once sent a review to *Il Primato* ['The Primacy']
[31] – if they want it.'

Contini lived in Domodossola and taught Romance philology at Fribourg. His note rendered the poet, who was just making his début, happy and was to remain the most important literary fact of his life. Contini too remembered it:

> ... partly because of an interest in archives, partly for what I shall call postal reasons, it is true I was the first to notice the existence of P.P.P. He made it part of his own legend – in part, certainly, for the reasons which Aristotle too attributes to the unforgettable nature of first love with the high-flown rhetoric that accompanies it . . . [. . .] I was teaching then at a foreign university and went backwards and forwards from that chair to a little city on the frontier. One of people who supplied me with books, whose craftsman's way of running his business (wrappers and bills entirely in his own hand) was reflected in the scantiness of his earnings, was a little antiquary in Bologna called Mario Landi. I never knew him personally and only much later my dear friend Giuseppe Raimondi[32] was to describe him to me as 'a Bolognese character', distinguished, among other things, by being an albino. One day in 1942 the post brought me an envelope inscribed with the beautiful archaic hand of Mario Landi but it did not contain a few liras' worth of Bodoni[33] or Romagnoli-dell'Acqua[34] but for the first and only time a small volume with the imprint of Landi himself. The author unknown, Pier Paolo Pasolini, the name having the unmistakable appearance of someone from around Ravenna, and unknown to me the linguistic garb of these *Poesie a Casarsa* – Friulano but *di cà da l'aga* [from this side of the water] (that is the Tagliamento), hence an exception among exceptions. The smell was that unmistakable one of poetry of an unusual species, moreover in one of those languages which I do not know whether to call quasi-languages or minor languages which it was my passion and profession to study . . .

The poet Giorgio Caproni[35] also remembered the little volume from Casarsa:

> After Contini I was one of the first – along with Alfonso Gatto – to review *Poesie a Casarsa*. I read them in 1942, the most hopeless of years, and still

remember vividly the emotion they awoke in me while my knapsack – that of a soldier called to the colours – was full of hand-grenades and darkness.[36]

The preparatory stage of the review *Il Setaccio* was finished and in November the first number appeared as 'An order of the day from the headquarters of the Gil in Bologna'. A piece by Pasolini, *I Giovani, l'attesa* ['The young men, the waiting'], was a projection of his personal experiences as being the general fate of young poets, with a request for the maximum amount of freedom and of solitude. Proposals so much in contrast to all that sustained an institution like the Gil that, while they might be accepted through laziness and muddle, did not fail in the long run to throw into continual crisis the relationship between the contributors and those responsible for the review:

> Rarely in its short life was there agreement between the attitude desired by the editors and the point of view of the official hierarchies because there was no possible communication between them, given the distance separating those who saw a reality in movement – and that everything was therefore to be read problematically – and those who trusted solely to an authoritarian bureaucratic vision of things.
>
> (M. Ricci)

What appears extraordinarily challenging is the piece in the third number of *Il Setaccio* on the meeting in Weimar in which Nazi propaganda is written off as being greatly at odds with European culture. Another anomaly – the publication in the very first number of a poem in Friulano, *Fantasie di mia madre* ['Fantasies about my mother'], accepted by a publication which depended on a regime that was hostile to dialects (and to the reality they represented, which had to be kept hidden) and was the safeguard of a national and Roman language. In this first naïve anti-Fascism – all ideals and culture – one can perhaps also see a first unconscious impulse to challenge society.

The managing editor of *Il Setaccio* was Giovanni Falzone, the celebrator in verse of the 'Fascist Era'. Pasolini was assistant editorial adviser. Various friends of his were members of the editorial board or contributors: Fabio Mauri, Mario Ricci, Giovanna Bemporad (who concealed her Jewish name under the pseudonym Giovanna Bembo), Fabio Luca Cavazza, Riccardo Castellani, Luciano Serra, Sergio Telmon, Cesare Bortotto. Of the *Eredi* group both Leonetti and Roversi stayed aloof; Pasolini on the other hand also contributed to *Architrave*, the review of the Bologna Guf, some articles, the last of which is 'Filologia e morale' ('Philology and morals') of 31 December 1942.

25

The story of his collaboration on *Il Setaccio* was chiefly in the correspondence with Fabio Luca Cavazza and Fabio Mauri. Bortotto remembers:

> The interest in and the discussions around *Poesie a Casarsa* had spread
> even to local groups, but then they narrowed down to a 'triangular'
> meeting which lasted a long time – Pier Paolo, Castellani and myself.
>     The discussion had widened to include neo-Latin readings and
> literature taking in Ascoli,[37] necessarily, and then Friulian philology. Pier
> Paolo's entreaties – particularly towards autumn – led Castellani to write
> some articles for *Il Setaccio.*

Before Pasolini left for Casarsa, Serra dedicated his small volume to him:
'Tomorrow I shall have short hair, in two days' time I shall be posted to a
regiment, you will see Casarsa again, will write verses, paint . . .'

# 1943
'1943 remains one of the finest years of my life.'

Among the thousands of volumes which now occupied his grandparents' old
kitchen there were many monographs on contemporary painters. For some
months he had been busy writing his thesis on Italian painting of the
twentieth century to be presented to Longhi. Not a casual choice, given that in
this period he published in *Il Setaccio* articles of art criticism, while in the
preceding period he was thinking chiefly of this activity in the context of the
review *Eredi.*
    He had entered an 'adult childhood' and Casarsa – 'all morality and no
beauty' – although it had lost a little of the mystery that surrounded it when
he was a boy, acquired a new magic. In the article mentioned above from
*Architrave* he wrote:

> If today on many sides – and privately too – one notices a lack of mature
> and lofty civilization capable of bringing us together, we shall be able to
> rediscover this civilization at its distant and immutable origins, which is
> why fresh energies continually renew it and protect it, as happens in
> nature.
>     We shall be able to rediscover it by shutting ourselves up for a long
> period in ourselves and by moving within the narrow circle which family
> life – which has become extremely close – reserves for us, in the shadow of
> our hearth, under the leaves of our gardens, in the gestures of ingenuous
> men, which have not changed for centuries. This ancient civilization will

not be able to deceive us, if from it we are able to make new springs gush out; this is a private task which concerns each one of us . . .

From Casarsa he continued the collaboration on *Il Setaccio* following its perilous vicissitudes, urging others to contribute and to stand up to the managing editor and to defend their 'child', which he considers the only medium for the 'educational mission of our generation'.

The recurring crises and travails of *Il Setaccio* were born of a basic misunderstanding: the conviction of the Fascist regime that it could bind young intellectuals to itself by offering them an adequate space for debate and the refusal of the latter to accept a view of politics in which they absolutely did not recognize themselves. Hence new clashes over the line taken in individual numbers, compromises of various kinds, permanent discord between the most stupid positions (Falzone) and the most enlightened (Pasolini, Mauri, etc.). Points of near rupture were reached with the threat to suspend such publications; and probably it would have come to this had Fascism not died of its own accord in July 1943.

(M. Ricci)

The expected review by Contini appeared on 24 April in the Swiss daily *Corriere del Ticino*; it's author's premonitions had been correct – *Il Primato* did not accept it.

. . . to this end I used a paper in the Ticino, partly because the Italian editorial offices were falling apart as disaster, which was coming to a head, approached – and partly because the censorship was watching carefully to see that no one said too much good of anything written in dialect. It was basically my only discovery . . . Then a long friendship began . . . a friendship the true meaning of which was to be, as he said, quoting Jaufré Rudel,[38] *de lonh* [Provençal: from afar].

(G. Contini)

The censorship exercised by *Primato* was experienced by Pier Paolo as a personal insult by Fascism. 'His visceral and cultural anti-Fascism,' Cesare Bartotto remembers, 'was a recurring note in his talk; sometimes it was the mocking and grotesque tone (referring to the external aspects of the Fascist hierarchical structure) common to much of student youth.'

In this period a young woman joined the friends in Casarsa – Pina Kalč, a Slovene violinist who had also taken refuge at Casarsa in the house of relatives.

She was thirty but looked like a young girl, thin, pale, with wild but sparse hair . . . She was healthy, agile; she talked like a child: I met her in February 1943. She immediately became necessary to me because of her violin; first she played me the *moto perpetuo* by Nováček [Janáček] which became almost the motif of our meetings, and was repeated on many occasions. I remember her perfectly in the act of playing it with her blue skirt and white blouse. But soon she began to make me listen to Bach. It was the six sonatas for solo violin from which there rose to desperate heights the Chaconne and Prelude of the 3rd; the Siciliana of the 1st. The hundreds of evenings we spent together from 1943 to the summer of 1945 when, the war being over, she left for Yugoslavia, caused me the usual despair over something which cannot be expressed and is too unique; but at all events the music remained as something solid, something that happened without ambiguity and which sums up all our tempestuous friendship. I do not know if she felt love for me right away (certainly she must have felt a certain painful emotion from knowing me); later in her naïve Italian she confessed she had been afraid of me.

(*Quaderni rossi* of 1946)

On the evening of the last day of carnival, relatives and friends gathered in Susanna's kitchen for an improvised play – a sketch in Friulano, *Carneval e Quaresima* ['Carnival and Lent'] – based on a plot put together in a few minutes. Pier Paolo played the part of Carnival, Bortotto, in female costume, that of Lent. Pina played the violin.

Bortotto remembered, among Pier Paolo's reading, works by Pascal and Chateaubriand and related them to a 'powerful religious crisis' on Pasolini's part. Three years later he was to write in *Quaderni rossi*: 'In these last years I have sometimes drawn close again to religion: to begin with because of a sort of sense of history which led me to feel Christian and Catholic. It was at this time that I made some offerings to the parish priest for good works.'

After the religious zeal of infancy, the nostalgia of the 'present time' was tinged with an archaic peasant religiosity. In May he attended the Rosary every evening and listened to the singing of the litany, mingling erotic desires and poetic mysticism. 'I should like to throw myself on others, be transfigured, live for them.'

The young peasants met in church, the smell of incense, the singing of the litany, the sound of the words and the inflections of the language which were interwoven as if in a wood from Romance literature; the hope of new friendships; the colours of the spring: everything flowed together to stimulate his heart, which was still 'full of joy and goodness'. He drew some sketches for frescoes of the saints – Stephen, Sebastian – for an 'Ecclesia

Reginae Martyrum dicata' [a church dedicated to the Queen of Martyrs] which he intended to erect after the war.

Leaning at the door or near the font or standing upright, round about me sang those who had caused me to come to church. And that year, too, the boys had thought up a game, which seemed made deliberately to torture me. Coming out of church, shouting and happy, they set fire to certain pieces of transparent mica, stolen from goodness knows where, which they threw into the air [blank space] in a rain of joyous little flames. The days around Easter were particularly sad (the procession was over): I vented my feelings in particular on my friend, Cesare B. [Bortotto] who had to hear from me, if I am not mistaken, very moving recriminations against boredom, death, etc. I was desperately eloquent although the arguments were merely rhetorical pretexts (to which, however, I abandoned myself with the maximum sincerity), and one evening when I was accompanying him along the big tarred road to his house, I almost came to the point of weeping. But I have to say that in the night, which was already mild, there reached us – corrupted by the distance – choruses of trumpets and accordions . . . It was Jacu, Milio, Rosa, who in the distance were trying out their instruments, leaning against a willow perhaps, sitting on a kerbstone . . .

(*Quaderni rossi* of 1946)

In the morning he spent many hours reading, writing and drawing, in the orchard. In the afternoon he went to play football; life was as it always had been but now there was deeply imbedded in it the secret of an enormous desire, long resisted, which was attempting to cross its own desert until it met the life of others.

I remember a Sunday evening in 1943 when I was twenty-one. Boredom had brought me out of doors. It was raining, it was dark; all afternoon I had been tortured by my unrealizable desires; at five I left home, trembling, but desperation made me walk straight ahead, furious, as if there were no sure way out. I went to the station and walked along the railway line by a muddy road; I was thus deliberately approaching the zone of death, the dramatic game of my body mangled by a train. I went over the level-crossing and so was in front of the old cemetery. I climbed the low ruined wall and pushed on into it, always with the sureness of someone in a trance; I sat on a tomb and there gave myself up without any further restraint to my amorous thoughts.

(*Quaderni rossi* of 1946)

29

*Introduction*

Long bicycle rides in the surrounding countryside, from one village to another, seemed an attempt to prevent this desire from being so desperately solitary and the long hours such an obsessive time of waiting.

Must I speak of the 'blond boy' – the nth creation of my imagination – whom I ought to have found at Casarsa at last, with all the delicate ways and mysteries of a little adolescent student, who would be capable – how absurd that was! – of understanding my desires and of sharing the sublime joy of an embrace? I made him mine in my eternal, unbearable daydreams; I caressed him, finding in him all the most excruciating and subtle of seductions – a certain languour – a certain abandon – and those fascinating lines which sketched the beauty of an ephebe from the curve of the lips to the convex designs of belly and thighs . . . I was fated to torture myself for months and months with fantasies of this kind and besides it was already at least five years since I had been initiated into them.

I set out on my bicycle in the early hours of the afternoon and went away from the village, making long trips through the surrounding hamlets – I was searching, I repeat, for love, even lust . . . With the naïvety of a boy who had grown up in the city I sought my 'divine' presences of boys disposed to sin precisely where I would never find them – along the springtime roads, in the semi-deserted fields, by farmsteads or places sunk deep in limitless boredom. I passed again and again through Bannia, Fiume, Orcenico, Castions . . . continually, invariably cheated of the meeting [blank space] seeking an inevitable impossibility. There is no point in recalling the thousands of *forms* of youths which brushed past me, fascinating me, and which I tempted with inadequate means, like a novice and – what was more – a desperate one. I did not dare to risk being shamed, to take some step simply to stop on my way one of those boys who ignored me pitilessly, riding along on their bicycles or working among the intertwined mulberry trees and vines. I returned home at the hour of vespers in the twilight interrupted by some yellow [illegible] on the horizon, in the damp, sepulchral loneliness of the fields. Passing by a house or village the smell of the fire surrounded me, along with the confused and tranquil shouts which announced supper; some boy would appear near a pump, on the steps to a door, totally absent-minded, in the state of angelic indifference of a person, tired with work, who savours a rest, and I, abject, guilty, was not even worthy of a glance, while I pedalled desperately through the village towards distant Casarsa of which one could hear only the bells . . .

(*Quaderni rossi* of 1947)

At the end of May, Giovanna Bemporad was the first of the Bolognese friends to come as a guest to Casarsa for a few days. Giovanna, who was in love with the moon, saw its light gleam freely on the vast countryside during the nights of blackout. She shared willingly the village friendships of Pier Paolo and was already thinking of a possible move to Casarsa where threats of war and of racial persecution seemed remote. While Pier Paolo continued to keep up contact by letter with his friends in Bologna, even after publication of *Il Setaccio* had ended, his thoughts dwelt on the dearest of them, Ermes Parini, of whom there had been no more news from Russia for months and whose fate was to be that of so many missing men. Pasolini wrote in *Il Setaccio* of March 1943:

> I and my mother are sitting in the room which protected first her infancy and then mine. And here in this room, from the darkness of the night, a voice can be heard echoing – it is a boy, who has stopped at the door of our house, and is calling a friend. And that cry does not – as once upon a time – awaken in me nostalgia for the past, for myself as a child, or vague tremors, but summons me with new pain to the moments we are living through. For a second it shows me before my eyes more vividly the faces of my father and of my dearest friend whom the war has taken from me. It is two years since I saw the former. Of the second I know nothing more and I pass my saddest hours imagining him in Russia, wounded, missing, prisoner . . . And here in front of me I have my mother's sad look – and I should like to express all this but it is impossible; it is too acute, violent, painful . . .

In letters to Serra and Farolfi he told the story of his life. On 24 June he wrote to Serra: 'I cycled there [to the Tagliamento] yesterday, a young native along with a younger native called Bruno.' The name of this boy reappears in the second and third of the *Quaderni rossi* and his footprint runs across many pages of *Atti Impuri* ['Impure acts'].

> He had very dark hair but little [blank space], two eyes the violet light of which would strike me only later, a discoloured and irregular face much burned by the sun. His chest, half-naked because covered only by a singlet, was tanned and gave off a smell of dust and river water, which somehow I found slightly revolting – all the more since it mingled with the smell of a 'milit' [a cheap brand of cigarette] . . . Bruno was destined to play a large part in my experience. I lay in wait for him an infinite number of times; when I saw him appear with that gait of his – what shall I call it? slightly animal (his right foot was a little damaged) – I felt myself grow faint. A whole complicated arrangement came into being which bound me through infinite tricks and subterfuges to this boy who had not yet come to puberty. But finally I was lucky. When the blinding heat of summer

brought back the season for bathing I could see him when I wanted. We went to bathe in a gravel-pit among the fields behind the cemetery; immediately after supper a crowd of rowdy boys invaded the banks of that pond, trampling the grass which gradually withered and became dirty. It is really incredible the internal disorder, the lack of conscience, the shamelessness of these sons of share-croppers or labourers. There was continuous impure laughter, a rush of senseless words – worthy of a herd of monkeys. When they left, the surrounding grass looked like the abandoned encampment of a family of gypsies. Mostly they bathed naked, even those who had passed puberty, and often they masturbated each other without even bothering to go among the stalks of the maize. Bruno was one of these and although rather serious and indolent, by no means one of the least arrogant. His family must have been of plebeian stock and one felt in him an animal insensibility; he was violent, rude, and therefore was successful with his contemporaries. The moment I had finished supper I rode to the pond on my bicycle carrying with me useless books and lay down on the dirty grass, waiting for him, while the crowd of other boys milled around me. He would arrive, taciturn, smoking the remains of a cigarette: downright brutal. I was overcome by humiliating tenderness. He did not even look at me (or pretended not to?), threw down the empty sack which he would later fill with grass for the rabbits; on the sack he threw in disorder his miserable rags and, naked, went to plunge in. For me up to then boys had been basically sexless Angels – I had never seen them. At the time I did not realize it but now I would be able to say that in Bruno, in his sex, there was something – what shall I say? – priapic . . . One day three of us were left by the pond: Bruno and another slim comrade of his. Both had to go and cut grass and I accompanied them, noting right away in them a certain complicity. I remember that a strong wind was blowing and the sky was three-quarters black. When we reached the top of a bank, to my great astonishment, forgetting about the rabbits, they lay down on the grass, hinting at unconvincing games, and I lay down between them. Must I also say that Bruno's clothes were unfastened and that, having been jokingly made aware of this by his friend, he shrugged his shoulders? It was natural that we should begin a friendly fight as a result of which we embarked on an initimacy that knew no further restraint (in spite of my lack of initiative); and they gradually mastered me. But the bank was too exposed, so they took me into the labyrinth of the maize-field and laid their sacks down for me on the damp earth of the furrows.

*Quod factum est infectum fieri nequit!* [What is done cannot be undone] But I know my guilt is aggravated by speaking of it with such insouciance (and with the [blank] intention of not showing myself altogether in a bad light). But must I say these things in front of someone?

If this someone should in any case be myself, well, let me at least open the door on my privacy with a little golden key.

My tradition where feelings are concerned is too honest: in fact I never wished to betray him – that sensitive and generous boy I was for so many years – even when lying desperately. It is the nostalgia for that uprightness and that candour – a tenacious nostalgia – that lends this confession of mine a tone that is still insincere. But sympathize with me, pass over [illegible] the lack of delicacy in my writing in which I have not wished to commit myself: every style is a judgement. And I do not wish to pass judgement on myself. I helped Bruno and his friend to pluck the grass for the rabbits and when the sacks were full I wanted to accompany them home: they certainly did not imagine that behind my guarded gestures and my hoarse words, in the excessive politeness of my behaviour, there was concealed, alas, emotion at my first amorous contact so recently savoured. Nor did they imagine (but perhaps they guessed it later) that I was behaving as if I were at their service, as if I must 'serve them'. (Often later I would help Bruno to carry his sack of clover and would humiliate myself in a thousand ways when faced by his [blank] absence. Later I saw him some days, always near the gravel-pit; it was he who thought up a plan whereby he and I would run off and two other boys would look for us. Naturally we could not be found in our hiding-place ... Bruno was already naked like the others and I saw with a shudder of joy that he was impatient for me too to loosen the knot fastening my drawers.

We met often in that summer of 1943. The enchantment was broken; for me too the miracle had come true which had seemed to be denied me for ever. Every day we met, no longer at the gravel-pit but near the railway, beyond the hamlet delle Aguzze, on the banks of a pond whose [illegible] is Li fondis [The Deeps]. I am not saying that I did not suffer a great deal and desire a great deal at that time; Bruno, reserved and rude – with childish perversity – never gave an inkling of what he was thinking and too often gave obvious signs that he cared nothing for me, disappearing for days on end. I grew mad with jealousy for the places which saw him, for the grass he trod with his bare foot. Then he would reappear and with cold and lecherous condescension would come with me into the maize. Do not believe (nor is it to excuse myself that I say so) that I initiated him into an operation about which incidentally I was ignorant. Rather it was he who, coldly, without a shadow of scruple [blank]. I remember one day when I took him down to the Tagliamento. For years I had been pursued by the dream of embracing a consenting body in the wild, immensely peaceful solitude of that boundless river-bed. I was prey to an irrepressible joy when, with Bruno on the bar of my bicycle, I turned off from the tarred road down along the lane on the dyke and reached the bank of the river.

We undressed in a wonderfully fresh meadow and, leaving the bicycle and our clothes, made our way towards the middle of the shingle of the river-bed, a whole [illegible] of incandescent stones. Having got completely out of sight in an expanse of sand, I tried to have him and he consented without more ado. But my dream was completely ruined so miserable was that youth's embrace. How a sudden hurricane that chased us away then raised a grey wall of sand over the Tagliamento; indeed I still see, as we fled, with Bruno on the bar (his smell of mud and [blank]), the two bright blue gypsy caravans amid the whirlwinds.

(Quaderni rossi of 1947)

Some days after 25 July,[39] while Pier Paolo was writing to Serra to inform him of the changes that had taken place in Bologna following the deposition of Mussolini, Guido with his friend Renato went out at night to write on the walls of Casarsa: 'Long live liberty'. Both were stopped by the carabinieri and during the interrogation Pier Paolo was forced to restrain Guido's impetuosity which threatened to have them arrested.

'In the following days,' writes Bortotto, 'Pier Paolo came into possession from Bologna of the first leaflets of the political parties which we read avidly.' Other memories of Bortotto's refer to the events at a date a few days before 25 July [the date when Mussolini was deposed].

The events of the war which were moving fast (the Allies had landed in Sicily) brought to maturity in Pier Paolo the arrogant idea of the 'Little Fatherland' of Friuli which was ideally to be rescued from the collapse of the Fascist state.

The text of the proclamation to be sent 'to the mayors and parish priests of Friuli' he wrote in a few hours while we were sitting in the little wood at Le Aguzze in a sheltered nook of ours. The typewriter to write the three hundred copies was the one from the Fascist club. The work had scarcely got under way when it was interrupted on the morning of 25 July when Pier Paolo, who had been listening to the radio, came in jubilation to tell me of the fall of Fascism.

On 1 September he was in Pisa for his first summons to the colours. With the rank of corporal-major he attended the course for officer cadets of the reserve. The 8 September [the date of the Italian armistice] surprised him in Livorno where his unit, after a gesture of resistance to the Germans, was taken prisoner. During the confusion of a burst of machine-gun fire, Pier Paolo and a comrade threw themselves into a ditch and hid till the column of prisoners moved away, then they fled for many kilometres on foot. The next day he reached safety at Casarsa, with two odd shoes which had tortured his feet, and without his baggage which contained among other things the first three chapters of his graduate thesis – on Carrà,[40] De Pisis, Morandi – now irredeemably lost; perhaps fortunately so for he did not attempt to reconstitute it but, as soon as he could, asked the lecturer in Italian literature, Carlo Calcaterra, for a totally different subject: an anthology of the poetry of Pascoli with commentary – a magic world, highly artificial, falsely naïve, very close to his own taste.

Contini writes:

> ... If I remember rightly (the information, in the dramatic wrappings usual with that very great actor, came to me from Roberto Longhi) Pasolini's thesis at Bologna dealt with Pascoli. He was in fact the only one of his predecessors he could bear among all the pomp (and above all the aspiration to pomp) of the recent tradition. The poor backcloth of San Mauro [Pascoli's birthplace in Romagna] finds an echo in the initial poor backcloth of the barren landscape around Delizia, which an Alexandrine and 'convivial' vein of poetry – it would be concentrated (beginning with the *Poesie a Casarsa*) in the moving symbol of the violet – could not but cultivate.

When the Germans descended on Friuli and subjected it to their martial laws governing the 'Adriatic Littoral', the Tagliamento became a no-go area: the two bridges over the river at Friuli were the targets of Allied bombers and Casarsa was no longer an island of peace. As it lies on the road leading to Austria, every day saw the passing of trains laden with Italian prisoners on their way to the German concentration camps. Bicycles were requisitioned or became unusable because of the impossibility of replacing tyres. So the last summer was enjoyed on foot among the fields. During one of these walks Pier Paolo reached Versuta, a hamlet of a few houses less that two kilometres from Casarsa, through which there ran an irrigation canal called the Viersa and a single road: its centre – a small patch of grass on which there rose a little fourteenth-century church. The houses had external staircases, wooden balconies and house-fronts, orchards and courtyards with big roofs which isolated them within the rural world.

Ernesta Bazzana was a young mother who was doing some jobs in the courtyard when Pier Paolo, attracted by the cleanliness of her little house, asked her to rent him a room. Agreement was quickly reached because the sense of something unusual, together with the hope of some small earnings, conquered the peasant woman's distrustful heart. Some days later, pushing a handcart laden with books, Pier Paolo reappeared in Ernesta's courtyard and took possession of the room; for the moment it was dedicated to poetic dreams but there was the prospect that it would soon become a refuge from the bombing and the German terror.

The bombings created difficulties for the children of Casarsa who had to travel to school at Pordenone and Udine, and there was talk of a little private school. Two kilometres from Casarsa, on the other side of the railway, lay the village of San Giovanni beyond which was Versuta, the more distant as one went towards the Tagliamento. In an abandoned house, which had a certain bourgeois dignity, with two central corridors on the ground and first floors and rooms laid out on either side, Pier Paolo and five of his friends opened a school at the end of September with all the usual rules about enrolment and timetables. The chaplain at San Giovanni, who had a degree in literature, merely lent his name as cover to the request for permission from the school authorities. Pier Paolo taught literature and history, Cesare Bortotto science, Riccardo Castellani mathematics and Giovanna Bemporad, summoned at once from Bologna, Greek and English. The school at San Giovanni, as a first experiment in teaching, lasted a very short time because halfway through November the director of education at Udine sent an official 'warning'. The school was closed and the teachers decided to continue the lessons in their own houses.

Pasolini's pupils were boys from the fourth class of the *ginnasio* who every day attended his lessons held in the little dining room of the house at Casarsa. Dante, Petrarch, *The Songs of the Greek People* translated by Tommaseo, Leopardi, Virgil, Ungaretti, Machado, Marlowe, Wordsworth were the authors studied before and after the hours dedicated to Latin syntax, to Greek and English: five hours of lessons each day. The written work of the pupils were real exercises in historical and stylistic criticism of the texts. In the educational programme Friulian poets made an unexpected appearance which was to arouse the annoyance of the examiners at the *ginnasio* in Udine.

All the pupils – some ten of them – were drawn by these lessons far beyond the limits of school programmes to the point of being happily fanatical about becoming authors themselves, composing poetry in Italian and Friulano, reading them to their teacher, following him in the things he was writing, which were read out in class just like those of the boys. For all of them – teacher and pupils – it was an apprenticeship during which naïvely the Academiuta de lenga furlana [the Little Academy of the Friulian Language] took shape.

One evening in October, Pasolini, Bortotto and Castellani discussed the project of a review of Friulano poetry, *Lo stroligut di cà da l'aga* ['The little almanac from this side of the water']. The Friulian Philological Society of Udine each year printed an almanac, *Lo strolic furlan* ['The Friulian Astrologer']; the Casarsa review was – perhaps ironically – the diminutive version located *di cà de l'aga* [on this side of the water], that is to say, on the right bank of the Tagliamento.

In 1943 Pasolini wrote in Italian a small book of religious meditations which were to form the first part of *L'usignolo della Chiesa Cattolica* ['The nightingale of the Catholic Church'] and completed in Friulano the second edition – 'twice the size' – of *Poesie a Casarsa.*

## 1944
'The war stinks of shit.'

Of the two brothers, Guido was the one more tempted to take part in the Resistance which was being organized in Casarsa against Fascists and Germans. In the days following the armistice, with his friend Renato and other boys from the village, he got into a barracks to seize arms and ammunition which he then hid in his bedroom under the flagstones. Other arms and ammunition they took from the wagons of a waiting train and hid in the funeral niches of an abandoned cemetery. He was attending the scientific *liceo* in Pordenone and at the end of April 1944 was to take his final examinations.

On 5 March he wrote to his father:

We are all well. Pier Paolo is still quietly at home and I am at home too but not too 'quiet' (although I haven't received the postcard [his calling-up paper] ). I cannot – in spite of my good intentions – keep out of politics, in this I am terribly hot-headed (ideas and attitudes changed very much lately); and I am truly very worried at the thought of acting contrary to your way of thinking. Yet I am convinced that if you were here you would have no hesitation about which side to take . . . Pier Paolo does all he can to restrain me and I admire him for his generosity (I am sure he does it solely to avoid making Mother unhappy) and I feel I love him very much but unfortunately I am often carried away by strong feelings . . .

When the Germans occupied the barracks and airfield at Casarsa, Guido and Renato managed to get close to the planes – the big Ju 52 transports – escaping the survelliance of the armed soldiers, and remove arms and ammunition. All the arms and ammunition procured in this risky way later passed to the partisans.

In these same days propaganda leaflets against Fascism were distributed secretly in Casarsa. The investigations of the carabinieri again directed suspicion at Pier Paolo although once more Guido was the author of the propaganda. Pier Paolo was arrested for some hours along with various friends including Pina Kalč. From that day he often slept at Versuta and one night a band of Fascists searched the house and arrested Guido. The grandmother, Giulia, knelt before the soldiers, begging them to free him, but their commander pointed a pistol at her back until Guido was made to climb into the truck. He returned on foot from Pordenone after some days of interrogations and beatings. A few days later the grandmother died, overcome by all the excitement. Guido, too, went more and more often to take refuge at Versuta and from there made contact with the partisan formations in the mountains. He left at the end of May with a haversack full of real rolls of bread on top of other imitation ones in which were concealed hand-grenades, a dictionary the pages of which had been hollowed out to accommodate a Beretta pistol and a copy of the *Canti orfici* [Orphic songs] of Campana.[41] At the station in Casarsa he took a ticket to Bologna, where he pretended to be going, while Renato took one to Spilimbergo; from there Guido went on through Pielungo in the Carnic Alps to the headquarters of the Osoppo-Friuli division. He enrolled 'with enthusiasm' in the Partito d'Azione [Action Party].[42]

Pier Paolo remembered in *Quaderni rossi* the first months of 1944:

At this time I was very friendly with P. (Pina Kalč); we had become inseparable and she continued to be a burden to me because of her too obvious preoccupation with my inner life. At this time she felt – behind my moral maturity, my availability, my moments of abandon – that dead area which she perhaps confused with my secret (the secret seen as 'innocent beauty', heedless virtility, etc.) and which she therefore wished to explore. I cruelly allowed her to offer herself to me; I did not exclude a single one of her thousand assumptions . . . One Sunday, before the football match, which I did not want to miss, and I need not tell you why, we went together far into the sacred loneliness of the fields. It was truly an error to violate that vegetal and earthy essence, while all other men were enjoying the rainy Sunday together. The immense plain with the two solitary oaks – an exceedingly rare tree in these parts – saw us really suffer – I (at least on the surface) from boredom, she from desire. My [illegible] fault consisted in thinking only about Bruno and not at all about her and beyond that of not being able to abandon the youthful demeanour which – as I knew – was what chiefly bound her to me. We left the useless meadow with its totally indifferent oaks and although we had stuck a flower in our lips (my God, I seem to remember that under the oaks she combed my hair . . . and put a flower on my head) our return to join the rest of the people was no longer cordial. It was raining. The people in the sports field were shouting, impelled by a passion which was far removed from our minds, as one might imagine. But between her and me there was this difference that there, in the playing field, I was at home – I knew perfectly how to play the part of the sporting youth (which in any case I was) while in her the pain was increased at seeing me distracted. In reality I was looking and searching about to find Bruno. I saw him at last under the cold lines of the rain with his elegant turquoise blue Sunday suit and his white shorts.

This was my first experiment in love. No one who lives in a normal way can imagine what sense of the miraculous I attributed to what was happening to me. For me it was really the absurdity of eternity cut in two which was taking concrete forms . . . It was a wonderful day in late spring; the grass absorbed a burning sun; the first birds – a few scarce voices – were singing with shrill discords and among the mulberries the already almost mature leaves shone. In the abundance of light, so liquid and pure, I left home for my adventure in which I did not wish to believe; and the very books under my arm threatened to become the true reason for my midday spent in the countryside while the closer I came to Bruno's village the less hope I had of realizing the unrealizable. I turned off stealthily once I had left the dripping tunnel along the dyke, among bushes, hoping internally that no one was able to watch me and make guesses about my odd behaviour. There were no sheep; there was no Bruno. In the brutal and impassive silence everything seemed naturally arranged for my disappointment or my punishment – I don't know which – certainly for my punishment. Among the ugly bushes, on the dirty grass, I found myself concretely, no longer notionally, alone. As the symbols of a destiny being fulfilled, coming punctually true, I heard the whistles and puffing of a locomative wandering along the embankment . . . and the voices of the railwaymen and even the smell of the faeces that spread treacherously among the rubbish and dirt of the slope. But that day was not to be like the others; preceded by his sheep Bruno arrived with his chest bare, his thighs and legs covered with a pair of greasy, heavy shorts and a pair of big clogs on his feet. With his irregular way of walking and his unlovable burnt face, he came close to me and let himself be clasped by an arm and then by a thigh; for it had been miraculously established by him that there was to be no more shame between us. On the dry bed of the canal, which was still muddy however, we walked in delicious complicity towards a hidden place. Bruno insisted on the maximum secrecy and was very sure in the way he found the hiding-places where he could give rein to his lusts. The bed of the canal brought us to the heart of that wild spot which bordered on the railway embankment. That sunny day the brambles which hung down over the canal were already thick with buds and formed what were almost lairs, hiding-places against the cracked bank. But Bruno was in no hurry – so much so that he lingered to climb a poplar to take a blue tit's nest full of eggs. Then he rolled one of his cigarettes, allowing himself to be caressed all the time by me, taking advantage of that absurd freedom. Perhaps it was this amorous [blank] that made me lose my head sufficiently, when at last we lay down between two thick bushes, for desire to free itself from its conscience and I could almost know the fullness of abandon.

That hour was not the first of a series of hours (as I so avidly hoped); Bruno was capricious and nasty. Once again he very frequently fell into his habit of evasion: every day I passed and repassed through his village, obstinately scanning the path between the dyke and the canal where his sheep must be grazing, a sign of his presence; for weeks and many times a day I went far along that path to explore it. Bruno was not there; he was absent in a visible, provocative manner. I passed whole hours in that desolate spot while the whistling of the engines shunting and a vague, disgusting stink of faeces lulled my fits of jealousy, my burning protests. Then the scene where I had to play such a humiliating role changed: it was summer. People came back to swim at The Deeps. The unbearable, belittling uproar of the boys was there once more. Bruno showed himself often; but he rarely obeyed a knowing look from me or allowed himself to be overcome by my insistence. Mostly I waited for him for hours sitting with my Tommaseo or my Tasso on a marvellous meadow surrounded by a row of vines and a ditch overflowing with trees. There summer accomplished its silent miracles; it heaped flashing lights on the surface of the tops of the trees, with enchanting softness and artificiality, while lower down against the empty spaces of the canal it made golden shadows [words scored out] flow past. Thousands of birds sang in different scales alternating with or superimposing on each other, and sweetly pierced the silence, now with human modulations and now with animal trills and melodies. All this distracted me; but it was a distraction quite incapable of taking me out of my constant state of waiting and my envy of the meadow which Bruno trod with his feet.

Often I seemed to hear a human voice in the ambiguous network of the birdsong; and then I rose up trembling on the absurd pretext that it was Bruno calling me. Later, about a year later, I learned from her own lips that Pina often came during these days to look for me round about The Deeps; the excuse this time was that she was coming to see the meadows I so greatly praised; and from this interpretation I learned this detail of her life – and I imagine that the call I heard in the fields (a call that dissolved like a falling star, so very plaintive that in reality it seemed to be born only in my breast) was Pina's. Certainly in this naïve discovery of mine there is a reality – at least a poetical one. But at that time all that mattered to me was my closeness to Bruno.

When the first air-raids began, with sirens that were repeated day and night, the inhabitants living round the village square fled, making their way down a lane between the fields far from the main road and the railway station. Susanna and Pier Paolo found a safe place for their belongings: a handbag full of jewels which they did not yet know were of little value and Pier Paolo's leather briefcase with his 'Rough Notebooks' – the last containing a play in Friulano, *I Turcs tal Friul* ['The Turks in Friuli'], and the notes for his thesis on Pascoli. In the crowd fleeing by night were always Pina and her relatives.

In moments of calm Pina came every day to the Pasolinis' to give Pier Paolo violin lessons and after his lessons they played together a few duets which they finished with visible emotion; then Pina played Bach:

It was the Siciliano above all that interesed me because I had given it a content, and each time I heard it again it brought me face to face with that content by its tenderness and pain: a struggle sung impassively between the Flesh and Heaven, between certain low notes, veiled, warm, and some strident, terse abstract notes. How much I was on the side of the Flesh! How I felt my heart being stolen by those six notes which, by a naïve superimposition of images, I imagined to be sung by a Sicilian youth with a bronzed and ardent chest. And how much I felt myself refuse to surrender to the heavenly notes! It is clear that I suffered, even here, from love; but my love, transported into that intellectual order and camouflaged by sacred Love, was no less cruel.

He wrote a study on the sonatas of Bach with many literary comparisons – almost a search for equivalents, for instance between some notes from the sonata and the opening of the *Canto notturno di un pastore errante dell'Asia* ['The nocturnal song of a wandering shepherd of Asia'].[43]

With Pina he organized a little popular theatre with the boys of the village. They taught a choir old and new Friulian *villotte* [a type of traditional song]; other boys performed the dialogues in Friulano by Pasolini published in *Il Stroligùt*. Pina and a pianist played pieces of classical music. Rico De Rocco painted the backcloths. Thus a show was mounted – *An Afternoon of Art* – which was put on in front of the peasant public – twice in the little theatre of the nursery school in Casarsa and once in the one in Zoppola.

I felt the need of a more direct contact with rustic customs and rustic life, with the 'parish pump' and the need for a more immediate and filial expression – all things that later turned out to be mistaken and which in any case amount to a brief period. This experience – a sort of dialectal one – helped me however to identify better what Casarsa stood for and to locate its virtues . . .

(*Quaderni rossi* of 1946)

41

To make him feel the need for identification with the world of Casarsa there was also the war with its alienating terrors; and the desire in the moments of calm to feel popular strength and merriment spread – something of which these *spectaculs* [performances] were in those years the humble banner, events in popular life which at last illuminated one of Pasolini's inclinations:

. . . The quality Pasolini possessed in rare measure was therefore not humility but something much more difficult to discover: love of the humble and what I should like to call competence in humility . . .

(G. Contini)

Every so often Guido managed to get letters to his mother signing himself, as a precaution, Amelia:

My thoughts return with a strange insistence to Pier Paolo – in the last days too I have thought intensely about him . . . what is he doing? Why does he never write to me? Sometimes I am obsessed by the idea that he thinks of me with a certain bitter irony. It makes me shudder. Is it possible that I should suffer like this, so much?

I got the book. I am very pleased with it, send me another and above all, if you can, something written by Pier Paolo.

It seems so unreal to me to find myself sitting here among friendly faces after such wanderings. But it will be a brief parenthesis. I am free until tomorrow just after midday. Up there where 'I have decided' to go in for winter sports it will snow in a few days; I have an absolute need of winter gear – jumpers, a balaclava, woollen gloves, stockings and another pair of boots (the ones I have are in a pitiful state). So either you or Giannina along with Signorina Pina should bring all these things you know where as soon as possible! The journey presents no difficulties for a woman.

Pier Paolo should keep calm . . .

Between September and October the bands of the Fascist army with their threats of death for those who did not report to join up, the air-raids which came now almost daily and a sweep by the Germans which kept the village in a state of siege for some days, made the Pasolinis decide to take refuge permanently in Versuta. Before moving Susanna and Pina Kalč went up into the mountains to find Guido who had assumed the *nom de guerre* of Ermes in memory of Ermes Parini.

After this meeting, which was to be the last, he wrote other letters which, passing from hand to hand, reached Versuta clandestinely:

Dearest Fatty,

At last I have got round to you with my famous smile on my lips.

I have a feeling of well-being and peace in my whole body. In fact I am sitting among dear friends (whom you know well and who have been extremely nice to me, which has embarrassed me a great deal because I have become very primitive and rough), etc., etc.

If it was up to me – you must believe me – I would write to you every day but I have been forbidden by the 'doctor' ('the doctor' who's not a doctor). I got Pier Paolo's letter. It gave me great peace of mind; I am really very grateful to him for it. The poem interpreted in an extraordinary way my state of mind on certain windy days tempered by the sun. I was up there on a high peak and under me was the plain all the way down to the sea, to Istria, and the villages (the roofs of the houses – red) lay thickly on the plain which was still green (but a pale green). With eager eyes I followed the white bed of the Tagliamento. At a certain point the countryside became obscured in a thin blue mist. You were perhaps there thinking of me. Ask Pier Paolo to write again when he has time – it gives me great joy.

On 27 November (1944) Guido wrote to Pier Paolo a letter* which was to remain the most important document about his hardships and about the happenings which were to become known as 'The Events at Porzus'.

Dearest Pier Paolo,

What I shall write in this letter will amaze you. 'But it has nothing to do with me!' you will say at the end, making a disconsolate gesture with your hands . . . I entirely agree. But since a very painful and serious situation produces a state of mind which makes one feel the absolute necessity of confiding in someone and besides we are convinced that you could be a great help to us with an article or two and on the other hand, having been authorized to do so, I shall inform you forthwith of our situation as it presents itself on today's date – 27 November. Say nothing to Mamma. She would get alarmed for nothing . . .

On 7 November, the anniversary of the Russian Revolution, in all the Garibaldini units they celebrate the union which has taken place with the Slovene troops. The agreement had been signed before the famous denials!!!

---

*The bulk of the letter is an account of the difficult mountain fighting against superior German forces and of the problems arising from the political situation. The Communist partisans (Garibaldini) were allied with the Slovenes and had signed an agreement to fight under the Communist flag rather than the Italian one; Guido belonged to the Osoppo brigade which was strongly nationalist and fearful of attempts by Tito to annex Italian territory. (Translator's note)

But a large number of the Garibaldini troops did not support the agreement (which had been decided by a few men); many wept with rage and did not wish to substitute the red star for the tricolour star. Some got permission to join the ranks of the Osoppo Brigade and tell us that the Garibaldini commissars have begun a progaganda of threats among the units…

One of the clauses of the agreement with the Slovenes is the following: the Garibaldini units undertake to carry out loyal propaganda in favour of the Slovenes and to mobilize the male population in the areas under their control. Those mobilized cannot join the Italian formations but must join Slovene units.

Four days ago the famous commissar, Vanni, presents himself at our headquarters. He declares to our commander, Bolla: 'By order of Marshall Tito the 1st Osoppo Brigade must evacuate the area' (territory under Slovene influence) unless it agrees to join the Slovene formations. Things have come to a pitch – how will it end? Udine is 12 to 16 kilometres away.

Our watchword for the moment is to reply to treacherous anti-Italian propaganda with more convincing propaganda. We have among other things founded a new newspaper, *Quelli del Tricolore* ['The men of the Tricolour']. You should write some articles making our case (it's not that we are short of arguments nor do we lack 'writers'; I am convinced you could help us greatly), with some poems perhaps in Italian and Friulano (with translations), some songs to well-known melodies, also in Italian and Friulano, etc., etc.

In the articles try just to touch on the themes referred to above – you must be an Italian speaking to Italians.

I was forgetting – the Garibaldini commissars (the news comes from a source we have not checked) intend to set up the (armed) republic of Friuli – the first move towards the Bolshevization of Italy!

I am sending you a copy of the programme of the Partito d'Azione which I have joined with enthusiasm (all those whom I have got to know in the P.A. are very honest, gentle and loyal people – true Italians. Enea very much resembles Serra.)

Naturally all this has bored you very much but it is well that you should know the situation – also because I need your advice if nothing else.

I perfectly understand that very probably you will not have the time or the inclination to compile the articles referred to above, but if you do mean to write them, do it as soon as possible and give them to Berto in a sealed envelope and inform (Mamma can do it) Elda Paravano when you have handed them over and she will go and pick everything up in Udine, etc., etc.

If nothing else at least write me a line or two . . .

I kiss you with the greatest affection,

Guido

PS. Tell Mamma that in case she has anything else to send me (gloves, socks, naphthalene), she should add a tricolour scarf and a green one . . . Greetings to all and if you see Renato give him an idea of what I have written.

I haven't time to reread my letter I must leave for the mountains *immediately.*

On 16 October Susanna and Pier Paolo installed themselves in the little room at Versuta.

Our neighbours were called Ciol; they were the first to give us the joys of exile by presenting us with fruit and pork, etc. But what we found moving was the interest taken by Felice, the head of the family, a very odd big-bellied man, a past-master at telling tall stories, with the face of a poacher – archaic I would say if I might express myself in literary language – an interest which he pursued goodhumouredly but with a suggestion of terror: the homuncule, the chicken-thief whom as a boy I dreamt of at dawn. With his ogre's voice he sang for us – in these first days – the introduction to that poem which our meeting with the peasant soul was to be. An extremely difficult soul, produced by a civilization different from our own, which lives alongside us without any possibility of exchange! We approach it with too much warmth (when we manage to avoid the usual perversions based on the *Georgics* [Virgil's pastoral poems]) and it is inevitable that our loving weapons are blunted by their inveterate indifference. I have never met more coherent sceptics than the old peasants; they voluntarily abandon that form of dignity – that is to say their sceptism – only in the name of two habits which are almost a passion with them: the Church and wine. To all the rest they oppose their laughter which looks like diffidence but is merely consciousness of their own incapacity which has become a hypertrophied organ of their life. 'We are ignoramuses' – this is their montonous refrain, their recurrent, mechanical relapse. In fact their decline is rapid. At fifteen they are delightful idols, graced with instincts of modesty, with tender feelings, with inexpressible vivacity; at eighteen the charm with its promise (but one without a future) which gave them a thirst for life is already finished and their lovely timidity has taken on darker, monotonous tints. It remains for them to satisfy the curiosity of the flesh and this renders them more vulnerable; but at twenty-two the game is up – they realize that what they could know of this sweet world they have already known and they are incapable in their disillusion of finding new sources of illusion. They let themselves fall into the cynicism of 'we are ignoramuses' without moving a finger further to save themselves. And with maturity they will be able to overcome their absolute state of apathy in only two ways: with the merriment of the drunkard or the seriousness of the bigot. When I landed in Versuta from the heaven of my habitual life I did not yet know any of this. So I committed an infinity of errors; fortunately errors of this kind have no consequences and besides I redeemed myself for ever by the candour of my behaviour.

I was at the age therefore at which the young peasants begin to fall off, to lose the last stirrings of the heart and the last feelings of shyness; but I did not have enough clarity of mind to tell myself so. I was in a complete crisis and I was experiencing it without defences, because my *conscience* was taken up with sorting out other matters in my mind which at that point I had good reason to consider important – for example, poetry. That crisis was due to the loss of my virginity; now I must confess that I would be unable to give a satisfactory definition of what a man's virginity consists of, but it seems to me that it is no other than the solitude of adolescence – narcissism as a fact common to all adolescents. However much they seek the impurity of an accomplished [?] pleasure of the flesh, sometimes more sometimes less conditioned by the fantasies of an excited brain, they never manage to sin. Through the hours of important desires, in their enactment [blank] there is always an unshakable, imperturbed purity.

So I had finally sinned, had suffered that loss which is impurity; I began to become hardened. But so-called experience is merely a matter of habit; whereas inexperience, life, has inexhaustible ways of disorganizing things. The world continues to have its fascination for me but a fascination which is beginning to crumble. In fact the beauty of the countryside, of the moon, of the river, was nothing other than the transposition of the one and only beauty: the mysterious nature, of certain songs heard in the summer evenings, of certain lights (I would get up at dawn only to see the sun's pink flooding out), of certain landscapes set in an ideal frame, in a way long poetic habit had made me skilled at, was nothing other than a form of the one and only mystery. Now that I had partly gone beyond this point, now that I had thrown a glance at least behind the confines of that beauty and that mystery, nature began to withdraw, to shut itself away in its pure functionalism. This process of decomposition was long; it is only now, in the summer of 1947, that I have merely cool feelings for the fascination of the natural world but then – during the crisis – the beauties that surrounded me, modest ones it is true but, for me who had discovered them, priceless ones, began to have splendours which were more physical, more intrusive and impure. The human beauty (for me – Greek) of the boys' bodies had become as it were naturalized, with the result of rendering my desires more tenacious and imperious; in fact no relief had come my way from the famous loss of my solitude, from my miraculous experience in short. Now the necessity of love was less intense, less desperate but more dialect; I knew the taste of the beverage and was committing the sin of gluttony . . .

That solitude in which my intelligence easily triumphed over the defenceless Pina and over my friends was the situation most apt to make me worse. Naturally the worsening was only marginal; but I still blush and become furious at the thought of that victory circumstances won over me . . . Do I have to say that the result of all this was verses mediocre in their language, mediocre precisely as language, if the state of complete, internal self-identification gave me so many guarantees of being very much more than mediocre? I wrote, it is true, some good verses in Friulano but mixed with the excessive, overflowing production of a Friulano that was over-inclined to emotion.

(*Quaderni rossi* of 1947)

Pina and her relations, too, found temporary lodgings in Versuta and together with their friends, the Pasolinis, prepared themselves – giving reciprocal consolation – to face the unforeseeable, perhaps interminable risks of the last phase of the war.

While a dark series of days began which would place our whole past in a new light, while all this was happening so openly, my real (only) feeling was that of pain at the loss of the chance to meet Bruno. It was moreover a suffering to which I was [blank], around which my life was co-ordinated, the very system of my life. The interruptions of the brutal act, in which I felt brutally – almost theoretically and that is to say outside of time – the loss of what was necessary for living, no longer made me despair because of themselves but for what caused them. It was my custom to throw myself on my camp-bed with my face against the red silk of the bed-cover, which was slightly impregnated with dust; in the best of cases I succeeded in having fantasies, as in adolescence; but mostly I kept myself in the presence of my pain, which had become almost visible. Bruno was on a road which no longer crossed mine. The reconstitution of my purity came about unexpectedly. In Versuta there were about a score of children who could not because of the danger attend school at San Giovanni. I and my mother became their teachers – with what trepidation, with what real interest I prepared for that enterprise . . . I remember the first hours of school so suffused with a virginity [blank space] in which I cunningly played with enthusiasm and made of emotion some sort of rhetorical figure of speech which might serve to [blank] my discourse, which was made up of pauses, of reticences, of secret exclamations – all juices that led, in the end, to the fermentation of a deliberate note of scandal that would arouse curiosity. This tension of mine communicated itself to the scholars who for the first time tasted the ambiguous flavour of irony and with it the compelling safety of facts clearly stated. They became so enthusiastic that ours was no longer a school but a kind of literary gathering to which I offered the best of those energies that had remained pure in me. I began from pre-history. I was thinking of Vico[44] and they of certain ideal fables; thus we were in agreement, seized by an identical excitement. With calculated cunning, which was however far from cold, I underlined the insignificant details, allowed to fall into the void of stupefying indifference the essential data, played with their attention, deceived them, discouraged them in order to catch them at a moment of their attention that was still a virginal one. In short, I made my lessons almost dramatic, sometimes actually simulating unjust fits of bad temper beneath which I allowed to boil, intact, the [blank] gaiety with which I related to them. Even the arid grammar lessons had become a complicated game of those clashes (good and evil, conqueror and conquered) which the children, with their adventurous natures, never gave up even when they were eating or washing themselves.

I taught, as I have said, in our one room where they crowded round the desk and two little tables. There were eight or nine pupils and then Gianni joined them.

He was, as I was saying, a great distraction for me and ended by being a joy. I do not believe I ever gave myself to the others with such dedication as to those children (who were by the way extremely grateful for it) during the Italian and history lessons. There I introduced a kind of jargon – that of a 'clan' – made up of poetic revelations, of moral teachings (even if somewhat too liberal ones). I ended up by amusing myself greatly, even when explaining grammar! Imagine then the reciprocal enthusiasm at reading poetry – I dared to teach them (and they understood them very well) lyrics by Ungaretti, by Montale, by Betocchi . . .

An experience of absolute solitude had refined my spiritual life in an extraordinary way – when I found the mystical name for this state of interiorization of mine I began to expect Grace: that is to say, the ability to conceive of the Other, God.

(*Quaderni rossi* of 1947)

The school at Versuta and the reworking of peasant mysticism with more direct contact, the pedagogic passion for the children which in a passage that sounds sentimental became an enormous passion for two of them – metamorphoses of a crueller form of sweetness – form other stories which recur and intertwine in the hand-written pages of the *Quaderni rossi* and later were to be transfused 'with greater liberty of invention' in the pages of *Atti impuri.*

While even intimate matters changed in the setting of Versuta, impelled by the tempo of peasant life, friendship with Pina was held back by the usual uncertainties and refusals, which turned in on each other. Pina was living in a house not far off on the other side of the Viersa. Her person too continued to be present in *Atti impuri* and – with more significant implications – in the diary:

In Versuta, a tiny hamlet lost among the fields, I had entered into an inhuman condition; solitude, pride, horror of death, were a superstructure which transformed me for the worse. For this reason I made Pina suffer more than necessary. I have to add as well the recent loss of my adolescent virginity which had robbed me of much of my candour and of my desire for goodness. I remember certain terrifying evenings in which every slightest object seemed to be immersed in a funereal atmosphere. It was winter. The half-melted snow froze in the night thus imprisoning everything in a fragile dress of glass. When the last alarm had passed, we ate supper, terrified by the thought that soon we would hear the first noises of the nocturnal planes. As soon as supper was finished I went downstairs from the one room in which I lived with my mother to go into the kitchen along with the owners of the house, other evacuees and some neighbours. The women span. An oppressive and corrupt atmosphere developed in which fear of death mingled with the most banal gossip and talk that was sometimes openly obscene. Living for days and days without moving about, passing from one fit of terror to another, had made us all worse and our natural little ambitions had become miserable. Often Pina, who lived not even a hundred metres away with her sister's family, came to visit us bringing her violin. One evening I, who nevertheless loved her, anticipating her visit, went down into the kitchen earlier than usual and sat with the others near the hearth. I was in a corner and a little in the shadow and had Gianni on my knees. I was talking and laughing with him – that evening he was less wild than usual. He responded to my jokes and stared at me with those eyes of his like two turquoise lakes. She arrived; I followed her step by step, word by word, while in the room above she talked with my mother. I felt the icy coldness of her flesh, her desperation, the shadow into which she felt she was falling headlong, to drown. I imagined perfectly her fettered gestures, the excessive prudence of her talk, the smile attempted in vain for a witness who did not exist. At all events I was too tied to Gianni and pretended not to have noticed her. Gianni was tremendous with his cheeks ruddy from the fire in the hearth and his eyes which stared consciously at me. That evening I had invented a game with him which consisted of looking into each other's eyes without smiling. I was completely a prisoner of the senses. And suddenly I heard one, two chords from the Chaconne – they were from the 14th variation, plaintive, lacerating, like a human voice. Pina was calling me. I continued to look into the boy's eyes and to clasp him to my breast.

Even when she was playing Pina did not feel free of me; I require cruelty to be able to affirm this, when I think that she thought she found in music her solitude and her independence. I behaved to her in the way certain of my childhood companions had behaved to me, making me suffer with their cruelty at certain 'breaks' of theirs – outside my life – when I saw them eating a snack or laughing with relatives who made me shy: all things by means of which they kept the mystery halfway between annoyance and absentmindness. But I was too involved in the difficulty of living from one hour to the next, with the threatening uncertainties of my existence. (I wondered – very rarely – how I might judge my conduct from the point of view of the Church. It is immediately clear that I would have to get to the bottom of this question, to the elementary level; and there I would at once declare my sympathy for the Christianity of St Augustine, omitting without many scruples the Catholicism of the Counter-Reformation and Thomism . . . In a state of mystical nudity, that nakedness of the spirit which inspires terror, I would perhaps be able to find some way of justifying myself: I had to sin – that is follow the Christian road backwards. It is well known that the convert normally has a point to overcome – the state of guilt. I would have two of them in order to arrive from a forced innocence to a voluntary innocence. It is enough to discourage one.) But Pina would certainly have pardoned me for my cruelty if she had been able to assess the difference between her state (in which she saw me, heard me, talked to me) and my state – a state of absolute deprivation in which from time to time treacherous chance threw into my arms a [illegible] phantom.

(*Quaderni rossi* of 1947)

## 1945

On 2 February Guido Pasolini died in 'a fight against irregular forces'. Pier Paolo recalls his end:

In January 1945 he was with Bolla and Enea at Porzus where the Osoppo forces were reorganizing after the disastrous enemy sweep of November. Meanwhile Guido had joined the Partito d'Azione. On the day when Bolla and Enea were murdered he was at Musi with his friend D'Orlandi, on some mission or other, and they were returning together towards Porzus.

Suddenly some of their comrades (who being stationed in an Alpine meadow further down had seen the act of treachery and were withdrawing) warned the two boys of the danger. But the latter did not wish to think of turning back and instead rushed towards Porzus to bring help to their friends . . . I often think of that piece of road between Musi and Porzus which my brother went along on that tremendous day; and my imagination is made radiant by some sort of burning whiteness of snow, by some purity of the sky. And the person of Guido is so alive.

Guido and his comrades were killed by Italian partisans backed by the Slovenes. After trying to absorb the remains of the Ossopo Division, which had been decimated by the enemy sweep, into the Garibaldi Division these Communist partisans then decided to abandon their opposition to the plan to annexe the territory of Friuli to Slovenia.

Guido's fate was to remain unknown for many weeks after the end of the war – until the first vague news of the events, still veiled by much reticence.*

Susanna, who woke at dawn all that winter, heard a tit singing and dreamed that this song was bringing her news of her son's imminent return.

On 18 February, the Academiuta di lenga furlana was founded at Versuta. Its members were the friends Cesare Bortotto, Pina Kalč and Rico De Rocco, together with a group of students some of whom had been at the little school in Casarsa. The badge was a sprig of corn with the motto: O cristian furlanut/ plen di vecia salut [Oh Christian little Friuli/full of old health]. The poetic language adopted was western Friulano with a spelling which made changes in that laid down in the written tradition. Later Contini advised against this and it was quickly dropped.

'The absolute essence of the Friulian spirit, the Romance tradition, the influence of contemporary literature, freedom, imagination' were some of the aesthetic starting-points of *félibrisme*[45] in Casarsa. The meetings took place every Sunday in the little room in Versuta and each of the academicians read his latest poems; Pina played the violin and Pier Paolo reads verses from a poem in *ottava rima, Il Tancredi* – one of the many works that ended up in the familiar chest.

But what lovely Sundays we passed that winter and spring thanks to Friulian poetry and Pina's music. I and my cousin Nico** remember them, I hope, as the most beautiful we ever spent (in spite of the fact that every time we could reckon on at least six dangers to life, accurately counted, imminent and capable of happening from hour to hour). We met in my

---

* This event is still (1992) a debated and delicate topic in Italian politics. (Tr.)
** Editor of the Italian edition and author of this introduction. (Tr.)

room or in the Cicutos' little back kitchen, where our friends were lodged, or, finally, in the hut where I taught.

No one can drive out of my mind what this *Decameron*[46] of ours was like or, more concretely, the [illegible] of that den of mine where we were able to take refuge and upon which not even the echo of those tremendous explosions, which shook the earth day and night, impinged. We argued about music, about poetry; but with extreme gaiety, with much laughter, with many interruptions to talk maliciously about our mutual bourgeois friends in Casarsa. We helped each other greatly, Pina and I, to find a way into the cluttered heart of the peasants whose guests we were; it is strange – this is what we talked about above all. In matters of poetry I was the accepted guide and I loved to talk about it because while usually my shyness (caused by my melancholy) makes me speak badly, when I am happy on the other hand I possess all the elements of eloquence – I even become brilliant. I like to remember those poetical meetings of ours as a kind of Arcadia or, with much joy, a kind – in truth a very rustic one – of literary salon. Just think that it was on one of these Sundays that our Friulian *félibrige* was born! At these meetings there was my cousin Nico who came from the mill at San Giovanni where he is evacuated with his family; braving by no means negligible dangers on a long stretch of road, he would arrive calmly with his black overcoat and Ungaretti under his arm. He was only sixteen at the time and at the fullness of his tranquil precocity; his readings of his own poems (which were not in the least boring as adolescents' poems usually are) formed one of the most serene moments of our meetings. There were Ovidio Colussi and his brother Ermes, belonging to that race of strongly Catholic 'small landowners' which is so uneasily settled at Casarsa – two sensitive and open boys; there was De Rocco, my old friend from San Vito and a solid painter, and many other students. The joy with which we met therefore gave a particular stamp to our Sunday noonday meetings, which was quite simply moving; and all this confirms for me once more that I would live (oh, this conditional tense) in a state of unchanging gaiety.

On 5 March a night bombing raid caused half the houses in Casarsa to collapse and the Colus house was also half destroyed.

With the good weather the little school at Versuta moved to a hut in the middle of the fields.

It was very small and there was scarcely room for us; but often we went to have classes on the grass under two enormous pines barely brushed by the winds. Now everything about that time seems perfect to me – even the air-raids (protected by my presence the children were amused by the frightening circling of the fighers, and tremendously excited by the blows which shook the roots of the countryside; Ponte, Madonna di Rosa and Casarsa, which was so close at hand, were continually hit, destroyed, struck by the bombs whose plumes of smoke obscured the horizon). I don't even find unpleasant the memory of the formations of bombers which at least seven times bombed Casarsa, little more than a kilometre from us, under our very eyes – and we looked on from the door of our little school. But beginning in January we rehearsed together for a performance of a dramatic fable by me, *I fanciulli e gli elfi* ['The children and the elves'], which we kept promising (and I leave you to imagine their passionate [blank space], to put on after the war. Gianni, Pina's nephew, Alfredo and Cesare Spagnol, were the children. Beppino, Dante Spagnol and Tonuti were the elves. I was going to play the Ogre.

Pina, after taking part in the *spectaculùs* at Casarsa, collaborated in setting-up this children's theatre; and this memory prompted another in the *Quaderni rossi*, leading to a further attempt to describe their sentimental relationship.

She was very intelligent and expert but she still had the spirit (or the body?) of a girl. By now the common terms of sensible or not sensible, of naïve or confused, no longer applied to anything she did to enter my life. One evening she handed me a letter in which she declared her love. It was not a common love letter. She had learned from me a kind of literary Italian from the number of poetry readings we had done together; she spoke of me, of my body, as I might have spoken of a youth who disturbed me. She spoke of my brow . . . I did not reply to that letter for this reason: I imagined that she knew how useless that letter had been and therefore thought of it – as I did – as some sort of a way of comforting herself. But 'useless' in two senses – first because the love she declared to me I already knew of; second, because I could never have returned it. She suffered terribly because I not only did not reply to it but behaved as if I had never received it. But this is certain – that she did not repent nor [space] for having handed these pages to me. It was a gesture like all the others she made to me – a gesture suddenly carried off by a wind and cast away behind us.

Other pages of the *Quaderni rossi* go back over the first months of 1945:

I lived with the continual risk of losing my life – for several months it appeared *certain* that to emerge alive from that hell was only an absurd hope. This gave me a continual sense of my dead body – something that certainly did not have a beneficial effect on the development of my inner life, which had become paralysed. It is at this time that I had the sense of that threshold beyond which there was no longer myself but another. Such was my religious crisis (not that earlier naïvely Pascolian and aesthetic one of 1943) that it led me to feel *hic et nunc* – as the existentialists say – that in these months I had rediscovered one might say the meaning of the word 'mystical'. This will be understood better if one bears in mind the real solitude in which I lived; since my thoughts could not achieve any sort of resolution they piled up on each other forming a kind of humus where I lost the feeling for reality; which is moderation and resignation (and also hypocrisy). I was excessive in everything.

It was a real sickness of the spirit – but my spirit was extraordinarily refined by it. I passed hours in front of a leaf or a hand in order to understand them, that is to cross the threshold or the suture where I ended and the other began: the leaf, the tree trunk. I did not think directly about God but about the Other – something much more important to me. With the discovery of this new dimension I ended up by believing in miracles and prophecy.

The end of the war increased the anxiety about Guido of whom all news had been lacking for many weeks and this period also brought – as if life had a false bottom – happiness in the form of love for another boy from Versuta.

At the end of May the official news of Guido's death arrived and a memorable polemic over the 'massacre of Porzus' immediately began – one which was transferred to the law courts with two trials, one in Brescia, the other in Lucca, held to pass judgement on the guilt of the murderers.

Susanna and Pier Paolo stayed shut up in the house for some days; the whole village lived through their sorrow and each family sent its children to bring baskets of food and other presents. Guido was to be buried at Casarsa on 21 June.

I have decided to write today about the happiest period of my life; it merges in my lonely memory with the innocent splendour of the moon flooding the fields at Versuta and San Giovanni. This memory is the most confused of all my affair with T. I do not remember whether those evening walks took place before May (all that happiness is naturally set against the horrors of the war which had reached its peak) or after May (that happiness would be irreconcilable with the death of Guido). I no longer remember if they were repeated often or if not more than three or four times; I cannot make out whether T. had already been mine or not yet . . . Those walks of ours to the first houses of San Giovanni, close together (T. used to rest his head on my shoulder), represent the symbol of a happiness that lacked perfection but for that very reason was all the more exciting.

(*Quaderni rossi* of 1947)

After some days of mourning Susanna and Pier Paolo resumed their lessons with the pupils and, on the grass by the hut, the rehearsals for *I fanciulli e gli elfi*. Two years later he wrote in the *Quaderni rossi*:

> I certainly do not dare to speak of our mourning faced by which I still feel an insurmountable difficulty – that of infinity. Yet as happens – although it may seem absurd and cruel – we continued to teach our pupils from Versuta, which was a distraction. I loved these boys very much; they in their turn had become passionately fond of me.

While the rehearsals for *I fanciulli e gli elfi* continued the old choir of children from Casarsa was being reorganized under Pina's guidance with a view to the forthcoming performance which was to be divided into two parts: the Casarsa choir and the show by the children from Versuta.

They rehearsed the scenes, the costumes, the make-up, and in July the play had its first performance in the little theatre in the nursery school at Casarsa, which had remained intact among the ruins of the other houses, and then in the one at San Giovanni. The second performance was more beset with difficulties than the former because Pier Paolo barely managed to keep Pina who, having received an offer of work in Yugoslavia, wanted to leave as soon as possible. 'She wanted to rid herself of that burden I represented in her life, of that cancer, born in my body, in my eyes perhaps, which had slowly spread over the whole landscape and all the people of Versuta.'

From the time Pier Paolo's new love became obvious to Pina, there were no more restraints or distractions to make their relationship tolerable.

> I was used to hating myself, so much so that there was no difference in time between my hating and pitying myself: the two things happened at once. What I naturally made a display of was my innocence (an imprecise, diffuse innocence which had remained from the time of my virginity or, rather, from the time of my adolescence) while I hid the rottenness. (Only women sense this rottenness and do not allow themselves to be greatly moved by my boyish charm . . .)
>
> The ignorance of Pina, who was nevertheless so expert and 'civil' concerning my true state of [space], unexpectedly awoke in me feelings, fears, prejudices which I had thought by now were dead within me. I rediscovered the meaning of the word 'corruption'; I could reexamine my probable future and that of that boy. I was terribly alarmed by it. Up to then I justified myself by saying to myself that my sin was in me before I was born, that it was unfair that I should have to pass my life alone . . . But from that moment these two arguments did not seem sufficient to me because they did not also take into account T.'s life. I am not the only living person

in the world. Then T. fell ill and I was so terrified by this that, for the first time for many years, I was seized by qualms about God.

Merely seeing T. ill, I thought inexorably of God's presence. I saw things rushing down a slope angled with such precision and coherence that I had no doubt that this was due to divine supervision. It was neither goodness nor justice, it was pure destiny, logic. T. had to be delivered from the incredible [?] guilt into which he, who was so healthy and religious, had been dragged by my passion. And God was freeing him by making him die, by taking him from me, but without rejoicing at it.

I behaved with Pina like a character in a play who already knows his future. Whereas she – even in the last months when she knew of my love for T. – that is to say, when she lost any possible hope – continued to need to have me give her long, detailed explanations, to need me to speak to her with tact, and to need me to declare all my feelings to her.

In short she wanted something from me – if only my gratitude. One day when she already knew everything, she went to the length of proposing to me that she should become my shield against people's gossip. It is not possible to imagine a more absolute and impossible sacrifice. Had I been more hypocritical I would not have held back the tears which shone in my eyes at that proposal. But in this case too I left it to her to imagine.

Pina left at the end of July and shortly after her relatives followed her. In August the first number of *Il Stroligùt* appeared; the numbers started from the beginning again to distinguish it from the two preceding issues of *Stroligùt di cà da l'aga*, being thus the first of the publications inspired by the new principles of the Academiuta di lenga furlana, which were proclaimed with the appearance of this issue. Besides the poems and prose of the usual contributors, translations into Friulano of Tommaseo, Wordsworth, Verlaine and Jimenez were included.

In the same period the collection *Poesie* appeared; it began the series of 'diaries' in Italian verse: a little volume printed – like the review and the following little volumes, at the author's expense – in 105 copies, none of them for sale, plus a score intended for his closest friends with an appendix of three love poems to the boy from Versuta.

In September he was in Bologna, staying with Serra, for the last examinations at the university; on 26 November he graduated *magna cum laude* having defended his thesis on Pascoli: 'An Anthology of Pascoli's Lyrics: Introduction and Commentary'.

In Bologna he met up with Carlo Alberto, back from prison in Kenya, and together, after the graduation, they returned to Versuta. Old Pasolini – 'a powerless tyrant' – reembraced his wife and settled down to live in the new situation, exchanging the prisoner-of-war camp for Versuta, to all intents and purposes another prison. His physique was beginning to feel the effects of so many years of strictly circumscribed life and of the adulterated whisky drunk in prison. The hardships of the war, his sorrow at Guido's death, all had forced on him comparative resignation.

Immediately after his return the Pasolini family moved to the rooms Pina and her relatives had occupied to wait – it was to take two years – for the house in Casarsa to be rebuilt.

The peasant world of the post-war years was still much the same as it had been a century or two earlier, with a few superficial changes brought by the new times. Each village has its dancing booth where they danced boogie-woogie and slow waltzes, and the young people went from one festival to another as if they wanted to make up for lost time. Little groups formed for evening expeditions which met other groups in a chain of Sunday happiness. The group from Versuta, composed of some grown-up schoolboys and other youths from the village, never set out without Pier Paolo. They cycled to San Giovanni but then went further afield to more distant villages. The 'native, collective *eros*' was everywhere, jubilant and late at night drunk, on the way home on the frozen roads.

Sometimes the evening trips were extended as far as Udine to see the first neo-realist films; *Roma città aperta*[47] was for Pier Paolo 'a trauma which I still remember with emotion'.

At the beginning of autumn, in the council chamber at Casarsa, rehearsals began for a comedy in Friulano, *La Morteana* [a folkdance], which was never to be performed because of various technical difficulties.

On 30 October he joined the Association for Friulian Autonomy.

By setting up that region on the borders of Austria and Yugoslavia the frontiers would be strengthened and not weakened. There is in fact no one who does not see how a Friuli stronger ethnically and linguistically (were its dignity recognized and consecrated in practice) would be much more solid, more Friulian and therefore more Italian, than an anonymous, drifting Friuli, lacking in consciousness and corrupted by the Veneto . . . There is no better course than to oppose to the sly spread of Slav influence a Friulian Region, conscious of itself, electrified by the dignity conferred on it as a right by its language, its customs, its economy, which are all clearly differentiated.

With the end of the war the correspondence with his friends in Bologna – Serra, Farolfi, Silvana Mauri – resumed, and that with some Friulian writers began – the Gorizian poet Franco De Gironcoli, Mario Argante in Udine, the philologist Gianfranco D'Aronco and his contemporary, Sergio Maldini, writer of short stories and novels.

Silvana had moved to Milan where she was working in the publishing house of her uncle, Valentino Bompiani. Urged by Silvana, Bompiani became interested in Pasolini's poetical work and, at the end of the year, Pasolini sent him a new manuscript of *Poesie a Casarsa*, 'corrected and twice as large'.

With the beginning of the new school year some pupils from Versuta enrolled in the local schools but most of them finished their studies and went to work in the fields with a great feeling of nostalgia for their companionship with their teacher. Tonuti Spagnol remembers:

> We were still young lads when the war set the frontiers of Friuli on fire and the schools were deserted because of the bombing. Pasolini, who was evacuated too among the rustic families of Versuta, collected us in a little hut which served as classroom, lost and hidden in the green fields. Without any means, helped by his mother, he taught us in a wise way, not only as schoolmaster but as a friend who wanted to save us from the fate of ignorance. We will always remember him among the fields of Versuta or in that wild classroom which was tamed into being a nest of culture.[48]

## 1946

In January there appeared under the imprint of the Editions of the Friulian Academy the little volume *I Diarii* ['Diaries']. Montale chose a text from it and reprinted it in *Il Mondo* [a literary and political weekly] in Florence while the wait for a reply from Bompiani about the *Poesie a Casarsa* became prolonged into a tacit rejection.

In the same month he wrote to Contini asking him for permission to reprint the old review of *Poesie a Casarsa*. It appeared in No 2 of the *Stroligùt* with a note: 'This article, which appeared in the *Corriere del Ticino* on 24 April 1943, is reprinted here in its entirety; but we should like Friulians to take more interest in its convincing discussion of the prehistory and possible future history of a literature of our own rather that in the lines which concern the *Poesie a Casarsa*.'

In an appeal 'To the Friulian reader' the little story of the Casarsa reviews was recalled; there followed the news of the founding of the Academy, with the new programme designed to extend its philological and poetic interests to other minor Romance languages, along with renewed confirmation of Friulian autonomy as a problem 'strictly connected with the poetic one'. And finally: 'In this volume, which is no longer reserved for the reader in Casarsa or Friuli, we announce that our Academy is named after a martyr, Guido Pasolini, killed when he was not yet twenty on the mountains of Venezia Giulia, who is an example to us of inconsolable heroism, of mute enthusiasm.'

Immediately the small volume appeared Carlo Alberto set in train work for the construction of a small hall on the ground floor inside the walls of the house in Casarsa, which was to become the seat of the Academy.

In April, for the first time after the war, Pier Paolo was in Rome as guest of Gino Colussi, his mother's brother. From Rome he wrote to his mother and to Tonuti and all the trip was nostalgically linked to what he had left behind at Versuta.

Upon his return, he began to hope for the promised visit by Contini.

In May he began to write the *Quaderni rossi.*

The first opens with a dedicatory letter 'To Stendhal': 'Dear Sir, exactly one hundred and sixteen years have passed since 1830, that is to say, a period of time sufficient to make the events of that epoch appear ridiculous to our eyes...'

There are three pages, immediately crossed out, which end like this: 'May the date and the place where these lines were written tell you through an allusion, the tragic significance of which you cannot grasp, how worthless they are and how much loneliness they presuppose. Casarsa, 20 June 1946.'

The fourth page opens with a title in capital letters, 'PAGINE INVOLONTARIE (romanzo)' ['INVOLUNTARY PAGES (novel)'], and a date intentionally left incomplete: 23 May 19 . .

There follows the diary which takes up the three successive notebooks (the fourth has writing only on the first four pages), dated from May 1946 to 8 August 1947: 'Diary which I write against my will (would that this, nothing else, were the divine punishment).'

At the beginning of the fifth notebook there is another title in capitals: 'IL ROMANZO DI NARCISO – terza parte – CON ALCINA' ['THE NOVEL OF NARCISSUS – part three – AND ALCINA'], and the date 7 October 1947. These five notebooks are, admittedly with a few disguises – such as their definition as a novel and the names of places and persons sometimes given initials – Pasolini's sentimental diary for the years 1946 and 1947 with recollections of infancy, of the first years at Casarsa, of the war, of evacuation to Versuta and of the death of his brother Guido. Most of the pages set down the reality of the moment:

*24 May 1946.* It is striking midday. The low grey clouds allow feeble beams to escape. How often in my life I have found myself in a condition like this. My head tired with too much reading, my senses full of the smell from the kitchen, the sky and the countryside which stretch all round with a heavy and colourless veil. It is horrible: like a flash an association passes through my mind – the title of the book on the crumpled cover (*Sagesse*) [by Verlaine], Sunday, my friendship with some young peasants. Is this what my life is made up of? Fortunately it is not possible to distinguish or isolate every fact – much remains confused in the trusting mystery which, hurriedly and only to ourselves, we call 'my existence' or, more simply, 'I'.

*31 May.* There is no longer anything irrational in my life except the links between the things that constitute it. I listen to the confused voices in the courtyard, the occasional shouts, the delicate song of the birds, which weave a continuous, pleasant murmur. I hear within me an entirely intellectual thought. Then T.'s voice calling me; I see him from the window, he is pale and melancholy, with his books under his arm; today his mouth is too like his mother's. It is more than a year since . . . He is almost sixteen. How can these things co-exist?

*1 June.* What a perfect day! I have confused my fleeting calm with the calm of the created world. Was it not a chance that I was on the bank of the river – the waterless river, a whole boundless scorching bed of gravel? I was lying naked on the cement of the bank. The [blank] solitude had slowly torn me away from any human norms. I was mad; that is certain and I savoured, gesture by gesture, my calculated madness. I could cry out loud 'Scarlet flowers . . .' and get up, make my way along the bank between ocean-wide stretches of grass. I began to pick flowers. 'Here is my poetry,' I thought. I pulled every tiniest leaf from the stalks so that the pure flower remained at the top. First I chose red and violet flowers. Then I decided to disturb their rocky perfection by mixing with them yellow and white.

*2 June.* This continuous road takes me into the heart of what from time to time we call 'the present'. Now I am so far into my life that to see its horizons I have to get on tiptoe. Besides nothing touches any more 'this exceedingly indifferent "I" of mine' (Foscolo).[49]

A festival at San Giovanni, a crowd of familiar faces. In Casarsa, which is half-empty, its ruins rising against the stormy sky, absolute boredom . . .

Now in my gloomy room I hear the groaning of a pump which is drawing laborious jets of water from the earth. It is the only sound; it is joined by lowing and a tiny noise of chains from a byre.

It is raining as if in autumn. Perhaps I shall not be able to go to the dance. Yet I am light, sociable – even in this inhuman boredom – and I feel that in me [blank space] of my nature, which was originally calm and almost gay. I hear from the courtyard the usual voices, which in the silence have a sidereal sound – the sound of other worlds. Now the light, the [blank space] of the rain, the voices of the people at supper, link me to an infinite number of similar hours in my past and suddenly the image of T. presents itself to me with immeasurable sweetness. What can I recall of him? We have lived together too much – really too much; I cannot risk attempting a memory. There is such a sense of the absolute and the unique in our friendship that by retracing some details of it I would risk ruining it.

Certainly, over everything, his innocence floats like a vision of snowy mountains above the plain – that innocence which shows itself above all in his face when he smiles at himself.

In August he was in Macugnaga, the guest of the Mauris who asked him to be there to exert an influence on the state of mind of his friend Fabio, who was wracked by a religious crisis. '. . . It is true, he had been the occasional special envoy to anxious families, rejected by me each time as the representative of secular ambition' (F. Mauri).

From Macugnaga he continued through the Dolomites to meet Gianfranco Contini:

> . . . he came to visit me for the first time, if I recall rightly, in 1946 (long after the caesura produced in his life, which was full of tragedy, by the death of this brother Guido, murdered in the partisan war; and this time too what brought him was a dramatic event – namely, a visit to a mentally ill friend in the neighbourhood of my city). I do not think I have ever seen such a display of shyness – so much so that at a certain moment, to ease the burden of the conversation (we were in my house in the country), I proposed to him to explore our natural surroundings – surroundings which today have greatly deteriorated ecologically but were then still unspoilt. At that time I was unable to understand it exactly – and basically I understand it fully only now when a total balance can be drawn up; but either chance or instinct had suggested to me the solution most suited to Pier Paolo's extraordinary virtue, which was the love of the humble and the authentic – and such was the landscape that surrounded us; 'if, having spent there a large part of my childhood and boyhood as well as the autumn holidays of my first youth, I did not reflect that it is impossible to pass a dispassionate judgement on the places with which the memories of these years are associated . . .'*
>
> (G. Contini)

Contini put him in contact with the Catalan poet Carles Cardó, whom Pasolini asked to undertake a short anthology of Catalan poetry to be published in the next number of the review of the Academiuta, the title of which changed from *Stroligùt* to *Quaderno romanzo* ['Romance journal'] to indicate a programme not only of poetry but also of philology covering all the minor languages of the Romance-language territory. And in fact, immediately after the Catalans and still with Contini's help, he tried to make contact with the Romansch poets of the Grisons in order to recreate at the heart of his

---

* A quotation from Nievo, a nineteenth-century author with Friulian connections.

review that ideal and abstract region of Ladin languages defined by Ascoli. While he sent Contini the typescript of the Friulano poems which made up the *Poesie a Casarsa* in the twice-as-big version, towards the end of the year he entered for the poetry competition of the Lugano daily *Libera Stampa* – Contini was one of the judges – the Italian collection *L'usignolo della Chiesa Cattolica*, with its second part, *Il pianto della rosa* ['The tears of the rose'], also complete.

Still in 1946 he wrote a three-act drama, *Il cappellano* ['The chaplain'], which he sent to Contini to read the following year, saying that he hoped some man of the theatre would stage it. This drama was eventually staged in 1965 under the title *Nel 46* [In 1946] as a *répêchage* of acts of imagination which had had their day.

The poetry publications of the Academiuta and the theoretical propositions which underlay them aroused – as well as support – the first polemics in the cultural life of Udine, which had not greatly changed since Pasolini cast a glance at it in 1943, devoting a few lines to it in an article which appeared in *Il Setaccio*:

No one could claim that the Friulian capital can boast of being, culturally, an outpost of the avant-garde, with its meagre and backward group of literary figures (who go on putting forward in the *Popolo di Friuli* [a local paper] their thin and confused ideas) and with its old philological centre which has outlived a rigorous tradition and is now at a low ebb.

For the moment these polemics centred on the symbol represented by Pietro Zorutti,[50] the eighteenth-century poet from Udine who was very dear to vernacular ears. Pasolini did not refuse the task of evangelizing with gentle tenacity and, while he debated on the one hand the rational bases for Friulian administrative autonomy against the sentimental, regressive claims of local prejudice, on the other he asserted the poetical progress made by the *félibrisme* of Casarsa as compared to the vernacular traditions.

On 31 December an article published in the daily of the CLN [Comitato di Liberazione Nazionale (Committee of National Liberation)] in Udine, *Libertà*, dedicated precisely to the question of autonomy, opened with this declaration: 'We too being Communists . . .' The Communist Party branch in Udine immediately published a statement which, while expressing its pleasure at this declaration, pointed out that Pasolini was not a member of the Party. His formal membership took place some months later – probably at the beginning of 1948.

If the district of Casarsa remained the linguistic base for his poetic language, Pasolini had picked up the variations in local speech throughout the district of western Friuli, from village to village, from hamlet to hamlet, in which the varying temperament, physiognomy and social conditions of the peasant world of the small proprietors and the agricultural labourers were mirrored. This world, after having surrendered some of its mysteries to be reflected poetically, now presented itself once more in its social reality as well – one where the class struggle had begun after the war. It found Pasolini totally unprepared politically but, unlike other intellectuals, he had an extraordinary understanding and experience of the differing modes of existence – in terms of mentality, spirit, sexuality – of the peasants of Friuli. Faced by this class war, which would never assume dramatic forms because of an old tradition of submissiveness which limited the ability to rebel of even the youngest peasant, the old cultural and aesthetic anti-Fascism of Pasolini was complicated by a new passion which came to be defined as populist and humanitarian, a passion which had roots going far back to his earliest childhood, to his rivalry with his father and with all the petty bourgeois world. 'My hatred for the bourgeoisie cannot be documented or questioned, it is what it is.' And this passion, even if it could act only externally, was made authentic and validated by love for and knowledge of humble people – by that populism, in short, which Pasolini many years later continued to feel positively as the initial impulse for a future history: 'For me populism and humanitarianism are two real facts in history . . . they are simply parts of an inevitable transition of the middle class into which one is born and in which one is formed, to the adoption of a different ideology, the ideology of a different social class.' From this there sprang an increased poetic dedication which led to greater political involvement.

The big occasions were still the summer ones when the trips to the Tagliamento started again along with the rambles on bicycles from one village to another along the infinite dusty roads of the countryside, following voices, names, presences, each of which added a perspective and a meaning to the great design of reality. It was a condition that exhausted him happily with complicated situations – an all-pervasive condition but also a bored one, fearful at any symptoms of change, of novelty, patient enough to endure the harshest truths. Poetic language and political consciousness had the same strong impulse and the same sense of direction – to determine the future.

His break with the dullest circles in Friuli did not lack support, even from those historians of the language and its traditions who were grouped round the Friulian Philological Society and its periodical bulletin *Ce Fastu?* – Gianfranco D'Aranco for one and poets like Franco De Gironcoli who became known after the war and who were later invited to contribute to the Casarsa reviews. Pasolini also became friendly with other young writers in Italian – the poet Dino Menichini, the narrative writers Sergio Maldini and Elio Bartolini. He got to know the painters Anzil and Giuseppe Zigaina with whom he also had in common his new political commitment. In this period he became active as a journalist – he was to become increasingly prolific in the following years – on the themes of autonomy, of Italian and Friulian poetry, on social developments, along with his first examples of narrative. He finished the first two *Quaderni rossi* which traced the outline of the novel *Atti impuri*, a diary of his love affairs in Versuta which was already intensely narrative;

> ... the spring earth may be flowering or caught in the grip of the winter frost or shaken by bombing – love affairs remain the only reality with their 'tremendous' (the adjective continually recurs) unfolding of rejections and tender surrender. The result is a celebration with a noticeable pedal note of masochist moralism, but not such as to change the music of the 'unutterable magic' of pagan-catholic nights and days – which is ardently participatory and already nostalgic – in the fleeting festival of youth. The 'green heavens' or the 'green hells' ...
>
> (A. Bertolucci)

On 21 November he wrote in the second of the *Quaderni rossi*:

> Time has passed again, I am still at Versuta, day after day, increasingly 'astonished to see the general rule exemplified in my own case'.
>
> It is autumn – here is the rain sighing in the muddy courtyard, some owls which utter vague cries as they fly.
>
> Today there was a festival at San Giovanni – a gloomy mistake of a festival. And now it is night and I am in my room, desperate, no longer having the energy to think of myself, to move or to weep, because in my despair there is no longer any purity, any ingenuousness.
>
> Too often I have found myself in this state, always seeking a minimum of hope if only by abandoning myself to despair ... Now I am a desert that has been fully explored – there is no longer any means to save me. I am all conscience.

He painted some pictures and made a lot of drawings. He wrote the text of the catalogue for an exhibition of paintings by a family friend, Paolo Weiss. He published in the Editions of the Academiuta the little volume *I pianti* [The laments]. He wrote the short poem 'Europa'. In October he made a second journey to Rome where he met some writers and literary people, among them Ennio De' Concini, editor-in-chief of *Fiera letteraria* [a literary review].

This time Rome attracted him with its 'intellectual and social life which in Versuta, alas, is simply impossible'.

# 1947

On one page of the *Quaderni rossi* he drew his self-portrait as if seen through the eyes of a boy:

He was a youth of about nineteen or twenty with a navy-blue jacket – double-breasted, as I have said – and a white polo-neck. He was rather short in stature but he moved and bore himself with elegance like a well-bred person, although he laughed almost like a child with his companions. His hair was chestnut, wavy, and under the light had blond and dark lights; a strange face which, seen from the front, was almost beautiful with an affectionate and direct look in his chestnut eyes – seen from the side the face was transformed with its prominent cheekbones and its little nose – it took on the look of some sort of Pirate or Collie-dog. His voice was sweet with strange inflections which left people curious and enchanted.

Further on in the third *Quaderno* where the autobiography evolves from the period of *Atti impuri* to that of *Amado mio* ['My love'];

I am twenty-five, the age at which Gozzano[51] said farewell to youth; but I can say that I do not find myself passing through that cruel necessity [scored out] if my appearance continues to be that of an adolescent. Certainly a similar [blank] is not included in what is defined as the normal order of things; but the surreptitious sweet pleasure of my state is greatly compensated by a real sweetness – the curiosity, the availability, the lightheartedness with which [space] even in my days. If my eternal adolescence is an illness it is indeed a very slight one; the hateful side of it is its obverse – that is my contemporaneous old age. In other words the avidity with which, in the role of a young person, I devour the hours dedicated to my existence, with the result that – carrying along behind me my tender and gleaming baggage of youth – I have entered upon a stage of precocious experience and therefore of indifference. One day I said to myself that all men have an equal quantity of life before them and that therefore, since I devour it with greater avidity than some of the others, it is in the logic of things that I should die very young.

This punishment has perhaps come true – not in the body of the chronology but in its system; the present indifference caused by that operation which destroys itself and life – the experience gives me a kind of death and I am, in fact, very young. This is 1947 – this was the year in which nature would lose its value for me. Here are the veins of sand all along the interminable perspectives of the gravel which, rising towards a horizon tinged with dark blue, end up by lapping against the sky. Here, around me, is the bank with its withered grass, its dust, its poplars gasping because of the lack of breeze. All this is not sufficiently mysterious to seduce me again – it is as if I had drawn it so many thousands of times that I can repeat its forms with my eyes shut. The agitation due to the Sunday sounds of the bells, floating from the various church-towers, which rise here and there in a radius of several kilometres round the river and arrive here to echo in the immense river-bed where the blinding burden of the sun lies stagnant – that agitation is simply notional – I do not bother to take note of it. So after so many ambitions and aspirations towards the absolute I find myself becoming nothing other than a 'case' – the fame I was to have built on such a serene image of myself is stranded in this river of stones.

I am like a traveller who, having lost himself in the midst of a desert, having come to the end of his provisions and nothing being left to him but statues, finds his hunger whetted for the limbs of porphyry or alabaster.

Except for these statues of mine I no longer love anything, not even T. I have long known this, but each time I repeat to myself I have to make a great effort to overcome the resistance of my baseness. 'I do not love T.' And even this negation – rather this negation above all – is full of impurity – my lack of love for him does not seek to be such by not loving him, specially if my relationship to him has not changed, if I still ask of him loving acquiesence. No discretionary power could bring it about that anyone could conceal matters in order to defend me – everything between him and me has taken place under the sign of guilt. It is three years since I saw him for the first time on the bridge over the Viersa – two and a half year since in that [blank] hut he yielded to me, more than a year since I dared to tell myself for the first time that my love had ceased. Nevertheless I did not lift a finger to bring things to a resolution, to procure for them a moment of chastity which might end up by dominating things; I allow, on the contrary, hardened as I am in delays and equivocations, the affair to run out without the least pity, except mental pity which is silenced, for that boy who has had to bear all the burden – of which I had lost the concept – of my life in which there is no relief.

*L'usignolo della Chiesa Cattolica* after having 'warbled' on the banks of the Ceresio[52] received only one vote – the winner was Sereni[53] – but it was awarded a mention in the report drawn up by Contini. And Contini himself offered to find him a publisher, perhaps Vallecchi.

He took part in the Cesena poetry competition with the little poem 'Europa', putting his hopes on the favourable judgement of Montale, who was on the jury.

On 19 January he signed, with Gianfranco D'Aranco and others, the manifesto for the founding of the Popular Friulian Movement for Regional Autonomy.

During the 1947 carnival Silvana Mauri was a guest in the house at Versuta:

I took freezing trains to meet him at Casarsa, twelve and sometimes twenty hours of travel from Milan. I got out on to the grass of the plain, which was hard with frost, and then in his mother's warm kitchen at Versuta there were two camp-beds beside the fire. By day, drunk with happiness, winged, heedless, we cycled along the frozen banks of the Tagliamento to find some little parish cinema in the neighbouring villages or to dance with abandon (indefatigable and highly skilled dancers) tangos, polkas, fox-trots, in the popular dance-halls, or to watch the women's religious plays of Carnival (a girl dressed like a man who carried on a dialogue with a boy dressed as a woman), disturbing masks, going from house to house to drink wine and eat polenta.

I was the reflection of everything he owned and I felt I did not live in a real country but in his very heart. Even Pier Paolo was still happy then: 'Perhaps I must emerge from this ineffable (and ridiculous) serenity of mine to which the fields of Casarsa and my excessively young looks contribute.' Even his homosexuality was still a sweet affair between boys, a red notebook which stuck out of his pocket and which we played at snatching from each other. But his face was suddenly devastated by the urge to follow the clumsy movements of tender young peasant boys, the stripling 'poplars' as we called them among ourselves, as opposed to the 'king-trunks', which were the black, knotted mulberries and the black old peasants.

(S. Mauri)

They met again in Rome in mid-March but 'the sweet games between boys' confessed to in the *Quaderni rossi* had still to be spoken. With Silvana he could trust to the complicity of pure friendship and intelligence, even if precisely with her more painful questions were to arise.

How did it come about that I, a middle-class girl, without dialect, without country roots, heterosexual, and he who was then entirely taken up with Casarsa, maternal poetry, unpractised in the world, afraid of what he did not know, so afflicted by 'his unknown inner self' with his strong, brilliant mind, that of a studious student, homosexual – how did it come about that we tracked each other all our lives, writing to each other, meeting, whenever it was at all possible, being inside his life which became more and more separate from my own – his life which was frenetic with work, with a thousand other encounters, with persecutions and provocations?

Rereading his letters I now understand. Alongside his mother, the only love of his life, but a fixed and symbolical figure, which had crystallized in infancy and the childish innocence of which he always trembled to protect, I was the site 'of his vital confidence', the red thread of total acceptance.

(S. Mauri)

In Rome he met other literary people – Falqui invited him to contribute to the review *Poesia*; Giorgio Bassani[54] offered to find an editor for his poetry. He began to contribute to *Fiera letteraria*.

Whether going or coming he always stopped in Bologna – 'how beautiful and sweet it seemed to me' – to meet old friends again and to take some examinations in the faculty of philosophy in which he enrolled immediately he graduated in literature. He had in mind a thesis on 'the relationship between existentialism and contemporary poetics' but after the first examinations he broke off the course.

Then he returned to the 'gloomy' little room in Versuta. On 29 March in Venice his poem 'Vea' ('Veglia') ['The wake'] won a prize in a competition for dialect poetry from the three regions of the Veneto. He showed three self-portraits in Udine at a collective from the Veneto. In July he was in Florence for the meetings of the Youth Front [a Communist youth organization]. In the section 'Dramatic Art' he presented the first scene of the third act of *Il cappellano* himself taking the part of Eligio, the boy loved by the priest. On 18–20 August he wrote to Contini that he would perhaps enter for the competition held by *Libera Stampa* the novel *Pagine involontarie* under a different title, *Casarsa*. By this he meant the *Quaderni rossi*, which were already at a stage where they were being transcribed in a version halfway between the autograph notebooks and the text which would be published under the titles *Atti impuri* and *Amado mio*.

It was the last Versuta summer. The wing of the Colus house which had been destroyed by the bombing had been rebuilt and after three years was ready for the Pasolini family. Next door was the little hall of the Academiuta, which had already begun its cultural activities with meetings, showings of classical films, a little library; in a small display window the publications of the Academiuta were laid out. In June the *Quaderno romanzo* No 3 came out (the number followed on from the last *Stroligùt*) in which, among the texts in Friulano, there appeared the anthology of Catalan poets edited by Carles Cardó: '. . . The direction given to it . . . was something in the nature of a Félibriste International to set which up I had been a link with the Catalan poets who were still forced to be in exile . . .' (G. Contini).

Pasolini wrote in the *Quaderni rossi* of 1947:

7 *October.* Yesterday evening the boys from Versuta, my friends, came twice to call for me and not finding me set out for Rosa without me. I had been at the station in Casarsa to accompany two of my friends – the poet Menichini and the painter Zigaina – who had come to spend Sunday with me.

I had a hurried supper, I brushed my clothes and went down into the courtyard where T. and Alfredo, forgetful of their comrades, were waiting for me. We left together for the festival at Rosa. I was in one of my joyous moods when I place myself in a world which seems made especially for me – the metallic night with a moon that broke up the clouds with its pink liquids, the long road thrown across the whiteness of the dust. . . . I talked gaily to T. . . . T., prompted by some turn in the talk, suddenly remembered the day of his confirmation on which, when he came out of the church, he saw the stall with sweets, the one that comes back every year to San Giovanni for the feast of the Madonna, and bought himself a *colas* (a sweet).

'Why,' I said to him, 'don't you write a poem?'

He became confused, replying, I believe, 'I can't, I can't manage.' But I reassured him saying that, after myself and my cousin, he was the best writer of verses in Friuli. All three of us laughed about it; but I hope T. understood that I was telling the real truth. The little stall, confirmation (that is, T. as 'a child'), the *colas* . . .

Rosa was at the excited height of the festival. After crossing a bridge the road splits – the fork was at the heart of that Sunday happiness; along with the little road on the left was the big platform where they were already dancing. A mass of weak lights illuminated all that wooden stage with the couples whirling and the real crowd that pressed round the fence to watch.

Some boys seated on the fence near the orchestra had nothing seductive about them except their age. And in any case how little notice they took! You could read in their eyes the integrity and liveliness of their interests; they were violent ones. But mingling with the crowd, although alone, there was a boy whom I scarcely noticed the first time I passed close to him as I danced. The second time round he had already conquered me. I would have said he was an outsider – a Roman or (my unbridled imagination!) a boy from Syracuse . . .

My little Greek from Syracuse stood there with his elbows leaning on the fence and I understood his silence immediately. No, it was not a normal silence – it spread around him like a violet and [illegible] mist, which at once coated my heart with ice . . .

In spite of my past experiences, I did not take the advice of that silence and approached him, waiting patiently till the youth who stood beside him went away in order to take his place. He left at last because my manoeuvre aimed at and demanded it; my boy's guardian angel was perhaps absent-minded. When I was near him I too was silent and observed him. He at once felt in me the Enemy – my silence protected him like a desert at the heart of which he still attempted to invest in the dancers and the music his previous attention. Shyness became despair within him. So my little Greek was ill! But not even this discouraged me – besides all I wanted of him was to look at him . . .

Dear reader, I now find myself – in October 1947 – totally untrammelled, utterly pagan, unless having taken Angelo Dus for a boy from Syracuse is without significance. It is not true – rather than being a layman, irreligious, I am continually taken up with an interminable religious crisis. A few days ago I finished writing the last section of a book of poems, a section of which is called 'Un'anima' ['A spirit'] – I tell the angels that I mean to be left in peace, that I want to be the culprit who is unpunished and a backslider, that the intervention by the God who sends them [blank] and so if he really wants me let him make himself feared in me and not in his innocents; that if he has endowed me so greatly with enthusiasms, with credulity, with intransigence, then let him surprise me now with them; that the only thing I really fear (because my sole attention is directed elsewhere not at Him) is that when the present youthfulness and candour no longer exists in me I may lose the threads of joy, and that my ghost, my automaton, will be let loose in me – then in my life – in this life – there would be the *dies irae* for me and I would beg God only for my days, my past. All this has been written in any case with only one aim – that of obtaining *authorization*. I asked God to help me to sin! It would be a monstrous piece of naïvety if it were not so human. I am tired of being so untouchably exceptional, beyond the law. All right, I found my freedom, I know what it is and where it lies – I have known since the age of fifteen or even earlier . . . In the development of myself as individual, of my difference, I was extremely precocious and it did not happen to me (as it did to Gide) to cry out suddenly 'I am different from the others' in unexpected distress. I always knew it. Authority is what I seek now – perhaps (at least for the time being) an authorization . . . As for God he should be logical, should explain it all to me: what an effort it must be for him to think about it! I prefer to abandon the attempt to explain things to myself and to take an interest in the matter – so I fall back into the tremendous horizontality of the life of a person who resolves the innumerable facts of life not outside of but within life – perhaps in the enchantment of a 'different form', or else in the rhythm of my life which is becoming a legend. So I silence everything. I have passed after a brief visit to Calvary from the garden of infamy to the garden of Alcina[55] and I like it there.

*9 October.* Yesterday I went with Nico to Casarsa – being Wednesday there was only the cinema there and this was the pretext for our romantic evening. In fact what seduced us was the idea of the public, of the crude silence, of that oleograph of heavy and heedless love which arose from that crude audience – those boys and girls, who during the intervals sweetened their turbulence with certain splendours in their hair and certain kindnesses in their glances . . . The expectation of all this did not cause me the usual discomfort (or fear of excessive or ill-directed flutterings of the heart): I had Angelo. With Nico I could not help talking about him; I told him about my trip to Rosa and the discovery of Angelo as a painter. I was overcome with emotion as I exposed to him my hopes of making an artist of Angelo, perhaps a great one. 'My Giotto!' I exclaimed, laughing. Nico encouraged my hopes and talked to me about the way I was capable of emanating a sort of poetical game which touched certain internal chords in those close to me and aroused in its turn grace and poetical aspirations. He offered himself as an example and quoted many others. This (which is probably true) inevitably raised my secret feeling of well-being to a degree of pleasant fervour; and in that state Angelo quite simply sang and [illegible] within me.

The new accommodation in Casarsa gave a definite shape to the future.

At the beginning of the scholastic year, Pier Paolo was appointed to teach literature in the lower middle school in Valvasone, which was a detached department of the middle school at Pordenone.

From Casarsa to Valvasone was six kilometres by road, and this he travelled each day by bicycle along with his colleague Sergio Vaccher. With the boys of Valvasone Pasolini had his third experience as a teacher – this time governed by timetables and programmes under the control of the education authority. But this class, too, immediately resembled the previous groups of pupils.

Andrea Zanzotto, a colleague of these years, writes:

. . . One thinks of Pasolini in school, of his didactic passion, of his scrupulous and ardent desire to apply 'active methods' in the post-war days – the methods which may be described as those of Carleton Washburne[56] and of the Deweyite[57] 'honesty'. Drawing the attention of his colleagues to Pasolini's experiments, the headmaster whom he served under described him as 'a marvellous teacher' and always described him as such when he remembered him later. There was sadness at the thought of the enthusiasms of those times, with the motto 'education and democracy' which so many young teachers (a bicycle, one meal a day, an unheated room) shared. They were teachers who had all sorts of different approaches but who – almost astonished at receiving money from the government with which to buy themselves bread and cheese, and dazed with joy at feeling themselves alive in a Free Country – put all their energies into repaying the democratic state, born of the Resistance, in order to distribute 'active and democratic education'. To bring to life even the stiff and frozen bit of Latin grammar, to turn into real roses the *rosa-rosae* – which was so naïve – of those grammars. Pasolini tended the little garden in the schoolyard and taught the Latin names of the plants; he drew posters with coloured figures (he had always drawn and painted well – one remembers a mysterious saint) and invented fables like the one about the monster Userum, so that the boys would be amused and learn the endings of the nouns of the second declension – *us*, – *er*, – *um*. It was what was called a pedagogical vocation which flourished on the restless gifts of the young master. It was a disarmingly 'calm' pedagogical attitude. Water running down to the others, helping them but only following the slope. In that atmosphere of love – *agape, philia, eros* – on which those who write theses on the subject insist so much and which is of course necessary for pedagogy to conceal and transmit its power to subject others – which in the more 'devout' masters', that is those who had less mastery, tended to drop to zero but still persisted even if in the shape of a pointed upsilon. A love which however must spread out, persuading and involving at all levels, and which in more than one civilization was accepted even in those of its aspects which are linked to sex.[58]

He joined the Communist cell in San Giovanni.

Unlike Casarsa where small properties predominated and the peasants were strictly Catholic and divided the fruits of the fields among their children without too much hunger and poverty, at San Giovanni and in the villages round about, and still more at San Vito and its surroundings, there were large estates with share-croppers, agricultural labourers and a tiny fraction of working-class sub-proletariat. This act of joining the Communist Party, which had come about from his position as a petty-bourgeois intellectual modelling himself on Gramsci, he thought of as a hinge – a means of mediating between the classes – and it was projected on to the revolutionary perspective of the peasant world. Of that world of which he by now had so much experience and knowledge that he thought he could introduce it into the heart of his universal theories without trying to hide its sentimental side, which bound together reality and his dream of this world.

To anyone who reminded him of his brother's death at the hands of Communists he replied with a knowing silence. It was his deepest conviction that that death remained something exceptional, alien to the logic of everyday facts where Communism was the only thing 'capable of providing a new "true" culture which is both a moral system and a total interpretation of existence'.

Many years later, in 1971, he recalled once more the exceptional nature of the events which led up to the murder of his brother and his idealistic, intransigent world:

> I believe there is no Communist who can disapprove of the work of Guido Pasolini. I am proud of him, of his generosity, of his passion, which obliges me to follow the path I follow. That his death should have happened thus, in a complex situation which it is clearly difficult to judge, does not cause me to hesitate. It merely confirms me in the conviction that nothing is simple, nothing happens without changes and suffering; and that what counts above all is the critical lucidity which destroys words and conventions and goes to the bottom of things, into their secret and inalienable truth.

He contributed to various regional dailies – *Libertà, Il Mattino del Popolo, Il Messaggero Veneto*, with short stories, reviews, linguistic notes; to the *Fiera letteraria* with reviews of books. He published in Number VIII of *Poesia* the essay 'Sulla poesia dialettale' ['On dialect poetry']. *L'usignolo della Chiesa Cattolica* was completed with its third part 'Lingua' ['Language']. The book of Friulian poetry, enlarged with his most recent lyrics, was now called *Ciants di un muart* [*'Songs of a dead man'*]. In July he sent the manuscript to Contini, having given up hope of finding a publisher. To the competition for the *Libera Stampa* prize he submitted, instead of the autobiographical novel *Pagine involontarie*, the collection of Italian poems *Diarii* ['Diaries'] and this was given a mention and a verbal assessment by the jury – an anonymous one but one attributable to the great critic who had for years been reading his unpublished works:

> It is admirable how Pasolini, burdened by narcissism – indeed by what the clinics technically call infantilism – has gone on progressively identifying this, his constant theme (which might not seem capable of yielding much) by a series of approaches which have been encouraged by the most varied literary experiences (dialect poetry, poetic prose, epigraphs, dramas, rich lyrical techniques drawing on Pascoli and the *crepuscolari*[59] and on to Saba[60] and Penna[61] but with an abundance of inspiration which is far from ordinary.

## 1948

Carlo Pasolini had spent two years in Versuta busying himself with sundry household activities to relieve the boredom.

With his return to Casarsa, amid arrangements made for him, the bitterness, the boredom, the unresolved relationship with his wife, tormented him. He passed lonely hours in the inns of the place with half a litre of white wine on the table, chewing over his obsessions. At night he had never-ending bouts of rage which forced Susanna to abandon the matrimonial bedroom. A psychiatrist from Udine, summoned by his son, was brutally ejected. The psychiatrist delivered a diagnosis, based on what little he had been able to observe, of 'a paranoic syndrome' and 'ethical decadence'. The tension in the family was often intolerable for all and Pier Paolo made some references to it in letters to his friends.

It was the only gloomy note in his existence because the school in Valvasone was a 'considerable source of amusement' while he led his 'usual life with obsessive joys' and 'radiant Sundays'.

On 7 January in San Giovanni there was a demonstration organized by the trade unions and the parties of the Left to apply the 'De Gasperi award'[62] which promised jobs to the unemployed and help to the share-croppers who had suffered losses owing to the war.

The youngsters stormed a palazzo belonging to aristocratic owners who lived in Rome. After a few hours they were chased away by the police; some were arrested and tried. Pier Paolo, who meantime has been appointed secretary of the Communist branch in San Giovanni, was in the piazza in San Vito. In the pauses between clashes with the police, there gathered round him as usual the group of friends from the Sunday festivals, who today had the red handkerchief [of the Young Communists] round their necks. Never so much as on this day did the prospect of peasant revolution seem a realizable dream. On this emotional crest Pasolini began to write a novel about the events.

But like a realist novelist from another time, it was not enough for him to have seen with his own eyes the little revolution in San Vito, to have spoken with the leaders and their supporters, to have discussed it for a long time afterwards in the cell. In the following years, during the various versions of the novel – its first title was *I gironi del lodo De Gasperi* ['The circles of the De Gasperi Award'], later changed to *La meglio gioventù* ['The finest youth'] (a title later relinquished to the collection of verse in Friulano) and finally *Il sogno di una cosa* [*A Dream of Something*] – he continued to ask for recollections from protagonists in and witnesses of that day.

Dino Peresson, one of the boys in *Il sogno di una cosa*, relates:

He would visit me or someone else who was there – he was always at San Vito – to and fro to San Giovanni, Casarsa, San Vito – but more San Vito than Casarsa because I think he had loved these peasant struggles because I know he loved the peasants. He loved them in a way all his own – and naturally he was present at these things . . . I really couldn't say the reason why he loved the peasants so much. But, to my way of thinking, through the studies he had made of peasant life I think he had come up with something special about the peasants – that is to say, that they needed someone to help them, to encourage these people and give a hand to these peasants . . . In us young people, as I say, what pleased him was the sincerity and the meekness we had . . .[63]

Bertolucci observed:

. . . *Il sogno di una cosa* which stands by itself but, if you like, expands that Friulian saga from a diptych to a triptych, tells of the boys of *Atti impuri* and of *Amado mio* who, as Penna says, have grown a bit older . . . and of their families involved in the peasant struggles – which, if one thinks of them today, were mysterious in their simplicity – to obtain the application of the De Gasperi award. In Pasolini's papers they laugh about that poor Friuli which is determined to have justice – 'the peeling walls of the houses, the rusty metal of the bicycles, the crumpled cloth of the banners'.

In February Pasolini informed the secretary of the Popular Friulian Movement of his resignation after seeing petty provincial tendencies to look inwards and to sentimental autonomy win the upper hand over the entirely logical and functional character he would have liked to give to the movement.

The elections of 1948 required organized militancy both in the Party cell in San Giovanni and throughout the province, with meetings, debates, interventions in the papers, electoral strategies, and the hostility of his enemies grew. Even his friends changed – some distanced themselves, repelled by his political ideas, others argued over them publicly. New friendships were formed, with Zigaina and other Communist intellectuals. Zigaina remembers:

The first time he came to see me was in March 1948 (I remember that the buds of the violets were sprouting and so say March with certainty). Together on our bicycles we went over again all the routes of my nocturnal trips during the wartime blackout: the banks of the Torre and of the Isonzo. We stopped in the little hamlets and he went up to the children to talk to them in Friulano. Then when we got home he noted down all the endings, etc., etc. He came back several times and on one occasion we went to Ruda to hold a meeting on Peace (organized by the PCI [Italian Communist Party]). It must have been in the autumn of '48 or April '49. Pier Paolo talks about it in *Quadri friulani* ['Friulian pictures'].[64]

There were frequent meetings of the San Giovanni cell in the room over the ENAL bar [a workers' club]; around the broken table, under the crucifix and the portrait of Stalin, the meetings were organized and the posters to be put up in the loggia of the village were copied out by hand.

Some boys from Ligugnana, in the aftermath of the demonstrations in January, clandestinely emigrated to Yugoslavia. Dino Peresson relates:

> We went over the mountains on foot. We were looking for the dream of something but unfortunately it didn't come true because we came back very disillusioned. Pasolini came looking for me and told me he wanted to write about this adventure – if we want to call it that – and even quite a nice adventure because at that age it's not easy to have certain adventures. So I gladly said 'Why not?' I told the story of the short time I spent in Yugoslavia. This is the basis of the book, according to me.

Woven into *Il sogno di una cosa* were other real adventures that took place at this time. Archimede Bortolus (to whom the poem 'Viers Pordenon e il mond' [Towards Pordenone and the World] would later be dedicated) emigrated to a Swiss village from which he made a trip to Fribourg to convey greetings from Pasolini to Contini and on his return, after a few months at Pasolini's request, wrote an account of his adventures which appeared with slight modifications in the novel.

If the making of *Il sogno di una cosa* mirrored the *chanson de geste* of the 'finest youth' of Friuli, other and more secret events were concealed in this summer: they too were destined to have prolonged echoes in the writing of a novel.

*Amado mio* was the chronological and existential continuation of *Atti impuri* and, like the latter, had its first traces in the *Quaderni rossi*, which were broken off at the end of 1947. It is another summer tale of bathing, of festivals and of cordial friendships 'which are always linked by threads of bitter-sweet sympathy to one place' and these places emerge from distant memories of Nievo.[65] There was a large natural fountain and waterhole – the Pacher. In the early afternoon hours its banks were alive with groups of boys from the villages round about and each of their ways of speaking had its pecularities. Learned in this way, from one bank to the other of the Pacher, these ways of speaking went to make up the linguistic mosaic of 'El testament Coran' ['The testament Koran'] which opens the first part of the collection of lyrics in Friulano.

He wrote a series of 'Friulian pictures' – narratives which reproduced some pages of the *Quaderni rossi* – and gave them the title *I parlanti* ['The talkers']. He published at his own expense for the Edizioni dell'Academiuta the little volume of Friulian poems and translations of Spanish poets by Nico Naldini: *Seris par un frut* ['Evenings for a child'].

## 1949

Replying to the question of a French interviewer, Pasolini stated in 1970, 'Both to resolve certain misunderstandings and to remove certain labels, I wish to say that I belonged to the Communist Party for about a year in 1947–8... Then, like a certain number of other comrades, I did not renew my Party card when it ran out ...'

This was a summary statement which rendered his relationship to the PCI vague and imprecise. Chronological exactitude eluded him on this as on other occasions, while he tended to draw a veil over the reasons for his expulsion from the Party, which at this time were very close and real. Perhaps because at a distance of more than twenty years he considered them a simple incident on the way towards what was in any case the final outcome – or perhaps because he considered that explusion an anachronistic ghost unworthy of being recalled.

His militant period in the Communist Party continued with much zeal for a large part of 1949; he drew close to Marxist thought by reading a short and simplified version of *Das Kapital* but more important than Marx was his reading of Gramsci.

Pasolini became a public figure in the social world of Friuli – he took part in political congresses as the most prominent intellectual of the Left and, firmly in charge of the cell in San Giovanni, prepared to draw up the cultural line of the Party in the regional context. In February he took part in the first congress of the Communist Federation at Pordenone; in May he went to Paris for the Peace Congress.

He had grand plans for the school at Valvasone after the headmaster had drawn the attention of the director to him with the proposal to turn his class into 'a kind of experimental school'.

'I write, I work, but for whom?' His literary work was in crisis. His last entry of poems for the *Libera Stampa* competition won him another mention while the publishers remained deaf to requests to publish his verses; all three novels were *in fieri* [Latin: on the stocks]. Yet even from Casarsa he managed to form some literary relationships. Vittorio Sereni invited him to contribute to the review *La Rassegna d'Italia*. 'When I read *L'usignolo della Chiesa Cattolica* for the first time I suddenly thought of a Rimbaud come to life again. I will not take up more space to justify what was at the time an impression – partly literary and partly not – and what is today no more than the memory of an impression ...' (V. Sereni).[66] And Giacinto Spagnoletti,[67] having tracked him down 'in the depths of the darkest province', asked him to send him his Italian poems to appear in his *Antologia della poesia italiana*. To Contini he sent as usual his collected typescripts.

In 1949, *Dov'è la mia patria* ['Where is my native land?'], verses in Friulano in various dialects of the right bank of the Tagliamento, appeared and later went to make up 'El Testament Coran', the first nucleus of the second part of *La meglio gioventú . . .* The Casarsa edition was illustrated by drawings by Giuseppe Zigaina.

After the 'marvellous spring', the summer of 1949 ran its course in the same settings as previous summers: bathing in the pool and in the Tagliamento; and then the festivals, the dances, new friendships. 'I live on delicious subterfuges, perfectly happy to be hidden.'

In reality this summer was under attack from vague threats, from attempts at blackmail by his political opponents, to which he attached no importance; rather they excited him like a challenge and made the happiness of *eros* even more obsessive.

At home his father's moods were unalterably at their worst – a recurring soliloquy full of delusions which provoked outbursts of exasperation.

On the evening of 30 September, at Ramuscello during the festival of Santa Sabina, Pier Paolo met a boy whom he knew already, along with two of his friends. During the festival they hid in the bushes.

On 22 October he was reported to the carabinieri of Casarsa for corruption of minors and obscene acts in a public place. Our 28 October the papers published the news and next day *L'Unità* [the Communist Part daily] announced his expulsion with a comment written by Ferdinando Mautino of the Party headquarters in Udine.

We take as our cue the events which have brought about a grave disciplinary measure involving the poet Pasolini to denounce once more the deleterious influences of certain idiological and philosophical currents represented by various Gides, Sartres and similarly decadent poets and literary figures, who wish to pose as progressive but in reality are a sum of the most harmful aspects of bourgeois degeneration.

At the beginning of November Nico Naldini wrote to Fabio Luca Cavazza:

This morning I have had a very alarmed letter from Serra – which means the bomb has gone off in Bologna too. The situation is this: we are waiting for the legal charge to take its course and for the investigation to be opened by the magistrate's court in a little town near here (San Vito). Probably the outcome will not be serious because it is hoped that the parents of these boys will sign a statement withdrawing their suit. So perhaps everything might die down; I say 'might' because there are naturally unknowns. If all goes well Pier Paolo will go to Rome in a few weeks to our uncle where he will look for work.

This is how events occurred then: On the evening of a festival in a village not far from Casarsa PP found himself with three boys whom he knew already and without any venal proposal went off with them into the fields and there there were some very simple erotic exchanges.

There was a case of masturbation. Now to an outside observer this fact may seem almost monstrous but for anyone who knows our village boys, it cannot either arouse amazement or be judged severely. Some days later the boys quarrelled, it's not known why, and brought up this contact. Someone who was present wrote an anonymous letter to the sergeant [of the carabinieri] in the village who, since the matter had become public, drew up a charge after having questioned the boys. PP has several enemies among the Christian Democrats for his political activity and they have taken the matter up and have done everything to see that this event, which – and I say it with my hand on my heart – is of no importance, should cause scandal which would then ruin him for the rest of his life. All of which has happened. They have been diabolically clever.

The sergeant at Casarsa, having received the charge, questioned PP, who thought it best to confess and to put forward – apart from having been drunk – the reasons which you will know from *Candido* ('I remember having tried an erotic experiment which was literary in character and origins and heavily influenced by the reading of a novel with a homosexual subject by Gide'), which must have been enough for the sergeant who showed himself to be very understanding of erotic, literary oddities in the D'Annunzian style. PP's statement quickly reached the Christian Democrat Party in Udine, which saw to it that it was sent, along with the text of the charge, to all the editorial offices of all the papers in the region. Notice that three months before the event a very important prelate in Udine had conveyed to PP that if he did not stop his political activity he would do everything in his power to ruin him – intentions which were later confirmed to me by a Christian Democrat deputy who is a friend of mine. These are the facts; their consequences are very grave. PP has in fact lost his teaching post and I do not think he has much chance of getting it back. You cannot imagine the propaganda that has been made out of it in Friuli and the grief of all of us.

Excuse the confusion of my account – I should have liked to give you a better idea of the subtle perfidy of the organizers of this scandal.

With this double catastrophe – the loss of his teaching post and the expulsion from the Party – 1949 came to an end.

In all this the father had finally found something objective on which to vent his obsessions and, up to a certain point, assuage them. But once the first effect of the scandal had passed, they reappeared more stormily than before. Susanna was overcome by despair, which led her to associate the injustice of Guido's death with this other injustice which was being visited on Pier Paolo. She stayed in bed for a whole day in long conversations and weeping fits with her son, while the relatives went to and fro between the lawyers and the parents of the boys to make them abandon the lawsuit.

Pier Paolo passed the last three months of his life in Friuli working by day, going out sometimes in the evening in a strange forbidden world, without the festive crowds of another time. The old friends, boys who were now twenty, had almost all emigrated – some to Australia, some to South America. The villages, too, were changing now that 'the finest youth' had scattered.

Some contemporaries came to see him – Zigaina, Bartolini – others wrote to him encouragingly; the bulk of his acquaintances vanished into silence while some unknown persons, but perhaps not very many of them, pursued him with anonymous letters and satirical pieces.

Paolo Volponi afterwards wrote: 'He was loved by the whole village, considered truly a little prophet. But suddenly there exploded what was to be the drama of his life. Then the whole place, which had loved him very much, arose, upset and furious with him.'[68]

It was true but this has to be added: the boys remained his faithful friends. Casarsa was enclosed in a silence that consisted more of pity than of scandal. Ferdinando Mautino later had ample time to repent his condemnatory article and for many other Friulian Communists this condemnation was a source of guilt which had its effect in the years that followed. As for the literary figures and politicians in Udine who were congratulating themselves on his ruin, oblivion has long overtaken them.

While he was working at *Il sogno di una cosa*, other texts were completed: the short poem 'L'Italia', which was to see the light in Spagnoletti's *Antologia*; the last three sections of the *Usignolo* – 'Paolo e Baruch', 'Tragiques' and 'La scoperta di Marx' ['The discovery of Marx'] – which in this first and fullest version was called *La ricerca di mia madre* ['The search for my mother']; some compositions in Friulano, which complete the Suite Furlana of *La meglio gioventú*.

For the third time he gets a mention at the *Libera Stampa* competition for the collection of poems *L'unica divinità* ['The only divinity'] as well as at the Saint-Vincent Poetry Prize.

# 1950

'If ever I have had a certain vitality I feel it on me now like a new suit.'

At five in the morning of 28 January, Susanna and Pier Paolo went to the station at Casarsa to take the first train to Rome. Susanna was like a young girl on her first journey as she walked down the street arm-in arm with Pier Paolo. The happenings of the recent past seemed almost cancelled from her face and the future did not worry her – in any case it was to be a life lived with her son. The way in which they had left the house where Carlo remained alone, ignorant of their sudden departure, was a first sign of the relief after his father's latest crises. They took with them only what was indispensable and Susanna's bag of jewels, which were to be of no help. Following a programme they had talked over with great uncertainty, they reached the house of her brother Gino in Rome.

After a few weeks Susanna found work as a governess – a sacrifice which she immediately offered her son. Pier Paolo was put up in a rented room in Piazza Costaguti, a few metres from the house where his mother would be working.

The letters which came and went in this period were all taken up with the aftermath of the misadventure in Casarsa and the difficulties of the present. Silvana Mauri looked for means of support for him and Susanna. Sereni and Spagnoletti, who were aware of events, brought help in the form of increased interest in writings to be published. After a renewed attempt with Bompiani, Pasolini had sent the typescript of *L'usignolo* to Mondadori where Sereni, adviser on the poetry series *Lo Specchio* ['The Mirror'], recommended it warmly. Spagnoletti, after choosing 'L'Italia' for his *Antologia*, excited him with the prognosis of a 'future adventure' as a poet.

Piazza Costaguti was in the Jewish ghetto, a few steps from the Tiber, and it was from there that his Roman life began, even if he was still not sure whether to look for work elsewhere. Every evening he met his mother and they walked about hand in hand with a child. On Sunday afternoon they went to the cinema. When they came out Susanna, dazed and happy, seemed to be back in the days in Bologna with her ironical heedlessness of fate's surprises.

The shame of his disgrace – 'I am struggling in a miserable life, in a chain of shames' – prevented him from immediately forming relations with literary figures whom he already knew.

In the rented room he lived alone, reopening the scrapbooks and working up to ten hours a day on his Friulian dreams, which he felt, without regret, were now shut away in their time. He was engaged upon a third, more novelistic version of *Atti impuri* and *Amado mio*; at the same time he continued to write *Il sogno di una cosa*, asking his friends in Friuli for additional information – proper written accounts – on the famous peasant revolt.

Instead of literary figures he met a poet who walked along the Lungotevere every evening and 'crossed over the bridges' with infinite openness to nocturnal surprises. A bitting gossip, sometimes nasty to the point of malice, he was the poet Sandro Penna. He went out every evening from his house in via della Mole de' Fiorentini, knew all the boys to be found at the river, dealt in everything from paintings to fountain-pens, and never worked. Penna's poetry caressed with inimitable magic all those aspects of the city Pasolini had longed for and which were now concretely before the eyes of the 'exile from Friuli' who found in them what he sought: a Mediterranean climate and pagan liberty.

With his head buzzing with the cries from the Campo de' Fiori, in a Rome 'bleeding with absolute novelty', in a world with a 'different' taste, the trauma of the passage from the past to the present was extremely severe: the sharp air of Friuli and the baroque lights of Rome; the greetings in Versuta which were flutterings of the heart and the shouts of the Roman plebeians; the hidden sex of the Friulian boys over which tears were shed and the serpent which at the height of the Anno Santo slithered along 'as viscous and muddled as a perfume'. The Lungotevere with its swimming pools, the Janiculum with its boats, the Port black with excrement and contraceptives, Ciriola with its cheeky boys who gave themselves at a single glance, made up his Rome of 1950, which was both visionary and musical. 'A life all muscle, turned inside out like a glove, absolutely stripped off sentimentality, a human organism so sensual as to be almost mechanical.'

After Penna he met the poet Giorgio Caproni:[69]

For a long time we saw each other almost every day. He came to visit me in the tiny Incis [state employees' housing association] house where I had found accommodation a short time before, opposite Bertolucci's luxurious appartment, and I was irresistibly attracted by his angular, drawn face and by those eyes of his, which were extraordinarily bright and yet very gentle, in which it was easy to read a certain unease – yes – but also extreme resolve.

He was as poor as me – perhaps poorer than me who did not even have a chair to offer him.

He showed me his tram ticket, reading omens into the serial number, but without complaining about his poverty. In fact he had an iron faith under his apparent hesitancy and timidity.

He hoped I might find him a little work, I who had not been able even to find any for myself.

To his correspondents he cried, 'Rome is divine', but without the means to survive he was torn between the temptations of that divinity and suicide. He joined the Extras Union at Cinecittà. Ennio de' Concini recommended him to the head of a troupe 'for walk-on parts' but he had to wait a long time before getting even two days' work. Without success he made inquiries about giving private lessons, corrected proofs on a newspaper and, as an extreme measure, had recourse to selling his books to the second-hand bookstalls.

After vague offers to contribute to the newspapers, from the month of May onwards he managed to publish a few articles – reviews, stories and 'bits and pieces' – in the extreme right-wing Catholic dailies *Il Quotidiano, Il Popolo di Roma, Libertà d'Italia.*

Triggered by the discovery of Rome, and with that 'violent charge of vitality' which sustained his existence and his writing, as a unique experiment his new narrative vocation was born: 'I wrote my novels late because I found myself in 'new situations' in which the setting was first and foremost 'novelistic' for me. To write novels for me remains to live out in the writing the novelistic situation – the recognition of elsewhere.' He wrote the first sketches for *Ragazzi di vita*: 'Squarci di notti romane' ['Slices of Roman nights'], 'Il biondomoro' ['The blonde brunette'], 'Gas', 'Giubileo' ['Jubilee'].

Rome was not only an object to be described but was in a certain sense the world. To travel over it needed much energy: by day on the rafts at Ponte Garibaldi and Ponte Sisto, in the evening on the Lungotevere with Penna, who was its first poetic transposition. From the crystalline memories of Penna, which are those of the Borgo and Trastevere, Pasolini quickly moves on to the unexplored territories of a different city 'which only a person who lives it with total lack of responsibility is capable of expressing'. While he pursued this discovery it is interesting to note the names he gave to himself with a rich metaphorical synthesis: Villon, Cacarella, Inusitato farlocco, Je, Pecora, l'Appassionata, Lautréamont, il Reporter, François. Taken separately and together they were: 'This blowhole, this outfall, this receiver and transmitter through which the Rome that cannot be named finds its way of expression.'

From 'the feverish Lungoteveri' he pushed on towards 'fabulous San Paolo', the Testaccio, Monteverde, Primavalle, 'a scum of consumptives, thieves and idiots'.

It is the Holy Year and 'the whores burned in pyres of joy their papal veils'. The boys have their hair combed *alla ghigio*, are brown 'like statues cased in mud'.

During the summer he met them on Orazio's raft at Ponte Sisto:

Half an hour later, back on the sand, I saw Nando clinging to the side of the raft calling to me. 'Aoh,' he said, 'can you carry the boat?'

'I can manage,' I replied.

He turned to the attendant. 'How much?' he asked.

The attendant did not even look at him; it seemed as if he was talking to the water over which he was leaning and angry into the bargain: 'One hundred and fifty for an hour, two persons.

'Damn it,' said Nando with his little face still laughing. Then he disappeared into the dressing rooms. He reappeared alongside me on the sand like an old friend. 'I have a hundred lire,' he said.

'Lucky you,' I replied, 'I'm completely flat.' He did not understand.

'What does "flat" mean?' he asked.

'That I haven't a penny,' I explained.

'Why? Don't you work?'

'No, I don't work.'

'I thought you worked,' he added.

'I'm studying,' I said to simplify things . . .

Besides energy, one needs great good health to roam the world day and night and in fact to his first Roman story he gave this epigraph from Sainte-Beuve: 'The finest, most blessed, most poetic thing in the world is to be healthy.'

In August he won second place in the competition for 'Catholic Poetry – the people's calendar' with his Friulian verses 'El testament Coran'. Susanna was in Montecassiano in the province of Macerata in a villa belonging to the family for whom she worked. She wrote to him on 27 August:

You should see what a lovely village Montecassiano is! It is like a city in miniature. It rises on a hill, is surrounded with high walls and has two great gates, a fine little square. From the terrace you can see, about ten kilometres off, the hill on which Recanati [birthplace of Leopardi] rises.

Now it is close at hand. Every evening I see the light go on there. I'd like to go there. At this time I'd be walking with you, perhaps a little dazed if the film was boring, but happy for a few more hours. I hope, as you say, that your business will be sorted out in September. Please write to me before leaving and when you are in Casarsa go to see Guido and kiss his grave for me too and, if you can, take him a bunch of flowers. Do you need money?

The 'business' to which Susanna referred was the trial for the 'incidents at Ramuscello'. In December at the magistrate's court in San Vito the trial was concluded with a suspended sentence of three months for the obscene acts while the charge of corrupting minors was dropped because no charge was offered.

Distance had improved his relationship with his father with whom he was perhaps already discussing a reunion in Rome shortly.

After the early days when he shunned literary circles he now established relationships with – among others – Enrico Falqui, Giorgio Bassani, Attilio Bertolucci and Carlo Muscetta.

Bassani tried to help him by suggesting him as librarian to Princess Marguerite Caetani, who edited and financed the literary periodical *Botteghe Oscure*, but his youth advised against his appointment. Muscetta asked for the Friulian poems in order to present them to the publisher Einaudi.

He wrote the poems later collected in *Roma 1950 – Diario*, published by Scheiwiller in 1960.


## 1951

He celebrated New Year's Day 1951 at Chioggia with the writer, Giovanni Comisso, and his cousin Nico Naldini. Victim of the theft of his wallet by a gang of drunken youths, he was shut up in the cell at the carabinieri post. His recent sentence had made him a person 'persecuted a wanderer, an outcast'.

Having returned to Rome at the beginning of January, he was forced to stay in bed for a month because of a fracture of the pelvis resulting from a fall.

His letters to his friends continued on the anguished notes of unemployment and poverty as he faced the second year of Roman life. 'This adventure, so new that it makes one cry out with amazement' was carrying him from his wanderings in the centre to the periphery of the city:

> . . . As for the city, its parabola is one of the least publicized imaginable. We were used to the conquerors from the provinces – as in Balzac (or D'Annunzio) – who seeing the capital lying at their feet resolved to throttle it and to tame it: 'A nous deux, maintenant!'
>
> Pasolini arrives in Rome like a person rejected ( I remember his letters from Ponte Mammolo, poverty sustained by the sacrifices of his mother) and learns to know the city from the degradation and dereliction of the outer suburbs . . . obeying the Flaubertian law 'sublime from lower depths' which Pasolini meanwhile was putting into practice by descending with irreproachable cleanness quite simply to a sub-human level, the Pasolini of the novels of the slums of the periphery encloses himself rigorously within a horizon of 'garbage'. It should be noted that the knowledge of this depressed cosmos, of this frontier of the human, is facilitated by glossaries which are perfectly comparable to the lexical lists drawn up by Pascoli for his rustic material from the Garfagnana [a wild mountainous region on the borders of Tuscany]. It is a rupture with the norm, a gap radically similar to that formed by dialect.
>
> (G. Contini)

In June, in *Paragone*, he published *Il ferrobedò*, which with variations would later appear as the opening chapter of *Ragazzi di vita*. Ferrobedò was the contorted version in Roman dialect of the Società Ferro Beton [The

Reinforced Concrete Company], a big factory in the Borgata Donna Olympia, 'the matrix, the surroundings in which the infancy of Riccetto and of the others lurked'.

The plan of the first novel, which was taking shape against an increasingly wide horizon and which was gradually encompassing all the Dantesque circles of the world of the *borgate* [the slums on the periphery of Rome], for the moment consisted – apart from stories and the sketches already written – of a series of jottings and lists, mnemonics rather than writing, of language, places, physiognomies, stored away day by day immediately after the experience.

Thus while before I had used dialect for subjective reasons, as a purely poetic language, on the contrary when I arrived in Rome I began to use the dialect of the Roman sub-proletariat in an objective way so as to obtain the most exact description possible of the world I had before me.

The dialect words of slang are absolutely necessary for me to write . . . it is they that give me the joy necessary to understand and describe my characters.

So the work of mimesis is the work that requires the most skilled and daring stylistic research (given the necessary corruption of the modes of speech – that of the narrator and that of the character, of language and dialect, etc.) . . . certainly one must let things speak physically, immediately; but to 'let things speak' one has 'to be a writer and even ostentatiously a writer'.

In the *borgate* were the people of the periphery, mingled with the recent immigrants; twenty years ago part of this population was the nerve centre of Rome. Its story is that of violence suffered at the hands of Fascism which uprooted it from its ancient seats – Borgo Pio, Trastevere, San Lorenzo – and dispersed it in the *borgate* where it survived with the old spirit of Belli [Gioacchino Belli, the great nineteenth-century Roman dialect poet], its codes of honour and the nobility of a caste within which its ordinary people have enclosed themselves with an arrogance that 'a member of the bourgeoisie cannot even imagine'.

A fugitive and rejected like those of that world, he spent days and nights in the *borgate* where there was 'a lot of sunshine, a lot of joy' and where the plebeian narcissism of the boys had its erotic counterpoint, joyfully unconfined.

On a summer day, on the shingle of the Aniene [a tributary of the Tiber], he met Sergio Citti, an eighteen-year-old house-painter. Citti recalls:

This meeting, when I think of it, seems like a dream. We stayed together all evening, we spent the whole night talking, sitting on the steps of a school. Pier Paolo talked and talked and I talked too; he talked about life and I understood that I had these things within me too but I realized that if he had not said them I would never have understood that I had them too.[70]

If I had not met Paolo, what would I have done? I was already fed up with being a worker . . . I would certainly have become a thief![71]

Pasolini recalls:

I think he had done only the first three classes of middle school in a boarding school (those boarding schools which generally train really dangerous delinquents; claiming to re-educate them, they teach the bourgeois morality so as to exploit it or to simulate it). Sergio had been untouched by that kind of re-education naturally. Perhaps the only negative trace left in him by that aborted education is a certain heightening of sadism, which – if you like – is as far as he goes. Sadism moreover born of those tragedies of his which are common to working-class families about which, however, he quickly became philosophical . . .

He lives the life of his social class which is that of a Roman proletarian in very close contact with the sub-proletariat whose ideology he adopts, accepting the world of work as an irrelevant necessity and yet conscious of this because of an atavistic illumination (grandfather and father anarchists).[72]

Sergio quickly became his 'living dictionary of Romanesco', a source of thieves' slang and the slang of the gangs of the *borgate*, with the readiness of his acute intelligence and an authenticity which it was impossible to manipulate.

The house where the Pasolini family was reunited in July 1951 was at Ponte Mammolo – a rather more civilized *borgata*, inhabited by workers and white-collar employees.

When he moved to Ponte Mammolo, in a pitiful *borgata* kilometres away from my house, I got to know there that very sweet person, Susanna, his mother, who took to having undeserved faith in me.

When we visited each other, Pier Paolo and I, being hard up, walked all these kilometres not talking much but seeing a lot in a landscape still smashed from the war.

(G. Caproni)

After renting the little hall of the Academiuta to a photographer, the father moved from Casarsa furniture, books and household goods. Age and solitude had depressed his character. 'My father is always there, alone in the poor little kitchen, with his elbows on the table and his face on his fists, motionless, bad-tempered, suffering; he filled the space of the little room with the bulk that dead bodies have.'

Outliving himself, he unexpectedly allowed his better sides to develop. From now on – although with recurring crises – he became his son's secretary, dealing with daily chores and playing an obstinate part in every act of his growing fame.

On 13 September Giacinto Spagnoletti wrote to Pasolini:

I was thinking again about our meeting, of the hours spent together in that house of yours, of your mother and your father – and they are the nicest things Rome offered me. I'd like to see you calmer and happier. What wouldn't I give to hear that you have got a job of some kind. But you mustn't lose heart.

The poet Carlo Betocchi[73] wrote to him on 23 September:

Seeing the article and your name you came to mind – most vividly as I met you in front of Lombardi's in via della Gatta . . . and the exclamation from my wife when she saw you holding your bicycle and she suddenly recalled the beauty of the plains of the Veneto and said – 'a real Friulano'.

Meantime I had read, in the nocturnal calm of a journey to Milan, all the little volumes you left me and of which until now I had not even read the extremely nice dedications. It reawoke in me the desire to write that article – and now this is the first day I have free since the one when you came here. After reading your poems and the notebook, which is so richly interesting, and confronted by the evidence of such an intelligent civilized mind, I would hope to write an article which will draw not only on my feelings and the long habit of affection which I have for your part of the world and for its people, but which might put renewed life into the arguments which I share with you concerning dialect and languages. Your initiative was very lucid and fine – a pity that it should have had to lie silent in its legitimate site, the little volumes of Casarsa.

Among the few friends from Friuli who remembered him, Luigi Ciceri, a doctor from Udine with literary interests, offered him economic help by proposing the printing of a small volume of verses in Friulano which saw the light two years later under the title *Tal cuor di un frut* ['In the heart of a boy'].

In August he went to Puglia and wrote for the usual skimpy journalist's fee a reportage from Bari. In October he won *ex aequo* the poetry prize Sette Stelle Sinalunga. Spagnoletti wrote to him on 19 October: 'They're never going to give you a prize of half a million, damn them! I read about it and had a fit. The essential thing would be for you to get a job, employment, whatever it is. It is really incredible that in Rome today nothing is offered to you.'

While he continued (with much scepticism) not to give up hope of seeing his Italian poems published by Mondadori, he proposed to make a 'more mature and concise selection' – but the result, in spite of interventions by Sereni and Spagnoletti, was worse than negative. It was to be held over for ever.

In December came the long-wished-for appointment as a teacher of Italian in the recognized middle school at Ciampino. His protective intermediary with the school authorities had been the dialect poet from the Abruzzi, Vittorio Clemente.

The journey from Ponte Mammolo to Ciampino took three and a half hours each day – an undertaking which to begin with had its pleasurable moments in the bus and the local trains. During the journey he read the most significant works of the dialect poets of the nineteenth century. Having obtained the first editorial contract of his career he set about putting together an anthology of dialect poetry for a series published by Guanda, which had Bertolucci as editor.

He visited Ungaretti and got to know, at the offices of Rai (Italian Radio), Carlo Emilio Gadda. Gadda, who was writing *Quer pasticiacio brutto de Via Merulana* [*That Awful Mess on Via Merulana*], was attracted by the language of the new outskirts of Rome and sometimes ventured out to Ponte Mammolo as a guest, together with Bertolucci and Caproni, at Susanna's little dinner parties.

He wrote the short poem 'Appennino', which opened *Le ceneri di Gramsci* ['Gramsci's ashes'] and the Roman stories which appeared in *Alì dagli occhi azzuri* ['Alí with the blue eyes'].

## 1952

He sent the publisher Guanda the collection of Friulian verse with the provisional title of *Romancero* which was later changed to *La meglio gioventú* [*The finest youth*].

Spagnoletti wrote to him on 9 January: 'I got hold of Guanda by the jacket a few days ago and told him he must at all costs publish your marvellous Friulian poems. I saw them on his desk and read them. Bravo Pier Paolo!'

The Parma editor remained deaf even to gestural incitements. In April a more concrete proposal was made by Anna Banti[74] for the *Paragone* series.

He commuted to Ciampino; in the afternoon he worked in 'the sad, building-site room suspended over the mud' of Ponte Mammolo. In the evening he saw his friends Bertolucci and Caproni or else met Sergio Citti

and asked him innumerable questions about language and situations in
Roman low life.

> Sergio Citti's is always low and hoarse and his lines are always spoken as if
> in parentheses or in a scarcely breathed clause (to the void, which is the
> only interlocutor worthy of him – the void which is generally to the right of
> the real and adjacent interlocutor). One has to have a practised ear to
> understand these lines whispered by inspiration, amid the hoarseness and
> quiet laughter, in the direction of the airy person who is on our right and a
> little below our shoulder – to whom Sergio's black putto's eye turns with
> bewitching and cruel electrical flashes: unwavering testimony to a state of
> aridity which is both stocial and epicurean, which is curious about life and
> lacking in any illusion about itself.[75]

Sergio's answers were not used by Pasolini to link two incommensurable
worlds – his own and that of the boy from the *borgate* – and thus to reflect
these replies as a mosaic of popular aesthetics. Sergio is not even a *tranche de
vie* but the subject which at once anticipates and immediately deciphers a
reality which reaches Pasolini by way of the complicated psychological and
environmental networks, both in the air and underground, of the world of
the *borgate*. And after he has established with this world infinite complicities
and these complicities – which are his entire aesthetic principle – come
about between his own internal 'degeneration' (but not a total perdition)
and 'the brutal external vitality (the sub-proletariat environment): two strains
of pus which mingle with gleams of gold.'

In April at Pordenone there was the last stage in the legal *via crucis* for the
events at Ramuscello, with a verdict dismissing the charge for insufficiency of
proof, including the obscene acts in public.

The image of the old Friulian places glimpsed during the journey to the
court was split between two contrasting emotions: visionary nostalgic
longings airborne by the countryside in spring, and boredom, resentment at
the provincial culture whose pettiness still poisoned his memories. On
this alien aspect of real life – a permanent and obsessive one however –
Pasolini was writing a strange narrative pamphlet called *Il disprezzo della
provincia* ['Provincial contempt']. A story made up of dialogue and actions, it
projected with careful objectivity the outlines of the milieu and the profiles of
known persons. The project, which was quickly dropped after the writing
of the first chapter, carried this inscription drawn from Ascoli's youthful
*Diary*:

> Often we are so careful of appearances that we even sacrifice the substance
> and this so that others may not be aware of what it is we suffer from. This

must be based on the artrocious doubt that the others may rejoice in our pain; do not make our enemies laugh, my mother wrote to me recently, and these tremendous words found a prompt echo in the depth of my heart. But one needs strength – contempt or compassion for wickedness – and these are acquired by turning to virtue.

In May he won the Taranto prize for the short story *Terracina – Operetta Marina* ['Terracina — a marine operetta']. During the 'unsalaried summer' – because the school at Ciampino paid only for the months of teaching – he entered for other literary prizes, pulling whatever strings he could. He entered his essay on Ungaretti – 'Un poeta e Dio' ['A poet and God'], written between 1948 and 1951 – for the Premio delle Quattro Arti [The Four Arts prize] at Naples where, among the judges, there was Luciano Anceschi.[76] I hope to see you winner of the competition for critical essays,' Spagnoletti wrote to him on 26 June. 'It should not be difficult for our friends to pick out your great abilities above all the others. I have already spoken to Anceschi in this sense.' He won, along with Leone Piccioni and Franco Rizzo. He contributed to the review *Paragone-Letteratura*, edited by Roberto Longhi and Anna Banti; to Rai's talks series *Approdo letterario* ['Literary Landfall']; to Mario dell'Arco's little reviews of dialect poetry articles on Horace and Belli;[77] he wrote the introduction to the anthology *Il fiore della poesia romanesca* ['The flower of poetry in Roman dialect'], edited by Leonardo Sciascia. He passed 'the red and squalid' months of summer going about in the slums of the periphery, in the mud of the Tiber, while continuing to work on *Ragazzi di vita*: 'When all life has been consumed all still remains.' At the end of the year he had the end of his novel in sight; after two years of work, two more years of corrections and polishing awaited him. 'I have been able to start working again and to believe in my work.'

At the beginning of the scholastic year he began commuting again from home to Ciampino for 'the school's miserable pay'. In December, the anthology *Poesia dialettale del Novecento* ['Dialect poetry of the twentieth century'] appeared; above his name on the front-cover was the name of Mario dell'Arco but the work had been his 'even in the manual sense'. A great welcome was given to the 'massive anthology' which brought together forty-four poets from all over Italy with a long introduction. Among the reviews was a memorable one by Montale in the *Corriere della Serra* of 15 January 1953:

A citizen of Bologna, Pasolini writes verse in his maternal dialect, which is that of Casarsa in Friuli, as well as verses in Italian – among the most interesting today – which have not yet been collected in a volume... Only a young poet could bring to a conclusion a work of this kind with such sure intuition and such an unshakeable conviction that poetry – cultured or uncultured, in Italian or dialect – has far from vanished from the world.

He began *Il canto popolare* ['The popular song'] which was to be published two years later in a series edited by Vittorio Sereni.

# 1953

After the dialect anthology, Attilio Bertolucci, on behalf of the publisher Guanda, commissioned him to prepare a second anthology on Italian folk poetry which appeared in 1953 with the title *Canzoniere italiano* ['Italian lyrical poems'].

In 1953 the little volume of verses in Friulano *Tal cour di un frut* was published in Tricesimo by Luigi Ciceri with a dedicatory letter from Pasolini 'to the Editor' dated 22 December 1952.

From February he contributed to the new magazine edited by Gianfranco Vigorelli, *Il Giovedí* [Thursday], with reviews and essays on poetry which would later be partly collected in the volume *Passione e ideologia* ['Passion and ideology'].

In April he met the publisher Livio Garzanti to whom Bertolucci had shown the short story *Il Ferrobedò*. Garzanti offered to publish the novel.

He continued with the collection of texts of folk poetry which he managed to obtain after laborious requests for loans of books from libraries all over Italy.

Among his radio contributions there was a proposal, which unfortunately was never pursued, for a dramatization of the stories of Bandello[78] in collaboration with Carlo Emilio Gadda.

He took part unsuccessfully in the Viareggio prize with the introductory essay to the dialect anthology. In September he won the second Pordenone prize with 'Lied', a short story set in Friuli, later to appear in *L'Approdo letterario* (April-June 1954) and then, reworked, in *Il sogno di una cosa*.

He entered three Friulian poems for the poetry competition of the Friulian Philological Society but they were turned down the following year with specious arguments. On 12 November Sereni wrote to him:

Spagnoletti should have written to you about that series which in agreement with Solmi and the two editors I am supposed to look after for *Meridiana*. I should like to do not more than four *notebooks* (of not more than 12 to 20 poems each) a year. I also think one should pick out in the totality of a work one aspect or a group of lyrics which can be referred to a precise and well-defined period – *not* a little general anthology. I should very much like (and the others agree) to have things by you as soon as possible. The edition should be one of not less than three hundred copies with a percentage to the author (of 10 or 12%, I'm not sure; but I would try to have a *tantum* discreetly paid). The series will be quite different – in format and paper too – from the rest of *Meridiana.*

I was counting on it but I see Spagnoletti doesn't give me the answer I was expecting. So I have decided to write to you (I should have done so sooner) asking you to accept.

Having once more taken up the *Diarii* written from 1945 on and having sent a selection to Sereni, he decided to publish *Il canto popolare*, 'a composition in the form of a ballad' composed between 1952 and 1953, and it appeared the following year. The blurb of this little volume announced a forthcoming collection of poems: 'Some little poems, published and unpublished, will appear as soon as possible, thanks to a Milan publisher, under the title *L'umile Italia* ['Humble Italy'].' This meant *Le ceneri di Gramsci*, which came out in 1957 with those poems composed up to 1956.

He wrote the short poem 'Picasso' inspired by the great exhibition of the collected works in the Galleria d' Arte Moderna in Rome, and it was published in Number XII of *Botteghe Oscure. Il canto popolare* and 'Picasso' appeared with variations in *Ceneri.*

He wrote two groups of poems *I Colus* ['The Colus family'] and *Il vecchio testamento* ['The Old Testament'] which would appear in the section 'Romancero' with which *La meglio gioventú* would end.

In October he published in *Paragone* the story *Ragazzi di vita* – 'a formidable thing' Contini would say – which would be published with some changes as the fourth chapter of the novel which in December was almost finished, 'very clear in my head'.

New correspondents were the dialect poet from Grado, Biagio Marin, and his Bolognese friend, Francesco Leonetti, found once more twelve years after the *Eredi* group – 'overcome by the sense of the years' they almost wept.

## 1954
'When I accepted the first film-script I was literally dying of hunger.'

In March, along wih Giorgio Bassani, he began to collaborate on Mario Soldati's[79] film *La donna del fiume* [*Woman of the River*] with a reconnaissance of the waterways of Comacchio.

A writer's work for the cinema can be marvellous – indeed, in abstract, I consider it to be marvellous. Unfortunately one works with ignorant, stupid people, who don't know what they want. A scripwriter shouldn't

even know that there is a production or a distribution – he should work
with the director and that's all . . .

This unexpected work, which he had been dreaming of for years 'for lucre',
gave 'some relief to my family's exhausting life'. The improved family
conditions allowed them to leave the mud of Rebibia to set themselves up in
'a lovely and decent' place – a flat in Monteverde Nuovo in via Fonteiana 86:

> Where I then had the luck to meet and get to know him [writes Paolo
> Volpini], also visiting his house and forming ties of affection with his
> parents. Even with the father, distant and severe, but always very proud to
> show me the poems Pier Paolo had written or translated.
>     Often on Sundays we would happen to go together to certain vegetable
> gardens kept by people from Le Marche beyond Torre Pignata, simply
> because Pasolini was interested to see and understand certain milieus,
> words, language, directly; to get hints and names, for example, which he
> then used in his first novel *Ragazzi di vita*. There he had got to know the
> Citti brothers, who would later become his pupils and collaborators.
>     . . . At that time, as he gradually emerged, he led a life that was not
> unhappy, indeed very serene and quiet, with that characteristic gentleness
> which always accompanied him.

And Giorgio Caproni:

> When, already in better shape, he went to live in via Fonteiana, in the same
> block as Gadda and a few steps from his via di Donna Olympia, the haunt
> of wide boys, it was easier for us to meet and I was able to get to know his
> father, the colonel, his face shut away in silence like a helmet.
>     Among lively paintings by himself and others, and alongside his gentle
> Susanna, who sat in a corner, he was then writing *Le ceneri di Gramsci* and
> I enjoyed watching that incredibly little black cast-iron typewriter of his,
> almost as old as a pyramid, a real museum piece.
>     Every so often he would read me a verse or two, typed – as was his
> custom – on paper no bigger than the pages of a notebook.
>     He became more sure of himself, while still keeping his very discreet
> and I might almost say reserved manner, diving avidly into the city (into
> life) and affectionately rebuking me for my remaining, deliberately,
> outside the great birdcage.
>     Once when he saw me post a letter in a box at the Quattro Venti where I
> lived and where at that time sheep still grazed 'Oh no,' he said, 'you must
> post it in the Centre, you mustn't shut yourself up in the outskirts.' A phrase
> that reveals his determination, even then, to spend in all things *la*

*monedita del alma* as a protagonist and not as a simple extra.

To Caproni, four years later, Pasolini addressed this 'little epigram': 'Soul harmonious because mute and because dark, pure; if there is another like you life is not lost.'

In June the whole corpus of Friulian poems *La meglio gioventú* came out in the *Paragone* series, dedicated 'To Gianfranco Contini with *amor de lonh*. This is to be considered my first published work.'

On 7 August Giacinto Spagnoletti wrote to him:

When I saw your book I asked myself if it was true or was I making it up with the eyes of the imagination. That book which I have seen appear and disappear more than once on the horizon was there, full and solid – it seemed to be of flesh like a child. And you will see – my heart tells me so – that it will have the eternal youth of an ephebe.

*Il canto popolare* and *Dal Diario (1945-1947)* both appeared.

Before leaving Ponte Mammolo and before finishing *Ragazzi di vita*, one evening the plot of *Una vita violenta* was outlined 'in a flash'.

There is a point on the Tiburtina, level with Pietralata and a little before Tiburtino III and Ponte Mammolo (where I was then living), which is called the 'Fort'. You can see a barracks, a bar, a factory, a hillock, a bald and infernal hummock – 'Monte Pecoraro' [Shepherd's Hill]. There was a dirty and mournful air with that dark blue, funereal, too clear, which one finds on the horizon when the weather gets better towards evening and it is already too late. I was walking in the mud. And there at the stop where the bus turns off towards Pietralata I got to know Tommaso. He was not called Tommaso but he was identical, in his face, to the way I described him repeatedly in the pages of *Una vita violenta* and was dressed in the same way as well: a wretched ragged suit but 'proper' with a white shirt that was maybe dirty and a little tie, purplish and worn. As the Roman youths often do he quickly became friendly and in a few minutes told me his whole story: the episode I later told in the first chapter and his illness in the Forlanini hospital.

Then he disappeared. I never saw him again. Neither at Pietralata nor at Tiburtino – in none of those miserable streets which surround the city of Dis.[80]

At Marina di Pietrasanta he won the Carducci Prize for *La meglio gioventú* along with Paolo Volpini.

On 3 August Sereni wrote to him:

Before leaving I saw Bo[81] who told me about the Carducci and about Mondadori having promised you a contract for *Specchio*. These publishers of ours! As if your stuff had not been presented to them four or five years ago, and moreover warmly supported by the undersigned to whom they had been given to read!

In September, along with Giorgio Bassani, he had a marvellous trip by car through Central Italy in the footsteps of Giotto and Piero [della Francesca] – a journey which inspired the second part of the short poem 'La Richezza' ['Wealth'].

After an 'arid and truly unhappy' summer, at the beginning of October the Calvary of school began again; but this year it was shorter than usual because at the end of December he resigned for good.

On 28 October Francesco Leonetti wrote to Pasolini: 'Eleven years on and this lapse of time is also partly an indication of my frightening seriousness (but in the meantime I have become a "man of the world"). I say: this is the point where one has to set up a review.' It was the first mention of *Officina* [Workshop] and Pasolini answered him: 'I think it will be something interesting.'

He wrote the short poem which appeared in Number XIV of *Botteghe Oscure* with the title 'Notte a Piazza di Spagna' ['Night in Piazza di Spagna'], 'L'umile Italia' which was published in the April number of *Paragone* and 'Le ceneri di Gramsci' which was later collected with variants in the volume *Le ceneri di Gramsci*. The short stories *Dal vero* ['From life'] and *Mignotta* ['The tart – a story for a producer'] were later collected in *Alí dagli occhi azzurri*. William Weaver translated 'Appenino' which appeared in the American review *Folder*. New correspondents were the poet Vittorio Bodini, editor of the review *L'esperienza poetica* ['The poetic experience'] of Lecce; Antonio Altoviti, a film producer in Rome; and the publisher, Livio Garzanti.

---

1. The *Quaderni rossi* ['Red notebooks'] are five unpublished autographed notebooks which have two different titles: the first, at the beginning of the first notebook, is 'Pagine involontarie (romanzo)' ['Involuntary pages (novel)']; the second, at the beginning of the fifth notebook, is 'Il romanzo di Narciso' ['The novel of Narcissus']. In fact it is one autobiographical diary for the years 1946-7 written straight off, with blank spaces left waiting for the right expression, in which the daily journal alternates with memories of previous times right back to early infancy. Reworked with clear novelistic aims – but the autobiography is nevertheless always transparent – they became the narrative text published posthumously as *Atti impuri* ['Impure acts']. They were published by Garzanti in 1982 together with *Amado mio* ['My love'] and with an introduction by Attilio Bertolucci.

*Introduction*

**2.**\* Carlo Emilio Gadda (1893-1973), novelist, one of whose best known works is *Quer pasticciaccio de via Merulana* [*That Awful Mess on Via Merulana*] in which he makes remarkable use of Roman dialect.

**3.** Anteo Zambini fired at Mussolini and was stabbed to death by members of the crowd. It was probably a police provocation leading to laws for the defence of the State, the dissolution of political parties, the setting up of the OVRA (secret police), special courts and death sentences.

**4.** Salgari, author of a well-known textbook.

**5.** Giuseppe Carducci (1835-1907), major poet, Nobel prizewinner.

**6.** Giorgio Morandi (1890-1964), metaphysical painter famous for his still lifes.

**7.** Guerrin Meschino, hero of a medieval epic.

**8.** Giovanni Pascoli (1855-1923), lyric poet, patriotic socialist.

**9.** Gabriele d'Annunzio (1863-1938), poet, dramatist, novelist, adventurer inspired by the Nietzschean idea of the superman, intensely nationalistic.

**10.** This and the successive quotations are from an unpublished statement by Cesare Bortotto.

**11.** See 'Questi ritorni per me sono una vera pena' [These goings back are a real pain for me] by L. Serra in *Bologninconti*, No 9, September 1985.

**12.** Giuseppe Ungaretti (1888-1970), the most radical experimental Italian lyric poet of the twentieth century.

**13.** Alfonso Gatto (1909-76), hermetic poet and translator.

**14.** This and the following quotation are taken from the introduction by L. Serra '*Eredi, Setaccio, Stroligùt*' to Pasolini's *Lettere agli amici (1941-1945)* ['Letters to friends'], edited by L. Serra, Guanda, Parma 1976.

**15.** Pre-Littorals were the preliminaries to the *Littoriali*, such as the *Littoriali* for Art and Culture, which were national university competitions in social sciences and humanities. Their aim was to raise social consciousness. Pasolini and others used them for critical discussion of social topics.

**16.** Salvatore Quasimodo (1901-68), leading hermetic poet.

**17.** *Quai des Brumes*, film by Marcel Carné (1938).

**18.** Vincenzo de Bartholomaeis, philologist and student of medieval Italian literature, held the chair of Romance philology at Bologna until 1937, founding a very lively school.

**19.** This and the succeeding quotation are taken from the article 'Lettere a Franco Farolfi' ['Letters to Franco Farolfi'] by A.B. (Attilio Bertolucci) in *Nuovi Argomenti*, No 49, January-March 1976.

**20.** This and the following quotations are taken from 'Gioventú di un Poeta' ['A poet's youth'] by R. Roversi in *Bologninconti*, No 11-12, November-December 1975.

**21.** This and the successive quotations are taken from 'Testimonianza per Pier Paolo Pasolini' ['Testimony for P.P.P.'] by G. Contini in *Il Ponte*, No 4, 30 April 1980.

**22.** Gianfranco Contini (1912-90), Romance philologist, at this time teaching in Fribourg in Switzerland. Later Professor of Romance Philology at Florence University.

**23.** Pirona, nineteenth-century philologist. Compiled a dictionary of Friulano.

\* Bold figures indicate translator's notes throughout.

*Introduction*

24. Juan Ramon Jimenez (1881-1958), Spanish author of intensely private poetry expressed with preciosity of style.
25. Saetti Bruno (1902-84), Bolognese painter.
26. Filippo de Pisis (1896-1956), painter much influenced by French Impressionism.
27. Silvana Mauri, a close friend of Pasolini, niece of the publisher Bompiani.
28. *koiné* (Greek) - the spoken version of a language or dialect.
29. Antonio Machado (1875-1939), great lyric poet. A Republican, he died in exile from Franco's Spain. Soria was a region of Spain he celebrated in some of his best known poetry.
30. Attilio Bertolucci (b. 1911) poet, father of Bernardo Bertolucci (b. 1941), the film-maker whose first film *La commare secca* ['The Skinny Woman' (i.e. Death)] was a subject taken from Pasolini.
31. *Il Primato* ('The Primacy'), a review founded in 1940 by Bottai, a leading Fascist who had differences with Mussolini over policies. *Il Primato* published dissident views and used some anti-Fascist contributors.
32. Giuseppe Raimondi (1898-1985), writer and critic.
33. Bodoni, famous eighteenth-century typographer.
34. Romagnoli dell'Acqua, also a typographer
35. Giorgio Caproni (1912-90), poet and translator.
36. This and the following quotations are from an unpublished statement by G. Caproni.
37. Graziadio Ascoli (1861-1907), famous Italian philologist, held chair of linguistics in Milan. His studies included Friulano.
38. Jaufré Rudel, twelfth-century Provençal poet who celebrated his love - *de lonh* - for a princess only to die in her arms when they met.
39. On 25 July 1943 Mussolini was dismissed by the Fascist Grand Council.
40. Carlo Carrà (1881-1966), painter, one of the founders of the Futurist movement.
41. Dino Campana (1885-1932), radical poet, a rebel against literary institutions.
42. Paritito d'Azione - a political party, supported largely by middle-class liberals, which did not survive in post-war Italy.
43. One of the most famous poems of Giacomo Leopardi (1798-1837).
44. Giambattista Vico (1668-1744), historian and philosopher.
45. *félibrisme* - derives from the Félibrige, a society of prose writers and poets founded in 1854 by the writer Mistral to preserve the Provençal language. Hence *félibrer*: to meet among such people. Extended by Pasolini to writing in Friulano.
46. The *Decameron*, a collection of tales put together by Giovanni Boccaccio, the fourteenth-century writer and humanist.
47. *Roma, città aperta* [*Rome, Open City*] (1945), film by Rossellini secretly planned under the German occupation. Blends documentary and fiction. One of the major examples of neo-realist film-making.
48. From an unpublished statement by Tonuti Spagnol.
49. Ugo Foscolo (1778-1827), lyric poet.
50. Pietro Zorutti (1792-1867), satirical writer who used a kind of Friulano which was merely the dialect of the petty bourgeoisie of Udine.
51. Guido Gozzano (1883-1916), one of the crepuscular poets.
52. Another name for Lake Lugano.
53. Vittorio Sereni (1913-83), one of the hermetic poets. Later was instrumental in getting Pasolini's poetry published.
54. Giorgio Bassani (b. 1916), novelist and scriptwriter. Editor of the influential literary periodical *Botteghe Oscure*.
55. See *Il romanzo di Narciso e Alcina*, p.xx.

**56.** Carleton Washburne, director of schools in Chicago in the thirties – a pioneer of progressive education.

**57.** John Dewey (1859-1952), American educationalist who advocated child-centred education.

**58.** See 'Pedagogia' by A. Zanzotto in *Pasolini, cronaca giudiziaria, persecuzione, morte* ['Pasolini, judicial history, persecution, death'], Garzanti (Milan, 1977).

**59.** *crepuscolari* – literally 'twilight' poets, a school of poets born in the second half of the nineteenth century, defined by G.A. Borgese, an influential critic, as 'the twilight of Italian poetry'.

**60.** Umberto Saba (1883-1957), Triestine lyric poet.

**61.** Sandro Penna (1906-77), a hermetic poet.

**62.** De Gasperi (1883-1957), the Christian Democrat prime minister who dominated post-war Italian politics.

**63.** This and later quotations are from a filmed interview with Dino Peresson, one of the boys who figures in the novel. Reproduced in 'Il sogno di una cosa e i contadini' in *Reporter*, 26-7 October 1985.

**64.** From a statement by Giuseppe Zigaina.

**65.** Ippolito Nievo (1831-61), poet and novelist brought up in Friuli. Took active part in the Risorgimento. Wrote popular poetry. His best known works are *Le confessioni di un italiano* ['The confessions of an Italian'] and stories of peasant life.

**66.** See 'Quelque chose d'autre que la littérature' by V. Sereni in *Le point de l'Epée*, No 56-57, 1976.

**67.** Giacinto Spagnoletti (b. 1920), poet, anthologist.

**68.** This and the following quotation are from 'Pasolini maestro e amico' [P. teacher and friend] in *Perché Pasolini* ['Why Pasolini'], Guaraldi (Florence, 1978).

**69.** Giorgio Caproni (1912-90), one of the hermetic poets.

**70.** See 'Tutto Pasolini' ['All Pasolini'] by L. Cavicchioli in *La Domenica del Corriere*, 21 February 1979.

**71.** From the cover of *Ostia, un film di Sergio Citti* ['Ostia, a film by Sergio Citti'], Garzanti, 1970.

**72.** From Pasolini's introduction to the above.

**73.** Carlo Betocchi (1898-1985), poet and contributor to the Catholic literary review *Frontespizio*.

**74.** Anna Banti (1895-1978), distinguished novelist and publisher.

**75.** From Pasolini's introduction op. cit.

**76.** Luciano Anceschi (b. 1911), professor of philosophy at Bologna.

**77.** Giuseppe Gioacchino Belli (1791-1863), poet who wrote in Roman dialect a famous sequence of 2,000 sonnets.

**78.** Matteo Bandello (1485-1561), writer of novellas. A source for Shakespeare.

**79.** Mario Soldati (b. 1905), film-maker who considers himself primarily a writer, author of *America, primo amore* ['America, first love'] and *Lettere da Capri* ['Letters from Capri'].

**80.** Dis, the god of the underworld.

**81.** Carlo Bo (b. 1911), literary critic, essayist and senator.

# 1940

## 1 To Franco Farolfi
Parma
[*In possession of addressee: autograph*]

[Bologna, June 1940]

Dear Franco,

However did you suspect that I wouldn't reply to you? That same evening I wrote you one of those famous long letters – but this is what happened: I couldn't remember if the month in your address was October, November or September[1] which is why the letter waited on my desk until I could ask some-one. I asked Guigiallini;[2] when I got home I couldn't remember it properly any more but the only doubt remaining was between November and September (evidently the Bison was wrong) and that is why I sent the letter to this address – 20 via November, 13 – leaving to the intelligence of the postman the choice between 4 November and 20 September. This teaches one not to write the address right away. Amen.

Marks: It 7, Lat 7, Gk 7, histy 7, phil 7, maths 6, sc 7, art histy 8, military cult 8, gym 7.[3]

In the other letter I had written a lot of things of a sentimental nature and of an almost practical nature – the first I won't repeat because they are trees that have shed their blossom, the second are as follows: Pariah[4] will go into an office for a fortnight (he's started already) from 9 to 12 and from 3 to 7 or something like that. (This is something that gives me nightmares.) I got 27 in Romance Philology and 28 in Geography. The trip to Riccione is disappearing behind dark clouds. Very very probably we shall go (I, Ghezzi, Bignardi,[5] etc.) to the Venice Biennale; I'll write to you about this, in fact much more probably I'll talk to you about it, in more detail, the first time we meet in Modena, on Sunday 16th June, if circumstances do not prevent it, between 9 and 9.30 under the Ghirlandina;[6] so answer at once. Things are going somewhat slowly with the girl at the C.S.;[7] at the exams I met lots of girls, nice too, and I have very friendly relations with them. *Bis in die.*[8]

A hug,       PP

Space for Pariah
I have to go to the office and can't write you anything. Am very . . .

As you see Pariah had begun to write but it was very late and the pen had no more ink; in any case what he had to say to you was of little importance.

1 Many Italian streets are named after important dates in Italian history.
2 A schoolfriend, nicknamed 'the Bison'.
3 Farolfi's marks in the classical finals.
4 His friend Ermes Parini, nicknamed Paria (Pariah).
5 Agostino Bignardi.
6 La Ghirlandina: the tower of the cathedral in Modena, so called because of an ornamental feature like a garland.
7 The Casa del Soldato (Soldiers' Club) which Pasolini went to as the son of an army officer.
8 *Bis in die*: until that day.

## 2   To Franco Farolfi
Parma
[*In possession of addressee: autograph*]

[Bologna, June 1940]

Dear Franco,

What happened to you? Astonishment and other feelings. We were at Modena under the Ghirlandina from 9.20 till 10.40; there was no sign of you. How come? We even waited in vain for a letter from you with the explanation but the letter hasn't come either; it is only because I'm afraid something serious has happened to you that I am writing to you to tell you off severely. On the way back from Modena to Bologna it rained all the time and we got some aches and pains, perhaps rheumatic ones.

All this is not very cheering for many reasons. Write to us at once and fix an appointment with us with solemn oaths – and quickly because today is Thursday 4th and we are leaving for San Vito.¹ I shall stop in Venice to see the Biennale. It's raining and it's boring; the thing with the girl in the C.S is beginning to drag on in a tiresome way; I almost don't like her any more – I prefer Bianca whom I went for a walk with twice alone. Everything else is a provisional shadow[?] which weighs on me and bores me; I can't wait to leave and to build a life and a relationship with other completely new people and one that will be subject to my will. I don't want to let myself be dragged along any more by the hours and by habits. Let's hope I succeed.

I read Goncharov's *Oblomov* recently, which has nothing like the fascination of Dostoevsky and Tolstoy. I also read Calderón de la Barca's *Life is a Dream* which, although flawed sometimes to the point of obsession with Gongorism,² is of a surprising modernity; it had an extraordinary effect on me and I even wrote notes for a possible production of this work. If you want, as you said, to work up a contemporary culture, buy the last two numbers of *Primato*[3] where there is a very interesting discussion of hermeticism.[4]

Tell Constantino that I am full of praise for his shoelaces and tell Nini to buy a puppy.[5]

The fields are muddy and one can very seldom play football. How I shall enjoy myself in San Vito I don't know – perhaps not very much, perhaps I shall be bored as almost always happens with me, but in any case there will be Emilietta and in all probability lots of other girls. Today Pariah insisted that I leave him room to write to you and I'm leaving it for him. I hug you (hitting you hard over the head a few times as well).

Pier Paolo

Dear Franco, you won't be pleased for long to see my handwriting for if Pier Paolo has been nice to you I shall tell you off with sarcasm and nastiness: bow wow.

You don't come to Modena for some reason or other – the most comprehensible is fear of the rain. No others can exist and you will have thought it was much better to stay in Parma and go mad about girls rather than risk a soaking to see Pier Paolo and Pariah who, having come to Modena, could in any case very well go away again. You should be ashamed and, if you can, try to prove your innocence. I don't know if we shall see each other. You should be pleased to have a job; but listen to me because I know but haven't become a man at all.

Affectionate greetings and good wishes to your mother.          Pariah

1 A holiday resort in the dolomites.
2 A florid style which derives from the Spanish poet, Luis de Gongora (1561–1625).
3 *Primato* (Primacy): a review founded by Giuseppe Bottai (1895–1959), Fascist Minister of Education, which gave some space to dissident writers.
4 An inward-looking tendency in modern Italian poetry.
5 Schoolfriends.

## 3   To Franco Farolfi
Parma
[*In possession of addressee: autograph*]

[Bologna, June–July 1940]

Dear Franco,

I read in your letter about your mother's illness with great apprehension – I don't need to tell you with how much anxiety I wait for your news and it is impossible to say how many good wishes I send you and how much I hope your news is good.

In these days things of such great importance have happened that compared to them all our private affairs disappear and become grotesque; I live in a cloudy provisional state and am constantly expecting something different. I'd like to see you again first of all and together to put things back in place again. But that it not important now – what is important is that your mother recovers as soon as possible and as well as possible. Everything seems to be a prey of the wind these days! Everything rises and sets more rapidly than the sun. There's Pariah who it seemed would have to stop going to the office and now apparently he'll go there all the holidays; we who have changed the plans for the holidays two or three times; the girl in the Soldiers' Club who one evening makes me feel faint and another evening is like a piece of wood; I who had decided to join the University Battalion as a volunteer and now, naturally, no longer; the Ghirlandina which was to have seen us together and instead who knows how long it will miss us! But forget about that, there's nothing more to be done, because the wind turns everything upside down. And you, write to me at once and often because every so often I feel something wrong with my heart, I examine it and find it is worried about you and your family.

Pariah is in the office (I can assure you that this too is a great affliction) and naturally sends you greetings and hugs you as I do.

Pier Paolo

PS In case you're interested I got 30 in Eng Lit and in Philosophy.

## 4   To Franco Farolfi
Parma
[*In possession of addressee: autograph*]

[San Vito di Caldore, July 1940]
Dear Franco,

Forgive me if I have delayed a little before writing to you but I had to give precedence to Pariah and Melli[1] – to Pariah because I haven't seen him for longer and to Melli because I had important things to tell him about the diaries, etc. I can tell you almost nothing about myself. About the self you know because in many senses I am lost – in the vastness of the mountains which have a smell so powerful and so nostalgic that it produces very strong sensations in me; but above all because I have lost myself in surroundings and in a mentality which is not mine.

It is not a setting for middle-class holidays as Riccione was and neither is it a rustic and peasant place like Casarsa but is halfway between them; I find it difficult to get used to it. I don't know either how to dress or how to think within myself, or how to behave with others. The hours, the things that happen and habits – things I wanted to destroy – begin to draw me into their cycle again and what I put off from one day to the next – not knowing what it is – always passes me by in the distance. Yet I feel very lighthearted and am very light in the flesh – my thoughts are light too and have lost that emptiness which made me so sad in Bologna. I am light and hope while always never hoping anything important. Emilietta, physically, strikes me as less beautiful – but she is always very nice and is for me the only company. To begin with I wondered if my feeling for her was tenderness or friendship – it is the latter. There are some other girls of average calibre. More are going to come. But in any case thinking about girls is less important here than you would expect of me.

Talking of girls and of Emilietta, my aunt[2] had put about in our house the worry that I was in love with Emilietta and everyone – painfully with looks and half-sentences – hinted all sorts of things to me ('Ah poor Pier Paolo! So he's in love, the young man! Isn't it great to be young! But there are lots more good looking than that girl') I felt completely ridiculous. When my father left I went to the station with him and this conversation took place between us: He . . . 'and not too much poetry!' I: 'What do you mean – not too much poetry?' He: 'With that girl, with that Emilietta!' I: 'Dad, surely you don't believe all my aunt's talk and guess-work!' (silence) He: 'In any case remember, not too much poetry; all women are the same – with women you must only think about having fun.' And I said Yes.

The weather is rather nasty but I have a patience that rivals that of the mountains, which always stand there waiting for the clouds to pass, stop and do as they please on top of them.

I won't tell you anything about the Biennale because I am tired of talking on and on about it with Pariah; write me your impressions as soon as possible.

All good wishes to your family

Pier Paolo

c/o Ulisse Fiori, S. Vito di Cadore (Belluno)

1   Elio Melli, a friend from the *liceo*.
2   Giannina Colussi.

## 5   To Franco Farolfi

Parma

[*In possession of addressee: autograph*]

[Casarsa, August 1940]

Dear Franco,

I won't make my laziness an excuse for my long silence, given that laziness is excusable as an excuse only between elderly relatives. I put off answering you first of all because of our departure for Casarsa, then because of my cousin Annie's wedding,[1] then because of writing to Pariah and Emilietta, to whom I had more urgent things to say.

I am empty and without will-power. As always, things happen uninterestingly, sometimes they are moving. The wedding was marvellous but it only confirmed me in my ideas, which are opposed to matrimony itself. Casarsa had disappointed me but then everything disappoints me while it is there and when it is past I regret it. Now everything the countryside can give me I can have - peace, girls, concentration, meadows, leisure, drinks, and in reality all this is in my possession but it is sporadic, watered by a flood of empty and arid hours. And how much I shall regret the present days this winter - as always happens with me! Let's hope Pariah comes - when one is with a friend even the most ordinary and empty minutes can be used.

In any case it's a fine thing to be confused by a dream - I had one: the journey from San Vito to here by bicycle (130 kilometres - that's one of those events that cannot be recounted without the help of the voice and expression. Dawn, the Dolomites, the cold, the men with yellow faces, the unfamiliar houses and churches, the unfamiliar accent, the peaks and the misty valleys lit by the sun.

I am reading a book which interests me intensely - Hölderlin's *Hyperion*;[2] it deals with problems and a growth of feelings and spiritual situations which are a burning reality to me. Very often I seem to hear myself speak.

As for girls I'd merely have to pick and choose - you go down the street, see a couple of dark-haired ones, you look at them and they say to you: 'Ciao, good-looking boy.' Some of them are really pretty; but my lack of will-power and my scepticism triumph over all other feelings and I am waiting for something or other - maybe Pariah.

I go as usual and play football but even this does not amuse me as once it did.

It might look from what I am writing to you as if I am sad, lonely and pessimistic, whereas I have never been so gay and so full of appetite - perhaps it comes from the fact that I am becoming less and less intelligent (in the usual sense of the word) and more aerated – at least that's what it feels like to me.

A hug,        PP

Greetings to your family

1   Annie Naldini.
2   Johann Christian Friedrich Hölderlin (1770–1843), German Romantic poet.

## 6   To Franco Farolfi
Parma
[*In possession of addressee: autograph*]

[Casarsa, September 1940]

Dear Franco,

I am writing to you but cannot imagine where and when you will be able to read this letter. Are you in Milan or in Mantua? I say this because I still have a vague idea about something you wrote to me about your bicycle trip.

You must have been very nice – you and the baker's girl – did you kiss her with your tongue? Perhaps it's because you didn't do that that you didn't enjoy it very much. Perhaps Pariah has told you how things ended up with Giovannina – she isn't Giovannina but almost a Giovannino, that is to say halfway between a Giovannina and a Giovannino. Her friend described her to me without keeping anything back – I can't describe it to you again. Can you imagine anyone with worse luck than me? It is something that happens to one man in three million or more. She is still in love with me, Claudia tells me, and I am water [?] and stone when I get near her. The fine thing is that now that she absolutely can't be mine I feel I desire her more than before. All this has disgusted me and for now I can't start up over again with someone else.

Now my life in Casarsa has dried up; I keep feeling that it is almost time to leave and that I can't finish anything I begin . . . It is very sad to leave here – another summer is over and another period in my life, I am impatient to see once more the things I am leaving, at the same time hope that moment may be very distant because in between there must come a year of my life, and I very much hope that it will be the longest possible because one's nineteenth year will not come back.

Meantime life here will continue, they will harvest the grapes, they will sow the seed, they will sing as they go after the girls, and I will be absent from all that, as if I were dead. On the other hand, my life in Bologna attracts me – I have plans for some good things to be brought to fruition during the year (books, pre-Littorials, sport).

Now I am only studying and reading. I read *Le Occasioni* ['Chances'] by Montale[1] which I liked although it didn't excite me, what did excite me were Quasimodo's[2] translations of the Greek lyric poets.[3] 'Oh crowned with violets, divine, sweetly smiling Sappho!' I read Kleist's extraordinary *Penthesilea*, Strindberg's *The People of Hemsö*, very fine. I am painting too and have got better at it. I shall arrive in Bologna on the 20th; on the first Sunday after I get back we shall see each other in Modena. So it is not very far off the moment when we shall meet again.

A hug,      Pier Paolo

Many regards to your family

1   Eugenio Montale (1896–1981), major lyric poet of the 'crepuscular' school.
2   Salvatore Quasimodo (1901–68), the outstanding poet, founder of the hermetic school, and master of the new Italian lyric; Nobel prizewinner 1959.
3   *I lirici greci* ('The Greek lyric poets') by Salvatore Quasimodo, Edizioni di 'Corrente' (Milan, 1940).

# 7   To Franco Farolfi
Parma
[*In possession of addressee: autograph; incomplete*]

[Bologna, autumn 1940]
Dear Franco,

As is my usual terrible habit, I have waited perhaps a little too long before writing to you. In this period nothing particularly interesting has happened in what goes on in my head – that is to say, nothing definitive and therefore nothing one can put on paper. The usual problems, the usual enthusiasms, the usual sudden setbacks. Only my ability to speak is more fluent than usual and I find it a great relief to be able to speak about it with my friends here. The poetic vein is very dry; and in that connection I don't know when I shall be able to type out my poems. I don't have time for the following reasons:

1) I must get down to finishing that little book on Italian contemporary art for a series of monographs brought out by the Gil[1] (editor Cantelli). I have just begun this short essay; I must finish it and then type it.

2) I have to do a paper on Ardengo Soffici[2] for a girl at the University of Florence. (I'll earn about 200 lire for it, which together with the great sum of 200 I shall get in payment for the book on art, will come to a nice little sum!)

3) I have to begin working for the Latin exam which covers a lot of ground.

4) Over and above the usual tasks which fill up my day in a terrible way I have others – at the Guf[3] as usual and now at the Gil as 'adviser to the youth committee on art' – a bit funny?

*1940*

Now I should, as usual, talk to you about things of another kind, by their nature more ours and more intimate. I shall therefore write for you the first short chapter of a little treatise I am writing and which I call:

On life
as the constant transformation
of dream into reality

1

Introduction

We do not wish, friends, to number swine among those who live in the exile decreed by the ephebes. Joyously these pass along our island – pass like the waters surprised by a river, surprised by the immature happiness of living. But we are not afraid, we are not the fantasticating poet who is content with the *reality* of men as he is wont to change it in his dreams. This fantasticating poet is like the *false* man who listens to music and thinks of it as a pretext for his own sluggish dream. Oh sluggish dream! How you sustain us in the luminous sea of existing-together! But we are not like the fantasticating poet who humiliates himself, contents himself with reality transformed into idea, by the tension of the spirit itself. We, friends, are tired of the tense spirit, of intense life – thought burns us like a feverish sickness, we are like children who cannot be still and listen to those who speak to them. We seek distension – we want to slacken the bows of the . . .

1  Gioventú italiana del Littorio: a Fascist youth organization.
2  Soffici (1879–1964), avant-garde painter and poet.
3  Gioventú universitaria fascista: the Fascist organization for students.

## 8   To Franco Farolfi

Parma

[*In possession of addressee: autograph*]

[Postmark: Bologna, 1 November 1940]

Dear Franco,

I am very happy that you have decided to come.

I *absolutely advise* against the bicycle – think what a bore it would be to have to do ninety km alone, how little – how minimum the baggage you can take with you (and you might, just as an example, tear your trousers). Then there's the rain (a fortnight's rain day after day would not be unusual in November).

Come by train, send us a wire with the time of your arrival and we will be at the station waiting for you. If you need a bicycle here in Bologna there would be my brother's.

On the days when you are here I warn you that for about two hours a day I shall have to study (2 hours isn't much, in fact, and I'll do it early in the morning).

I await you with great impatience.

Long live Italy.

Affectionate hugs,     Pier Paolo and Pariah

## 9   To Franco Farolfi
Parma
[*In possession of addressee: autograph postcard*]

[Postmark: Bologna, 26 November 1940]

Dear Franco,

Yesterday I wrote you a letter but I don't remember if I posted it or if someone else posted it – the fact is I can't find it any more.

So as a precaution I am writing to you again that I am back in Bologna, that I have nothing to do and that I am therefore only waiting for you to write to me – so do it right away.

So let's hope we see each other again as soon as possible – my greetings and thanks to your family in anticipation.

A hug,     Pier Paolo

## 10   To Franco Farolfi
Parma
[*In possession of addressee: autograph*]

[Bologna, autumn 1940]

Dear Franco,

For the millionth time I ask someone to forgive me for having put off writing to him. You know my habit – but perhaps your parents will be surprised at my laziness – give them warm greetings and also many thanks.

I went to camp with the Militia – you can't come to that camp. So I wrote at once to my aunt in S. Vito di Cadore – the moment she replies I'll let you know.

I don't attend the University – I'm fed up. Manzoni is still sociable and nice. Melli bores me to death by beginning a sentence at the University and finishing it (after innumerable parentheses and regressions) at the Soldiers' Club – he had to finish it perforce with dots . . . Cloudy Elio!

Pariah comes and goes to the office: Pariah-the-Office. Where is Pariah? In the office.

*1940*

Give my greetings to my new and old friends. I haven't seen Basso yet, tell him I'd like to see him, but I don't remember what day he is in Bologna.

We too are becoming basketball players for the Guf – so we have to give ourselves airs and I shudder to think of the pitiful figures we will cut.

I should talk to you now about what I am feeling like – but I am very tired (even if I haven't...) so I am copying two poems for you which will perhaps give you a good idea of my general and prevailing state of mind; I don't know whether they are bad or passable, because I have just finished them.

*The snake-charmer*

Boredom, solitary worm.
I feed your hunger in my guts
and you embrace me.
Despicable tapeworm, I clasp you
round my heart
and you joyously stretch out a veil
before my eyes;
then the human faces are distorted
and the mouths open like caves
the bellies are swollen like casks.

My solitary worm, I hate you
and despise you and dream of cursing you ...
and instead my voice enchants you
and you dance moving your head

With your tail you poke at my stomach:
so sing and so we will console each other.

*Invective*

I shall drive you out, stupid fat beasts,
burning your houses.
I shall burnt the churches, the theatres.
the dwellings. You will flee, moaning at first.
Then enraged you will pursue me
sniffing out my footprints.
I will come back through thickets raving
I shall trample the mud biting my fingers ...
But when the most beautiful of all,
the fittest, the proudest, reaches me, then,
I shall turn round and brown with blood
he will weep at my feet.

For if my heart is a crippled fugitive
It is also a bearded raging hero.

It seems to me they are somewhat unorthodox in their musicality; they are all in jerks but I like them – they made me get things out of my system.

Down with offices, down with the bureaucracy, down with reaction, down with puritans, down with Carmine Gallone.[1]

I'm breaking off because it is late and I want to go to the Soldiers' Club.

An embrace,        Pier Paolo

PS. Thanks to your parents.
Down with C.G., De Stefani, Cantini, Forzano, etc.

1   Carmine Gallone (b.1886), film director of elaborate spectacular films.

# 1941

## 11  To Franco Farolfi
Parma
[*In possession of addressee: autograph*]

[Bologna, winter 1941]

Dear Franco,

Naturally I shall begin by giving you all the reasons why I have put off replying to you for rather a long time: they are two in number – 1) I have been writing like mad at an article for *Architrave*[1] and a radio entry for the radio pre-Littorials.[2] I had influenza for a week with the usual nasty feelings of indisposition which prevent and inhibit all mental and physical activity. Now that I am convalescent I feel I have come out of a frozen tube.

I am as happy as a lamb because I feel quite well physically, if I felt very well I'd be as happy as a reindeer. Talking of reindeer, I saw a Nordic film *Laila* which combines marvellous qualities with irremediable defects. The director is a poet who does not know how to use the camera – he has an intuition for splendid sequence and sometimes achieves them. The cutting is clumsy. Altogether the film disturbed me greatly and opened up vast new spaces in my imagination (I dream about reindeer, thaws, fiords, packs of wolves and the folklore life of the young people who in spring dress themselves up with necklaces and, clad in furs, sing with the sweetest voices as they splash with their feet in the shining mud).

Thank Umberto for the greetings card which I haven't replied to, not knowing his address. Arrange things with him, ask him when he is going to be in Bologna, at what time, etc., and tell him to come to see me at home, provided naturally that he has time. Write to me when he can do all this and I shall wait for him.

Today I had decided to write to you and tell you to come to Bologna; but a postcard arrived from the Militia which asks me to go to the office on the 17th to hear about the camp which I have put my name down for. I shall give you more news about all that. My life in the last three weeks – apart from the last one – influenza – has been peaceful and – why not? – enjoyable. We have formed a nice group I, Pari, Manzoni (who has become more intelligent and nicer than he used to be) and Melli (who has come back to literature and is in a better humour). Together we began by taking up basketball which we still like very much. Then we made the theatre into the idol of our thoughts – we have decided to get together a company and possibly to act in the Soldiers' Club. Things are still undecided – so far we have only acted pieces of tragedies and comedies among the four of us (two by two alternately). I am often a prey to concupiscent thoughts but as for doing anything . . .

I saw Pirandello's *Tonight We Improvise* (as perhaps I told you) and *Our Town* by Wilder. The last a most interesting play and one that would be worth very long discussions, because it deals with original and necessary problems specially concerning the technicalties of staging. If you have seen it too we could talk about it at leisure.

Lately I have taken up music enthusiastically. An event of exceptional importance for me – Beethoven. In the last few days I heard on the radio the 4th, the 6th, the 7th and the 8th symphony. I listened to them with almost complete attention, experiencing pleasure and immense consolation: feelings which I used to experience from a play or opera or work of art, etc. and which finally I have also experienced with music. I have elevated music from being a purely hedonistic concept – a casual, fleeting one – to a vision which I could define as 'spectacular'. And I have changed certain convictions radically – e.g. I no longer, as I once told you, seek in music objective, descriptive music but music with a life of its own; a spectacle not of human figures or characters nor of the beauties of nature but a spectacle which lives through the counterposing of purely musical feelings. All this naturally goes for symphonic or chamber music, etc., not for opera. Now I am unable to express myself properly because it is the first time that I write about musical things and the right expression escapes me – but I should like to tell you how much finer it is to be conscious of understanding in a piece of music what the composer wanted to express, not making our pictorial or sentimental ideas correspond – more or less gratuitously or in a dilettanteish way – to the musical idea of its creator but allowing the feeling to vibrate within us under the fascination of musicality, without having recourse to too facile flights of the imagination. Because if in a painter one admires his painting and not those moral, representational commemorative aspects which his picture may contain (see Croce),[3] in a musician should we not admire simply his music in itself, leaving to one side what he may possibly wish to describe (something which, by the way, never happens with the great musicians)?

I have noticed that whereas before, to stay and listen to music and understand it, I had to have recourse to images and sentimental ideas, now there is actually no need for them; inside us there is something musical which becomes directly feeling, without the need of sentimentalism, remaining music without the need of images. I have been able to test this by listening to Beethoven – listen to any movement of any symphony of his, you will feel such a power of feeling, such a passion that you are moved and don't know why. (Certainly you don't imagine seduced and abandoned girls or a jealous lover on an ill-treated child or a loving mother); and yet you are moved by the succession of questions and answers, by that sequence of sounds, you are moved although you don't see anything being described (described in the ordinary sense of the word). The fact is that the pain, the problem, the yearning – call it what you like – of the Beethovenian soul has expressed itself in music and the music causes to vibrate again in you (by means of that purely musical something which exists in us and which must be cultivated) that pain, that problem, that yearning.

That is why simply descriptive music is not great music, but only mediocre or average hedonism – that is why nothing is more unpleasant than onomatopoeic music which is rampant in the concerts of mixed light music organized by the EIAR[4] with exasperating frequency.

And that is why Beethoven's 6th is, of those I have heard, the one that pleases me least; in fact whatever people say, there are in it some vestiges of description not transformed purely and fully into 'music as such' (the cuckoo, the thunder, a tree blown down by the tempest, etc.); while the one I prefer of them all up to now is the 7th – 'the apotheosis of the dance' – the most equivocal, the least definable. Everything is uniquely music and rhythm (the second movement is for me the greatest page of music ever written).

As for the music of opera (which engages me less however) I would have to start a long discourse: I shall tell you briefly that it seems to me that in it the opposite to symphonic music happens, since song, over and above being beautiful music, beautiful melody, must serve to depict a character and express a passion; the musical accompaniment must therefore describe a climate and describe as well human feelings and passions. That is why people are wrong who say that it is better to listen to opera on the radio so as to enjoy the music more; opera is born to be seen, as well as heard, because the music is not born by mere musical self-creation, not as expression as such, but as the musical interpretation and expression of visible action. All this is true more in theory than in practice since very often the musicians rely on the mere musical inspiration, forgetting their own characters and everything else (a defect specially in Italian music in a fluent vein). I am sure I have fallen into some contradictions to which you could reply but I don't have time or room. Keep this letter because one day I think you will want to look at it again, because these are the first seeds of a musical thought which is being born in me. Margherita's lament in Boito's[5] *Mefistofele* is very beautiful. How rhetorical, arid, short of ideas Puccini is!

Greetings to your family, to my friends.

An embrace,      Pier Paolo

1   A paper of the Guf in Bologna, published from December 1940.
2   Littorials: competitions organized by the Fascist Youth organizations.

3  Benedetto Croce (1866–1952), idealist philosopher and literary theorist.
4  EIAR: the Italian state broadcasting organization.
5  Arrigo Boito (1842–1918), composer who collaborated as librettist to Verdi in *Otello* and *Falstaff.*

## 12  To Franco Farolfi
Parma
[*In possession of the addressee: autograph*]

[Bologna, winter 1941]

Dear Franco,

I got your letter yesterday and today I saw Umberto – your letter made me burst with laughter – poor Franco, are you really so cold?

I talked quite a long time with Umberto but not easily because Serra was there with me, then we met Sgardi, etc. etc.; I hope to have more frequent talks with him in the next few days.

I don't know Debussy well but the little I do I like very much – that's all I can say.

As Umberto will have told you, it is impossible to go to San Vito because of the huge price; I advise you, if you can, to go to the Parma Militia. That is what we shall do, very probably (but that way the pleasure is cut by at least half). Emilietta wrote to me and I replied. The Gazzotti girl is boring me to death, as they say; I shouldn't be indifferent to her. Franchina is in Rome and I have asked the Gazzotti girl for her address. The Magri girl (remember?) has died.

For my first moment of goodhumour and leisure I have a plan ready for approaching a girl: I go up to her (any girl), greet her by taking off my hat and put it in front of her mouth saying 'Spit into it'; naturally she doesn't spit and I thank her for the favour she does me by not spitting into it. Then I show that I feel obliged to her and have to return the favour, and I pretend to stand on her foot but at the last moment I don't stand on it. 'Now we are friends,' I shall say, 'because those who exchange courtesies and favours are friends.' And so we shall go off along the avenues singing and whispering words of love.

Umberto talked to me about Ibsen and Benassi; I only partly share his view on Memo's poor interpretation – at any rate it is better than the classical one by Zacconi:[1] the former's is less guilty because of aestheticizing slickness than the latter's is by psycho-physiological staging.

I don't like my two poems[2] any more – they are some of the ones I most dislike – only the first and last two verses seem good in their 'invective'. Perhaps seeing that you are reading Baudelaire it is right that you should find a *poète maudit* in me; but between me and poetry like that there is a substantial difference. In me *maudite* poetry only represents occasional chance moments whereas in the *poètes maudits* it is their basic stance, their substance, their essence. As for Soffici and the Futurists – there's absolutely nothing there – in the first (not in the ideas but in the sound) there is a trend that recalls Ungaretti. But they simply do not merit any further talk.

Pariah hasn't been very well for 3 or 4 days – I didn't see him today which means he isn't better yet.

I am now engulfed in the whirl of a new job – using the Italian language – Tasso's *Rime* ['Rhymes'] after S. Anna.[3] The bibliography is immense – up to a total of four hours' work so far in the library just taking notes and seeing what books there are on this subject. This is classical university work done out of a pure sense of rhetoric and erudition, which I have a horror of and which is an act of courage I shall demolish to Prof. Calcaterra's[4] face when I give him my report. What importance can these thousands of yellowed and toneless verses of a minor poet like Tasso have for me, who idolizes Cézanne, who responds so strongly to Ungaretti, who cultivates Freud?

I often go to play basketball – I am hopeless but I have a lot of fun. Sport is truly my most pure, continual, spontaneous consolation. Now I have a desperate desire to go skiing – I dream of the Dolomites as a lofty world, above the clouds, sunny, loud with shouts and laughter. Do you remember how on the top of the peaks the wind raises clouds of fine snow when everything is clear? The little wooden bedrooms, the village children, and all the other magnificent things? And think too that we are reaching our twentieth year without a [celebratory] ball. It's sad – not to say disgusting – but we are virile and warlike.

I enclose in this letter a poem I wrote about a month ago. You're not obliged to read it but I think it will probably interest you; and then what interests me above all are your fresh and spontaneous judgements. I wrote it in one of those moments which the classical writers are wont to call 'poetic furore'; I was writing without knowing what I could write and how I would go on and yet the verses came to me clearly as if worked out beforehand. I was sad and full of unfamiliar desires – by writing I found relief. Rereading this poem at some distance in time I rediscovered the state of mind that inspired it in me. It is only a state of mind – the title and the logical meaning I gave it later: the logical, narrative meaning is given by the legend of the flute-player who has himself followed – by enchanting them – by the children of a village and then shuts them up in a cave – the allegorical meaning is: the flute-player represents the transition, a secret one, from naïvety to cunning, from before puberty to adolescence.

All that, I repeat, is secondary and subsequent – it is the parallel to the principal meaning that gave birth to the poem which is a lament for lost childhood and the exaltation of violent and sensual youth.

*The magic flute*

Here is winter, hear it coming!
the wind blows; the clouds, the disturbed sea
open their eyes, fleeing ceaselessly;
they cover my face my hair with those naked dreams
icy and elusive! On the hills there is mud,
the damp ravines bow their backs, the caves
and the mosses smell of death.
Oh, to flee from here and go off
to the benign backs of those mountains
where, crowned with green lizards and dripping buds,
the sun may lead spring by the hand,
waving branches and leafy peach-trees.
Oh for me to hold in my firm hands
the pierced cane, and thus make music
over the plains and piazzas, the ravines and the thickets,
the laughing countryside and the sown gardens,
the villages, the streets, and on through the green dewy
    orchards,
make such sweet music, and for my body of an adult child
to go so beautiful that the boyish tribe will not hestitate,
neither scornful nor hostile, to follow me with uncertain
    steps.
Let them sing them with me,
the melodies, let them dance then with men garlanded
    with wreaths and chaplets, all troubled by new love.
Play, oh my tender dancing flute!
Boys, do you wonder at my easy stride?
On my sea-green back I carry the smallest;
there your hands play among the wreath I fasten on me
of white flowers. Let us go, my tender flock:
the mountain is wide, the wood damp.
I shall make you my slaves, and the most beautiful
(which of you?) with shining air
shall stand upright beside my goblet.
It is spring. I am the prince. Let us go.
The March of your limbs is sweet,
tender birds that have fled from the woods!
Do you not hear the weeping of your mothers?
They are weeping over the empty beds!
But let us go! it is spring, and the thunder rolls,
at each step time leaves us . . .

Unripe virgins, do not dare to look me in the face:
the shameless secret of my adult life is shamed!
I shall tell you by the music of my flute
of the hungry violence of the nocturnal nakednesses I have
    lived.

Many greetings and good wishes to your family

A hug,        Pier Paolo

PS. I think your family want you to spend Christmas with them; if not I'd say to come quickly to Bologna – in fact, for us the camp begins in January. And if none (of us three) goes skiing we shall pass happy days together just the same, here in Bologna.

PS. I'm pleased for you because you have found a nice new friend in Umberto.

1    Zacconi, actor, contemporary of Eleanore Duse.
2    See Letter 10.
3    Torquato Tasso (1544–95), author of the epic *Gerusalemme Liberata*, was confined in the lunatic asylum of Sant' Anna in Ferrara.
4    Carlo Calcaterra, lecturer in literature at the University of Bologna to whom Pasolini was to present his thesis on Pascoli.

## 13   To Franco Farolfi
Parma
[*In possession of addressee: autograph*]

[Bologna, January–February 1941]
Dear Franco,

Before replying to you I have waited a few days to see if I received the letter you promised me on your postcard.

It was very wrong of you not to send me the very long letter you told me about! Don't do it again.

I'd have a tremendous number of things to tell you – from the Camp on. I don't know where to begin – there is no distinction in chronology or importance. We would have to meet to be able to have a long talk about it.

In this immensely arid life of mine there is not a single flower which speaks of living humanity. I am getting more and more like my *spectacles* – my brain is a garden planted with tulips. I have got to such a point of agnosticism that I not only don't – as they say – go after girls but don't even look at them so as not to be upset – offended, bored, humiliated, like a foal without teats.

But now, as you know, I am exaggerating, impelled by a particularly negative moment. Besides I have got to this point – I dreamt that I split into two very beautiful versions of myself and embraced myself (but without the slightest sexual impulse, indeed I am experiencing a chaste and sour sensation – let me point out to you, on the other hand, that lately I have been able to give myself over to a severe bout of abstinence).

I need sun, good weather, friends. (Pariah is always in the office, now he will join up – that's tremendous!); above all I ought to deprive myself of my greatest and only consolation – reading. But in these last weeks I have perhaps exaggerated in this sense – I have read a book and a half a day. My culture has been entirely given fresh blood and has extended into new regions which are still partly obscure; they have all the virgin fascination of the unknown which must be discovered. (Modern contemporary literature naturally.) But we'll talk about that more when we meet.

As for music – three events of unequal importance: Benedetti-Michangeli, Semprini, Agnelli.

I don't feel like expanding now on these matters – we'll talk about them when the time is more propitious.

The provisory state of affairs *in pendente* – created in the last few weeks by a volunteer spirit, by the call-up of students born in 1921, the proposed closing of the University, the possible suspension of the Littorials to the preparation for which I have given body and soul – all this has thrown me into a stormy state. And to think that up to a few days ago I was the most flourishing, fat, bright-eyed, happy, self-assured of young men! Melli is a locust-mole; Manzoni I like more and more and is a consoler – we have a plan for a very pleasant drunken session in the very near future.

Prepare the ground, in any way, to be able to come here to Bologna at the very beginning of March.

I won't re-read this bad letter – for two reasons: 1) because I have suddenly become good-tempered again (today after dinner I shall go and play basketball); 2) because seeing how ungrammatical and unpleasant it is I would not send it to you.

Many greetings to your family

A hug,       Pier Paolo

*1941*

## 14   To Franco Farolfi
Parma
[*In possession of addressee: autograph*]

[Bologna, January–February 1941)]

Dear Franco,

I apologize and recognize I am in the wrong in the way that is more than serious – stupid. But for me this has been more than a month – a period in my life. I have been swept by such a storm that I could barely speak to myself – now I almost feel that I am on the shore but I don't dare to turn my head round and look for fear that the world I have left might call me back with its allurements. I am on the edge of the beach – I am now almost sure of being safe on solid ground. When I shall have victory in my grasp without hesitations and regrets I shall explain all this better to you.

Have you ever heard in some philosophy or other of the concept of breaking the chains which tie one to the past by an act of pure will? That is what I am trying to do. I want to kill a sick and hypersensitive adolescent who tries to pollute my life as a man as well – and he is already moribund – but I shall be cruel to him even if basically I love him because he has been my life up to today's threshold.

Apart from all this other things have assailed me and almost stopped me breathing – some initial manias (to learn to play the banjo, to take up athletics, to join Virtus), then the exams about which, I don't know why, I am very worried and if this letter is so hurried it is because in a few minutes I have to go and deal with, go through all the thousand bureaucratic complications at the secretariat, and then ask as well when the next exam will be.

But another very important event has taken place in my family – my father left the day before yesterday for Rome from where he has to go on to Italian East Africa. I won't describe to you – because you'll imagine it very well – the state of affairs that arose between us.

I think that until I have fixed the exams we won't be able to meet – a pity because your presence in the struggle I have told you about would have been very helpful to me.

Better still I have decided that as we had arranged you will come here to me in Bologna for two days – then as soon as I can I shall come to Parma too.

If you can come, come quickly – send me a telegram. I expect you at least before the first of the month.
Try and do all you can to come.

I embrace you affectionately,        Pier Paolo

## 15  To Franco Farolfi
Parma
[*In possession of addressee: typewritten*]

[Bologna, spring 1941]

Twice and thrice dear Franco,

Today is Tuesday and today I got your letter saying that this morning at the latest we will meet under the Ghirlandina. As you see it is astronomically impossible. On the other hand we could not have met in any case for two reasons: 1) because I have an exam on the 3rd and am very badly prepared; 2) because for two days I have had an unspeakably sore stomach which obliges me to stay shut up at home with body-belts and taking all sorts of precautions.

Farewell, Modena! But before our respective summer holidays we can see each other all the same and say hello so on your way to Ancona you can stay with us for a day or two (I'd like to say a week – but with these ration cards!). Write soon and fix the day and time for your arrival here.

Pariah left yesterday. Serra was leaving at three. Carlo will leave tomorrow. We will leave on the 10th; Melli (as usual) doesn't know when he's leaving.

I am marvellously idiotic – but in the way the gestures of someone who has won a lottery are idiotic – at least the stomach-ache is beginning to go away and so I feel myself prey to euphoria.

As for virginities I pass long hours of languor and extremely vague dreams which I alternate with mean, stupid attempts at action and with periods of extreme indifference. Three days ago Pariah and I went down into the den of a merry prostitute where the big tits and the breath of naked forty-year-olds made us think with nostalgia of the lidos of innocent childhood. Then we peed dejectedly.

Friendship is a very nice thing. The night I am telling you about we ate at Paderno and then in the complete darkness we climbed up towards Pieve del Pino – we saw an immense number of fireflies which made clumps of fire among the clumps of bushes and we envied them because they loved each other, because they were seeking each other with amorous flights and lights while we were arid and all males in artificial peregrinations.

Then I thought how beautiful friendship is and the bands of twenty-year-old youths who laugh with their innocent male voices and take no notice of the world around them, continuing along their lives, filling the night with their shouts. Theirs is a potential masculinity. Everything in them turns to laughter, to bursts of laughter. Never does their virile enthusiasm appear so clear and overwhelming as when they seem to have become once more innocent children because their complete and joyous youth is still present in their bodies. Even when they are talking about Art or Poetry. I have seen – and saw myself in the same way – young men talking about Cézanne and it seemed as if they were talking about one of their love affairs, with a shining and troubled look. That is how we were that night – we clambered up the sides of the hills among the undergrowth which was dead and their death seemed alive, we made our way through orchards and trees laden with black cherries and reached the top of a high hill. From there one could see two very distinct and fierce searchlights very far off – mechanical eyes from which there was no escape, and then we were seized by terror at being discovered while dogs barked and we felt guilty and fled along the brow, the crest of the hill. Then we found another grassy patch – a circle so small that six pines a little apart were sufficient to encompass it. There we lay down wrapped in blankets and talking pleasantly together we heard the wind beating and raging in the woods and we did not know where we were nor what places were around us. At the first signs of light (which is something unutterably beautiful) we drank the last drop from our bottles of wine. The sun was like a green pearl. I stripped off my clothes and danced in honour of the light – I was all white, while the others wrapped in their blankets like *peones* [Spanish peasants] trembled in the wind. Then we wrestled in the light of the dawn until exhaustion came; then we lay down, then we lit the fire in honour of the sun but the wind put it out ... Other things have happened which I don't have time or room to tell you – I'll do so as soon as possible. See you soon. Greetings to Umberto and your family.

I embrace you,       PPP

## 16   To Franco Farolfi
Parma
[*In possession of addressee: autograph*]

[Bologna, spring 1941]

Dear Franco,

I am as usual a bit confused and have a bad conscience about my usual detestable and highly deplorable silence. Naturally there is no excuse that will hold up because I could always have had time to write you a couple of lines.

I have been living through sad days:
1) Departure of Pariah and Melli. Very sad hours which do not encourage hopes – I have been downcast and without the will to do anything, very undecided whether to ask to volunteer and leave as well. Before their departure we indulged in a little orgy and to the intoxication of alcohol – something which led me to piss repeatedly that night against the doors of the cafés. (Something that is now distant and lost.)

2) Cultural pre-Littorials. I took part in the pre-Littorials for Literary Criticism, winning first place, praised by eminent critics like Bertocchi, Guidi, Corazza, etc. I was to have gone to San Remo to take part in the Littorials but this year they have been cancelled, to my great annoyance.

3) Best of all – the inter-Faculty football tournament. I was captain of the Arts Faculty team. A wonderful one. I am in better form than ever before in my life. The Faculty of Letters ended up fourth out of six teams – we were very unlucky. We shall take part in another tournament very soon where I hope we get a better placing.

On all these matters I would have an infinite number of observations to make but I don't have the patience to write and lose myself in particulars. Let's hope we can soon speak – as soon as I know definitely about the near future (I shall perhaps have to go into camp for the Officer Cadets' Course). I shall write to you to fix when we shall meet – I'd propose Modena now that the good weather has returned.

This week or next I had decided to go to Padua to see Pariah – always provided that circumstances permit – would you like to come too? (By bicycle as far as Bologna, etc., etc.) Tell Basso to come and see me as he did about a month ago and give him my warm greetings.

What a tragic sense of this life I am having! My only consolation were my friends and you are all so far away from me. I wish those hours spent together on our bicycles – me, you and Pariah – would return. It hurts me to see the leaves budding on the trees as when we were happy students from the *liceo* on holiday.

An embrace,      Pier Paolo

## 17   To Franco Farolfi
Parma
[*In possession of addressee: typewritten*]

[Bologna, June 1941]

Dear Franco,

Having got your letter I went through a long period of indecision because I was uncertain if I should keep trying to persuade you not to postpone our meeting or to postpone it forthwith. I'd very much like to see you and to spend a few hours together – just in these days I was struck by violent nostalgia for our past (the good weather coming back, the trees putting on their leaves, the little café tables in the open, the boys cycling about on what look like new bicycles) – everything reminds me of our long-ago (but not so long-ago) last days of school. I remember Sasso, the caves of the Farneto, the Calanchi.

But never mind – we know by this time that all one can do is to remain in a continual state of discontent.

But as for our meeting, I think too that we should wait till the exams are over – up to now I have done absolutely nothing for school. I am taking three exams for which I must do a lot of preparation. I am very fed up with this university culture which consists of dust and palimpsests. But in the midst of the extreme opacity of that culture, and still in the cultural area, I have been – to tell the truth for more than a month – very excited by an idea/a passion we have. I, Serra, Leonetti, Roversi are hatching a review (title *Eredi* ['Heirs']) which will come out after the war. We are preparing its programmes, topics, etc. with immense joy. With a little less joy we are finding out about things and making contracts from an economic point of view. (This was something else I wanted to talk to you about when we met – and to Umberto too because of the music criticism.)

Unfortunately I won't finish my exam until about 15 June and so do you, I believe. How far off our appointment is!

In any case Umberto I could meet even sooner – tell him to visit me often. I'll introduce him to the co-editors.

Now, as I usually do, I should talk to you about my reading – but I have been reading too much and just to give a list would take up the whole letter. Together with the above-mentioned friends I shall go to see an extremely interesting revival of *Oedipus Rex* directed by Fulchignoni.[1]

Pariah: I went to see him in Padua – in barracks, and I was filled with fear and fatigue – I'll tell you more about this unlucky visit. There are no words for Pariah as soldier. Last Sunday he came on leave.

Very soon we shall be called up, to my great joy – joy for various reasons (just as if I could ask to volunteer) – I no longer have fantasies about private glory, but military ones.

My father is still in Gondar[2] and yesterday we had a reassuring telegram.

I enclose some 'odelets' which I have finished typing to try out the typewriter.

Greetings to your family and Umberto.

An embrace,     PPP

> *The preferable pain*
>
> I do not wish to fall asleep
> because after sleep
> comes waking . . .
>
> Oh that this eternal vigil
> would last, this
> completed suffering!

*Terror of dreaming*

Up to the margin of sleep
the long-drawn suffering
and hence the terrified dreams.

I do not wish to be lost in the night . . .
Mamma, sleep close to me
and hold my hand tight.

*Moonlight night*

There were two of them:
him and his shadow.

*Spring*

It is something stronger than me, it is terrible
to smell once again the perfume of the wistaria.

**1**   Enrico Fulchignoni (b. 1913), editor of *Fiera letteraria*, film and stage director.
**2**   Gondar in Abyssinia was the last mountainous position held by the Italian army which surrendered there in June 1941.

## 18   To Franco Farolfi
Parma
[*In possession of addressee: autograph*]

[Bologna, June 1941]

Dear Franco,

You will naturally be wondering a lot about my long silence. But you might also have thought about the fact that I didn't know your new address! You only wrote it to me once on a postcard which unfortunately got lost. So I waited a long time to see if it would occur to you to write to me again.

Have you taken your exams? I haven't taken a single one so far – very soon I shall take Roman History – two more at the beginning of July. I'd say that we wouldn't lose much time if we met one Sunday. We could do it without much harm. Fix the Sunday you want and I'll send you a telegram with a positive response.

I am impatient to see you again – it has been so long.

How is it that Umberto has never turned up? It's a long time too since Pariah had leave – now he's in camp (he'll certainly have written to you a few times.) He'll come soon to take some exams.

These weren't bad months for me. On the contrary – pretty good – I might almost say nice. No women, naturally, but all the same I am at peace with myself as far as that goes because of some promising undertakings of mine. Then there's a girl in an ice-cream parlour (I see her in the evenings) who looks at me with very sweet shining eyes.

I have read a lot of books of poetry, modern as usual, hermetic. Now I have almost got to the bottom of it and have an almost precise critical view of it. The programmes of *Eredi* are going well. We 'Editors' read the poetical parts to each other in turn. Lately I was very pleased by the very favourable reception a little prose poem of mine ('The nocturnal errors – To my brother') received. I'm sure it will please you too for its well-turned form.

But one serious thought never leaves me and continually weighs on me – my father. Yesterday we had a telegram from him which says: 'Decorated for bravery. Am very well.' I may not be very heroic but I cannot wait for them to surrender. Or else I should like very much to be in his place. I still wish they would call me up.

Write to me very soon because for one reason or another it is a long time since you did. Greetings to your family and to Umberto.

I embrace you,      Pier Paolo

## 19   To Luciano Serra
Bologna
[*In possession of addressee: autograph with corrections; also addressed to Leonetti and Roversi*]

[Casarsa, 18 July 1941]

Dearest friends,

I love you in Ciceronian style and send you first of all information that is in a certain sense bureaucratic.

You, Luciano, will have to go as quickly as possible to the University Militia with this invitation, which I am sending you, in your hand. Ask what you must do – I think you will be able to give me the information asked for. Whoever you wish of the three[1] should also go to Capelli [*sic*][2] to chase up my books.

Very soon, Luciano will get a book for the Archiginnasio with further instructions.

* * *

A lot has happened to me and I don't know where to begin – some things that seemed important to me when they happened, seen in the light of subsequent events appear trifling to me. As, for example, a storm that broke out the day before yesterday on 16th July. The 16th of July – one of those days which happen very seldom in any year, I don't remember for what reason. In the morning I woke up feeling bad – there was thunder – the thunder went on for three hours until the middle of the morning – the clouds were very light and almost invisible. In the middle of the morning the bells suddenly began to ring because of the bad weather. It began to hail – it was country hail, the kind of hail that make some think of millennia. We ran to save the youngest ducks in the orchard – I was laughing and Nico[3] was very worried. Annie was in the last stages of pregnancy – her pains had begun during the night (Annie whom I had known as a little girl and used to play with, I have seen pregnant and her face had got fatter too and her mouth very big). In the afternoon while I was at the stationmaster's talking to him and looking at his gallery a baby girl was born whom I ran at once to see. I could not think of anything else but only this: 'Imagine when in twenty years' time I tell you that I saw you when you were just born!' I don't remember what else happened that day – I am sure that something else did happen but now I can't remember – I'm a bit numbed by the things that are happening.

I should like to proceed in an orderly way and say one thing at a time, subdividing them according to categories: 1. (accommodation) – I didn't want to sleep in the usual room as normally happens. But in my grandmother's house there is what is called 'a big bedroom' which doesn't communicate with the rest of the house but which you reach by an external staircase such as one often sees in houses in the country. There I am alone in the company of the noise of the geese. I have had it swept out and cleaned, have put two ugly red curtains on the window, have carried in a bed, a bedside table, two little tables, chairs and, on the trunk, my books – an attic-room for a rustic Bohemian. Unreachable. 2. (reading and art) – I have reread Sereni[4] whom I liked very much, I felt very close to him when he talks about Lombardy or girls, I feel he is one of us; all this may be a judgement based on content or worse, a sentimental one, but never mind: I advise you to read Sereni. Moscardelli is terrible. De Pisis,[5] alas, unpleasant. Malaparte's *Sangue* ['Blood'][6] very good, especially some short stories. Very bad Calcaterra, who is not teaching me anything about the seventeenth century.

Buso[7] the painter so greatly praised and discovered by the stationmaster (whom I have discovered to be probably a sexual introvert or pervert) I don't like much – wait a minute – he has marvellous possibilities but exceedingly little culture; he is a provincial painter whose great masters, alas, are the Macchiaioli.[8] So I had it in mind to introduce him to our art – but unfortunately this year I shall be at Casarsa only for a few days and won't have time to do anything. A pity – he is an unscreened member of the 'heirs'[9] and I think by now irredeemably so. I am a bit fed up with the stationmaster because I let him know some of my opinions. He was very upset and we said goodbye to each other. (He can do what he likes him and his Tito, Milesi, Silvestri and Martina!) The only Macchiaiolo in his collection who is a real painter is Cima by whom he has a great number of pictures, big and small, which are very valuable. To make up for this, yesterday in the cinema I found De Rocco, a very nice boy who won the pre-Littorials for frescoes at Venice; we probably met in San Remo. This afternoon we shall be together and tomorrow we shall go together to paint.

But Carta[10] has painted almost nothing and is a bit aimless. 3. (various events which have already taken place or are about to do so) – It will be possible only when talking to you to describe the serenade which I, Paolo, Galante and Tunin[11] went to perform under the windows of two girls – the most poetical and disturbing thing that has happened to me so far. I think things will go well with my little fiancée. I shall play football in the Cararsa team. Sunday next, a match against a place nearby.

I'd have a lot more to tell you but I am tired and impatient to do things, not write. I am adding, below, a poem I wrote the morning after I arrived. I haven't written very much – filled a lot of pages with drafts and re-draftings as with this lyric, which is still provisional and perhaps will always remain so.

*Return to the village*

Nico has wakened and goes to cut grass
under the eaves of dawn for the geese.

(1)      To me it is a prize, this alien
           sun, which I recognize.

(2)              Of the many years
           I have spent here
           all that remains for me
           is the screeching of the housewife's hen.
                And in the mist of the sun
           I don't know if I am in my old
           nest, heavy with time that does not pass,
           or in sad exile.

           My village is of a confused colour.[12]

Notes. Verses marked (1) and (2) are temporary, in fact I think it would be better to take them out altogether, leaving the rest as they are in that order.

So I greet you and embrace you Luciano and Franco and Berto.
Pier Paolo

*Ode to a flower at Casarsa*

Forlorn flower, outside the circle
of our houses, where in the open
the families make a din,

on the stones of day you burn
humbly where one sees around
fields and sky like sky and sea.

Forlorn, flower of the fields,

not evening dripping with lights.

Not shepherds soaked with dew.

tenuous fire of the hedges.

Not marigold, bilberry, bog violet,
or flag or gentian or angelica,
not grass of Parnassus or the myrtle of the swamps.
You are Pieruti, Zuan
and Beppi high on the stilts of their bones,
thin at the shaft of the cart,

flower of the meadow.

You become hay. Burn, burn
sun of my country, forlorn little flower.

Over you the years pass
and I too pass, with the shadows of the acacias
with the circling of the sun on this calm day.

Am sending you this poem as well, written at the last moment.

1  Francesco Leonetti, Roberto Roversi, Luciano Serra.
2  The Cappelli bookshop, in Bologna.
3  Nico Naldini, a cousin on his mother's side.
4  Vittorio Sereni: *Frontiera* ['Frontier'].
5  This probably refers to the volumes *Canto della vita* ['Song of life'] by Nicola Moscardelli, Vallecchi (Florence, 1939), and *Poesie* ['Poems'] by Filippo de Pisis, Edizioni di Modernissima (Rome, 1939).
6  Curzio Malaparte (1898–1957), Tuscan novelist, journalist and essayist.
7  Armando Buso, a Venetian painter.
8  I Macchiaioli: a school of Italian painting (1860–80).
9  i.e. a supporter of the programme of the review *Eredi.*
10  Paolo Carta, a painter from Casarsa.
11  Friends in Casarsa.

12   This verse, translated into Friulano was to become the second verse of 'Canto delle campane' ['The song of the bells'] in *Poesie a Casarsa* and, later, in *La nuova gioventú*.

## 20   To Luciano Serra
Bologna
[*In possession of addressee: autograph; also addressed to Leonetti and Roversi*]

[Casarsa, July 1941]

Dear friends,

I am sending this solitary little poem – I take the opportunity to thank you for the paint and for the opera omnia. But I was surprised at the latter's delay. As for 'letters' I have entirely regained my calm. Death to touchy letters and those who are touchy about touchy letters.

Otherwise everything is going well and I find myself at a most pleasant turning-point in my life.

An embrace,        Pier Paolo

PS. I call your attention to the fact that the poem on the back must be really read, must be examined and its meaning must be grasped. I added a marginal poem for you.

*Importunate voices*
Constellation of the Crab, look down
from the precipices of the sky
on our ruins.
                              Life is dead,
down here horrid old women shout
ululate against our joy.
Only one who is young, a green isle,
floats in this filthy world.

I am of the black tribe of Cain,
men, guilty victims!

*Nostalgia for the present time*
Super flumina Babylonis, illic sedimus
et flevimus, dum recordaremur tui, Syon.
In salicibus, in medio eius, suspendimus
organa nostra.
                              Old Testament[1]

My footsteps are a skyblue error and obscure
the sense of my words to those who know me
from other lives. Near the hedgerows, white in the distance,
untouchable fire burns my body
for the one who is a boy and looks at me from afar.
And to myself, I shall be a spirit living
under the blue vines and the treeline shade
when drifted away, lost, distant,
new life and a new day will hold me.

When I shall be far from these spots
and from the sad breathing I hear
from the countryside and from myself
(now a lost image in this dream of life)
perhaps I shall weep, suspended above the plain
blue with mists, its bitter smoke rising to heaven
from the hearths; and I shall be old
to time, which stands still and is consumed.

Lost Elysium, Casarsa, on my path
which turns back on its footsteps and goes away.

1   By the rivers of Babylon there we sat down, yea, we wept when we remembered Zion.
We hanged our harps upon the willows in the midst thereof. (Psalm 137, vv. 1–2)

## 21   To Luciano Serra

Bologna

[*In possession of addressee: autograph; also addressed to Leonetti and Roversi*]

[Casarsa, July 1941]

My very dear friends

Your letter eludes any response. I shall begin *ex novo* – that is to say by telling you nothing because I have nothing *ex novo* to say. In fact I have said a lot as you see from the size of the letter.

But note one thing: that I was almost cross at your way of judging my country poetry – allusions are always a bit stupid and so are wisecracks when they are written in a letter, because they freeze on the paper and lose all their native vigour. So next time, I beg you, be witty if you like but not on such a burning topic as what one writes; if another time my poems are bad, say so without beating about the bush, and follow up the judgement with some

little notes that have a critical flavour and not a jokey-allusive one –
particularly when there are tardy second-thoughts.

*Our poems*: 1st prize – Luciano Serra, 2nd prize – F. Leonetti.

Very good, dear Luciano. The poem 'Our hour' is your masterpiece – the
other two are also very fine, especially 'May'. As I read them I clapped my
hands with pleasure and I thought that you are now undoubtedly on the true
road of poetry. That one can't say of Leonetti (the poems of his I have read
here are incidentally good and his best). But in fact, Franco, in poetry you are
still not yourself – although very rigorous, very studied, full of good taste and
even inspired, it is still poetry made from the echoes of other poets – as
incidentally you admit. I liked 'At the window' very much but at the third or
fourth reading – to begin with it seemed to me to be botched work and full of
commonplaces. As you see, then, if I had followed your example I would
have written for you that 'habet noctes suas' which perhaps unjustly you have
tagged me with. (In fact it's not a question of night but of dusk – that is to say
the transition from one form of poetry and inspiration to another, which in
the enclosed poems you will see are maturing and yet, I think, still
extravagant.)

Put more pressure on Cappelli from whom I have received the
first package. Send me your 'opera omnia' (you, too, Serra, since unfortunately I have lost the notebook with the Tasso bibliography your poems
were in).

I have made a rather solid number of drawings and one painting (my best)
called 'Veiled summer' – it's not a question of an allegory but of a pure and
simple landscape a bit in the style of De Pisis.[1]

I still like the life I lead here very much but I don't feel like stopping to
describe it.

Here is the fairly solid number of my latest poems – I didn't want to make a
selection. I have included even those which are clearly abortions. Those I
have faith in are marked with an asterisk.

With regards to the publication by Cantelli[2] (I don't understand very well
what it is about and what one is supposed to write). I would certainly advise
you to write – it is always a very useful experience. And it can't hurt *Eredi* to
make our name buzz a bit in the ears of the public. As as far as my
participation goes, I wouldn't be against it – I'd like you to make things clear
to me.

In the last poem I have sent you, 'Nostalgia del tempo presente' ['Nostalgia
for the present time'] – in the last two verses a word has to be changed thus:
Lost Zion, Casarsa on my path . . .

On the back of this I have transcribed my latest poem which is still very
fresh and therefore not absolutely finished. It is on the same theme and has

the same tone as the preceding one – a song, that is to say, of premature nostalgia (cf. also 'the premature adieux' and many other passages in the preceding poems).

*Places in the memory*

When I shall recall, my song suspended,[*]
the slow days and the gentle solace
of these gestures accomplished, intact and past,
of a living man and of the summons
of nostalgia there will return with him sadly, a flood of tears,
my places in winter descending and in the icy
snows, heats of perennial summer,
blossoming among the dead trees!

Within my plaint and the supine errors
and the jumbled voices I shall be
more and more serene in myself, more and more
clear my life. Remote distances
will keep my body under trees in blossom
and the sunny house of this dead day.

Oh my country, in the languid flood of the sun
which tempers its rage with the mild winds of September
I see that space sets no limit to you nor does time. In
     memory
I shall rise up weeping for the sweet yokes
of your plain!

*Suspendimus organa nostra[3]

1a  *Waters of Casarsa[4]*

Fountain of water of my village.
No water is more fresh than in my village.
Fountain of rustic love.

2a  *Night dog*

I
Dog, you are dead. Faintly the fear
of your ancient terror besets me
in the shadowy nights.

I clasp in my fingers
my child's body.

II

Dog, dog, you are dying of fear,
you are counting the nights,
the lost nights, you dig me up.

Dog, dog, you awake me,
you fill the room with gloomy trees and hedges.

III

You are the threat with raised finger;
mother and sons; the respect of the sons
and their straight road;
death.

3   *Two thoughts about infancy and youth*

I

Your mother is calling you, Dilio,
we say goodbye, Dilio.
I am the one who is not called.
I still remain in this mystery, Dilio.

In the depth of the night
the travelling women will come.
I shall be with them, the hedgerows . . .

II

Now it is night. I do not see
the stars. There is lightning.

Night and day I never cease
to breathe. The naked grasshopper

also takes the air apart for me;
the girls by the river sweet and hostile.

4   *Cry of the Tagliamento*

Pretty blond boy
strong on the cart, on the bridge, by the river
tormented by sun

the power of a lightning flash
fixes you
among the people of my past.

5    *The frontiers of day* (poetics)
Having reached these frontiers
I do not know whether to go back again
over the sweet sayings of day or to give up,
immerse myself in the night.

*6    *A man like you*

My hand is the friendly light
that is born, my mind is that
light which gives body to the dead.

The summer counts my days; they pass
my nights; my hours come with the pace
of oxen. My awakenings, dawn of carts.

Sleep, we are lost; only the day
rallies us, we walk with wooden shoes,
we rest in the shadow of our powerful sex.

You, Bepi, hand that holds in the oxen, Pietro's
smiling eyes, you Dilio, senses wide awake.
and you billiards-players,

and the huddle of males by the nocturnal hedge
whom a common woman loves, Primo,
the passing of carts and footballer Manlito.

my body does not fear encounters nor that
sphere which sets me apart from you. Day's
serenity holds me. My flight has wings

to be a man like you.

7    *To the distant friends*[5]
(especially for Elio M.)
Pariah the sergeant, who laughed
ancient laughs, comfort of past times,
Franco, libation of human innocence,
resigned force of the wind, Luciano,
and you friends, Elio, Carlo and Francesco and Berto,
I warn you here that the time for the gloomy vesper
is over; night is the friend of sleep
and of late not solitary orgies.

Sleep of the just is good. The day peoples
my past; gives opportunity and the eternal
with serene power.

8    *Life in summer*

From the heat the silent
ancient wind roars, ancient summer,
mist of the old sun with its sad
fury.

Guido shifts the sea of geese
in a grey horror of hunger
you hear his cry 'Viri, viri',
the goose is snuffed out of life.

I do not complain of the heat. I have put up with
the frost. I accept everything from you, life.
Continue, day.

9    *Fragments*

I
Luminous evening, in the ditch
the water rises, a pregnant woman
walks through the fields.[6]

II
(On the bank)
Languor of this
my time in Friuli,
wind from the acacias
gently you strike
the presage
of evils close at hand.

*10    *Casarsa*

Now the sepulchre of the sun, the morning,
the unshared work of the fields,
which I suffer through the unsung songs
of the peasant,

bushes of the swamp are
my armpits, I raise a song to you,
desperate Mimnermos,[7] sun.

Oh people of the rosary, May
is past. Friendly
people I am one of you.

Ahi, ahi!

Apollo, your eye is sad
mist, you reflect the sign of the sun;
as always you escape me but flee
now with the passing of carts and oxen.

A landslide of carts loses itself
towards unknown fields.
You steal people from me,
I see no faces. Only
the hen.
Late the evening will
return, it will be an evening of songs.

Note – I'd like to call the eventual book of my poems *I confini del giorno* ['The frontiers of the day'] or simply *I confini* ['Frontiers'].

I don't read much – much less than I intended. To make up for this my empirical life is very varied and nice. I played with considerable skill left-wing in the Casarsa team, having lost 4–10 against Azzano Veneto. Tomorrow – Sunday – a match with Camino.

1   Filippo de Pisis (1896–1956), poet and painter influenced by French Impressionism.
2   A bookseller and publisher in Bologna.
3   From the passage in the Old Testament used on p. 130: 'We hanged our harps. . .'
4   Translated into Friulano, under the title of *Dedica* ['Dedication'], it was to be the first poem in the collection *Poesie a Casarsa* now in *La meglio gioventú*.
5   They are his friends in Bologna: Ermes Parini (Pariah), Luciano Serra, Elio Melli, Carlo Manzoni, Francesco Leonetti, Roberto (Berto) Roversi.
6   Translated into Friulano with the title of 'Il nini muàrt' ['The dead child'] it was to be the first stanza of the second poem in the collection *Poesie a Casarsa*, now in *La nuova gioventú*.
7   Mimnermos, Greek poet who celebrated sensual passion.

## 22    To Luciano Serra
Bologna
[*In possession of addressee: autograph; also addressed to Leonetti and Roversi*]

[Postmark: Casarsa, 1 August 1941]
Dear and afflicted friends,

This letter of mine will be a cry of sweet optimism – it isn't important if the review[1] will have to come out at an undetermined and very distant date – all the better for our preparation, our seriousness, our maturity. If it comes out in two years Serra and I will be teachers and will earn a living; we will all four have our own personalities at least 15 times more developed. Think in two years (or even in one) how much adolescent cultures like ours can develop! We will penetrate further and further into the heart of the problems of present-day Italian culture, we will be able to see more clearly and more profoundly. Besides – we must tell ourselves clearly, were we prepared to bear the burden and responsibility for a review for a year and more? You, Serra, for literature, myself for art, etc.? No, not without having recourse to bad faith or to throwing dust in people's eyes.

But there is one thing I wish to insist on particularly – constancy – as far as I am concerned I can assure you that I shall have it since this is now my ideal, in fact more – the point at which my empirical and superior ideals meet – and let it be the same with you. We shall have to be patient, to grind away, and to prepare ourselves. We shall have to purge ourselves of every particle of dross of egoism and personal ambition, which up to now – let us be honest – has upset our perfect equilibrium; where *Eredi* is concerned we must be four but in purity only one.

My certainty and my optimism have not been shaken – I felt myself ready for this and for other things. All this does not – unless there is another ministerial decree on the subject – prevent our books from appearing;[2] besides we had already agreed on this – that is to say to pay each time a quarter of the sum needed for the publication of a book. In any case we shall come back to this subject with more positive arguments in September. (In fact an idea has just sprung to mind, of a book – a kind of anthology – a critical/poetical one – to be called, for example, *concerning the concept of heritage*; but let's postpone discussion on this too till later.) To finish, I incline to think that each one should work on his own without worrying about obligatory articles, etc.

[There is a paragraph at this point taken up with a discussion of points of style and language in the poems of his friends.]

Concerning my own poems I was very grateful for your opinions, more for the observations than the praise, since all of them hit the mark – almost all the points you advised me to change had already been altered by me. I won't send you the corrections except one – 'Casarsa'[3] which is a radical one – because it would take too long. To Bologna! To Bologna!

Here is the packet of the latest ones, transcribed without distinguishing between those which have come off and those which have not.

1 *Life in the summer*

Thunder of the heat, silent
and ancient wind, ancient summer
mist of the sun old with sad
fury,
      Guido stirs up the sea of geese
in grey horror of hunger,
his cry is heard: Viri,
viri! the goose is snuffed out of life.

I do not complain of the heat. I have borne
the frost. I welcome everything of yours, life.
Continue, day.

2 *Rustic sense of comedy*

Oh rustic joy, you disturb and call
harsh voice to praise:

here is courtyard, threshing-floor, hedges of green,
dust, the race of geese, here
arid in life, mute on the pond,
the ducks circling impetuously.
'Viri, viri' for the former is the cry
of 'loving' recall, 'buti,
buti' for you, duck of the water.
Here, here, you do not inspire me,
Apollo of the green cloak,
friendly at last, do not flee
with painful steps but stop
and laugh with me, happily,
at the sound of these rustic cries.

3 *Elegy*
(for my friends in Casarsa)

Today you are fresh to me, light of my village,
steep slopes of light, serene rivers, and the pace of things

friendly and clear under the distant mulberry trees and the
vines.

If I walk on the threshing-floor I tread on you,
oh freshest of lights, come down to restore us,
peaceful as never before.

              Water of the ditches,
we are sweet things in your hands,
on the bank the duckling is conscious of you
and raptly sings to you and the goose is silent.

And already it was night, night was lightnings
and in the fields the threat of clouds and dogs,
night, drunk, we were happy,
I thank you for giving me
friends from the village and wine and the hoarse embers of
    laughter.

Wine, you married me to life;
and now that the storm of the dark
has resolved itself into fresh light,
night so far off, I no longer live distantly
above the labour of men, which scattered and various
makes music around me;
friendship unites me, the heart, and this light
which is not lost on our most ancient fields.

4 *Mornings in Casarsa*
(reworking)

Now that the sepulchre of the sun, morning
unfamiliar work of the fields, weighs for me
on the songs the peasant does not sing.
                        ahi, ahi,
sad mist, Apollo, is in your glance,
you reflect the ensign of the sun,
as always you elude me, but you flee

now at the pace of carts and oxen.
            Landslide of carts is lost
            towards the unknown fields
            You steal the people from me
            I see no faces. Only
            the hen.

The man who splits the wood, the man who guides the cart
exchange greetings, the day
proceeds, the scattered sounds of toil
beat out the time I raise a song to you,
desperate Mimnermos, o sun.
> Oh people of the rosary, May
> is over! friendly people
> I am one of you! and earth
> you are not like me
> and for this I love you.

> Evening
will return, it will be an evening of songs.

5 *Maria*

Time was when, the arch of the day
standing still – and the cry of the cockerels was thin –
I spoke to Maria

'Maria, are you the dear shadow
this evening rain brings to us?'

And in the balconies lightning
was the cries of children.

But bare gardens, oh evening
that rains down from the bitter clouds and wind
on the roofs of our houses
it is not my time for love!

Serene lightnings, cries of children,
wreath of cries for you who do not hear me,
Maria, I despise love, I am
high up on the rush of the slow wind
which retards the flight of the eyes and grows
the mosses on the (spent) lips.

6 *A girl's journey*

Maria, oh take with you on your journey the sign
of your most lovely eyes and the halo
of your hair, and the soft calm of you,
woman from the bitter countrysides.

Far off I shade my eyes,
oh lady of the rosary,
I let you go on your way,
I do not wish to make you the slave of my words.

Forgive the terrible writing. I am impatient to see your opera omnia. Tell Roversi to write something too, for heaven's sake.

Matches: Azzano–Casarsa 4–1; Camino–Casarsa 1–14. I have lost the newspaper in which I was noticed as the left-wing in the game against Azzano.

Long live Serra the hop-step-and-jumper.

Long live sport and heritage.

Do you know what a CA 3213 is? A 'Macchi'?[4] Do you know what the longerons, the ribs, the flaps are? I could swear you don't. I am completely immersed in the study of these things which are, if you don't know it, things to do with aeronautics.

1    The review *Eredi*, which could not appear because of ministerial measures concerning paper consumption.
2    Volumes by all four – including Pasolini's *Poesie a Casarsa* – were published in the following year by Antiquaria, the bookshop in Bologna.
3    A reference to 'Mattini casarsesi' ['Casarsa mornings'] which in the first version in the preceding letter was called 'Casarsa'.
4    An Italian fighter-plane.

## 23   To Luciano Serra
Bologna
[*In possession of addressee: autograph; addressed also to Leonetti and Roversi*]

[Casarsa, August 1941]

Dearest friends,

I have received: 1) the Serra-Leonetti letter; 2) Serra's letter; 3) Roversi's letter. I am terrified at the idea of the enormous answer I should give; I'm not sure whether it will be a synthesis or prolix. We shall see.

1) the Serra–Leonetti letter: [The succeeding paragraph is a discussion of linguistic details in the poems sent by Pasolini.]

About the word: I'd like to insist above all on this fact that since the word is a point, or rather one of the many points that form a line or a circumference, it has a particular value. The poetic nucleus of a poem cannot therefore ever be made up of a single word but of a circle of words, whose validity rests, rather than on the particular beauties of every single word, on the mysterious links and harmony by which the words are united with each other. I think that you, Franco, have got yourself into a muddle. In fact your search for 'the word' is a search for 'the phrase' and so for harmony and general tone. It is for the sake of this harmony and general tone that you are looking for words, and sacrifice one word for another – if you substitute 'road' for 'cobbled way' you do not do it in order to substitute what you call a 'general' word for a 'particular' one but to give a particular tone (or to improve it) to what you mean. I immediately come to the conclusion – if you agree with what I have said up to now (which seems obvious to me) – and my conclusion is this: that one cannot make distinctions between 'general' and 'particular' words. The value of a word is unique for each word and that's that. The 'virginal tremor' is given to the words by the 'tone' – that is to say, by the inspiration, that is to say by own's own particular achieved poetic style. You won't find a 'virginal tremor' obviously in the words themselves, detached from the text ('river', 'road', cobbled way'); the word is not sacrificed or sought for itself but for the text. The text is formed by the various words and at the same time suggests them. So I would advise you to forget your distinctions between words into 'general' and 'particular' since that carries you on to the characteristic confusions of 'a priori' assertions – that is to say, does not allow you to distinguish whether, on the one hand, 'in the evening they rolled the cobbled way' (particular) is better than 'in the evening they rolled the road' (general); on the other hand, 'no one on the side of the road' (general) is better than 'no one on the banks' (particular).

I read little, but paint a lot to make up for it – 6 pictures up to now of differing value, of which at least two seem good: my best. I have arrived at a palette of my own and in my own way. I hope to continue in this way without stupid dilettanteish changes. I am fed up with the classics: those I read for myself and those for the University (Angiolieri, Belcari, Manzoni, Folgore, Tasso, Alfieri). The only one that hasn't wearied me is Petrarch who has risen very much in my estimation. I read an elegy and a half by Rilke then I gave up, very bored: Rilke is like Rimbaud and Juan Ramon[1] – one of those poets who are venerated like gods and considered the very reverend fathers of modern poetry whom I cannot digest. That depresses me to some extent. A. Grande[2] is very bad. I have read half Fichte[3] on whom, obviously, I cannot pass judgement.

Dear Serra, it seems to me that you are getting a little too fastidious with others and with yourself over those 'ands', these 'commas', those hendecasyallables. Hasn't Franco, stupidly called Lenzio, told you yet? *Beh!**
[Well] this can be a sort of literary telling-off for you. And the letter by Franco and yourself, as you point out, is really a bit of a ticking-off.

* 'Beh – characteristic noise of sheep, stupidly adopted by men.'

[There follow two short paragraphs of detailed criticism.]

2) Serra's letter: I am not going to thank you for that horrendous photograph you sent me which makes us look like two conscripts – in fact just yesterday I saw a rabbit-skin merchant who looks terrifyingly like me. Then what a horrible idea to read Stecchetti[4] – how do you manage to stand it? I very much liked the pieces from Ravegnani[5] you copied out for me.

I have to tell you the truth, Luciano – your Sonnet I don't like at all in the quatrains – the terzinas are a bit better but – not what you say it is. You mustn't give way to outpourings which are always inexorably prose. The first stanza of 'Scherzo' is bad, there's no getting away from it – even the wit has frozen on the paper. The other two are good – indeed very good, forget about the title and the first verse – it will become one of your most interesting poems.

3) Roversi's letter: I haven't read *Ritirata del Friuli*[6] but I shall certainly read it since it talks about Casarsa. All Soffici's other works I have read more or less well and in general agree with you. I make note here of the mediocre impression *Kobilek*[7] made on me; I actually prefer his 'lyrical chemisms'.[8] Soffici is neither artist nor critic – he is a popularizer, the best of popularizers. Italian culture should be very grateful to him. (And painting even more so.) You put the poetry of De Pisis and Solmi[9] on the same plane; to me Solmi seems much, but very much superior to De Pisis – not in his prose pieces (which I don't like at all) but in his poetry . . .

I find Bartolini[10] very original – so much so as to appear artificial and to turn out to be a bit unpleasant; his sincerity is too much and comes close to lying. He wants to make the impression of being too humanly nice and that does not help – it feels as if he was trying, with his virulence, of which he makes too much display, and with his masculine simplicity to hide something that is not on sexually. Besides *The Prostitute*, I liked two or three other stories. It seems to me in any case that he is worth more than all the various American Saroyans. I have also read a number of books – especially classics. I particularly liked Caldwell's *Tobacco Road*.

As for the University of Florence for me it would be bristling with boring bureaucratic difficulties. As for you, see you don't get too far away from Bologna – that is to say from us.

4) My poems: All the poems I am copying out for you are previous to the Serra–Leonetti letter and the others since in the last few days I haven't been very well (5 or 6 days ago I seemed to be at the peak of physical and spiritual well-being and the collapse was sudden); but now I am getting better. Faced by our poems I ask you to note many interesting resemblances which are notable above all because we are far from each other and therefore reciprocal influence is a little dampened – that means that our spiritual unity and our unified method of feeling are very marked; that we form, that is to say, a group already and almost a new school of poetry, or so it seems to me.

*Note to be read after the poems*

One thing then for Luciano: 'Vita in estate' ['Life in summer'][11] is not a reworking – no poem has ever come out in the final version as it was in the first idea. The fragmentation was something I wanted to achieve – the various separate pieces should together give a feeling of 'calm excitement' which is what I should like to happen also in the poem which follows, entitled 'Senza fronde' ['Without leaves'].

All the poems I am sending you are, so to speak, minor and marginal with one exception – 'Immagine d'amore' ['Image of love'] which, because of some inspiration or witchcraft or other, came close to being my best piece and, instead, has got stuck halfway. Or so it seems to me.

1 *Pain of love*
(classical influences)

Not lily of sun which falls in whirlwinds
of exhausted petals of amorous fire not the moon
which so gently grows with violets and pours
over your rills and the hills and the pomegranates
and the mist and the ponds and the sweet May
of the lagoons,

               oh body of the rash women
on the paths of love, of this my furious
onrush of days, will rust the dry,
lofty sword of honour.
               Only your lights,
oh my sweet Jesus, will keep me, innocent Magdalen,
whom I wish to martyr sweetly on the cross.

2 *Madrigal*

Come with hoarse flowers in your hand,
I shall draw you with lowered head,
sad hair, strength in the lips,
intent, just like the moon
which sadly lingers over the brooks.

3 *Loving image*

Idol of tender flesh, you torture me.
light dies away, the shadow lengthens
on the labouring vines, your warmth of love
lights up under your hair and round about
has sweet echoes in the sounds of things,
within the closed horizon: birds, springs
and houses and hedges and the cries of children in love.

*1941*

The meadow keeps you, your face takes fire
with the earth, your heavy breathing is the wind,
and the (peaceful) labour of men.

And I am shut off, meanwhile, from the divine
circle of these things. I feel and do not live.
On you the shadow of evening sweetly
settles . . . But then I find myself again
and in my face is strength.

4 *The dead child*[12]

Luminous evening, in the ditch
the water rises, a pregnant woman
walks through the fields.

I remember you, Narciso, you had the colour
of evening when the bells
ring for a death.

5 *Calm morning*

Life is not always tense,
even the sun has ashes and the reed
is silent to the calls of the wind,
                        But occasional cries
now lazily corrupt the sky,
they are stones scattered in the flood
of the days.
                        Once life burned
with many cares but now vaguely rests
in the gentle wound of the sun.

6 *Without leaves*

Chaste of mind and lazy tumult
of the sun and the piety
of white cicadas relieve me.

I see myself chaste, within the closed
horizon, moving, against the old houses
among the hearths and fields, the obscure women
and the lowing of the cows.

And then to fill the naked walls
with hard-wrought canvases, to rule the paper,

go to the river and swim there
                              to seize the words
and reply, to fill one's belly with darkness
with the bitter wine and the wake. Pier Paolo
they call me, life is certain, oh naked,
leafless, noon.

7 *Fragment*

You wake, rise from the bed, flee,
it is raining, and you are all water.
                              You seek refuge
and run and then the wind freezes
the water in your body.
                              Red the sun
pours down behind the curtains and the Plough
trembles like rain on the branches.

You dry yourself then and the distant thunder
above the orchards raises you. The wind burns
the mud on your body
and carries from twig to twig
the gentle alarm of the evening.

8 *Betrayal*

Now the carts return. The dusk
brings back the cud-chewing of the heifers
from the fields and puts out the day's
suffering gleams.

                    She has eyes of ice
and a pale call and while deep
in other tasks . . .
                    In the sunk evening
I go through the silent streets
in sweeter company.

‘   I embrace you,          Pier Paolo

1   Juan Ramon Jimenez (1881–1985), Spanish poet of intensely private lyrics marked by preciosity of style.
2   Adriano Grande (1897–1972), poet, literary journalist.
3   Johann Gottlieb Fichte (1767–1814), German idealist philosopher.
4   Stecchetti, pseudonym of Olindo Guerini (1845–1916), poet who championed *verismo.*

5   Giuseppe Ravegnani (b. 1885), literary critic, authority on Ariosto.
6   *La ritirata di Friuli*, Vallecchi (Florence, 1934).
7   *Kobilek: a Battle Journal* by A. Soffici, Libreria della Voce (Florence, 1918).
8   See *Bïfsszf + 18. Simultaneità. Chimismi lirici*, Edizioni della Voce (Florence, 1915).
9   Sergio Solmi (b. 1921), writer, journalist, film-maker.
10  Elio Bartolini (1908–66), novelist and short-story writer.
11  Transcribed in Letter 22.
12  cf. first three lines of the poem 'Fragments' in Letter 21. This is the complete transcription of the poem.

## 24   To Franco Farolfi
Parma
[*In possession of addressee: autograph*]

[Casarsa, summer 1941]
Dear Franco,

As usual I must apologize for the delay. I have so many letters to write – to you, to Pariah, to Melli, to Serra, to Manzoni, to Roversi, to Leonetti, that I am going mad. I have taken on too much this year and – as happens – I do less than I could. Lately I have painted a lot and have got much better. I read too but with a less intense rhythm and with little inclination. Every day I curse this idiotic Italian examination, which fills my head with these monograph texts on Tasso, Alfieri,[1] etc. which read a little at a time are all right, but their 'opera omnia' read one after the other bore one to death. Lucky that I have with me many modern Italian poets and modern critics and monographs on art – it's no small consolation.

And you must excuse the stupidity of the present letter – in fact have chosen this moment in which I am neither happy nor sad to write to you, which produces mediocre results for the recipient. (I am so fed up with the 'prose' of Alfieri and Tasso's courtly lyrics that, by way of reaction, I am writing sentences that aren't just bad syntax but ungrammatical as well.)

I lead a very pleasant life here – it unrolls lazily but the days pass rapidly. Each day I find I am a week further on. I tremble at the idea of leaving.

One of my many companions are the geese – the discontented geese, always famished – there's no more discontented and *anxious* animal than the goose. You see them and think they are lying idly in the sweet light but if you go near them they immediately get up and come towards you yelling, with their beaks open and wagging their behinds: which shows that they were not lying there quietly resting but were continually a prey to agitation and one thought – food.

There could be girls but, as always, I am lazy – and then I have so many other thoughts, as always, what with art, social life and sport, which make me see too many resemblances between the girls and the geese (see the preceding description).

I think there is nothing as fine as life in the country, in one's native place, among simple friends.

You who have less correspondence than me, I think, write to me more promptly than I do.

Many greetings to your people.          Pier Paolo

1   Vittorio Alfieri (1749–1803), dramatist, author of a remarkable autobiography.

## 25   To Luciano Serra
Bologna
[*In possession of addressee; autograph; also addressed to Leonetti and Roversi*]

[Postmark: Casarsa, 20 August 1941]
My very dear friends,

I haven't had a moment of low spirits all the time I have been here – I'm sorry that one has been brought about and that very profoundly by Luciano's last letter. At a certain point he states that I am '*in bad faith*' when judging his poems – that is simply stupid. I'd like to point out to you, Luciano, that when I am hurt I say it at once without beating about the bush and don't hide behind a swamp of protests and reticences as you do in your last wretched letter.

The opinion on your sonnet[1] I gave you after my usual long meditation – Berto and Franco, you will see, will sooner or later be in agreement on this: that the only valid verses are the last two of the second terzina and the last verse: all the rest is fog. And I tell you this with the same frankness and critical thoroughness with which I told you, on the other hand, that 'Canto di memorie' ['Song of memories'] and your other lyrics are very fine and true poetry. But take a good look yourself at 'Sonnet' and 'Song of memories' – there is, over and above a difference in merit, a very great difference in inspiration, tone, *language*.

But let's forget about your wretched compositions and try to proceed in an orderly way:

It's good that you are reading novels and wretched works which 'are all right for most people'; I mean to do that too (and am doing it now in the case of certain classics.) Good your verdict on Bacchelli.[2]

Your shitty accusations: my poetry crepuscular! I call you to witness, Franco and Berto! Tell Luciano that crepuscularism lies in the language and not in the content; because if humble things (little things in life in Casara, geese, etc.) are expressed in a humble and modest way ('bastone' [stick]

149

rhyming with 'stazione' [station]) you have crepuscularisms. My language has never been humble and modest – if anything it sins by being overloaded and high-flown. You protest that 'crepuscularism was not your intention', that 'you can't be Leopardi, etc.' – but this is such naïve stuff that it is self-contradictory. Your defence of Carducci,[3] Luciano, seems out of place to me – I actually *love the classics too much, including Carducci*,[4] for you to come praising them to the skies to me. As for the poem you quote to me, there's no point in discussing it – it's one of Carducci's worst in my opinion and if you want we shall continue the discussion more easily when we speak to each other.

About Caldwell, Soffici, I am now very indifferent – in any case I see that you take certain paradoxes (*Chimismi lirici* is better than *Kobilek*) too literally in a naïve way.

[There follows a paragraph analysing the language of Franco Farolfi's poems.]

As for my poems, you are perfectly right to say that they are my worst – I had drawn your attention to this by calling them, in a nicer way and perhaps more accurately, 'marginal'. The 1st ('Pena d'amore') ['Pain of love'] is simply terrible. The 2nd ('Immagine amorosa'[7] ['Image of love'], dear Luciano, I beg you to reread because it is undoubtedly among my best things. About the 3rd ('Madrigale') I don't know what to say to you but I don't know how to change the tone of the last two verses – send me some advice. The 4th ('Il nini muart') ['The dead child'] is undoubtedly one of the best things – I am copying it out for you here with the translation. The 5th ('Mattino sereno') ['Calm morning'] is a characteristically marginal poem – *sparse* – *arse* – *ansie* – is a sound I sought for so that the resolution at the end would turn out to be broader and sweeter. The 6th ('Senza fronde') ['Without leaves'], a mediocre poem but one which you have interpreted in an entirely wrong way: crepuscularism is '*uncertainty*, mist, cloudiness, nuance – *one's ego which encloses itself in its surroundings and there abases itself tenderly*: what happens in this mediocre poem is the opposite – the 'I' is *sure of itself* (repeated thrice) – the setting is 'a closed horizon', 'sombre women', etc., because here where I live the setting is like that; but my figure 'moves' with certainty and is very detached from the setting. Beside Pierpaolo is the complete opposite of the 'Guidogozzano' character,[5] who withdraws into himself, humiliates himself, becomes anonymous, *a thing among things*, whereas 'Pier Paolo' detaches himself, is a shout, is *the certainty of being different from the others and from the milieu*; and another shout follows 'life is certain' and then yet another invocation 'oh noontime, naked without leaves'. One dies if one goes further from crepuscularisms than this. (And then let me say something here in parentheses: don't let us send up each other's poems; you will surely know how extremely easy this is; Luciano, especially, has this bad habit. For my part I have decided this – that since I confide my poems only to you who are my friends and otherwise cloak them in the deepest secrecy, if I see my poetry being made fun of again – even if it should fully deserve it – I shall not let you read them any more and will always keep them near me and secret as is my old ideal). The 7th ('Frammento') ['Fragment'], this too is characteristically fragmentary. The 8th ('Tradimento') ['Betrayal'] is an experiment that did not come off.

Dearest Franco,

I am replying to you even more directly – in fact I would have thought you and Luciano would have replied together to my last triple letter. I should have liked to have had a more balanced judgement from you in general and in particular. I got your letter of the 15th from Porto, etc. Congratulations on your literary activity and I envy you for it: I haven't even looked at Momi,[6] Contini,[7] etc. I have given myself up entirely to the classics – the marvels of *Pentecoste* and *5 maggio* ['The 5th of May']. Petrarch's *Canzioniere*! The Tragedies of Alfieri are exciting revelations to me. But above all Foscolo:[8] – he is my author, my master and guide.[9] I don't know how often I have read his odes and his sonnets, *I Sepolcri* ['The sepulchres']! Now I am madly addicted to the *Grazie* ['The graces'] of which I am reading every smallest fragment, every first draft, every revision, etc. – I am very enthusiastic about this work.

Quasimodo[10] – 'Preghiere alla pioggia' ['Prayer to the rain'] seems mediocre to me – the first strophe is common. The second is better. The third – the first two verses good, the second two mediocre. The last leaves me cold. The 'Elegos' is something superior although it has a shadow on it here and there.

That final 'Anadyomene' made me tremble and the last 5 strophes in general. I have an immense desire to read all Quasimodo, whose tone seems to me more valid and lasting that our contemporary poetry because of its more classical scope (pardon the naïve and hasty judgement).

My life here proceeds happily as usual. I am enclosing in the name of our extremely youthful doctrine of heritage this short paragraph from the *Popolo di Friuli*, which incidentally is inaccurate and should be corrected as follows: 'The first point was scored by Cecchet from a penalty 20 minutes in; there follow uproars on the field between players, referee and spectators, but peace having been re-established, a few minutes later, Pasolini, with a personal initiative, scored the second goal. In the second half it was again Cecchet who scored the third point, etc., etc.'

I continue to paint and to be very pleased with the pictures with which I fill the bare walls of this *à la Bohème* room of mine.

I embrace you all affectionately,      Pier Paolo

*Funeral Announcements*

---

The Bolzini family and relations
profoundly moved by the demonstration of affection
paid to their beloved
LUCIANO
warmly thank all those
who participated in their great grief

---

PS. Important – go and look in all the shops in Bologna and find me two small tubes of *Indian red* and please send them very quickly. See that from now on all of you write me letters together.[11]

1 *Memory in the morning**

Once you were a fearful leaf
which dawn tints with red, moon,
but first you were lost in that
which does not extinguish life, but renews it
in the ample wonder of sharp and fading lights,
most brilliant circle of the night.

What was I pursuing in the icy desert
of the streets, of the brambles and the silent
birds? I was cold from the serene
breeze, the silence was complete
in the whistling of the crickets.
                    The lonely
houses were in the wind and silently
the moon pressed on the windows.

2 *Second elegy**

August is at the point of death and is still
unborn: the light is blue, candid moon,
the cries are hoarser.
                    San Giovanni,
at night, gleams with white mists,

sad summons amid the horror of the fields
and of the moon.
                    Not far off is the cemetery
and the evening martyrdom of the frogs
wrings the heart.

Oh, my village, I already feel your leaves
are ready to fall. Trees already familiar
look how they are taken from me by the trembling silence
of the snow. Every door shuts, already across the grey fields
the smell of the smoke and the calls die away.
Although you look at it and hear it still, the cold
is stealing from time and obscure forebodings and the
thought that you will not end your life here. But I shall not know
laughter, labour and falling snow . . .
                    Oh nostalgia
for the present time! Friends, I walk with you
and already you tremble, ghosts, in the depth of memory.

*It was born in a period of nasty weather which made me foresee the bad
season ahead and my departure from Casarsa. Note the numerous assonances.
It seems to me my best thing.

### 3 *Meditation*

The girls come, they leave
red clots like evening on the walls
the taut cloud stretches out once more
and the fine weather returns.

Naked bodies struggle,
they fight to win, in the river
they are mirrored, evening comes
and solitude returns.

Just as doves cut through the sky,
springs are troubled, carts
run under damp clouds,
but everything flees, remains behind
trembles in the forgetful memory.

I am transcribing for Franco who asked me for them the *Three notes at the
frontiers of day*

*1941*

1   *(I become evening)*

Sensitive the evening
leans over the violets of the gentle
wind after the dark day
and opposes trunks and hedges
to the current
and the sweet step of the trees.

I am far from myself
not an obstacle to the wind
not a youth who talks
oh hedge.

Nor does the light grow dark in me.
But my name is now the dry
leaf, which joyfully rattles
in the terraces of evening.

And in me who am now the windblown
and dark and fresh shore of the evening
men's joy is terrified
is lost.

2   *(Berenice's lock)*

Whether you sing
or unravel
the auspicious song of the wind

or are blinded by the black
tempest of the sun

high up, o lock, you change;
I do not stop you.

I am the one who speaks.

3   *(Apollo's poetical laugh)*

Remote in the evening foliage Jove
reveals himself and hedges and shadows
and secretly closes laughter.
                    If you are disturbed you do not know
the evening on the wounds of the wind
or if pale with dewy frost
joyous light rains on the village.

If the wreath of dark air shifts to the gardens
sweet to the men's encampment.

But the one who looks does not live
and a bulwark against alien sadness
is laughter to Apollo.

I am writing 'El nini muàrt' ['The dead child']¹² out again with its
translation so that you, Luciano, can translate it into the dialect of Reggio
Emilia and let me see it.

[The text is in Friulian dialect, followed by the translation.]

### Awakening

I awoke, with silent steps
I crossed the valley which now
separates me from the risen morning.
I stood by the window and was one
of the pale things the sad
light pointed out.
At the foot of the walls
I saw disaster tremble and the ruin
of the yellow stones seemed anchored
in the lives of men. In the duck
which gulped the dark remains of the night's
rain I saw the indifferent threat of the years.

### Nights in Friuli

On those evenings the grasshoppers sang
on the meadows of the Tagliamento, in the vast
death of the countryside. And Casarsa on the horizon
was a fire of voices and cries, the closed shelter
of its people.
                    Deserted churches and cold
hearths and abandoned gear, I saw
Friuli, the complaints of your sons set free!

With them I spun the ancient plots of love,
I ran though the streets in the scattered secret festival
of the vast plain; here San Vito with white houses,
there Prodolone warm behind the hedges.

I knew that time does not fly and the years
are always the same on the unchanging face

of these holiday people, on those loves
which are adorned only by the clamour of the crickets
among old walls and enclosed solitude.

Thus, trembling at a guitar or the cry
of a boy suddenly close at hand
I gave myself up, oh my place, to the nights
of your history.
In the remote shade
of the mountains lightning flowed the while to remind
that even the rain and the storm and the hard
winter are not ungrateful gifts.

*Things said after the holiday*

Old children go
through the village. They drink
at the pumps and do not know
our holiday yesterday.
The one who drank a lot of wine
is happy today.

'Boys in our joyful youth
we are; the extreme sweetness
veiled in the sarcasm of the eyes
distracts the trembling glances.

A frost of shudders and laughter
points to us at once – the youths.
Each innocent glance hints
at overwhelming secrets of love.'

. . . . . . . . . . . . . . . . . . . . . . . . . . . . .

Today the sun is out.
I have in my eyes, still,
the shadow of the wine. I am
so blissful.
                        (The geese, light
in the wind, croak with happiness.)

Fly to my friends,
wandering song!

*The end of love**
(To Maria)

Under the pale ramparts of the so-distant mountains
the howls of the household dogs having died away
I looked at the green castle of the plain.

The wind, immense in the morning,
comes close to me in the shadow of a bough.

Since the face of the one who loved me
has faded in the white indifference of strangers
I feel you are my only companion in love.

Blessed is he who mows on the side of the road
and who on the horizon drags along the sacrifice of the cows.

* It is the end of a love never begun.

*To free oneself of song in the morning**
Solitude sacred to poetry
look how for me you change in the sweet ardour
of the morning into one who burns
and languishes for love, a youth who dances
over the villages.
                    Dances over the village delle Aguzze
native pond of such green snows,
hints with flying hands
at premature farewells.
                    Touches in Idria
the beaches lost in the dream
of memory, bitter with
my childish cries. Oh morning
divine footstep over the dead things,

the lighting of new lights, and the thunder
of new tender voices, under the trees
joyously identical.
                    The sistrum
hisses in the bitter heart and you, laughing,
fly above the shady panoramas
of memory; you waken dead
mornings above my dead places.

* I entrust completely to your judgement this poem which was born to me in a way very different from the others and which for that reason is new and closed to myself. The manner in which it was born is entirely explicable by that 'freeing of one's self' that makes me suspect that none of my poetry is born of itself but lives by a reflection not only of memories of other poetry but of human events! (Compare it, for example, with Quasimodo's *Elegos*.)

1  See Letter 23.
2  Riccardo Bacchelli (1891–1985), historical novelist, Catholic and conservative.
3  See Letter 23.
4  Giosuè Carducci (1835–1907), poet, senator, Nobel prizewinner.
5  Guido Gozzano (1883–1916), one of the crepuscular poets.
6  'Momi': Francesco Arcangeli, assistant to Longhi, Professor of Art History at Bologna.
7  Gianfranco Contini (1912–90), critic and scholar, expert on Romance languages.
8  Ugo Foscolo (1778–1827), major poet, died in exile in London.
9  A reference to Virgil's relationship to Dante in the *Divine Comedy*.
10  See 'Preghiera alla pioggia' ['Prayer to the rain'] and 'Elegos per la danzatrice Cumani' ['Elegy for the dancer Cumani'] in *Quasimodo's Poesie*, Edizioni Primi Piani (Milan, 1938).
11  Probably some of the following poems were transcribed in previous letters which have not been found. The editor chose to insert them here so as to connect them to references in later letters.
12  See Letter 23.

## 26  To Francesco Leonetti
Bologna
[*In possession of addressee: autograph*]

[Casarsa, August 1941]

My very dear Franco,

After the two big missives I sent yesterday I am sending you these, my two last things which are – to put it stupidly – as fresh as bread just out of the oven. Tell Luciano that I haven't yet got over the anger his letter caused me, but that I am already much calmer and that I am trying to drink as much of the water of good humour and good memories as possible so as to swallow down this very tough morsel of 'bad faith'.

I don't know what I shall think about this 'tempest' a little time from now but for the time being it seems to me to have a very elevated tone and to be among my best things. I hope it may please you.

I am going to ask you two favours – in fact more than two: 1) to reply at once since your last letters were so scattered, detatched, distant, that I have lost any sense of being one with you all – see that you write to me *together*; (2) send me these famous opera omnia; (3) as I said in the other letter, buy

me two little tubes of *Indian red* and send them to me at once; 4) buy me a
packet of paper in that shop where Luciano and I bought that magnificent
grey notebook.

Give Berto and his fat laziness a bit of a shove – pull him out of his den.

I have on the stocks (as Luciano says) 'a little lyrical poem' (let's call it by
this horrendous name) entitled 'Canto amoroso d'una Amazzone' ['An
Amazon's love-song'] – I have a draft of it already but it is still very unformed.

Put pressure on Cappelli.

I am renewing myself under *very changed* guises.

I embrace you affectionately,      Pier Paolo

### The tempest

Black foliage migrated from earth
to heaven, the air froze and was obscured.
The houses stayed on earth, naked, alone,
their deception ceased.
I found there virgins,
houses, white above the troubled vines.

The walls were lights under the hissing
flight of the sky, broken the silence
by the lament of the bells.
But wind fell
drops hastened up, were silent.
Relieved voices sighed and there was heard
the cry of a child.
Now in this
wind that burns and parches, under the dull
sky, I should like to slide, flesh
that I love, with you in the cold grass.

But after I shall see you like those houses
humiliated by the spent hurricane, left
on the ground, overwhelmed by the brief sin,
have a pale light among wandering waters.

I do not find in you what I seek,
you are an ardent flame that does not burn.

Where do I find myself? In the arbour, under the sad
unrisen moon, under the dead
tempest which has not destroyed me?

Now the earth has odour. New,
the light trembles with waters.

> I lose myself
> and, still the same, already cannot find myself again.

*Translation from Alcaeus*[1]

At the time when among the white mountains
Sirius burns the days and rules them
I saw you in Orcomeno.
                    There
the sun knows how to wound so sweetly
it does not rob man of his pride;
and from the boy it snatches melodies
with the flute which are sweetly painful.

1  Alcaeus (fifth century BC), Greek lyric poet.

## 27  To Luciano Serra

Bologna

[*In possession of addressee: autograph; incomplete; also addressed to Leonetti and Roversi*]

[Postmark: Casarsa, 28 August 1941]

My dearest friends,

As is my custom I will reply in an orderly way to your letter dividing it into topics.

1) Water under the bridge is water under the bridge. Our friendship is beyond literature, otherwise it would not be friendship – the literature we produce together exists in so far as a friendship which binds us exists. And it is in the name of the latter that literary squabbles are 'gone with the wind'.

2) My poems: I am pleased, as they say, that you liked them – but I am expecting in your next letter a verdict with wider and more particular views. I'd like you to refer also to 'Fine d'amore' ['The end of love'][1] which you have not even mentioned so far, although I am curious about your opinion of it. (The 'Traduzione' ['Translation'] I hope you have realized is not a translation but is entirely invented.)[2]

3) My reading: Ugo Foscolo, dear Luciano, has other magnificent polemical sentences which might be useful – he is the only writer of epigrams whose wit can still cause loud laughter – and they are very clever and varied. I am busy now with two things: the tragedies of Alfieri and my year's numbers of *Frontespizio*[3] where I am reading magnificent things which I can't wait to show you. I recommend a very interesting essay by Luzi: 'Notes on Italian poetry'.[4]

I am doing almost nothing for the University and am beginning to be frightened by how little time I have left.

4) Serra's poems. 'Elegia di fine autunno' ['Elegy for the end of autumn'] is not altogether good but does not deserve to be discussed as you discuss it, Luciano. The second stanza is good ... there are excellent points from which you can begin a revised version. The 'Poesia per Anna B' ['Poem for Anna B'] surprised me very much. Are you mad that you say bad things about this poem of yours mixing it up with the other two and calling the whole lot 'terrible rhymes'? This poem is among your three or four best. 'Human sweetness' and 'My silence is like a prayer' are the two central nuclei of the poem around which swampy landscapes of words coagulate; the effect is that of a damp coolness which suddenly becomes the sensation of finding oneself in front of true poetry. The symmetry of the two verses is remarkable: a central nucleus at the beginning – swampy landscape at the end – where the 'baying of the dogs among the junipers' corresponds to the 'reed the wind caresses' of the first stanza. The end is very fine with that 'unlucky hares' which becomes the synthesis of the 'physical sensation' one has when reading the lyric. The rhymes are very light – their weight so slight that one only notices their presence as something secondary and a little at a time; I have rarely noticed such successful and unforced rhymes in a modern poem.

The 'Canzoncina' ['Little song'], as you have noticed and rightly draw attention to the fact, is a trifle which one need not spend time on.

5) Various: what did you write to Domani and Corrente? I have not written to Matacotta – perhaps I shall write to him, perhaps not.

6) So let us come right away to your poem, dear Franco. I have been thinking a bit to find a title for it – two have occurred to me which I am writing down for you more out of curiosity than anything else: 'Love song for a lost summer' or else 'Lament for a lost summer'. It is undoubtedly your best and you hit the mark in your short preface when you say that 'you feel you have not so much made progress as made a point, etc., etc.'. It really seems to me that what we have here is a more daring step than the previous ones in our continous and irrepressible evolution – one doesn't feel the break with your other compositions – one notes a dawn of new inspiration and deeper maturing of the old. Your 'point' is and still remains 'I was beyond the hedge' – but here you are already much higher. Besides you say yourself that it is 'a refinement on your former way of writing'. But all this is not important and I have said it only to make clear the position of this component which I wouldn't like you to become confused about, being (rightly) seized by the joy of having created something fine which therefore strikes you as new. This poetry is the result of ripening, not of discovery, and if I stress this it is so that you don't go off the rails and get confused, and because to say this to you

161

is, as it were, to dedicate you to the road of 'the poetic mean', which is ripening, and which alone leads to true poetry, which is the discovery of ripening. Excuse the long digression which you didn't ask for, but by that means I also wanted to lay hold of (unfortunately somewhat undisguisedly) an idea which I had vaguely in my head. Now your poetry, Franco, which is on a high level, has a good many obscure moments and I am going to tell you all of them since they are all very easily remedied . . .

[The rest of the letter is an analysis of poems by his friends.]

1  Refers to the poems transcribed in Letter 25.
2  The 'Translation from Alcaeus' transcribed in Letter 26.
3  *Frontespizio*: literary periodical of Catholic tendency.
4  Mario Luzi (b. 1915), critic and prose-writer, leading representative of the hermetic school of poetry.

## 28  To Luciano Serra
Bologna
[*In possession of addressee: autograph*]

[Casarsa, end of August 1941]

My dearest Luciano,

I am very nostalgic for you and all of 'us' – I shall come back on 15 September without fail. This is a letter in which initially I had nothing to say to you except stupid and perhaps whining and disagreeable things. The disagreeable things derive specially from one fact: Roversi, about whom you say very just things in your last letter. In fact I would be even tougher – we will get nothing out of him. His culture is only superior to ours in terms of volume and his character is something I cannot grasp. He is one of the few people to whom, if I had to have a conversation by ourselves, I would not know what to say or what to talk about. I always thought this but never wanted to say so – not even to myself.

It will be best to face up to the situation. Meantime begin to attract Leonetti to us, detaching him from Roversi. Perhaps this will be going too far but compromise situations are what I hate most. Then there had to be Meluschi,[1] ignorant and plebeian as he is, in his literary circle in which I very nearly got bogged down. In fact this winter I was going to be introduced to him by Della Casa but fortunately after going to his house twice we never found him in. It is a lair of a house – there's an old woman who could be his mother or a bawd and instead is his wife,[2] who writes verses for some women's paper. Besides even Della Casa admits that Meluschi is very uncultured. Keep clear, keep clear, dear Luciano, don't even get a whiff of these people! By the way, Della Casa had already proposed that I take part in those monographs you are telling me about now. I gave him a vague answer. But now I wouldn't collaborate even if they begged me. Della Casa is a poor chap, good-natured but deluded, a liar, full of airs – someone who always gets things wrong. Meluschi must be the same. *Architrave* does not accept their writings. The Guf takes a poor view of them; Bignardi talks about them with biting irony.

These are not people for us, Luciano. We are much superior – don't let on about your poems to them. I really beg you, Luciano, in the name of our friendship.

If anything we'll let people like Rinaldi,[3] Arcangeli, etc. read our poems.

Stop Leonetti – again in the name of our friendship – from approaching them.

Everything you are doing worries me enormously. I feel I must be near you and so I shall be there by the 15th. Remember the *Eredi*, our days together. I sacrificed a lot of friendships for you – I decided not to take many acquaintances further out of fear of being deflected. Do the same, you people – one never knows how the things one begins are going to turn out.

And tell our very cold Roversi not to talk about 'exaltations' – a person who does not know what the word means except in the sexual–hermaphroditic sense. Leonetti's poems and mine too are not the fruit of exaltation; the deficiency lies elsewhere. They are the fruits of meditation and ripening and study.

I am ending this chaotic letter – as for letting Leonetti and Roversi read it – do as you like. If you like, only read them the principal bits about Meluschi.

I can't wait to embrace you again and to be with you, dear Luciano. Meantime I embrace you affect[y],     Pier Paolo

1 The Bolognese writer, Antonio Meluschi (b. 1909), who was believed to have Communist sympathies.
2 Renata Viganò.
3 The poet Antonio Rinaldi, who taught Pasolini at the 'Galvani' *liceo.*

## 29  To Luciano Serra
Bologna
[*In possession of addressee: autograph*]

[Casarsa, 1 September 1941]

Dearest Luciano,

I am writing to you in haste because this is the day when I have decided to begin my Italian assignment – as you see I have very little time – in fact please do me a favour right away so as not to forget – find out whom I have to hand the assignment in to and by when.

I have just this minute received your express letter which filled me with tenderness where our relationship is concerned but which alarmed me about Leonetti and Roversi. You mustn't show my outburst of a letter[1] to Franco because if, as you rightly say, he is bound by old friendship to Roversi – just think how wounded he must have been by what I wrote about Berto! All the more since as always I went over the top – but it is that wretched Meluschi who is to blame for my excess. I felt very bad that he read my 'Tempest'[2] and found the second part of your 'canto' very poor. Idiot! . . . let's not think about it – I am very grateful to you for having taken my advice and not going to that poor creature.

Tell Leonetti to be very forgiving for my outburst about Berto – some phrases of that outburst must be completely suppressed – but the general conclusion concerning the impossibility of reaching a literary agreement between him and us remains. As for Leonetti himself he can keep up both friendships ('Roversi' and 'you and me') and so would not compromise himself either way. I must point out that my friendship with Franco has by now taken on the general characteristics of an extra-literary friendship because I feel close to him not only because of matching ideas and literary ambitions but for real bonds of human sympathy which I am sure will become increasingly strong in a short time. And insist to him that he must break entirely with Meluschi.

About what you tell me of the pain which emerges when – left on the margin of life away from the joyous circle of your colleagues (who are stamped in your mind with the image of their laughing faces and so you mock them) you feel alone and shut up in yourself – this is the situation, dear Luciano, which I have felt most deeply and which has been the bedrock of my poetic feeling – but remember my myth (to me it's old by now) of the night and day where 'night (as I wrote) in my myth is the same as me aware of myself' and that comes about (let me make clear) because of an exasperated feeling of solitude among the men who live around me (day).

I have expressed myself confusedly because I am in a hurry – in any case I hope you have understood – but you can be sure of this, that I understand you very profoundly and when you feel lonely think of me and you will see that I shall be very close, passing time sadly with you. (True liberation, it is true, would be love – Sappho had the first sense of solitude (very like our own) and expressed it because of amorous pain 'καί ἐγὼ μόνα χατεύδω'.[3]

I have read a very interesting article by Betocchi, *Ritorno al canto* ['Return to song']. And I have re-read Luzi's poems which pleased me more than the first time but still don't enthuse me, and I cannot consider him one of our best poets as Bo[4] does.

I am enclosing without enthusiasm some poems which seem to me to mark a turning point in my poetry itself (a break with the theme of Casarsa towards feelings and explorations in a more general and universal direction).

*I was warrior in the orchards*

Happy the one who now the rain is pouring
shimmering down from the sky and now, now,
the clear sky emerges, the wind slices
down over the damp piazzas.
Bitterly the shadow of the smoke
rises to my eyes from the lit fires. A morning
this of sweet confidences.
    But the wind
that strikes the windows and makes drip
the willows and this pale ray
of sun is a call
to the familiar myths: and already I see
in the sunny arbour that strong
life which every day I win
outside these walls.
    Already new
worlds the dead blue of the rain
throws open in the sky, weeping
of downpours, the blue death
of the rain; my warrior infancy returns
in the fresh tumult of the orchards.

*Event after the tempest* (marginal)

The tree collapses in the wind,
the houses are back
in their places after a long
journey and are daydreaming.

Sadly the spirit moves towards
dreams; the room is left
empty; I am far away.

*The youth* (is unfinished and since I shall never
  be able to finish it, it remains one of my
  marginal works)

Now many seasons ago
at this hour I was a child.

My brow was earth-coloured at play
in this light of the tempest that had passed.

But behind the spaces of a tree
which curved vastly, I discern trembling
the untouchable worlds, sure goal of the present,
dreamt of by the boy.

        Was this
the landfall of my trusting game?

(*Untitled*) (you could suggest one to me)

Severina in the dark air
cleanses the threshing floor
of the muddy remains of the storm.

        To strip
fear from the branches leaves,
long sunsets, the sordid
evil of life
that begins again.*

        Severina,
extinct, why do you survive? Death (it is true)

like this
suspended rumble of the thunder
looms over you who live
and I who contemplate you.

*Here again there is adumbrated, or rather reborn, the myth of the day (you who live) and of the night ('I who contemplate you'). But the vision seems to me to be ennobled in the face of death, and I think I have never found accents stronger in their continual sombreness. Further a new feeling is born here (is born in so far as I am clearly aware of it, it having inspired without my theorizing it many other poems: 'Second elegy', 'Nostalgia for the present', 'Places of the memory', etc., etc.); this feeling is the 'Fear of the future' which one can identify, precisely, in the expression 'nostalgia for the present'.

1  See Letter 28.
2  'The Tempest'; see Letter 26.
3  'and I lie alone'.
4  Carlo Bo (b. 1911), literary critic and essayist.

## 30   To Luciano Serra

Bologna

[*In possession of addressee; autographs also addressed to Roversi and Leonetti*]

[Casarsa, September 1941]

Dearest friends,

I got your letter a little late – hence mine of yesterday turns out to be useless since I could have answered your last ones at one go. This I am saying because I have very little time and when I begin to write I don't stop and always lose an hour of very necessary study. I only began to study for the assignment on the first of the month and haven't written a single line. I don't know what I shall do. I'll make it short and nasty – but it doesn't matter. I shall arrive on the 20th or 21st in time to have it typed and hand it in. I have postponed leaving: 1) because I want to finish the above in peace; 2) because here in Casarsa I and my friends are putting on a theatrical show 'For those on active service'. I am the director and the thing interests me tremendously. I'll tell you about the rehearsals, the choice of the actors, my dictatorial position as director. The play is Sartorio's *Fallen Angel*.

I shall return alas with less than 20 paintings – a dozen. I shall start one tomorrow of great size and ambitious intentions. My latest literary discovery is Michelangelo about whom I am morbidly enthusiastic – I put him among the first 4 or 5 Italian lyricists; as for Tasso, I like him but I think there is no other Italian author who is subject to judgements of greater disparity and indecision.

Your opinions on those three poems[1] of mine are very just – but I'd have liked you to look a bit more closely at 'Untitled' which seems to me one of my best. Read it aloud letting yourselves be guided by the words you read – it seems to me that in this way that tone of 'gloomy contemplation' which seems to me one of my greatest achievements will become evident.

I await with impatience your judgement on the poem 'To the Virgin', to which one of those I am sending you is almost an appendix. The other – the ballad – I don't know where it comes from – certainly the concept of life-death is the classical one I am continually reading about these days (Michelangelo, Tasso). At any rate both are entirely marginal . . .

[The remainder of the letter is an analysis of poems by Serra and Farolfi.]

I embrace you,      Pier Paolo

PS. Send me immediately – get it at Cappelli's (or somewhere else) – the Tasso anthology by Flora.[2]

*1941*

> You only are good; your supreme pity
> succours my lost wicked state,
> so close to death and so far from God
>                               Michelangelo

Uninterrupted, if I listen well,
is within me the nocturnal
cry of the dogs.
                    It brings back to me
nights not spent
which already I regret; it recalls
the frontier where alone
I held up
the weight of the earth.

Oh voluntary exile
where torn from men
I have not even tears
but feed and, uncertainly, elude
my pain!

### Ballad of my brother³

You are right, brother, that evening
I remember when you said:
In your hand is the sign
of love and of death.* You joked
thus but I saw the future clearly
and certainty crept into my heart.
Now let the sound of the guitar
continue and let day accompany it!

*This little episode really happened.

### To the Virgin⁴

> Virgin, if with lips still soiled
> and full of, strewn with apples and absence
> to praise your name I am unworthy
> instead I ask you for the lament of song . . .
>                               Tasso

You do not welcome me, oh life of man
renewed with the new evening,
in your circle of sad ruins,
obscure trees and lonely walls,
in the dream of the living. But an enemy

semblance, you overwhelm me with the pale
things which, when the hour changes, daydream;
and as I am wont I lead them to the limit
of the infinite; see the fearful terror
of their weak (in the vast
life that follows) their imminent deaths.
    O you to whom I do not trust myself, Virgin,
it seems that in you they rise again
to gentle ardour and true semblance.
Perhaps the blue evening
is full of you, perhaps the prayer does not touch me
where the dying sun
wounds the lime-trees and
the footsteps of men and their voices are sweet.

*Merchant*

He who was no more a man
but a stripped pine, had his chin
burnt with tenderness,
and to the sold horse said:
'You're braw.'[5]
It neighed,
that stallion.

*Mother*[6]

In the years she has
ancient roots, that mother,
she has lived long.
Querulous women console her
in the sad shadow,
she who has been cheated by her son.

PS. I was in Cortina on Tuesday but the 'Exhibition' was shut already because
it had moved to Belluno for the 1st of September; so I went to Belluno
(Wednesday); but I don't know what the reasons were for its not being open.
I came home frustrated. I shall go back to Belluno on Tuesday.
    Two main things: 1st – a certain very vague move towards the Catholic
faith; 2nd – a certain very vague aversion to contemporary poetry in which I
find the defects which those who oppose it find there (Croce, etc., etc.)

1   Transcribed in Letter 29.
2   In the original MS the postscript is written at the beginning of the letter, before 'Dearest
friends'.

3  Translated into Friulano it appeared under the title 'To my brother' in *Poesie a Casarsa*. It was dropped in later editions.
4  The last three poems were probably transcribed in a previous letter now lost.
5  In dialect in original: Tu eris biel = Tu sei bello.
6  Rewritten in Friulano it reappeared with variants under the title 'The deceived one' in *Poesie a Casarsa*; it was dropped in subsequent editions.

## 31  To Luciano Serra
Bologna
[*In possession of the addressee; autograph; also addressed to Leonetti and Roversi*]

Casarsa – last days
[Postmark: Casarsa, 16 September 1941]

My dear friends,

For at least four days I have been expecting your letter every morning – absolutely certain I would not get it. And every morning I am very fed up at not getting it. It is the only link to the 'sordid evil of life that begins again' – I had an absolute need of it in these days – now that I see the colour of death distinct and clear on everything that surrounds me.

This is the last letter I shall write you from Casarsa – on Saturday I shall be in Bologna and after supper will come and fetch you as of old from your house.

So expect me at your house on Saturday after supper.

These poems I am sending you are my harbingers – I don't know what to think of them – maybe they too bear the imprint of the colours of death.

I feel detached and alien to everything that formerly was an occasion of confidence and gaiety – in fact forgotten. Yesterday evening, a cold, miserable evening, not yet dark, I heard the military band playing in the square and the din of the people round about and the anxiety in the laughter and I felt that I was physically touching death.

I feel torn and remote, wandering here like a shadow, while the normal run of life here continues totally unheeding and precise.

But even Bologna where I have put down roots and memories for many years and have long-standing habits and things that repeat themselves according to a habit which has by now become dear and a source of nostalgia, is a very sad goal for me – these returnings, which have been the same now for many years, in summer days that are not yet over, in the sweetly squalid September sun, are a real torture to me. And I do not even have hopes for my poetry since, from long habit, the weather in September puts me into a state of aestheticizing sentimentality which resolves into plays upon words, which are tamely stupid.

Fortunately I have you – but you too, I don't know why, are tardy in replying to me.

Until very soon

I embrace you affectionately,      Pier Paolo

PS. Even if one of these days – or even tomorrow I receive a letter from you I shall not reply because it would be too late – I'll do it verbally.

*Prayer of love*
to Luciano\*

At that pious fountain\*\* whence we all are
is assembled every beauty that here is seen,
more than any other thing, by those aware;
nor have we any other proof nor any other fruits
of heaven on earth; and whoever\*\*\* loves there with faith
transcends to God and makes death sweet.
                                        Michelangelo

A hard martyrdom encloses me
but I do not despair; if you were not
living stone to me you would split
the emptiness that holds me. \*\*\*\*

For you sweet colours on the leaves;
for you sounds felt; wind that suffers
over enclosed walls and says
its reiterated death, wind that flattens
the sky with sad lights and prints
colours of ill fortune, to us would be
a gentle handmaiden among the flowers remote
icon of cold grasses.
            Draw near. Break the solitude
of the waters, of the villages
and of the lands,
cut into my thought
with your smile. Where no friend
can reach (but only understand from afar),
where every human being
lives in another life, you alone,
you, can stand by me, be
my companion, here among these meadows
and houses where I try in vain
to bind myself with the lives of others,
to have in Christ a brother.

\* Diogenes searched for man; I should like to
      look for Woman
\*\* The divine origin
\*\*\*Loving beauty
\*\*\*\*These three verses are to be printed in a
      different font

*Dawn in childhood places*\*

Conegliano, light with years
on the hill, with wandering steps I climb
your roads and am repelled
by the tender cowardice of childhood

which, shy boy,
I exhaled in this air.

I have returned to the deserted dawn
of the hearths and tread on the dew
here near the old gate
of the Ginnasio.

Was it a dream that time
when I did not see this sun
being born, this hill
on which laborious herds graze?

Ahi, but it is not new to me, the bell
which now rings for other children!

\*A very marginal poem, written standing up, on the esplanade of the castle of
Conegliano, on top of a hill. It was very early in the morning and I was up here
waiting for the connection by train for Belluno.

*Prayer for the one not believed in*

I am speaking to you, Lord, man is not made
blest by any test of mine save for your blood;
have pity on me since I was born to your law;
and it will not be something new.
                                        Michelangelo

Not to watch with absent eyes
what is dying now is important to me
nor how each season is nakedly consumed,
to know that time arriving
brings cold return to calm
and the death of birds on the boughs.

Not to weep with crude laughter
for time, with absent eyes,
while above and around you
you note how cold grasses are trodden.
Why the water trembles
in the dry earth, and the hard sky
penetrates faces,
I do not regret, nor the cries
that pierce the roofs, or the back
of the land which recedes
and weeps, the insensible throng of human beings.
Do You, Alone, unite these discordant
remains, which I cleanse lovingly,
and with too much love hate. Reign over me,
Thou, govern me, nail me on the cross,
obscure my future. Forget me in Thyself,
cease to feel the wounds at each sight,
thus time may not wound me as it alters,
the imprint of human beings' hostile laughter.

*In Thee let me repent*

Grant that I may return to you,
almost garbed in heavenly plumes,
Lord, feed me and shelter me.

Tasso

With bitter laughter I escape the boughs
where pain hides that slashes me.
But I do not notice it and it forces me
to feel myself always elsewhere. Oh body,
oh love, oh unknown altar,
oh you who remain upright as a man,
pray and bow down!
Dissolve it, so that in the din
of these human beings I may sprinkle more
and ask for and think less
and let life give more than I seek.
So that I do not go deserted
searching for the dead in the stony dawns
and am dead, and being dead, I am reborn
to brief light and in me day lights up
once more with a painful dark light.
Let night not be night where with

a sky that clears I have lights of new
ill-fortune and, the more I recognize myself, real desert.
            Arise to new life since if I find myself
enraged at my sin (perhaps that is Thy name)
where, if not in Thee, can I repent? And do Thou humiliate
        me
so that, lost, this passage of others
over the earth may not be a desert to me.
But I awake and in this cold light
which has emerged among the trees and between the walls
I burn and turn to sin,
and do not repent. I follow that flame
that sets me ablaze – fallen – with enclosed silences.

*Evening of storm*
(Time returns to past autumns)

Bare fields and deserted by the pallor
of the air, here even your only friend,
the peasant, abandons you.

I remain alone and am a thing where evening grows dark;
peace did I ever ask of you, trees?
Did I lament at your joyfulness?

Now that the wind cuts into your happy
branches! Happy in the silence
of the tempest.

But above me the dark rotates,
sky, where I fall uncertainly
among the grass trod
by my child's feet*

*Among the grass I trod when I was a child.

PS. I waited another day before posting this letter – so I got yours but the reply
would be too long and so I shall give it verbally.

I was alarmed by the news that I have to hand in my assignment by the
20th; in another letter Luciano had told me that the 25th was all right. Now I
shan't be able to hand it in before the 23rd (on Monday 21st I shall give it to
be typed). Let's hope they accept it just the same.

Up to now I am rather pleased with it.

## 32 To Franco Farolfi
Parma
[*In possession of addressee: autograph*]

[Bologna, autumn 1941]
Dearest Franco,

Now I understand the mystery of your silence – you didn't get the letter I wrote you from Casarsa. I posted it with another addressed to Melli and he didn't answer either.

All this time I have lived, alas, as always – I haven't been untrue to any of my positive or negative faculties. And that, it seems to me, is what you have done too – it is characteristic of you to have done badly in the chemistry exam not because of lack of knowledge but because of contingent superstructures. And the same goes for what you say about the piano.

I am studying like mad too for the exam in Italian – but I won't talk to you about that because I would be forced to break out into the usual recriminations. Once more I have had to interrupt my beloved studies in poetry to which I had given myself over entirely during the summer. And – talking about the summer – I would have a lot of things to tell you – but there are too many of them and they are too full of nuances to be written down. All you need to know is that this has been the best summer and one of the finest periods of my life. Positive and tangible results – 15 pictures in which I have improved immensely – a complete series of poems dedicated to Casarsa, of which I shall perhaps send you some samples – football matches with reports in the *Popolo di Friuli* which I have kept. But the results which I hold most dear are those which one cannot list. I see now that my life will have to renounce what men call 'living' and withdraw entirely into a poetical vision of events of my own and thus savour the smallest things, continually transforming into something fantastic what goes on even in the most banal manner.

As for girls, things were going marvellously for me with a certain Nerina, a typist – with exceptional blonde hair – slim – a good family. I had quite a crush on her. For many evenings I took her home from her office. I revelled in the most tender amorous promises. But then – just look at the prosaic selfishness and laziness which govern me – I gave her up because of her office hours – impossible – they made me miss basketball, the Soldiers' Club, study. Perhaps she will change her office and consequently her time-table; then I shall start up again finding some excuse or other.

I think it will soon be calling-up time. The moment I have finished the exams (29th) we'll make an appointment in Modena. I can't wait to see you, dearest Franco, and as usual have a lot to tell you.

I embrace you,         P.P.

## 33 To Franco Farolfi

Parma

[*In possession of addressee: autograph*]

[Bologna, autumn 1941]

Dearest Franco,

I too very much want to see you – tomorrow, Wednesday, I have the exam – then for another two or three days I shall be happy putting various things in order (my books, because I have bought a new bookcase since they have increased beyond all limits, my pictures to frame, some poems to be typed, etc., etc.). On Sunday there's a football match which I don't want to miss. I suggest we meet on Monday without fail – if the weather is good we shall go on to Modena by bicycle and if it is nasty by train. Dear Franco, you will have to give in to the weather if it is bad and put up with the train because otherwise goodness knows how many months we'll need before seeing each other if we do what you amazingly suggest in your postcard. Our appointment is at the Ghirlandina between 9 and 10 as usual.

Now that I have told you these practical matters I have run aground. I have nothing touching to add and the exam, which has taken over all the grey (and not grey) matter in my skull, is to blame.

My sentimental life has either died away or is going on in the depths of my heart. But, basically, apart from the empirical worries of the exam I'd feel magnificently well as I am; in fact, I'd get fat. In the moments study leaves free I am in tremendously good spirits – a little of it is also the pleasure of doing my duty with mathematical precision.

My passion for music – and I feel desolate at my ignorance – takes me by the throat. And along with that, many other passions – that for Spanish, for Latin (!), for Art (a consequence of these passions will be immense expenditure on books) and above all my passion for girls.

But we'll talk about all this in Modena* on Monday. I beg you – endure the train if the weather forces you to.

I embrace you aff/y.     Pier Paolo

*Maybe Umberto could come to Modena too – greetings to your family.

## 34   To Franco Farolfi
Parma
[*In possession of addressee: autograph*]

[Bologna, autumn 1941]

Dearest Franco,

Yesterday, Serra, who works at the Censor's, brought me your card a day early. At last I have your reply.

I am very excited over your invitation to Parma – I shall certainly come on one condition – that you won't keep me there more than two days. I have absolutely no wish to put you out longer than that – and we know very well how difficult life is these days, etc., etc. In fact I feel I am exploiting your hospitality by even coming for two days – these two days will be Thursday and Friday of this week. I'll send you a telegram giving the time of my arrival on Thursday morning – and I'll send you a telegram if some unexpected obstacle arises.

Probably I shall arrive at Parma limping and with a stick. I sprained my ankle racing the lift downstairs at Roversi's – but I hope it will be better by then since it is something quite slight.

I don't remember whether I wrote about the result of the exam in Italian – at all events I got a distinction.

Naturally I have lots of things to tell you and will do so when we talk. Now I am going to break off because I am in a great hurry.

Thank your parents in anticipation and greet them from me.
Greetings too to Umberto.

I embrace you aff/y.      Pier Paolo

# 1942

## 35   To Luciano Serra
Bologna
[*In possession of addressee: autograph*]

[Postmark: Casarsa, 22 April 1942]

Dear Luciano,

I have taken a long time to reply to you – I have been here for two weeks but time has gone by very fast. I work all day and at a certain point am very tired. When I am tired I should write to my friends from a scruple of conscience so I am sending you this miserable letter.

I shall tell you so much the moment we meet.

Meantime you should know that: *Oedipus at dawn* is finished and done with (I can't wait to hear your opinion); I have written another 3 or 4 poems in Friulano; a poem in Italian; 4 or 5 pictures with two of which I am *very pleased.*

Shall arrive on Thursday or Friday. I have taken a very long time to write to you – forgive me – but I have not written to anyone else.

PPP

Greetings to your parents.


## 36   To Luciano Serra
Bologna
[*In possession of addressee: autograph*]

[Postmark: San Vito di Cadore, 31 May 1942]

Dear Luciano,

I got your bibliographical letter right away – you are amazing.

It is almost supper time. I shall start writing again shortly. It's not true that supper is ready (I wish it were!) so I shall go on.

Let's deal with business first. You should go quickly to Cap(p)elli and make them give you right away the books they were to get to me, and send them to me without any loss of time. All this, however, only if the books (or book) can reach me by Wednesday at the latest. In fact I shall arrive about Sunday.

Life here would be nice and particularly recommended for long calm periods of literary leisure if a continual bitter agitation – which sometimes turns into a sort of panic fear or depression – did not constantly undermine me. Pier Paolo Vergerio[1] and Leonardi Bruni[2] are a consolation to me for two reasons: 1) because they praise extended reading and the sweet humanistic studies; 2) because they say that poets are the only great educators of humanity. The latter is what above all elevates me to a sure hope – you will remember my stupid doubts about the use not so much of art as of artistic labour not for ourselves but for others.

But what I want to tell you today in a few dry words is about my morning run to the Forcella Grande – I did in 2 hours what they assured me ought to take 3½ – I am speaking about walking or marching.

The crunch of my boots on the stones and the scree of the mountain, but above all my silence and my solitude, together with the desire to climb to the top, had kept me company during the killing march. But when I reached the peak (now from down here it is a tiny ochre element[?] of rock, lost and strange among the clouds and the evening) I lay down among snow-covered meadows on a grassy ridge (the grass was almost warm) but, lying like this, the Noise of my boots and my Fervour came mechanically to a halt, but I was not yet aware of the terrifying solitude. But I was no sooner shaken out of my torpor by the sudden way the air turned grey, the sun having been eclipsed among the clouds, than I suddenly became aware of my untenable position. I rose up and, frightened like a child in a dark room, I began to run down the rocks like a goat. I felt as if I had the threatening eyes of the Spirit of those places on my back, impressive, drifting in the silence, impenetrable, and in their perfect tranquillity, hostile. I had experienced the same feeling as a child when, having stayed on alone in the green waters of the Tagliamento, when the surroundings were completely deserted, I felt as if I had been seized by the feet by the ferocious and deeply silent numinous spirit of those pools. I got quickly out, naked, dripping with barely repressed cries – happy ones.

So there, dear Luciano, I am happy, we are all happy, happy even in our pain provided it has been clearly defined within us. Long live poets like us. Long live even the stupid ones like Cicciarelli, to whom I would reply coldly as if I were throwing a pail of icy water over his cordiality – which is that of a bad poet.

I embrace you,        PP

1  Pietro Paolo Vergerio (1370–1444), scholar and historian.
2  Leonardo Bruni (1370–1444), humanist and politician.

1942

## 37   To Luciano Serra
Bologna
[*In possession of addressee: autograph*]

[Postmark: San Vito di Cadore, 6 June 1942]
Dear Luciano,

Up to now I have waited in vain, anxiously, for the books – those I brought with me I have drained to the last drop. I am left with *Dedalus*[1] but I am keeping it for the journey. Perhaps you will see me before this missive containing my poetic production. Let's hope the latter has the weight and the stature of my voice so that it will reach you as a faithful herald of myself.

### Portrait of the Mountains
For me San Vito is not dear with memories. The children who lead the cows to pasture and the girls who look out from the little balconies have not been known to me since childhood. Yet I love these parts in the way a man can love the rocks and the woods – but not the oleographs. An icy breeze blows but it is mild, it is warm. The Pelmo, up there among the clouds, is not alone but seems to be so; it is like a crucified Christ – a Christ painted by the Beato Angelico, not afraid but almost smiling, while Serdes and Senes,[2] full of woods, are sacred to the Virgin and San Domenico who, silent and kneeling, meditate on the cross in the great silence.

### Night time
Where has the dark of evening caught me,
that thins out the voices, and the infinite
sloping away of the hills.

To the north
everything becomes blue. Where the moon
is born the light unfolds and sends out its beams.
From the village to the valley the cry of children
sadly replies.

Where
does the course of life hold me? And when
did I reach these places? At the perfume
of the meadows the white ray
of the last bright patch sinks; in the evening
it is sweetly cancelled; it is peace that reigns.

### Birth of the day
Dawn is born with noonday peace
and in the valley morning emptiness,

180

it is a noon of greens. The hen,
light in its feathers, releases
shouts of quiet. A song – a summer one – of birds
from so high up falls on the sun-drenched plains
as if from other skies. On the road,
look, an old man passes and makes no gesture,
lost in his enclosed dream. Then
he is gone; already lives elsewhere,
leaves no trace of himself in the powerful
silence of the meadows.

*Morning in San Vito*

Glassily in the breath of the breeze
the mountain lights up its snows. The high green
freezes in the meadows and the pasture,
now that the cloud driven back into the sky
changes its colour. Now the wood lights up,
now it darkens. And the fear
of the fine sky blue, of the fine weather,
in the wind and in the silence, almost
fences one man from the other. Each one
is alive in another life, in the circle
of the unsteady woods, of the illuminated
peaks.

I shall add no more because I am neither joyful or downcast. These have been days of innocent and sunny peace. I have studied a great deal and willingly. But I long for our anxious life.

I embrace you,          PP

1  *Dedalus* (*Portrait of the Artist as a Young Man*) by James Joyce, translated by the novelist Cesare Pavese, Fratinelli (Turin, 1933).
2  A hamlet and an Alpine refuge hut above San Vito.

## 38  To Luciano Serra
Bologna
[*In possession of addressee: autograph postcard*]

[Postmark: Porretta Terme, 2 July 1942]

Dearest Luciano,

Am writing you a few lines in great haste out of a sense of duty. I am tired and rather ill-tempered (but always alive to good humour). For news more or less for the record I shall copy out the beginning of my postcard to my mother: The usual confusions on the journey – army food and mess-tin – camping on the grass among young trees. Leave, walking-out pass, tattoo, as always. Otherwise (20 days!) an unknown quantity.

I beg you do all the things I asked you to do. And write often.

I hug you, my distant Luciano.          PPP

Address: P.P.P., University Detachment Camp, I Bn, 3 Coy, 1 Pl, Porretta (Bologna)

## 39   To Luciano Serra
Bologna
[*In possession of addressee: autograph*]

[Postmark: Porretta Terme, 10 July 1942]

Dear Luciano,

I am overwhelmed by existence – this is one of these delightful moments when poetry returns like a distant memory and the only feeling present and certain is that of one's own solitude. I see a boy carrying water from the fountain in two pitchers – he is walking in the clear air of his village which is a village unknown to me. But he, the boy, is a figure I know extremely well as I know the sky which is fading with funereal sweetness and the houses which are abandoning themselves little by little to the dark while everything in the little square is overwhelmed by the disturbing sound of a trumpet. The day is about to end and I remember the infinite number of days I have seen die in this way as far back as those distant times in Idria and Sacile which you, Luciano, will never know. Then I was a boy and now I am a dead man. But the evening does not cease to lap at the villages of the world, their little squares, chaste and almost solemn, in a sharp perfume of grass and stagnant water. And now a woman appears on the balcony and utters a long-drawn-out shout that makes me shudder: 'Son!' That is how it was in the little square at Sacile when I lingered there with my friends.

Here I am now as if I were distant and mute – my life apparently devoid of sorrow and on the margins of existence.

Today my mother came to visit me and left a little while ago. Thinking of her I feel a pang of love – she loves me too much and I do too. I am a poet to her. She wrote me a letter the other day that brought a burst of weeping into my throat.

I laugh and suffer with the utmost decisiveness. The laughter is true, the suffering is congenital. You and I believe in laughter – in life with sails spread – to the future on a calm sea. We are poets. Ambition is awareness of ourselves. The future is certain. I have two days' dirt on my hands. The camp is a hell but I live it for the memory. I wash the mess-tins – something horrible! Being awake all night on guard – something horrible! These are – from the point of view of comfort – the worst moments in my life. But life puts down its roots everywhere and the tail grows again as it does on lizards. I am alive.

With the proofs I am quite pleased[1] – I shall make some typographical changes and in the text too (where the translations are concerned).

I liked Berto's slim volume a lot[2] – we'll talk about it at length together. Write to me. Now I'll give over because sleep is killing me.

I embrace you,        Pier Paolo

1    Refers to *Poesie a Casarsa.*
2    Refers to *Poesie* by Roversi.

## 40   To Luciano Serra
Sassuolo
[*In possession of addressee: autograph*]

[Bologna, end of July 1942]

Dearest Luciano,

Here is the slim volume.[1] I am very tired – it is late in the evening and I have been busy all day because tomorrow morning I am going to Casarsa. I am very sleepy as well – I am almost befuddled – but I was awake and so this will be a miserable poor sort of letter.

In these days I have been extremely lonely and – as always in solitude – melancholy was hypochondria and good-humour perfect serenity.

You left me at a moment of great tension that was mental more than anything else. I wanted to invent for myself a dualism to set against the idealistic monism and intuition of Croce. I am immature – but the fact of ethical research as something that transcends aesthetic research is a theme that recurs often in my meditations.

Alas, this is not even a poor sort of letter for as I write I am getting excited and would like to go further – but my laziness is immense. I have kept on going to the Reno[2] which is more gentle and white than ever, and spent there one of the longest noondays of my life. A bell was ringing (while I was lying on the warm shore) and its sweetly laboured peals came from the direction of my left knee, from hills that were misty and almost Cimmerian.[3] . . . Alas, laziness has made me talk of marginal matters which have nothing to do with you or me. I should have liked to talk about our friendship, about your hypocrisy and my overbearing nature, about the infinite number of nights we have passed together on the benches in the avenues, under the chestnuts, drunk on what sufficed to make us feel proud and almost divine, about our violent joy. Life has separated us – one here and the other there – without pity. Our recent life is already a memory that, although it does not yet touch us, has all the signs of a most painful future sorrow.

I kiss you,     Pier Paolo

1   A copy of *Poesie a Casarsa* with a dedication.
2   The Reno is the river at Bologna.
3   Cimmerian: the Cimerii were a fabulous people who lived in perpetual darkness.

## 41   To Luciano Serra
Sassuolo

[*In possession of addressee: autograph postcard sent to the University Military Camp at Sassuolo*]

[Bologna, July–August 1942]

Dearest Luciano,

How are you? I am not at all well since I am the victim of a – not very serious – state of exhaustion. Hurrah for my slim volume.[1] I have had a number of letters in praise of it, among them this from G. Contini: 'Dear Pasolini, yesterday I received your *Poesie a Casarsa* – I like it so much that I at once sent a review to *Primato* in case they should want it.'[2] I was happy for two days – and now I am beginning to become aware of the shadow of 'excelsior'. Write to me, oh dear and irreplaceable monster, but not about fruit-shakes.

I embrace you,     Pier Paolo

P.P. Pasolini, Nosadella 48, Bologna

1   *Poesie a Casarsa* (see above).
2   It did not appear in *Primato* but in the Swiss *Corriere del Ticino* of 24 April 1943. Official Fascist disapproval of regionalism meant that the article could not appear in Italy.

## 42   To Luciano Serra
Sassuolo

[*In possession of addressee: autograph*]

[Casarsa] 12th [August 1942]

Dearest Luciano,

I am in Casarsa in my room at the little desk I like so much and everything here is set up for my existence as a scholar.

I began to write to you because I remembered when reading a book by

Tecchi,[1] which I still have fresh and open by my left hand, something very important. It is as follows:

We perhaps possess a soul as a possibility and this possibility makes man in general superior to the animals. But this possibility is realized only in those who 'in life, by making an effort, reached upwards' and only in them can it be immortal, or at least a divine spirit perhaps subsists for a few brief instants or an extremely short time and then it dissolves and falls to the ground, extinguished for ever.

This is rhetoric, a useless construct, and a fragment – but it is also one of the sweet myths which, here in Casarsa, are born in me more generously and more spontaneously than in any other place on earth.

Here in Casarsa I find myself in a perfect mean in which sadness and joy are balanced in themselves and balance each other. A mean of affection (compared to my mother's) for my parents – a mean of solitary life – a mean of life in common. The books snatched from the bookshop in Bologna live in a different air here which is dark compared to them, and they shine there like austere constellations.

What a pleasure I experience at seeing them like that – chosen and arranged. I have truly made a marvellous choice! How I love to touch with expert hand those intact, rough and shining pages, full and succulent with ideas that are clear and documented, each of which will contribute to enlarging something in my soul, so that each day I may feel myself superior to the previous one.

The mental stresses and strains – like exhausting and arid research – have come to an end almost by magic – I listen to myself living more and more sweetly and am always clear-headed as when one awakes from a benign afternoon sleep in summer and it is not yet evening and the air is brilliant and festive with distant noises.

I go from one hour to the next, from one thought to the next innocently, as if turned into a child again. But this is a very wise and thoughtful childhood! I measure the time that passes and the life that accompanies it – not my life but that of all the people I know and do not know who live around me. My balcony open to the sky, the roofs, the courtyard, is like a pulse in which I hear beating the existence of the entire village.

A day has passed and I get your card. I was broke or nearly so – I shall tell my mother to send you the money.

It is Sunday morning – remember Part III of *The Litanies*.[2] That time has returned – but it is destiny that all should undergo changes (fractures, Montale would say) but though here in Casarsa changes do take place things remain true to themselves and fundamentally unaltered. What a horrible place Casarsa is! There is nothing. It is all morality and no beauty – the peasant ignorance of the boys, the nastiness of the women, the thick grey dust of the streets. Everything has lost the mystery with which childhood surrounded it and is naked and dirty before me – but this is a new enchantment, a new dream and a new mystery. I have entered upon an adult childhood now that the other has lost my regrets.

I embrace you,      P.P.

1  Bonaventura Tecchi (1896–1968), novelist, poet, Germanist.
2  'Li litani dal biei fi' ['The litanies of the handsome boy'] in *Poesie a Casarsa*; now in *La nuova gioventú*.

## 43   To Luciano Serra
Sassuolo
[*In possession of addressee: autograph*]

[Postmark: Casarsa, 23 September 1942]
My dearest Luciano,

I read your letter with trepidation – for us even the lines thrown down on a piece of notepaper are poetry and of the most moving kind. I understand your condition perfectly which is a little like my own although the external circumstances are immensely different – Professor Cinti,[1] when I expressed a profound sense of human suffering and of the parallel impossibility of expressing it, advised me to write short pieces of prose in which the responsibility of the poetic form would not alarm one before setting about composing and yet which are not merely an outlet for emotion – what he called the prose of waiting.

Poetry will return, Luciano, all the more so since I saw clearly in your little volume[2] that you have struck poetry and the true kind. A poetry apparently delicate and almost transparent but in reality of extreme purity – in my memory certain passages are close to, and of the same stock as, certain Greek fragments. I have read your poems to Franco Farolfi who was completely overcome by them – I have read him – in the capacity of a kind of spiritual educator – many things but he was never moved as much by anything else as by your poems. Pay no attention to the horrible syntax of what I write – but I am still full of sleep. It is raining here. Autumn has begun. But now it causes me no pain. My conscience is at peace with me. I have not lost the summer. I shall come back to Bologna with a very long piece of poetry – 'The last poem to Casarsa'. It is the most complete and mature I have composed up to now and, at least for the time being, I am proud and sure·of it. I shall type it and send it to you as soon as possible. For you – since you lack books – it will be a sweet, and above all long, letter. Naturally I won't expect a critical judgement from you – I am not able to criticize your things either – I wanted to review you in *Architrave* hoping to do something decent which would please you without making you feel that it was propaganda. But I did not manage.

Of my stuff in the next number of *Architrave* I shall send us article on Italian poetry in general[3] – very short but very meaty and strongly felt, called 'on an old composition by C. Betocchi' (*Return to Song*).[4]

Forgive me if I do not write often and regularly – but it is my old anti-epistolary illness which some days I find it absolutely impossible and painful to overcome. And to think that I know how marvellous it is to get mail when you are doing time in the army.

My life here continues to be very pleasant – but I shall tell you about it another time – or perhaps you already can imagine it perfectly.

A kiss,     Pier Paolo

1   Italo Cinti who was to be one of the moving spirits of the periodical *Setaccio* ('The Sieve').
2   Serra: *Canto di memorie.*
3   Not published.
4   Carlo Betocchi (1880–1985), Friulian poet.

## 44   To Franco Farolfi
Parma
[*In possession of addressee: autograph*]

[Bologna, October 1942]

Dearest Franco,

Under my impenetrable silence I am writing to you in great haste.

I am overwhelmed by exams – but above all what concerns me is the founding within the ambit of the Gil of the review *Il Setaccio*[1] from which my real career will perhaps begin.

The exams will be over and done with on the 30th and then I am free. I naturally accept your invitation to Parma with enthusiasm and will arrive at your house, I believe, on the 12th – if that is all right with you. Then we shall tell each other everything.

I embrace you,

PS. Please send me right away the book with the reproduction of the kiss of Judas because I want to do a picture for a competition in Piacenza and I have in mind, precisely, Christ's face. I'll bring the book back if necessary.

1   The first number appeared in November 1942.

## 45  To Guglielmo Petroni[1]
Rome
[*In possession of addressee: autograph*]

[Bologna, November 1942]
Dear Signor Petroni,

Thank you warmly for the nice things you say about my small volume which you have undoubtedly sized up accurately in spite of any difficulty of vocabulary. Thank you.

Yours,       Pier Paolo Pasolini

1   Guglielmo Petroni (b. 1911), anti-Fascist writer and literary editor. This letter was in reply to a letter from Petroni, to whom a copy of *Poesie a Casarsa* had been sent.

## 46  To Luciano Serra
Bologna
[*In possession of addressee: autograph postcard*]

[Postmark: Bologna, December 1942]
My dear Luciano,

When I write to you I inevitably write briefly. But in these times I have too much to do and write. I am sending you the first number of *Setaccio*,[1] which isn't as we want it yet. Now I am working like mad on the second, which will be very fine.

De Roberto[2] has sent me an invitation to contribute to *Signum* as a result of my piece on Weimar.[3]

Arcangeli has seen my drawings and liked them in a way I found flattering. My little volume continues to reap successes which I find moving.

But the best thing would be to talk, to see each other, damn it, and to sleep together and dream together sweetly mingling our solitudes as once we did. And sending each other up which was such fun.

I give you a really big hug,       Pier Paolo

1   Six numbers in all appeared of *Il Setaccio* – 'the order of the day of the Bologna HQ of the Gil (politics, literature, art, cinema, theatre, music, radio, sport, notebook)' – between November 1942 and March 1943. The second number already changed the subtitle to 'monthly review of the Bologna Gil (politics, literature, art, notebook)' and so remained. The editorial group under the editor, Giovanni Falzone, included Pasolini and Fabio Mauri. Contributors included Giovanna Bemporad (G. Bembo, to conceal her Jewish origins),Fabio Luca Cavazza, Luciano Serra and Sergo Talmon. Its illustrations were particularly interesting because they were avant-garde in style, or at least not tied to the political line of the publication.

**2**  Federico De Roberto (1861–1927), novelist, essayist, friend of Verga.
**3**  'Italian Culture and European Culture at Weimar', in *Architrave* of 31 August 1942; republished in *Il Setaccio* in January 1943.

# 1943

## 47   To Fabio Mauri
Bologna
[*In possession of addressee: autograph*]

[Casarsa, January 1943]

Dear Fabio,

Here are some things for *Il Setaccio*. I shall send you the long introductory article in two days' time and it will be called instead of 'Presentation of an anthology, etc.', ' "Dino" and "Biography to Hebe" – two important texts'.[1] Have you had articles from Telmon and Serra? and go and see Leonetti (via Rubbiani 1). Write at once – if necessary I'll send another article myself. Try to get a lot of drawings from Ciangottini – and always fill up the gaps with drawings. *Il Setaccio* III has some *awful* things: the Summary, the fillers (who on earth is responsible for this low flame?), the page of poems with the translations mixed up so stupidly. And the contents also have awful things. Theatricality and Youth! Direction! the Mediterranean! Ludwig van Beethoven! Poor old Fabio, try not to have any more. I leave here on the 7th. I have had a temperature for three days but now am almost better – I felt I was living in Bologna – I wrote some of my finest poems. Tell Cavazza to be a little less presumptuous – ah the youth but mature!

I beg you, Fabio, work well for *Il Setaccio*.

A big hug,        Pier Paolo

Greetings to your people and to Cianetti.

1   A review of two books in *Il Setaccio*, 4 January 1943.

## 48   To Luciano Serra
Bologna
[*In possession of addressee: autograph*]

[Postmark: Ortisei, 22 January 1943]

Dearest Luciano,

Two words in reply – I have neither the time nor the disposition to write.

Life is very beautiful and dream-like – I am not a commendatore but Kurikala.[1] *Architrave* is terrible. What about *Primato?* I know nothing about it. I am waiting for *Il Setaccio* with enormous impatience. By the way, remember that for the fourth number I expect from you an article of 4 foolscap pages on a poet (Betocchi or Gatto, etc.).[2]

About *Eredi*, I charge you.

Take it then or send it to Ricci.

I'll write at more length another time.

A hug,        P. Paolo

1  Finnish skier: world downhill champion.
2  Alfonso Gatto (1909–1974), a left-wing hermetic poet.

## 49   To Fabio Luca Cavazza
Bologna
[*In possession of addressee: autograph*]

[Casarsa, January 1943]

Dear Fabio Luca,

I got the express letter – catastrophic. Then I waited in vain for some details. Silvana has written telling me that she brought you my article (Dino and Biography). I can't tell you how much ill-will I feel towards the person who took away our child.[1] These are the things which can bring about changes of opinion that last a lifetime – and which above all will rebound on whoever is responsible.

Write and give me the details – and then that bit about 'hoping it was a joke' – what a thorn in the spirit.

Try to put together the fourth number as well as possible – and send me *ten or so copies of the third number as well.* I'll refund the cost of the postage the moment we meet.

And do me a favour and go to Ciangottini, give him my greetings, and tell him that it was not my fault if in the third number the report on the activity of the Gallery is incomplete. And ask him who a certain Massimo Rendinia[2] (or something like that) is, what he does, and if he has any good points or not – he's the new editor of *Architrave.*

I lead a sweet and painful life here – I am sad and happy and lose a lot of time. Dear Luca, we passed good very full days together in Bologna – who knows when they will be repeated.

Write to me at once. A kiss.        Pier Paolo

1  Refers to one of the recurring crises between the editors and the political direction of *Il Setaccio.*
2  Massimo Rendina, co-editor of *Architrave.*

*1943*

## 50 To Fabio Luca Cavazza
Bologna
[*In possession of addressee: autograph*]

[Casarsa, January 1943]

Dear Luca,

I thought I would be able to bring the stuff myself in time. But my calling-up card still hasn't arrived. So I am sending everything by post. The piece on the Temptation should take up two pages. I didn't use the two verses from *Le Cid* because I left the book in Bologna.

See you soon. A kiss.  Pier Paolo

Tomorrow I shall send a political article by Bortotto[1] – also fairly mystical in tone.

1  Cesare Bortotto, a Friulian poet.

## 51 To Fabio Mauri
Bologna
[*In possession of addressee: autograph*]

[Casarsa, February 1943]

Dear Fabio,

I am writing you a short, sharp letter. Why have you not sent the material for *Il Setaccio*? To abandon it at a moment like this is the kind of irresponsibility which only a 'laddie' can commit. I am very upset by it – your face returns to my memory not wearing the fine colours of trust and of open affection. Why do you always disappoint me like this? Naturally you will have your own good reasons and the one to be wrong as always will be me.

My life – at this luminous time of year, among the fields which, being leafless, offer no protection from the light and so the distances seem infinite, amid good and warm friends and so many little things dear to me – is no longer as calm as once it was. A continual disturbance without images and even words beats at my temples and blinds me.

Dear Fabio, for you, whatever you do is gratuitous – you have the hope of a future. For me it is a duty to give results; there is no future any more. There is the life which will be mine – one of the infinite number. It has an enormous weight, I am incapable of exploring it thoroughly and I let the days go by – at twenty I am in the same precarious state as at seventeen. Have I lost my serenity? My faith in myself? Perhaps it is only a phase – and then we are cowards and I shall learn to repress even these reasons for pain – which is a laborious task. But I believe that the principal reason for my state is the continual cruel, insistent, painful thought of Pariah's fate.[1] Every time I say that name I have to bite my lips or to look hard at something to swallow my tears, I am still watching for news of you.

I embrace you, dear Fabio, write to me.        Pier Paolo

PS. I am buying from someone (no name) an etching by Bartolini for 200 lire. If you want to go halves with me I won't pay you back the 100 lire I owe you and we shall be joint owners of the work. Write.

1   Ermes Parini was on the Russian front.

## 52   To Fabio Luca Cavazza
Bologna
[*In possession of addressee: autograph*]

[Casarsa, February 1943]

I have had your latest news about *Il Setaccio* – and also a postcard from Ricci. So I am replying to you, to Ricci and Falzone.[1]

I have thought a long time about what to do – and I am convinced of this: that we must not give in. We talked a lot – and Vecchi will remember this – about our generation's educational mission and now that we have a vehicle to be able to achieve this – a drop in the ocean – why should we give up?

There is still one attempt we can make and that is to accept the compromise with nobility. If this 'nobility' also does not find favour, then we shall be silent. If instead we succeed in contenting them then – little by little – subtly we shall retrace our steps until we arrive more or less at the level of our present position.

Anyway I do not believe that 'the noble compromise' will be demanded of us given the various expressions of approval which *Il Setaccio* has elicited.

Finally, a 'noble compromise' can in no way diminish our dignity if one turns one's mind to the really serious and – I would dare to say – anti-literary moment through which our Fatherland is passing.

In short, do you remember what I said in my piece on Weimar[2] – which is that we Italians will never be overwhelmed by things imposed from without but, while not demolishing the barriers, we shall cross them just the same by infiltrating ourselves under them like water? Ours must be a subtle and diplomatic operation!

In any case to have attempted it will be entirely to our advantage. Now it remains to define what our noble compromise should be:

1) Not to allow new collaborators to write who are rhetorical and stupid youths.

2) To dedicate ourselves to the problem of education and – let us call it that – of faith.

3) Dr Falzone should write – in the next revised number – a editorial in which to define his view that ours should be not a journal for young people but *by* young people but that nevertheless since we must stay within the ambit of the Gil – that is to say, have to be dedicated to the problems of youth – the journal *by* young people will deal with precisely such problems but in the most elevated manner possible, because it is natural that a young person feels obliged to give the best of himself, not compromise himself and limit himself to a task of popularization, for which all the wisdom and experience of an [illegible] is required.

4) To publish a lot of drawings which have the virtue of taking up a lot of space, thus denying it to various boring pieces and of being in themselves works of popularization. (The drawings will still be by Ciangottini, Mandelli, along with mine and Fabio's.)[3]

5) To do away with the divisions into politics, literature, art, etc., which give it too literary a tone. Naturally the literary articles will remain, reduced in size, and the first political–educational part will be more important.

6) We will even go in for some polemics with other bulletins just to show that they don't interest us.

7) The Diary could be preceded by a kind of Chronicle of one or two pages (done by Ugolini for example), commenting on the events of the day with some good photographs of ceremonies – not only in Bologna – or of the war.

8) As ideas like these come to us, put them into practice.

Soon I shall send you: 1) The page-proofs of the new, revised *Setaccio*; 2) Articles of mine with signature and pseudonym and an article by Castellani,[4] very well researched, on the relationship between school and the Gil in country schools with proposals, etc.

Dear Fabio Luca, please do me the favours I asked for in the preceding letter – you should also send me the latest bulletins of the principal federal headquarters[5] and the bulletin from Rome with the famous article. You should also go to the editorial office of *Architrave* and get them to give you my article 'Comment on an anthology'[6] which Rendinia (?), whoever he is, is not publishing because of a divergence of opinions. Write for *Setaccio* No 5.

I embrace you,      Pier Paolo

1   Dr Giovanni Falzoni, editor of *Il Setaccio*.
2   Refers to 'Italian Culture and European Culture at Weimar' (see Letter 46).
3   Fabio Mauri.
4   Refers to 'Fascism as Spirituality' by R. Castellani in *Il Setaccio* No 5.

5   Of the Fascist Party.
6   Comment on an anthology of 'New lyrics' in *Il Setaccio* No 5.


## 53   To Fabio Luca Cavazza
Bologna
[*In possession of addressee: autograph*]

[Casarsa, February 1943]
Dearest Luca,

I got your triumphant letter this moment. I won't stop to tell you how much enthusiasm I feel for the idea of the firm of Arcangeli-Gatto, etc., etc.[1]

As I wrote to you and Ricci, it was already decided that I should come to Bologna on Friday and I shall be in Bologna on Friday afternoon.

For the 5th number of *Il Setaccio* I sent off a lot of material express yesterday.[2]

See you soon,

A kiss,      Pier Paolo


1   The programme of this 'firm' proposed the publication of poetry in the original; the first was to be *Les fleurs du mal* by Baudelaire but police headquarters in Bologna intervened with a ban.
2   Articles and drawings by Pasolini and others.


## 54   To Fabio Luca Cavazza
Bologna
[*In possession of addressee: autograph*]

[Casarsa, March 1943]
Dear Luca,

If Falzone really wants to play the capricious bully, well, we'll give him tit for tat. If *Il Setaccio* is not going to be as we decided together in all particulars tell the Doctor that I want nothing of mine to be published. And you do the same. Let him learn, that boring ass.

I shall come back to Bologna on Monday 6th about midday like last time. I shall speak to Facchini[1] and let's hope the usual complications haven't arisen.

Is there anything new? I feel well here – well in the way men are well – that is to say a prey to perpetual discontent.

A kiss,      Pier Paolo


1   Eugenio Facchini, co-editor of *Architrave*.

## 55 To Fabio Luca Cavazza
Bologna
[*In possession of addressee: autograph*]

[Casarsa, March 1943]

Dear Luca,

A couple of lines in haste because I have written ten letters this morning seized by great joy at having news of Parini.

Splendid, the last *Setaccio*[1] – I'd like to kiss you all on the forehead. For you three or four kisses more than the others for 'The End of Guerrino'.[2] When did you read Freud?

Congratulations on your cinematographic fantasy.

I shall come to Bologna towards the 12th or 13th to sing our swan-song together. Meantime you should send me – no more of the disgusting bulletins – but ten copies of the 4th number. And send a copy to Elio Melli (Albergo Centrale, Riva del Garda, Trento) and to Serra (Infantry Officers Training Course, 2a Cadet Company, Casagiove, Naples) – one copy should go to Gatto (S. Petronio Vecchio 39) and the editorial office of *Primato*.

A hug,      Pier Paolo

1   No 4 of February 1943.
2   A film script by Cavazza in *Il Setaccio* No 4.

## 56 To Luciano Serra
Casagiove di Caserta
[*In possession of addressee: autograph*]

[Postmark: Casarsa, 8 March 1943]

Dear Luciano,

I am copying just as it is the letter I wrote today to Carlo, Franco, Elio.[1] I am so happy!

'I had meant to write to you with such painful news that for many days I have been almost stunned. It was about Pariah[2] who, according to a letter from Tarcisio, was wounded and then perhaps made prisoner if not worse. I went to Costa – his colleague who got away – in Tricesimo, who – as witness – confirmed the news.

'This morning a letter from Tarcisio informs me that an Alpino,[3] who is wounded in a hospital in Bologna, told him that Pariah escaped from the Russians as well, at the last moment, and is in Poland where he has been operated on for a wound in the shoulder and is soon to be repatriated. Dear

Carlo, Franco, Elio, Luciano, I have suffered and been afflicted in a way that I could not have imagined.'

In the second last number of the dying *Setaccio* your 'Elegie brevi' ['Brief elegies'] seemed to me very pure, sweet, refined. If you have anything for the last number send it, because then – on orders from Rome and to save paper – all Bulletins will be suppressed.

A big hug,       Pier Paolo

1   His friends in Bologna: Carlo Manzoni, Franco Farolfi, Elio Melli.
2   Parini did not return, and died in Russia.
3   A soldier from one of the Alpine regiments.

## 57   To Luciano Serra
Casagiove di Caserta
[*In possession of addressee: autograph*]

[Postmark: Casarsa, 30 March 1943]
Dearest Luciano,

The months are mounting up between us and I am constantly changing my thoughts, my bitter meditations, in a swift and unhappy ripening process – and so are you. What longing to have you near me! To cancel out with one afternoon and evening of talk that tiny bit of mutual mystery which has arisen between us.

Instead of screeds, I am writing two poems on the back of this for you. I still know nothing precise about *Architrave*. I shall be back in Bologna on the 6th and shall speak to Facchini. *Il Setaccio* has finished its short but not entirely distasteful or unworthy existence. The 5th number will not come out[1] thanks to Falzone and his whims and bullying.

In your last poem the first line and the last two are very fine – I'm not at all convinced by the middle – in the end do you remember or not? Are you or are you not a man 'who does not have sweet memories'? The argument proceeds almost dragged along by the words – hence their sensual and aestheticizing gesture of consolation. I'm inclined to feel that your brief elegies were more clear and more honest – closer to your true life. At all events there remain these three very beautiful verses and if you work – I mean logically – to develop with clarity that approach and that conclusion you will perhaps pull off one of your best poems.

Hoping that army bullshit is being kind to you.

I embrace you and kiss you,       Pier Paolo

*1943*

### The rain

In the orchard the rain breaks
with a magical harping
light, uninterrupted,the long murmur.
The cries of my cousins
come back from the Marches of childhood
while the water – it is evening already –
is not placated

on the old tiles and the roads.

Evening was arriving in the silence
of our games that had died. Why did we

sadly bend our heads almost drawn away
far off by the rain?
Now I pay
that ancient sadness and in the noise
which drags itself from the roofs to the countryside

I breathe my past. And those magic things –
the fire lit in the house, the smoke
heavy in the fresh air, the melancholy
lights, the tired voice of my mother –

are brought to life again by this smell
and this arcane play of drops on my roof.

### Song

The fire crackles quietly, already it breathes
the nocturnal sadness of the house.

It is cruel songs the moon asks for.

And such I listened to as a boy
and such as in other times my mother
also heard as she lay awake.

Oh sweet choirs
of my village, today I sing you.
With my friends along distant roads.

And still children – from the house –
hear youth passing
as they lie awake late at night. Their sweet body
will grow to a destiny

like ours and when we fall silent
with chaste and light lips they too will go,
oh God, singing to this same moon!

1  In fact No 5 came out (March 1943) as did No 6 (May 1943).
2  The two poems – 'La pioggia' ['The rain'] and 'Canto' ['Song'] appeared in *Poesie* in 1945.


## 58  To Gianfranco Contini
Domodossola

[*In possession of addressee: autograph*]

[Postmark: Casarsa, 24 April 1943]

Distinguished Signor Contini,[1]

The interest you have taken in the fate of my first slim volume[2] is truly a great consolation to me. You will understand that what I cherish is your critical opinion, your esteem – not that the review should be printed in *Primato* or elsewhere.

Having returned after a long absence to my village I am continuing to write I hope with a clear consciousness of what I am doing – in the meantime experiences and sorrows very different from those of a year ago have intervened!

I must thank you too on behalf of my mother who is certainly more ambitious and desirous of recognition – for me – than I am myself.

Thank you again and best wishes.

Cordially yours,          Pier Paolo Pasolini

PS. Could you let me have the address of the *Corriere Ticinese*? I should like to get them to send me the issue with the review which I naturally very much wish to read.

1  He uses the very formal mode of address: *Egregio Sig. Contini.*
2  *Poesie a Casarsa*; See Letter 41.


## 59  To Luciano Serra
Casagiove

[*In possession of addressee: autograph*]

[Postmark: Casarsa, 24 April 1943]

Dearest Luciano,

It must be ages since I wrote to you. It is Easter – the pigeons continue to shit on the roofs and the hens to lay precious eggs. Very soon all these things will look very different to us – either because we will be dead or because these hens will be more precisely Friulano and the ones from Romagna more Romagnolo.

Life is becoming more and more difficult and writing is an enormous burden – I am tired of my thoughts which have been giving birth to each other for a thousand years and are mine. I want to throw myself on to other people, become transfigured, live for them.

Don't be afraid, Luciano, it is still me – nothing has changed. Now we could very well be in Piazza Malpighi[1] in one of our cafés talking about *Eredi*. Did you see the last *Setaccio* – it's very good?

Facchini has made me literary editor[2] – for the time being – but we'll see.

I have lost a considerable number of letters, among them yours too, with your poems – you should send me both of them. (The second you sent me I don't much like – it is too Quasimodian. Quasimodian, Luciano, is terrible! Be like me and hate that verbal masturbation – get it out of your memory. And be logical when you write, Luciano; in your last poems there is always a logical contradiction, and it's not clear if you want something or not.)

The first I hope to publish in the next number of *Architrave*. I am always writing ten letters at a time, contriving to discharge only superficially the duty of remembering but not of writing letters that say something. I have worn myself out by dint of writing. Here instead of words is a drawing for you.

1   Piazza Malpighi in Bologna.
2   See No 4 of the review *Architrave*.

## 60   To Franco Farolfi
Parma
[*In possession of addressee: autograph*]

[Casarsa, spring 1943]

Dear Franco,

Evidently we speak two different languages. By now I am so immersed in my dream that I do not know how my voice can reach those who do not accompany me. Now I am fairly calm – the acts of putting on the light and looking for paper have put a stop to the fury of my thoughts – but I am still cool from the Casarsa night which I passed, suffering, on those roads which I have tramped for years. I should like to speak to you now – but all that will reach you is words distorted by the frankness I feel forced to use with you.

Your whole reply to my letter follows a path which I know already like the thousand others I can foresee – *but I cannot resign*. Stop for a minute over these words and imagine that in a moment of absolute frankness, without emotion and without posing, I am shouting them to you with all the voice I have in me. And instead you speak to me – like all the others with whom I touch on these topics – about a possibility of resigning oneself and of not thinking, which men it seems have been granted by nature. Your whole letter hinges on this illogical possibility of resignation. Well clearly, just as in matter all disequilibriums are compensated for, so it is in things of the spirit – perhaps such an equilibrium does exist whereby something not thought or not clearly thought, let us say, must be thought and suffered by a minority but with such intensity and fidelity as to make up for the imbalance. You will not believe this but if, as you think, Schopenhauer did not have many moments of stasis (to eat, take a wife), I have no such moments. Every image in this world, every human face, every peal of bells, is hurled against my heart wounding me with a pain that is almost physical. I do not have a moment of calm because I live always being thrown into the future – if I drink a glass of wine and laugh loudly with my friends I see myself drinking, I hear myself laughing with immense and deeply felt desperation, with premature regret for what I am doing and enjoying, a consciousness of time that is continually alive and painful.

But I am neither ill nor mad – I am normal and calm not only in looks and external gestures but also inside myself. And I thought – as I wrote to you – that such 'calm' was due to fundamental and healthy balance of my spirit. But probably I owe my salvation (not becoming mad, not consuming myself) to my imagination which is able to find a concrete image for every feeling and – as it seems to me – imprisons it, prevents it from working away frantically in my brain.

Thus in me, to the painful pressure of feelings, which I suffer continually, there methodically corresponds a poetical rearrangement which, if nothing else, serves to put between two banks, to render harmless the constantly moving current of my emotions. Last time I told you more or less the subject of my thoughts. You will not believe me if I tell you that I force myself to weep . . .[1]

. . . You see how all the things that the possibility of resigning oneself and accepting makes obvious to you, for me are abstrusely and painfully open to thought – my existence is a continual shudder, a fit of remorse or sense of nostalgia. I have even spent a whole hour looking at my hands because I was overcome by the qualm that at the point of death a man does not know what hands he has had – he has always resigned himself to having them, has been too used to them – does not think that among the infinite number of hands these are his.

I have wakened up rather happy and will finish. As for searching for a logical – that is to say a philosophical – justification for existence, I shall not even look for one. Those abstract things like God, Nature, Word, do not interest me. The philosophers do not interest me in the slightest except in certain poetical passages. I find nothing more useless and painful than to borrow a language used for centuries and to use it for a newly abstract philosophical construction. All the more since I find a kind of consolation and equilibrium through poetical images, as I said. The only philosophy which I feel very close to me is *existentialism* with its poetical (and even more close to me) concept of 'anguish' and its identification of philosophy as existence. (Read the book by E. Paci, *Existentialism*, C.E.D.A.M. Padua, where you will find a bibliography I think.)

Yesterday evening I saw – goodness knows how it turned up here – *The Tragedy of Yegor*, which must be the film you and Umberto told me about. I wasn't very well and seeing that film made me completely better. It is a long time since I felt such pure and disinterested enthusiasm for the works of others – not even for *Gli angeli del male*[2] or *Quai des Brumes*[3]. The ingenuity and rhetorical quality of the contents, which are often almost ridiculous, are redeemed by a technique so original, free, poetical (almost all close-ups) such as I haven't chanced to see for a long time.

Write soon, I embrace you, my greetings to your family.
Pier Paolo

1  Page missing.
2  Probably *Les Anges du Péché*, directed by Robert Bresson (1943).
3  *Quai des Brumes*, directed by Marcel Carné (1938).

## 61  To Franco Farolfi
Parma
[*In possession of addressee: autograph; incomplete*]

Casarsa, 4 June [1943]
Dearest Franco,

This ought to be a wonderful moment for me. Had I imagined it a year ago it would have been with emotion and joy. Gatto's presentation in *Ruota*, a review in the Friulian philological bulletin[1], and above all a marvellous article by Contini 'At the limits of dialect poetry';[2] the invitation to contribute to various reviews – *Eccoci, Spettacolo, Signum*, etc. – a whole bunch of successes should make me happy. But instead I am very sad, unwell, disappointed. Dear Franco, *we* – *we* of all people to be twenty-one – it is a miracle, a cold shower to which I cannot get used. The whole of life has changed – we are no longer adolescents; now our gestures, those gestures of ours are the definitive ones – ours among the infinite number we could have and hoped to have. For eternity this brief and precarious appearance of ours on earth has taken on the garb of our eyes, our hair, our words, and should we not use these attributes in an absolute sense? Now I am at my desk writing – are these the gestures of mine at twenty-one which will remain in the story of my life, so terribly short, declining towards DEATH, the gestures of the green and joyous season? But where is their true sense, what separates them from their absolute state? I cannot resign myself to having arrived – not to have to grow and improve still more. My body. Do you remember it when we were at the *liceo*, along the roads of Emilia? . . . and here we are too remembering and mourning, miserable things which I scorned in others as things which would never happen to me, to me eternally a boy. And instead, Franco, you are a gentleman of 21 years, my friend, and together we remember past times, the times of the *liceo* . . . But don't you see this is ridiculous, that this isn't right for the two of us? How we have betrayed ourselves, Franco, this is not our life, this is not how we were to talk to each other according to the promises made at Sasso, in via Nosadella. Yesterday I saw the fountain at Venchiaredo where the youthful body of Ippolito Nievo[3] crushed the grass and breathed – then *he* was young, *he* laughed, *he* did not think even remotely – and wouldn't it have been ridiculous if he had thought it? – that for him too death would come? And in fact it came. I cannot live because I shall not be able to get used to the thought that for me too there is a time, a death.

Scribbled down amidst these thoughts, which, mark you, do not leave me.

1   *Ce Fastu?*
2   Contini's review appeared in *Corriere del Ticino* on 24 April 1943 and was republished in *Il* [*sic*] *Stroligut* (the literary periodical dedicated to Friulian writing, founded by Casolini), No 2, April 1946.
3   Ippolito Nievo (1831–61), writer, active in the Risorgimento, who spent part of his youth in Friuli.

## 62   To Luciano Serra
Casigiove di Caserta
[*In possession of addressee: autograph*]

[Postmark: Casarsa, 4 June 1943]

Dearest Luciano,

We should meet and talk – I have an infinite number of new feelings and sorrows to tell you about. My life has been entirely renewed – I have advanced again. A new miracle to see the faces of the men, the boys, the hours of the day. I have never suffered so much as in these last months for nothing. But these are general statements which could fit you or me or anyone. I should like very much to talk to you – I would have a whole new system of pain to open up to you. About 'Via Appia', which I shall send to

*Architrave* about which, by the way, I have heard nothing more either as concerns myself or Facchini, etc.

I am continuing to work a lot and I can't wait to read you my latest Friulian notebooks; I can confess myself to you, Luciano, and can tell you that my imagination has greatly matured in these last months and I have arrived at a clarity of invention which strengthens me to live and often fills me with enthusiasm. I have invented a huge number of myths. I have constructed a legendary history of these places here which did not exist before; and I hope that one day it will be accorded a certain value . . . But never mind. I have been invited to contribute poems to the Friulian philological bulletin; Paolo Grassi has invited me to contribute to *Eccoci* and *Spettacolo*. But the best news I can give you is that an article about me by Contini called 'At the limits of dialect poetry' has appeared in the *Corriere Ticinese* (and will soon be republished in a university paper). I hope to let you read it soon.

Giovanna Bemporad[1] came here to Casarsa for a week – six days passed together.

As for you, as a physiognomy and as poetry, you seem to me to be put on ice – military service being the ice, so to speak.

I embrace you very strongly,      Pier Paolo

1   Giovanna Bemporad, a literary prodigy who, being Jewish, suffered under the race laws.

## 63   To Luciano Serra
Casigiove di Caserta
[*In possession of addressee: autograph*]

[Postmark: Casarsa, 24 June 1943]

Dear Luciano,

Here I am for you as fresh as a rose. I have ten minutes free – I am waiting for the news on the radio, because then I am going to the Tagliamento; there, black and almost naked, I shall throw at the sun my youthful gestures of a boy bathing. I shall trust the sun; I shall tread the grass as if it were alive and trying to prick me, mown and tender.

I am free and healthy – it is a week of serenity, of carefreeness, of cordiality. This is a face of mine that I love very much but which does not correspond to the true reality of my nature and you know it, I don't need to tell you again. Serenity has taken on the face of a girl from Valvasone, fat and attractive, who is something between a magnolia flower and a tomato. I kiss her and take away her breath every evening and all she asks of me in return is to keep her happy.

These are beautiful evenings, Luciano. But I do not weep – as, wretched creature, I always do – over their beauty which is there, their well-known fleeting nature. The days no longer pass over my head like shadows but it is one infinite day in which I swim happily. My anguish, which lasts for days on end, is terrible but my serenity is also not usual.

I am working a lot, not with excitement but almost with irony.

But don't let us think about such things! When I began to write to you I was singing

<blockquote>
let the sky be clear<br>
the sun without clouds.[1]
</blockquote>

Now I don't want to sing any more. Your fault. You made me think of Renato Fucini.

I long to be in the Tagliamento, to throw my gestures one after the other into the shining concavity of the landscape. The Tagliamento is very wide here. An enormous torrent, stony, white as a skeleton. I arrived there yesterday by bicycle, a young native with an younger native called Bruno.[2] The foreign soliders[3] who were washing themselves there listened with amazement to our rapid and incomprehensible talk. And they saw us dive without delay almost bashfully into the cold water, which they find mysterious. We were left alone and the storm caught us in the midst of the immense stony bed. It was a storm as livid as an erect penis. We fled – dressing in haste – but half-way across the bridge the wind stopped us. The Tagliamento had disappeared as if in the midst of a mist. The rage which the wind raised up furiously in the sky blinded us. And the sky from black and yellow had become very white. Everything died down almost unexpectedly. When, with difficulty, we reached the end of the bridge the Tagliamento behind us was still somewhat ruffled with sand. Bruno gave a sigh of relief. Three or four gipsy caravans were fleeing like us from the storm, which was still roaring, with some shudders of raindrops, towards Codroipo. In a sky-blue caravan a gipsy boy was lying playing a trumpet.

I kiss you,     Pier Paolo

1  In Friulano in the original.
2  For Bruno see Pasolini's novel *Amado mio*, Garzanti (Milan, 1982).
3  German troops.

## 64  To Franco Farolfi
Parma

[*In possession of addressee: autograph; incomplete*]

[Casarsa, 19 June 1943]
Every time I hear the funeral bell and I ask about the dead man or reconstruct

his life (child, youth, bathing in the river, the Procession candle in hand) and I feel it is impossible not to see the whole of life from beyond the point of death, to see it past and finished, gesture by gesture, a chain of days all unimaginable: to find oneself at the point of death and not have had the time to bring to a perfect close the period of childhood.

This morning at dawn I was wakened by some voices; warm, precise, clear, sweet. They were the voices of eighteen-year-old youngsters who were paying amorous compliments to my cousin's daughter, born yesterday, the child of a day, and already dreamt of by me as a young girl, and with her my old face. Not to be thought of? Ridiculous? But don't we have before our eyes the clear, cruel examples of people who saw us being born and now a little apart watch us being youths. *I cannot resign myself.* Never, not at any moment of my day: the summer which is passing, the wheat, yesterday and the day before turning yellow, and now cut and threshed; the sudden memory of Sergio, the boy who used to bathe with me in the river and now is an ugly and grey youth. We sink in a swamp of faces, hands, curls, voices. The relationships which bind men to each other are enormous, illogical, inexpressibly absurd; imagine, for example, what relationship can pass between a dead officer (whose funeral I saw with its fanfare and wreaths) and the two children who are playing in a meadow (whom you see at one and the same time). It is the same relationship as binds me to a wasp.

A moment of truce – everything is new. Each gesture those who are around me make is a pang in my heart: demands a new setting in my picture of the world. Each funeral bell makes me suffer as if a dear one had died, so much respect do I cherish for life that I even see that of an unknown person, directly as if he were concretely close to me. I see him as a child, a youth, and on feast days seeking amusement as if that moment were eternal and the most important of all moments; and now he has grown old and died. The war has never seemed to be so disgustingly horrible as now – have they never thought what a human life is?

I have not replied directly to our letter – you are one of the two or three to whom I can pour out my feelings and I do it with all my heart. I think your discontent has the same sources as mine and is clothed with different attributes. I very much believe that a woman truly loved can take up much of our time, assure us of a support which not even our mother or brother could be. The naked body is the truest and its embrace is the one bridge which can be thrown over the abyss of solitude which divides one from the other.

Meantime 'I am of a sadness beyond compare', as I was writing to my uncle, continually struggling with the events of life, which are too beautiful and sweet to be enjoyed. I get no help from the hope of any sort of future because I love the present too much, I love it with a violence that equals remembrance, memory. Whatever happens to me I shall be happy because I should like to remain without moving in these days, in this age, in this unhappiness. And instead the days are passing under my feet without touching me, more like the clouds which pass over the stones of the Tagliamento than anything concrete *to be lived*. At certain moments if I do not fall into a kind of enchantment or madness I have to thank my make-up which is by nature healthy, serene and happy . . .

The official news of Pariah is that he is a prisoner. His image, there in Russia, cut off from his life as in another world where they only suffer and lament, causes me constant anguish. I embrace you affectionately.

Regards to your family,     Pier Paolo

## 65   To Fabio Luca Cavazza
Bologna
[*In possession of addressee: autograph*]

[Casarsa, end of July 1943]

Dear Fabio Luca,

I never imagined that one day I would set about writing to you so seriously. Reply immediately, will you, because the anxiety to have news of you and all my friends is wearing me out. Add to the list of common friends: the Serra family, Leonetti, Signor Landi (S. Domenico 5), Bertani (Loderingo degli Andalò 1), Meluschi, my neighbours at via Nosadella. Let me know about these as well as about your own people.[1]

Find out and tell me something too about the Bolognese political scene – what, in short, was that party Morandi, Rinaldi and Arcangeli supported.[2]

Lately I had gone over in an absolute fashion to politics with very decided and revolutionary ideas but events have anticipated our intentions, filling us at first with unspeakable joy and then leaving us feeling empty and useless. We – I and my friend from here, Bortotto – want to work, act, be with someone.

Forgive my ignorance – but *Il Setaccio*? Had the printers not been paid yet? And in that case could a new number not come out with a new title and new material? Then I would immediately come to Bologna.

Write to me at once, dear Luca. Long live liberty.

I embrace you.     Pier Paolo

1   Mussolini had fallen from power, having been dismissed by the Fascist Grand Council on 14 July.
2   Il Partito d'Azione – the Action Party, a grouping of mainly liberal intellectuals.

*1943*

## 66   To Antonio Russi
Pisa
[*In possession of addressee: autograph*]

Casarsa, 28 July [1943]
Dear Sig. Russi,

It was only yesterday that I saw *Primato* of the 1st of July and that by chance. Here one is cut off and moreover in recent times has had other things to think about.

A kind of reserve keeps me from thanking you in the words I could wish. But you can imagine them. Besides your piece is so close to the origins of my little volume – and everything it intends – that I felt as if I had a new lease of life. Thank you again from my heart.

Cordially yours,      Pier Paolo Pasolini

## 67   To Fabio Luca Cavazza
Bologna
[*In possession of addressee: autograph*]

[Casarsa, August 1943]
Dear Luca,

From your long letter only one thing has remained in my mind, growing all the time as thought follows thought: Ornella's[1] illness. I hope that it is a case of Fabio's usual alarmist behaviour because I don't know how to adapt to an event so strange, unexpected and fierce.

Do you remember when we saw Ornella in Bologna? How full of life she was. Let me have news of her quickly and of all your family – tell me what Silvana[2] is doing. Write soon because I hope you can imagine my anxiety.

About *Setaccio*. I have heard that as a result of some demand or other the journals of the Guf and the Gil can continue. Luca, please look into it thoroughly because I intend to make of *Setaccio* something marvellous and ours at last.

My greetings to all. A hug,      Pier Paolo

1   Ornella Mauri, Fabio's sister.
2   Silvana Mauri, later an important figure in Pasolini's life.

## 68   To Luciano Serra
Casigiove di Caserta
[*In possession of addressee: autograph*]

[Casarsa, August 1943]

Dear Luciano,

I think you are the victim of a tremendous process of becoming an idiot. I will blame army bullshit. What is this talk you give me about 'guerrillas' and 'guerrilla actions'[1] – I don't know whether to laugh or to have a fit of anger. Although you set so little value on your own blood take great care of it for the time being and if possible save it up for something better than guerrilla actions against these good Croats. Italy will need blood, that's for sure, but it is my country that must be bathed by it. It needs to be inundated with blood – or with tears – that may destroy a whole century of errors – monarchist, liberal, fascist and neo-liberal ones.

Italy needs to be remade completely from the bottom up and for this it needs – but needs desperately – us who, amid the frightening lack of education of the ex-Fascist youth, are a reasonably prepared minority. And in this connection I accuse you (or must I, as I hope, accuse the long months of the military process for turning people into cretins?) because in your letter there is not a hint of anything savouring of politics, not one comment of pain or of joy at the coming of liberty. And to think that for me, on the other hand, even for my singular and most intimate poetic experience, these days are of immense importance.

Freedom is a new horizon, which I dreamt of, longed for, yes, but which now in its extremely bitter realization, reveals aspects so unforeseen and moving that I feel I have become a child again. I have felt something new rise up and affirm itself in me with unexpected importance: the political man whom Fascism had wrongfully suffocated without my knowing it.

Now my life seems longer: the rhetorical 'youth' of Fascism is in fact no more than a state of inexperience and therefore all 'we young people' who used to be enrolled in the Guf find ourselves, rightly, with a whole new education to go through again. And History seems closer with its events of half a century ago than we recognized with such insouciance and uncertainty. Do you believe me, Luciano?

I feel in my nostrils a fresh smell of dead men – the earth of the cemeteries of the Risorgimento has just been turned over and the tombs are recent. And we have a real mission amidst this terrifying Italian misery – a mission not of power or of wealth but of education, of civilization.

I kiss you.

My dear greetings to your family,          Pier Paolo

1   'The initial rebuke refers to the news I had given that at the school for officer cadets we were being trained for guerrilla warfare; my letter dated just before 25 July reached him – fortunately, I would say – with some delay, because from P's resentment at me (who was innocent) was born his admirable statement of his political position.' L. Serra in *P.P. Pasolini, Lettere agli amici* (*Letters to his Friends*), Guanda (Parma, 1976).

## 69   To Fabio Luca Cavazza

Bologna

[*In possession of addressee: autograph postcard*]

[Postmark: Casarsa, 29 October 1943]

Dear Fabio,

Since those days what a series of events.[1] I am here unscathed – have been for two months now and my life is as before. But what an adventure that military fortnight was! Now I am so much back on an even keel that I am even opening a private middle school for the pupils from here.

A big hug,        Pier Paolo

1   A reference to his military service at the beginning of September until the Italian armistice with the Allies, and to the German take-over in Italy on the 8th of that month, and his long journey home on foot to Friuli.

# 1944

## 70   To Luciano Serra
Bologna
[*In possession of addressee: autograph*]

[Postmark: Casarsa, 26 January 1944]

Dear Luciano,

What an immensely sweet feeling you have given me! Today is Sunday and I have just got up, all warm with sleep; who would have thought that I have caressed your image with such friendship? After so long, so many months, so many Sundays. Each of us is lost in his own life, one here another there, two bodies living in the flower of a sad youth. What gestures do you make when I am walking in the fields or stand near the stove or go to the Rosary or laugh among faces you do not know? Dawns, vespers, evenings, noons, my gestures here, your gestures there, allowed to show themselves uselessly day after day in the vale of the light or the silence of the night.

But now what I find most painful is your distance from me – at this moment I think only of our sweet interrupted friendship, of your company which I miss, of the confidences – such long and joyous ones – which caused long hours together to pass. I think how alive we were at that moment and how now our two bodies which talked together as if that moment must last for ever no longer exist in our memories, two images which have the sole aim of making us sad and regretful. I have not changed in any way and this sometimes frightens me – when we meet again you will see in me the identical adolescent whom you found in the first years of our friendship. My friend here, Bortotto,[1] (who is now also far from me), playing one of our games, called me 'the eternal day-dreamer'. It is something which I think is very accurate – I don't know whether to my advantage or my unhappiness. Giovanna[2] came here only because there was a need for a Greek teacher; she was the only one of my friends independent enough to be able to come. Now our little private school has more or less broken up and she has gone home. I spent many fine poetical days with her and had good discussions but in return how many awkward situations she put me into in the village!

During this year I have worked a great deal – but in a very different way from that of the past. More calm, more constancy, more serenity, more fruitfulness to my fantasies which are less violent and numerous and much

211

more concrete. I have finished three small volumes in Friulano: the first, the second edition of the poems from Casarsa; the second a little book of dialogues ('Friulian dialogues' – dialogue between the clouds and Fruili; dialogue between a native of Casarsa and a pilgrim or snail; dialogue between a young girl and a nightingale; between a child and a chaplain and the tempest; dialogue between an old woman and the dawn).[3] I have written out the titles for you so that you can have an idea. Thirdly, a book of religious meditations: *The Nightingale of the Catholic Church.*[4]

I have done a lot of work in Italian too but with fewer results. Up to now, of the dozens of Italian poems I have written this year only five or six are presentable: you know two or three of them ('Tear', 'The rain . . .'),[5] three – the latest ones – I shall show you now. What a wonderfully sweet feeling I had reading yours, old Luciano. At a first reading they strike me as very fine, specially 'To the memory of Fabio and Sirio'. In the others it seems to me that the minor Serra is still there – the one who is too fond of syllabic encrustations of words (a harmony more rationalizing than musical) and altogether one is back with Quasimodo – a bad mark in poetical education.

My God! when shall we be able to talk about these things, happy and absorbed in them as before? When will the days return when our poetry will be the nicest and most important thing in life?

I lost my thesis in Pisa. The flight from Livorno (where I had my rifle with the safety-catch off to fire at the Germans) was like a novel. But now it is a useless appendix to my life – it has passed as the fatigue has from my limbs after the hundred kilometres on foot.

Give my greetings to everyone, your family, Carlo, Odoardo, Cavazza.[6]

A big hug,     Pier Paolo

PS. Along with the thesis[7] I also lost my student card – could you do me the favour of going to the secretariat and ask what I must do? I know nothing about the University. What does one do to be an external student. Does one have to matriculate? Try to let me know something and help me in this connection.

I have to teach about 5 hours a day.

Listen, ask Calcaterra too, if you can, if, in my situation, he can accept a thesis on 'Giovanni Pascoli'. In my next letter I shall take up these practical matters further.

1   Cesare Bortotto taught mathematics and technical subjects in the 'little private school'.
2   Giovanna Bemporad taught Greek and English.
3   Published in *Stroligut*: '*Il Stroligut di cà da l'aga*' ('The little almanac from this side of the river') was first thought of in October 1943 by Pasolini and some friends. It was a review of Friulian poetry to match the annual *Lu strolic furlan* ('The Friulian astrologer') produced by the Philological Society of Udine.

4  A reference to the first group of poems of *L'usignolo della Chiesa Cattolica (1943–9)*, Longanesi (Milan, 1958).
5  cf. Letter 57.
6  His friends in Bologna: Carlo Manzoni, Odoardo Bertani, Fabio Luca Cavazza.
7  The thesis on nineteenth-century painting which he should have submitted to Longhi.


## 71   To Luciano Serra
## Bologna

[*In possession of addressee: autograph*]

[Casarsa, February–March 1944]

Dearest Luciano,

Who knows why I am writing to you this evening; the last thing I would have thought of was writing to you this evening. The bell is ringing to say it is night, the stars are crackling in the sky which is deep dark in the centre while down towards the horizon it is pale. The moon will rise. A day past, a youth past. What aridity! With the burning sensation on my skin due to staying long in the sun among the dry mulberry trees and the damp primroses I feel in my body the aridity of an almost adolescent boredom, the sense of having lost the years. I don't know if we shall see each other again – everything stinks of death, of end, of shootings. What is Telmon coming to do in Casarsa?[1] You know he told me a very odd piece of news with an ineffable tone of voice? Every time I think of it my amazement grows. Sergio in Casarsa? Is he coming or not? Why does he not write? I would welcome him with open arms.

The war stinks of shit. Men are so disgusted that they could burst out laughing and say, 'It's not worth it.' But they are waiting for something or other – for the rottenness to fall away. There is not much rottenness but it stinks of shit. And I often go walking in the empty fields with a few little primroses here and there, a few patches of piercing green, against the snows of Monte Cavallo hanging with its white crests in the blue air. Alone I go through the fields and walk and walk in Friuli which is empty and infinite. Everything stinks of firing, everything makes one sick, if one thinks how that lot[2] are shitting on this earth. I feel like spitting on this earth, this idiot, which keeps on bringing out greenery and yellow and blue flowers and buds on the alders; I feel like spitting on Monte Rest, so far off, at the other end of Friuli on the Adriatic Sea, which is invisible behind the low hills; and also in the faces of these people of Casarsa, of these Italians, of these Christians. Everything stinks of shootings and feet. What ties me to this earth? Don't be afraid, Luciano, that I am enough of a stinker myself to be capable of not feeling myself to be tied to all this shit. Tomorrow (in sixty years' time, I insist) we shall have a hole – it wouldn't be anything new if I had not with THESE eyes

213

seen them lower into it a woman of whom I knew that she had been alive;[3] and then in that body which sank down I measured all this shitty humanity. Someone (death) comes and stops up your nose and you don't smell anything any more. In my country spring is being born.

    A kiss,        Pier Paolo

1    Sergio Telmon, the Head of the Partito d'Azione.
2    German troops.
3    Refers to the death of his maternal grandmother, Giulia Zacco, who inspired the poems of *I pianti* ['The laments'], published in Casarsa in 1949.

## 72  To Luciano Serra
Bologna
[*In possession of addressee: autograph*]

                              [Postmark: Casarsa, 25 March 1944]
Dearest Luciano,

I wrote to you a little time ago and have nothing new to tell you. Only to let you know that Calcaterra has accepted this subject of mine: 'Prolegomena to an anthology of Pascoli's lyric poetry'.

I'd like to get to work right away; please send me right away an essential bibliography of Pascoli; the best editions of all his works and the principal general works on P.

On the other hand I shall do a lot of work 'investigating the subject within myself' as the great man advises me. And I shall use the critical work of others to bring myself up to date. I think that my choice of his poems will be rather new.

What are you doing? I heard that Bologna had been bombed again. Here the planes pass continually and lots of bombs have fallen round about, on airfields, etc. One goes from one fit of fear to another.

Apart from that I continue to teach in my little school and to walk and *look at the peaks of Monte Rest white with snow and slender in the sky.*[1]

    A hug,      Pier Paolo

1    The passage italicized here is in Friulian in the original.

## 73  To Federico De Rocco
San Vito al Tagliamento

[*In possession of addressee's heirs: autograph*]

[Casarsa, May 1944]

Dear Rico,

Last night they came to arrest me but I was at Versuta hiding there for fear of round-ups. Today I, Pino, Gastone, etc.[1] were interrogated, etc. on the charge that we had put leaflets in the streets. But, thank God, our innocence emerged and now we are free. I shall tell you the story with its tragicomic details.

Please do me a favour – speak to the teachers in San Vito about these two boys, Ovidio Colussi and Giovanni Cappelletto, two good boys, serious and diligent. I'm not asking you for a run-of-the-mill recommendation. You just need to refer to the seriousness of the youngsters and the ambitious nature of our training at least.

A hug,        Pier Paolo

1   Friends from Casarsa.
2   Pupils at his private school.

## 74  To Luciano Serra
Bologna
[*In possession of addressee: autograph*]

[Postmark: Casarsa, 29 May 1944]

Dearest Luciano,

Since we shall meet again in a few days I won't tell you anything important in this letter. I only don't want Telmon to come here with you. In fact the day after you left, Pina, Luciana, Gastone[1] and I were arrested with a great theatrical production, accused of having scattered those leaflets of which you saw one that was found in my aunt's shop.[2] Do you understand what a horrendously humiliating thing they accuse me of! To think that we laughed so much and deplored the rhetoric of that manifesto!

Never mind – the evidence of guilt consisted only in the fact that we were the only ones to have permits and so to go about after ten o'clock. Our innocence emerged so fully that now our customers are apologizing and accusing each other.

But I learned so much – among other things that I am considered by the authorities some sort of dangerous element who is plotting goodness knows what against them. Poor fools! In any case they cannot understand that the most important thing for a person can be himself or his poetry. I cannot return their ill-will – but they annoy me.

That is why I don't want you to come with Telmon (because you must know that they had grave suspicions about you as well) – besides the danger from bombing is growing and so are the German round-ups.

A big hug,     Pier Paolo

1   Pina Kalč, Luciana and Gastone: friends from Casarsa.
2   Enrichetta Naldini.

## 75   To Federico De Rocco
San Vito al Tagliamento
[*In possession of addressee's heirs: autograph*]

[Versuta, October 1944]

Dearest Rico,

How are you? Where are you? I'm in Versuta definitely evacuated. As for my health it's not bad – indeed good. As for my morale, that too, when everything is calm, which is to say rarely. Otherwise a lot of fear. Fear of being done in, do you understand, Rico? And not only for myself, for the others too. We are all so exposed to fate, poor naked men.

Here is *Lo Stroligut* for you – that is a moment of calm and aesthetic pleasure – is it not the only pleasure that remains? And then *Stroligut,* sweet, little and beautiful, will not have been something useless.

The costs are still high – could you buy a few copies for me and do a bit of publicity? Certainly you with your gloomy pessimism will laugh at all these childish matters. But, in short, Germans or no Germans, death or no death, let's hope to meet this spring in the trees of your orchard eating cherries with the world at peace.

A hug,     Pier Paolo

**There is a long unexplained gap in the letters at this point.** (Tr.)

# 1945

## 76  To Luciano Serra
Bologna
[*In possession of addressee: autograph*]

Versuta, 21 August [1945]

Dearest Luciano,

I got your most dear, most consoling letter of 14 July. Try to write to me
often even if the post is so slow. How much you tell me about yourself – and I
have nothing to tell and that one thing you know.[1] The misfortune which has
struck my mother and me is like an immense, terrifying mountain which we
have had to cross and the more hours we move away from it the higher and
more terrible it seems to us against the horizon. I cannot write about it
without weeping and all my thoughts arise confusedly within me like the
tears. At first I could only feel horror, a repugnance at living, and the only
unexpected comfort was to believe in the existence of a destiny from which
one cannot flee and which is therefore humanly just. You remember Guido's
enthusiasm and the sentence which has pounded away within me was this:
he was unable to survive his enthusiasm. That boy was of an unbelievable
generosity, courage and innocence. How much better he was than all of us –
now I see his living image with his hair, his face, his jacket, and I feel myself
seized by such an unspeakable, so inhuman an anguish. I think I won't be
able to tell you anything about the article[2] you are thinking of writing – my
mother is here busy in the kitchen and I have to make painful efforts not to let
her see me weep. Now the only thought that consoles me is the idea that we
have to be wise, that we must overcome and resign ourselves; this
resignation is egoism; it is cruel, inhuman. That is not what we must give to
that poor boy who is there lying in that terrible silence. We ought to be
capable of weeping for him always, without end, because only that could be
some small thing equal to the immensity of the injustice which struck him.
And yet our human nature is such that it allows us to go on living, even to be
cheerful for some moments. Therefore the only thought that comforts me is
that I am not immortal; that Guido has merely preceded me by a few years
into that void toward which I am bound. And which now is so familiar to me –
the terrible obscure distance or inhumanity of death has become clear to me

since Guido entered it. That infinity, that nothingness, that absolute opposite, now have a domestic look. There is Guido, my brother, you see, who was always near me for twenty years, sleeping in the same room, eating at the same table. So it is not so unnatural to enter that dimension which is so inconceivable to us. And Guido was good enough, generous enough to show it to me, sacrificing himself for his elder brother whom he perhaps loved too much and believed in too much.

So I can say to you, Luciano, that he chose death, wished it – and that from the first day of our slavery. On 10 September he and a friend of his had already risked their lives many times to steal arms from the Germans on the airfield at Casarsa and so through the whole autumn of 1944.[3] His friend, Renato, during one of these extremely risky undertakings, lost a hand and an eye; but they did not stop for that; instead for the whole spring[4] at night during curfew they scattered propaganda leaflets and wrote on the walls (on the wall of a ruined house in Casarsa one can still read his writing: The hour is near). And, Luciano, you will remember our arrest during which I was accused of being guilty of that propaganda; instead it was Guido. From that time on the surveillance of us was continuous and exasperating. We often went to sleep at Versuta; meanwhile Guido had long taken the decision to go up into the mountains. And at the end of May 1944 he left without it being possible to persuade him to stay hidden in Versuta as I then did for a year. I helped him to leave early one morning. We had taken a ticket to Bologna telling everyone that that was his destination. These were days of great terror and the most rigorous surveillance. And his flight was somewhat dramatic. We said goodbye and kissed each other in a field behind the station; and it was the last time I saw him. He left for Spilimbergo and finally arrived in Pielungo, joining the Osoppo division.[5] That is when his legendary actions began which I do not know much about. At that time the patriots were still few in number on the mountains of Carnia – Guido's unit was of six or seven men who had to pretend to be a company by dint of furious, incredible marches in the mountains. In September Mamma went to see him – now he was at Savorgnano del Torre above Tricesimo. He was all right there – the partisans were well organized and their morale very high. Then came the offensive of October and November by the black brigades[6] and the Germans – a memorable offensive which the people of Friuli will never be able to forget. In that horrible confusion Guido must have lived through tremendous moments – and letters addressed to me bear witness to them. Finally the partisans reorganize; Guido finds himself at Musi with his friend Roberto d'Orlandi, 'Gino' and 'Aeneas'. His most heroic action is from this period (we are in January 1945); his commander 'Gino' has urged me that if I were to write about Guido not to be sparing of the most extraordinary adjectives. He saw him at work and I am repeating to you what he said of him without being able to convey to you his admiration and emotion. In short Guido and Roberto alone had held out against a hundred or so Cossacks[7] who had come to make a sweep of Musi; retreating up the mountain they fired with the calm and coolness of veterans, they who were nineteen-year-old boys; and although they were almost hand-to-hand they did not lose their heads and held out until the Cossacks withdrew. A month later, that is on 7 February,[8] Guido was dead; and he could instead be here happy, glorious, with his flag, close to his mother. but events presented themselves is such a way that he had the choice between his life and liberty. For some months a group of traitors had been busy betraying the cause of that liberty; the Osoppans of that zone, headed by De Gregoris (Bolla) with his staff, to which Guido belonged, did not wish to give way to the requests of the Slavo-Communists to enter the ranks of our enemy, Tito. That was the end of November '44; now things had become tense when, without any plausible reason except hatred and a repugnant selfishness of theirs, a group of unemployed and troublemakers who were fighting in the ranks of the Garibaldini[9] of that zone, pretending to have escaped from a round-up, had themselves accepted as guests by Bolla and his men; then suddenly, throwing down their masks, they shoot Bolla and take out his eyes; they massacre Aeneas; they take prisoner all these other poor boys, about 16 or 17, and one by one will murder them all; this took place in some Alpine meadows near Musi.[10] That day my brother was at Musi with Roberto and others and was going to Bolla to bring him some orders; then suddenly they hear the first shots and see a fugitive who tells them to escape, to go back, that there is nothing they can do. But my brother and Roberto, no – they want to go and see, to bring help, poor boys. But faced by a hundred or more traitors they had to surrender. After a few days, these truly heroic youths, having been asked to serve in the ranks of the Garibaldino-Slavs refused, saying they wanted to fight for Italy and liberty, not for Tito and Communism. So they were all murdered barbarously. The burial of their exhumed remains took place in Udine with great solemnity some months later after the Liberation; now Guido is in the cemetery at Casarsa.

Guido had joined the Action Party. And from that letter I mentioned to you here is a piece, Luciano, for you that concerns you: 'I am sending a copy of the programme of the Action Party which I have joined with enthusiasm. All those I have got to know in the A.P. are very honest, gentle and loyal – true Italians. Aeneas greatly resembles Serra!' He loved you very much, Luciano, and I write this to you weeping. He called himself 'Hermes' as a *nom de guerre* to remember Parini, about whom you still tell me nothing. Now all the love this boy had for me and my friends, all that admiration of his for us and for our sentiments (for which he died) continually torment me; I wish I could return them in some way. His martyrdom must not remain unknown, Luciano. Try to write something yourself meantime; it would give the greatest pleasure to our poor mother as well who wants at all costs to know the reason why her son died. I cannot continue in this vein because I feel distressed.

Aeneas (Gastone Valenti), the one that resembled you, was from Udine; he died shouting 'Long live Italy and long live liberty!' and then, struck down, had still the strength to murmur: 'Tell my parents that I am dying for the Action Party.' Impelled by this circumstance I too have joined the Action Party.

Write to me soon, Luciano, and meantime show this letter to all our friends for I do not feel able to write to each of them. Tell them that it is for them as for you and to forgive me. If you can, send a summary of it to Farolfi and Mauri.

I kiss you and with you all of them,     Pier Paolo

1   A reference to the death of his brother, Guido, on 1 February 1945.
2   See Ricordo di Guido' ['A memory of Guido'] by Luciano Serra in *Giustizia e Libertà*, the Action Party's weekly in Bologna of 18 September 1945.
3   Should be: 'autumn of 1943'.
4   The spring of 1944.
5   Formed by the Partito d'Azione.
6   The black brigades were notorious Fascist formations.
7   The Cossacks had been recruited by the Germans and were responsible for numerous atrocities in northern Italy.
8   Later information established the date of Guido's death as 12 February.
9   Communist formations.
10   A spot called Malghe di Porzùs (Udine).

## 77   To Franco Farolfi
Parma
[*In possession of addressee: autograph*]

Versuta, 22 [August 1945]
Dear Franco,

In your letters you are not entirely sincere. You ask me what my shadow is but it is easy to reply to you – it is the absence of my brother which makes me measure our stupid and never resolved life no longer intellectually but concretely. I always look at myself from your point of view and see myself rushing in a train from Casarsa to Bologna, up and down, like a madman inside a body. But I tell you nothing else of myself because everything is out of proportion to the enormous silence which has separated us and I do not see the use of restarting an interrupted discourse when death takes over my thoughts so exclusively. You ask if I am happy. And I answer by asking you if you are out of your mind. I am unhappy but not bored. Life has a precise meaning and it is that my being is infinite – I go no further than this thought neither with respect to men nor with respect to God. I see everything as so infinite, that I cannot take anything up seriously unless I look at it from the point of view of the infinite.

But what I do not know is what *your* shadow is. Since you felt like confiding in a certain Pier Paolo – one who has remained absolutely the same as the person you knew and loved in Bologna – you could have done it completely without so much scribbling and so many marble words. Oh, don't think I bother about you out of goodness – I am doing it only because I am alive. I am sorry instead not to be able to talk to you in a sensible way – but it is the fault of your epistolary style which makes me greatly regret your effusions and uncertainties of another time. But I still hope to hear you muttering through your hair with your comb in your hand or to see you eating birds and spitting out the little bones one by one. The affection that binds us has shown itself to be absolutely out of proportion to the infinite nature of our egoism and in this sense I advise you to read the Maxims of Rochefoucauld.[1] Yet 'il faut tenter de vivre' one doesn't know for what reason (or rather I wouldn't know if I didn't have to write verse), and so we shall have to cultivate our affection which has truly much that cannot be replaced, that is to say necessary. But in accordance with the 'status quo'?

You have changed in your way of writing and consequently in what makes you live. It is an aesthetic premiss in which I believe (moreover an absolute, intransigeant, delirious aestheticism is the last fixed point for the mystic who is losing himself in nirvana: words, dear Franco, are like a leaf or a face, are colour and sound, a material datum, are the thing that links us to the unknowable forms, the metaphor – $\mu\epsilon\tau\alpha\varphi\acute{\epsilon}\rho\omega$ – which takes us into the beyond, that is to say outside of ourselves – into the sweet world).

Your disquiet is of a moral order; I think what we are talking about is a matter of a sole desire (and I believe this because I feel it myself), the desire to be sincere. I should like to be so. Indeed I would be so without more ado if I had more esteem for men; I am afraid that to reveal myself to them because of a superior moral impulse might make my stay among them uncomfortable. To confide a secret puts the one to whom it is confided in more danger. If it were not so I would not fear to speak clearly of the rottenness I have inherited from my ancestors.

But it was you who brought me back to these thoughts which I had left for a while in the sphere – it can be disregarded – of the life of others.

The origins of my poetry – which is the only sense in my absurd and most ordinary days – are very deep, but for some time it has been cut off from them. Recognizing them has taken them away from me. I have entered a savage world with no more formulae; I am within myself in an atrocious, inhuman solitude and I go further and further into this desert from which, when I turn round, I once again see the world restored to its original and terrible objectivity.

There I am talking to myself, miserable creature that I am, and you who are the friend from whose eyes I perhaps have removed the most bandages, the friend who looks at me the most shamelessly, pardon these effusions, which I no longer need but which come from my pen for the one and only reason I am writing to you, that is to say for a reason of brotherhood [?]. When it has been renewed and we take each other's arm and I tease you about your eternal girls, let us hope the matter will present itself in simpler terms, and so from now on begin to pretend never to have read this letter which I have written to you to observe the conventions.

A kiss,      Pier Paolo

Fond greetings to your family and thank your mother very much for me.

1   La Rochefoucauld (1613–80), moralist and epigrammist.

## 78   To Luciano Serra
Bologna
[In possession of addressee: autograph]

[Versuta, September 1945]
Dearest Luciano,

Thank you for your kindness. If you find the French university texts buy them because I shall come two days early and so I shall be able to look at them. I think I shall be in Bologna on the evening of 29 September. You must tell me first of all, without being polite, if I am a great nuisance to your parents; so that I can make arrangements.

The question of Dante is extremely important, Luciano. It is a question of surrendering, so as to be able to understand each other, our particular rhetorics or illusions which are our hopes for the present. I have been too brusque with Dante and you, perhaps, insincere. In fact there is no way in which you will be able to prove to me for the present that he has been a stage on our way, a help, an influence of some kind on our poetry.

For the future, no one can say anything: certainly Dante's inimitable qualities, the solitude of his poetic conscience, the inaccessibility of his terzinas are matters that have been demonstrated. What gratitude can I have towards him? And why regard him with false veneration in my writings which are absolutely private? The freedom in which I live is enormous – Gide's *Immoraliste*[1] is in chains compared to me. When I push on into the unexplorable desert which is truly infinite, which is truly a void, and it opens up immeasurably within me, and it casts me down, I am no longer anything for you men. And what should I expect from you? A distraction? In fact we can do nothing but distract each other as we wait for death; but for me the disquiet of my own life is enough. 'It is only and always the single one who succeeds in reaching the light,' I read in K. Fielder – and similar things in Schopenhauer, in Maritain[2] ... These are dead people who help me truly and in their being finite, inexorably unique, I find a little of my infinity.

    A kiss,       Pier Paolo

1  *L'immoraliste* by André Gide (1902). The hero gives in to any impulse, regardless of morality.
2  Jacques Maritain (b. 1882), French neo-Thomist philosopher and man of letters.

## 79  To Luciano Serra
Bologna
[*In possession of addressee: autograph*]

                                  [Versuta, November 1945]
Dearest Luciano,

    Two words to tell you the terrible urgency I am seized by; the dates of the exams and the degree are ghastly. I don't know whether I shall finish the thesis in time. You must please find me the typist or two typists who could type the thesis between the 10th and the 15th. It isn't long. *I shall be at your place on the 9th, in the evening,* and shall have to stay at least 11 days; I shall try to bring with me as much stuff as possible and to put you out as little as possible. You are my providence, dear Luciano, and I very much hope to be able to do the same for you. For now I am most grateful to you and your family.

    A big hug,      Pier Paolo

## 80  To Franco De Gironcoli[1]
Conegliano

                                 [Versuta, 3 November 1945]
I read with very great pleasure your two small volumes. I should like to write to you at length – but to begin a discourse, a colloquy is so difficult because everything is out of proportion to the enormous silence that precedes it. The silence must be broken little by little, and I am always very much afraid (in such delicate matters) that an incapacity to communicate, and an excessive presence of the body may disturb the relations which arise from poetical reasons. [...] Will agreeable poetics succeed in taking the place of a natural

friendship? And I speak of friendship because I have echoing in my ears that word which I and my friends always say to each other and which you too said at San Daniele[2] – *félibrige*.[3] Reading your small volumes I once more ran over ardently all the ideas which have occupied my heart for three years – I do not know whether they are exactly the same as yours but this is certain that if I set your 'E l'e restade un'olme' alongside my 'Vuei a e Domenia' ['Today is Sunday'] or 'Piardisi tal mar dai siuns' ['To lose oneself in the sea of dreams'] alongside 'Ti jos, Dili' ['You see, Dilio'] I see that it is the same linguistic search in order to penetrate into a same colourless and infinite time. I think that they are considerations of an inferior order our references to *félibrige*, to *trobar clus*,[4] to the Laudi ['Songs of Praise'] of Iacopo;[5] I think it is a matter of lesser importance to consider Friulano as a kind of Greek or Christian dialect close to the moment when Adam pronounced the first word; and it seems to me now also a consideration of lesser importance to understand poetry in Friulano as a limbo granted to those who wish to flee from a moral impulse of too great and absolute sincerity. For me now writing in Friulano is the means I have found to fix what the symbolists and musicians of the nineteenth century so much sought (and our Pascoli too however badly), that is to say, an 'infinite melody' or the poetic moment in which one hears the infinite in the subject. In practice we ought to come together, a poetic movement of a certain interest could arise but the first to enjoy it would be ourselves . . .

1   A partial text published in *Corriere del Friuli*, November 1976. Franco De Gironcolo, a Friulian poet from Gorizia.
2   A reference to the Congress of the Friulian Philological Society held at San Daniele on 21 October 1945.
3   Félibrige: a term invented by the nineteenth-century French poet Mistral (1830–1914), who wrote in Provençal, to describe the group of poets writing in the old Romance languages.
4   *Trovar clus* (Provençal): a style of writing used by the troubadours.
5   Iacopone da Todi (1230–1306), poet, author of some hundred religious poems.

## 81   To Susanna Pasolini
Versuta
[*In the Pasolini Archive: autograph*]

[Postmark: Bologna, 11 November 1945]
Dearest Fatty,

Has Father arrived? As we said I hope to see him in Bologna. Today I was at Aunt Dora's – so if Father goes to her place he knows where to find me. The journey was interminable (from Venice to Bologna) because the bridge over the Po was damaged and so we had to have a boring change of trains.

I wonder if Father is there with you. How I should like to have waited for him together.

I can't write more, first of all because I feel I'm in Versuta, secondly because the written exam in Latin lasted from 8 in the morning to 4 in the afternoon without a moment's break. I hope it went reasonably well. But it was something idiotic. I hope to be back between the 22nd and the 25th – but if Paroli were to invite me to Parma I might stay right on till I get my degree.

But everything depends on Father's arrival. If he is there give him a big kiss from me.

Kisses,      Pier Paolo


## 82   To Susanna Pasolini
Versuta
[*In the Pasolini Archive: autograph*]

[Postmark: Bologna, 17 November 1945]
Dearest Fatty

Today I met Father here in Bologna in via Castiglione. He had been in Rome at Uncle's to whom I had sent an express letter to tell him that I was here. Think what an enormous joy! All the greater because Father seems full of health and vigour, young. Shortly we shall all be together. We shall arrive, as I wrote to you between the 22nd and the 25th. Let us hope that a slightly more human period will begin for us. Many many kisses, Fatty, be brave.

Pier Paolo

Adored Susanna
Pier Paolo wants me to be with him and he is to blame that I shall delay my arrival there. We hope to be there on the 23rd.
I so much want to see you again. Many many kisses.
Carlo Alberto


## 83   To Gianfranco D'Aronco
Udine
[*In possession of addressee: autograph*]

Versuta, 29 November [1945]
Dear D'Aronco

Perhaps you will have been surprised at the silence on my part which followed your article on *Lo Stroligut*[1] but it was due to chance – that is, to a stay in Bologna from which I returned yesterday. I take the opportunity to thank you for your elegant article which you dedicated to my little poetry anthology. I shall be in Udine on Saturday so we shall perhaps have an opportunity to discuss it together. Now I should like to ask you for a favour hoping that you will be able to excuse my extreme tactlessness – I should like, that is, to ask you to re-read the two translations from Jimenez and the poem 'Spring' by Naldini.[2] Perhaps because of their character which is so timid and candid they escaped you at a first reading. Once more I ask you to excuse this intervention of mine. My *Poesie a Casarsa* have been published by the 'Libreria Antiquaria', Bologna.

For the theatre I have written a one-act comedy *La morteana* (the title is taken from a verse by Colloredo)[3] and a play *I Turcs tal Friuli* ['The Turks in Friuli'].

The first will very shortly be put on by my little Company of the Academy here at Casarsa; the second, which is perhaps the best thing I have written in Friulano is lying in a drawer and will lie there I don't know how long.

Cordial greetings,      Pier Paolo Pasolini

1   Refers to an article in *Libertà* of 4 November 1945 discussing the first number of *Il Stroligut.*
2   Pasolini's cousin, Nico Naldini, editor of these letters.
3   Ermès di Colloredo (1622–92), considered to be the father of Friulian writing.

## 84   To Silvana Mauri
Milan
[*In possession of addressee: autograph*]

Versuta, 6 December [1945]

Dear Silvana,

After so many months I am making the incredible gesture of writing to you. But I assure you that not a day has passed when I have not had this intention. In fact I remember that this September I was on the point of writing to you an extremely poetical letter about harvesting the apples which was really something extraordinary. Not to have written that letter is a continual remorse.

Now there isn't another harvest of apples, or of figs, or of grapes, nor do I have any pupils any more, nor do I find myself in that absolute solitude which constituted a precise and communicable fact. I ought to tell you about myself, that is, about something infinite. I shall limit myself to telling you something the interpretation of which is really easy – that is, that my father's return has put me in a confused state of mind but one less unbearable than in past months.

Instead I should like to be closer to Fabio.[1] I am not able to write to him – there are an infinite number of ways of addressing him and our friendship has been so broken off that I am unable to choose the right one. Assure him, however, of something he knows very well: that I consider our friendship to be one of the most precious things I have found during my life. And that I keep him inside me touching his image with enormous tenderness almost out of fear of breaking it. He is so fragile, that Fabio who walked along via Castiglione! He was as light as a fan. Now the passing of the years which has made him a man (I like to think of his religious crisis as no other than this) has placed him for me on a kind of distancing pedestal from which I must nevertheless make up my mind to take him down some time or other. Inviting him here, to my place, as we used to say; now my father's arrival will prevent me from doing so for some time but I hope to be able to write to Fabio in a few weeks asking him to visit me in uncomfortable Versuta, if he wants to. It will be very useful for both of us.

I behaved in a rude way to your uncle.[2] I should have written to him thanking him for his kindness, sent him some manuscripts. Instead nothing – but the thesis for my degree is to blame – a work in great depth on Pascoli (a selection of his poetry which I think has never been published). Now that I have got my degree on the 26th, with honours, I have once more found my confused freedom. I shall send your uncle my *Poesie a Casarsa* corrected and abundantly added to, because they tell me on all sides that they should be published. Your uncle will perhaps be afraid of a bad commercial outcome but I think they would sell in Friuli. I shall explain myself better about all this to your uncle when I write to him in a few days and send him the typescript.

Warm greetings,      Pier Paolo

Remember me to your family and to Michele.[3]

1   Fabio Mauri, Silvana's brother.
2   The publisher, Valentino Bompiani.
3   Michele Ranchetti, a childhood friend of Silvana and Fabio Mauri.

## 85   To Franco De Gironcoli[1]
Conegliano
[*Incomplete*]

[Versuta, 7 December 1945]
[. . .]

As for my Friulian poetry I am going through a slight crisis of lack of confidence; I think that here in Friuli very few, even those who are animated by the greatest good will, possess cultural assets to allow them to interpret exactly what I am doing. They live outside the Italian and European poetic climate in a kind of philological sentimentality which leaves them cold when faced with the disinterested act of poetry. In my poetic production they see only an elegant document of the actual state of the spoken language of Casarsa or the possibility of a renewal of Friulian literature in a vaguely 'modern' sense. They do not grasp the principal fact, which is that my Friulian language (and yours) is a language without a history, with no roots in custom, a kind of Lethe, beyond which we find a momentary (but in itself absolute) peace. I very much hope that you are working, that you are soon to give us a new little collection – yours is a voice that reassures me, the only one in all Friuli . . .

1 Published in *Corriere del Friuli,* November 1976.

## 86 To Mario Argante
Udine
[*In possession of Gianfranco Ellero, Udine: autograph; published in 'Pasolini in Friuli',* Corriere del Friuli, *Udine, 1976*]

Versuta, 12 December [1945]
Dear Sig. Argante,

I hope you have chanced to have in your hands a *Stroligut* or that you will have heard something about it.

I have seen your poems in *Ce Fastu?* and *Lo Strolic*[2] and will not say that they convinced me completely yet they seem to me, certainly superior to all the rosy and useless stuff in the style of Zorutti[3] which infests Friuli. Above all there are some touches, some initiatives which have an enduring quality of pure lyricism:

> When the child was born
> fate went to and fro
> between the last snowflake
> and the first violet

in which I find such a sweet felicity of rhyme and the graceful movement which transposes into a poetic area the common way of saying 'between the first and the last'. I hope you may be able to grasp precisely the duration of the poetic emotion so that it does not become thinned down into too many little 'occasional' verses.

Forgive me if I interfere in this way but I who have had an entirely poetic experience of Friulano (and in no way a vernacular one) by means of continual and suggestive appeals to the poetry of our origins, to the least sentimental kinds of Romanticism, to symbolism, would like all those who write in Friulano to feel in this way now.

Therefore I should like to ask you the favour of knowing your poems better. Could you send me some? Those you have written in greatest intimacy with yourself. If I were to find in them something corresponding to my own poetics or, in short, to the taste of *Stroligut* I would print them in the next number.

Forgive me once more. Warm greetings,

Yours,      Pier Paolo Pasolini

1   Friulian poet.
2   Friulian publications.
3   Friulian poet.

## 87   To Sergio Maldini
Udine
[*In possession of addressee: autograph*]

Versuta, 20 December [1945]

Dear Maldini,

I finished your book[1] this morning. To speak to you about it I would need to let at least a year pass to see how your pages last in the memory. But a certain practice as a reader causes me to have optimistic previsions – I know that the aristocratic delicacy and a certain youthful candour will remain with me. I shall tell you my immediate and concrete impressions. There is a 'quiet' in your pages which is in contrast to a sensuality which is in no way unhealthy but very marked, the insistent nature of which spoils almost half the book. It makes you show your cards a little – all your girls seen with the montonous eye of a twenty-year-old have an aprioristic animality, a grace that is too sure of itself. Who to blame? The excessive naturalness of your desire? The best female figures, therefore, are two elderly women, Silvia and Sonia. Their interrupted mystery and the joke played on them by the years renders them human; and so you let us see them more concretely, with a richer and more secret substance and, finally, with more mystery. I shall not talk about your male characters; they are inexorably pervaded not so much by your character as by your sensuality. As characters (but I don't know if you clearly had this ambition) they have not worked for you. Just as the most specifically poetic pages do not work; their poetry you have identified as something strangely allegorical (The talk in the mountain; The journey; The two streets; A stay by the seaside; Sunday – which seem the least good things to me). As you see I am discarding for you the pages which tried more than the others to be 'artistic prose', which in your case has a particularly gratuitous effect – here more than anywhere else your candid youth shows through. And *à propos* style or rather form, apart from a trifling amount of disparate influences (you can tell their names yourself), I note as the most obvious that of the crepuscular style of writing,[1] that abandonment to Proustian memory which, curiously, is linked to a Leopardi–Cardarellian[2] clarity of expression, the manner of the young Florentine writers (Revolution)[3] and Bilenchi.[4] And also, note, a certain American influence which was in the air two or three years ago (short sentences with 'he says'). These are the influences I would advise you to get rid of at once along with the poetical–allegorical pages and certain inversions which I cannot understand ('no one I saw' 'behind they found themselves'). In your best things (The bigger boys; A useless meeting; Circles of water on the river (with some reservations); the first 2 or 3 pages of Ace high; An ambitious woman; some pages of Stay by the seaside), I come to notice once more that quiet which allows you to conduct narrative and form at the same pace. Indeed there results a work so chiselled, so light, that it attains the impartial naturalness of true narrative. When you have freed yourself from the little matters I have been talking about (and also of certain landscapes which are too soft, too pervaded by the physical feelings of the characters – those hills, those rivers, those skies without bad weather) I shall see in you, without further reservation, one of the best prose writers of today who, even if he does not have extreme psychological penetration, will be able to catch exactly the average sensations of an exceptional person (yourself) and his links with our common world. For the rest, as you will have understood, I conclude by saying to you that you are on the right road and that I read you with a rare abandon because of a rare sympathy which emerges from your pages – even the most exposed ones.

An embrace,　　　　Pier Paolo Pasolini

1　*Racconti* ['Stories'], Sergio Maldini, Mario Cozzi (Trieste, 1944).
2　Giacomo Leopardi (1798–1837), the famous nineteenth-century poet; Cardarelli (b. 1887), lyrical poet who took Leopardi as a model.
3　Florentine publishing house.
4　Romano Bilenchi (1909–89), novelist and journalist.

## 88　To Sergio Maldini
Udine
[*In possession of addressee: autograph*]

Versuta, 27 December 1945

Dear Sergio,

I read your letter in instalments with great interest. I congratulate you on your critical spirit – everything you could grasp in my poems you have grasped. They are only a tiny part of my daily work in which there is not lacking even for an hour the sense of the infinite that is in me and of the lack of proportion between my experience and everything else in the world. To feel myself alive and as such different from everything I could have been – that slight displacement which I have accentuated to the Rimbaudian 'dérèglement de tous les sens' (long, immense, illogical) sets me in an initial commanding position which I do not wish to betray by any concession to the senses which in me are, however, monstrously developed. At this point I could insert a speech about my Friulian poetry which represents an abandonment of the senses to the most ingenuous and perhaps deepest breath of the flesh confronted by the ineffable nature of certain mysterious relationships (of names, times, images, feelings and other things that do not exist in the vocabulary). But Italian poetry, my diaries[1] which represent the furthest extent of my poetical effort, are born of a maturity which you perhaps do not imagine. Together with my experience of absolute macabre solitude, which led me to find my way to certain unexpected mystical overtures (the Augustinian going into oneself, into the unextended space of one's own *life*, deep into such profound deserts out of which the world, when re-examined, reappears in its original and terrible objectivity), an aesthetic experience has kept pace with this, which represented a continuous, last possible salvation from 'nothingness'. Like all the poets from Novalis[2] to Baudelaire in whom consciousness of poetry as poetry is affirmed, from mysticism I continually emerged into aestheticism, so that the activity of poetical *writing* slowly assumed for me an absolute, almost disproportionate function. Such being the case how could I possibly have had moments of abandon? I can now only aim at perfection – I know I cannot write except in what you rightly call 'the second half', and which is precisely the *serenity* of all great Italian poetry. Of this serenity – which is, by the way, one and the same as the capacity for style, for form, I am perhaps excessively conscious (I was writing verses when I was seven) and consider null and void any attempt which contents itself with an expression of a lesser nature however accepted (Montale and lower down Pascoli). Therefore a just sentence on those verses of mine which you have read should be positioned historically and be inserted in a kind of study which might be entitled something like 'The evolution of the smooth style in Italian from Leopardi to Pascoli to Ungaretti . . .' This you may consider to be one of those odd ideas authors usually have when they consider their own work. But it seems to me to be something essentially accurate. It isn't for nothing, you see, that I am perhaps the only person in Italy – and I hope it will be agreed – among those who are writing poetry who does not imitate Montale or Saba,[3] nor the other minor figures Betocchi, Penna,[4] etc., etc.), nor the French symbolists nor, finally, the best Romantics, in whose case one can mention the names of Leopardi, of Foscolo, perhaps, and also of a certain ambitious Pascoli in some of his excellent hendecasyllables.

I see I have done what I didn't want to do – that is, I have held forth somehow about my poetry and I have done it *currenti calamo*,[5] schematizing in an intolerable way. I hope it may be the first and last time; that depresses me.

As far as your book is concerned, perhaps from a kind of shyness in my other letter[6] I did not make it clear enough to you that I certainly consider it to be positive, that I consider it to be an excellent sketch for a future novel, and at the same time a complete and satisfying piece of writing. I repeat that it is a long time since I read contemporary narrative prose with so much interest. The phrase 'naturalness of your libido' must not hurt you – it is perhaps a misunderstanding – let me explain: for me naturalness meant normality, health, tranquillity.

Menichini's[7] poetry disappoints me – it seems me to lack bite. It is the first time that I don't have the courage to give my exact opinion to the author – I am sure I would give Menichini a bitter blow if I said to him that his poetry seems mechanical to me, that he has not yet come to the point of thinking over why one writes; he is too enthusiastic, expansive, ambitious and a cold shower would hurt him. What am I to do? Pay false compliments? I don't feel like it. That uprooting of common human feelings from their course to reduce them to a forced course of the intelligence has been applied in Europe for several decades; and he has all the air of being a follower of that trend. Yet he is able to make beautiful images, his thirst for poetry, which is so avid, sometimes helps him. What is your opinion?

You complain about your life – you give me hints of a certain winter 'spleen'[8] of yours. I have come to have almost no feeling about all this in so far as it seems to me to be unheard of. It feels as if I know too much about these sufferings, these discomforts, these congestions of the senses. Can it be that there is no other road than this? I am trying it. Perhaps this is why you see *too much* order, to much detachment in my poetical images . . . we live, dear Sergio, we *are* living, do you understand? And yet as Rilke says: 'How is it possible to live if the elements of this life are entirely out of our reach? If we are nevertheless always inefficient in love, uncertain in our decisions, and helpless in the face of death, how is it possible to live?'

Warm greetings,     Pier Paolo

1  See *Diarii*, Edizioni dell' 'Academiuta' (Casarsa, 1945).
2  Novalis (1776–1801), German Romantic poet and essayist.
3  Umberto Saba (1883–1957), Triestine lyric poet.
4  Sandro Penna (1906–77), one of the hermetic poets.
5  *currente calamo*: Latin for 'with a running pen'.
6  See previous letter.

7   Dino Menichini, poet from Udine.
8   In English in the original.

## 89   To Gianfranco D'Aronco
Udine
[*In possession of addressee: autograph*]

Versuta, 27 December [1945]

Dear D'Aronco,

I am very happy that you are in agreement about the timeliness of an exclusively poetical mission. I see it as one of the essential things the Philological[1] should apply itself to; everything else is fleeting and easily forgettable. Don't you think you find a lack of moral sense in all those vernacular versifiers who *always* set about writing according to an aprioristic scheme? Then unfortunately the model remains poor Zorutti[2] – that is to say the representative of the most contigent and cloying Romantic taste.

Certainly all these 'sentimental' and unredeemable rhetorical versifiers (the rhetoric of pure, simple, sober Friulano, etc., etc.) are totally unprepared for a turn in a modern direction, that is to say live, that is to say thought over, in their way of setting about to write. Yet by speaking, by arguing, by getting angry, some seed may be scattered and our young contemporaries confined within the calm provincial darkness may gather some of it.

As for the evenings at the artistic club[2] you must forgive me but I shall not mix my words. First of all it is of no importance to me to win consensuses or applause in that sad city of Udine – nor yet in the rest of Fruili. Just as my nature is uprooted from the common habits of living, so in these literary relationships I feel I can behave in an absolutely gratuitous manner.

Do not put down to presumption, therefore, my refusal to confuse our poetry with that of those versifiers, dead or alive, to whom I referred; nor my refusal to make of the evening at the Academiuta an appendix to the other four.

Since, I repeat, the bourgeois consensuses of Udine are of no importance to me, I would be willing to do something only if I were allowed to do it with absolute dignity and coherence with my difficult ambitions.

Forgive me if I have expressed myself a little bluntly but, you know, it is better that in our relationship, which began with warmth and I hope will become more intense, these matters should not be left out or misunderstood.

Warm greetings and good wishes,          Pier Paolo Pasolini

1   The Friulian Philological Society of Udine.
2   Pietro Zorutti (1792–1867), Friulian poet.
3   The Friulian Art Club of Udine.

# 1946

## 90   To Franco Farolfi
Parma
[*In possession of addressee: autograph*]

Versuta, 12 January [1946]

Dearest Franco,

I would never have imagined that our life would be so miserably destroyed. The pain does not get better, in fact it gets worse. The lack of my brother, if it does not cause me that insufferable astonishment of the first months, has now entered into me, it has spread through my mind, depressing all the impulses and moments of my existence. Everything around me has taken on a squalid and frightened colour. I see to the bottom of everything – so you must forgive me for that nasty letter[1] which made you so cold towards me. Try to understand that act of mine as one of those characteristic impulses which you know of and that now it has happened the other way round. I need to be with dear friends – to talk and laugh.

Try to write to me in a relaxed moment using our old language. I embrace you with the utmost affection,

Pier Paolo

1   See Letter 77.

## 91   To Silvana Mauri
Milano
[*In possession of addressee: autograph*]

Versuta, 14 January [1946]

Dear Silvana,

I at last decided to write to you three weeks or a month ago but I am afraid my letter may have got lost.[1] I had written to your uncle too asking him if he could publish my *Poesie a Casarsa*. But perhaps this letter has got lost too. Must I attribute a metaphorical sense to the word 'lost'?

Give me an answer, please, if for nothing else than to give me news about you, about Fabio. I should so much like Fabio to write to me; perhaps it would be easier for him than for me. Besides the two images of Fabio are slowly merging one with the other, forming a single one, dearest, as his 'conversation' gradually acquires less importance and novelity.

Many greetings also to Michele (tell him Del Piero has written to me) and all your family.

Warm greetings,        Pier Paolo

1   See Letter 84.

## 92   To Pina Kalč
Opicina (Trieste)

[*In possession of addressee: autograph*]

[Versuta, 17 January 1946]
Dear Pina,

It is the feast of Saint Anthony, I am the same as ever, at my desk in Versuta. You,[1] better than anyone else, can imagine me in this solitude.

It is a dark day dug into by an agonizing wind which comes down from the invisible mountains, hinting unfeelingly at those distances. Carmela is singing through the wall that divides us with a child's voice; the thud of the pump and that cold peal of the belfries of Versuta mingle without echo with that slight sound. A pity that the idea of writing to you came to me this morning – I noticed a little late that it is a festival and suddenly that disgusting poison which you know of filled me like a colourless liquid and all my feelings float there motionless.

You know the infinite number of things which we still have to give each other, that the conversation begun more than a year ago still continues by certain invisible roads, unloading or loading itself with arguments or memories according to a regular process in time. Only our death will interrupt it at some point or other (but if God exists it will not be a chance point!)

Certainly as our talk unwinds in time I feel that something is resolving itself naturally. That we renounced the idea of saying certain things to each other over and above the things – perhaps too many of them – we did say to each other is probably a good thing because thus our reciprocal images have not been consumed but retain an inexhaustible residue of enchantment.

Cowardice, shynesses, obstacles, now reveal themselves to be the

235

instruments of an unfeeling necessity which, like a torrent, has over-whelmed, divided, isolated us within a vortex. That is why I still feel strongly moved by the image of you playing Bach – you built an extremely solid edifice into my life.

Forgive me, Pina, I cannot (and do not wish to) abandon myself to the full flood of memories or evocations. In all our special friendship that side of my character with which I react to my excessive sensibility in fact predominated; and naturally the reaction, even if it too cannot be called excessive, proves to be at least incoherent, disordered.

Write to me. I send you greetings – from my mother too – who will write to you, affectionately,

Yours,      Pier Paolo

1  He addresses her with the formal third person 'Lei'.

## 93   To Luciano Serra
Bologna

[*In possession of addressee: autograph*]

Versuta, 17 January [1946]

Dearest Luc,

The usual hitches. I had sent Montale for *Il Mondo*[1] an Italian poem ('On earth, I am witness to it...') and one in Friulano; he replied that he preferred two in Italian. So I sent him the *Diaries* for him to choose two. Now I have heard nothing more. So I am waiting to put the little volume on sale and haven't yet sent you the twenty copies – wait a day or two more.

I had asked you for that page and the article[2] on Nievo.[3] Nothing from you. It looks to me as if you've gone a bit soft in the head.

I am sending you the photographs for the engravings. Apart from that, I am in a state of desperate insensibility. Greetings to Sonia and everyone. Very many regards to your family.

I embrace you,      Pier Paolo

1  An important literary and political weekly published in Florence.
2  For publication in *Stroligut.*
3  Ippolito Nievo had connections with Friuli.

## 94   To Gianfranco Contini
Domodossola

[*In possession of addressee: autograph*]

Versuta, 22 January [1946]

Distinguished Sig. Contini,

Do you remember me, my Friulano? I am showing a sign of life again to ask
you a favour – to publish your piece 'On the frontier of dialect poetry'¹ in
*Stroligut* of which I am sending you the first three numbers. Please bear in
mind that it is a modest thing, written in the first place for the inhabitants of
Casarsa alone and then only for Friuli.

I should like to write to you about other things – but I am rendered
apprehensive by your double image as unknown person and friend. Please
forgive me and I send you my warmest greetings.

Yours very truly,        Pier Paolo Pasolini

1   See Letter 58. The review of *Poesie a Casarsa* appeared in *Stroligut* No 2, April 1946.

## 95   To Luciano Serra
Bologna

[*In possession of addressee: autograph*]

Versuta, 22 January [1946]

Dearest Luciano,

Allow me to tell you with our usual sincerity that you are a swine. Why
don't you do the article on Nievo for me? The other little reviews, yes,
because they pay you. Well *Stroligut* too will pay you modestly. Just think that
my little review is the finest thing in literary terms in Friuli and has an assured
resonance. To write for us would be more rewarding for you than to publish
wretched little articles in the Jesuit papers. If you really can't do me the article
(swine) written with critical abandon (2 pages of foolscap with your
signature) at least send me *immediately* the famous page by Nievo
discovered by Momi.

I have heard that *Il Mondo* has been discontinued – so farewell to
publication.¹

I am very sorry. I shall send you perhaps this very day 20 copies of my
*Diaries.* Will you be able to place them all for me? The moment I have
finished *Lo Stroligut* I shall give Primon your poems,² as many as you say.

Greet everyone for me with great warmth,

I embrace you,        Pier Paolo

*1946*

1   Inaccurate information: cf. Letter 93.
2   See I.A. Serra, *A Sonia* ['To Sonia'], Edizioni dell' 'Academiuta' (Casarsa, 1946).

## 96   To Franco De Gironcoli[1]
Congeliano

[Versuta, 22 January 1946]
[. . .]

I continue to hope to bring to birth in Friuli a living current of poetry, modern, not vernacular; in this you are closest to me [. . .]

1   Part of text published in the *Corriere del Friuli*, November 1976.

## 97   To Luciano Serra
Bologna
[*In possession of addressee: autograph*]

[Versuta, end of January, 1946]
Dearest Luciano,

You have hardly received my chaotic letter of some days ago than you are getting another skimpy one.

At the same time I am sending my *Diaries*, 20 copies, which you must take to Capelli [*sic*] so that they are all sold. (15 lire each, 25% as is usual for the bookseller.) In three weeks yours will be ready and then those of Arcangeli. Try to see if someone could do a review of them. The article on Nievo[1] (and the page by him which you are to ask Arcangeli for) I need for this number of *Lo Stroligut*. The paper with the letterhead is not ready but since I am in a hurry put the books you need on my account.

To work, Luciano, do a splendid article for me in the shortest possible time (10 days).

I embrace you,      Pier Paolo

Lots of greetings as usual to your family and Carlo

1   See *Il minor Friuli di Ippolito Nievo* ['Lesser Friuli of Ippolito Nievo'] and *Da una lettera a Matilde Ferrari* ['From a letter to Matilde Ferrari'] by Ippolito Nievo in *Stroligut* No 2, April 1946.

## 98   To Gianfranco Contini
Domodossola
[*In possession of addressee: autograph*]

Versuta, 25th February [1946]

Distinguished Signor Contini,

I received your card with the greatest pleasure and would have an infinite number of things to reply to you. The fear of appearing naïve, my youth, restrain my pen with difficulty especially because of the way you declare yourself to me 'a friend although (and partly because) unknown'. That is a kind of sentiment which is particularly dear and familiar to me.

The danger my Friulian poetry runs in the numbers of *Stroligut* (naturalism, crepuscularism . . .) is very clear to me and therefore I have risked it solely so as to be understood by those good people of Friuli. The things I have written for myself are, at least so I hope, ones like 'Misteri' ['Mysteries']¹ and I have added them to *Poesie a Casarsa*. This little book, corrected and copied, is now with Bompiani who had asked me for manuscripts – and I am awaiting its fate.

To Falqui² I had sent 'Il nini muàrt'³ ['The dead child'] and three other new poems ('Lied', 'La Roja ['The rose'], 'A me fradi' ['To my brother']) and he had answered me hesitantly saying 'one would need a guide'. I know no more. In any case I am sending those poems so that you can see them along with this little book of Italian verses⁴ which I would never have had the courage to send you if Montale had not reassured me by publishing a *Diary* of mine in *Il Mondo*.⁵

I am also sending you the proofs of your article (the only copy of the *Corriere del Ticino* is too crumpled) so that you can look it over and think it over; but I hope you will not have difficulties in granting me permission to publish it.

The Friulano in the next *Stroligut*, which is already almost ready, will appear in that arbitrary spelling which I invented;⁶ but in number 3 it will return to normal. My real danger is the excessive solitude in which I live, a state of being abandoned to myself, a kind of imperfect mysticism; just when I delude myself to have attained a freedom or inner calm, I commit the most naive errors. The t, the q and the c cedilla of that spelling perhaps are included among that kind of error. So you see how valuable your advice, which I fear not to deserve, can be to me.

I thank you and greet you respectfully

Your most truly,      Pier Paolo Pasolini

1   See *Il Stroligut* No 1, August 1945; now in *La nuova gioventú*, p. 67.

2  Enrico Falqui (1901–74), literary critic, editor.
3  For 'Il nini muàrt' see Letters 21, 22 and 25. For 'Lied' see *La nuova gioventù*, p. 45.
4  Refers to *Diarii.*
5  See Letter 17.
6  See article on some rules of spelling in *Il Stroligut* No 1, August 1945.

## 99  To Luciano Serra
Bologna
[*In possession of addressee: autograph*]

Versuta, 9 March [1946]

Dearest Luc,

I am extremely worried at your long silence. I don't know how to explain it to myself. Has something happened to you? You who are usually so thoughtful and affectionate . . .

I am anxiously waiting for the article – all of *Il Stroligut* has been ready for two weeks and there it is held up. Try to understand me. Aren't you concerned about your little book?[1]

For the rest, I get along in a continual anabasis towards the centre of myself amid ever more absolute deserts. Contemporaneously there coexists a life – practical as usual – among whose feelings nostalgia for you and all Bologna is notable.

I embrace you affectionately,     Pier Paolo

1  See Letter 95.

## 100  To Franco De Gironcoli[1]
Conegliano

[Versuta, 18 March 1946]

[. . .]

I learn with regret that you do not know what poetry is. I hoped that you would continue to write in that ineffable language of yours so full of humour and unexpected perfections. The thought of not being alone comforted me on an unknown and unpopulated road. But I always hope that sooner or later poetry will have its revenge on you – then it will be a sunny holiday, an enchanting voyage by train, which will make you get out your notebook and fix on the blank page a moment of sadness of gaiety – a countermelody [. . .]

I do not hope to cause a school of poetry to arise – I know everything is always imperfect and provisory, how only memory purifies events.
[. . .]

1    Partial text published in *Corriere del Friuli*, November 1976.

## 101    To Gianfranco Contini
Domodossola
[*In possession of addressee: autograph*]

Versuta, 27 March [1946]

Distinguished Sig. Contini,

Here I am again to thank you for your last letter[1] and for your latest opinions. I am in that state of mind of someone who must begin all over again and now knows how it will all finish. It is a brutal thing to say but I delude myself only in those feelings which tell me I am alive, direct and corporeal feelings, moments of abandon which lead me to the accuracy of the diary. This solitude, I wanted to tell you, is therefore not enforced but voluntary although I know that it is a blind alley or, let us say rather, sin, selfishness. It is impatience with a limit, an agnosticism which is not resigned, an excessive habit of Proustian experiments. But there is no use my telling you these things – I know that you imagine them, that they are part of an obligatory burden.

I laughed over my poor Simplon – it is a name so laden with geography that it seems to have been invented by Cattaneo.[2] But I am not very gentle with my poetical discoveries and I will see that I suppress it, although I think I am not the only one to believe it is a mountain.

The others members of the Academiuta *exist* – at least physically; but they are very young pupils of the secondary schools with one or two exceptions. But if you have time try to look at the things by my cousin Domenico Naldini and those of Bortotto – perhaps there is the start of something original there. How very useful your help would be to our little *félibrige* – in fact, here I am throwing you an idea which with time, who knows, could turn out to be not so gratuitous and infertile; what would you say to the *Stroligut* (maybe with a changed name) becoming a little review, but more poetical than philological, of all the Ladin tongues? I am thinking of that huge volume by Ascoli[3] in which an ideal curve united the Engadine and Friuli, in which all 'those final s's, those palatals, those diphthongs' are, as it were, impregnated by a disturbing aroma of the high mountains. Coira and Cividale undoubtedly have a new charm. You would be the only one who could edit a review of this kind, whose tone could change from that of conventional philology to that of the most refined avant-garde reviews. The material would not be very extensive, but unknown, exciting. Thus from the heart of Switzerland to the mountains of Gorizia that ideal and abstract region whose presence was indicated by Ascoli could be drawn. In the same number of those invited the other minor languages of the Eastern Empire could figure ... There you have the idea I have been hatching for some years and which I could not make concrete by myself. Now it is up to you to see whether it is so absurd.

I have written to Falqui telling him that you would be willing to have his article published in *Poesia.*[4]

Forgive this long letter. Unfortunately I have a lot of free time but I make absolutely no claim to rob you of yours.

Cordial greetings,

Yours very truly,      Pier Paolo Pasolini

1   Not found.
2   Carlo Cattaneo (1801–69), historian, economist, politician.
3   Graziadio Ascoli (1861–1907), Italian philologist, professor of linguistics in Milan.
4   A review edited by Enrico Falqui.

## 102   To Gianfranco D'Aronco
Udine

[*In possession of addressee: autograph*]

[Postmark: Casarsa, 27 March 1946]

Dear D'Aronco,

I will not be able to take part in the Council[1] because tomorrow I am leaving for Rome. Besides I am not at all necessary.

Some time ago I handed over those forms to the headmaster here.[2] If you want to know my opinion of this research I will tell you that I am somewhat pessimistic. Ignorance of the teachers, indifference of the children ... Well. Then forgive me if I meddle in this matter too – of my poems in the numbers of *Stroligut* does 'Misteri'[3] not seem the best to you? It would certainly be the most significant.

In *Ce Fastu?* there is a little piece about me – and it is the compliment paid to Primon for the edition of those Berries.[4] Castellani, when dealing with the cover of that little book, made a fool of me as usual and – of his own accord, along with good Primon – added that horrible black line under the greenish title. Once again excuse my hasty frankness.

Best wishes and warm greetings,      Pier Paolo Pasolini

1   The council of the Friulian Philological Society of which D'Aronco was secretary.
2   D'Aronco was carrying out research on popular poetry in the secondary and elementary schools of Friuli.
3   See *Il Stroligut* No 1, August 1945.
4   See R. Castellani, *Bacche di ligustro* ['Laurel berries'], Primon (San Vito al Tagliamento, 1945).

## 103　To Tonuti Spagnol
Versuta

[*In possession of addressee: autograph*]

Rome, 3 April [1946]

My dear Toni,

Perhaps you will be interested to know where I am writing to you from: at this moment I am in a little room full of shadow among an infinity of pictures hung on the walls: madonnas, gentlemen, cribs, crucifixions, holy families, in violent and delicate colours. The furniture is antique, and everything is antique and precious. There is a silence so tranquil and dreamy that it feels like being in the middle of the fields in summer after a meal. But instead of the grasshoppers here one hears a distant and muffled concert of horns, of whistles – it is the traffic of the capital, a constant stream which you cannot imagine.

Do you remember when I left Casarsa? (I think a month has passed . . .) Well, at Sacile I found a seat and arrived in Venice comfortably – from Venice to Bologna too the journey was comfortable. In Bologna I found so many old friends and we had a nice evening together. How beautiful and sweet Bologna seemed to me! You know I arrived there when I was your age and passed seven years – perhaps the finest – there. Now the city continues to live calm and sunny as if lying lazily between the hills and the rich plain; now, walking through its streets, I feel that it does not remember me.

From Bologna to Rome I was also comfortably seated; but you will understand that to pass the night sitting on hard wood is not really very comfortable. But what an unending series of stupendous spring landscapes was imprinted on my eyes! because from Romagna on everything is green by now, everything is reborn. I saw half Italy framed in the glass of a little window. And on Saturday I arrived in Rome. By now I have seen so many things that it would take too long to tell you about them. I shall only tell you, haphazard, some things which may impress you a little. Just think that from my house to the Vatican one has to take 40 minutes by tram and almost half-an-hour on foot – and that is only a short trip compared to the size of the city. I go to the Vatican to visit the museums. Imagine that from the entrance to the Sistine Chapel (the ceiling is painted by Michelangelo – do you remember that I showed you the figures in school?) there is a corridor as long as from Colonel's house to Versuta, all painted and decorated with great pains. But that is nothing compared to the beauty of the Sistine Chapel and the Raphael rooms. But perhaps I shall tell you about this when we talk.

What are you doing? Do you get up early in the morning? How is your diary going? And your Latin?

I don't know the precise day yet when I shall return. But I feel that in a few days I shall have had enough of pictures, of concerts,of plays, I shall feel strongly nostalgia for my peaceful countryside. Now it seems impossible to me, while I am immersed in the dazzling splendour of a theatre, that in the world there is someone who sees to the cows, who sews in the evening by the fire, who grafts the trees . . . And yet that is man's true life. Give many greetings to your family and everyone in Versuta.

A hug,      Pier Paolo

## 104  To Luciano Serra
Bologna
[*In possession of addressee: autograph*]

Rome, Monday [9 April 1946]

Dearest Luciano,

Here I am in Rome in a variation on my humble Roman adventure. I have used my senses to imprint on them a general Roman landscape (in spring) but above all certain colours and certain ineffable gestures by Caravaggio, by Giovanni di Paolo, by Lorenzetti, by Piero della Francesca . . . I tell you them, these names, in the natural order in which they emerge from my memory. I have seen such a quantity of pictures that I have to leave it all to the mechanism of the memory, hoping that it will keep whatever was truly of value. On Friday evening I shall leave Rome and on Saturday, about 11, I shall be in Bologna. Tell Luca[1] at once, that he should write to Giovanna[2] that I shall leave again for Venice on Monday morning where I shall stay until Tuesday afternoon. Don't let this coming and going drive you mad. Give my greetings to your family and apologize to them for the disturbance I am causing. I don't know how to thank them and show my gratitude. Shall we have a nice evening of poetry readings? Try to organize it.

A big hug,      Pier Paolo

1  Fabio Luca Cavazza.
2  Giovanna Bemporad.

## 105  To Gianfranco Contini
Domodossola
[*In possession of addressee: autograph*]

Versuta, 7 May 1946

Distinguished Sig. Contini,

I know a long talk with you would be more necessary than ever for me; and

I leave it to you to imagine how much I want it. I was in my first or second year at the *liceo* when I began to read your things and still remember the immense, febrile impression that flowed to me from them. It was an inconceivable world that opened before me – more 'different' still from that of Montale or of Cardarelli, whom I was beginning to read in those days. But forgive me these memories. I only wanted to tell you that now I really wanted to talk to you, to know you as a person.

Two or three days ago I sent you the latest *Stroligut* with your piece;[1] if you want other copies tell me and I should like you to advise me on a certain number of persons to whom the reading of the review might prove interesting so that I can send it to them.

I have written to the Catalan poet Carles Cardó, asking for his collaboration and for that of other poets, fellow-countrymen of his. And the Romansch ones?[2] Could you find something? Besides verses there could be room in *Stroligut* for philological writings or essays on Romansch popular poetry.

Probably the next number of *Stroligut* (whose title I shall change) will try to set up a little society which, by establishing a fund, can entrust the publication of the review and its distribution to a publishing house.

If in this connection you have any advice to give me I should be very happy to follow it.

Warm greetings and good wishes,

Yours very truly,     Pier Paolo Pasolini

1   See Letter 94.
2   Romansch: Swiss French dialect.

## 106   To Gianfranco Contini
Domodossola
[*In possession of addressee: autograph*]

Versuta, 8 June [1946]

Distinguished Sig. Contini,

Although you are afraid that being forced to reply to me briefly is 'disastrous' for you, I assure you that I receive no more welcome letters than yours. (My friends after three years of absence have fallen away somewhat and besides my dearest friend[1] is still in Russia and I feel by now that he is fated not to return.)

But then, whether because of your habit as a critic or because of my habit as a reader, through your lines I can read much of what could still be written. Now I am waiting till you decide to go to Venice; I leave it to you to think with what joy and with what apprehension. You would find here a village ugly by nature and now half-destroyed. Among the ruined houses there is also ours and we live camping in a peasant house in the middle of the fields. If you decided to make a trip here amidst so much misery perhaps you would find two things pleasing – the little hall of our Academiuta and my father's tagliatelle, for he is a most hospitable native of Romagna. I won't sing the praises of the rustic life because the beauty of this plain is so hidden away that one must live here for many years to grasp it; but then it ends up by being one with the habit of poetical thoughts. (Have you read *Varmo*?)[2] Now because of these little discomforts I feel that the joy at your arrival would be all mine and not yours at all. And this I tell you out of a scruple of conscience – besides, it is pointless for me to write to tell you that by mentioning a probable visit you have given me *extraordinary pleasure*.

Warmest greetings from yours very truly,

Pier Paolo Pasolini

PS. If, as I ardently hope, you come to Casarsa you will get to know another *liceo* student[3] who is reading your things – the translator of Jimenez. Do you have occasion to go to Rome, Bologna or Parma? These would be the three cities to which I could go at any moment.

1   Ermes Parini.
2   'Varmo', a story by Ippolito Nievo (1831–61).
3   Nico Naldini.

## 107   To Sergio Maldini
Udine

[In possession of addressee: autograph]

Casarsa, 19 July [1946]

Dear Sergio,

I have received your letter which is as dirty as an apron and I am replying with this one which has no need to envy a soiled handkerchief. It is my usual frankness in which the frontiers between falseness and naturalness are indefinable. Between the 25th and the 30th I shall perhaps be in Udine because invited by Falqui to a talk with a certain Signora Astaldi[1] whose guest he is at Cortina. Apparently it has to do with advising her about a publication of posthumous writings by her father (Costantini).[2] Something which, I bet, would make your mouth water. But perhaps this lady will come to Casarsa because I have written to her that I would prefer to avoid a stay in Udine which I have defined as 'the most depressing city in the world'. So if we don't see each other during those days it will be you who will come to Casarsa (a Saturday evening, etc., as we arranged a long time ago). I should like to write to you at greater length – you nice reactionary – author among other things, of a very nasty article called 'A discontented priest' which ran the risk of getting you excommunicated – but my father has filled our plates with tagliatelle and he can't bear it if I am slow in coming to praise his culinary virtues.

A hug,      Pier Paolo

1   Maria Luisa Astaldi.
2   Giuseppe Constantini, student of Friulian place-names, history and folklore.

## 108   To Gianfranco Contini
Domodossola

[*In possession of addressee: autograph*]

Casarsa, 20 July [1946]

Distinguished Sig. Contini,

No Allied permit is needed to come here.[1] By now I have the illusion that I shall meet you here in Casarsa, which is far from delightful but which is on the other hand the only place that justifies the obstinate fact that I look like an eighteen year old. I remember that my mother complained about herself when – already a teacher for many years – they took her for a child. I have received and read most of the Catalan anthology sent me by Carles Cardó – a stupendous thing. For me it has brought a throng of forgotten dreams, a return to the sources . . . A language and a civilization, both forgotten, caused me to remember the meaning of certain poetical terms which had become too familiar to me. I have had in my hands these last days a score of numbers of *Fogl Ladin*;[2] there I read some rather mediocre verses. In Rome the first number of *Italy of the Dialects* has come out (have you seen it?), which could hardly have been more pedestrian. Ah, I am afraid Falqui is right to be suspicious of dialects.

Please let me know the dates when you will be in Venice in the event – a very sad one for me – that you should be unable to venture up here, then I would decide to take a train myself to a Venice which is suddenly full of people.

I send you my warmest greetings.

Yours very truly,      Pier Paolo Pasolini

1   Contini will have thought that since a permit was required to enter the Free Territory of Trieste, which had not yet been returned to Italy, the same would apply to the province of Friuli to the north.

2   A publication in Ladino, the Romance language spoken in the Italian Dolomites.

## 109   To Gianfranco Contini
Domodossola
[*In possession of addressee: autograph*]

[Macugnaga, August 1946]

Distinguished Sig. Contini,

I am at Macugnaga at the house of a friend[1] who suddenly needed me to be there. It is not a pleasure trip but a real sacrifice.

On Wednesday or Thursday morning I leave and so shall be in Domodossola to see you; can I hope to find you? Forgive this hurried notice but I am extremely tired. I shall come to your house at about 10.

Forgive me and accept my warmest greetings.

Yours very truly,     Pier Paolo Pasolini

1   Fabio Mauri.

## 110   To Gianfranco Contini
Domodossola
[*In possession of addressee: autograph*]

Casarsa, 2 September [1946]

Distinguished Sig. Contini,

To rescue myself, to some extent, from the naïve and thoughtless picture which I inevitably gave of myself at our meeting I am sending you this all too scanty bundle of verses. But I doubt that they will be able to help me. The 'Ciants di un muart' ['Songs of a dead man'][1] I wrote in February 1945; the other two lyrics are recent (from May of this year).

I am thinking above all of the angel you *saw* in that little valley where the bells were ringing. But don't think that I am too serious or in a certain sense too Nordic; if I were not completely taken by the internal perfection which you showed in every word you spoke I might have been able to reveal to you a certain spirit. I would not have forced you, for instance, to drop the discussion of the double intepretation of morality and, still more, of Rosmini's[2] heresy. If, as I very much hope, you come up here I hope to find allies in my *fuejs*, in my *rios*, or to say it in plain language, in the expanse of my world about which I known an infinite number of things.

Warm greetings,

Yours very truly,     Pier Paolo Pasolini

1   Published in *La nuova gioventú.*

2   Rosmini (1797–1855), priest and philosopher whose writings were condemned by the Vatican.

## 111   To Fabio Luca Cavazza
Bologna

[*In possession of addressee: autograph*]

[Casarsa, September 1946]

Dearest Luca,

   After you left nothing new happened at Macugnaga. The journey by bus along with the two idiots was fairly comfortable. (But just think that at a certain point just before the terrifying curves a hunchbacked woman entered the bus and came and pressed her hump against my chest. Fortunately she then got out again because another coach had been announced.) Now I am once again eternally in Casarsa.

   Send the money when and how you like. I think I shall be in Bologna fairly soon.

   A kiss,       Pier Paolo

## 112   To Gianfranco D'Aronco
Udine

[*In possession of addressee: typewritten with autograph signature*]

[Versuta], 24 September [1946]

Dear D'Aronco,

   I have had your letter from the Philological Society in which it was announced that the new council had decided to take me on as an additional member or whatever. Yes, I accept, although you know by now that I shall be able to be of only limited use. I wanted to ask how the offices are distributed (I have received three letters with the signatures of three different secretaries); but now I remember that on Sunday I shall probably be in Spilimbergo[1] and there we can have a few words. I shall be there with my eternal *Stroligut*s.

   Warm greetings,

   Yours,       Pier Paolo Pasolini

1   For the annual congress of the Friulian Philological Society.

1946

## 113   To Gianfranco Contini
Domodossola

[*In possession of addressee: typewritten with autograph signature*]

Casarsa, 16 October [1946]

Distinguished Sig. Contini,

I am replying to you after an enormous delay only because I feared this answer; your last letter in fact awoke in me two feelings which give a discourteous picture of me. The first to which I confess is joy, just the joy of the scholar, for your appreciation of LENGAS [Language];[1] I hope to confirm you in your suspicion by telling you that those verses I already saw as living on their own without any further need of me. The other feeling is still that of a scholar and consists in the confused feeling, perhaps the anxiety, which comes from my not having understood with certainty your 'formula' (do you remember? 'he discovers his humanity a little beneath the human'). The consciousness of a dragonfly, of a violet . . . you say, but I am thinking of the differences one might list between 'naïvety' and 'naturalness'. In short, do you believe that consciousness of one's own naïvety prevents one from remaining naïve? I do not, and the explanation I find in any psychological textbook. Did you yourself not see that Angel in the little valley? For me to understand entirely that formula of yours (and that would be very necessary) you would have to explain if what I am for you (provided always that you do it with deliberation, conscientiously) descends from the human to below the human, or starting from the non-human *comes to rest* below that.

Casarsa awaited you in vain for this first fortnight of October; and now I must surrender to the idea of not having you here and I do it with great regret. Tomorrow I am setting out for Rome.

Warm greetings,

Yours very truly,     Pier Paolo Pasolini

To this letter Contini replies:

*Domodossola, New Year's Day 1947*

*Dear Pasolini,*

*Owing to the negligence of the doge (you know I was to have been the guest of the descendants of certain doges, by-the-by Genoese ones) I did not make the journey to Venice. So I missed that mysterious sector of the north-east and the dear félibrige of the ginnasio of Ca da l'Aga. Let us postpone it but it is a pity because the liceo is growing old even faster than me unless you manage to stop it with yourself, utinam.[2]*

*L'usignolo della Chiesa Cattolica [ 'The nightingale of the Catholic Church'] is warbling heedlessly on the banks of the Ceresio very seductively even for those who did not know your name. I have made a 'short list' of 20 (out of about 130 competitors) in which 'L'usignolo' naturally always figures. There should in this connection be an agency announcement about it but it certainly won't reach Casarsa. Very fine the lament for David and the last*

250

poem specially.

*Do not be worried – man's slightest movements are human. For millennia literature has been above the line. I like it to go below the line and, so to say, below the human yet without descending into the nether regions (which are, besides, hyperhuman, not hypohuman – I say hyper and hypo in the literal sense of verticality). Besides* 'L'usignolo' *sums up the attitude of the narcissistic hero but, so to speak, diffused over the others whom the* Poems from Casarsa *dominated. Everywhere* cherchez l'Es.[3]

*I wish you a good new year very affectionately*
*Yours,       Gianfranco Contini*

1   See 'Lengas da frus di sera' ('Language of the children in the evening') in *La nuova gioventú.*
2   *utinam*: would that it were possible.
3   The Es: German for the Freudian Id.

## 114   To Mario Argante
Udine

[*In possession of addressee: typewritten with autograph date and signature*]

Casarsa, 16 October [1946]

Dear Argante,

Once again I have fallen short of my duty as a 'civilized' person: will you forgive me? Circumstances oblige me to obey only in part the categorical imperative which obliges me to write to you and thus to send you the ghost of a letter, certainly not the one that was my intention. As for the Italian verses, from what you said at San Daniele I understood that you were conscious of their shortcomings (occasion, feelings) and I can only confirm them. Those in Friulano seem very prosaic to me; in the first group of poems you had sent me there were others much superior and in another letter[1] of mine I had indicated their good points to you. Please leave the largely Zoruttian tracks; derail yourself. There are possibilities of new poetic patterns in you – if you begin (innocently) to detest the Friulian dialect tradition you will see that you will set free inside yourself an original inspiration.

Cordial greetings and best wishes

Yours very truly,       Pier Paolo Pasolini

1   See Letter 86.

*1946*

## 115   To Sergio Maldini
Udine

[*In possession of addressee: autograph; handwritten address*]

[Versuta, 1946]

Dear Sergio,

In order to write to you I am breaking an incredible intimacy and solitude. It is eleven at night, an extremely late hour for Versuta, and I have come back from the cinema and then from a stop at the house of a friend of mine where, talking about absolutely commonplace things, we drank a bottle of wine together. Now I find my room silent and trusting. Three centuries ago, when I was a boy at this time of night, a sacred time, as in a sanctuary, I used to sit up writing verses. Tonight I am preparing to do the same thing – so you see what a break I am making with the rules in writing to you and into what kind of intimacy I draw your image. To think that I only wanted to say to you that I still know nothing about Sunday and the same for the next one. On the other hand I should very much like to have you here and to stuff you with tagliatelle. So on Saturday only Nico[1] will be able to tell you anything precise. But tell me – couldn't you come on some other day than Sunday? Wednesday, for example, or any other day? I think that you should be able to have a little leave. I hope you will make this decision, otherwise from one Sunday to another we shall arrive at the Sunday when you should have come for the second time and not the first.

A hug,      Pier Paolo

1   Nico Naldini.

## 116   To Silvana Mauri
Milan

[*In possession of addressee: typewritten with autograph additions, corrections and signature*]

Versuta, 1946

Dear Silvana,

Your letter – I got it on Saturday – threw me into a state of excitement, of impotent emotion. I should have liked to reply at once but the little experience I have ended up having in such matters prevented me from doing so. Today, which is a desert of a Monday, void of any possibility of amusement, and which renders the thought of a future unbearable, I feel myself incapable of effusions and so I take advantage of that to answer you.

You have no need of hints, of diagnoses – your intelligence is almost too keenly honed. That is why you came to the point of saying: I know nothing any more. All your arguments cancel each other out and it is natural that it should be so because you are too close to Fabio, whereas to judge – and a judgement is always finite, provisional – distance is needed. You so greatly fear the crudity of the doctors, the 'imprecision' of their treatment; but it is precisely that which you must hold on to. Look, I am far away – in space and already in time – from you, and Fabio's condition has become simplified in my eyes and therefore perhaps falsified, I admit. I think you must resign yourself to the thought that Fabio is talking nonsense – that is to say, that he is ill. But following immediately on this thought there must be another, that Fabio will get better. I am very convinced of that – I find it in the nature of things. You still have the doubt that it is unfair to have entrusted him to the doctors – but think, if Fabio were 'sane' what hopes could we have for the future? In what sense could there be an evolution? A holy mystic? But I am in no way a believer, I have no inkling of the existence of a Heaven and so I have to tell you that to call him 'saint' in this sense would be exactly like calling him lost. And so we are back at the beginning – to entrust him to the doctors was the only thing to do. On that score you can be at peace. I know if I too were with Fabio for an hour I would have the thought a hundred times that he is our usual Fabio dragged far away from us by an irresistible experience because I would watch his every smile and would recognize the true, the old one, I would weigh up each word of his and would recognize the pitiful one . . . But from afar, remembering things I was present at, and examining what you have written to me, I would be cowardly if I hid what emerges so clearly. You see, the smile of intelligence which he exchanged with you before leaving you, his lucid talks with the religious persons, are – I am finally convinced – the purest signs of his confusion. It is in no way humanly explicable that he does not talk to his father and that on the other hand he speaks to a stranger only if he wears a habit. Tears come to my eyes as I write this to you, but in the end it is the only way to think of Fabio with a minimum of tranquillity that isn't cowardly. It is the only way to hope; in fact my conviction, a deeply rooted one, is that this is not a serious case – and this conviction is yours too – and that one must only be patient for some time. Where the vagueness of the medical treatments is concerned forgive me if I give you a little example drawn from my experience. In 1944, that is in the midst of the war, I had ended up not believing in anything which was not the *hic et nunc*[1] of my existence, I had ended up attributing an immensely greater importance to my finger-nail than to any other entity which existed outside of me; it was obviously an aberration due to the solitude, to the continuous danger of dying; a real sickness of my feelings which had all taken a turn for the worse. Of this I was partially conscious but the trouble was that I remained convinced of the philosophical validity of resting my only faith in my existence. I have explained myself very badly but in short the conclusion is this, that the moment the war was over and I had made contact with the world again I saw that all that I had thought had already been thought, and that there was a name – existentialism – which could (but how loosely) be applied to my case. I had a somewhat bitter laugh over it and quickly began to get better. Fabio too is a case for which a label already exists, even if it is an inexact one; the treatment is a corollary of this, also an inexact one but one which cannot but give the expected results. In any case that treatment will be a help, a push, because I am convinced of this too, that Fabio will get better on his own.

Will you accuse me of the same things as you do Pippo² and Michele? I am in any case not afraid of this because everything I think about Fabio is due to the affection I feel for him. Indeed I was astonished at the reference you make to me of 'serious and delicate matters'. I simply do not know what to think.

I am unspeakably sad, Silvana, and the only consolation would be to let myself go with someone; here there are only fields and horizons which are beginning to be as hateful to me as Monte Rosa. Since my return from Macugnaga I have written almost nothing more because I have gone into one of those states which are full of unease in which, when writing, one wishes only to be sincere; it is an arid crisis from which I can only expect boring fits of despair; I am unhappy with myself and don't know what to do about it. It is a terrible condition this, which perhaps you do not know because it seems you still believe in God – that is, in someone who judges you and punishes you. By now I am too much at home with my conscience, I deal with my fits of remorse in the family, and the sense of being in error rather than making me feel better makes me feel worse.

It was the contact with Fabio that took me out of my state of being fairly at peace, in which everything came down to translating myself into hendeca-syllables; I detached myself from myself by studying myself continuously. Now that is no longer enough. 'Fabio is right' I repeat to you now as I said so often up there; one must hate oneself and suffer as he does; in fact if he had the least pity for you and *were able* to sacrifice to you a little of the love which he has for his mad God, it would remain for me only to wish to imitate him. Please answer at once giving me some news of him. Don't be afraid of speaking to me about yourself as well. (Then I am going to ask you a favour – it is to send me as soon as possible these books: *The Personality* by Richmond, *Introduction to Existentialism* by Abbagnano, *The Ego and the World* by Berdayev (all by Bompiani). Forgive me for putting you to this trouble.)

Affectionate greetings also to your family,   Pier Paolo

1    *hic et nunc*: here and now.
2    Pippo Ponti, friend of Fabio.

## 117   To Franco Farolfi
Parma
[*In possession of addressee: autograph*]

Rome, 20 October [1946]

Dearest Franco,

After an infinity I am writing to you from a place where you certainly did not imagine me. Some months ago, just after the war, we wrote to each other but in a wrong way. We must set free inside ourselves, as far as possible, the boys who loved each other in Bologna – well, I finally feel myself relieved and think of you with joyous affection and without the scruples of that time. I don't want to argue with you but to laugh with you. The pain, as I told you, had brought me down, but now that it is receding, that it is becoming something experienced, it is beginning to bear some fruit too, that monster. I have a desire to embrace you once again, to say nasty things with you about Carmine Gallone, etc.

I shall be in Bologna on the 28th and 29th, at Serra's; please don't fail this time.

I embrace you, many greetings to your family,

Pier Paolo Pasolini

## 118   To Sergio Maldini
Udine
[*In possession of addressee: autograph postcard*]

Rome, 25 October [1946]

Dear Sergio,

It is no use giving you news of me, there would be none. Just know that I can't bear that terrible place, Udine. Do you see how, as foreseen, I send you unknown addresses?

A hug,        Pier Paolo

*1946*

## 119   To Tonuti Spagnol
Versuta
[*In possession of addressee: autograph*]

Rome, 25 October [1946]

My dear Toni,

I would have liked to write to you sooner also because you would have been able to reply to me. But I haven't had a free moment – that is, a moment of calm.

This time I have nothing great to describe to you – in fact I got to know men and not works of art. I met some writers and literary people from here and this meeting is simply not to be compared to that with Michelangelo or Piero della Francesca. Yet yesterday a touching thing happened to me. While I was waiting for some friends on a bridge over the Tiber (it was night) the idea came to me to go down a flight of stairs that led to the level of the water. I immediately did what I thought and found myself on a strip of sand and mud. It was very dark – above my head you could make out the arches of the bridge and along the banks the lamps, an infinite number of lamps. I was about twenty metres below the level of the city and its din reached me deadened, as if from another world. I simply did not believe that in the heart of a metropolis it was enough to go down a flight of steps to reach the most absolute solitude. The trams passed screeching over my head but I was face to face with the Tiber, the age-old Tiber, which was dragging its muddy waves and its reflections down to the Tyrrhenian sea. But the odd thing was this: that I did not think I was near the Tiber of today but that of two thousand years ago, and I seemed to see with amazing precision Horatius Coclites[1] swimming across it.

It seemed impossible to me that Versuta exists and that in a few days (Wednesday) I shall be there too. I enjoyed myself a lot this time and got used to an intellectual and social life which, alas, is simply not realizable in Versuta. If you could know how microscopic and absurd it seems to me when I think about it here! But in any case it has for me irreplaceable merits. Here one lives too much with the brain and very little with the heart – here people's only feeling is ambition, in the best of cases, and in general, the desire for pleasure and money. So goodbye for now.

Many greetings to your family,        Pier Paolo

1   Horatio, who 'kept the bridge' against the Etruscans in the very early days of the City.

## 120   To Silvana Mauri
Milan
[*In possession of addressee: autograph*]

[Rome, October 1946]
Dear Silvana,

I am in Rome and this will explain to you my delay in giving a sign of life. I cannot write you a long letter and will do so in a few days as soon as I am back in Casarsa. Meanwhile I beg you, don't wait for a fuller letter before replying to me – all I need from you are some lines giving me news about Fabio.

You ask me in your letter to be 'true' but this is precisely the insurmountable difficulty which has always made a polite correspondence difficult for me. You will laugh but one also needs an 'epistolary style' (I am not talking about Cicero's) which makes it possible to be sincere. When speaking to you I can tacitly be pardoned for certain odious compromises between absolute frankness and a half-sincerity – but by letter it is much more difficult. Try not to be strict, then, with some of my 'little letters' in which I shall end up by describing to you the landscape of Casarsa or of some village or other. I like you very much, Silvana, that is certain, so with you I am not afraid to seem uninteresting and don't feel the need to show myself to be intelligent.

Once again please let me have news of Fabio as soon as possible but make an effort for it to be very precise, 'scientific'. If you don't feel like it get Luciano[1] to do it.

If I have some money I shall perhaps come to Milan for a day in November.

Affectionate greetings to all your family as well,       Pier Paolo

1   Luciano Mauri, Silvana's brother.

## 121   To Ennio de'Concini
Rome
[*In possession of addressee: typewritten with autograph date and signature*]

Casarsa, 18 November [1946]
Dear de'Concini,

I hope that your cordial feelings did not explode all at once at the moment of our meeting but have instead left you with sufficient residues to accept this letter. Certainly now that my face is protected by the Po valley and the Appennines I feel more at ease than when offering it to you defencelessly, so conscious of its unutterable anachronism. I have to confess to you that during my brief stay in Rome the only person I got to know (or got to know again) was Horatius Coclites – I saw him swimming across the Tiber under the Ponte Cavour, etc.

But you were a surprise – exactly like one of those unexpected and delightful surprises one finds in Easter eggs. You did not communicate your expansivity to me because it was too complete and beautifully finished in you – for the moment I could only be its spectator. And, since you probably like to hear yourself being talked about, I will add that it gave me the impression of liking laughter as such – something very rare here in the North where people love laughter but confuse it with amusement (I am talking about the essential amusement which is a diversion from the Life Line). That is why they drink more in the North than in the South – the innocent (and too good) wine that you went to drink shouting 'Long live Timoshenko'[1] was nothing compared to the bad and aprioristic wine they drink up here. And then you live in Rome where Scipio and Lelio played at ball.

But really I had decided to write to you to talk about FIERA.[2] Gradually, as it has become familiar and close, it has shown some of its shortcomings, some of its tics. This happens with people who love each other – and the finding in them of some *natural* defect gives rise to at least a moment of great upset, or of bitterness. The fact that the defect is natural gives rise to two opposite theories: that it is curable or it is incurable. I hope that 'our inquests', the 'polemics on the Twenty Years of Fascism' are curable ills . . . A little more deeply rooted, more radical, is a certain perhaps involuntary 'atmosphere' – don't be angry – which is anti-communist. Well, in any case it is not very important.

Seeing that, on due consideration, the poems which have appeared up to now in *Fiera* are not masterpieces but have almost all had a youthful or experimental character, I have decided to send you my *Diaries* so that you can see whether they are possible. I have also sent some bits of writing[3] from that time which we agreed upon at the printers, do you remember? I should like you to give me news of them. So I am waiting for your answer which I hope will be in line with the image you left with me.

Warm greetings,      Pier Paolo Pasolini

1  The famous Red Army Marshall.
2  The Rome weekly *La Fiera letteraria* of which Ennio de'Concini was editor in chief.
3  *Dialetto e poesia* ['Dialect and poetry']: unpublished.

## 122   To Fabio Luca Cavazza[1]
Bologna

[*In possession of addressee: autograph*]

Casarsa, Christmas 1946

'Giovanna, what shall we write to little Cavazzino?'

'Let's write that the hens are all housewives, that they have feelings and emotions and the terror of death like men, that they shit themselves like us.'

'Don't let's say these nasty things to Luca because, otherwise, this evening he won't be able to swallow his braised chicken.'

'Then let's talk about the future.'

'The future of Fabio Luca, in fact, has no cause to be jealous of that of the hens: he'll end up in a pot too.'

'Oh yes? Perhaps because being fat and red he may be tasty to eat. I am keeping for myself the best – and leanest part – the backside.'

'That depends. You see, if we roast him we cut off the backside and put it aside to make stock next day.'

'No, please, we might be dead tomorrow – it's better to fill our bellies. But let's put him to roast in any case; he seems just made for that, Luca. And who shall we invite to the banquet?'

'Well, we'll invite Fabio, Gigi, Ricci, Silvana.[2] And Falzone too, what do you say?'

'Of course, poor thing. In any case he died with a number of Setaccio on his pate. And shall we invite Vighi too?'

'No, Vighi told me he wants to fast. Listen – what shall we have to go with it? I think mushrooms would go well.'

'No, I don't like mushrooms, especially the poisonous ones. Potatoes are better with a lot of gravy or else fried. But wouldn't it be better to let this poor boy live?'

'Pooh! What a smell of burning! It must be Cavazzino who's burning in the pot. Wait while I go and stir him. Well, what were we saying? Ah yes, mushrooms. Yes, let's put in mushrooms, Giovanna, and let them be poisonous so that we all die.'

'No. I don't want to die so young and beautiful; you can die if you like, because you're ugly and hairy and I wouldn't want to eat you even if you were dead.'

'Well, shall we send him greetings?'

'Yes.'

'Greetings and kisses.'

'A hug and a very gentle smack.'

1   Dialogue between Pasolini and Giovanna Bemporad.
2   Old friends of the periodical *Il Setaccio*: Fabio Mauri, Mario Ricci, Silvana Mauri.

# 1947

## 123　To Fabio Luca Cavazza
Bologna

[*In possession of addressee: typewritten with autograph signature*]

[Casarsa, beginning of 1947]

Dearest Luca,

I am late in replying to you but it is Giovanna's fault. By this time you will have seen her and she will have told you already about her hard-drinking stay. You should have seen her when one evening she went into the byre at the Cicutos'[1] and touched a cow asking: Can one touch it? The women were spinning and sewing and she went mad with amazement in their midst and began to rave, saying she was drowning in a sea of milk, and then quoted Theocritus.[2] All these poor people looked at her in utter amazement and I had to save the situation. But that is nothing – you should have seen her when she was dancing with Miotto, etc., etc.

Has Giovanna told you that I am waiting for news of my exam results from you?[3] You must contrive to tell me immediately if there is a session in January and, if there is, to send me the timetable and the date of the philosophy exam. It is a little bit of a bore, I know – but I can't deal with it any other way.

I have become decidedly famous and very respected in Friuli – but I am ashamed to talk about it; tomorrow I have a lecture in Udine.

Your letter gave me tremendous joy where Fabio is concerned – let's hope you weren't deceiving yourself! I wrote a long letter to Silvana but she hasn't replied yet – if you have recent news, send me it immediately.

An affectionate hug,　　Pier Paolo

1　A peasant family in Versuta who were hosts to the Pasolini family.
2　Theocritus (third century BC), great Greek pastoral poet.
3　In the Faculty of Philosophy.

## 124   To Gianfranco D'Aronco[1]
Udine

[*In possession of addressee: typewritten with autograph addition and signature*]

Casarsa, 9 January [1947]

Dear D'Aronco,

I wanted to reply to your letter so as to join;[2] but today, Thursday, I have to be in Udine – the trip has been postponed and so my membership will reach you with a slight but unwarranted delay – and from this delay you must not draw conclusions about a possible coolness on my part. On the contrary, I am definitely with you and resolved to do things for our Region – but do things, not beat about the bush.

Tome, the lawyer, agrees to participate – perhaps he has already written to you. I am glad you accepted without the least protest the historical and naturalistic arguments which I attributed to you in an article of mine[3] . . . You will certainly have seen that I did it above all (over and above an exclusive love of frankness) to get at Rosso better.[4]

So keep me informed – I am entirely at your disposal.

Warm greetings,        Yours, Pier Paolo Pasolini

1   A scholar living in Udine, secretary of the movement for Friulian autonomy.
2   i.e. to join the 'Friulian People's Movement for Regional Autonomy' set up in Udine on 19 January 1947.
3   See 'Le opinioni valide sull'autonomia friulana' ['Valid views on Friulian autonomy'] in *Libertà* of 31 December 1946.
4   Lawyer in Pordenone, an opponent of regional autonomy.

## 125   To Gianfranco D'Aronco
Udine

[*In possession of addressee: typewritten with autograph date and signature*]

Casarsa, 19 January 1947

Dear D'Aronco,

On Thursday at 4 I shall certainly be with you. For the future, however, neither the time nor the day suit me very well – it would have to be brought forward because I have a train at 6. I hope the meeting today, Sunday, went well; I am sorry I could not take part and had to be absent. At this moment (if this doesn't seem irrelevant to you) the bells of San Giovanni are ringing, from my window I see the mountains and imagine the sea. Nature is with us, dear D'Aronco, even if it is only a question of a landscape.

Warm greetings,        Pier Paolo Pasolini

## 126  To Ennio de'Concini

Rome

*[In possession of addressee: typewritten with autograph date and signature]*

Casarsa, 19 January 1947

Dear de'Concini,

I was born a liar and will die truthful. Believe me I never got a reply from you to my first letter and that is why I have been so silent. That is how a horrible postal misdirection (I have no other theories) awoke in me a certain distracted bitterness, in you your pungent liking for Proverbs. So let the postmen blush and let us forgive ourselves for the non-existent blame. As for the 1000 Swiss francs of *Libera Stampa*,[1] alas they are not in my possession – I believe I was merely mentioned for a very short collection of lyrics dating from 1943. What about my 'Inspiration in contemporary writers',[2] which I sent to *Fiera* instead of 'Dialect and poetry'? If it was no good you could at least say 'No' and not offend me with this blanket silence!

Cordial greetings,

Yours,      Pier Paolo Pasolini

1  Refers to the *Libera Stampa* ['Free Press'] prize of Lugano for which he had competed with the first nucleus of *L'usignolo della Chiesa Cattolica* ['The nightingale of the Catholic Church']; see Letter 113.
2  See 'L'ispirazione nei contemporanei' in *La Fiera letteraria* of 6 March 1947, and Letter 121.

## 127  To Giovanna Bemporad

Venice

*[In possession of addressee: typewritten with autograph corrections, date and signature]*

Casarsa, 20 January 1947

Dear Giovanna,

I did not welcome your pictures – this wish of yours seemed too selfish to me. Did it really not occur to you to ask me to give greetings to the poor group of our New Year friends in Capodanno?[1]

Do you absolutely refuse to forgive them for not writing poetry?

I know – now you feel insulted – forgive me. People are stupid, nasty, confused; but in this there is an aspiration, an inferiority complex which can still be considered a remnant of abstract goodness. That is valid and must not be neglected by those of us who have a conscience. Basically you have a very romantic idea of the poet and want to be forgiven too much because you write verses, that is to say, have something godlike in you. You are still not so superior to others not to be upset if they do not forgive you. I am saying this to you because I am a friend and I am sorry to see you falling short – not where I am concerned but where you are concerned. Since you are important to me I am tired of seeing you the prey to secret and inhuman sadness. Has your intelligence really no other resources than those of poetry? Why do you not exploit it to overcome your complexes which are such a burden to you? But you are too proud to listen to me and will say to yourself: 'What does this person want, what does he know about the infinite things within me?', in fact you know that *the other* is always infinitely less important than the 'I'. But it is the others who make history. Do forgive me – I hug you and send you greetings from my family.

1   See Letters 122 and 123.

## 128   To Gianfranco Contini
Domodossola

[*In possession of addressee: typewritten with autograph date and signature*]

Casarsa, 26 January 1947

Distinguished Sig. Contini,

I am replying very belatedly to your postcard giving me news about 'L'usignolo'[1] – the printer is to blame, being intent on postponing from one day to the next the birth of that little white book[2] which by now you will have received. If you have read it there is no point in my saying that it is well above the line[3] if one overlooks perhaps a few disrespectful shouts of rebellion.

Do you think, at any rate, that I could send it away from Friuli without excessive damage to that poetic image – a minor one certainly, not a domestic one – which I want to try to present of myself?

As for 'L'usignolo', I feel a certain affection for it since it represents me at twenty-one and still a virgin who, having been back in Casarsa, has allowed himself to be influenced by a kind of peasant Christianity, not without finding however in his frustrated Eros sweet and equivocal sources of heresy. But 'situations' do not find solutions, they are consumed; so I am happy that the nightingale, which no longer has anything to say to me, produced on the banks of the Ceresio a few convincing trills. I greet you warmly and, may I say? affectionately.

Yours,      Pier Paolo Pasolini

1   Refers to the first collection of *L'usignolo della Chiesa Cattolica* sent to the *Libera Stampa* poetry competition in Lugano. See Letters 113 and 126.
2   See *I pianti*, Edizioni della' 'Academiuta' (Casarsa, 1946).
3   See Contini's answer to Letter 113.

## 129  To Giovanna Bemporad
Venice

[*In possession of addressee: typed with autograph correction, date and signature*]

Casarsa, 31 January 1947

Dear Giovanna,

Thank you for your nice letter. When you seem lost in a troubled and fatal darkness here you are emerging again with frankness and ingenuousness; you make lovely recoveries. When will these recoveries be reflected on the outside? When will your face, your glasses, your stockings, also shine with goodness? When will you sing the Seventh[1] silently without insulting the others by declaiming it at the top of your voice? There will be a time, I am sure, when all this will come about. What you are hatching 'inside' is naturally destined to resolve itself, to be consumed, to become less important; in short, you will stop being 'adolescent'. Forgive this hymn which I have let loose on your future and try to give me the huge satisfaction of seeing my prophecies come true.

An affectionate embrace,        Pier Paolo

1   Beethoven's Seventh Symphony or the Seventh-day Requiem Mass?

## 130   To Gianfranco Contini
Domodossola

[*In possession of addressee: typewritten with autograph date and signature*]

Casarsa, 5 February 1947

Distinguished Sig. Contini,

I confess to you that your letter[1] gave me a moment of irresistible joy. Now I owe you a great deal: you have a decisive role and that in my most secret and presumably most jealous existence. My great fear is not knowing how to touch with the necessary delicacy the mechanisms of this friendship of yours – something so difficult for me precisely because it is so keenly desired.

I should be very happy to see 'L'usignolo' published if only in order to get rid of it from the drawers of my desk and of my memories; however if your 'activity as impresario' should fail it would still remain for me a symbol of my good luck. As for the Cesena prize, I took part with a little poem 'EUROPA';[2] now I am faced with two suspicions – the first (the lesser) that the manuscript has been lost, the second (really alarming), that Montale did not recognize in it the author of *Poesie a Casarsa*; in fact the 'connection' is there – a little academic, somewhat traditional. Please inform Cardò[3] that *Stroligut* under the new name of *Quaderno romanzo* ['Romance Notebook'] will come out in a month and a half; that all his Catalan anthology will be there.[4] If he were then to send me some information I could write an article on Catalonia, inserting the argument into the debate on the problem of Friulian autonomy.

Hoping still to have you in Casarsa some day I send you my warmest greetings.

Your very truly,        Pier Paolo Pasolini

1   Not found.
2   See *Dal Diario (1945–1947)* ['From the Diary'], Sciascia (Caltanissetta, 1954).
3   The Catalan poet; see Letter 105.
4   See 'Fiore di poeti catalani' ['Anthology of Catalan poets'] in *Quaderno romanzo* No 3, Edizioni dell' 'Academiuta' (Casarsa, June 1947).

## 131   To Fabio Luca Cavazza
Bologna
[*In possession of addressee: typewritten with autograph date and signature*]

Casarsa, 11 February 1947

Dear Luca,

For many days I have been anxiously awaiting a letter from you telling me the dates of the exams. Perhaps you did not get mine in which I included the request?

Please reply immediately because I must know that I am in order. I am sending along with this 20 copies of *I pianti* so that you can give 10 to Cappelli, for him to put on sale, and the others to the following friends: Arcangeli, Meluschi, Adriana, Vighi, Pancaldi, Vecchi, Manzoni, Telmon, Lorenzetti. If I should have forgotten anyone, warn me so that I send other copies. Yet another little favour – get me from Cappelli, with whom I still have an account, subscriptions to the following reviews: IL PONTE, LETTERATURA, L'INDAGINE, SOCIETÀ, PSICANALISI (if it is still coming out).

Forgive me these boring matters and send me news about all of you.

I hug you affectionately,   yours,        Pier Paolo

1   See Letter 128.

## 132   To Luciano Serra
Bologna

[*In possession of addressee: typed with autograph date, signature and postscript*]

Casarsa, 13 February 1947

My dearest Luciano,

For more than a month I have been putting off writing a letter to you from day to day to give you an account of what has been happening (very little practically) recently. But the moment does not seem to have come yet – I am in fact full of haste and above all of excitement because I have to prepare a lecture on contemp. poetry to be given tomorrow at the People's University of Udine. But I decided to write to you all the same to ask you the favour of preparing for me immediately a note (about a page and a half typed) about Percoto;[1] it will appear in QUADERNO ROMANZO (the new name for *Stroligut*) which will be very fine. But I have a great sense of urgency because in it that famous letter by my brother[2] will also appear and the circumstances now are such that the time is ripe for its publication. So I beg you to be quick. I should come to Bologna for the exams[3] but Luca can't get round to sending me the date. Are you writing poetry? I should so much like to read something of yours, I feel it with the spring.

A very affectionate hug,   yours      Pier Paolo

PS. Shall I get a note from you within a week? Tomorrow or the next day I shall send you the headed notepaper.

1   See 'Racconti della Percoto' by Serra in *Quaderno romanzo*.
2   The letter was not published: see Letter 76.
3   In the Faculty of Philosophy.

## 133   To Fabio Luca Cavazza
Bologna

[*In possession of addressee: autograph*]

[Casarsa, February 1947]

Dearest Luca,

As you see, the questions were already prepared, one only has to change the dates (if possible). So I shall be in Bologna very soon and we shall embrace again, talk again. Life here is the same as usual – monotonously varied. I am not ungrateful to fate – should I not perhaps (?) thank it for what in giving me it does not give me?

A hug,      Pier Paolo

The moment you have news of Fabio let me have it, please. And write to tell me the date of the exams at once.

## 134 To Ennio de'Concini
### Rome
[*In possession of addressee: typewritten with autograph date, signature and postscript*]

Casarsa, 15 February 1947

Dear de'Concini,

The pleasure you give me by telling me that my little book will be reviewed in FIERA[1] is made a little bitter by the dilemma it confronts me with. I must confess that as critic I have more respect for Petroni,[2] on the other hand Caproni[3] knows me personally and has read my poems in Friulano. I really do not know which to choose. You do it – and don't laugh at this conclusion.

And forgive my provincial naïvety but if the proposal came from them, Petroni and Caproni, could one of them not deal with it in the same way, e.g. in *Lettere d'oggi* ['Letters of today']? But I really have to tell you that at this moment I feel guilty . . . How are you? Your letter hinted at the onset of influenza; but my diagnosis (taking advantage of the 'distance' which separates us: the Appennines, the Po, etc.) suggests a name: spring. Thus I leave you, spring-like, amid the perfume of the stones of Rome.

Warm greetings,  yours     Pier Paolo Pasolini

PS. As far as the review is concerned, I put my trust in you, send me the book that seems most appropriate. Here in the midst of the fields one does not catch the niceties needed in the choice of a book to review.

1  See the review by Caproni in *La Fiera letteraria*, 20 March 1947.
2  Guglielmo Petroni (b. 1911), novelist and poet.
3  Giorgio Caproni (b. 1912), hermetic poet and critic.

## 135 To Silvana Mauri
### Milan
[*In possession of addressee: typewritten with autograph corrections, date and signature*]

Casarsa, 19 February 1947

Dear Silvana,

While I am writing in the corner of the room that you now know, you are in the truck which has already almost become a ghost. Let me go on lamenting rhetorically the absurdity of this fact; two hours have not passed since I left you! I have found my solitude again (you know that familiarity, that cretinous nausea which one no longer wants to deal with) and have begun to play on the huge drum of my existence. Since you will get this letter in a moment not analogous to the present I shall offer an exchange for the little bag of gleaming details which you are now giving me: instead of your scarlet pullover, of the movements of your speech, of your forehead, etc., *voilà* you can hear Sior Anzul[1] calling Oriente, the rustle of the *Gazzetino* which my father has moved.

Doesn't it seem monstrous to you if I say to you that the memory has already 'set'. Your handkerchief waving under the stars of Macugnaga has no reason to be envied by the forest kings or by the two of us unravelling the skein of a samba.

Forgive me this 'little epistle' which is due to the good spirits that come from sleep – you see I am all rosy with sleep, nibbled at and grazed all over by paper teeth. But, as you see, I am keeping you company (I am talking about that Silvana who is abandoned to the journey in the truck in a damp and dark corner without any glimmer of light except hope for the huge apple of arrival); I am keeping that Silvana company who, if she knew, would be afraid I might be bored! Let me tell you instead that I shall not go to sleep before 10 or 11 so as to keep you company until you arrive; as you see I run the risk of being ridiculous – but in this case I would only be imitating you (the broomstick). This strange mystical courtesy must be my rhetorical pretext for recognizing in myself the youth whom, I don't know how, your nearness awakened. I feel 'good' – but perhaps, as I told you, this may be due to sleep.

Tomorrow or the day after I shall write to you more seriously. Who knows what that seriousness will be like? It makes me suspicious – I think however that in any case before Rome, if Rome is not to be a betrayal (but I don't know whether I want it to be so), it is not possible to do without an inauthentic language. No, don't feel hurt; it is not a Sibylline phrase, just think of it as stupid. I should like to end now with a soundless sentence, all hidden goodness; but let us laugh at it together, resigned and, above all, gay.

Affectionate greetings,     your          Pier Paolo

PS. Why am I so suspicious of the epidermis of the heart? You are right – let Freud go to the Devil and long live De Amicis;[2] the latter would have advised me better how to express what is after all only natural – friendship, sorrow at the flight of the hours, etc., etc . . . But do you see how I detest these 'names'? The objects are there – but how can you know if I am ashamed to talk of them? Now I have chased you into an infinity of planes (like a barber's mirrors one opposite the other) and you will curse me. On the other hand, you must imagine that I am speaking to your empty picture of Milan towards which you are being carried by a truck running across the plains of the Po.

1  Sior Anzul, a peasant (*Sior* = *signor*).
2  De Amicis (1846–1908), a sentimental nineteenth-century writer, author of *Cuore* ['Heart'].

## 136  To Ennio de'Concini
Rome
[*In possession of addressee: typewritten with autograph date, addition and signature*]

Casarsa, 22 February 1947

Dear Ennio,

I shall return the affectionate tone of your letter by replying to you with sincerity. Do you know why I did not send you a copy of my little book right away? It was the fault of my reserve which I often curse, which more or less unconsciously – that is to say in a cowardly way – prevented me from letting you have *I pianti* so that I would not take advantage, even in the most indirect and remote way, of our friendship which is by now so well launched … Take advantage in the sense that you might suspect a hidden desire on my part to be reviewed. But now that I see that you liked the book for its own sake and not just because of me, I willingly send you a copy and indeed will write a dedication in it – something I have never done for anyone (again because of my habit of telling the truth). Don't be astonished at these 'complexes' – just think that I am nordic, provincial and 'childish'. You know, for the review I had thought of Radiguet's *Devil in the Body*.[1] Would that be all right?

On 15th and 16th March I shall be in Rome with Silvana Mauri, Bompiani's niece. I hope we shall see each other sometimes.

I embrace you,      Pier Paolo

1  *Le diable au corps* by Raymond Radiguet.

## 137  To Sergio Maldini
Udine
[*In possession of addressee: autograph*]

Casarsa, 24 February 1947

Dearest Sergio,

I am writing you the nastiest letter imaginable but perhaps you will laugh at it: it is a question of taking part in a shady game. Lately I have spent a great deal of money and I need a lot; so I should like to pay the insert in LIBERTÀ with the money the paper owes me. I have already written this to Bianchi. Now my father thinks I have already paid, leaving the 1300 lire with you with instructions to give them to LIBERTÀ. Are we agreed then: when you come here, etc. I have handed you the 1300 lire and in any case they have to form a fund for 'Confidenza'. Laugh.

All this because my father has the pleasant habit of reading my correspondence and I wouldn't like a revealing bill to arrive from LIBERTÀ while I am in Bologna.

So I have found a way to tell you that on Wednesday I shall be in Bologna and will stay there till 9 March. On the 13th I shall be in Udine for a lecture; then we shall see each other and maybe the next day I shall take you to Casarsa with me. In fact on the 16th I leave again for Rome and will stay there till the beginning of April. From down there I shall write to you with more calm and good humour.[1]

A hug,         Pier Paolo

1   'humour' in English in the original.

## 138   To Tonuti Spagnol
Versuta
[*In possession of addressee: autograph*]

Bologna, 6 March [1947]

Dear Tonuti,

This time I don't have time to write to you because I am very busy with the exams and other business. But I was hoping to get a letter from you to bring me the perfume of Versuta!

Affectionate greetings,         Pier Paolo

## 139   To Silvana Mauri
Milan
[*In possession of addressee: autograph*]

Casarsa, 11 March 1947

Dear Silvana,

I came back yesterday evening from Bologna and found your letters and your parcel. Do I need to thank you? Let me dump the expression of thanks (which I should so much like to be able to do without reservations) in the gilded pool of our etc. I cradled in my hands for a long time the weight, the solidity and the splendour of the German Theatre and for two hours skimmed the illustrations and the frontispieces, a prey to fits of aesthetic excitement. For the cover[1] I think I shall follow your advice – finely lined in black with two white strips above and below and in the centre, background, the scene with the Siren flying away from the castle (reduced to tiny proportions by the engraving). As for Radiguet, de'Concini writes to tell me that it has already been reviewed in FIERA (and you yourself sent me the review). So I shall talk about it in LIBERTÀ as soon as it comes out with four pages.

I am very pleased about the Solmi affair; but as you know these are feelings of pleasure that last a minute in their true splendour and have an extraordinary tendency immediately to become pale memories.

But let us talk right away about Rome: I shall certainly be there on Wednesday 19th and will leave again on 2 April because on the 3rd I absolutely must be in Bologna for a conference at the I.A.S. So please try not to be later than 20th. You know, I am sure they will be 'inspired' days which will not evaporate like a kind of dream like those in Versuta. The reason is that our surroundings will be equally available to both of us: in any case you will be my 'Cicero' not my Ras[2] (as I am in Versuta). Even without *tremors* we must still admit that the days passed together here were not mediocre: for the time being we shall still remember all too well the little miserable things of the present but just think what splendour the baroque and infernal rags of the masqueraders in Versuta will acquire later on in contrast to the frozen sweat of the sky. And think of the possible enchantment of your talk of Siberia which *happened* in that lane flooded with cold. In the memory the inhibitions of the slush and of the wind will lose a little of their consistency, allowing themselves to be overcome and cancelled out with the greatest ease by our two distant images.

Tomorrow morning I shall write to Fabio telling him to come here at the beginning of April. Did he go to Rome then as you wrote to me? 30 in Aesthetics, etc. seems like a miracle to me for whom the last image of Fabio is that of Macugnaga. I seem to see your family in an atmosphere of *après le deluge* although it is natural that your alarm and distress are not yet over. I hope that in Rome you will have to admit to me once more – in spite of your fear – new facts which may demonstrate to me Fabio's continuous and sure recovery during his convalescence.

About Bologna I have little to tell you; Giovanna[3] is still the same somewhere between hunger and poetry. She actually wears 'proper' men's trousers; I feel that I find her in a state of involution. Otherwise I have spent macabre days over extremely boring books and tremendous 'idealistic' texts of lectures. The thesis I have got out of Battaglia is very good however: 'The relationship between existentialism and contemporary poetics'.[4]

But we shall talk about all this in a week's time in Rome. Do send me your Rome address right away.

A hug,     Pier Paolo

1   Probably refers to a proposal for the cover of *Quaderno romanzo*.
2   Ras: an Abyssinian chief but used in the sense of 'boss'.
3   Giovanna Bemporad.
4   For a degree in philosophy – a thesis that was never presented.

## 140   To Sergio Maldini
Udine
[*In possession of addressee: autograph*]

[Postmark: Rome, 27 March 1947]

Dearest Sergio,

First of all a serious word of thanks; your review[1] is worthy of Stendhal (you are a swine!); certainly apart from all the parentheses and allusions which make up our friendly blood-bond, it is in critical terms one of the most to the point. Here is the schedule round which I shall weave my talk the first time we see each other.

Friday: Falqui
Saturday afternoon: Angioletti and de' Concini
Saturday evening: reception with De Chirico, Isabella Far, Bartoli, Velso Mucci, etc.
Sunday: reception with Leonetta Cecchi, Scarfoglio. Pellizzi, Bartoli, etc.
Sunday evening: reception with Falqui, the Manzini woman, Ferruccio Ulivi, Caproni, G. Petroni
Monday: arrival of Fabio Mauri – reception at Saffi's
Tuesday: arrival of Silvana,[2] etc.

Have learned that I have won the first prize in the All 'Angelo competition: about 40,000.[3] As you see, good days for me.

A hug,     yours Pier Paolo

1   Review of the volume of poems *I pianti*
2   Silvana Mauri
3   First prize for poetry in the competition 'All' Angelo' (for vernacular poetry from the three Veneto regions) for the poem 'Vea' (*Veglia*) ['The wake'].

## 141   To Luciano Serra
Bologna
[*In possession of addressee: autograph*]

[Rome] Thursday night [April 1947]

Dear Luciano,

I am a sponge full of sleep. It is two in the morning and I am writing to you now because tomorrow I want to find the letter ready to be sent off express.

I shall arrive in Bologna at an impossible time, that is to say, 3 in the morning: I don't know if I shall have the courage to come and ring your bell at that hour; in any case, if, impelled by desperate sleep, I should do so would you come and open to me? I know you are a great sleeper but after all you wouldn't lose more than five minutes of sleep. This is the utmost disturbance I shall cause you and your family but for some years I have been training to disturb you and it is right that I should finally get a prize.

I have just come back from an evening spent with Falqui, the Manzini woman, Caproni and Bodini. So till we meet soon and probably at an early hour.

I embrace you. Many greetings and apologies to your family. Try to arrange a first get-together for Monday evening. I shall leave again on Wednesday morning.

A hug,      Pier Paolo


## 142   To Silvana Mauri
Rome
[*In possession of addressee: autograph*]

Casarsa, 8 April [1947]

Dearest Silvana,

Here I am by now in the heart of my Casarsa atmosphere. I am assailed once again by all my habits, by all my miasmas and the unexpected traces of perfumes.

I should like to write to you at length, detail by detail, about my return. I shall do it in a week's time when I have dealt with the bundle of post which has piled up on my desk. It is true I could send to blazes all my other boring correspondents, dedicate an hour to you (an epistolary hour); but I am in a nervous state and my pen is jumping in my hands. You see there is the usual problem of the infinite. And then there is a quantity of recollections, of lazinesses, of moments of exultation, which absolutely prevent me from committing myself. I shall only give you an introduction to my return.

# 1947

Near Conegliano (which by the way last night I dreamt of full of hills and castles) a lament, a distant and metallic song, came and inserted itself in the meshes of the thunder of the train. I realized that it was the bells; but that merely gave me a musical pleasure. That it was to do with Saturday of Easter Week was a detail that left me cold. You should have seen the colours of the horizon and of the countryside! When the train stopped at Sacile in a deep, deep silence like that of Ultima Thule I heard the bells once more so painfully cold, just tinged with melancholy; and in a pond near the station hundreds of toads were singing uninterruptedly, very violent, very clear.

There behind the station at Sacile a road pushes its way into the countryside; I do not know whether I have gone along it or if I have dreamt it. I ought to talk to you at length about it: there was a company of ladies, friends of my mother, with me, then you see a farmhouse with a threshing floor, geese; you reach a bigger road . . . You cannot imagine the deadly feeling of unease this memory gives me. One day I shall have to go to Sacile to destroy it completely. At Pordenone too, the noise of the train had barely ceased, in a heavenly silence, when I heard a bell ringing, solitary, at once out of breath and cold. The passengers, who were struck by it, were silent, tracing on the little opal windows, which gave on to an unending sky, their profiles of wounded animals. About these places I knew everything with monstrous subtlety; they were rotten with familiarity. That bell was accusing me. Then the train moved off for Casarsa.

Forgive me for this bad letter but my hand is shaking because of some anxiety or other. I know that if I stepped out of generalities I would produce a disagreeable effect at this time.

Let me tell you that I keep turning over in my hands a jewel of the purest water: our 2nd of April. I have written a score of hendecasyllables for that little poem I told you about (a false gem).

In Bologna I found them all well, Lionella[1] very sweet. Here I found a letter from Fabio asking me to send him what I had promised. I shall do so as soon as possible, you know, Silvanuta,[2] although the lack of any typewritter causes me great difficulty.

Write to me soon from your room in via Belsiana among the cries of Rome. Very many thanks and an affectionate greeting

Yours,     Pier Paolo

1   Lionella Calcaterra, daughter of Carlo, a friend of the Mauris.
2   A dialect diminutive of Silvana.

## 143   To Gianfranco D'Aronco
Udine

[*In possession of addressee: autograph*]

[Postmark: Casarsa, 30 April 1947]

Dear D'Aronco,

I have written to the F.d.G.[1] accepting willingly the invitation to take part in the jury, etc.[2] Many thanks for your courteous pimping: you really are disconcertingly active and punctual! The one and only number[3] has also reached me: alas, I don't like it. Don't say so to Ciceri, it would be indelicate. But with you, however, I feel I can always be sincere because you have a real sense of humour[4] – that is to say you are urbane. But, that one and only number – what a jumble!

Many cordial greetings,

Yours, Pier Paolo Pasolini

PS. Could you send me the Christian name and address of Francescato?[5]

1   F.d.G. = Fronte della Gioventú: Youth Front, a Communist-based organization.
2   For a poetry competition organized by the Front in Udine.
3   'La regione Friulana' ['The region of Friuli'], edited by Luigi Ciceri in *Movimento populare friulano* (Udine, 1947).
4   In English in the original.
5   Giuseppe Francescato: see article on resemblances between Friulano and Albanian in *Quaderno romanzo.*

## 144   To Luciano Serra
Bologna

[*In possession of addressee: autograph*]

[Casarsa, June 1947]

Dearest Luciano,

With a great delay I am replying to your long letter. I too should like to tell you a lot of things about myself; but to tell the truth there are too many of them and they are too suffused by that *intimacy* which is difficult to express, so I shall refrain from exchanging 'the examination of conscience'.

We shall talk about it the moment I am in Bologna, where I shall turn up for the exams (by the way please send me as soon as possible the usual dates of the two exams and the two sessions for Theoretical Studies and Psychology) and where I shall also turn up probably on my way to Florence. I shall go to Florence to *act* at the Festival![1]

Tell me – by when have I to do an article on Pascoli for Calcaterra and what is the point of it?

*1947*

For *Il Progresso* I include this article, hoping that it isn't absolutely awful.[2]

Please greet everyone from me very warmly: I am very unhappy but always with my zone of emptiness, that is of cynicism or of serenity, whichever you like.

A big hug,          Pier Paolo

1   The festival of the Youth Front where Pasolini and a friend acted a scene from *Nel '46* ['In '46'], later called *Il cappellano* ['The chaplain']; see also Letter 152.
2   'I dispetti' ['The nasty businesses'] in *Il Progresso d'Italia* of 22 June 1947.

## 145   To Sergio Maldini
Udine
[*In possession of addressee: autograph*]

[Postmark: Casarsa, 6 June 1947]

Dear Sergio,

Who would have imagined that I would write to you? I am doing so because of a momentary state of good-humour due to fatigue. I have just come back from Pordenone – or rather from the sun. My father is preparing supper with a pan in his hand (but the sun continues to come into the room with incredible tranquillity; it colours everything with an ethereal yellow as if it were never going to set again). You cannot imagine what a calm there is! You know one can hear from the sunlit courtyard the voices of some men (happy because they will shortly have supper and because their bodies are warm) mixed with the naïve songs of the birds. It is a moment that is not mine, which is why I am talking to you about it so crudely. But was it necessary for me to describe what *hic et nunc* surrounds my body? I did it so that you will not think that I am an image. I am alive, do you understand, Sergio? I shall give you the ultimate proof: I have a sore stomach, I hear the tick-tock of the alarm-clock.

You are too intelligent to take it that my poetic game can be confined to these stupidities, to this useless state of wonder. But then how to explain that I was writing poems at the age of seven? The relationship between me and the blank page has not changed much since then. The illogical element which can be reduced to the one 'desire to play the poet', the pure *furor poeticus*[1] has remained the same in me since these times – very recent ones, I assure you, not distant. The logical reasons have undergone various changes and perhaps even profound, essential ones; but only if expressed with common and consecrated words. If another word existed I would be able to show you how even these changes in my poetic consciousness are basically very slight. Now, in these days, I have said to myself that the aesthetic is useful to me to make the illogical function. Autocriticism, instead of impelling me to follow a normal life, helps me to abandon myself to the abnormal, to get excited with the play of analogies and alliterations, the most illogical things.

But do you know why I started to write you this letter? To tease you about *The Mark of Zorro*,[2] a film I haven't seen. But the reason why I wanted to tease you was the smug way you talk about Mamoulian.[3] Had the news really not got to you? I am warning you that Mamoulian is deservedly popular and is to be put on the same level as a Capra.[4] Watch out, Sergio, and try to read the not inconsiderable pile of volumes on cinema; there are already classical texts and the bibliography on the cinema could fill pages and pages closely written.

The inauguration of the Academiuta[5] will take place on Sunday 16 June. You know that a coach taken by the Philological Society will leave from Udine. Try and tell the other two or three men and a dog who are interested in poetry. In any case I shall come to Udine myself before then.

A hug,     Pier Paolo

1   *furor poeticus*: poetical inspiration.
2   Remake (1940) by Rouben Mamoulian of a classic film about a Spanish–American folk-hero. Douglas Fairbanks starred in the original 1920 version.
3   Rouben Mamoulian (1898–1987), born Tbilisi, Georgia, distinguished Hollywood director.
4   Frank Capra (1897–1991), distinguished Hollywood feature film and documentary director.
5   At the premises in Casarsa, via Guido Pasolini 2.

## 146   To Gianfranco D'Aronco
Udine
[*In possession of addressee: autograph*]

Casarsa, 14 June 1947

Dear D'Aronco,

On Thursday it was impossible for me to be in Udine because I was busy with the *Quaderno romanzo*[1] which is being laboriously brought to the light of day by the Arti Grafiche at Pordenone.

I am not sure what you decided about the future of the M.P.F.[2] but now we shall have to see what they come up with in the Constituent Assembly where the Region is concerned. As for MONEY MONEY MONEY, I shall be able to lay hands on a little as soon as I am back in Casarsa, as I told you. Meantime I am now going to Florence for a week. I am pleased with your polemical piece on

*1947*

our *félibrige*. Publish it! (Wait perhaps till the QUADERNO ROMANZO comes out.)

Many greetings,      Pier Paolo Pasolini

1    *Quaderno romanzo* No 3, Casarsa, June 1947.
2    Movimento Popolare Friulano (Friulian People's Movement)

## 147   To Gianfranco Contini
Domodossola
[*In possession of addressee: autograph*]

[Postmark: Casarsa, 23 July 1947]
Distinguished Sig. Contini,

I am venturing once again and with a great deal of fear into the lake of silence and of distance which divides us, preceded fortunately by the little white flag of the *Quaderno romanzo*, which will at least announce to you that I am still alive and that the Friulian countryside, simply as a pure geographical datum, has not yet absorbed me into the dense network of meridians and parallels.

Along with this letter I am sending you a packet containing the *Ciants di un muart* ['Songs of a dead man'] [1] – that is to say, my collection of poems in Friulano which, were we not living in Italy in 1947, I might dare to hope to see published. I am sending it to you as a way of giving vent to my feelings but also because for some time you have been in my imagination. You are my only reader. Along with the verses in Friuliano there is something which will perhaps surprise you, that is a play, *Il cappellano* ['The chaplain'], which cost me two years of desire. I am sending it to you hoping that you will face up to the hour and a half of reading which it requires and that you will say something about it to me: only following on from this could I try to let somebody in the theatre (but who?) have it.

I am going through a bad period (twenty-five years old, the age at which Gozzano [2] said, farewell to youth: do you remember the appendix to 'L'usignolo'?); I cannot say that I am *disheartened* because my pride will not permit me; but in short I am betraying poetry because of certain naïve youthful aspirations. These solitary fields are not full of what you called my 'complexes'; on the other hand, the affection which ties me to them is by now an incurable illness – mortal. The last stage of my narcissism was therefore indifference! I imagine that you have overcome all these things; and I imagine you will smile if I tell you that after an interval of some years the deeply, passionately felt wish to escape to the Caribbean Sea as cabin-boy in some pirate ship now presents itself to me as the wish to flee to a city, in the most civil sense of the word, perhaps to Venice, to die there and that *exactly* like Thomas Mann's literary figure. Forgive me. Now with extreme impudence I have to ask you for two more little favours, that is to give me news of Carles Cardó, to whom I wrote about a month ago and to whom I sent the *Quaderno* without his giving a sign of life. I hope nothing has happened to him! The second favour is to tell whom I could ask to return to me a copy of the typescript of my 'Usignolo'. When copying it for the competition I made certain changes in it which I no longer remember; and now I would need to have the typescript, polished in this way, to give it to Bassani[3] who promised me to talk about it with a view to eventual publication by the 'Astrolabio' publishing house. Vallecchi in fact, as far as I am concerned, is sunk in a deep silence. In the event of the Nightingale's being published (which I do not believe) would you be happy with a dedication of this nature: 'To Gianfranco Contini with subtle *amor de lonh*.'[4]

Very many warm greetings,

Yours,        Pier Paolo Pasolini

PS. Forgive me for this letter which is so indelicately frank.

1   It was published with the addition of poems in Friuliano written towards the end of 1953 and entitled *La meglio gioventú* ['The best youth']
2   Guido Gozzano (1893–1916), one of the 'crepuscular' poets.
3   Giorgio Bassani, novelist and film-maker with whom Pasolini was to collaborate.
4   Provençal for 'love from afar': the title of a famous song by the twelfth-century Provençal poet Jaufré Rudel.

## 148   To Sergio Maldini
Udine

[*In possession of addressee: autograph*]

[Postmark: Casarsa, 23 July 1947]

Dearest Sergio,

Are you still in Udine? or has Prague swallowed you up by now? In the latter case I would curse fate. In fact if I have sent an article to a reactionary paper,[1] causing the most lively disappointment to my friend Bianchi,[2] it is simply because of the money which you had promised me as a reward. Now there is no sign of that money, and if you have not died in the geographical hell of Prague (meridians, parallels, Carinthia, etc. . . .) please look into it and let me have it as soon as possible.

A hug,        Pier Paolo

1   The *Messaggero Veneto* of Udine.
2   Oliviero Honorè Bianchi, a Triestine writer, editor of *Libertà*.

## 149   To Gianfranco D'Aronco
Udine
[*In possession of addressee: autograph*]

[Postmark: Casarsa, 23 July 1947]

Dear D'Aronco,

I read in *Fogolar*[1] the defence of *your* Zorutti by a certain 'Blanchis'. I am sorry for you but you have found a really fifthrate advocate.[2] Among other things, after having been – to say the least of it – rude where I am concerned, he did not sign it. This all speaks against him, seeing that he boorishly calls me ignorant and presumptuous.

The offensive by the anti-autonomists[3] is taking on dramatic hues! What should one do apart from telegrams? I handed in to LIBERTÀ a fortnight ago a fairly weighty and sharp article. But it simply hasn't appeared in *Libertà*.

Listen, you ought to send me as soon as possible a list of a dozen or so deputies to whom it would be a good idea to send the *Quaderno romanzo*; it would be a new voice, the sign of a conscience and one that's not superficial. Along with the names I naturally need the addresses as well.

Many warm greetings,       Pier Paolo Pasolini

1   An Udine review.
2   Refers to a polemic stirred up by an article on Friulian literature in *Quaderno romanzo*.
3   The opponents of Friulian autonomy.

## 150   To Gianfranco D'Aronco
Udine
[*In possession of addressee: autograph*]

[Casarsa, 7 August 1947]

Dear D'Aronco,

I am writing to you even if from the circular dated 1 VII '47[1] I learn that you are away from Udine, because I hope that in one way or another this letter will reach you.

First of all our argument about Z.:[2] you say that Z. represents everything that is Friulian; but it is precisely this that I question and you must document 'critically' or at least 'psychologically' this gratuitous assertion of yours if you are then, by drawing conclusions from it, to come to suspect that I am against everything Friulian. If you were to insist, then I could insist on my opinion that Z. represents nothing more than Friulian parochialism and that you, by defending him, merely defend that parish pump! Am I illogical?

As for my unjustified absence from the meeting of Thursday 31st, I hoped you would remember that my train leaves Udine precisely at 6 and so I did not think of warning you.

The circular of 1st VII '47 is very intense: I would insist on the need for the Meeting at the Puccini but I would try to get the other parties too to take part officially if only to receive their public opposition, that opposition to which it is so easy to reply.

What is of capital importance then is the compilation of the Statute and I hope that you will not want to have the discussion of it at 6 in the evening. Finally I fervently hope that 'our weekly' can be included among the list of living things.

Many warm greetings,        Pier Paolo Pasolini

1    Refers to a circular from the Movimento Popolare Friulano for Regional Autonomy.
2    Pietro Zorutti.

## 151   To Silvana Mauri
Milan
[*In possession of addressee: autograph*]

Casarsa, 15 August 1947

Dearest Silvana

Yesterday your letter fell on my desk like a stone; on the one hand I found it so inexplicable so illegible (Fabio's typhus) and on the other hand so sweet (the signs of your friendship) that I was bewildered by it with the pure and simple reaction of a long fit of anxiety. Even now I do not know to which of your two letters to reply . . . But I am saying right away – and you will have imagined this – that the news of Fabio's illness disturbed me greatly; not so much for the illness (which one can hush up by considering it quite certainly curable) but because of its threatening hint of a fierce and hostile destiny. I who feel myself so involved in Fabio's fate felt this new blow strike at me from within and not from without. And the first impulse that came to me was to risk coming to this absurd Etruria where you have hidden yourselves away and to run to embrace my poor Fabio.

With you, Silvana, I won't be able to get away with a few words – at the risk of making this letter a source of hurt rather than of consolation; but I need in some way, that departs from my unspeakable (and ridiculous) serenity to which the fields of Casarsa contribute, to salvage for you my over-youthful looks, etc. That absurd serenity which made us pass so many moments of inexplicable and cruel unease: do you remember our conversation in the waiting-room at Casarsa while we were missing the train? And those hateful silences of mine on the steps in Piazza di Spagna? And the red corner of my notebook[1] which stuck out of my pocket causing you that pang? All forms of that silence of mine, of that unknown interior of mine, of that desert zone in which you lost your bearings, perhaps offended sometimes that I did not act as your guide by freeing myself from that kind of persistent cowardice.

But let us take a step back: do you remember my last letter in which I described to you that horrible dream?[2] Well, now I have once again overcome that kind of sadness and protest; I have gone back to my happiness ... to my serenity. The reason for this return is that famous little red notebook in which I was describing, I am not sure for whom, the facts of my ferociously private, intimate life, the unconfessable nature of which made me behave with you in a way that was so unmanly and dishonest. Now I have resumed the thread of my narrative with a new awareness; I have seen that the *involuntary nature* of my pages[3] was not so much due to a psychological mechanism but to a very marked though not very conscious moralistic aspiration. It is for this that I decided today to be explicit with you, perhaps at the cost of losing you. From my first meetings with you will have seen that behind my friendship there was something more but *not very different*, a liking that was quite simply affection. But something that could not be overcome, let us say it, something monstrous interposed itself between me and that affection. Remember something else, Silvana, and you will have understood at last; do you see the two of us again in that restaurant in Piazza Vittorio over our 'calzoni',[4] and remember the heat with which I defended that homosexual woman-friend of yours. Don't be alarmed, for goodness sake, Silvana, at this last word; think that the truth is not in it but in me, that in the end, in spite of everything, I am amply compensated by my joy,[5] by joy which is curiosity and love of life. All this has only one end for you – to explain to you certain restraints of mine, certain incomprehensions of mine, certain uncertainties and false innocences which perhaps (I say, perhaps) have hurt you. I cannot claim to have been so important to you as to have seriously wounded you; on this point I have only some suspicions. Yet I believe you will not blame me for this unexpected frankness and that indeed you will consider it necessary, is that not so? because I must add this as well which is also the true reason for all this speech: you are the only woman for whom I have felt and feel something very close to love, certainly an exceptional friendship.

Have I wounded you again, Silvana? Will you forgive me? Certainly this letter so rapid, precipitate, unexpected, can only make you bitter, perhaps make your blood run cold; but how could our relationship continue in the state in which it was? Everything was made false by it, even Fabio; there had to be recourse to this resolution, to his intervention, don't you think? Besides, how often have I not repeated to you that you would be the only person to whom I would read my notebook? And if I did not do this it was solely so as not to weigh you down with a weight which only I had to bear.

Now it seems to me that this is the propitious moment; in the shadow of Fabio's illness you will be able to think rather with sweetness than with the pain of a friend who has opened himself to you and with himself has opened up a true interpretation of all our common past. Now Silvana, willy-nilly, you have entered the little circle of my life's intimacy, the little room of the 'I'. And so I shall be able to direct towards you the love I feel for you without the confusion of the child caught in the act ... I do not know how you will reply to me, nor what you will think; but in any case remember that this letter after all tells you nothing: I am in fact the same person whom you saw in Bologna, in Macugnaga, here, in Rome ... When shall we meet? Then yes, at last, we shall be able to speak; we shall speak till we go mad with it. Oh how you must have hated that Pier Paolo who lied to you with his silences by the stove in the kitchen at Macugnaga while you put your fingers in the warm water, caught up in the vitality of what you were saying. That will not happen again.

Like a flash of lightning I remember that night when I dreamt of you: we were in Macugnaga in fact but in a Macugnaga happy and marmoreal, a Macugnaga without Monte Rosa or the stream. That corner of the living-room has, clearly, fermented in my poetic memory the smell of the wood, the colour of the divan and the little table ... until it made of it a kind of marble or ambrosial substance, in which you and I argued calmly and with enjoyment. What else must I tell you? Everything else has become so insignificant after the violent commotion which made me write this letter! Now I am thinking about Fabio, annoyed at not being able to do anything for him; try to talk to me about it at length, Silvana; I should like to know how he has been in these last months, his way of accepting the illness. Do you think he would like a letter from me? But if I don't know anything about him I can't write to him.

I am still worried for your mother and father – I see their images in my own parents. So I am expecting a letter from you very soon – one which will reach me in the heart of a life that is unchanged and often very sweet.

A hug,     Pier Paolo

1   For the *Quaderni rossi* ('Red notebooks') see note 1 on pp. 96–7.
2   See Letter 142.
3   See Letter 152.
4   calzoni: a kind of pizza.
5   In English in the original.

*1947*

## 152  To Gianfranco Contini
Domodossola

[*In possession of addressee: typewritten with autograph signature*]

Càorle, 18 August 1947

Distinguished Sig. Contini,

   I have transferred my researches for some days to Càorle from which I
would never have thought to write to you. It is a place between the mouths of
the Tagliamento and the Livenza, so anonymous and desolate that, if by
chance your imagination has ever thought of it, it will certainly have slipped
over it without finding the slightest roughness; I would not be surprised if I
were the first to give you a notion of this arc of the semi-circle between
Venice and Trieste (bearing in mind however your competence in matters of
geography and railways). Càorle is an extraordinary place; certainly the most
multicoloured place in Italy given that there the worn Venetian paint has
taken fire with the wildest colours: blue, brick-red, emerald green, scarlet
and black. The girls with earrings weave nets in the Calles, cutting the air, in
which the smell of fish is visible, with their sharp dialect. The boys have
arched necks, which gleam if they are seen against the sun, and from which
there springs a tuft of the most golden hair falling in a halo over their
wrinkled brows (do you remember de Pisis?: 'wrinkles on the beautiful
youthful face . . .') on a face where virility seems to do nothing but exhale in
an odour of salt and ropes. And those eyes with the oblong and intricate
eyelashes, those lips cancelled by the bronze of the skin: precisely the
Venetians of Saetti. On this arid crescent of sand facing an ugly Adriatic I am
now living in the etymological sense of vacation, so overcome by sensations
that I am writing almost as if I knew by heart what I must say to you. It is that I
am out of my orbit, of my atmosphere; you know the atmosphere which a
horse chewing slowly in front of *its own* manger gives off around itself or a
statue in *its own* corner of a museum. That animal atmosphere, the vehicle of
intimacy and the haunt of extremely private manoeuvres in which, amid the
provinical archaism of Carsarsa, I have contrived to excel! The atmosphere of
the *Cappellano*,¹ in short; and in this connection I could – now that I feel so
free of it – reply to you with enthusiasm but will tell you only one thing – that
is that in Florence,² at a youth rally, the first scene of Act II was acted, and
proved to me that the play was theatrically sound, something of which I was
in any case convinced. But that is not important: I wanted only to tell you now
that it was I who played Eligio . . . So let me have my joke, the reunion has
taken place! But why do you speak to me of 'a liberating act' of 'solution'?³ I
am by now so compliant, so confirmed in equivocation and in doing things
in the family circle by myself, that a commonplace remark of this kind – 'the

284

events of life are not revealed, they are consumed'[4] – leaves me completely satisfied.

Casarsa, 20

And I have absolutely no intention for the time being of lifting myself out of this abject state of mine because I know that the only way to do so would be unique and final: a crisis which would turn my life so upside down as to make me unrecognizable, the thought of which disgusts me – almost as much as the remorse. Naturally a crisis of a religious kind, the threat of which continually appears on the horizon of my life, which is so perfectly secular... Look for example at what happened to me (and things of this kind are not infrequent with me): at the bottom of one of the copies of the manuscript of *L'usignolo*, which you got back for me, I find this poem:

> The seed remains arid:
> among those who seek you, Lord, am I.
>
> Mercy,
> I have cheated your love;
> loving the pleasure of the shade
> I have turned my back on your light
> like a bat.
>
> And I stumble in the dark
> and my hand caresses unhealthy
> loves and in the end
> is wounded by them.
>
> I call on you
> with a dead heart with words
> sought out, of ice.
>
> Warm my icy prayer;
> receive this spirit
> scan the words in syllables
> so that it too can hear
> your miserable hell.
> And so that it may know again
> pain for the comrades' death;
> and drink drunk with joy
> when dawn once again
> strikes the sail of the dark
> and the thunder of the dawn
> re-echoes.

Was it included by mistake? But if by mistake who will assure me that it was not fortuituous? it may be an unfounded assumption but it seems to me that the language of these verses, although more supple and flowing than that Italian of mine which is bound by dialect, still preserves something of its style, some feature.

Moreover a phrase like this: *I have cheated your love* is typically part of the orphic-confessional language used by certain intelligent priests … Could not 'I call you on you with a dead heart, etc.' be the epigraph to the whole of 'L'usignolo'? Then is the mistake that led to this page's being included in my manuscript really a mistake? In spite of certain ambitions of mine, am I so little medieval as not to believe that an Angel violated the 'registered' letter to add this sign? And yet, in spite of everything, I have had no hesitations in my behaviour: I ignored that angelic warning with a shrug of the shoulders.

Also I include in this letter what will – perhaps – be the introduction to *Pagine involontarie* ['Involuntary pages'] or *Casarsa*, the novel which I shall – perhaps – send to Lugano this year.[5] A preface like this is the answer (a somewhat deafening one, it is true, but please take into account that I am sending you the first draft) to the questions in your letter which, as you see, give unity to certain themes which I was keeping as the justification for the excessive sincerity of what I wrote.

Once more, meantime, thank you for the new assurances you give me concerning my Friulano, which owes so much to you; if I had not had your initial consent and support I do not know if I would have arrived at the freedom of *Lengas*[6] (by the way the second part of 'Ciants' [*Canti* – 'Songs'] does not belong to *Lengas* except through a simple faithfulness to chronology. Concerning the Venice prize,[7] I thought you knew about it because my father assures me that at the time he sent that piece from the *Gazzettino* which gave the news about it; here it is). But I must thank you still more for the marked expansiveness of your letter which as always has come to be one of the two or three little flags with which I mark my slow marches across the monotonous green of my Map. Very many warm greeting from yr most dev.ly,

Pier Paolo Pasoloni

*Involuntary pages*
Preface

This confession which has assumed the length of the novel by placing itself within it, in the body of time, was rendered necessary for me by the need to find some sort of way of satisfying my habit of writing. This way presented itself to me in the guise of a sincerity which is perhaps indiscreet, offensive, and which is moreover the exact opposite of that fantastic or purely linguistic manner which, up to about a year ago, had permitted me the minimum respite necessary if I were not to die amid the facts of my life (so long as that life was able to seem like a paradise to me or, better still, a reflection of paradise). These pages are not too involuntary (they are involuntary in the sense of a moral stance which is no longer secular but almost puritanical) if it has permitted me to save myself at least in part from the neutral and brutal indifference achieved by sating oneself with something in order no longer to feel the desire for it ... I have found no other way of writing, to leave hell [as] hell, than this which is so openly direct – almost a document, if the habit of what is called good writing had not always and always against my will taken me by the hand. A gratuitous documents perhaps to the point of inviting irony, certainly a smile: I am incapable of writing chronicles. This is the grave symptom of what an existentialist would call lack of manoeuvrability (a lack I inherit from my mother) because of which any practical connection, even at a high level like criticism, comes apart in my hands. It will be very noticeable, moreover, how the events of the war become puerile (innocuous poetic movements) in this narrative of mine; that humiliates me but what can I do about it? Consciousness of this can only help me to falsify it: something of which I have not taken advantage. I could have done so, it is true, but sometimes I have done it to make this confession-novel less unpleasant by aerating it with memory; but I, like everyone else, live in the continual state of malaise due to the imperfection of reality, which I should like to make perfect immediately in the real, and not later on in the ideal; this is why in effect I regard with scepticism attempts to redeem memory and the undeniable nature of the past.

Casarsa, 15 August '47

1  See Letter 147.
2  See Letter 144.
3  Refers to a letter to Contini which is missing.
4  See Letter 128.
5  For the *Libera Stampa* competition. He presented instead a collection of Italian poems: *Diarii*.
6  *lengas*: tongues, languages.
7  See Letter 140.

*1947*

## 153  To Antonio Russi
Pisa

[*In possession of addressee: autograph*]

[Postmark: Casarsa, 7 October 1947]

Dear Sig. Russi,

Thank you for your letter which found its mark in a way more lively and intelligent than you can imagine. And your judgement is very accurate; but I beg you with all the warmth an author invests in the matters of his craft to consider these choruses as quite simply the fruit of chance (in the old sense of the word) and that they therefore be placed very much in the margins of my poems. There is no need for me to tell you either how great the emotion is that suffocates me . . .

I am in no hurry for them to appear and so can await without the least impatience their turn in publications put out by *Strada*.[1] If in the meantime you wished to choose some for *Strada*, that would give me pleasure.

I do not know when I shall return to Rome – probably this Easter as is now my tradition. Do you know that I came to look you up in via Principessa Clotilde (but you were not at home)? However I am very doubtful about such meetings *de visu*,[2] at least I am afraid of them; people cannot get to know each other in a few hours and I believe Jaufré Rudel[3] died of disappointment.

Many warm greetings from yours very gratefully,

Pier Paolo Pasolini

PS. How could I not remember your review?[4] It caused me to pass one of the nicest days of my life.

1  'Solo lo spettro della Carnia affonda' ['Only the spectre of Carnia sinks'] and 'Le nuvole sprofondano lucide' ['The clouds collapse brightly'] in *La Strada* I, No 2, 1947 – a periodical edited by Antonio Russi.
2  *de visu*: face to face.
3  According to legend, Jaufré Rudel was in love 'from afar' with the Countess of Tripoli, whom he met only to die in her arms.
4  See Letter 66.

## 154  To Gianfranco Contini
Domodossola

[*In possession of addressee: autograph postcard with the heading* Quaderno romanzo]

[Postmark: Casarsa, 10 October 1947]

Distinguished Sig. Contini,

This note has simply been extracted from me by our Tommaseo[1] which caused me to pass an hour of immense pleasure. You must imagine that I read it in bed the other evening but had to get up and in order to subdue my excitement walk up and down my room. Certain passages in that article (the geographical and linguistic placing of Tommaseo, his *hatred* of himself, etc.), I repeat, compel me to thank you.[3]

You are certainly conscious of the difficulties of a person who because of a kind of plain speaking is unable to pay compliments and when he decides to do so proves intemperate and almost a little annoying so you will forgive

Yours must affect.ly,　　　Pier Paolo Pasolini

1　Niccolò Tommaseo (1802–74), Dalamatian poet and novelist who compiled a *Dictionary of the Italian Language*.
2　See 'Progetto per un ritratto di Niccolò Tommaseo' ['Project for a portrait of Niccolò Tommaseo'], published in *Fiera letteraria* of 2 and 9 October 1947; now in Gianfranco Contini, *Altri esercizi* ['Other exercises'], Einaudi (Turin, 1978), pp. 5–24.

## 155　To Gianfranco Contini
Domodossola

[*In possession of addressee: autograph postcard with the heading* Quaderno romanzo]

[Postmark: Casarsa, 20 October 1947]

Distinguished Sig. Contini,

You are in Cremona! But don't you know that this fact not only 'strikes me full in the breast' but devastates me? And into the bargain the roofs – the very ones which for three years (from ten to thirteen) I saw from the terrace of the house in via XX September where I was the old man in the last stages of impuberty. Perhaps it is because, as you say, in this my state of joy[1] I can set free within myself the unknown person, for to imagine you in the one place of my time which is still not deconsecrated, arouses in me an emotion that is almost loving.

Corso Campi, the public gardens, the 'Baldesio', the 'Ponchielli' – that is another illness to which your presence gives the kind of happiness with which these places appear to me in dreams.

Affectionate greetings,　　　Pier Paolo Pasolini

1　In English in the original.

# 1948

## 156  To Giovanna Bemporad
Venice

[*In possession of addressee: autograph*]

[1948]

Dear Giovanna,

I don't know what kind of sinful Angel deposited your card on my little table. Well, after Venice come to Casarsa, you will spend two or three of our typical days.

Have you any good news? I have very little. My life is a dance-floor where the dancers, when they go out to the W.C., don't come back because they have died from a kind of black ammonia.

Greetings. Till soon,     Pier Paolo

## 157  To Luciano Serra
Bologna

[*In possession of addressee: typewritten with autograph greeting and signature*]

[Casarsa, January 1948]

Dearest Luciano,

With what joy I saw your handwriting again! You are really someone back from the dead. And for other reasons as well I thank Flora for having been the Christ who revived my sleeping Lazarus. You lucky person, to have so many things to tell me – I have nothing that is of interest to either of us. I have my life which goes on according to its patterns; it is becoming more and more interior and clear, more and more necessary. But these are things that interest others only if expressed, certainly not if enumerated as I might do with you in a letter. I write articles for the *Mattino del popolo*[1] and other papers and little reviews; every so often, as you will have seen, my signature appears in some less provincial pages. As well I am teaching in Valvasone in a detached section of the secondary school in Pordenone, deriving from it the pretext for a continual, rich pleasure. The old friends write to me little, I know almost nothing about them any more. How grateful I should be to you if at least every fortnight you would write me a couple of lines giving me some news of our Bolognese world; I have, you see, a real need of this. But do not think that I am therefore very unhappy, in fact I would say the opposite, that I am serene and indeed almost a prey to an avid and dionysiac gaiety, were I not continually worried about the physical and, above all, the psychic condition of my father. Write to me soon, then, and unsparingly. Ah, I was forgetting, the article by Contini² is reproduced in the sky-blue number of *Stroligut.*

I hug you affectionately and give my greetings to your family,

Pier Paolo

1  Venetian daily
2  Contini's review of *Poesie a Casarsa, Il Stroligut* No 2, April 1946.

## 158  To Gianfranco D'Aronco
Udine
[*In possession of addressee: typewritten with autograph signature*]

[Postmark: Casarsa, 4 February 1948]

Dear D'Aronco,

I had seen your article¹ in that horrendous *Giornale dell'Arte* ['Journal of art'] (art indeed), which seemed to me to be very unfair; I replied to you therefore in a little article I sent to the *Rassegna adriatica* ['Adriatic review'] without hearing anything more about it. I have been frank, that is, I have not minced my words, which seems to me by this time to be in the tradition of our friendship.

When will the broadcast be?² Let me know in time because naturally the most important thing is to radio-auscultate it if that is what makes the novelty. And the M.P.F? In this connection I have to tell you of a decision I have taken but I shall do so orally since it concerns a slightly delicate matter.

Many greetings from yours,       Pier Paolo Pasolini

1  See 'Per una poesia "friulana" ' ['For a "Friulian" poetry'], in *Giornale dell'Arte* of 24 December 1947.
2  Refers to a cycle of poetry edited by D'Aronco for Radio Trieste.

## 159  To Silvana Mauri
Milan
[*In possession of addressee: typewritten postcard with the heading* Quaderno romanzo]

[Postmark: Casarsa, 5 February 1948]

Dear Silvana,

This morning coming home from Valvasone where I am teaching (it was spring already, a pure air, a sun to give one a migraine) I saw four people in masks sitting by the side of a field. They were four figures, sexless and ageless, with indescribable strips of blue, red, green, purple paper. I went up to them and felt the terror of that night in Versuta, do you remember?[1] I could not help writing to you even if after our last letters of this summer much more than a note would be required. My life is not very serene but would certainly be so if my father were not in a painful state; the doctors say he is a paranoiac. If you reply to me and tell me about yourself and your family (about Fabio) then I shall take back these few lines with their brutal haste.

Many affectionate greetings from your        Pier Paolo

1   See Letter 139.

## 160   To Gianfranco D'Aronco
Udine
[*In possession of addressee: typewritten with autograph signature*]

[Postmark: Casarsa, 25 February 1948]

Dear D'Aronco,

I am writing to you with a little delay because I was hoping to thank you by word of mouth. It felt a little strange to hear that gentleman read, or rather declaim, my 'Leopardine' lyrics with such casualness.[1] But it was a rather endearing effect; honey and ambrosia spread in my aunt's kitchen over the heads of my relations, who were very moved. Many thanks.

I saw the leaflet of the M.P.F. in *Patrie*;[2] naturally I don't like it – are you surprised? In fact although this thank-you letter is the least suitable place I must make up my mind to tell you that I have decided to resign from the Movement.

I shall explain myself better when we talk; meanwhile please do not be too astonished and do not think badly of someone who remains yours cordially,

Pier Paolo Pasolini

1   See letter 158.
2   Refers to an insert in Italian in the fortnightly publication in Friulano, *Patrie dal Friul* ['Homelands of Friuli'], edited by Giuseppe Marchetti.

## 161    To Geda Jacolutti[1]
Udine

[*In possession of addressee: typed with autograph addition and signature; postcard with heading* Quaderno romanzo]

[Postmark: Casarsa, 1 March 1948]

Dear Jacolutti,

I reach you with my ritual epistolary delay; oh, it is not something new among the traditions of my daily existence, rather it belongs to my psychological characteristics. Your postcard gave me a lot of pleasure; it was one of those resources which every so often this sleeping and cruel life demonstrates it possesses. If you see him greet Feruglio[2] for me and accept my warmest good wishes.

Yours,        Pier Paolo Pasolini

1    A (woman) writer from Udine.
2    Arturo Feruglio, editor of a Friulian almanac.

## 162    To Geda Jacolutti
Udine

[*In possession of addressee: autograph*]

[Casarsa, 1948]

Dear Jacolutti,

Menichini writes to tell me to let you have through Titute Lalele[1] an article of mine ('Valvasone'); since I happened to be in Udine today I thought of leaving with you not 'Valvasone' but something similar and unpublished.[2]

I hope that T.L. will not be disappointed. Thank your extremely nice father. (His little verse is delightful: it reminds me at one and the same time of Croquignole and Gozzano; I am talking above all of the cemetery.)

Many warm greetings from yours,        Pier Paolo Pasolini

1    The pseudonym of Arturo Feruglio. See Letter 161.
2    'Topografia sentimentale del Friuli' ['Sentimental topography of Friuli'] in *Avanti cul Brun!,* an almanac by Titute Lalele (Udine, 1948).

## 163  To Giovanna Bemporad
Venice

[*In possession of addressee: typed with autograph signature; postcard with heading* Quaderno romanzo]

[Postmark: Casarsa, 24 March 1948]

Dear Giovanna,

I don't need to tell you my impressions of your book;[1] you know I find your poems very beautiful. And the dress the publisher has given it is a happy choice. On the other hand I would have some criticisms to advance, not without a thread of nasty irony, concerning that pinch of modernity which you wanted to sprinkle over the volume with those dedications and little quotations. We shall talk about them soon in Venice. (But don't be sulky – these are butterflies under the arch, etc.)

De Rocco told me that Izzo is reviewing you in the *Mattino*; the *Fiera* has changed editor and publisher and I no longer know to whom to turn to recommend your book. Here in Friuli all the dailies are forbidden to me because, being reactionary, they do not wish the signature of a communist.

In a few days I shall write to you about your letter to the C.A.F.[2] in Udine and about a review of me in some papers. Excuse the haste.

An affectionate hug,    Yours,    Pier Paolo

1   *Esercizi* ['Exercises'], Urbani and Pettenello (Venice, 1948).
2   Circolo Artistico Friulano [Friulian Artistic Club].

## 164  To Giovanna Bemporad
Venice

[*In possession of addressee: autograph postcard with heading* Quaderno Romanzo]

[Postmark: Casarsa, 10 April 1948]

Dear Giovanna,

I imagine you raging at my repeated silence. In any case Tubaro[1] and De Rocco, although reticent, managed to give me a fairly exact impression of your just indignation. But listen: having just got your last letter and sent off my own, that is to say when everything seemed to be under way, my marching orders to Florence for the Cultural Alliance[2] arrived. So perforce everything had to be held over. Now all you have to do is write to me immediately whether you are staying on in Venice or not; in the first case I shall immediately organize your reading in Udine. As for the review, here too a doubt – also an unexpected one – has arisen: because the *Mattino del popolo* no longer wants my signature (perhaps for political reasons). In fact I sent in an article which has not been published; I would find it annoying to send your review as well as pointless. Could you investigate at the *Mattino* and inform me?

A hug,　　　Pier Paolo

1　Renzo Tubaro, a Friulian painter.
2　A Communist organization.

## 165　To Giovanna Bemporad
Venice
[*In possession of addressee: typed with autograph signature; postcard with heading* Quaderno romanzo]

[Postmark: Casarsa, 7 August 1948]

Dear Giovanna,

How can I hope for your pardon? But I have sat down at my typewriter at least fifty times to dash off the review of your poems; and I am never able to write anything decent. You see I almost feel as if I were writing about my own poems, your exercises[1] are so familiar to me; on the other hand criticism eludes me in the direction of a panegyric note. So I have decided not to do a proper review but an article about you,[2] our friendship, your vocation, etc.

I have nothing to tell you about myself except that I am leading my usual life dedicated to obsessive joys, and that on the other hand I am grief-stricken by the *terrible* state of my father.

A hug,　　　Pier Paolo

1　See Letter 163.
2　'Poesia della Bomporad' ['Bemporad's poetry'] in *Il Mattino del popolo*, 12 September 1948.

## 166　To Luciano Serra
Bologna
[*In possession of addressee: typed with autograph signature; postcard with heading* Quaderno romanzo]

[Postmark: Casarsa, 7 August 1948]

Dearest Luciano,

I have been meaning to write to you for days and I can't make up my mind because of the usual fact that I would have to write a novel at least; it is so long since we saw each other.

*1948*

I am maintaining myself in a state of joy between the erotic and the mystical and of not thinking about the future. My father's 'paranoid syndrome' makes our family life a hell; it is a problem without solutions; I simply do not know how it will end. Believe me there aren't words to express certain situations which arise in our house at my father's moments of crisis. Write and tell me when you feel like coming to see me; you won't spend happy days here, dear Luciano, and I am telling you so because of the conventional duty of a host.

A big hug,      Pier Paolo

## 167   To Giovanna Bemporad
Venice
[*In possession of addressee: typed with autograph signature; postcard with heading* Quaderno romanzo]

[Postmark: Casarsa, 17 September 1948]

Dear Giovanna,

After a long delay and not in its entirety I have read my article on you in the *Mattino*.[1] I felt very unhappy with it; I had already written to you about my scruples and now I see that I was less wrong than I thought. Because of these worries I lost all sincerity and all freedom in speaking about your poetry and because of a kind of compulsion and shyness together I underplayed to the reader the exceptional nature of the book. I should like to make up for my mistake (but there is the prospect of committing one that could be more serious), so that I shall think of reviewing your book for *Convivium* or some other periodical. Write to me soon.

An affectionate hug,      Pier Paolo

1   See Letter 165.

## 168   To Giovanna Bemporad
Venice
[*In possession of addressee: autograph*]

[1948]

Dear Giovanna,

This evening (it is a radiant Sunday) I shall go back to Ligugnana. I feel like that 'happiness' you know of. I didn't laugh on hearing that you lost the rest of the five hundred lire, in fact I was almost moved.

Fraternally yours,      Pier Paolo

## 169   To Franco Farolfi
Parma
[*In possession of addressee: autograph*]

[Casarsa, September 1948]

Dear Franco,

You don't know what a comfort and what sort of happiness you gave me with your letter. I have been on the point of answering a thousand times to the one in which you alerted me to your illness and have never been capable of doing so, not from cowardice but from selfishness. Perhaps I was happy, who knows, I don't remember. Now that at least potentially you too are at peace and full of life I can treat you as an equal and reply to you even in the maddest way. The first thing to say to you is this: I feel as never before my friendship for you, I very much desire to see you. It will not, I imagine, be as the last time in Bologna, a meeting weighed down by the responsibility of *having to find each other again.* Now we can give ourselves credit without securities; who knows what has become of us (at least of me . . . you have a very pure and, what shall I say? Dostoevskian air).

It has never been my luck to leave a hundred-thousand-lire note in a pocket (because of the simple fact that I have never possessed them: I am a teacher as poor as a church mouse), but I imagine our friendship is a bit like finding by chance a hundred thousand forgotten lire. What shall we do with them? Let us spend them in the most lighthearted way possible, without worries of nostalgia; come and see me or say if I can come and see you.

The second thing to tell you . . . is that I have come to the end of that period in life when one feels wise for having overcome crises or satisfied certain terrible (sexual) needs of adolescence and of first youth. I feel like trying again to give myself once more illusions and desires; I am definitely a little Villon or a little Rimbaud. In such a state of mind if I were to find a friend I could even go to Guatemala or to Paris.

For some years now my homosexuality has entered into my consciousness and my habits and is no longer Another within me. I had had to overcome scruples, moments of irritation and of honesty . . . but finally, perhaps bloody and covered with scars, I have managed to survive, getting the best of both worlds, that is to say eros and honesty.

Try to understand me at once and without too many reservations; it is a cape I must round without hope of turning back. Do you accept me? Good. I am very different from your friend of school and university, am I not? But perhaps much less than you think, in fact perhaps I have remained too like the Pier Paolo of that time (of my clinical case of infantilism). If there had not been an unjustifiable and strange drought in these last months I would tell you that poetry is still my job (not to say precisely my vocation or refuge or hygienic habit). My poems are in an incredible disorder and besides I don't like them; for these two reasons I am not sending them to you.

Dear Franco, thank fate for your reappearance (by the way are you bald? I warn you that you reappeared to me 'blond'), I am full of freshness and expectancy.

An affectionate hug,     Pier Paolo

PS. Re-reading my letter I noticed that I had been too brusque; it is a question of measure and civility: one cannot take advantage of the comprehension of others! Besides there was a walk we took on the Montagnola, do you remember? But then I was not human enough to accept humanity in all its forms. But that's enough because you would bore me if you talked too much about your pulmonary infiltration.

Perhaps it will interest you to know a bit about my family: my father is a little better; my mother the same as ever; I am a little worried waiting for my appointment; it would be terrible if I didn't get the post. In general, apart from the calm and terrible fits of conscience, a kind of monthly menstruation, I live in a kind of happiness, in fact entirely taken up by the obsession of this immediate, sensual happiness.

## 170  To Gianfranco Contini
Fribourg

[*In possession of addressee: typed postcard with autograph signature and heading* Quaderno romanzo]

[Postmark: Casarsa, 25 October 1948]

Distinguished Signor Contini,

Your new address contained in the letter to my cousin obliges me to address you directly even if, as you perhaps imagine, between us – on my side with trepidation and shyness, on yours, I believe, with slightly tender absentmindedness – the *line is always busy*. So you will not be surprised if I confess to you that your verdict on my *Diaries* presented at Lugano last year[1] entered my consciousness with the utmost fertility and continues to act and work like yeast. I should have liked to write to you often but never dared to confront the difficult topic. Now I am asking you for three little favours, namely: to give me a short biographical note on Ramuz[2] (about whom, alas, I know nothing and from whom I read an enchanting quotation in a number of *Il Ponte*), to write a couple of words for me about my presentation of the *Ottave* ['Octaves'] by Dell'Arco[3] telling me clearly if I have made some blunders, and finally to explain to me what is so terrible about the word 'utterance'[4] (which in any case I swear to you *a priori* I shall not use any more!)

Affectionate greetings from your      Pier Paolo Pasolini

1  At the *Libera Stampa* competition.
2  Charles-Ferdinand Ramuz (1878–1947), Swiss–French author.
3  See introduction to *Ottave* by M. Dell'Arco, Bardi (Rome, 1948).
4  Refers to the text on the cover of the little volume *Seris par un frut* ['Series for a boy']
by N. Naldini, Edizioni dell' 'Academiuta' (Casarsa, 1948).

## 171   To Luciano Serra
Bologna
[*In possession of addressee: typed postcard with autograph signature and
heading* Quaderno romanzo]

[Casarsa, 14 November 1948]

Dearest Luciano,

The usual two hasty lines, a telegraphic sign of affection. I am back from
Padua where I filled the regulation exam papers[1] with terrible Latin and an
Italian that was a little too modern. You, as always, will have managed to do
things more wisely and with more moderation than I and will go on to the
orals without more ado. Very many thanks for what you intend to write about
my poems; but sooner or later I shall repay you, it's true, Luc! I have heard that
Giuliano[2] has a job in the bank and that he is very rich; this caused me a lot of
pleasure on behalf of your parents who I imagine are at peace and happy with
their enviable sons.

An affectionate hug,      Pier Paolo

1  To qualify as a teacher.
2  Luciano Serra's brother.

## 172   To Gianfranco Contini
Fribourg
[*In possession of addressee: typed postcard with autograph date and
signature, headed* Quaderno romanzo]

Casarsa, 14 November 1948

Distinguished Sig. Contini,

I am back from Padua thinner and humiliated by certain competitive
examinations and find here the two volumes on Ramuz which reached me
with lightning punctuality.

You really want me to make an idol of 'Contini'. No, I am not exaggerating.
You are part of my mythology; and, voluntarily or not, I try to assimilate

myself to you; but what a difficult and dangerous attempt. Imagine that I even quoted you in the competitive examinations in a parenthesis dealing with the criticism of notebooks (fortunately the subject was Dante's *Stil novo*[1] and your name came up of its own accord because of the edition of the *Rime*).[2] Now smile as usual. As for the rest I am at work: what have yet to come are the proofs.

Affectionate greetings from your          Pier Paolo Pasolini

1    *Il dolce stil nuovo*: 'the new sweet style' – the manner of writing of which Dante was one of the main exponents.
2    *Le Rime*: Dante's lyric poems.

## 173   To Tonuti Spagnol
Magreglio (Como)
[*In possession of addressee: typewritten with autograph signature*]

[Postmark: Casarsa, 28 December 1948]

Dear Tonuti,

Thanks for your long and generous letter which didn't have to be waited for like mine. I am replying to you briefly because I have so much to do during these days and in any case we shall shortly be able to see each other and talk comfortably.

I expect to be with you on the morning of 3rd or 4th January; you should now reply immediately giving me instructions about the trip (in Milan does one get a ticket for Magreglio or Como? How do I get from Magreglio to San Primo? Let's hope there isn't a bus; I would prefer a bicycle!)

So I expect a letter from you at once.

An affectionate hug,          your Pier Paolo

# 1949

## 174   To Vittorio Sereni[1]
Milan

*[In possession of addressee: typed with autograph signature]*

[Casarsa, 1949]

Dear Sereni,

Your letter filled me with joy and worries because, having drawers overflowing with prose pieces and poems of which I, and that not by my wish, am the only reader, I find myself very embarrassed in the choice. I pass whole six months at a time without meeting anyone with whom to talk about poetry and I have no other opinion on what I write except my own and that of the jury of the *Libera Stampa* prize; this is not my wish, I repeat, for I am actually so vain that your letter of invitation, for example, for at least five minutes made me the happiest man in the world. I hope finally that you will not curse the moment you wrote to me if now I send you a whole package of verses from which you can choose: it is the only decision – in a certain sense a Solomonic one – that I could take.

I take this opportunity to tell you that I am one of your first readers (*Frontiera*) ['Frontier'][2] and often spoke about your poetry with Arcangeli walking along the Paviglione or in the deserted halls of the University at Bologna.

Cordial greetings, to be extended, with all due respect, to all the editorial staff of the *Rassegna* from your most grateful

Pier Paolo Pasolini

1   Vittorio Sereni (1913-83), one of the hermetic poets, who had written inviting Pasolini to contribute to the review *La Rassegna d'Italia.*
2   *Frontiera* (1941) was Sereni's first volume of poems.

*1949*

## 175  To Sergio Maldini
Udine

[*In possession of addressee: typed postcard with autograph signature and heading* Quaderno romanzo]

[Postmark: Casarsa, 20 January 1949]

Dear Sergio,

On Saturday afternoon we have to get together about the prize;[1] so try to be free. Between three and four I shall be at your house, looking in at the *Messaggero* first (running the risk of possible challenges to a duel), where you can leave word in case you should have anything to tell me.

Affectionate greetings from          Pier Paolo

1  Prize for poetry in Friulano inaugurated by the 'Academiuta di lenga furlana'.

## 176  To Sergio Maldini
Udine

[*In possession of addressee: typed with autograph signature*]

[Postmark: Casarsa, 25 January 1949]

Dear Sergio,

Since we shall see each other on Thursday I shall write you now a real telegram: See that the *Messaggero* publishes the news of the prize which has no jury – a ghost jury. It would be atrocious if the winners found the Club deserted.

A hug,          Pier Paolo

## 177  To Tonuti Spagnol
Magreglio (Como)

[*In possession of addressee: typed with autograph signature*]

[Postmark: Casarsa, 26 January 1949]

Dear Tonuti,

Two words, in great haste, to tell you that you have won the prize of the Academiuta with the poem 'Matina' ['Morning']. Your poems pleased the jury very much. Keep on writing with humility and sincerity. The prize is a very fine picture by the painter Anzil. The other winners (for a lyric in free verse) are Cantarutti and B. Vergili, equal. The prizegiving will take place publicly at Udine on Thursday; I shall tell your father to come and stand in for you. I shall write to you at greater length when I have a little time.

An affectionate hug,      Pier Paolo

## 178  To Silvana Mauri
Milan
[*In possession of addressee: typed with autograph signature*]

[Casarsa, March 1949]

Dearest Silvana,

You told me in Lerici that we two now have less need to speak. Yes, you are undoubtedly right but why admit it? I have found very often that when I no longer have a feeling or a need I can pretend it: and it is not hypocrisy but skill. It is a question of a kind of interregnum in which I, as ruler, take over power; then that feeling or that need becomes adult again and then it once more begins to reign. Naturally such skills are not applied if it is not worth while; and do you think our friendship is not worth while? I think it is; where the past is concerned you represent for me some of the most limpid hours of my life and above all my only trust; as for the future . . . Don't let us make forecasts and don't let us exploit our 'experience'; it is always possible that a little madness has remained. When we met we spoke little with all Lerici around us; besides we could not hope to work up artificially the necessary warmth and we lived on interest. But what a stupendous thing, that sea and those horrible narcissi.

It is almost two months since we saw each other but I assure you it was an eternity. Perhaps because of that slight change I have seen in you and in your family (Ornella's[1] son, Luciano, become 'grown-up' and disappointed).

What is the nature of your change? Perhaps it is like mine – I mean that experience we talked about, but I am not very sure about this because in spite of everything we two are very different. My sickness consists in *not changing*, you understand, don't you? And so if there is some change in me it is purely superficial, and if it is a question of moral decadence (but then we should have to talk differently) . . . but no, not even in such a case could I swear on the essential importance of such decadence. I have lost many scruples and many kinds of timidity; I have learned, for instance, to make love without love and without feelings of remorse. (There, confessed at last, is my change.) 'To become happy is a duty' (Gide), this has been the only duty in my life and I have carried it out zealously – the agony and the illwill 'duty' brings with it. What a miserable person this friend of yours, eh Silvana? But you really have changed a little and if only you knew how much I envy you! For almost ten years now you have been a kind of model of purity all the more authentic because habitual and inborn. Now I see you going away along a road flooded with a kind of sorrowful luminosity where I would be lost, timid and sacrilegious. No, it has nothing to do with the inferiority complex or my maniacal eros; these are things written off which have become humus, undergrowth, matters without any further direct value; it is the individual whom I have constructed on them, and who basically could have been a masterpiece, that does not satisfy me. Is it possible that to find oneself outside nature's pure functionalism should not provoke in the end a nostalgia for nature? Well, let's not talk about that, I am boring you.

Back in Casarsa my usual life engulfed me. Like a stone falling in the water I set up some concentric waves, then the surface flattened out completely. Under the water I live on delicious subterfuges, perfectly happy to be hidden.

I teach, I have big plans (a theatre and an infinite number of para-scholastic things to do: the Superintendent has decided to make the school in Valvasone a kind of experimental school).

I am working a lot in the political field; as you know I am secretary of the San Giovanni branch[2] and that takes up a lot of my time with conferences, meetings, wall-papers, congresses and polemics with the priests of the district, who slander me from the altars. For me, belief in communism is a big thing.

As for my literary calling, my inspiration is all too abundant; the usual verses in Friulano and Italian, a little criticism and the novel[3] which continues to keep me busy I cannot tell you with what agitation and what immense hours of work.

On Sundays I enjoy myself; now the weather is good, one blue gash. On Sunday I shall go back to Malafiesta. Moments of trepidation and sardonic laughter.

But answer me if only with two lines to the palaeozoic affection of your most aff.te

Pier Paolo

If you remember and haven't lost it send me the typescript of *Manuti*:[4] I need it for the novel. If you see Vittorio Sereni ask him if got what he asked me for (that is poems for the *Rassegna*). Warm greetings to everyone especially your dearest mother.

1  Ornello Mauri, Silvana's sister.
2  Of the Communist Party.
3  Probably *Il sogno di una cosa*, Garzanti (Milan, 1962).
4  Probably draft of *Il sogno di una cosa*.

## 179   To Luciano Serra
Bologna
[*In possession of addressee: typed with autograph signature*]

[Casarsa, March 1949]

Dearest Luciano,

I got *Il Progresso* with my article[1] and your postcards with the news of your courses. Magnificent, you have been allowed to take the orals; lucky you, that is something which will certainly not come my way. Next time I shall try to be more cunning and far-sighted.

Now I am going to ask you for a little favour: that is to send a number of *Il Progresso* with my article to Velso Mucci at Il Costume in Rome.

In a few days I shall send you another article (on the poetry in Romagnolo dialect by Antonio Guerra)[2] for *Il Progresso*; but since I wouldn't like to be an unwelcome contributor you should first write me a couple of reassuring lines.

Greetings from me to all your people and all our friends, if you see them, above all Arcangeli.

An affectionate hug,        Pier Paolo

1   'Conversazione letteraria' ['Literary conversation'] in *Il Progresso d'Italia*, 16 February 1949.
2   The article did not appear.

## 180   To Luciano Serra
Bologna
[*In possession of addressee: autograph postcard with heading* Quaderno romanzo]

[Postmark: Casarsa, 11 April 1949]

Dear Luciano,

A devil really does keep putting a stick in the wheels of the train which should bring you to Casarsa. I envy you for your oral examinations and your stay in Rome; I don't at all share your views on Penna and on Gide whom I admire unconditionally. Agreed about Sartre. Agreed to on the bad effects of my solitude in Casarsa; but if only you knew what advantages too.

I shall go to the Peace Congress in Paris.[2] It is a nice way to interrupt my solitude, don't you think? As for the rest, things go on still in the same way. I teach, I write (a great deal) and sin.

An affectionate hug,      Pier Paolo

Many good wishes for Easter – to your family as well.

1   A Communist-inspired 'front' occasion.

## 181   To Vittorio Sereni
Milan

[*In possession of addressee: autograph postcard with heading* Quaderno romanzo]

[Postmark: Casarsa, 11 April 1949]

Dear Sereni,

Many thanks for your frankness and, let me say it, for the kindness of your last letter.[1] The choice of my poetry, however made and whenever it comes out, will be fine: I have faith in you. As for the other proposals I don't know, but perhaps I shall have the chance to do some reviews and then I shall try to send them to you (only if the book reviewed should interest me specially). Has Anceschi[2] not spoken to you about a possible tiny Friulano anthology? He mentioned it by letter to my cousin Naldini and indirectly to me. And have you seen Lajolo?[3] Thanks again and warm greetings,

Yours,      Pier Paolo Pasolini

1   See Letter 174.
2   Luciano Anceschi (b. 1911), professor in Bologna, editor-in-chief of *Letteratura*.
3   Davide Lajolo (1912–84), literary editor, editor of the Communist daily *Unità*, poet and writer.

## 182   To Gianfranco Contini
Fribourg

[*In possession of addressee: autograph postcard with heading* Quaderno romanzo]

[Postmark: Casarsa, 5 May 1949]

Dear Sig. Contini,[1]

Since the evening when I heard about 'Loredana Minelli'[2] (in quotation marks because it is the rather Kafkaesque symbol of my regression to old despairs) I have really wept, and I can confess it to you, I have allowed at least a week to pass before writing to you. It is true that I have read since then something by Minelli in *Libera Stampa* and the quotation marks have vanished, and yet along with the relief goes the bitter curiosity to know – from you naturally, from no one else but you – if I can hope for some mystery . . .

As for the rest, if it interests you, you who are my model, my Nymph Egeria,[3] I can tell you that I am writing, that I am working. But for whom? Once my ardour sufficed but now, as you can imagine, not even this tremendous spring in the plains can convince me that I hope or live.

Yours,        Pier Paolo Pasolini

1   For the first time he addresses Contini as 'Caro Sig. Contini'.
2   Probably refers to not getting the *Libera Stampa* prize.
3   The nymph Egeria: a source of inspiration and advice for Numa, the legendary king of early Rome.

## 183   To Gianfranco D'Aronco
Udine
[*In possession of addressee: autograph*]

[Postmark: Casarsa, 10 June 1949]

Dear D'Aronco,

Here you have with a shameful delay the little article;[1] I hope I haven't come too late.

But in the third number of *Panarie*, Ermacora will publish the one against you . . .[2]

Warm greetings,        Pier Paolo Pasolini

1   'Motivi per una poesia friulano non dialettale' ['Reasons for a non-dialect Friulian poetry'] in *Tesàur* I, 2, September–October 1949.
2   'Poesie d'oggi' in *Panarie*, May–December 1949, in reply to D'Aronco's 'Poesie moderna ma friulana' in the same publication, January–May 1949.

## 184   To Gianfranco Contini
Fribourg
[*In possession of addressee: autograph*]

[Postmark: Casarsa, 7 July 1949]

Dear Sig. Contini,

Some time ago I happened to read in a Swiss paper a little article by Benda[1] which filled me with remorse; it said in fact – very pessimistically – that men write letters only to ask for something, that there is no such thing as a 'pure' correspondence. And Benda is certainly right but it is equally certain that Benda cannot prove his bitter rule by the exception of which I am aware. I hope you will once more forgive me (I have a blind faith in your historical analysis) if I reply to your so disinterested letter with the most typical display of egoism.

In '43 when I wrote 'L'usignolo' (which should be considered to *belong more to the Friulian side than to the Italian one*) I was also writing the *Poesie*, which were then rejected and which I am now sending you so that you can see the phyletic line that led me to the *Diaries* and the *Unica divinità* ['The only divinity'] and which, as you see, belong entirely to the Italian side (with a stench of literature as you rightly say). Is it a case of orthogenesis? Now that you have in your hands the authentic progenitor, you will be able to judge better.

It is certain however that I shall continue to write diaries for a while – and, please note, I have laid my hand on my conscience – that is to listen to the monotonous and obsessed note of my one-way biography.

How could it turn out otherwise? Have you perhaps forgotten that 'mortgage' of which it was precisely you who spoke?[2] For the first time – you who are so perfect – let yourself be caught in a tiny lapse of attention and led me to believe, with despair, that your demand on me was only a statement of good wishes, a *flatus vocis*.[3] In fact I have had to accept that the NO, first of all of Lugano[4] and then – the one that counts – yours, did not produce salutary reactions in me and merely confirmed a certainty which I already had.[5] For me now it is a failure, defeat. The only consolation (and leave me it, please) is that I am still sitting on the point of the sword knowing that sooner or later everyone is removed from such an uncomfortable position. What kind of renewal is that?!

For the time being I see nothing in my existence, which has practically become mad between extreme ugliness (a paranoid father, a suffering mother, a hard life in school, life among stupid and treacherous people, political hatred and a conspiracy of silence) and extreme happiness which you know where and how to diagnose . . . Now I feel like collapsing into confession, like giving in, at the very end of this letter, to that impulse which – what joy! – you envy me. But what about your permission? Would it not really be a little too irrational?

Warm greetings from your most affectionate

Pier Paolo Pasolini

1   Julien Benda (1867–1956), French critic and essayist.

2  Refers to the *Poesie* of 1945.
3  Refers to one or more letters from Contini, which are missing.
4  Refers to taking part in the *Libera Stampa* prize with the unpublished *Diaries*; see Letter 182.
5  Refers to a missing letter from Contini; see Letter 195.

## 185  To Gianfranco Contini
### Fribourg

[*In possession of addressee: typed with autograph signature*

[Casarsa, 1949]

Dear Sig. Contini,

This morning I got a little book by Antonio Guerra[1] (a name which I think is not new to you), *La S'ciuptèda*. I know that nothing escapes you (not even that terrible article of mine in *Il Tesàur* to which you referred in a letter to Archimede)[2] but I should like to avert the one in a thousand possibility that Guerra's gunshot has not reached your ears.

I read the book at once, in one go, and don't yet know whether I can tell you flatly that it is good; yet I should like to have done for these places in the Friulian plain what Guerra has done for his part of the country.

Perhaps in a few months I shall have to ask you for a new favour, that is to say, for topographical information about the surroundings of Fribourg and precisely about the road between Fribourg and Morat (?) about which Archimede talks to me with the utmost lack of linguistic interest. A chapter of a novel on which I am working (and of which up to now the only thing certain is the title: *La meglio gioventù*)[3] is dedicated to the stay in Salvenach of Archimede, who has become Milio. For this I shall perhaps need you, apart from the fact that while I write I always feel your eyes on my pages.

Many warm greetings from your        Pier Paolo Pasolini

1  Antonio Guerra, a poet from Romagna.
2  Archimede Bortolussi, a young Friulano who emigrated first to Switzerland, then to Australia, and who under the name of Milio became one of the characters in *Il sogno di una cosa*.
3  This title was transferred to the collection of Friulian verse while the novel acquired a new one: *Il sogno di una cosa*.

*1949*

## 186    To Vittorio Sereni
Milan

[*In possession of addressee: typed with autograph corrections and signature*]

[Casarsa, 1949]

Dear Sereni,

I really don't know how I could find the choice of poems you propose to me wrong;[1] I naturally suppose that there exist many other possible choices – given also my incontinence in writing; however your point of view looks to me like the one with the best chance of guessing the right 'note' for the choice. Very probably the direction I am taking will have looked extremely 'out of tune' and I realize it only notionally and with a certain justifiable alarm, if you bear in mind that – in my solitude in Casarsa – I staked a great deal on *L'unica divinità* ['The only divinity'], in fact it is with this collection that I tried for the *Libera Stampa* prize again this year.

Certainly you were not required to give me an opinion on these latest verses of mine! Yet I seemed to read between your lines an opinion which, as I am telling you, alarmed me. At all events yes, the list of poems you propose to me has the great merit of being 'anthological' – that is to say not very compromising, and I of course give you my approval, regretting only a little not being sufficiently compromised. There is only one little difficulty: perhaps you know that Ungaretti as writer of the preface and Lajolo as secretary, are compiling an anthology of the poets mentioned at the Saint Vincent prize, one of whom I also am; but I do not know which of my poems they have chosen.

Now I do not know to whom to turn to learn about this anthology and since it would be absurd for someone like me who sees his things published so seldom to see the same poem published twice, I hand over to you the task of asking for information from Lajolo whom you probably have occasion to meet. Forgive me if I am indiscreet but since you are obliged to read so many of my verses you will already have understood all about me and will not be surprised at the indiscretion.

As for *the question of when* my verses will come out in *Rassegna* I assure you that I do not feel it to be at all a problem: you have already given me five minutes of great happiness.

Warm greetings from yours,        Pier Paolo Pasolini

1   See Letters 174 and 181.

## 187   To Vittorio Sereni
Milan

*[In possession of addressee: typed with autograph corrections and signature]*

[Postmark: Casarsa, 14 September 1949]

Dear Sereni,

I shudder at the idea of having formed however tiny a black spot on your conscience; if another time for reasons which I know very well, since I experience them daily, you should take a long time to reply to me, don't, please, think of me as 'one of the 25 people to whom one ought to write' – to be added perhaps to a review perpetually postponed; I give you permission not to imagine me angry at the wait but rosy and laughing and leading the most heedless of lives. Besides, I had already warned you of my ascetic patience. I am very happy about the review by Caproni (whom I imagined to be still in Rome and to whom I had sent the little book at La Fiera.)

On the other hand a quick word with Lajolo would be urgent because I imagine that the Saint Vincent anthology is about to appear.

Affectionate greetings from yours      Pier Paolo Pasolini

## 188   To Gianfranco D'Aronco
Udine

*[In possession of addressee: typed with autograph signature]*

[Postmark: Casarsa, 14 September 1949[

Dear D'Aronco,

Here you have a collection of verses for *Strolic*.[1] I have been somewhat unsure about sending them given that, as you well know, I possess no verses 'suitable for *Strolic*'; now it is up to you. If the poem to be published were the only one then I would naturally go for the 'Lied'. How is the *Tesàur* doing? And the Movement? Have you recovered from the traumas of Gorizia?

Warm greetings from yours,      Pier Paolo Pasolini

1   The popular almanac of the Philological Society, edited by D'Aronco. The 'collection of verses' did not appear.

*1949*

## 189   To Ferdinando Mautino[1]
Udine

[Postmark: Casarsa, 31 October 1949]

Dear Carlino,

About three months ago, as perhaps you know, I was blackmailed by a priest: either I gave up communism or my scholastic career would be ruined. I answered the priest as he deserved through the intelligent lady whom I had made my intermediary. A month ago a Christian Democrat deputy, a friend of Nico's, warned me very indirectly that the Christian Democrats were preparing to ruin me; from pure *odium theologicum* – they are his words – they were waiting like hyenas for the scandal which some gossip led them to expect. In fact the moment the manoeuvre about Ramuscello, still from *odium theologicum*, had succeeded (otherwise it would have been a question of a little unimportant matter, an experience of some sort which anyone can have, in the sense of an entirely internal matter) the Sergeant of the Carab.[2] in Casarsa probably carried out the orders given him by the DC[3] by immediately informing the members of the ruling class, who in their turn caused the scandal to burst in the Superintendent's office and in the press. My mother nearly went mad yesterday morning, my father is in an indescribable condition: I heard him weeping and groaning all night. I am without a job, that is to say reduced to begging. All this simply because *I am a communist.* I am not surprised at the diabolical perfidy of the Christian Democrats; but I am surprised at your lack of humanity; you know perfectly well that to speak of an ideological deviation is idiocy.[4] In spite of you I remain and will remain a communist in the most authentic sense of that word. But what am I talking about, I who at this moment have no future? Until this morning the thought sustained me of having sacrificed myself and my career to loyalty to an idea; now I no longer have anything on which to lean. Another person in my place would kill himself; unfortunately I must live for my mother. I hope that you may work with clarity and passion; I have tried to do so. For this I betrayed my class and what you call my bourgeois education; now those betrayed have taken their vengeance in the most pitiless and terrifying way. And I am left alone with the mortal pain of my father and my mother.

A hug,      Pier Paolo

Published in *Pasolini: cronaca giudiziaria, persecuzione, morte* ['Pasolini: judicial history, persecution, death'] by various authors, Garzanti (Milan, 1977)

1   An official of the Communist Party in Udine.
2   Carab. = Carabiniere. The military corps of the Carabiniere is also a police force with detachments in all towns and villages.
3   DC = Democrazia Cristiana: the Catholic party.
4   Refers to the article by Mautino (Carlino) published in *Unità*, 29 October 1949.

## 190   To Antonio Faleschini[1]
Osoppo

[*In possession of Gianfranco Ellero: typed postcard with autograph signature and headed* Quaderno romanzo]

[Postmark: Casarsa, 10 November 1949]

Dear Sig. Faleschini,

Thank you from my heart for your letter; it was a comfort to me and you cannot know how slender the trickle of friendly voices is in this ugly, tangled mess. The hyenas and jackals of Udine have revelled in my bankruptcy after, naturally, having prepared it with devilish skill. Need I tell you that in spite of everything I remain substantially unscathed?

Thank you again and affectionate greetings,

Yours,       Pier Paolo Pasolini

1   Friulian scholar.

## 191   To Teresina Degan[1]
Roveredo in Piano (Pordenone)

[*In possession of addressee: typed postcard with autograph signature and the heading* Quaderno romanzo]

[Postmark: Casarsa, 10 November 1949]

Dear Degan,

I shall tell you about the background,[2] which you can imagine in any case, when we meet. It was a perfect job, meticulous and frighteningly well timed: we have a lot to learn from them.[3] As for me I stand guilty of downright indecent naïvety. It is perhaps late for learning but the seven or eight friends who have survived keep repeating that I am very young and can put myself together again. A fine consolation! There was a moment when I could have drowned in the dungheap of bourgeois hatred but now I am recovering and if ever I had vitality I feel it on me now like a new suit. What you say about having made myself a defender of the working classes is by now an element in my thinking which is absolute and, do not fear, nothing will change it.

Warm greetings from yours,       Pier Paolo Pasolini

1   Communist Party member.
2   Reference to the accusation of corruption of minors.
3   Reference to Catholic bourgeois circles in Udine.

*1949*

## 192 To Giacinto Spagnoletti
Milan

[*In possession of addressee: typed postcard with autograph signature and headed* Quaderno romanzo]

Casarsa, 13 December [1949]

Dear Spagnoletti,

I also think we can say 'tu' to each other right away: apart from anything else we are the same age (I was born in '22 and you in '21 if I remember rightly). And having established a certain intimacy, almost like that of members of the same club, I can tell you right away without feelings of shame the great joy your letter gave me by tracking me down miraculously here in the depths of the blackest province where I would never have imagined you knew I existed.

Two years ago (in Cappelli's in Bologna) I saw your anthology[1] and with some reservations, especially with regard to Pascoli, on whom I did my degree and so pride myself on having a certain competence, it looked to me like a good job and I should have liked to buy it; and I did not buy it only for the eternal reason of cash which you will know about. To appear in an anthology of modern Italian poetry edited by you[2] simply makes me exult. In a few days I shall send you what you ask for; unfortunately my publications in Italian are almost nil; I shall have to send you a lot of typewritten stuff, indicating to you the reviews in which they appeared; not a great deal by the way. Thank you again, dear Spagnoletti – and as for considering you a friend, to me it is obvious and natural after a period of almost ten years during which I know you have been working in the circle of my closest interests.

Many warm greetings from yours,       Pier Paolo Pasolini

1  See G. Spagnoletti, *Antologia della poesia italiana contemporanea*, Valecchi (Florence, 1946).
2  See G. Spagnoletti, *Antologia della poesia italiana (1909–1949)*, Guanda (Parma, 1950).

## 193  To Franco Farolfi
Sondalo

[*In possession of addressee: typed with autograph signature*]

[Casarsa, 31 December 1949]

Dearest Franco,

I shall write to you at length in a few days; meanwhile two words. I have lost my teaching post because of a scandal in Friuli following a charge made against me of the corruption of minors.

Fortunately we wrote to each other this autumn so the business will cause you less surprise. The thing that cost me the ruin of my career and this tremendous biographical jolt is not in itself very serious; it was all a put-up job due to political reasons. The Christian Democrats and the Fascists seized the occasion to get rid of me and did it with repugnant cynicism and skill. But I'll tell you about that another time.

Today is the last day of the year; I have nothing before me, I am unemployed – absolutely without any hope of work; my father is in the physical and moral condition you know of. A suicidal atmosphere. I am working furiously at a novel[1] on which I am building all my hopes including practical ones; I know they are mad hopes but in a kind of a way they fill me. In my condition I naturally could not come to Parma. Who knows now when we shall see each other again and I am very sorry because I still feel that I am very fond of you.

A kiss,       Pier Paolo

1   *Il sogno di una cosa.*

# 1950

## 194   To Silvana Mauri

Milan

[*In possession of addressee: typewritten; a page from a lost letter*]

[Casarsa, 18 January 1950]

... Milan gave me too heedlessly and too incompetently for me to feel sure of being happy about it, that Fabio is getting better. Perhaps you will have read in the papers about the Brescia trial;[1] I was there too as a witness and came back to Casarsa yesterday evening. I was tempted at Brescia to come and visit you but then I thought that by now I am too much of a Giovanna Bemporad.

My future, more than being black, is non-existent. I am giving myself another month or two to finish *La meglio gioventú*,[2] my novel (which I mentioned to you in Lerici), and then I shall go away – where to? To Rome, to Florence, perhaps also if things turn out in a certain way, to Lebanon. I realize that I have understood nothing about the world and that I am going further and further away from it; I do not find – not the strength but the reasons to rehabilitate myself, to redeem myself, to resign myself, to camouflage myself: one of these actions, in short, which people carry out who have some idea of what sort of a world it is in which they live – and go more and more off the rails, Rimbaud without genius. Please write and tell me something about your life and about Fabio.

Affectionate greetings from yours,      Pier Paolo

1   Dealing with the massacre of Porzus where his brother Guido was killed.
2   See Letter 185.

## 195   To Giacinto Spagnoletti
Milan

[*In possession of addressee: typed with autograph signature and postscript*]

[Casarsa, January 1950]

Dear Spagnoletti,[1]

Forgive my long delay but making a choice of my poems[2] has been a much more difficult and complicated operation than I imagined; and then I unexpectedly had to leave for Brescia for the Porzus trial because my brother is one of the Osoppan martyrs and I was called as a witness.

As you see the manuscript parcel is thick while the number of published poems is slim and almost insignificant. In the selection I have made (which is almost a quarter of my work from '43 to today) I preferred to be indulgent here and there since down here I have no friend to consult and, anthologizing myself alone, I was afraid of discarding things which someone else might have found passable. I was particularly undecided about 'Alla ricerca di mia madre' ['In search of my mother'][3] which should perhaps be entirely reworked and about many diaries. I don't know what else to tell you if not to repeat that I am immensely grateful, that you have caused me the greatest joy.

Most warm greetings from yours,      Pier Paolo Pasolini

PS. I have put a little red mark against the poems already published for your greater convenience. As for more precise information on the number and date of the journals in which they appeared I cannot give you them because I have not kept them.

1   Curiously, in spite of what was said in Letter 192 to Spagnoletti about using the familiar 'tu', in the present one Pasolini uses the formal 'lei'.
2   See Letter 192.
3   The seventh section of the collection *L'usignolo della Chiesa Cattolica*; it was later called 'La scoperta di Marx' ['The discovery of Marx'].

## 196   To Vittorio Sereni
Milan

[*In possession of addressee: typed with autograph signature*]

[Casarsa, January 1950]

Dear Sereni,

You wrote in your last letter, if I remember rightly, that if I had some other poems which I felt it worthwhile letting you read for possible publication in *Rassegna*[1] I should send them to you. Now Spagnoletti has asked me to send him a collection of my poems for his new anthology which will come out from Guanda; this finally decided me to collect and correct my output from '43 to '49 and I have made a parcel of it which I have sent to Spagnoletti. I think that if you still intend to publish anything in *Rassegna* you should certainly take a look at that parcel; there is for example a section, 'L'Italia', written this September, which I think you could consider.

Do you ever see Spagnoletti? In that case you could ask him for my typescripts for two or three days.

Forgive me this unexpected reappearance and accept my most warm greetings,

Yours,      Pier Paolo Pasolini

1   See Letter 174.
2   Fifth section of the collection *L'usignolo della Chiesa Cattolica*, Longanesi (Milan, 1958).

## 197   To Giacinto Spagnoletti
Milan
[*In possession of addressee: typewritten with autograph signature*]

[Casarsa, January 1950]

Dear Spagnoletti,[1]

The joy your letter gave me I leave you to imagine – and do imagine it in the most elementary and naive form. And let me tell you at once that I am very happy to go along with the idea of choosing 'L'Italia'[2] for your anthology: I could not have hoped for anything better.

About my poetry you say things which are very true and very clear; not only about its values – which I am too inclined to doubt – but also about its reasons. They are ten years of work and – I realize it now – of desperate work. I am one of those people who began to write verses at the age of seven; then in adolescence I committed all the errors of taste imaginable (Carducci, D'Annunzio . . .),[3] actually filling a chest with manuscripts. And so I continued until yesterday like someone condemned to forced labour. Contini wrote to me a little time ago asking me to put my hand on my heart and wonder if it was really possible for me still to live 'on the point of the sword'. He evidently expected a negative answer, but after laying not one but two hands on my heart I had to answer *Yes*. That is why I am a little – no, very – frightened by what you call future adventure, that is to say by your expectation. You see, I don't know if living like this, *à la* Rimbaud, without his genius, can still be resolved in the literary calling; I have atrocious suspicions about my future.

But they are suspicions; I have practically never been so rooted in the habit of writing, in the penal servitude of my calling.

Forgive me for talking so much about myself; perhaps it was the wrong thing to do and I had begun to write to you only to thank you and to express my gratitude to you. It will be rather difficult for me to come to Milan and the idea of your bar[4] gives me goose-flesh; I am shy with that shyness that makes relationships difficult. But I should like very much to get to know you just as I should like to know Sereni – the person you call 'Vittorio the best' around whom I have built a whole Proustian framework; since I am now unemployed and kept by my father I shall have to make up my mind to go out into the world; probably for the moment to Florence, and hope we shall be able to meet there.

I have to thank you also on behalf of my father and mother who want me to ask you when the anthology will come out.

The most warm greetings from      Pier Paolo Pasolini

1   In this letter Pasolini reverts to the familiar 'tu'.
2   Gabriele D'Annunzio (1863–1938), poet, novelist, dramatist, adventurer.
3   The short poem from *L'usignolo della Chiesa Cattolica* which appeared in the *Antologia della poesia italiana* (1909–49).
4   The 'Blu Bar' in Piazza Meda, a meeting place for Milanese writers.

## 198   To Vittorio Sereni
Milan
[*In possession of addressee: typewritten with autograph signature*]

[Casarsa, January 1950]
Dear Sereni,

At the announcement of the death of *La Rassegna*[1] no one will have cried with a sadder voice than I: Long live *La Rassegna*. Not that its loss is serious for me; but it is one of the little strokes of bad luck which, as the saying goes, make one's cup overflow. And I think that fewer cups were so likely to overflow as mine. And it is impelled by desperation and by the upsets of these last months that I have decided for the first time to send my verses to a publisher;[2] this is Bompiani with whom I have some connections but up to now I have had no reply.

Could you, directly or indirectly, get a sympathetic word or two to him? You see I don't know what I am asking for because to me what goes on in Milan has no *tertium comparationis*,[3] it is Greek to me; I ask you for this help more or less nominally – more out of a scruple of conscience and a sense of duty towards my mother and my father than anything else.

*1950*

Spagnoletti has written to me with much liking for you and much dislike of literary circles in Milan; he has promised to publish 'L'Italia' in his anthology and all that remains is for me to hope that Guanda[4] doesn't blow up.

Warm greetings from yours,     Pier Paolo Pasolini

Sereni replied to this letter on 18th January 1950:

*Dear Pasolini,*

*A good idea to send things to a publisher; but I am not sure that Bompiani is the best choice. He very seldom publishes books of poetry and it cannot be said that those which have appeared show much flair on the part of this same Bompiani: Father D.M. Turoldo, the Masino woman... You will remember Erba, one of the people from Libera Stampa. He had a good deal of support but found he was given the answer that this publisher only rarely publishes poetry.*

*It is probable however that your book has been sent out to be read by someone who has a high regard for your things. I shall find out and try to be of help to you.*

*But if it did not work out why not try Mondadori?*

*There is a fifty-fifty chance that the book has been sent to me to read.* Specchio *is at a turning point. There is the risk – with the ways things are going – that they will put in new people but who? It would really be a pity if someone were to come in – the kind that write poems on the lines of* The Waste Land *packing them with little progressive bits (I am of the Left but not in this sense) and that you were to be left out, whereas the opposite would be desirable.*

*However we shall write to each other again about how to deal with the situation.*

*Affectionately, yours     Vittorio Sereni*

*Spagnoletti was over the moon to me about* L'Italia. *I imagine that the Pasolinian measure has shown itself at its best in this case (your rose, your periwinkles, your pansies – which are peerless – relate to my first reading of your things) and I am anxious to read the work.*

Latest!

30 January 12 o'clock

*Spoke this morning to Mondadori; they are* favourably interested *in the matter; expect further news from me.*

This letter Sereni followed with another on 31 January:

*Dear Pasolini,*

*Following on my latest of yesterday I am writing to tell you that this morning they phoned me to say that a person you can trust has taken the text from Bompiani and passed it to Mondadori.\* It is a result of yesterday's conversation (but they tell me that Bompiani, as I foresaw, was not inclined to publish your things for reasons that are of a purely administrative-economic nature). I have also been given the job of writing the usual opinion for the publisher and the text will be passed to me in a week's time. I intend to suggest and back up the view that it ought to be published in* Specchio.

*I hope the business pleases you from every point of view. And this seems the right time to me, always excepting any hitches of a bureaucratic-economic nature.*

*So wait for further word from me and be of good cheer.*

*Affectionately yours,     Vittorio Sereni*

* *You ought to know also – so that you don't think that I did something out of order – that the person with whom I spoke was already well disposed towards you and knew – I don't know how – that the text of your things was in Milan.*

1   See Letter 174.
2   This is a collection of Italian poems divided into three sections: *L'usignolo della Chiesa Cattolica, Diario, Lingua.*
3   *tertium comparationis*: a third term which allows one to make a comparison between two others.
4   The publisher for whom Pasolini was to work on an anthology of popular song.

## 199   To Silvana Mauri
Milan
[*In possession of addressee: typewritten with autograph signature*]

[Casarsa, 27 January 1950]

Dear Silvana,

Forgive me for writing to you again but my last letter was too important to me. It was the last absurd thread of hope, wasn't it? Meantime my situation has got tremendously worse although a worse state of affairs was not even imaginable. My father, caught up in one of his usual crises, of wickedness or madness, I no longer know which, has for the nth time threatened to leave us and has entered into agreements to sell all the furniture. You have no idea what my mother is reduced to. I can no longer bear to see her suffer in this inhuman and unspeakable way. I have decided to take her to Rome tomorrow, unknown to my father, and to entrust her to my uncle; I shall not be able to stay in Rome because my uncle has led me to understand that he cannot keep me there but I hope that for my mother things will be different. From Rome I do not know where I shall go, perhaps to Florence; as you see I am in a very sad state (bear in mind the trial and the state of my father when he will find himself alone) and a friendly voice may be the thread that binds me to some reason for living. Why do you not answer me? I may have acted badly – I say so because I cannot think of any other plausible excuse for your silence – and in that case forgive me; it is very difficult to behave well, to be reasonable, when one finds oneself in my condition. So if you want to write to me, my address for some days at least will be c/o Gino Colussi, via Porta Pinciana 34, Rome. Then I do not know where I shall go or what I shall do; my life is at a most decisive turning-point. I hope that in some part of the world there will be a little work, even the most humble, for me. They say one does not die of hunger. So on the eve of my adventure I send you my most affectionate greetings, also to your family.

Pier Paolo.

*1950*

## 200   To Franco Farolfi
Sondalo

[*In possession of addressee: typewritten with autograph signature*]

[Casarsa, 27 January 1950]

Dearest Franco,

Two lines to let you know what I am facing. My father, after thousands of similar scenes, has said he is leaving us and going away; meantime he has made arrangements to sell all the furniture. The situation is so desperate that I have decided to leave tomorrow for Rome with my mother; I shall leave my mother at my uncle's hoping he can keep her and I shall leave again at once perhaps for Florence or for Milan, to do what? I really do not know; I shall have at my disposal at most twenty thousand lire; I shall look for work; I have to find it. Will it be possible in ten days or so? But at this point I have no other alternative. Write to me, if you have anything to tell me, c/o Gino Colussi, via Porta Pinciana 34, Rome.

A big hug,      Pier Paolo

## 201   To Vittorio Sereni
Milan

[*In possession of addressee: autograph*]

Rome, Feburary 1950

Dear Sereni,

I have been in Rome for a week and that is why I have taken so long to answer your letters which I received here. They are letters which gave me a comfort such as you cannot imagine and more even than the wonderful news for the way in which you gave it.[1] I felt the breath of kindness and do not know how to tell you my gratitude. Concerning the publication I am very pessimistic, when one is reduced to the tragic and humiliating conditions in which I find myself today one cannot but think that some economic–administrative snag will come up. *The person whom I can trust* you speak of is perhaps Silvana Mauri: if you meet her she will be able to give you some information about me, past and present.

I greet you with a warmth that is already affectionate and thank you very much also on behalf of my mother who is here to share my misfortunes and hopes.

Yours,      Pier Paolo Pasolini

To this letter Sereni replies on 8th February:

*Dear Pasolini,*

*There is no need for thanks; to believe in certain things rather than in certain others and to do one's best for their success is also a way of defending one's self. Yesterday I got the manuscript which I shall read in the next few days. I hope my intervention may be more successful than it was for* Rassegna [. . .] *Be brave and think that things are on the right track.*

1    See Letter 174.

## 202    To Silvana Mauri
Milan

[*In possession of addressee: typed, with autograph corrections, date and signature*]

Rome, 10 February 1950

Dearest Silvana,

I had decided to write to you again this morning because I was sorry about my last letter,[1] which was a little too full of despair; I hope you have forgiven me. Today for no reason I was less oppressed, I had a little bit less unhappiness. Now it is already evening and I am here with your letter before my eyes. You know I am living near the ghetto a couple of steps from Cola di Rienzo's church;[2] do you remember? I have gone over again, two or three times, our walk in '47 and even if I have not found once more that sky and that air – from the tremendous grey of the ghetto to the white of San Pietro in Montecitorio; the Jewish woman sitting beside a chain against the dark doorway; the storm with its smell of resin and then via Giulia and the Farnese Palace, that Farnese Palace which will never be repeated again as if the light after the storm had sculptured it in a veil – I was amazed and consoled.

Even now my head is buzzing with the cries in the Campo dei Fiori while the rain stopped. But this warmth which floods me like a moment of repose I owe to your letter; it is here soiled with lipstick and cream, from the carnival at Versuta and the flowers in Piazza di Spagna. In those days in '47 my descent which became a precipice after Lerici[3] began; I cannot yet manage to pass judgement on myself not even, as would be easy, to give a negative judgement, but I think it was inevitable. You ask me to speak to you truthfully and *with a sense of shame*; I shall do so, Silvana, but when we *talk*, if it is possible to talk with a sense of shame in a case like mine: perhaps I have partly done it in my poetry. Now since I have been in Rome I just have to sit at my typewriter for me to tremble and not know even what to think; the words seem to have lost their meaning. I can only tell you that the ambiguous life – as you rightly say – which I led in Casarsa I shall continue to lead in Rome. And if you think about the etymology of ambiguous you will see that someone who leads a double existence can only be ambiguous.

For this reason I sometimes – and lately often – am cold, 'nasty', my words 'hurt'. It is not a 'maudit'[4] attitude but the obsessive need not to deceive others, to come out with what I *also* am. I apparently did not have a religious or moralistic education or past but for long years I was what is called the consolation of my parents, a model son, an ideal scholar . . . This tradition of mine of honesty and uprightness – which had no name or faith but which was rooted in me with the anonymous profundity of something natural – for long prevented me from accepting the verdict. You must imagine my case as being a little like that of Fabio without psychiatrists, priests, treatments and symptoms and crises, but that – as was the case with Fabio – I distanced myself, absented myself. I do not know if there are any longer ordinary measures for judging me or if one should not rather have recourse to the exceptional ones adopted for sick persons. My apparent health, my equilibrium, my unnatural resistance, can be deceptive . . . But I see that I am looking for justifications once again . . . Forgive me – I only wanted to say that it is not possible for me nor will it ever be possible to speak of myself with shame: and instead it will be necessary often to stand in the pillory because I do not want to deceive anyone – as basically I deceived you and other friends who talk about an old Pier Paolo or of a Pier Paolo who has to be a new self.

I do not know what to understand by hypocrisy but now I am in terror of it. Enough half-words – the scandal has to be faced, I think St Paul said . . . I think in this connection that I want to live in Rome precisely because here I shall be neither an old nor a new Pier Paolo. Those who like me have been fated not to love according to the rules end up by overvaluing the question of love. A normal person can resign himself – that terrible word – to chastity, to lost opportunities; but in me the difficulty in loving has made the need for love obsessive: the function made the organ hypertrophic when, as an adolescent, love seemed to me an unattainable chimera: then when with experience the function had resumed its proper proportions and the chimera had been deconsecrated to the point of being the most miserable daily matter, the evil was already inoculated, chronic and incurable. I found myself with an enormous mental organ for a function which by now is so negligible that only yesterday – with all my misfortunes and my fits of remorse – there was an uncontainable despair for a boy sitting on a low wall and left behind for all time and in all places by the tram as it went along. As you see I am talking to you with extreme sincerity and I do not know with how much shame. Here in Rome I can find more easily than elsewhere the way of living ambiguously, do you understand? and at the same time the way of being entirely sincere, of not deceiving anyone as I would end up doing in Milan: perhaps I am telling you this because I am discouraged and place you by yourself on the pedestal of someone who is able to understand and feel for me: but the fact is that up to now I have not found anyone as sincere as I would wish. The sexual life of others has always made me ashamed of mine: is the wrong all on my side? It seems impossible to me. Understand me, Silvana, what I have most at heart is to be clear to myself and to others – with a clarity that has no half measures, is ferocious. It is the only way to make me forgive that terrifyingly honest and good boy which someone in me continues to be. But about all this – which will continue to be a little obscure to you because it is said too confusedly and rapidly – we will be able to talk in a more leisurely way. So I think I shall stay in Rome – this new Casarsa – all the more since I have no intention either of knowing or meeting literary people, persons who have always terrified me because they always ask for opinions while I have none. I intend to work and to love, both desperately. But then you will ask if what has happened to me – punishment, as you rightly call it – has been of no use to me. Yes, it has been of use but not to change me and even less to redeem me; but it was of use to me to understand that I had touched bottom, that the experience had been exhausted and I could begin from the beginning but without repeating the same mistakes; I have liberated myself from my iniquitous and fossil perversion, now I feel lighter and my libido is a cross, no longer a weight that drags me down to the depths.

I have re-read what I have written to you up to now and am very unhappy with it; perhaps you will find it a little chilling again like the letter after Lerici, but bear in mind that then my descent into distrust, incredulity, disgust was beginning, while now I am rising up again, or at least so I hope. You will be able to guess how much of the pathological and febrile lies in my words, what traces my despair of these days has left there. Other phrases you must not take at their face value. For example, 'Rome, this new Casarsa' is a phrase which mustn't make you throw up your hands even if it is rather nasty; there was also a good Casarsa and it is the latter I wish to regain. This latest crisis in my life, an external crisis, which is the trace of that internal one which I postponed from day to day, has, I hope, re-established a certain equilibrium. There are moments when life is open like a fan, you see everything in it, and then it is fragile, insecure and too vast. In my statements and in my confessions try to catch a glimpse of this totality. My future life will certainly not be that of a university professor; by now I bear the mark of Rimbaud, or Campana[5] and also of Wilde, whether I want it or not, whether others accept it or not. It is something uncomfortable, annoying and inadmissible, but that is how it is; and I, like you, do not *give in*. From certain of your words ('. . . among things which have caused you pain if they really caused you pain') I seem to understand that you too, like many others, suspect some aestheticism and some complacency in my case. But you are wrong, you are absolutely wrong in this. I have suffered what can be suffered, I have never accepted my sin, I have never come to terms with my nature and have not even become used to it. I was born to be calm, balanced and natural; my homosexuality was something additional, was outside, had nothing to do with me. I always saw it alongside me like an enemy, I never felt it within me. Only in this last year I let myself go to some extent; but I was exhausted, my family situation was disastrous, my father raged and was nasty to a sickening degree, my poor communism had made me hated, as one hates a monster, by a whole community, a literary failure also loomed; and then the search for an immediate pleasure, a pleasure to die in, was the only escape. I have been punished for it without pity. But this too we shall talk about or else I shall write to you about it more calmly, now I have too many things to say to you; I shall add right away in this connection a detail: it was at Belluno when I was three and a half (my brother was not yet born) that I felt for the first time that most sweet and violent attraction which then remained within me – always the same, blind and sinister like a fossil.

It did not yet have a name but was so strong and irresistible that I had to invent one myself: it was 'teta veleta' and I write it for you trembling, so much does this terrible name invented by a child of three in love with a boy of thirteen frighten me – this name which belongs to the fetish, the primordial, the disgusting and the affectionate. From then on it is a long story which I leave it to you to imagine if you can. Getting on for nineteen, a little before we met, I had a crisis which was within a hair's breadth of being identical with Fabio's; but instead it resolved itself in a neurosis which was not very serious, in a state of exhaustion, in an obsessive thought of suicide (which often comes over me still) and then in recovery. In '42 in Bologna, do you remember? I was as strong as a horse by then and sound as a tree. But it was a flourishing state that was not to last.

You have been something special to me and different from all the rest; so exceptional that I can find no explanation for it – not even one of those spectral explanations which are so concrete, which we seize on in our internal monologue: in our astute manoeuvring of our thought. From the time when you opened the door to me in Bologna, a few days after I met Fabio, and appeared to me in the shape of a 'thirteenth-century madonna' (I think I said this to you) at the Malga Troi,[6] in Milan, after the war, at Bompiani's, in Versuta, in Rome, you have always been for me the woman I could have loved, the only one who led me to understand what a woman is, and the only one who up to a certain point I have loved. You know what that point is: but now I have to tell you that sometimes I know neither how nor when I passed it timidly, madly, but I did pass it. If you want to think of a similar situation think of *Strait is the gate*;[7] but I have never said anything to you about my tender feelings, because I did not trust myself. Don't make me add any more, understand me. In my last letter I wrote that you were the only one among my friends in whom I was able to confide; and this simply because you are the only one I truly love, to the point of sacrifice. For you, to be of help or a comfort to you, I would do anything without the least shadow of indecision or of selfishness.

Now here, your letter if I look at it, moves me ferociously, I feel tears in my eyes; I think of what I have lost, at the waste of my life into which I have been unable to welcome you.

I cannot go on with this letter; the other things I have to say to you I shall write tomorrow. I could continue only if I could let myself go, but I cannot, I have to melt so much ice within me. Forgive me if I have written you another nasty letter but if I could write nicely, with all the niceness of another time, then this letter would not have been necessary. I am furious with myself and my impotence, while I would like to tell you of all my tenderness and my affection.

A hug,      Pier Paolo

This letter is a reply to a letter from Silvana Mauri posted on 2 February 1950 which contained another written on 23rd January:

Letter of 2 February

*Pier Paolo dear,*

*Do you see this letter all grubby with lipstick and face-cream? It is the one I wrote in reply to your first letter immediately after getting it so as to cheer you up before your journey and which I mysteriously found yesterday in a wastepaper basket. While I was already busy about the poems I was at least calm because that letter would have reached you. Now I am writing in haste to tell you: 1) you must not show that you know but it is almost certain, read that as certain, that Mondadori will publish your poems; 2) to send me the novel when the time is ripe; 3) to give me notice of your movements so that I don't lose track of you and can write to you; 4) to go in my name to Brianna Positana Carafa, via Principessa Clotilde 7; don't tell her anything about yourself; she knows you through me; go there because she can perhaps help you to set your mother up.*

*I shall soon send you other addresses of people who are outside the literary scene, trustworthy people who can be a support to your mother. In the meantime write to me immediately. In a few days I should have the definite answer about the poems and will write to you at once, so that you could come up and meet your editor and maybe have a bit of money. But now, in the meantime write to me.*

*Ciao, a hug,      Silvana*

*And give an affectionate hug to your poor dear mother.*

Letter of 23rd January

*Pier Paolo dear,*

*Since your dear and lovely visit last year to Lerici (exactly a year about now) I have always and sometimes passionately wanted to write to you to give you excellent news about Fabio, about myself (I am getting married in April), to keep better track of you and your work and not to give in once again to that silence which is quick to bury any impetus. But to your letter, I don't know if you remember, the one that was so chilling.[8] I did not know what to reply. Words one can always find but to what end? If it becomes a game which by now we know how to play only too well, I was grieved because it seemed too easy an examination of*

*1950*

*conscience, too definite, too obscure for me who am still used to talking about feelings, hopes, fits of remorse and pain, and could not get rid of the impression of seeing you as lost, false, in a blind alley, everything having become you – that dear Friuli, the sorrow of your mother, your communism, the model school, your conscience, highly literary matters, well-exploited material for your intelligence but static now (the material, not the intelligence) on the point of becoming desiccated like a dead leaf.*

*What happened then in the summer merely pained me to see you so brutally punished, a clamorous result which will, however, manage at last to prise you free from the ambiguous conditions of your life – now over and done with – in Casarsa to which you were so absurdly attached. Dear Piero, if you only knew the difficulty I find in speaking, in doing something at such a distance in matters which caused you pain, if they really caused you pain and in what way I do not know. But how can I not react, not fear, if I love you? In the evening, before falling asleep, I mentally write you very long letters, and it may be the confused clarity of the letters of a half-waking state but you know how it happens, sensibility and love have no limits and obstacles then to understanding; I seem to identify perfectly your mistake, not your guilt, and the beginning of a new Pier Paolo. But then by the light of day I see that I know too little to be able to write to you with conviction. Why didn't you come to Brescia? Every day I read the reports of the Porzus trial, I read your name among those of the witnesses, and I was expecting you. Perhaps it does not matter to you, but I should like us to have a long talk with you there defending yourself, explaining to me without any more reticences; if time has taken so much from us it has at least presented us with this great and full and absolute possibility of talking sincerely and with immunity in affection and friendship, an immunity, dear Piero, which is, however, without resignation on my part. For if there were resignation (you know I am incapable of it for those I love) I would not even write to you. It is not redemption I am speaking about but only of hope, of a life which is not a miserable waste. I am only saying to you now that to me it seems a good thing that you should leave Casarsa, I don't know what the Lebanon offers you, but certainly I warn you against going to Rome, to Florence, to Venice, cities to be feared, where you would find once more the imprint of lives already dead and the scenery ready to receive you like a pale reflection, I see you in these cities killed without the shedding of blood; but go instead to Bologna, rather come to Milan, such an ugly city, imperfect, crushing, which does not indulge in anything, does not support anything and where you would find friends who love you. Meantime I shall see what can be done about the poems you sent me and I want to tell you right away how things stand. Although I have been back working at the publisher's [Bompiani] I have never happened to hear the name of Danilo Dolci[9] so much as mentioned – something that never ceases to astonish me. I have not been able to get to the bottom of things at once because I have been in bed with a high temperature and an obstinate bronchitis for three weeks, but I intend to take the matter up personally the moment I go back to the publisher's in a few days.*

*I think that the Anthology of Christian Poetry is part of a series of publications for the Holy Year – publications which so far as I know are still a little vague and 'à côté'. As I have told you, it is shameful, but for the moment I know no more. As far as the Usignolo della Chiesa Cattolica goes I have few hopes in Uncle Valentino,[10] who has an obstinate repugnance towards and a tenacious lack of interest in poetry – in fact the house has never published volumes of poetry except Father David and Paola Masino, for reasons which were unconnected with art. (Valéry, too, it is true but many years ago.) Do you authorize me to try elsewhere then? With Mondadori for example? The boy [Ottiero Ottieri][11] whom I am going to marry, who is your age and would like to teach rather than work in a publisher's, is, cursing, with Mondadori. And I can also try, perhaps successfully because it is you, otherwise it would be a waste of effort. Instead, as soon as you have finished it and if you*

328

*don't already have someone to send it to, let me have the novel. I urge you strongly to do this* [. . .]

*Now dear Piero, I leave you, I have a temperature and am a little tired of this stiff machine; write me a long letter please, with truth and shame, about yourself, what you would go and do in the Lebanon, if you like the novel at least, if you are suffering, if you are not suffering; please. As soon as I get back to the publisher's I shall write to you.*

*Meantime I hug you, Silvana*

1 See Letter 199.
2 Cola di Rienzo (1313–54), tribune of Rome, reformer, executed.
3 See Letter 178.
4 Maudit: refers to Verlaine's critical and biographical study of – among others – Rimbaud as a poet cursed from birth.
5 Dino Campana (1885–1932), sometimes described as 'an Italian Rimbaud', who challenged contemporary literary institutions. Died in a mental home.
6 *malga*: a mountain pasture.
7 A reference to Gide's novel: *La porte étroite.*
8 See Letter 178.
9 Danilo Dolci (b. 1924 in Trieste), poet and writer, interested in modern experiments in pedagogy and social integration.
10 The publisher Valentino Bompiani.
11 Ottiero Ottieri (born 1924), poet and novelist.

## 203 To Nico Naldini
Casarsa

[*In possession of addressee: typewritten with autograph signature, correction and postscript*]

[Rome, February 1950]

Dear Nico,

Still no news after what I wrote to you in my letter to Aunt Giannina. I have had one of the usual missives from my father in which he announces his unshakeable decision to sell the furniture and to leave.

It will be a good idea if you take steps, to be on the safe side, to save my books.

You could put them some in Aunt Giannina's kitchen and some in your room; bear in mind that the two sets of bookshelves were bought with my mother's money and so belong to us.

Silvana has written[1] to me telling me that the publication of my poems in *Specchio* is certain; but until I have signed the contract I don't want to have illusions; she also warmly recommends that as soon as the novel[2] is finished I should send it to Bompiani.

Write to me oftener. Greetings to all.

A hug, Pier Paolo

Save my typescripts at once as well – some in the right hand side of the desk, some in the desk and the notebooks of *Atti impuri* ['Impure acts'][3] in the second compartment of the bookcase.

1   See Letter 202.
2   *Il sogno di una cosa.*
3   These are the five 'red notebooks'.

## 204   To Vittorio Sereni
Milan

[*In possession of addressee: typewritten with autograph signature, corrections and postscript*]

[Rome,] 10 February 1950

Dear Sereni,

Allow me to thank you, and that repeatedly, for what you are doing for me and how you are doing it, above all because it is a very difficult moment for me and I could be, if that were to happen, altogether without hope; perhaps it is to the credit not only of yourself but also of the circumstances, but the air of goodness and of solidarity which blows from via Scarlatti[1] does me an immense amount of good.

If you are reading my poems (I tremble and not so much for the editorial reactions as precisely for your verdict), bear in mind that what is contained in those pamphlets is about a quarter of what I have written in verse since '40 but that it ought to be pruned here and there: 'Alla ricerca di mia madre' ['In search of my mother'] should all be excluded except for the 'Canzonette' ['Little songs']. 'Inferno e paradiso proletario' ['Proletarian hell and heaven'] is not yet finished. As for the *Diarii* I know that they have to be slimmed and in this I could also follow your advice or that of some other friends (for example Spagnoletti and also Mauri herself whose instinct I trust).

I have lived too much alone and out of this world in these last years to be able to make certain rather painful cuts on my own. Finally I could also count on the advice of Contini (or even on a preface?)

I thank you again and greet you with affection,

Pier Paolo Pasolini

PS. The other typescripts which I sent you [illegible] if I am not mistaken are stuff that has been discarded. You can burn them.

1   Street in Milan where Sereni lived.

## 205   To Silvana Mauri
Milan

[*In possession of addressee: typewritten with autograph date, corrections and signature*]

[Rome,] 11 February 1950

Dear Silvana,

I am continuing my letter of yesterday more and more strangely peaceful. The unexpected break with my world has isolated me in another world which seems to me empty and unreal. However, because of the complete lack of regrets, I see that Casarsa had been outgrown. Basically what concern me most now are the practical problems – and from the weight and difficulty of my letter of yesterday you will have understood how at this moment the essential problems come apart in my fingers or in my throat like a 'mea culpa' mechanically repeated.

It seems to me that everything has remained in Friuli, like the landscape. Rome stretches out around me as if it too had been drawn in an empty space but yet it has a strong power to console; and I immerse myself in its noises without in that way hearing my own out-of-tune notes.

Yesterday Sereni wrote to me,[1] he too encouraging me to hope: in these last two days the importance of being published by Mondadori has assumed its proper proportions; I hope for it so ardently and desperately that I don't dare to say it to myself. I must begin to give private lessons; since for the first months I shall be the guest of my uncle it is not really urgent to find a permanent job; but it is certain that the shorter this period of hanging about, full of worries, the better it is for all. You said in your last letter that you would send me some addresses; if the people you are talking about can get me some tutoring then please let me know soon; I cannot bear to be idle, because – as I told you – I am physically incapable of writing. Do you know Angioletti?[3] Caproni tells me that Angioletti is at the radio and can get work (cultural news, odd pieces, for broadcasting) which is well paid; it seems he doesn't find it easy to get contributions of this kind (in fact Caproni got tired of it right away), but for me in these days it would be an ideal job. If you can put me in contact with Angioletti please do so. In the other letter I said I didn't want anything to do with Roman literary figures; I was exaggerating. I shall make a connection with those who seem 'good' to me. You understand, the ones that confront things. Caproni and Angioletti seem to me to be two of them. My mother will perhaps get fixed up with a lady from Ferrara who is very nice; it would be an excellent arrangement; but should things not turn out well I shall turn to that friend of yours forthwith. How can I thank you, Silvana? I shall never be sufficiently grateful to you. Moreover I have to ask you for advice because I trust your instinct and your experience very much.

331

There are three novels I am writing. Don't be afraid. In these last months I have done nothing but write even ten hours a day. Do you remember the little red notebooks[3] which stuck out of my pocket that night when you missed the train? They were the diaries of my love for Tonuti. I began them in '46 when I had already finished with it, and continued to write off and on until '48; there was a little volume of about a hundred pages.

But I was not happy with it. Chronologically I went from poetry to prose and the things in prose were my stammering attempts. In these last months I have taken the book up again, I have alternated the diary with narration in the third person: in short I have objectivized (in the secondary sense of this word, perhaps also in the primary sense) what happened, changing the names of the protagonists and the places, reconstructing everything with less commitment to confession and greater liberty of invention. But the book, which should come to 200–250 pages still lacks two or three chapters. The title is *Atti impuri* ['Impure acts'].[4]

The second book is entitled *Amado mio* ['My love']; it is a kind of sequel to *Atti impuri* but still more liberated in terms of fantasy from biography. The protagonist resembles me even less than the one in *Atti impuri*; in fact is very different from me as a character. For him condemnation is implicit; yet his love for a youth is told like a legend, exactly at the short-story length – even if its typographical length will be about two hundred pages. It is my 'nasty' book, the one that hurts. The action takes place partly in Friuli (remember what I told you about Malafiesta?), partly in Rome, the Rome of the suburban cinemas, of Trastevere, of the building sites and also of via del Tritone. I think this is my lesser book but, within its limits, the most successful. But for this too the last three chapters are missing.

Finally there is the novel on which I am staking everything: *La meglio gioventù*,[5] which is very different from the other two and very complex: just to give you an idea you must think of a strange cross – in the direction of Dostoevskian narrative – between Proust and Verga,[6] not without some elements of that Babylonian, eccentric and composite language which in Italy has a magnificent model in C. E. Gadda.[7] The plot is very complex and very ordinary. Do you remember *Cronaca di poveri amanti* [*A Tale of Poor Lovers*]?[8] It is a little like that but with the presence of time which is lacking in Pratolini's tapestry. The events I think I told you in Lerici, but in these last months they have been enriched and finished. Three young men from the people are added to the main characters (one emigrates clandestinely to Yugoslavia, another to Switzerland,[9] another works in a quarry and will end up by dying – the other two return discouraged and starving). These are true facts (even if I have put them together) like the love story of Don Paolo (who loves a boy, Cere, who goes off to America with his father and then during a strike Don Paolo shields Cere's brother, Nello, with his body and dies), the spiritual experience of Renata (who loves Don Paolo); but bear in mind that neither the love of Don Paolo nor that of Renata are spoken of and the reader has to imagine them completely – and finally, because he is a communist he is chased out of Friuli where he teaches and before going away organizes a *festa*, the takings from which are for the trial of Nello, an amoral liar and fanatic, and the religious business with Aspreno (in which I shall hint at Fabio simply because of the experience I had then, since Aspreno, as a case, is very different from that of Fabio): these things being immersed in the experiences of all the peasant youth of Friuli (the class of '27, 'the love-stricken class' as people wrote on the walls of S. Giovanni).[10]

I have barely sketched the events which, as you can imagine, are much more complex and detailed.

I have already written more than half the book; I expected to finish it before leaving Casarsa. Instead here I am, incapable of writing a clear sentence. But I hope my asthenia is temporary. Should the ability to write return, what book do you advise me to finish? By now only an editor's commission can give me the power to work and finish what I am doing. I would never have thought that things would end up like this; on the other hand, in this I discover an unexpected dignity.

I should like to say a great deal about Fabio and ask you a great deal; but I am afraid, the same kind of fear as the one I feel when I think of Mondadori; my brain does not respond and wraps itself in darkness to ward off bad things. I confess that I cannot imagine the new Fabio and that the thought of him in that extraordinary village[11] causes me more worry than joy. But I am happy for you, for your relief, which is mine as well. Time will give Fabio a future as it will give one to me. Let's hope so.

I hug you with much affection,      Pier Paolo

1   See Letter 204.
2   Giovanni Angioletti (1896–1961), journalist and writer.
3   See Letters 151 and 203.
4   *Amado mio*, preceded by *Atti impuri*, Garzanti (Milan, 1982).
5   Title later changed to *Il sogno di una cosa*.
6   Giovanni Verga (1840–1922), Sicilian novelist, a major nineteenth-century realist.
7   Carlo Emilia Gadda (1893–1973), novelist whose best-known work uses Roman dialect.
8   A novel by the Florentine neo-realist novelist Vasco Pratolini (1913–91).
9   See Letter 185.
10   Don Paolo, Cere, Renata, Don Aspreno: these characters did not appear in the final version of the novel.
11   The 'Children's Village' at Santa Marinella on the coast north of Rome. 'Fabio is at peace, he is active, he is alive, he is living among the ex-street urchins of Santa Marinella who love him, he is painting . . .' (from Silvana Mauri's letter of 25 January 1950).

## 206  To Franco Farolfi
Sondalo

*[In possession of addressee: typewritten with autograph signature]*

[Rome, February 1950]

Dear Franco,

I have taken a long time to reply to you and am now doing so because it would be shameful if I postponed it again. But I do not feel like talking to you about my case, I am fed up with it, overburdened. Perhaps you are dramatizing the scandal a little too much; its importance is purely practical in that I am left without a job, without hope of work, and with my family in the condition you know of. Yes, the most serious problem is now that of finding any kind of job, even as a worker. In a month or two I shall leave here, perhaps for Florence, and there I shall work out something or lose myself completely. You do not know what hellish darkness my future is. As for the scandal, I have digested it; after all I had a right to this scandal, didn't I? In this world incredible things like this happen. Think what a frightening mechanism can form in the brain of an unfortunate like me: sex-prison, love – having one's face spat at, tenderness – the brand of infamy.

And you know, in temporal and spatial terms, how much of us sensuality, that dragon with a million heads, occupies; this division from the rest which never ends.

I am writing two long stories, *Amado mio* and *Atti impuri*, in which I now, naturally, with no hints any more, speak of my loves.[1] But I am writing many other things – now I am definitely sentenced to my vocation for life. In a few days I shall send you my poems from '43 to '49, but on condition that you send them back to me shortly because it is the only copy I possess.

And you? Your girls, about whom you talked to me so candidly without knowing that for me every word on the subject was a mortal wound? Have you solved it, the insoluble problem of sex? It is a figure which increases in a geometric progression with each unit you substract from it; only with death will the zeros turn up.

I think my sentence is that of living among insincere people.

I wanted to tell you so much but I see that I am getting muddled; we really ought to talk. And I love you more and more, feel more and more bound to you and to our true years,

An affectionate hug,      Pier Paolo

1   See Letter 205.

## 207   To Nico Naldini
Casarsa
[*In possession of addressee: typed*]

[Rome, February 1950]

Dear N.,

Do you remember the main character in *Sotto il sole di Roma* ['Under the Roman sun']?¹ Well, his brother, seventeen years old, much more beautiful than him, has become my friend. We met yesterday evening through the actions of a god. I have not slept at all, I am still all trembling. I shall need money – take a parcel of books (Laterza editions, philosophers) and with some excuse go to Padua and sell some of them for 3 or 4 thousand lire immediately, and then send me the money express by the end of next week; not a money order but a registered letter.

Professor Vaccher² must also let me have a thousand lire from the school; try to get that as well, perhaps through Scodellaro. By the way how are Sco. and D. Rossa?³ So I beg you. Rome is divine. I absolutely must work and make a lot of money.

Ciao,          P.P.

1   *Sotto il sole di Roma*, neo-realist film by Renato Castellani (1947).
2   Sergio Vaccher, colleague at the school in Valvasone.
3   Pupils at the school.

## 208   To Sergio Maldini
Bologna
[*In possession of addressee: typewritten with autograph signature*]

[Postmark: Rome, 20 February 1950]

Dearest Sergio,

A letter to tell you that I am not at Casarsa but in Rome. You won't expect me to write you a volume as my situation would demand. The day before yesterday a young man between 25 and 30 with a black overcoat threw himself into the Tiber; it could be me. Imagine everything that lies under and around a candidate for the disgusting 10 metres deep Tiber under Ponte Mazzini.

Your tirade against human wickedness, with which you are trying to tell me something in your letter, is a bit weak; words like shit are missing which are irreplaceable when referring to certain of our acquaintances. You are a bit contrite for not having written to me during the scandal: I am for not having ever spoken to you earlier about my homosexuality, something which being

335

two friends I could *also* have done; but put your hand on your heart and ask yourself if your behaviour was the most suited to such a confidence.

Now in Bologna with my friends try to be a discreet advocate for me, something of which after all I think you are capable.

It remains for me to say that I like you, in fact am very fond of you, and that I am happy that you have disentangled yourself from that little jungle of cobras and hyenas which is the province, yes, the province, of Udine.

A hug,      Pier Paolo

## 209   To Nico Naldini
Casarsa

[*In possession of addressee: typewritten with autograph signature*]

[Rome, February 1950]

Dear Nico,

Nothing's more anachronistic than your Casarsese depressions. A name? No, at least four names, one more Trasteverine than the next. I finally got some good out of the various Fichtes and Hegels, to hell with them![1] Armando or the angel, an idiot like all angels. (Are we finally legalizing *trobar clus*?[2] Never has a figure seemed more natural to me. Now for our relatives we have become people under special surveillance.) If you want some geographical hints about me, imagine the Tiber, shamelessly irrational, amid all those domes so severely 'laden with history'.

And here we are on the edge of suicide: nothing new, neither work nor some arrangement for my mother nor news from Mondadori. According to what Zigaina and Bartolini[3] write to me, you are somewhat optimistic, you keep on believing in the future. Tell Aunt Giannina that I got 30,000 lire in a rather mysterious way, and thank her.

Write to Carron[4] asking him from me to forgive me for not having yet replied to his letter, and as excuse indicate to him my present conditions.

I urge active niceness – they deserve it.[5] Greet all my friends and comrades for me: give Susanna[6] a bit of a lecture.

A hug,      Pier Paolo

1   See Letter 207.
2   *trobar clus* (Provençal): a kind of love poetry.
3   The artist Giuseppe Zigaina (b. 1924); the writer Elio Bartolini.
4   Giovan Battista Carron, Christian Democrat deputy, had tried to come to Pasolini's aid at the time of the charge over the incidents at Ramuscello.
5   Refers to his ex-pupils at the school at Valvasone.
6   Giuseppe Susanna, secretary of the Communist Party cell in San Giovanni di Casarsa.

## 210   To Vittorio Sereni
Milan

[*In possession of addressee's heirs: typewritten with autograph signature*]

[Rome, end of February 1950]

Dear Sereni,

I devoured your 'critical prose' which you call a modest report; but in that case long live reports. I saw myself facing my poetical identity as if it had been detached from me for the instant that sufficed for me to catch sight of it, something which has never happened to me with such surpassing and indisputable objectivity.

With all the sympathy that runs between the lines, very warm and visible, and very contemporary, you have managed to be a kind of person of tomorrow: the editor of a future encyclopedia. I would have an infinite number of things to tell you, dealing with what you have thought, supposed and guessed about me; but in these days I have always been so excited and with my heart in my mouth that I am unable to write except by continually being untrue to what I want to say.

I am searching desperately for work, there is an enormous family gangrene to be cured, and, over and above that, this Rome dripping with the blood of absolute novelties, which is the drop that makes my cup run over.

I shall write to you at length shortly or, better still, will talk to you; that is to say provided that when sooner or later we meet I am able to speak! Given that perhaps it is not even necessary. As for Mondadori we have now reached the bureaucratic–administrative stage; but by now I am pathologically discouraged; I give in when faced by the knot in my shoelaces, never mind when faced by that Gordian knot, Mondadori. It may be to avert bad luck but I never turn my thoughts in that direction.

Affectionate greetings from yours          Pier Paolo Pasolini

This letter was written in reply to a letter from Sereni of 23 February 1950 where he writes:

*This very evening I am sending to Mondadori the report on your things. I imagine you will like to have a copy and so I am enclosing one which I have taken directly from the transcript of the text addressed to the publisher. Please do not be too hard on my critical prose seeing that it is merely a report to the publisher, as explicit and legible as possible. And lastly, I beg you not to let anyone else read these few lines (except your mother, naturally, given that she follows you with so much affection).*

In the publisher's report to Mondadori, Sereni writes:

*From* L'USIGNOLO *to* DIARIO *and* LINGUA *(the most recent and most committed collection) the story of a soul is sketched; the story of an original purity corrupted step by step in a process the symptoms of which are caught time after time in the moments, in the climates and in the*

*villages, in unquiet and disquieting forms, with a courage, an acuteness and a faithfulness to the most intimate feelings which cannot fail to catch the attention. Is there a touch of complacency? In reality many things which might disturb a suspicious reader (instances of narcissism, decadentism, luciferism, etc.) are to be forgiven and accepted because they bear, in an undeniable manner, the mark of a spirit, an accent easily recognized as theirs, the delicate vibration of a landscape which will make itself remembered.*

## 211   To Luciano Serra
Bologna
[*In possession of addressee: typewritten with autograph signature*]

[Rome, end of February 1950]

Dear Luciano,

I have had an incredible letter from you – incredible because I thought you knew I am in Rome, having fled with my mother from Casarsa. Before leaving a month ago I had written a letter to let you know; the business could even end very badly. And indeed it is ending badly. My mother is in service: I find no work, I feel alone, unable to do anything, in a terrible condition. For the moment my uncle is keeping me.

The flight from Casarsa is due to the fact that my father was by now intolerable; my mother would have ended up by dying. In fact I hide from her my suicidal state of spirits – she has recovered in such a way that she seems to me to have returned to the Bologna days. It is the only consolation. Yesterday in one of my inconclusive and desperate attempts to find work I met a certain Prof. Borrello, who was supposed to find me lessons (lessons which I am waiting for like a miracle, wearing my nerves out and destroying myself); this Borrello had sent to *Convivium* an essay, 'Some themes in Pirandello', and had received from Calcaterra an affirmative reply; try to do something about it, I beg you, so that I may have the chance to return the favour and in a certain sense to force him to give me effective help. If then you should know anyone here in Rome who could get me some tutoring, let me know without delay, by immediate return of post.

I would never have thought one could be so tired.

I hug you with much affection,       Pier Paolo

## 212   To Silvana Mauri
Milan

[*In possession of addressee: typewritten with autograph signature*]

[Rome, 6 March 1950]

Dearest Silvana,

As you feared, your silence had really frightened me; but I blamed only myself, the sick person's rashness with which I wrote you those letters:[1] I never for a moment came close to suspecting that there was any shortcoming on your part. Now I am relieved, do write to me when you can or feel like it; it is enough for me to know that our friendship has not been damaged or finished by my betrayal, by my mistakes, by my blind obedience to my unfortunate case. You who have remained entirely on the other, on our side, in the same place as my passive nostalgia, are for me a continual consolation and – forgive me if I speak to you about yourself as if you weren't there – something positive, pure, and sweetly resolved – a way of escape which always remains open towards the light, even if I will never emerge – which rests at some point in my consciousness and which I can always find again the moment I turn my thoughts to it. By now I have got you a little used to my inopportune and shameless sincerity of recent times . . . – so you will forgive me if I tell you that the thought of you is the dearest thought I have. Contrary to what I believed in these last days I have thought a lot about Fabio: perhaps because I talked about him with the Positanos (whom I went to visit. Giuseppe I already knew; they were very nice and promised to help me in some way although I did not have the courage to tell them explicitly the desperate conditions I find myself in). I think Fabio has really reached a zone of definite tranquillity: the crisis was terrible but if there is a scale of proportions, of compensations (and it does exist, I know with certainty, for I try it out on myself with precision that is measured in millimetres), it means that Fabio suffered all at once what I suffer a little every day. As you see, I persist in considering my case and Fabio's as parallels although our two natures are very different – except that Fabio can get better and I cannot. I have a little joy, a little feeling of health each day (which merely makes me more abnormal) while Fabio by now has entered a definite state which, if it has robbed him of much, has given him just as much. I now envy him; I envy his purity, his God, who is so little 'Father' in Freudian terms, so spiritual. Meantime I struggle in a miserable life, in a chain of shames. But as you say, it is the punishment not so much (I believe, have the presumption to believe) for the bad I have done or for my impure attitude, as for the good I have not done, for the purity which I knew where to find and how to love but which I did not reach.

One thing which I do not understand and which does not fit into the calculations, into the accounts between me and whoever is punishing me, is the fate of my mother. I will not write much to you about it because I already have tears in my eyes. She has found work with a little family (husband and wife with a small boy of two); and with a heroism and a simplicity which I cannot tell you has accepted her new life. I go to see her every day and take the little boy out for her to help her a little; she does everything to show that she is happy and carefree; yesterday was my birthday and if you knew how she behaved . . . these are things that cannot be expressed. I cannot go on writing to you about them.

As for the rest: I do not find work, not even miserable private lessons.

Either I do not know how to ask or the people to whom I turn do not want to bother with it. I have vague offers of contributing to papers. In short, the oppression continues and I do not know when I shall rejoin life as it is lived normally. From Mondadori I have had no news: but I do not have very good presentiments, because I am so disheartened that for me the whole of existence has only one colour: that of misfortune. Forgive me these depressing pages, my natural gaiety is a yellowed photograph.

An affectionate hug from your        Pier Paolo

1   See Letters 202 and 205.


## 213   To Nico Naldini
Casarsa

*[In possession of addressee: typewritten with autograph signature]*

[Rome, March 1950]

Dear Nico,

I can only think that you did not get my last letter in which I asked you to get Marangoni[1] to send me my Friulian poems *by immediate return of post* because I need them for *Botteghe Oscure*.[2] If it is a case of confusion and apathy on your part, try to remedy it, so too if the confusion and apathy are the railway's.

Try to understand the terrifying conditions in which I am living: for ten days I have been going to my uncle's to see if there is post: nothing, no one writes to me any more, I pass the rest of the day dying of demoralization. I have not managed to get even one lesson. By now I am reaching the very limits of despair. Did you by the way see the atrocious joke of the Premio Roma?[3]

Please, do not keep me waiting, I have no patience left.

A hug,        Pier Paolo

1   Vittorio Marangoni, editor of a review in Udine.
2   Literary review edited by Giorgio Bassani.
3   A reference to the prize awarded on 12 March 1950 to G. Ungaretti, a well-established poet, for 'La terra promessa' ['The promised land']. Pasolini had sent in the poem 'Italia', obtaining a mention.

## 214   To Nico Naldini

Casarsa

[*In possession of addressee: typewritten with autograph signature*]

[Rome, spring 1950]

Dear Nico,

Shall I manage to stir you from your deep sleep? Meantime I am waiting with particular anxiety for the translations of Theocritus. Then, although you despair profoundly, here is a new task: send me forthwith the 'Notebooks', the ones you found in the righthand drawer of my desk, to put them in a safe place. In the last or second last of those notebooks there should be translations of Verlaine. Before sending me them all, check this.

The etching by Bartolini[1] must be either in the cupboard in the room where my mother slept or in the cabinet in the Academiuta or, finally, among my papers in the trunk or on top of the bookshelves. If you find it you will see it is in a rather bad state; have it put right and cleaned and perhaps frame it at Rico's.[2] Then if instead of 25,000 it is only 10,000 that is still all right.

The rest as usual. Forgive my peremptory tone; but one has to shout at the deaf. Put a hand on your heart and accuse me if you can. Besides there is not even a shadow of the Friulian poems from Marangoni.

An affectionate hug,      Pier Paolo

1   Luigi Bartolini.
2   The painter Federico De Rocco.

## 215   To Nico Naldini

Casarsa

[*In possession of addressee: typewritten with autograph signature*]

[Rome, spring 1950]

Dear Nico,

I wrote to my father today but I forgot to tell him about Bartolini; tell him to begin a methodical search.

I got the little translation. Bah. Did you send the notebooks right away? Let's hope so.

The business of the trial[1] worries me; why all these postponements? Go to the lawyer and tell him to try to get a clear view of things. Here – blue sky and a Kafkaesque spring. I am overcome.

You never say anything about Scodellaro and Della Rossa;[2] have you thrown them over? Before you answer this question allow me to call you a swine: you would always have deserved it (hand on my heart).

Rome-the-trauma is beginning to wear off: there remains the acute, intolerable desire to be a millionaire. It is ages since I had a line from Aunt Giannina: greet her and kiss her. Further, lately I had written to your mother about two salamis, half a kilo of butter and a dressing-gown: is nothing happening about them?

I end this 'letter of Van Gogh to his brother' with good wishes for palpitating haloes and since we are (help, help!) in the middle of Easter, maybe for eggs which you know about.

Pier Paolo

1   A reference to the trial for the events at Ramuscello.
2   See Letter 207.

## 216   To Gianfranco Contini
Fribourg
*[In possession of addressee: autograph]*

[Rome, 12 May 1950]

Dear Sig. Contini,

Since February I have been in Rome with my mother and for long I have been wanting to write to you about my latest experiences, which are very sad. I did not do it only because of inhibitions which you know well, but now the circumstances, which are increasingly painful, and the kindness of Ulivi[1] compel me to break the silence to ask you for some help – which I hope with all my heart will not be in the slightest way a burden to you.

In Rome I have been looking for work for months: yesterday at the Ministry of Education where Ulivi is employed they told me I could perhaps get a job as 'salaried employee' in the Fine Arts administration but for this the request from a Superintendent, e.g. Cesare Brandi, would be necessary. Now I remember that about a year ago you mentioned to me your friendly relations with the Director of Painting: could you today write me a letter of recommendation for him? How much it costs me to ask you for this you can well understand and not because I lack in the slightest degree reason to count on your kindness.

Forgive me and accept my most affectionate greetings,

Yours,       Pier Paolo Pasolini

c/o Colussi, via Porta Pinciana 34

Replying to this letter on 18 May Contini writes:

*Dear Pasolini,*
*Here is the note for Brandi for you* [...] *I did not know where to reach you. Some time ago Bortolussi wrote to me about serious 'moral' troubles which had forced you to leave Casarsa; although so vague the news made me very sad. I wish you all possible relief and ask you to remember me even when my own troubles will prevent me from maintaining consistent, continuous relations with the external world.*

1   Ferruccio Ulivi (b. 1912), lecturer in Italian literature, critic and writer.

## 217   To Giacinto Spagnoletti
## Milan
[*In possession of addressee: typewritten with autograph signature*]

[Rome, 22 May 1950]

Dear Spagnoletti,

For a month I have been putting this letter off from day to day; and now I have given up hope of its reaching you in time to be of use. It is about 'L'Italia':[1] in the fourth last stanza one should replace 'twelve-year-old' with 'schoolboy' and in the third last 'splendid as poplars' with 'splendid as horses'. There has also been a biographical blow in the last few months so that the little note on me should, to be accurate, end with 'now lives in Rome'; without a guarantee that by the time the anthology comes out I shall not find myself in Mexico or among the Cimmerians.[2]

Again many thanks and cordial greetings,

Yours,       Pier Paolo Pasolini

1   See Letter 197.
2   In classical mythology, inhabitants of a gloomy northern region.

## 218   To Gianfranco Contini
## Fribourg
[*In possession of addressee: typewritten with autograph signature*]

Rome, 23 May 1950

Dear Sig. Contini,

Given Brandi's difficult nature, to which you referred,[1] I thought I would get an appointment with him through a common friend, who is very trustworthy, very irreproachable, whom Brandi told by telephone, however, that he was busy all this week.

So I still cannot tell you anything except that I am grateful for what you have done for me, which is much and more perhaps than you imagine: a real ray of light in this gloomy Rome of my moral troubles. Concerning which it was my wish – beside being almost a duty – to speak to you: I shall do so in the next letter and perhaps in a most thankless way, given the tremendous difficulty. Meantime allow me to be lavish – in such dramatically reduced circumstances – in suffering, while knowing nothing of them except by instinct, because they are 'private woes' – those of someone who is very dear to me.

Thank you again and an affectionate greeting,

Yours,       Pier Paolo Pasolini

1   See Letter 216.

## 219   To Giacinto Spagnoletti
Milan

[*In possession of addressee: typewritten with autograph date and signature*]

Rome, 31 May 1950

Dear Spagnoletti,

I wasn't joking when I spoke in a somewhat dramatic tone about my biography: I am really in the midst of upsets and depression which have not given me a moment of serenity for almost a year; and I must tell you that you with your letters, which are so affectionate and open, have represented one of the very rare exceptions to the rule of my misfortune.

So I hope to see soon – although I do not hope to be able to buy it – the *Anthology* which, my personal satisfaction apart, will undoubtedly be for me a special and extremely interesting read. As for the poems for the *Quaderno della Fenice*, first of all thanks again: the choice seems to me three-fifths good; I would be a little unsure about 'La mia camera ha incanti . . .' ['My room has enchantments . . .'] which I actually thought of leaving out of the collection, and also perhaps about 'Ah, non è piú per me questa bellezza' ['Ah, this beauty is no longer for me'] which, coming immediately before 'La crocefissione' ['The crucifixion'], does not foretell it. But don't trust me who am naturally the worst anthologist of myself, as can happen.

Here in Rome, in a muddled way, I still work. Of literary people I see only Caproni who is splendid.

Affectionate greetings,

Yours,       Pier Paolo Pasolini

Many greetings also to Sereni

This letter is a reply to a letter of 26 May 1950 in which Spagnoletti writes:

*I have been wanting to tell you for some weeks that I and Vittorio Sereni, along with Carlo Bo and Attilio Bertolucci, have chosen some of your poems for the first number of* Quaderno della Fenice *(a weekly poetry review which we shall put together for Guanda). The review will be sent to you – I hope – before the end of September. Here are the titles of your things and let me know if we have made a good choice (if at all the blame is mine).*

*1) Vicina agli occhi* ['Near the eyes']
*2) Ahi non ha più fine questa notte* ['Ah, has this night no end']
*3) La mia camera ha incanti* ['My room has enchantments']
*4) Ah non è più per me questa bellezza* ['Ah, this beauty is no longer for me']
*5) La crocefissione* ['The crucifixion']

*You will see the Anthology in the shop windows, probably within ten days. Your poem looks very good there. Work!*

## 220   To Gianfranco Contini
## Fribourg

[*In possession of addressee: typewritten with autograph signature*]

[Rome, 3 June 1950]

Dear Sig. Contini,

That eternal, diabolical Person Unknown, Cesare Brandi, is *the least uncommon and difficult* man I have ever met. After the first alarming – indeed for me almost terrifying – minutes he showed a precision and warmth of language such as I have rarely encountered. He talked to me about Friuli, about its *villotte*[1] – immediately after the short bureaucratic dialogue which had a negative outcome (in the Ministry it seems they have given me inaccurate information, something about which Brandi showed himself to be sincerely sorry, promising however to give me some help). So, in terms of what came out of the conversation, I should be depressed and am instead particularly disposed to a flicker of hope, however slight . . . As for our letter and your article – Brandi said that it was literally Greek to him; he said he will write to you about it (can it be a simple case of postal misdirection?) and, finally, he seemed to me to be full of trust in and affection for you.

Thank you and many greetings,

Yours,       Pier Paolo Pasolini

1   *vilotta*: traditional song of Friuli.

## 221   To Nico Naldini
Casarsa

*[In possession of addressee: typewritten with autograph signature]*

[Rome, June 1950]

Dear Nico,

I have written about these matters to my father as well but since I am afraid he is still all at sea and will send my letter back to me, I am turning to you as well.

They are two very simple matters and I beg you to deal with them carefully if you see that my father is negative.

1) To go to Vaccher and ask for exact information about a rise in salary for the summer months of '49 to which I should be entitled; and for him perhaps to take up thus little matter with the secretary.

2) To send me a parcel with the fustian shorts, the white trousers and the green trousers. And what are you doing? I have become a Roman and can no longer bring out a word of Venetian or Friulian dialect and so say 'To hell with you' in Romanesco. I bathe in the Tiber and concerning the human and poetic 'episodes' which are happening to me, multiply them by a hundred in comparison with the ones in Friuli.

Write to me and tell me something about yourself, about your exams and the boys, etc.

A hug,      Pier Paolo

## 222   To Susanna Pasolini
Colleverde-Montecassiano

*[In the Pasolini Archive: typewritten with autograph signature]*

[Postmark: Rome, 22 August 1950]

Dearest Mummy,

I got your two cards and kissed them a hundred times. I didn't reply to the first one right away precisely because of the inhibiting lack of an address. I hope you really are all right as you say and that you can rest a little. Here I am leading the usual life: I spend all afternoon by the Tiber with Penna[1] and I spend the evening with him too in never-ending discussions. Maria wrote to tell me that Jus – an employee at the magistrate's court – told her that my affairs will come up at the beginning of September.[2] So who knows if I shall be able to come to visit you! But don't let us be sad – I had to go to Casarsa sooner or later in any case and we were bound to go without seeing each other for a little. And then the days pass so quickly. As for my health I am very well since I have been living so much in the open air and even where my morale is concerned I can't complain. A thousand kisses,

Yours,      Pier Paolo

His mother replying on 27 August writes:

*I think you will have started to laugh at something in the postcard before this one: confront everything with energy – you will say: What pulpit is this sermon coming from!... However, if you really think about it, I'm not really so weak, don't you think? But the little energy I possess, like a little candle-flame, comes to me from you. I walk in your footsteps and what keeps me alive comes from you.*

1   Sandro Penna shared Pasolini's interest in boys.
2   A reference to the forthcoming trial.

## 223   To Susanna Pasolini
Colleverde-Montecassiano
[*In Pasolini Archive: typewritten with autograph signature*]

[Postmark; Rome, 28 August 1950]

Dear Mummy,

Here is a nice piece of news for you. On Saturday I got this telegram: 'Your poem Testament Koran[1] has won second prize fifty thousand lire jury unanimous national competition Cattolica.[2] Would welcome if possible your presence Sunday afternoon. Congratulations.'

Are you pleased? I was happy above all for you and for the beneficial effects on father (at least temporary ones). It is a great success because if the winner was decided beforehand I won second place on pure merit as the unanimity of the jury tells us.

I did not go to Cattolica to avoid expense and fatigue – all the more since the journey to Casarsa is close at hand.

Your last postcard gave me a lot of pleasure, telling me about your rest; except, naturally, your evening melancholy which I felt in all its weight and its truth, like a rather painful shudder.

But have you seen how quickly the days pass, we are at the end of August already; almost half the time of our separation is over by now.

About sleeping don't worry. Penna gave me virgin wax to put in my ears (just think if we had known about this in Casarsa) by means of which in the morning, sunk in a very deep, visceral silence, I sleep as long as I want, unaffected by Paolo crying, the noise of the door and the news on the radio.

A thousand kisses,      Pier Paolo

1    Later included in the volume *La nuova gioventú.*
2    The literary competition held at Cattolica.

## 224    To Susanna Pasolini
Colleverde-Montecassiano
[*In Pasolini Archive: typewritten with autograph signature*]

[Postmark: Rome, 18 September 1950]
Dearest Fatty,

Forgive me if I haven't written to you for some days. You know the way I am . . . Time slips away from me. I am so pleased that you liked the idea of sending you the photograph: I matched all the kisses you gave it.

A few days ago Aunt Giannina came through on her summer tour: she was coming from Naples disgusted by the festival of Piedigrotta.[1] The bulletin on her health notes 'a veil in front of the right eye'. I passed on to her at once the new thing about the virgin wax: she wanted to try it out when she went to rest in the afternoon. But the wax had gone too far in and she couldn't get it out; she had to go to a doctor which cost her 1500 lire. Then with the same lightning speed as she came she set off again. She said to send you lots of greetings.

I have learned from San Vito that the magistrate has asked for a month's leave because of illness; so everything is in suspense again. They are talking about 6 October . . .

Just imagine that last Sunday I scored 12 at *Totocalcio*[2] . . . and won only 4000 lire.

That's our luck.

I give you an infinite number of kisses,         Pier Paolo

A reply to a postcard of 7 September 1950 where his mother writes:

*You can't imagine with what joy and how much joy I got your postcard with your picture. The peasant's daughter brought it, a nice little girl, who, thinking she would please me, brought it instead of her father. Then she stood and watched smiling as I kissed your loved image. How pleased I am to have you; every so often I take you from my bag and look at you and kiss you, then get on with my work again refreshed. The expression on the face is perfect. At first you look too serious then if one looks closely one sees that it is the expression not only of your genius but of your generosity of spirit. Don't laugh; I put things as well as I can.*

1    The annual Neapolitan festival.
2    The Italian version of the football pools.

## 225 To Susanna Pasolini
Colleverde-Montecassiano

*[In Pasolini Archive: typewritten with autograph signature]*

[Postmark: Rome, 27 September, 1950]

Dearest Fatty,

No – no disappointment about the 12:[1] that very Sunday evening I had thought there wouldn't be much money since to get a twelve had been very easy and foreseeable and so thousands of other people had got it.

Don't worry in the slightest about money: the 50,000 lire have arrived and over and above that I have the money from some articles. In general I am spending fairly serene days. Try to keep calm too; by now your distance from me is nearly over; soon we shall be together. The trial will perhaps be held before 28 October.

One of these days I shall ring Carron, maybe something can come of it.

I have had my umpteenth mention: this time at the Premio Soave (for an unpublished lyric: they decided to give the prize to a local poetess, you can imagine what an ugly creature).

Forgive the telegraphic style; but it is half past 10 and I am hungry. I want to go straight out and have something. As you see you can be at peace, I am following your advice.

A thousand kisses from your          Pier Paolo

1   See Letter 224.

## 226 To Gianfranco Contini
Fribourg

*[In possession of addressee: typewritten with autograph signature]*

[Rome, 7 October 1950]

Dear Sig. Contini,[1]

Not only have I not kept my promise to write to you at greater length about myself but with this letter I am putting it off again. Muscetta, whom I saw today, asked me for my Friulian poems to try to publish them in a new collection of poetry by Einaudi: now a friend of mine (if he still deserves this description) has lost the only copy left.[2] There are, it is true, the notebooks, but what a desperate thought to go back over them; so I thought I would turn to you who have the other copy of my *Romancero* ['Collection of romances'][3] (by the way do you think this is a good title?) asking you to lend it to me for some time. In the best of cases I shall return it to you published, in the worst – a most miserable gift – re-typed, revised and corrected. Imagine how sorry I am to give you this new trouble, and once more, for the nth time, forgive me.

What can I tell you about myself? I am living in the after-effects of the Roman trauma; still no work; I have become very friendly with Penna and, inseparable, we pass nights which are somewhere between being anguished and stupendous. Do you never come down to Rome? Meantime I look forward to good news from you of peace of mind restored.

Many affectionate greetings from yours,

Pier Paolo Pasolini

1  Pasolini's epistolary mode of address to Contini is now 'Gentile' which is still formal but less so than 'Egregio'.
2  See Letters 213 and 214.
3  This title was later changed to *La meglio gioventù*, Sansoni (Florence, 1954), the collection of verses in Friulano dedicated to Contini with '*amor de lonh*' ['love from afar'].

## 227  To Susanna Pasolini
Colleverde-Montecassiano
[*In Pasolini Archive: typewritten with autograph signature*]

[Postmark: Rome, 7 October 1950]
My little darling,

I got your two rather sad postcards: the first, while it wrung my heart, made me smile a little at the thought of your culinary apprehensions; the second on the other hand would have distressed me had it not reached me on a morning of good news. Muscetta, secretary to Einaudi (the publisher and not the president,[1] because you are capable of all kinds of interpretations!), wanted to meet me to ask me for my manuscript of Friulian poems: so a possible publication by Einaudi! Then there are other prospects which I shall write to you about when I am more certain. But I hope you will arrive here meantime; I have a terrible desire to see you again.

Meanwhile I shall tell you – I know these things interest you – that I have bought myself the material for a coat, very elegant, latest fashion, pure wool, all for 8500 lire, that is to say half price. It was a great bargain even according to Gigino and his wife. Aunt Giannina had said that together with my father she would give me it this Christmas; so meantime I have used my money and then, if they can, they will let me have it back. So it is a saving as well.

There is no other immediate news. Don't worry about the flowers – do you think anyone will have forgotten that the 4th is his birthday?[2] But the other things, the Germans, etc., one must forget, dear Fatty, one must forget them.

I kiss and hug you with infinite tenderness,

Yours,      Pier Paolo

In the second postcard his mother had written:

*Today is Guido's birthday. I wonder if anyone will remember to go and take flowers! Do
you remember how for his birthday he wanted me to make strudel with new apples and
grapes? Do you remember how six years ago today you were in the steeple at Casarsa hiding
because there were the Germans and the round-ups of men? What terrible and sad days!
And yet Guido was still with us and we were happy . . .*

1   Luigi Einaudi was the first post-war president of the Italian Republic.
2   A reference to the birthday of his brother Guido.

## 228   To Gianfranco Contini
## Fribourg
[*In possession of addressee: typewritten with autograph signature*]

Rome, 5 November 1950

Dear Sig. Contini,

There is no need for you to go looking in your drawers in Domodossola for
the notebooks about sending which I have a very unclear memory: those I
needed were the 'Ciants di un muart'¹ which were the first to jump out when I
opened your parcel. As for your slight delay, Penna is witness that I never
doubt your concern and that I was rather worried about you because of the by
no means good news you had given me about your health in the last letters.
As for me, I *must* be open with you and you will forgive me if I do it in the
most speedy and indiscreet way. So here it is: on 28 January I and my mother
fled, literally, from Casarsa and came to Rome.

My father – as I think I mentioned to you – came back from prison with a
'paranoid syndrome', an alcoholic, and in short in such a state as to render my
mother's life intolerable (take every word in its literal and absolute sense);
and for some time living with him had been impossible. Then came my
setback: a charge against me of corruption of minors because of my love for a
boy in a village near Casarsa, Ramuscello. The matter perhaps, indeed almost
certainly, would have passed unnoticed had I not been a Communist and not
therefore attracted the hatred of all the respectable citizens of Friuli. The
non-Communist papers caused a scandal without precedent to explode in
Friuli: I was immediately expelled from the Party, from the school where I
taught, etc., etc.

Now I am in Rome; for several months I have been looking for work
without success: I live on my uncle and my mother is working as a governess.

These are my 'moral troubles';[2] as you see they are very serious or downright desperate.

Thank you again very much for everything – for your friendship; you cannot perhaps imagine how much it means to me and I send you affectionate greetings,

Yours,     Pier Paolo Pasolini

1   They were published in the second section of *La meglio gioventú*.
2   See Letter 216, which quotes from Contini's letter of 18 May.

## 229   To Giacinto Spagnoletti
Milan
[*In possession of addressee: typewritten with autograph signature*]

[Rome, December 1950]
Dear Spagnoletti,

For several days I have been meaning to write to you but I am always so agitated, unsettled, discouraged that I simply postpone and postpone. And yet for me to thank you is not just an external duty. The very beautiful volume[1] gave me hours of emotions and satisfaction which were truly consoling. Here in Rome, at least going by these persons with whom I have literary relations, it seems that your production was much liked. And there is a strong feeling of gratitude and liking for your volume. I do not feel like embarking on a more logical statement; or else I shall do it later on if I once more find a little calm and confidence. Meantime thank you for everything and I shake your hand with affection,

Yours,     Pier Paolo Pasolini

1   A reference to the *Antologia della poesia italiana*: see Letter 217.

## 230   To Susanna Pasolini
Rome
[*In Pasolini Archive: autograph*]

[Postmark: Casarsa, 28 December 1950]
Dearest little Mummy,

The trial went as foreseen: that is to say the minimal sentence with remission which is of no importance for the future because my criminal record is clean. In Casarsa the usual melancholy; but it seems to me that there are still a lot of friends. I cannot write to you at great length because Father is walking up and down waiting for me to finish to go and post the letter.

A thousand kisses from your      Pier Paolo

Many kisses and greetings to Uncle.

# 1951

### 231 To Leonardo Sciascia[1]
Palermo
[*In possession of addressee: autograph*]

Rome, 11 January 1951

Dear Sciascia,

I received the two thousand lire and your letter the day before I left for Friuli; I took your address with me to write to you from up there but I did not have a free half-hour. Then I came down to Rome again just in time to write the rough copy of the review of your delightful fairytales[2] and to fall in such a nasty way as to fracture a bone in my pelvis: six days in hospital etc. and now a month in bed. So here you have all the reasons why I was failing in my duty to write to you and thank you. I hope my misfortunes will excuse me! The moment I am a little better I shall copy the review and send it somewhere.[3]

Forgive me and accept my most warm regards,

Yours very sinc/ly,      Pier Paolo Pasolini

1 Leonardo Sciascia (1921–89), the Sicilian novelist.
2 See *Favole della dittatura* ['Fairytales of the dictatorship'], Bardi (Rome, 1950).
3 *Letture di malato* ['Letters of an invalid'], *Il popolo di Roma*, 22 March, 1951.

### 232 To Leonardo Sciascia
Palermo
[*In possession of addressee: autograph*]

Rome, 25 January 1951

Dear Sciascia,

I am still pinned down in bed but only for a few days. As soon as I am on my feet I shall type the review of your book and take it to a newspaper.

As for the story[1] Dell'Arco has spoken to you about it is so daring that I fear it will need a lot of guts to publish it and then it is very long. I have, by way of narrative, other less violent things which, if you like, I shall send you for you to look at soon as I can.

Meantime, warm good wishes and greetings from yours,

Pier Paolo Pasolini

1   Refers to a short story 'set in Rome', probably *Ferrobedò*, which was to appear in *Paragone* in June 1951.

## 233   To Franco De Gironcoli
Gorizia

[Rome, March 1951]
. . . Unfortunately I shall not be able to be in Gorizia for the presentation. I don't even know where I shall be in ten days or a fortnight. To Friuli (you will know something about me and my reversals) I shall not be able to return; I cannot stay in Rome any longer because the person who has supported me up to now no longer wishes to do so. Forgive the brutality of my report; it is the obsession that breaks its banks in every way and in all directions. I hope to see your new book[1] (if in the best of cases I can stay in Rome to be an extra at Cincecittà, otherwise I do not know what my address will be). I have had a commission from Rai[2] for a cycle presenting dialect poems for the Third Programme . . . So think of my figure or my ghost as being present in Gorizia; don't think that I shall be far from you . . .

Part of a text published in *Corriere del Friuli* in November 1976.

1   *Elegie in friulano* ['Elegies in Friulano'], in Edizioni di Treviso (Treviso, 1951).
2   Rai: the Italian state broadcasting institution.

## 234   To Guglielmo Petroni
Rome

[*In possession of addressee: typewritten with autograph signature*]

Rome, 3 April 1951
Dear Petroni,

You must forgive me if, uninvited in this way, I present myself with this piece[1] for *Fiera*. I have had it in a drawer for months thinking vaguely of sending it to you; finally I made up my mind to do so, overcoming my scruples, hoping, that is, that you will not find my initiative too indiscreet. Then I hope to see you as well sometime in spite of the terrible picture of me Penna must have put before your eyes . . .

Many warm greetings from yours,        Pier Paolo Pasolini

1   Probably refers to an article which appeared in *La Fiera letteraria* on 3 June 1951.

1951

## 235   To Gianfranco Contini
Fribourg
[*In possession of addressee: typewritten with autograph signature and date*]

Rome, 11 June 1951

Dear Dr Contini,

Will you permit me this 'dear'?¹ You will have to put up with it however because it is so 'irrational' that it is impossible to take any measures against it. For a long time I ought to have written to you; I am still here in Rome, desperate, jobless (at last, after two months of waiting, I was an extra for two nights) and waiting for the new case-list of the Appeal Court in Pordenone which must continue to pass judgement on me. This is why I I have delayed so long in replying to your letter: in all these weeks I have never found the 'glimmer of happiness' necessary for doing so. Perhaps you will have had my greetings from a Capuchin monk whom I met at Ungaretti's, an afternoon in which they spoke almost exclusively about you with absolute and un-conditional liking, including in equal proportions respect and affection for your knowledge and your person. I tell you this with joy. And this happens in Rome often, infinitely more often than for any other man of letters.

Affectionate greetings and good wishes from yours,

Pier Paolo Pasolini

It is a reply to this letter from Contini:

*Domodossola, 21 April 1951*

*Dearest P.P.P.,*

*For I don't know how long I have been in your debt. I fear I have not even told you how sorry I was about your report (a very calm one, however) of the persecution you have suffered. (Does the human species perhaps want to have its revenge for its lack of imagination? I really do believe that a kind of aesthetic judgement underlies Pharisaism – let's say Pharisaism in good faith.) I am sorry that you did not get a sympathetic word. I am sorry not to have written to you when that famous story about Fribourg came out. It was not ill-will, of this you will be convinced, it was truly force majeur.*

*I no longer have the right to ask you – if these lines still find you in Rome – to send me news of yourself every so often. I am too much of a bad correspondent and that even at decisive moments. But do believe at least in the authenticity of my handshake.*

*Affectionately yours,     Contini*

*PS. I am writing to you still on holiday. I go back 'to my post' tomorrow.*

To Pasolini's letter of 11 June Contini replies:

*Domodossola (San Quirico) 20. vii. 1951*

*Dear P.P.P.,*

*I am in the big room where you visited me many years ago; it is dawn, the pensioner from*

*Valcuvia passes the whetstone over his scythe; exquisite botanical odours come in to delight and set off the usual hayfever again, I think: shades still invade the Ossola which you saw and which migrated (without inhabitants) into a verse in your 'Italia'; and I find myself thanking you for the letter you wrote me some weeks ago, an affectionate signal from the external world at a time when I was furiously angry with the external world. Curious, while one foams with rage against A, B, C... from all the other points of the horizon (M. N. P...) arrive - gratuitous or compensatory? - flattery and politeness. My pupil, the Capuchin monk, had already brought me your greeting; and this winter your cousin Naldini and Bartolini (i.e. Elio) had written to me, evidently reflecting your affectionate propaganda. (By the way, who is De Gironcoli? His little book is delicious but I should like to be a little more clear about the question of dates because it seems to me that he is strictly dependent on P.P.P. if not actually on the Academiuta.) In short, I am completely off my balance.*

*I am sorry that your life is what it is, and I have still more sympathy for you persecuted, exiled and struggling, than for you an insatiable conqueror. Sympathy, but what use is it? I send it to you precisely because it is in vain, unusable. And please keep me informed of your conditions. Do throw these bottles into the ocean: smelling of mown hay, family misery, primitive virtue.*

*Courage. An affectionate memory from*
*Yours,     Gianfranco Contini*

1   Pasolini had up to now used the formal mode of address 'Gentile dott. Contini'. Here he writes, 'Caro [dear] dott. Contini'.

## 236   To Nico Naldini
Casarsa

[*In possession of addressee: typewritten with autograph signature*]

[Rome, July 1951]
Dear Nico,

Have you finished the Pyrrhic dances? I have two new little jobs to give you: 1) (under dictation from my father) in a few days the Commune of Rome will ask the Commune of Casarsa for our documents to give us residence in Rome. You must ask Francescutti, who is now head of the Registry Office, to give you these documents the moment Rome asks for them so that you can send them directly to us - registered - so as to avoid hold-ups in the offices in Rome;*

2) to go to Signora Amodeo and take her the letter I am enclosing for you. I am asking her, in agreement with Carron, to go herself to Ridomi's mother; I have told her frankly my situation: if she wants other news from you tell her (and put on a bit of a tragic air, as Carron advised). I did not mention Carron's name in the letter; you can mention it, advising her, however, not to talk about it - not even to Ridomi's mother.

Have you understood all this? Do be good and careful as you have always been (let's keep our fingers crossed) up to now, seeing that in the end, if not actually directly, you are acting in your own interest as well. Meantime try to exude less Luther and to work for as many exams as possible. Learn from me: you see how important it is to have a job and how badly off one is without a job. Try to immigrate to Rome with a degree and beyond reproach. With a minimum of security and of money in one's pocket, life in Rome is marvellous.

A hug,      Pier Paolo

\* That is what the employee in the Rome office advised us to do.

### 237   To Nico Naldini
Casarsa

[*In possession of addressee: typewritten with autograph signature*]

[Rome, July 1951]

Dear Nico,

I am sending you back a copy of the contract and a receipt to be handed to Mario Verderi[1] who must give you the sum of 44,000 lire. With the aforesaid sum you will get at the Banca del Friuli a banker's draft for 43,800 lire made out to my father; this you will send registered to the following address: Lt Col Carlo Pasolini, via Giovanni Tagliere 3, Ponte Mammolo, Rome.

The two hundred lire less are for the postage.

Thus far the letter dictated by my father with a rider urging you not to indulge in your usual laziness. I shall write to you another day.

Up to now things have gone fairly well. (Get the official stamps on the receipt for the rent: another paternal rider.)

I hug you affectionately and all the others along with you,      Pier Paolo

1   Tenant of the little room of the Academiuta di Casarsa.

### 238   To Nico Naldini
Casarsa

[*In possession of addressee: typewritten with autograph signature*]

[Rome, August 1951]

Dear Nico,

I haven't yet had anything from Signora Amodeo – what about you? I beg you, go back to her, if she hasn't yet written to you. It is very important.

On behalf of my father: find out from the Town Hall the date of dispatch of the documents and the number of the protocol (because here in Rome they haven't yet arrived). Find out for us if the sign of the Academiuta has been taken down and if Pederoba (?) has done the work on the roof of the latter – and what he has to get.

Furthermore, the Verderis have not yet sent us the money for the rent. Try to get it from them in your interest as well (keep 1500 lire, 500 for trips to Udine).

Do my father a favour (he continues to get on very well): whenever you have a chance tell Sior Bianchi – as propaganda – and Emilio Filello and Dr Berlese – out of friendship – that my father got the silver medal for bravery 'in the field'. (Tell them at the Town Hall too maybe, tell Francescutti, if you can manage: my father is very keen for this to be known.)

Reply to this letter right away (*the same day as you get the news from the Town Hall*), I beg you.

I do not know what your 'arrogant happiness' is due to: it is extremely funny.

I have no new words to brush up the radiant image of the Roman pubes for you.

A hug,      Pier Paolo


## 239   To Nico Naldini
Casarsa

[*In possession of addressee: typewritten with autograph signature*]

[Rome, August 1951]

Dear Nico,

For a week my father has been coming back disappointed from the post office saying: 'Nothing from Nico'. You know what a delicate mechanism my father is and you are causing us serious difficulties by your laziness. Two lines at least about the Town Hall would be enough. Please this time answer immediately. Have the Verderis given you the thousand lire? The other five hundred we will send you the moment you reply.

A hug,      Pier Paolo


## 240   To Nico Naldini
Casarsa

[*In possession of addressee: typewritten with autograph signature*]

[Rome, August 1951]

Dear Nico,

Your silence is extremely hurtful. It has brutally brought shadows of old distresses into the family: my father could not understand your silence and we imagined new atrocities from Casarsa. Have a little remorse for it. And please reply about Pederoba and the tablet of the Academiuta: and if you have had the thousand lire from the Verderis. Not for me who don't give a damn, but for my father. As for Signora Amodeo, write to her thanking her affectionately from me; tell her that for the present it is better to leave things in suspense (for as long as the parliamentary recess lasts), and then perhaps I shall take advantage of the help she can give me.

On Thursday on the red network[1] my piece on Sbarbaro[2] will be transmitted: talk about it a bit there, e.g. to Maria,[3] but also to some others – as a first little revenge and piece of satisfaction at the expense of our enemies.

A hug,      Pier Paolo

1  One of the Rai radio-networks.
2  The poet Camillo Sbarbaro (1888–1967).
3  Their friend Maria Seccardi.

## 241  To Giacinto Spagnoletti
Milan

[*In possession of addressee: typewritten with autograph corrections and signature*]

[Rome, October 1951]

Dear Spagnoletti,

Forgive my long delay: there has not been a day when I have not felt a pang of remorse for the letter I was not writing to you; but you must know that I have been in Lucca for two weeks for the trial,[1] and then, was no sooner back in Rome, than I had to leave again for Sinalunga to pick up the fifty thousand lire of charity which were given me as a little poetry prize; and meantime I carried up and down the Appennines – either stormy or lunar – among many others, your tortured image. If the torture can be printed in your features – but I don't believe it is because it is too hidden by the boyish Ionic brightness of your expression, which is that of someone who is perpetually loving. My Calvary here in Rome continues: at this moment I have not the feeblest hope of a job.

Muscetta cannot be found at Einaudi. The newspapers do not pay me. It would be great good fortune if I could go and play a Mexican in a film Soldati[2] is shooting. You revived my hopes in Mondadori meantime, and I keep the little flame sceptically fed more for my father than for me and you know why. If there is even the most remote probability that Cantoni[3] might be interested write and tell me so that I can send a new, more concise and mature selection of my things.

An affectionate embrace from your          Pier Paolo Pasolini

In reply to this letter Spagnoletti writes on 19 October:

*I spoke at great length to Cantoni about your book and it was like discussing the immortality of the soul: they are all right. He was right to say: 'What can I do if that is what this publisher is like?' And I to say: 'It oughtn't to be like this . . .' With Mondadori all the results are negative, by the by, that goes for idiots, opportunists and personal friends; so he has a general policy.*

1  Of the events at Porzus where Guido Pasolini was killed.
2  Mario Soldati (b. 1906), writer and film director.
3  Remo Cantoni, consultant at Mondadori.

## 242   To Carlo Betocchi
Rome
[*In possession of addressee: typewritten with autograph correction, date and signature*]

Rome, 15 October 1951

Dear Betocchi,

At Sinalunga I seem to have been the one to feel your absence more than anyone else; I was alone all the time incapable of any relationship, looking with the ill-will of an exile at the valley of the Chiana or the gilded friezes of the Teatrino dell'Accademia. I got to the point where I was unable to thank the judges. But with you I do not have to do so; if the others are strangers to me you basically are not. Although I have seen you only twice I seemed to be united to you by many years of familiarity and your face, as it appears to me in the most affectionate area of my imagination, is a face ripened by long friendship. I think that many things about the prize remained unspoken in between the words of your telephone call just as many remain so between the lines of this letter of mine. But what I do not know is whether they really are important to you, whether liking, born at a first glance, can be buried because of the effects of *flatus vocis*,[1] because of abstract acts . . . As for the rest, things continue to take a nasty turn: no job, no hope of getting things sorted out (the fifty thousand lire from Sinalunga were providential) and heaven help me if everything should sink into that indifference which is part of a naïve and hardened vocation. Again many thanks and an affectionate handshake,

Yours,     Pier Paolo Pasolini

In reply to this letter Betocchi writes on 18 October 1951:

*1951*

*I am certain that you like me and I like you in this world of unhappiness. Thank you for keeping me in your sight, think of me also in its truth, and think that truth is one and one only, active and vehement; on the other hand each one of us is a supplicating multitude.*

    *I often look at your little books and you are right to think that between them and me that* flatus vocis *to which you refer has insinuated itself. Having unexpectedly reached me who live in ignorance of many things, I prefer to be sincere and tell you that it caused me great sorrow; and I began to think simply of your father and mother wherever they are. Forgive me for being so intrusive, forgive me if I touch you a little, not having the right to do so.*

    *Now I shall look more closely at your rights, denying my own non-existent ones; yours which are those of the creature facing its creator. I tell you that I am happy to bear witness to the inexhaustible hope which lies in this fact; and meantime I beg you to invite your naïve and hardened vocation to declare itself, to write poems which are by chance directed against itself; because what is naïve and hardened is precisely not the vocation but the delight in it (forgive me if I dare to refer to it).*

1  *flatus vocis*: literally 'the breath of the voice' – rumour.

## 243  To Tonuti Spagnol
## Monte San Primo di Magreglio (Como)
[*In possession of addressee: typewritten with autograph signature*]

[Rome, end of 1951]

My dearest Tonuti,

    I should like to write to you a long letter: it is so long since we spoke and wrote to each other, and how much life therefore we have to tell each other about. For me yours is shot through with images full of youth: you are in full *chanson de geste*, my dear Toni. Ski-lifts, smuggling and scooter (and girls, I imagine).

    But mine cannot be summed up in any way and certainly not in joyous and expansive terms; it is so enormous, neutral, a mixture – for good and ill – of acts of violence. It is a bit like Rome.

    Unfortunately neither today nor for three weeks do I have the time to write you a long letter: I am working like a dog on a story which I must finish by the end of the month plus all the rest. For now I shall say one thing to you; you were the most beautiful time of my life. For this reason not only shall I never be able to forget you but rather will have you continually in my deepest memory, like a reason for living. I say these things to you rationally, like axioms: but that is what they are by now and there is no other way of expressing them. There is nothing for which I am so grateful to fate as for having loved you.

    I embrace you with the greatest affection (. . . and who knows that they won't send you to do your military service in Rome or nearby).

Pier Paolo

1951

This is a reply to a letter of 11 November 1951 in which Tonuti Spagnol writes:

*Do you still have the little poems you took from me or have you lost them?*

*Instead I have learned to be a smuggler; it is the very nature of these parts which taught me to do it; it is a trade that I like because it is very tiring and dangerous but the plots and the things to do with smuggling cigarettes are also amusing. I don't really do it as a business because I have to think about my work here in the firm. In winter I work on the skilift for which I am responsible, I have learned to ski fairly well and this year if my knee heals and if military service allows me to stay on for another couple of months I shall take part in some small competitions.*

*To tell you how I hurt my knee I have to tell you that this spring I bought a motorbike, and the other day because of my lack of care I risked my neck in a frightening spill. I long to see you and your mother and if you happen to go to Casarsa let me know.*

# 1952

## 244   To Nico Naldini
Casarsa

[*In possession of addressee: typewritten with autograph signature*]

[Rome, January 1952]

Dear Nico,

You mentioned (in the obscene station bar?) that you were in touch with a certain 'Dialect Muse' or some such name which, if I am not mistaken, is based on Verona and further afield on the three regions of the Veneto. You should at once send me the address of the editor with whom I want to get in touch to get information and texts for the *Anthology*.[1] At once, I beg you. Then weren't you to let me have as soon as possible the text of my thesis which is at Maria's? Ungaretti's daughter is waiting for it.

For the rest, as usual (actually no, not at all as usual), I am working from morning to night because I have been working in that school since Christmas and then there is the *Anthology* plus an inextricable mass of other work (also an anthology of pedagogists). Am studying Latin.

An affectionate hug,        Pier Paolo

PS. And Annie?
Greetings to Aunt Giannina and thank her for her postcard.

1   A reference to *Poesie dialettale del Novecento* ['Dialect poetry of the twentieth century'], Guanda (Parma, 1952).

## 245   To Giacinto Spagnoletti
Milan

*[In possession of addressee: typewritten with autograph signature and corrections]*

[Rome, January 1952]

Dear Spagnoletti,

Thank you for your affectionate postcard: I shall certainly send, and that willingly (in view of the company), some poems to the anthologist you speak of. Unfortunately I have to limit myself to a skimpy letter because it is evening and I am exhausted; and I don't know when I shall be able to write more to you. I get up at seven, go to Ciampino (where I at last have a post teaching at 20,000 lire a month), I work like a dog (I have a mania for pedagogy) come back at three, eat and then have the *Anthology* for Guanda[1] concerning which I shall only say that I am in the state of mind of the old woman in Casarsa who one day, combing her daughter's hair, after the latter had lain sick for months on an old sack, found two hundred lice and said: 'Let's leave the rest till tomorrow.'

I hug you affectionately, dear Spagnoletti, and give greetings to Sereni (my companion in misfortune, for your compatriots, when it comes to paying us, seem to lack that exuberance which on other occasions is typical of them: an exile from Friuli, I understand a lot about you, the exile from Taranto).

Yours,      Pier Paolo

This is the reply to a letter of 19 January in which Spagnoletti writes:

*Now listen; a friend of mine, Piero Chiara from Varese, who is a critic on L'Italia, the Milanese Catholic daily, would like to get together a little book to present a group of young poets and to this end turned to me not only to ask me to contribute those crumbs I have written in these last years but also to advise him on his choice. I thought you could send him ten or so lyrics with a bibliographical note.*

1   See Letter 244.

## 246   To Piero Chiara
Varese

*[In possession of addressee: typewritten with autograph signature]*

Rome, 1 February 1952

Dear Chiara,

Some days ago Spagnoletti wrote to me telling me about the little anthology[1] you are working on and inviting me to send you ten or so poems.

*1952*

The choice is so difficult for me that, as you see, I am sending you two little collections instead of one so that you can choose whichever seems best to you. In any case I am expecting a letter from you in which you can perhaps explain things better to me (Spagnoletti's card is affectionate but not exhaustive) and meantime thank you very much.

Yours,      Pier Paolo Pasolini

1   *Quarta generazione* ['Fourth generation'], edited by P. Chiara and L. Erba, Editrice Magenta (Varese, 1954).

## 247   To Nico Naldini
Casarsa
*[In possession of addressee: typewritten with autograph signature]*

[Rome, February 1952]

Dear Nico,

I only got your letter – by now irredeemably late – on Sunday morning (the post takes at least half a day more to reach Ponte Mammolo).[1] On the other hand to put Edin[2] up here was impossible, there is no room: or rather there would be if there wasn't somebody like my father in the house, to whom all such things are unbearable. I am very sorry indeed; apart from everything else I leave at half-past seven in the morning for school and get back dead tired (to work on the anthology) at three, and I could have been very little help to Edin. If you see him again in Casarsa (and I haven't seen him today or tomorrow in Rome) give him many regards and explain my problem on the lines of this letter. I am passing horrible days because of my father, who is going through a phase. Send me the poems in Chioggian dialect. Many affectionate greetings to all.

Pier Paolo

1   A remote Roman suburb north-east of the city.
2   Edin Bortolussi, brother of Archimede, on his way to emigrate to Australia. The poem 'Verso Pordenone e il mondo' ['Towards Pordenone and the world'] was dedicated to the two brothers. See the dedicatory letter 'to the publisher' in *Tal còur di un frut* ['In the heart of a child'], Edizioni 'Friuli' di Lingua Friulana (Tricesimo, 1953).

## 248   To Nico Naldini
Casarsa

[*In possession of addressee: typewritten with autograph corrections and signature*]

[Rome, March 1952]

Dearest Nico,

Lovely – your two Chioggian pieces (but the Italian one as well: the blue has turned well into the festive). You should write a little collection of poems in Chioggian dialect. (Perhaps Ciceri[1] will finance a new regular *Quaderno romanzo*).

It is perfectly useless to send poems to Penna – he doesn't give a damn for anything. However, he has still a vague idea of writing about your Friulian work (note that for some years he has not written a line – so there's not much hope). Do you know that the hero of what is wrongly considered to be Tolstoy's finest story[2] died of a floating kidney? I see you have turned pale. But don't be afraid – it seems that, judging by the symptoms artistically described, it was a case of cancer instead. But Tolstoy did not know at that time that a floating kidney is something harmless. I am pleased about the outcome with *I pianti*; I don't know which of my ideas could be useful. If I were to mention one it would certainly be already out of date – one your friends had had already. Tell them however to try to do something radiophonic which I could then perhaps get on to the radio (to the benefit of all). I am very happy that you are coming to Rome this summer. As for me, I am working like a dog. In the letters you write me always make some reference to my father (seeing that he always ends up by reading them – some sign of interest, of greeting, etc. You know why.)

I hug you affectionately along with all the rest,

Pier Paolo

This was in reply to a letter of 25 February 1952 from Naldini in which he writes:

*I and my friends have have been thinking of putting on a theatrical performance of your* Pianti *in Venice. It seems that things are now far advanced – they have found a theatre, small but chic, the sets, the music.*

1   Luigi Ciceri, Friulian student, publisher of *Tal còur di un frut.*
2   *The Death of Ivan Ilych.*

1952

## 249  To Giacinto Spagnoletti
Milan

[*In possession of addressee: typewritten with autograph signature*]

[Rome, March 1952]

Dear Spagnoletti,

I had sent Chiara a group of poems – he chose four or five and is asking me for more to make a better anthology. If you see him try to keep an eye on things. All the more since I have sent him the only collection of my things I possess and am naturally very particular about them.

Now allow me to be shamelessly frank with you: I simply do not want to keep this back; although it is a very trifling trouble it is better to deal with it. I have seen your anthology for schools:[1] very fine, that I can tell you – and I can tell you that I like it all the more because I always made my students in secondary school study those poems with excellent results in the outward sense and in the sense of comprehension and interest; and I find it very right that I am not represented, naturally (believe me) by 'Italia' or some other Italian poem. But what hurts me a little is that, having had the idea of including dialect poets, you left me out: put a hand on your heart and think what I have contributed directly or indirectly to you so as to make you mentally inclined to welcome the dialect poets into an anthology of this kind. In the second place, if you had stopped at Giotti[2] or Trilussa[3] (who is worthless) I would have thought that you didn't wish to make bets in this field which is still so uncertain. But you bet on Dell'Arco – and to be precise on his worst book, the one that is worthy of Bocelli.[4] Without taking into account that Dell'Arco, before a certain year, was a dialect poet of the most second-rate kind. Now that I am making the anthology[5] with him I see who he is, I see that he has not the slightest dignity – to the point of consenting to put his name on a book put together completely (in the manual sense as well) by me. Here in Rome they have smelt a rat and you must pardon me this outburst; but I am exhausted by work, by my job, by worry, and have lost the innocence (in the midst of all these wolves), in which there was also a touch of cowardice, with which I would once have overlooked and forgiven things.

Don't take what I am saying too seriously; they are things which in our false literary liaisons[6] are usually not talked about, or else they become tinged with meanness and hysteria. I have spoken about them because of a scruple which is entirely mine, because of a moral casuistry which, in the midst of my perdition, still has meaning; I did not want there to be hidden thoughts in my relationship with me [corrected to 'you'].*

An affectionate hug,

Yours,      Pier Paolo

\*What a *lapsus calami*:[7] one could write a novel about it. I add as a postscript that Rizzo is 'ill' and of the money from Taranto, as you will know from Sereni, there is no sign.

In reply to this letter Spagnoletti writes on 5 March 1952:

*Never, my old friend, could you be lost from my heart because the heart is* one *and cannot forget its Pasolini. There are not two hearts, one for everyone and one for the schools. The simplest explanation is this: that I was about to withdraw the book after it was finished because of the outrageous behaviour of the publisher.*

1  *Poeti del Novecento* by G. Spagnoletti, Mondadori (Milan, 1952).
2  Virgilio Giotti (1885-1957), poet writing in Triestine dialect.
3  Trilussa (1871-1950), Roman dialect poet.
4  Arnaldo Boccelli (1900-71), journalist, critic, editor of the *Enciclopedia Italiana.*
5  The *Poesia dialettale del Novecento* for Guanda.
6  liaisons: in French in the original.
7  *lapsus calami*: a slip of the pen.

## 250   To Giacinto Spagnoletti
Milan
[*In possession of addressee: typewritten with autograph signature*]

[Rome, March 1952]

Dear Spagnoletti,

You wrote me a letter which you thought you would have to write to me sooner or later; you did not reply to mine. But I swear to you that your aprioristic letter was not necessary; it was right that I should not appear in the new anthology for schools, for excellent reasons, and it was equally right that the instinctive affection which binds us was not minimally obscured by this. Read my letter again and you will see that there are no logical justifications for my exclusion from the dialect section *if Dell'Arco is there.* But this trifling matter has already been fully dealt with – it is not important to me in the sense that it has really no importance etymologically, and don't let us talk about it any more . . . But Caproni charges me to tell you that he is very upset and that to his mind the justifications you give are not valid.

I am still up to my neck in work and that is what exhausts me, not really the Roman literary scene; as for attempts to adapt to the scene, I am by now a harmonica, while remaining essentially unadaptable . . .

But try to come to Rome: here in general there is enormous laziness, I am not lazy but am compelled to be so and think with longing of your enthusiasm. As for Chiara's anthology[1] it is not that I would not deign to accept certain approaches (for goodness sake, you misunderstood me); I told you to look after my typescript, which is the only copy I have, and perhaps to give Chiara some advice about the choice.

An affectionate hug from yours,     Pier Paolo

In reply to this letter Spagnoletti writes:

*This time, yes, you have upset me. I had not written you a letter 'with intent' to justify myself and regain your friendship. I had simply described to you how things went. Badly – that is because the first person to feel the lack of you in the book and that of Giorgio [Caproni] was myself. But I really could do nothing about it. Your names and those of others which they did not want they removed. That's all. So it was not because of Dell'Arco [...] You see, Pier Paolo, relationships are always accepted when they are good. There is no before or 'after'. Since I got to know you, you exist for me in only one way. But it seems to me you have not understood this otherwise you would not have written me that letter.*

1   See Letter 245.

## 251   To Giacinto Spagnoletti
Milan
[*In possession of addressee: typewritten with autograph signature*]

[Rome, March 1952]

Dear Spagnoletti,

I'm not sorry that you are upset[1] – the matter ought not to pass without upsets . . . But I repeat, with or without them it is over; there remains, it is true, the mystery of that character who imposed Dell'Arco on you while keeping me out, but all the better for Dell'Arco. Please don't speak about it any more; I still consider you in a certain sense guilty but this 'guilt' has entered into you, has become part of you, it is a (little) shadow which has quickly merged with the warm, friendly light which your image gives off when I think of it. And then I have a thousand ways of justifying you: first of all your critical freedom, then my lack of confidence in myself, then the circumstances . . .

Here life is as usual: I see only Bertolucci, Dell'Arco and Caproni (who has understood how things are and has completely pardoned you). I work like a black for this school and the anthology and in between times am aware from intermittences,[2] which smell of scrap iron and old rags, that there is something 'age old' the poetry says, which my scholars like so much, in the sun that beats down on Rebibbia[3] as it does on the province of Lecce or a Touareg encampment.

An affectionate hug,     Pier Paolo

1   See Letter 250.

2   In French in the original.
3   Rebibblia: a Roman suburb.

## 252   To Silvana Mauri
Milan
[*In possession of addressee: typewritten with autograph corrections and signature*]

[Rome, spring 1952]

Dear Silvana,

Sunday morning is here again, the only time when I can write to my friends without the obsession of work waiting for me. I have just opened the window on to the balconies of that room¹ where you came one Sunday, that sad builder's site of a room suspended over the mud in which you contrived to catch the 'thread of the sun', like some sort of intimist consolation (the kind of consolation one has in childhood with a shiver of fear in the stomach: to be secluded, alone, to reduce the world to the walls that surround you and to be overcome with joy at it, playing with the threads of the sun, writing a poem for one's mother's birthday).

Opening these balconies and colliding breast to breast with spring, which is already adult, almost faded, the true, tremendous Roman spring, which you know, and the scent is like an enormous mudguard baked in the sun, a piece of metal, of rags wetted and then dried in the heat, of old iron, of burning heaps of rubbish, I immediately thought of you with a choking flood of sweetness. Some tatter of adolescence remains attached to the skeleton: and all that is needed is the smell of the madeleine . . . In my case an atrocious madeleine of the outskirts of town, of the houses of the evicted, of warm rags. Altogether I feel the excitement (but without the abundant softnesses of childish fat, of sex ardent with freshness and unconfined violence) which I felt on Sunday morning in Bologna, when I had to go to the Imperiale for the retrospective screenings of the cine-club (Machaty,² Feyder);³ of Bologna, which is so civilized. In which you and I each plunged into a world full of resonances, a necessary world: the family in society.

Now I think how frighteningly alone we are: as if they had taken us, naked, and chased us for ever into the open. I am in an absolute sense alone, listening to a radio which is playing certain old songs ('Torna piccina mia') of the typical Sunday programme, and to boys playing football.

And I have before me a Sunday without prospects: I shall go dancing with Mariella.⁴ If not I shall go to the devil, going to Settecamini to see a match by adolescents from Pietralata, and then go and get drunk with them. So there, I have got it off my chest. About your visit still no ideas – but I confess to you that ideas do not come to me because I don't think about it, I have become discouraged. I am working a lot at the anthology;[5] I am making the last spurt (talking about dialect poets have you been in touch with Guicciardi?)[6] Guanda will probably soon publish my book of Friulian poems, the *Romancero*; I hope so, then I shall be able to work more freely, get ahead. Throw myself on Rome. Then in Milan there's a certain Chiara[7] who is supposed to be making an anthology of young poets (he is a friend of Spagnoletti): and he has asked me to send him my Italian poems. The person in charge of this venture is Anceschi: now since I do not trust Chiara much you should say to Anceschi if you see him, if that is easy for you, to take a look at the selection. I went to see Valeri's[8] performance: and I enjoyed it hugely. Then I went round to her dressing-room to thank her and behaved in a decidedly ridiculous way; that is to say, I complimented her like a chemist. She, as she told me, expected a critical judgement and will have taken it badly. But I had to catch the bus at Portonaccio, the bus one mustn't miss, the last one. And with me counting every second and with her straight from the stage who in short made me shy, so that I plunged into a complete aphasic syndrome.

Many affectionate greetings (convinced I shall see you soon, I feel that you will not be able to resist the attraction of this Roman spring) from yours,

Pier Paolo

1 Of his flat in via Tagliere 3, in Ponte Mammolo, Rome.
2 Gustav Machaty (1901–63), Czech film director, best known for his film *Extase* with Hedy Lamarr.
3 Jacques Feyder (1887–1948), French film director who worked in France, Austria and Hollywood (where he directed Garbo in *The Kiss*); best known for *Thérèse Raquin* and *La Kermesse Héroïque*.
4 Mariella Bauzano, who worked at the Biblioteca Nazionale in Rome.
5 The anthology of *Poesia dialettale del Novecento*.
6 Emilio Guicciardi, Lombard dialect poet.
7 See Letter 246.
8 Franca Valeri (b. 1920), actress specializing in intimate revue.

## 253 To Giacinto Spagnoletti
Milan

[*In possession of addressee: typewritten with autograph corrections and signature*]

[Rome, spring 1952]

Dear Spagnoletti,

I should like to ask you for a small favour provided it only costs you an even smaller effort. You should, that is, let Anceschi know that the essay on

Ungaretti ('A poet and God')[1] entered with the pseudonym for the Four Arts prize for criticism is mine. This, naturally, if you have not entered yourself and if you feel you can do so without the *slightest* effort on your part or that of Anceschi ... You will understand that someone who earns 21 thousand lire a month working in school five or six hours a day is to be pardoned if he bets on certain hopes and decends to certain transactions which once would have made him blush with scorn.

What are you doing? I had a card at Easter from you (a very sweet card and a source of emotion and gratitude for my parents), since when I have had only indirect news about the giddy whirl of your lively literary activity. About myself, about this shipwreck of mine in the shallows, I think there is nothing to add in these last months: I am waiting for summer to be able to work a little. It has never happened to me in my life before, not having time to write: and now I see what tremendous lack of balance this brings with it, what a depressing effect on the whole tone of life.

An affectionate hug,        Pier Paolo Pasolini

1  See *Passione e ideologia*, Einaudi (Turin, 1985), pp. 309–26.

## 254  To Nico Naldini
Casarsa

[*In possession of addressee: typewritten with autograph signature and postscript*]

[Rome, April 1952]

Dear Nico,

This is to let you and your mother know that a week today there will be the last (at least let us hope it is the last) station of the *Via Crucis*.[1] I shall be in Casarsa on the evening of the seventh at the usual time. How are things? Latin? Ferruccio Ulivi (who will write a piece about us) liked your poems very much.

The anthology is coming on well but I am exhausted. Many greetings to Aunt Giannina and everybody.

An affectionate hug,        Pier Paolo

PS. Write poetry in Chioggian dialect (but also in Friulano or in Italian). The two you sent me I shall give with one of mine and one by Guerra to Bertolucci for *Paragone*, where I hope they will do well.

1  A reference to the appeal over the sentence for the incident at Ramuscello.

## 255   To Fabio Luca Cavazza
Bologna
[*In possession of addressee: typewritten with autograph signature*]

[Rome, April 1952]

Dear Cavazza,

As you will know the train was six hours late; I therefore sat at the window so resigned to not seeing you that in fact I did not see you. But you have once more made the station at Bologna human – which for so long had been shut off in the hostility of a stranger. But I shall come that way again, I shall come that way again, the Methuselah of Justice on his way to Friuli the eternal;[1] and barely touching what is the dearest of all cities (and to which I shall dedicate my book which should appear in the *Paragone* collection).[2] I hug you for the nth time by letter. And I give you a job which should suit you very well: to make enquiries from the publisher of a Bolognese review (*Portici?*) so as to find out if it is true that a certain shit called Rino Borghello, who is editing a selection of Friulian regional work, has twice sent him two things of mine: without success because, according to him, the editor sent them back to him, the first being too long, the second having arrived too late. I know that lot up there; and I know how much lack of moral feelings is characteristic of them, how much limitless imbecility. A Friulian collection without my name seemed intolerable to my father, who became ill over it; so although I don't give a damn I am forced to see how things stand. Also to settle matters with the shit when I go to Udine: whether to greet him or to heap scorn on him. Today I am going to ring the Ottieris; where has Silvana got to? I am full of desire to see her. When are you coming down?

An affectionate hug, yours,      Pier Paolo

1   A reference to the trial.
2   *La meglio gioventú.*

## 256   To Piero Chiara
Varese
[*In possession of addressee: typewritten with autograph signature*]

[Postmark: Rome, 30 April 1952]

Dear Chiara,

Here are the other 'reserve' poems you ask me for. I don't feel like making a selection so I am sending you the complete packet of those against which you made a little mark in pencil and therefore imagine that you felt they were fit to be included in an anthology. I thank you again, really from my heart, and send you my most warm greetings.

Yours very dev.ly,     Pier Paolo Pasolini

## 257   To Giacinto Spagnoletti
Milan
[*In possession of addressee: typewritten with autograph signature*]

[Rome, June 1952]

Dearest Spagnoletti,

Thank you for your affectionate interest; there is still no news about the prize.[1] So much the better, so I continue to hope. One way or another I shall simply have to 'survive' the summer without a salary . . . And yet at this moment as I write to you I am happy, I don't know why. Tomorrow is Sunday, I shall go to Ostia, my mother is preparing a meal for me next door, the window behind me is open on the extremely warm and very ancient night of Rebibbia, and all the radios of the Carabiniere NCOs are making a din with accents that are atrociously and sweetly nostalgic. When everything in life is finished everything is still there. Will you come to Rome this year? You don't talk any more about your idea of moving here – are you giving up?

Many affectionate greetings from yours,     Pier Paolo

PS. Schwarz (is that how it is spelt?) has already sent me an invitation to contribute to the series you tell me about – I naturally think at your recommendation.

My father did everything conscientiously and sent it off. Perhaps you have seen the package; I chose that portion of my verses which I felt you would like best.

Replying on 26 June Spagnoletti writes:

The appeal which he [Schwarz] has made to many young people – the one you received – also implies, once the manuscript has been accepted (I have already refused about twenty), the acceptance by the author of this clause: to undertake to dispose of 100 copies of the special edition at 600 lire each . . . I know very well that this clause will seem unfair to you.

1   See Letter 256.

## 258   To Nico Naldini
Casarsa

[*In possession of addressee: typewritten with autograph signature*]

[Rome, 21 June 1952]

Dear Nico,

I am very pleased with your programme. Rome is at your feet. (By the way, could you find among your socks some other poems to send me? I am afraid your verses are a little scanty and an editor always has the weakness of wanting to make a choice; meantime the old *Letteratura* has reappeared and Ulivi likes your 'Seris' ['Evenings'] very much. On Thursday I shall see him at the Premio Strega – I am one of the jury and have already become a subject of gossip as you can see from an article by Vicari in the *Fiera letteraria* of today, 21 June – and I shall ask him about his article.) As for overtures to Aunt Chiarina I am not clear about them; Aunt Chiarina's authority is extremely limited as you can imagine. *Does my uncle know anything about them or not?* You must talk clearly to me about this matter otherwise you could be counterproductive. I disapprove of your grandiose programme for the trip: by all means take that most uncomfortable and particularly unsafe means of locomotion, Elio's[1] Lambretta, as far as Ravenna, but as for coming from Florence to here by bicycle – that seems to me to be a very bad idea. Your proud attitude towards your illness is admirable but a recurrence of jaundice etc. here in Rome would be very inconvenient indeed.

So write soon. I hug you affectionately and all the others as well (including Aunt Giannina – you don't tell me whether or not she got my poem[2] which cost me so much effort during atrocious days of marking, anthology, etc.).

Pier Paolo

1   Elio Bartolini.
2   A 'wedding poem'.

## 259   To Giacinto Spagnoletti
Milan

[*In possession of addressee: typewritten with autograph signature*]

[Rome, summer 1952]

Dear Spagnoletti,

I have been meaning to write to you for so long but I keep putting it off, having plunged into an obsessive holiday. If you only knew what Rome is like! All vice and sun, scabs and light: a people invaded by hunger for life, by

contagious exhibitionism and sensuality which fill the outskirts of the city …
I am lost here in the midst of it and it is difficult for myself and for others to
find me. I wanted to thank you for mediating with Anceschi[1] and to charge
you – if you get the chance – to thank him warmly. As for the editions by
Schwarz, why did you appear so worried about telling me the terms? They
neither surprised nor dismayed me; all that belongs to a world which I am
more than used to. But I do not have the money to order the hundred copies
nor the energy to have them ordered by others, so let's forget about it. And
don't be upset about it, just as I am not.

An affectionate hug from yours,     Pier Paolo Pasolini

1   See Letter 253.

## 260   To Silvana Mauri
Milan

[*In possession of addressee: typewritten with autograph corrections, addition
and signature*]

[Rome, July 1952]

Dear Silvana,

I need to ask you for your advice: that is to say, I should like to know from
you if you feel it would be right for me to write to Fabio to be involved in
taking a new boy into his village.[1] This is the situation: I got to know this boy
at the Villa Borghese on the evening of the Premio Strega* and, while chatting
to him, at once learnt his situation. His father died (I think in the war) then in
1948 so did his mother whom he loved very much but who had married
again; the stepfather had other children and completely ignored this
newcomer. So that now he has neither family nor house: every so often he
works as an electrician and during the period when he is earning he sleeps at
the house of a woman who throws him out when he has no money left. So he
spends three quarters of the year in the open in the sense that he does not
have a roof and sleeps and eats in the Villa Borghese or under some bridge
over the Tiber. You know what sort of thing poverty can force people into: I
know for example that he once stole a suitcase from a Swiss pilgrim. But I
assure you he is not a thief. He is a vessel of clay among vessels of iron, there
at the Villa Borghese among real thieves, real criminals. He has in him
something terribly serious, something 'moralistic'; he could become a type
like that blond boy from Frosinone (remember?) and is already 'refined'
within himself in the sense that he has within him his mother and the
memory of a normal life. This deprived him of the possibility of becoming
one of the Roman scum, a thief, a blackmailer; but it also robs him of his

liberty. I know a lot of thieves etc., who are happy even when they go for three days without eating and then in order to eat go and get filled up with a can of soup at some barracks; they are free, they have no memories, or else have that vague 'sunny' happiness we talked about. It can be said that I know hundreds of poor people like this; but it has never occurred to me to turn to Fabio so that they could have somewhere to sleep and something to feed themselves with or so that, above all, they could be reformed. Either they had no need of it or had too much of it, I don't know which. This one (he is called Cristoforo, poor boy) concerns me. Just imagine for example that he explained to me that what he found hardest to bear (on that extremely hot afternoon of the Premio Strega) was not to have soap to wash with. (You have to think of his wardrobe, Silvana, a T-shirt, a pair of trousers and a pair of shoes are all he has. He washes his clothes himself on the banks of the Tiber and waits, naked, till the clothes dry.) At night he sleeps on a bench in the Villa Borghese; clothed, naturally, and just think of this, one morning while he was sleeping, someone like him (but one of the other lot) stole his shoes slipping them off in his sleep. I could tell you a thousand other incidents or situations in his life, but I think you do not need them, that you have grasped what I wanted to say to you, which is basically very complicated because a person who lives in the midst of bourgeois life lacks the necessary information to grasp the truth of certain situations which they know only from the papers, from terrifyingly conventional notions in which however any feeling of truth is lost. You have sufficient imagination to sense these things in their truth even if you do not know them at first hand; in short you have the means to make them human even if you do not have some facts. What I am anxious to add however is that I am not in love (forgive me for speaking so clearly to you) with this boy; sensually he does not interest me; what interests me is his case and I don't know what to do to get him out of his frightening state, that of someone who when he wakes up at first light in Villa Borghese says to himself: 'Today if I do not steal or find some homosexual I shall not eat.'

I repeat – this is the sort of thing hundreds of boys say but Cristoforo says it full of anguish *as we would do*. Now I am waiting for a prompt response from you, Silvana, but don't take it too much to heart, don't exhaust yourself: quite simply think whether it is possible or not to take this boy into Fabio's village. If it is not possible, never mind: we shall abandon Cristoforo to his fate once again, I am hardened enough to accept this as well . . .

I have no news to give you about myself: my holidays began two days ago and now I am waiting to spend these red and squalid months like a mutilated animal wandering through the outskirts of the city in the mud of the Tiber. I hope to work a little on my novel[2] as well. What about you? and Ottiero?[3]

Many affectionate greetings from yours,          Pier Paolo

*I make this precise reference to the Premio Strega because the night before I had dreamt about you and Fabio. We were on the top of a hill (perhaps vaguely San Luca) or a block of flats; then we came down in a kind of lift – rustic and very grand, which came down in wide circles; since the lift was going too slowly Fabio and I got out and ran on ahead. Fabio was radiant and at a certain point while running ahead of the big vehicle from which you looked at us affectionately, Fabio and I started to play at football; it was a stupendous ball painted with all the colours of the rainbow.

Further, at the Premio Strega, I saw Luciano.

1  See Letter 205.
2  *Ragazzi di vita.*
3  Ottiero Ottieri, Silvana's husband.

## 261  To Silvana Mauri
Milan

[*In possession of addressee: typewritten with corrections and autograph signature*]

[Rome, summer 1952]

Dearest Silvana,

I have not written to you sooner for the reasons I have often told you about: writing to you is a serious business for me and I need a free morning to do so – something which has not happened up to now because, among other things, a cousin of mine[1] (the poet no 2 of the family) has come to Rome which keeps me very busy: I am in a state of continual, tiring tension. For me summer is a wager I must not lose: I reckon time not by years but by summers.

I dive in head-first with a disgusting and indifferent voracity: I eat nothing and die from indigestion, I eat continually and am empty. The first storms announce the tomb and I await them with a terror that is by now entirely mechanical. Cristoforo[2] has disappeared: I tried to make enquiries at the Villa Borghese but it was useless because the other people like him either don't know him or do not care at all what may happen to him or are afraid that I am interested in him because he had been robbed or something like that and so tell me the first lie that comes into their heads. For my part I have already forgotten him: one fate is always the same as another fate. And Rome has made me sufficiently pagan not to believe in the validity of certain scruples which are typically northern and which have no meaning in this climate; I now understand certain of your attitudes of pity, which are so different from mine, so much more heroic and positive than mine (even if they are a little ineffective): your roots are down here. Do you remember when (in what seem very distant times) we talked about your interest in the 'rapport' with others. It was something that had a mysterious flavour for me, bound up with 'the romance of the Mauris'; I shall explain. Anyone who lives because of ethnic tradition in a world inhabited by extroverts, whose secrets, whose weaknesses are sensual and not sentimental, cannot but be interested in rapport as the concrete form of a life lived on the external surfaces which are social in the primordial sense of the word. Perhaps it is from this that all the conventional forms that characterize both the conformist bourgeois of Rome and the South are derived (and the people too, but in a more poetic way; sex not religion, honour not morality . . .), and the forms of 'Franciscan' religiosity which is directed entirely to the external world, is active, curious (take Fabio too, whose vocation also began in the way you know, entirely interior). For two or three years I have been living in a world with a 'different' feel: an extraneous body and therefore defined in this world, to which I am adapting myself, and very slowly coming to terms with. Between the Ibsenite and the Pascolian (so that we understand each other) I find myself here in a life which is all muscles, turned outside in like a glove, which is always unfolded like one of these songs which I once detested, absolutely stripped bare of sentimentalism, in human organisms so sensual as to be almost mechanical; in which one does not know any of the Christian attitudes, pardon, meekness, etc., and selfishness takes permissible – virile – forms. In the northern world where I have lived there was always – at least so it seemed to me – in the rapport between one individual and another, the shadow of a kind of piety which took the forms of timidity, of respect, of deep anxiety, of strong affection, etc.; in order to break off a love-relationship only a gesture, a word, was needed. Since the interest in the intimate, in the goodness or wickedness that is within us had the upper hand, it was not an equilibrium between one person and another that was sought but a reciprocal impulse. Here among these people who are much more the victims of the irrational, of passion, the relationship on the other hand is always well defined; it is based on more concrete facts: from muscular force to social position . . . Rome, ringed by its hell of suburbs, is stupendous in these days: the unconcealed steadiness of the heat is what is needed to mitigate a little its excesses in order to strip it bare and so to show it in its highest forms. I thought we would have seen it together . . . But you have much better things to dedicate yourself to – something miraculous and inexpressible,[3] for me, who am so outside all the functions, so provisory and aimless; and my amazement is all the more profound and undefined since it is precisely you who repeat the miracle, who carry it out with all the symptoms of a terror and of an exultation which I know well, which plunges one into the plans of 'others' by way of that difficult thing – poetry. It is this now which is important in your life, which is important in our relationship (and which perhaps prevented me from replying to you immediately, because of a kind of confusion, of embarrassment of which I am the object, and of joyful anxiety of which you are the object).

All the rest has very little importance. Don't be discouraged if I take a little time to reply to you: write to me, keep me informed about your life and about that life (which, as you understand, seems stupendous to me in terms of its future) which is uncoiling in you.

I don't have much to tell you about myself (the poet on the prize is Ungaretti;[4] Anceschi, if you see him, can tell you something about it); my life is the same as usual.

Many affectionate greetings – also to Ottiero and your parents.

Pier Paolo

1 Nico Naldini.
2 See Letter 260.
3 Silvana was pregnant.
4 See Letter 253.

## 262 To Luciano Serra
Bologna
[*In possession of addressee: typewritten with autograph signature*]

[Rome, summer 1952]
Dearest Luciano,

Are you in Bologna? Or are you away on holiday as usual? It is true that now there is *Il Mulino* which at least indirectly gives me news about your active life; but it is rather a shame that we lose touch with each other like this. Why don't you decide to come to Rome for a few days – perhaps this September? The more time passes the more life in Bologna – clear and happy – sinks to the turbid bottom; and I have strong pangs of nostalgia. To speak about all this by letter is impossible now because there is a whole story to begin over again, there is the history of almost a decade to be told: one would need to write volumes. I wanted with this hurried note to ask you for news of that essay of mine on Ungaretti[1] which was to have appeared in *Convivium*; will it appear? Along with Piccioni and Rizzo I have won a prize for criticism at Naples with this essay (the Four Arts prize); but I had made additions and corrections; if Calcaterra were still thinking of publishing it, let me know, so that I send him the latest version. Have you any way of getting touch with Calcaterra just now? If you can and it isn't too much trouble, write him a note reminding him that I am competing for the 'Modena' poetry prize of which he is judge.

*1952*

You will find this story of the prizes ridiculous – so do I – ridiculous and without dignity. But I live that way ... You know very well that if you teach in a private school you are not paid during the summer and then how is one to make ends meet?

Many affectionate greetings to you and your family. Remember me to my friends in Bologna.

Yours,     Pier Paolo

1   See Letter 253.

## 263   To Carlo Betocchi
Florence
[*In possession of addressee: typewritten with autograph addition, date and signature*]

Rome, August 1952

Dear Betocchi,

Caproni has told me of your intention to take part in the Udine prize.[1] At this moment I cannot give you precise news because I have never got involved in it, knowing how much rottenness there is in the bourgeois, *bienpensant* (and, according to them, Catholic) circles of that province. I know indirectly that there are big arguments (a group of parish-pump patriots has taken umbrage because the prize is for Italian and not Friulano) and I know, still indirectly, from what I hear from my cousin, Naldini whom you know, that Don Marchetti (one of the two or three honest people there are in Friuli) has said that they already know the name of the person who will win the prize. That is the bad news; but you know that one has to keep it in mind only up to a certain point. I would definitely advise you to send the collection of poems. In the meantime I shall write a letter to Friuli in order to get more accurate news; thereafter I will be able to write covering letters (but if the jury is made up of people who know their job there will be no need ...) to the bigwigs who have organized the prize and whom I will certainly know more or less directly. Meantime I think one can mention the name of Tessitori, the parliamentary deputy, whom I know; and then that of the presiding genius of Friuli, Chino Ermacora (who never fails to be involved in these matters from the point of view of tourism and patriotism). I think moreover that in Friuli they will be very happy for you to be the winner; it is true that they are of such unimaginable ignorance that of contemporary poets they know only Ungaretti and Montale *by name alone*; but I have thought of a way of getting you known to the public; I shall write to D. Menichini[2] and get

382

him to talk about you in the *Messaggero Veneto* and – forgive the cynicism – stressing your Catholic origins, Bargellini[3] and *Il Frontespizio*.

Are dialect love poems of any use to you? I feel myself burning with guilt towards you, quite filled with bitter shame; but lately I have been overburdened with work between Ciampino[4] and Guanda[5] and I was also not very well (I was afraid I had something wrong with my liver, a threat which fortunately – that was all I needed – has disappeared); days have passed and, fearing that it might already be too late, I took refuge in cowardly absence. Do you forgive me? So meantime send the poems; in a few days I shall give you more accurate news. The only way to give a moral dimension to Friuli's million lire is for it to go into your pocket.

Many affectionate greetings from yours,        Pier Paolo

In reply to this letter Betocchi writes on 26 August 1952:

*I hope you may have been able in some way – as you intended – to give some support to the modest merits of the slight unpublished work which, also as a result of your affectionate urging, I have decided to send this very day: all I need is the time to finish the copies. I have made the decision or rather that compelling necessity for us to humble ourselves made it for me; and we do not even have the right to be melancholy about it. You know, and my friends know, that I don't presume; I am happy to be alive, and sad at my unfaithfulness to that wonderful gift. But then there is the recompense of letters like yours full of the fervour of profound affection and for which I am so grateful to you. It is not the hopes – the uncertain hopes – in your words (and the extremely uncertain ones of the chance my attempt will have) which cheer me but that extra something I receive. Thanks, dear Pasolini.*

*Your extremely precise letter informs me about that Friulian world which I know only through another love but which it was easy for me to guess at during my wanderings in Udine in other times, in the shadows of its squares and under the little colonnades... Your cynical tactic is very fitting! I can see the smile of the Saints burning and sanctifying the stones of the foundations which God himself wishes so heavy and rotten.*

1  The Premio Nazionale 'Friuli' for lyric poetry and organ music.
2  Dino Menichini.
3  Piero Bargellini (1897–1981), Catholic critic and essayist, contributor to *Frontespizio*.
4  Pasolini was teaching in a school at Ciampino.
5  Guanda was the editor of the dialect anthology on which Pasolini was working.

## 264   To Carlo Betocchi
Florence

[*In possession of addressee: typewritten with autograph, corrections and signature*]

[Rome, September 1952]

Dear Betocchi,

I read your letter and was moved by it – so dear, so full of the tension in which you live without interruption, without ever giving in. It is a miracle how this light of youthful ingenuousness which gives nobility to our world (so unworthy of being given nobility) endures in you; but everything is explained if one thinks that you see this world as Creation, but a Creation which takes places every instant. I remember that you quoted the English Romantics in the introduction to *Reality Conquers the Dream*[1] and I think that there is no one else to whom Keats' assertion that beauty is truth and truth beauty applies as it does to you. Your poetry and also your way of life derive from the confusion of those two terms . . . I am a little ashamed of my cynicism which you so gaily accepted. I have written to Menichini asking him to write a preparatory article about you in the *Messaggero* and he, with high praise for your poetry, replied that he was leaving, somewhat ill, to go on holiday, and that he could do nothing. I shall write again today hoping that he is back. Meantime I learned today that Baldini[2] is chairman of the jury. I think he is approachable in many ways. For example under the seal of the confessional, I could try through Dell'Arco who is frequently in touch with Baldini. But there might be better ways to try.

If you have any ideas on the subject write to me at once . . . meantime we shall learn the names of the other judges as well. In Friuli a little scandal has broken out. Don Marchetti has written in an article that 'the winner of the prize is already *in pectore*[3] of the person who pays him', and Senator Tessitori has started proceedings against him. That prevents me from writing to Tessitori who will have to act with the greatest circumspection and not compromise himself with the slightest word . . . As you see, things are not going in the most desirable way, but I foresaw it. The best and most important thing is to work on the jury: the indubitable and evident value of your poetry will do the rest.

Many affectionate greetings from yours,

Pier Paolo Pasolini

In reply Betocchi wrote on 9 September 1952:

*Dear Pasolini,*
   *Thank you for the trouble you have been to for me and for your very nice letter. Your*

commentary on my letter sums up briefly and in full the nub of a character – which is mine – on which the innocent imagination of my mother and (in part) the world collaborated; if those lines of creative energy which even science has begun to study have any meaning. As for my poetry, God knows what has happened to it . . . thank you for your other interventions in Friuli; the little scandal might, who knows, be in our favour. Alas I speak always and exclusively on the basis of my needs, and feel the deep anxiety for my weaknesses alive within me. So much so that if in '32 I would have been so pleased with a prize for Reality Conquers the Dream, if I were to get this one I would really feel I had come into a lost kingdom. Bear in mind, however, that my wager with life is so profoundly Catholic that it cannot lose; and if the poems which necessity has made me gather together to send off do not get my votes, as the little pages of filter paper in '32 did in full, the fact in itself has my full adhesion and responsibility and will also have the reward, whatever it may be. And you, my dearest Pasolini, for the pleasure which these letters have given me will have been a necessary witness because our brothers are chosen and are forgotten in this way, through letters which are written and then stop being written but are never ever lost. It would be beautiful too if of this business only this memory were preserved.

1  *Realtà vince il sogno* by C. Bettochi, Edizioni del *Frontespizio* (Florence, 1932).
2  Antonio Baldini (1889–1962), founder of *La Ronda*, writer and critic.
3  *In pectore*: literally 'in the chest'; i.e. like the secrets of the confessional, known but not to be divulged.

## 265  To Nico Naldini
Casarsa
[*In possession of addressee: typewritten with autograph corrections and signature*]

[Rome, Autumn 1952]
Dear Nico,

I have no news of you any more – why don't you write to me? Who knows why thinking about you fills me with emotion. And to think that once we were so happy. I am correcting the final proofs of the *Anthology*. Send me all your unpublished dialect poems in *Seris par un frut* ['Series for a boy']; they are useful to me to place here and there (*Fiera letteraria*, etc.) in articles devoted to dialect poets announcing the anthology. Besides Dell'Arco wants to start a high-class little review[1] on the lines of *Orazio* with fifteen regular contributors: but they, rather than being paid, would be the ones who finance it – two thousand lire a number every two months (it seems). I am not very enthusiastic about it – on the other hand it is necessary to have an organ, a little organ of our own, for the polemics the anthology will stir up. I know you don't have two thousand lire every month but you can try Uncle Gino whom I shall speak to as well for you – after all two thousand lire is a paltry sum. Write to me right away and above all send me the poems immediately.

385

An affectionate hug for you and for everybody,

Pier Paolo

1    *Il Belli.*

## 266   To Piero Bigongiari
Florence

[*In possession of addressee: typewritten with autograph date and signature*]

Rome, 4 October 1952

Dear Bigongiari,

Many thanks for our invitation to send my essay on Ungaretti[1] to *Paragone*; unfortunately, however (unfortunately because I rate *Paragone* above any other review), Anceschi had already asked for it and I had already promised it to him. But if there is no objection I should like to send you a 'Note' on 'Stanze della funicolare' ['Stanzas on the funicular railway'] by Caproni[2] in a few days' time because I am up to my neck in my *Anthology of Dialect Poets.*

Many warm greetings from yours,        Pier Paolo Pasolini

1    *A poet and God.*
2    See 'Giorgio Caproni' in *Paragone*, December 1952.

## 267   To Giacomo Noventa[1]
Turin

[*In possession of addressee's heirs: typewritten with autograph date and signature*]

Rome, 17 October 1952

Dear Noventa,

For goodness sake go back on your decision – I have already corrected the proofs of the *Anthology* – everything is ready. But apart from the technical reasons, your defection would be a severe blow for the *Anthology*. In the Introduction I talk about you at length as one of the major figures, one of the necessary ones; what would the reader say then if he did not see you in the text? I think that the problem you mention (the forthcoming publication of your poems in their definitive version)[2] would not be beyond remedy: all one would need is a little note at the end of the pages dedicated to you explaining the matter in the most rigorously critical way: you are too established a poet to be afraid of being confronted with variants – on the contrary . . . May I hope?

Many warm greetings from yours dev.ly,

Pier Paolo Pasolini

To the request to publish a selection of his poems in the *Anthology of Dialect Poetry of the Twentieth Century* Noventa had replied with a refusal in a telegram of 17 October 1952:

*I am profoundly grateful to you but I cannot agree to any publication or re-publication of my poems a definitive text of which I am preparing for another publisher Stop with many affectionate greetings Giacomo Noventa*

To Pasolini's letter of 17 October Noventa replies with one dated 20 October:

*Dear Pasolini,*

*I absolutely cannot – I have already given my word, I have already cashed a very large advance, I cannot, however sorry I may be; you as a gentleman and a poet must understand.*

*I understand your difficulties but I cannot. The poems I have published are among the very few which I shall hand in to my publisher; if you were to re-publish them and I were to consent, my publisher would be right in accusing me of a very grave lack of correctness and loyalty. There are, on the other hand, I believe, many dialect poets who deserve to be known as much as the poets in the Italian language. By replacing my poems with some poems by these poets you will therefore be doubly just.*

*As far as our introduction is concerned I do not believe that the silence about me would be an error; I myself have wanted – at least up to now – everyone's silence and that is what I deserve. But if you thought you absolutely had to talk about me – as a poet or not as a poet – which is not altogether clear – then speak about me and your reserve will justify my absence from the text.*

*Believe me, dear Pasolini, I am grateful to you, grateful with all my heart for the nice things you wanted to write about me; but do not run the risk of a positive verdict on me which would mean a negative verdict on three quarters of present-day Italian – and not only Italian – literature. Apologize to Guanda too for me, and believe me yours most affectionately and gratefully,*
    *Giacomo Noventa*

Pasolini's next letter has not been found. Noventa consents to the publication of only seven poems and on 29 October sends Pasolini this telegram: *Preface or postface my note if you think right with my little autobiographical note Assure me immediately integral publication of the note itself affectionate greetings Noventa.*

1  Giacomo Noventa (1898–1960), poet writing in Venetian dialect.
2  See G. Noventa, *Verse e poesie*, Edizioni di Communità (Milan, 1956).

## 268  To Nico Naldini
Casarsa

[*In possession of addressee: typewritten with autograph note and signature*]

[Rome, autumn 1952]

Dear Nico,

How are you? Is your system cleared out? I am in a bad way. I am working on the proofs with piercing headaches. Fortunately Graziella, who is delicious, is flitting around me. But let's get back to us: if by return of post you send me three lyrics, which I badly need, I'll let you off the other two (given my abundant inspiration . . .)*

Today I wrote your bio-bibliographical note for the anthology. But don't rest on this laurel – work and study for the university.

Ciao,      Pier Paolo

*but by return of post or it is no use.

## 269  To Leonardo Sciascia
Palermo

[*In possession of addressee: typewritten with autograph signature and postscript*]

[Rome, October 1952]

Dear Sciascia,

Thank you for your letter but this is not the end . . . I should like you to try to get the information I still lack; you will understand that in a series of bibliographical notes, all of them exact, gaps in the descriptive material[1] would be very serious.

[There follows a list of queries about Sicilian authors.]

I have re-read 'separately' the Sicilians in my introduction; they did not stand up at all well to that kind of reading because the argument is strictly bound up with the Neapolitans and by itself risks looking botched. So I ought to get it right – can you wait a fortnight? But I have a proposal which you should weigh up with the greatest impartiality; would you be prepared to publish in instalments in *Galleria* a long story of mine (almost a novel)? The title is *Il disprezzo della provincia* ['Provincial contempt'],[2] it is set somewhere between Friuli and Trieste and has a rather interesting plot even for a very average reader. I am making this proposal to you so as to make up my mind to finish and round off the novel – something I would otherwise postpone to infinity. As to whether it is a good idea to publish or not in a review like *Galleria*, remember *Rassegna d'Italia*, which published Piovene[3] in instalments . . . Think it over, feeling very free.

Many warm greetings from yours,     Pier Paolo Pasolini

PS. I told Giorgio Caproni to send you something being sure that a contribution from him would please you. Did you get it? I shall write very soon to Roversi to have things sent on.

1   A reference to the introduction Pasoloni wrote for Sciascia's selection of Romance poets, *Poesia dialettale del Novecento.*
2   Unpublished.
3   Guido Piovene (1907–74), well-known and successful novelist.

## 270   To Piero Chiara
Varese
[*In possession of addressee: typewritten with autograph signature*]

[Postmark: Rome, 10 November 1952]

Dear Chiara,

Many thanks for your letter and here is more material, in fact all the material; I no longer trusted myself to make a choice.[1] The things I have sent you were the ones that were liked best by my friends (e.g. by Contini – 'The names of the rosary' and 'The devils sermon'; by Sereni, who had made a selection for *Rassegna* when it was at its last gasp – 'The crucifixion' and other diaries (e.g. 'My room has enchantments of palms'); by Spagnoletti – who had made a selection for a review to be published by Guanda (which was stillborn). But many other things, the majority, only I know, because they have not been published but kept in a drawer: in short, I simply cannot form an objective idea of what they are like. The packet I am sending you is very precious because, of the majority of the typed poems, I have only that copy (of the final version) – precious to me, naturally. So please let me have it back as soon as you have finished your work, by registered post. I hope you may find something new (I know for example that the diaries of '49 you will not like and perhaps the last ones as well but read them as diaries rather than as poems – and that because, in any case, I value your opinion.

Many warm greetings from yours,     Pier Paolo Pasolini

1   See Letters 246 and 256.
2   These poems appeared in the collection *L'usignolo della Chiesa Cattolica.*

## 271  To Nico Naldini
Casarsa

*[In possession of addressee: typewritten with autograph date and signature]*

Rome, 30 November 1952

Dear Nico,

Your poem is good. And in general your letter pleased me.

Study and write poetry without getting discouraged. And try to get closer, as you say, to Italian critical works; you will see what splendid themes can emerge for dialect poetry from the XIV century to the Baroque, to Romanticism and southern Naturalism to Expressionism. Reply here to the questions for my little article for *Il Belli*,[1] which is supposed to come out by Christmas.

An affectionate hug,      Pier Paolo

1   See *Il Belli*, December 1952.

## 272  To Roberto Roversi
Bologna

*[In possession of addressee: typewritten with autograph corrections and signature]*

[Rome, December 1952]

Dearest Roberto,

I can't tell you how pleased I was to get your splendid little volume[1] and then to see how fine the short stories were too. I think I shall review you somewhere but it will take a little time because just now I am suffocating among the dialect poets who are about to appear for Guanda.

An affectionate hug,

Yours,      Pier Paolo

1   Probably refers to one of the five *pamphlets* (not for sale) printed at this time by Roversi for his friends.

## 273   To Tonuti Spagnol
Lucca

[*In possession of addressee: typewritten with autograph date and signature*]

Rome, 8 December 1952

Dearest Tonuti,

Unfortunately when your friend came I wasn't at home; my mother saw him and tells me he is a nice boy but he went away without leaving an address. Could you send me it? That way when I have some time I shall try to track him down. Forgive me for replying with such a delay and if in general I write to you so seldom; but I am terribly busy from morning to night what with school and literary work. Just now Guanda, the publisher in Parma, is about to bring out an *Antologia della poesia dialettale del Novecento* which I have put together (even if on the cover Dell'Arco appears as collaborator); in the introduction I have done for it, you are mentioned too. I naturally mentioned you because I hope you are continuing to write Friulian poetry with all simplicity and modesty as you have done up to now. The moment I have a little time I shall type it and send it to you. But I should so much like meantime to have other poems by you (for example I read one very nice one in last year's *Strolic*). Write to me soon and tell me about yourself. Do you have long to go before ending your military service? and then what do you mean to do?

I embrace you with much affection,        Pier Paolo

This letter is a reply to a letter of November 1952 in which Spagnol writes:

*Did you finish the novel you started in Versuta? Do you still paint? If you have kept the little jotter with my first poems you would do me a great favour by letting me have it back if for no other reason than because those verses remind me of the time when you taught me to write and it was lovely, that time.*

## 274   To Nico Naldini
Casarsa

[*In possession of addressee: typewritten with autograph signature and note to his aunt*]

[Rome, December 1952]

Dear Nico,

Very good about the article – it will come out in the first number.[1] About your thesis: the dialect literatures which have their origins in the XIV century are those in Friuli, in Genoa, in Umbria, in Sicily, in Venice. But in the

XIV century there is a whole body of 'macaronic' poetry which is very interesting. To get an idea of the dialects go to the library and take a look at Treccani;[2] for the 'macaronic' poetry read Contini's study 'Preliminiary thoughts on the language of Petrarch'[3] in the number of April 1951 (which is marvellous). Your thesis could be given the title of e.g. 'Texts of Genoese (or Umbrian, etc.) poetry from the earliest days' and consist of a critical edition of texts with philological and literary notes.* Keep in mind the anthology by Sapegno which appeared in recent months and for general help in finding your direction study the realist poetry of the XIV century in the footsteps of L. Russo (who has for example published with Laterza the poems of the Perugian lawyers of the XIV century – which we find very interesting, given their subject-matter, among other things . . .), meantime keep trying to see whether you manage or not. And also send Betocchi – why not? – Elio's book.[4]

An affectionate hug,      Pier Paolo

*It could be the basis for a future anthology by Guanda which we could do together.

Dearest Aunt,

Since you yourself gave me this chance I did not reply to your letter but my silence naturally meant consent. But nothing reaches me from Genoa, why ever not?

Many affectionate kisses,      Pier Paolo

1  See Letter 271.
2  Giovanni Trecanni (1886–1943), specialist in Friulian literature and folklore.
3  See *Paragone*, April 1951; now in G. Contini, *Varianti e altri linguistica*, pp. 169–92.
4  Elio Bartolini.

## 275  To Luciano Serra
Bologna
[*In possession of addressee: typewritten with autograph date and signature*]

Rome, 15 December 1952

Dear Luciano,

I am sending you a little note[1] for *Il Mulino*, hoping that it will be of use to you.

In about ten days' time my anthology on dialect poetry will come out (on the first page Dell'Arco figures as collaborator but it is a purely nominal collaboration due to previous undertakings between Guanda and Dell'Arco); could there be a discussion of it in *Il Mulino*? Could you do it?

As for the rest – the usual life but decisively better than a year or two ago. My father is pretty well now and so is my mother; and I have been able to start working again and to believe in my work. What about you? What are you doing? What are you writing? I would so much like to see you again and to see you all.

I embrace you with great affection,

Yours,    Pier Paolo

1   See *Il Mulino*, January 1953.

## 276   To Silvana Mauri
Milan

[*In possession of addressee: typewritten with autograph corrections, date and signature*]

Rome, 22 December 1952

Dearest Silvana,

What joy your letter brought me. I was very worried about your silence and did not dare to write to you; it is true that 'Silvana the mother' is very little different from 'Silvana the young woman' of Bologna, in fact is necessarily a postulate of her; but I feel lost and helpless when faced by these facts and altogether lacking in terminologies... What I do know is, I cannot wait for the time for the fruit to mature, a delicate happy fruit; you are to be envied hopelessly and with the best kind of envy – and more ready to transform itself into a hymn (I must tell you that the arrival of your son in this Italy presents itself to me as a reason for verses... which I shall not dare to make). As for me, my life continues to improve by degrees – externally and, what is more important, internally. But I am afraid to admit it; and think I can only do so to you. I am working a lot as usual for the poor school pay and also for myself; I am at last about to finish my novel (*Il Ferrobedò*)[1] but goodness knows how long I shall take to polish and correct it; I have finished the anthology for Guanda which should come out any day, etc. Do you see *Paragone*?

In December a poem of mine ('L'Appennino')[2] will appear and I should like you to read it; I think there is in it a little of your way of 'travelling', of which there is also a trace – easy for you to see – in the paragraph dedicated to Calabria in the introduction to the *Anthology*. And in fact, talking of Calabria, I keep turning over in my mind one of my six thousand stories... (As you see, my biography always ends up by identifying itself with literature; and I don't know whether that is bad or good). I beg you, now that the waters of birth have melted the massive silence, don't again lose the habit of writing to me! At least two lines of a pure and simple report on the condition of your health up to the marvellous news; and give me some news too about Fabio.

Many warm greetings to Ottiero and your family.

An affectionate hug from yours,      Pier Paolo

1   The first title of the novel *Ragazzi di vita* ['Ferrobedò' = 'reinforced concrete' in Roman dialect]. The title derives from Società Ferro-Beton (reinforced concrete), a large factory in the suburbs of Rome.
2   See *Paragone*, December 1952.

## 277   To Leonardo Sciascia
Palermo

[*In possession of addressee: typewritten with autograph date and signature*]

Rome, 27 December 1952

Dear Sciascia,

Forgive my delay in replying to you – but I have had a lot to do lately. Meantime I send you right away my best wishes . . . As for the parcel I sent you it is an indication not only of a certain distracted state of mind on my part but of the way things have become congested because of the dialect poets: but fortunately I am winding down. (Have you seen the *Anthology*? Guanda should have sent it to you already.) Do please send me back one of the two copies of *Voluntas tua*[1] which is not even mine and if you felt like including *Centona* as well I would be very grateful . . . I am sending you a piece for *Galleria* which can stand by itself, from the little thing I did for the Taranto Prize[2] and some poems by Naldini:[3] I hope you like the material.

Many cordial greetings from yours,      Pier Paolo

1   A collection of Sicilian poetry by Vann'Antò (Rome, 1926)
2   See 'Primavera sul Po' ['Spring on the Po'] in *Galleria*, January 1953.
3   See *Galleria*, August 1953.

## 278   To Giacinto Spagnoletti
Milan

*[In possession of addressee: typewritten with autograph date and signature]*

Rome, 28 December 1952

Dear Spagnoletti,

How are you? What are you doing? We haven't spoken for ages.

I am writing you this letter now first of all to give you my good wishes of the season and secondly to ask if you feel like including me in *Campionario*,[1] naturally on the famous terms (that is to say, the ordering of one hundred copies). I have had an unexpected burst of energy, due perhaps to some generous promises from relations and friends. And have you any news about Chiara's anthology?

Have you had the 'Dialect poetry' from Guanda?

An affectionate hug,      Pier Paolo Pasolini

1   *Campionario* [Samples], a collection of poetry published by Schwarz, edited by G. Spagnoletti; see Letter 253.

## 279   To Tonuti Spagnol
Lucca

*[In possession of addressee: typewritten with autograph signature]*

[Rome, December 1952]

Dearest Tonuti,

Here I am to give you my most loving wishes for the New Year. It is true you will spend it doing your time in the army but it can be happy just the same. I am enclosing a little article[1] in which you too are mentioned but which above all will remind you of our good times. I can also promise you (but it is not yet absolutely certain) that I shall add some of your poems to a little edition of my own.

An affectionate hug,      Yours,      Pier Paolo

1   See *Il Belli*, December 1952.

## 280   To Giuseppe Marchetti[1]
Udine

*[In possession of Andreina Ciceri: typewritten with autograph signature]*

[Rome, 1952]

Dear Father Marchetti,

I have suffered many disappointments and much pain at the hands of people from Friuli (and I am not going to say deservedly) but I would never have imagined that the worst would have come from you ... Your 'illustrative note' to Cantarutti's little book[2] was written – it seems to me – to say good things about Cantarutti in proportion to the bad things one could by analogy think of me. Are Zorutti and the Philological Society not enough for you? Did you need a new poet? And it was you who finished off Maramoldo's work with that underhand 'note'! Finished setting me apart, that is to say, replacing me. Forgive me if I write to you with such violence but I have always respected you. And if I have thought these things I felt it necessary to say them to you as well. What I do not understand is whether you acted out of cowardice or out of bad faith. Do you remember when you wrote across three columns of *Patrie* – talking about me – 'Blessed be his muse!'?

I do not understand what, in your critical capacity, happened meantime that was so important as to make you change your mind about me. But if your intention was to hurt me you have done so. If there is still a little of the old Father Marchetti in you – the one to whom I dedicated particular affection – please accept my most warm greetings.

Yours,      Pier Paolo Pasolini

1   Friulian historian and linguist, editor of the fortnightly publication in Friulano, *Patrie dal Friul.*
2   N.A. Cantarutti, *Puisiis* ['Poems'], Edizioni di Treviso (Treviso, 1952).

# 1953

## 281 To Giacinto Spagnoletti
Milan

[*In possession of addressee: typewritten with autograph date and signature*]

Rome, 1 January 1953

Dear Spagnoletti,

Eat your minestra or jump out of the window says a Venetian proverb: about Guanda I had come to understand a little, and felt a little of what you tell me and for which I thank you as a very precious proof of friendship, which moved me . . . But, in my extreme state of poverty, Guanda is my only meagre source and I am forced to content myself with those few thousand lire which flow from it and indeed to be pleased with them and thankful to Heaven. I shall take great care, following your warnings, and I shall work only if the terms and contracts are identical to those for the 'Dialect poetry': that is to say, a contract signed at once and with an immediate advance, however modest. Now Guanda is proposing 'Popular poetry' to me;[1] perhaps he is not wrong in commercial terms or in cultural ones but I am not very enthusiastic because I would have to work on it along with a specialist (e.g. Prof. Toschi) given the immense amount of material. On the other hand I would have my anthology of Pascoli almost ready and pathetically longed for. And here I would need your help and advice. Mondadori has the monopoly on Pascoli and Guanda is naturally not prepared to buy the very expensive rights; he would do it only if Mondadori suggested a special price and *not more than 30-40 poems*. Now one would have to get at Mondadori through friends, convince him that to stir up interest and fierce debates over Pascoli is also in his interest, etc., etc. Do you know of any way to do this? Think about it – you would really do me a great favour.

I am very happy that you liked my *Anthology*.[2] I need these injections of optimism if dialect circles are threatening to react in ways that are as distressing as they are ferociously stupid.

If you have time to talk about it do so; I say so with the apprehension of someone who has to build dykes against the threat of a flood . . .

Thanks again and many affectionate greetings and good wishes

Yours,      Pier Paolo Pasolini

1   *Canzioniere italiano*, Guanda (Parma, 1955).
2   *Poesia dialettale del Novecento.*

## 282   To Tonuti Spagnol
Lucca

[*In possession of addressee: typewritten with autograph note, date and signature*]

Rome, 1 January 1953

Dearest Tonuti,

Forgive me for the delay which prevents this letter from reaching you in the festive season but the blame lies with the season which has packed my days as full as eggs. But you know know very well that, even if late, my good wishes are most fervent and tender. Your letter made me think a lot and it also troubled me because, when it comes to it, I see that in practical terms I can do nothing for you, at least for now: all I can do is to give strong support to your study programme which seems to me to be very well planned. Do enrol at the Institute in Rome and begin to study right away; it seems to me that in Italian you are already far in advance of many teachers . . .

The essays you have to send to the Institute – send them to me at the same time so that I can give you advice; I shall also try to get you some books either for study or for cultural purposes and in general to put you on the right path. If, once you have finished your military service, you find work in Friuli, Nico can also be helpful. In any case don't hesitate – write to me, ask me anything you want and don't be alarmed if I take a little time to reply because there are times when I am drowned in work. As for the anthology, unfortunately I had to give all the copies I had a right to (very few of them) to the critics; however I am enclosing the order form to send to the publisher if you have two thousand lire to spend* . . . As for your spirits, try to be as happy as you can, not to think too much: and believe me, I too, the more I study and work the more I am aware of my ignorance; this is not something bad that troubles only you . . . I bet that even Croce, who in seventy years of study probably made himself the most cultured man in the world, at the hour of his death regretted only those things he did not know. I embrace you with much affection,

Yours,      Pier Paolo

* But perhaps it would be easier for you to get it in a bookshop in Lucca.

This letter is a reply to a letter of 20 December in which Spagnol writes:

*I still have four months of army bullshit; you ask me what I shall do when I am discharged. How often have I asked myself, Pier Paolo, without finding an answer. I am going to tell you something which you who know me better than anyone will understand: 'I am greatly worried over remaining ignorant, in fact it torments me'... When you were at Versuta, if they left me some time off work you would have got me to a good level. Then I went off to Como but did not manage to do anything; I just managed to get my secondary school certificate at the Institute because I had already learned everything from you and your mother. I had too much work up there and got too involved in what was going on in those parts. I hoped to make a little money to go on and study independent of my family but they, with the excuse that they were hard up, gradually ate it up otherwise they were going to behave too badly to my parents. Now I only have a small sum and a motorbike which I would be prepared to sell in order to study. I have found that the only way left to me would be to enrol at the Institute in Rome ... A few days ago I went on leave and felt bad about things: in Versuta I found a desert of almost empty houses and fields. My friends have almost all left and the few remaining ones are silent like after some disaster, I don't know why, and it was as if Nature was a burden on their backs.*

## 283   To Nico Naldini

Casarsa

[*In possession of addressee: typewritten with autograph date and signature*]

Rome, 1 January 1953

Dear Nico,

I am a little to blame too for the damp squib of the XIV century in Friuli because I took a long time to reply to you; if I had replied sooner I would have told you that the XIV century in Friuli consists of *only* four or five rather bad troubadouresque poems, which have already been published two or three times, and which therefore lack the interest of being unpublished: the great work of D'Aronco and Corgnali (in the very best of cases) perhaps consists of the discovery of a new text; but certainly as thin and useless as the others. So I would have inclined to advise the XIV century in Venice (which is equally close and familiar to you), which is very rich, already studied, but not yet (or so it seems to me) anthologized and looked at globally from a philological point of view and with modern aesthetic criteria.

But I could think of another idea which seems excellent to me and not difficult – indeed amusing – to carry out. Read carefully two or three times this study by Contini on the members of the *Scapigliatura*[1] in the volume of *Letteratura*[2] which I am sending you with the curious condition that it is returned to me in three weeks' time and preferably without a sock in it like a dried flower ... There are three or four lines in this article which seem to have been written expressly for you. Naturally, as you will see, there is immediately a plan for a trip to Padua to Contini. Did you get the copy of *Il Belli* and the *Anthology*?

1953

It would not be a bad idea to present yourself to Professor Roncaglia with them under your arm.

Give my good wishes to everyone.

An affectionate hug,      Pier Paolo

1   The *Scapigliatura* was a Bohemian artistic and literary movement in Milan in the 1860s. It aimed at an escape from tradition.
2   Contini's article appeared in *Letteratura* No 35, July–October 1947; now in G. Contini, *Varianti e altra linguistica*, under the title 'Introduzione ai narratori della scapigliatura piemontese'.

## 284   To Carlo Betocchi
Florence

[*In possession of addressee: typewritten with autograph corrections, date and signature*]

Rome, January 1953

Dear Betocchi,

There is no hurry for the note on Naldini[1] because *Il Belli* comes out every two months and so it is enough if you write it at the beginning of February: I shall ring you on the 22nd . . . Meantime thank you for your extremely nice, courteous letter; a document – a moving one – of the fact that among this load of horrible iron pots there is one terracotta vase which has survived by virtue of its gentleness . . .

So till soon and many warm greetings from yours,

Pier Paolo Pasolini

1   See *Il Belli* of February 1953.

## 285   To Giacinto Spagnoletti
Milan

[*In possession of addressee: typewritten with autograph date and signature*]

Rome, 12 January 1953

Dear Spagnoletti,

Our letters crossed; but while waiting for a comprehensive reply from you I am forced to write to you a third time to ask for another little favour; that is to say I should like you, if you can, to let me have the three volumes – Ungaretti, Luzi[1] and Parronchi[2] – to review in *Giovedì*.[3] If you can and if it is absolutely not difficult for you, because otherwise Bertolucci will lend them to me.

Have you thought of some way of approaching Mondadori about Pascoli? And above all forgive these requests from me for help and work. But I cannot wait to repay you . . .

An affectionate embrace from yours,

Pier Paolo Pasolini

1   Mario Luzi (b. 1914), Florentine hermetic poet.
2   Alessandro Parronchi (b. 1914), poet, art critic, translator.
3   See 'La nuova "Allegria" di Ungaretti' in *Il Giovedì*, 5 February 1953; and 'E dove andremo, Euridice', ibid., 19 February 1953.

## 286   To Luigi Ciceri
Tricesimo

[*In possession of addressee's heirs: typewritten with autograph date and signature*]

Rome, 13 January 1953

Dear Ciceri,

Look – you are wrong about my Introduction;[1] if you re-read it without aprioristic views you will find many of your perplexities about the use of dialect implicitly or explicitly explained. In simple terms: there is a linguistic institution (or 'inventum' or, according to de Saussure,[2] 'Langue') which is instrumental (that is to say used in practical and daily relationships) and a literary one (with all its various forms and techniques): the poet works on this institution, transforming its semantemes into stylemes, that is to say, creating a style of his own which is necessarily revolutionary and innovative; in this way one has the transformation of the *inventum* into *inventio* or of *Langue* into *Parole*.[3] Note that these are not my ideas – we are talking about the results of at least fifty years of European philology (witness, in Italy, Croce and his intuition). And note further that all this I am saying *a posteriori* – that is, *after* writing my verses: it is a rethinking, not a programme. When I wrote 'sblanciada da li rosis' ['made pale by the roses'] I was twenty, I was little more than a boy and, although already sufficiently educated and painstaking, I was following a mysterious instinct of my own: certainly no one in Casarsa said 'sblanciada da li rosis', but in the same way as no Florentine said 'quel rosignol che si soave piagne' ['that nightingale that weeps so sweetly'] (*si parva...*).[4] These are relations between words which the poet has to invent: in other words, the syntax. It is the syntax which has to be interiorized. So my syntax is not Friulian because it is mine; but it is the Friulian syntax that determines mine, as the Friulian landscape determines my painter's sensibility. As for the vocabulary it is perfectly and rigorously that of Casarsa;

after all, it doesn't take much to confirm this, all you need do is take the first train and in little more than half an hour you get out at Casarsa.

[There follows a list of examples of words in Friulano and a discussion of some lines and rhymes in dialect.]

Pay no attention to the Friulian pedants – they are ignorant and sectarian and want to reduce the Friulian vocabulary and syntax to a record of a cretinous, parochial moralism. They want 'polenta' to represent the morality of polenta[5] with this fine social implication: anyone from Friuli is content to eat polenta, asks for nothing better than to eat polenta. And the poet must be the bard of an epic of this kind.

Don Marchetti himself,[6] who is intelligent and knowledgeable, is shackled by this false moral judgement which comes down in the end to the most perfect lack of morality; because history teaches that acts of conservation are always immoral, being contrary to life which is never the same. And more immoral still are the compromises (on the lines of *Risultive*[7] – a fine recipe this with a little tradition and a little revolution, 'a wee bit of Philology and a wee bit of Academiuta' . . . worthy of the commonsense of a janitor).

As for our idea of making some change in the order so that I can say yes or no, you must tell me what it consists of; note however, I took a lot of trouble to put the book[8] together in this way, and note that all authors have little and tenacious manias in this area and I no less than the others . . . As for 'Damenia uliva' ['Palm Sunday'] it is true that it was already published in 1942,[9] but it is so much reworked and restored as to appear almost new; and as for the 'Suspir di me mari', etc. ['My mother's sigh'][10] I can tell you that it is there to complete the 'maternal' theme – that is to say the central theme of the book, and that it gives the book a certain balance of contents. Moreover, as regards the general arrangement (which is, I repeat, a little maniacal), bear in mind that there are *four* sections with *four* poems each. I have read the letter of dedication again:[11] I have not been able to pick out the obscure or involved points. You must point them out to me; where there are lists of names the text inevitably does not run well; in any case we are talking about a bibliographical note to be printed in small characters for the critic and not for the reader.

Hoping for a reply from you soon and with many warm greetings from your most grateful

Pier Paolo Pasolini

1   Refers to the Introduction to *Poesie dialettale del Novecento* and is a reply to a query by Ciceri in a letter of 8 January 1953 in which he writes:

*I am limiting myself to asking you a question because it interests me also as your future editor: is it true (and I have stated it in a number of articles as you know) that before the Academiuta in Casarsa Friulano was used only within the limits of its domestic and formal*

*possibilities, without any sense of the archaic sweetness of a Romance language that had remained close to its virginal state, and in attempting today by every means to bring it back to its pure sound one can commit the arbitrary decision to use constructions and syntactic passages which are not Friulian? To give you an example which is in front of me;*

> Lontan, cu la to piel
> sblanciada di rosis
> ['Distant, with your skin
> made pale by the roses']

2 De Saussure (1857–1913), Swiss philologist whose lecture notes, published in 1916 as *Cours de linguistique générale*, were a milestone in modern linguistics.

3 Saussure distinguishes between *langue* (i.e. the language system at our disposal) and *parole* (i.e. the use each individual makes of it).

4 *Si parva*: so small.

5 Maize porridge, a staple diet in Northern Italy.

6 See Letter 280.

7 Review of Friulian poetry edited by Novella Aurora Catarutti, Aurelio Cantoni and Dino Virgilio.

8 Refers to a small volume of Friulian verse *Tal còur di un frut*, published by Luigi Ciceri, Edizioni Friuli (Tricesimo, 1953).

9 In *Poesie a Casarsa*.

10 In *La meglio gioventú*, and republished in *La nuova gioventú*.

11 A reference to 'To the Editor', the letter of dedication of *Tal còur di un frut*.

## 287   To Nico Naldini
Casarsa

*[In possession of addressee: typewritten with autograph addition and signature]*

[Rome, January 1953]

Dear Nico,

I read with distress your distressed letter; try to be more explicit if you want me to be of some help – at least verbally.

From the way you express yourself I seem to understand that yours is a form of 'anxiety neurosis' (which I have had too, with the same symptoms, and which comes over me from time to time). You are going through an atrocious Calvary; but you should profit from my experiences ... You say that in these last months you have done nothing 'reprehensible' – but then *why* are you afraid of something precise? This 'something precise' could only be a charge and if it were a charge you would have known about it immediately. If it is a case of mere hints, don't be afraid: that is a foregone conclusion and the only thing is to be irreproachable in this area.

All the more since they have known about you in the village for years (probably including the Carabinieri). But enough of this disgusting, chilling topic. Read over again calmly, line by line, Contini's essay:[1] there you will find *explicitly* proposed my 'marvellous idea' (ah, Aunt Giannina) about the history of language.

Yes, *Il Belli* is not very good; but that swine Dell'Arco wanted to do it himself; that being his return for his presence in the title page of the *Anthology*.

He did it all by himself and, like the bogus creature he is, there you have the fine results he has achieved. Then behaving horribly to his financial collaborators, whose contribution is brutally collected in hard cash (and no one can get it out of my head that he does not make a bit on top).

I got back yesterday evening from a stupendous little trip to Naples. What stuff . . .

I shall go back, am expected, in a fortnight. The South, the South. Italy beyond the Rubicon can sink to the bottom of the sea. Did you get the *Anthology?* and the article by Montale?[2] What a success . . .

> A hug,      Pier Paolo

1   See Letter 283.
2   'La musa dialettale', in the *Corriere della Sera* of 15 January 1953; now in E. Montale, *Sulla poesia*, Mondadori (Milan, 1976).

## 288   To Sergio Maldini
Bologna

[*In possession of addressee: typewritten with autograph date and signature*]

Rome, 16 January 1953

Dear Maldini,

I swear that for two or three weeks I have been thinking of writing to you – as a result of the Hemingway, naturally.[1] To my great chagrin your extremely nice letter beat me to it. But I hope you will believe in my oath . . . During the summer I am thinking of coming to Bologna for two or three days; all my purest and most firm memories are there, my richest feelings. It is fate, now that you are there too as if there had not been plenty already.

> An affectionate embrace,      Pier Paolo

1   The Hemingway Prize awarded to Maldini's novel *I sognatori* ['The dreamers'], Mondadori (Milan, 1952).

## 289 To Biagio Marin[1]
Trieste

*[In possession of addressee: typewritten with autograph date and signature]*

Rome, 20 January 1953

Dear Marin,

Forgive the immense delay – but to reply to you immediately was due to a sentimental urge, not a practical one, and these days (I am ashamed to say) I have to give precedence to the latter. Your letter is extremely nice, it moved me in the best sense of the word and I treasure it. Did you see the article by Montale[2] in the *Corriere della Sera* of the 15th? After that I don't think you will refuse the little letter of introduction we spoke of . . .

Many warm greetings,　　　Pier Palo Pasolini

This letter was written in reply to a letter of 2 January 1953 in which Marin writes:

*I think it would have been great good fortune for me to have known you sooner. Your way of feeling is close to me and I understand what you write. It is not easy for me to understand other people. For two years I have been going out of my mind to understand Rilke's* Duino Elegies *and every time that I re-read them I find myself up against a wall which provokes me to furious anger. You are right when, in the magnificient Introduction to* Dialect Poetry of the Twentieth Century, *you write that the spatial limits of my poetical world are also internal limits.*

1　Biagio Marin, a dialect poet.
2　For this article, 'La musa dialettale' ['The dialect muse'], see Montale's *Sulla poesia*, Mondadori (Milan, 1976).

## 290　To Gianfranco Contini
Fribourg

*[In possession of addressee: typewritten with autograph date, corrections and signature]*

Rome, 21 January 1953

Dear Contini,[1]

You found in my book[2] an old, unexpected friend; but on the other hand all this year I have always had you at my side – that is, all the time it took to compile the anthology. And you will be very aware of it; obviously I could not quote the source every moment – if only because of the impossibility of defining certain of my attitudes which I owe to you, because of the impossibility of putting in inverted commas certain states of mind, including perhaps that of feeling myself fall so shamefully short of my model.

Yes, I did get – from those places where the people of Friuli have expunged and replaced me – your memorable postcard full of famous signatures; and I ought to have replied to you long ago. Do you know that it is ten years since you wrote your first note to me in Bologna informing me of the review of *Poesie a Casarsa*? All the war and the postwar times, and the sunset of the postwar period; and the two of us, immobile, moving with time, on two tracks as far apart as the Simplon and the Tagliamento and so close that there has not been a moment, one can say, when I did not feel your eye – pitilessly lucid and miraculously kind – scrutinizing the evidence of my mistakes and my tragedies. Forgive this rather impertinent feeling of a balance-sheet; but at the end of the decade I have on the credit side a feeling of friendship which is totally valid in every respect not only because of its tension, which is almost sad, but also because of its quality. The merit, naturally, lies with its object. Did you get my postcard from Naples? If I now tell you more precisely that it was a little trip 'for recreational purposes' there is no need of more to make you conclude that there has been a certain improvement in my condition.

Now I am living in Rome with my mother and father (who is partly cured of his illness, or at least is dealt with – in the ways one deals with an explosive charge – as his illness requires: now it is almost touching how he lives *on me*); I work like a black, teaching at Ciampino (20,000 lire a month!) from seven in the morning to three in the afternoon, and also work a good deal at my own things – that is to say, above all at a novel *Il Ferrobedò*:[3] Penna having been left a little to one side, betrayed, I am now very friendly with Caproni and Bertolucci (do you know them personally? they are what people call two pearls) and, although we meet rather less frequently, with Gadda (who intends when the good weather comes to make a series of visits to the outskirts of the city with my Arabo-Italian house at Ponte Mammolo as his base, to complete his *Pasticciaccio*.)[4] There you have the new picture, one that is a little less gloomy; but to avoid bad luck I am wary of singing a hymn of victory . . .

Many affectionate greetings from your      Pier Paolo Pasolini

This letter was written in reply to the following letter from Contini from Fribourg on 11 January 1953:

*Dearest P.P.P.*

*I have not been in Domodossola for more than two months. Passing through yesterday I had the very joyful surprise (like someone who comes home to meet an old friend) to find waiting for me there – with a dedication for which I am grateful to you – your monumental anthology. I did not take it with me to spare it my imminent move: I don't know whether you know but, having at last been appointed to a chair in Italy, I am about to return there with my household belongings and books. But it needed only a rapid glance to convince me that this is a very important book which I hope will be as effective as it deserves to be.*

*From Friuli, where I set foot for the first time last September (I also went through Casarsa*

*but it was late at night and I glimpsed only corners and yellow façades in the headlights)*
*along with other friends, I sent you a souvenir. But the address was the old one of via Porta*
*Pinciana and perhaps those greetings did not manage to reach you. At last I know where to*
*reach you and can send you my most affectionate good wishes (with the hope that being*
*close geographically may allow us to shake hands for the second time).*
   *Yours as always,*      Gianfranco Contini

1   In the last letter to Contini in June 1951 the mode of address was less formal than
previously: 'Caro dott. Cortini'. Here it is still less formal: 'Caro Contini'.
2   *Poesia dialettale del Novecento.*
3   Later retitled *Ragazzi di vita*
4   *Quer pasticciaccio di via Merulana* [*That Awful Mess on via Merulana*], Gadda's
Roman novel.

## 291   To Leonardo Sciascia
Palermo
[*In possession of addressee: typewritten with autograph date and signature*]

Rome, 26 January 1953

Dear Sciascia,

Thank you for the parcel with Vann'Antò and Martoglio.[1] I shall ask
Bertolucci about the 'thriller' but I fear without much success because he will
already certainly have had approaches which (alas) are more remunerative.
(And, by the way, the three thousand lire never reached me . . .) I do not
remember Roversi's home address (it is ten years ago . . .) but you can write to
him at the Palmaverde bookshop, 4 via Rizzoli, Bologna. Valerio Volpini was
already on the list of those who were to get the Anthology; did he get it? I also
asked for it for Vann'Antò and Guglielmino.

Many warm greetings from your      Pier Paolo Pasolini

This letter was written in reply to a letter from Sciascia of 12 January asking Pasolini to try to
get from Bertolucci '*that essay of his on the thriller which will be broadcast this week on the*
*Third Programme; I would like to publish it in* Galleria'.

1   See Letter 277.

*1953*

## 292   To Giacinto Spagnoletti
Milan

[*In possession of addressee: typewritten with autograph corrections, date and autograph*]

Rome, 26 January 1953

Dear Spagnoletti,

Thank you for your new long letter full of advice and suggestions. I give up without excessive pain the Schwarz edition and with great pain the Pascoli: I do not feel like writing an essay on Pascoli because it has spread so greatly inside me and become so gangrenous that I would not dare touch it except to reduce it to a 'critical bibliography' by way of preface . . . On the other hand I would not think of giving up the anthology of popular poetry – also because 'ideologically' I feel I could strike the right balance; and then besides if all the anonymous regional poems are like the ones I know (Friulian, Venetian, Calabrian, Sicilian), a delicious book would result. But I do turn down Toschi (although where collaborators are concerned I was well tested by Dell'Arco who unfortunately is not an idiot). In my letter I asked you for the poems of Ungaretti and Luzi – but the request has been overtaken by events, for Vigorelli[1] has lent me his copies and I have already written the review of Ungaretti which will appear in *Giovedì* this week;[2] but I beg you to let me have your next volumes since from now on I shall regularly review poetry in that weekly.

Many affectionate greetings from yours,

Pier Paolo Pasolini

1   Giancarlo Vigorelli (b. 1913), literary critic.
2   See Letter 285.


## 293   To Nico Naldini
Casarsa

[*In possession of addressee: typewritten with autograph date, signature and postscript*]

Rome, 26 January 1953

Dear Nico,

A couple of lines to tell you that on Friday at 2.15 Bellonci[1] will talk about the anthology on the national programme. Have you discovered the lines (which I marked in ink) where Contini indicates your thesis? I am glad 'the crisis' has passed.

A hug,        Pier Paolo

PS. Write me a letter praising my father.

1   Maria Bellonci: writer with important literary salon.


## 294   To Carlo Betocchi
Florence
[*In possession of addressee: typewritten with autograph date and signature*]

Rome, 29 January 1953

Dear Betocchi,

On the 22nd you were not in Rome and so *Il Belli* lost track of you but I follow you like a bloodhound . . . Here is the little book by Naldini,[1] in case it is of some use to you, for a little note which will take you the time to write a postcard.

Many affectionate greetings from yours,

Pier Paolo Pasolini


1   *Seris par un frut* ['Evenings for a boy'], edited by P.P. Pasolini, Edizioni dell' Academiuta (Casarsa, 1948). See Letter 284.


## 295   To Luigi Ciceri
Tricesimo
[*In possession of addressee: typewritten with autograph corrections, date and signature*]

Rome, 29 January 1953

Dear Ciceri,

My father has just come back saying all kinds of nice things about you . . . and bringing me the latest news from Udine and about *Tal còur*:[1] do I need to repeat that I am deeply grateful?

You ask me (as a politician) what can be done so that a language as beautiful as Friulano does not die? And I reply without hesitation: one must write poetry. As a man lives beyond his temporal death in his good works so a language lives on beyond its temporal death in its good poems. As for the temporal death, it is inevitable – there is nothing to be done about it: language – says Savi Lopez,[2] I think he was the first to do so – is a river that flows on: its life is a continual act of dying. But it is a question of centuries – and do not be afraid that the process will be more rapid for Friulano. In fact I can tell you that in Casarsa, for example, after the strong influence of Venetian dialect caused by the implanting in the peasant village of a railway station, the sense of being Friulian has been growing stronger again in recent years. In any case, to 'suffer' too much from these problems risks being no longer a sentiment but a case of sentimentality, that is to say a vice; that vice on which every kind of conservatism is based. Virgil's 'practical' language is dead and the 'practical' language of Zorutti may very well die. So work for Friuli but without precocious and inhibiting feelings of nostalgia; I am always with you for healthy administrative autonomy without mystical haloes.

Many affectionate greetings from yours,

Pier Paolo Pasolini

1   Refers to the printing of the small volume *Tal còur di un frut* ['In the heart of a boy'].
2   Paolo Savi Lopez, professor of late Latin literature, philologist.

## 296   To Carlo Betocchi
Florence
[ *In possession of addressee: typewritten with autograph corrections, date and signature*]

Rome, 8 February 1953

Dear Betocchi,

Thank you for your lovely little note;[1] it is obviously a piece, a sketch, inspired by your poetic morning with the cypress, the sunny space of your native Tuscany. I hope you went on and wrote one of those lyrics which are forming your high summer as a poet. And in this connection will your little volume come out?[2] My great delight as reader and my cross to bear as critic?

Many affectionate greetings from yours,

Pier Paolo Pasolini

1   Refers to an article by Betocchi on a group of poems in Friulano by Naldini ( *Il Belli*, February 1953) accompanied by a letter of 1 February 1953, in which Betocchi writes:

*Dear Pasolini,*
*    You maybe will be right to say that you don't like the piece (too much of a piece); I received your request – which was justified by the way – after my promise, and I took a moment's free space in the morning to satisfy you. But this morning I had a mood disturbed by other feelings and thoughts – of the same order as these things certainly, but there came into them a cypress in front of the sunny terrace of my pensione, an ilex, the cypress bent its top in the wind towards the east; religion, tradition, language made inextricable muddles, and the typed texts – with all your notes – I found obscure. I set about writing and what came out was this far from critical piece which is also too long perhaps.*

2   Refers to the collection of poems *Un ponte nella pianura* ['A bridge on the plain'],
Schwarz (Milan, 1953), which Pasolini was to review in *Il Giovedì* of April 1953. On
a postcard dated 11 February 1953 Betocchi writes:

*I have sent you the little book, accept it with saintly patience and don't worry about verdicts.
We are like the grass, here yellow, there green; the lawns are trodden less here, more there.
This book is a little Campo di Marte of when I was a boy in the evening with all my toys, old
and new, scattered on the ground. And since I have never been able to offer my dear wife
anything I dedicated to her a scattered memory of those years which are getting lost and of
my old people, whom she did not know.*

After Pasolini's review appeared, under the title 'Le estasi di Betocchi' ['Betocchi's
Ecstasies'], Betocchi wrote on 25 April:

*My dear Pasolini,*
    *It is the third time I have begun this letter on* BETOCCHI'S ECSTASIES; *I think you have written the
finest article I have ever read on my poetry. This possessive, which always had a marginal
importance for me (as for a king saying 'my people') your piece has placed still further, for
me, from any real possession – thank you! or more simply – thank you without an
exclamation mark. I set off calmly and got bogged down. I rushed off and talked nonsense.
Now I am trying, starting with the typewriter, directly, which obliges me to pause because of
my mechanical inexperience. You are a philologist – indeed an excellent one. The joy I feel
is this: that if your philological experience helped you to untangle the skein, the way you
talked, dear Pasolini, was a double confession and altogether beyond philology. There are
two of us confessing in what you write. For the moment I did not realize why reading your
article (I read it three times) I immediately felt the need to enrich the information you had
dug up about Betocchi; at the second reading I annotated the lines which required the
illustrative comments which are, please note, destined only for you; because where you had
probed, it merited further probing, it merited my saying to you* CORRECT! *and bringing you
the documentation. By removing the rubbish of presumed beauty, by rediscovering the
thread of guilt, the links between sin and honesty, dear Pasolini, how much good you have
done me and how I feel that I too have done you good. You simply had to go – leaving the
crimes on one side – looking for their origins; you simply had to realize to what an extent
the cry of liberty is fed by what is sadly guilty, weakly unworthy. And it will have been felt by
you as a comfort that you are not abandoned by God who knows us all in our misery, that
you are visibly guided, having received the aid of an intellect which is finely interwoven
with conscience, to discover in the work what it is that collaborates very clearly in you, how
much there is in man of guilt and innocence. Innocence! Nothing is innocent, touched as it
is with sin; but the knowledge, how necessary it is! The will is fed by this knowledge – ah
poetry, that ineffable attempt to awake! But then they come and tell you a load of useless
things. Until a youth who suffers on his own account and cannot stand it any longer takes
you by the navel and overthrows you completely. And then, knowing you, you can
penetrate to the bottom of things and invoke the instrument of innocence in the world of
sin – that is to say, the will. The secret sense of which, almost that of mutual confession,
binds us so subtlely to a common salvation! So that, once more, I find it impossible to reply to
you with nothing but a string of information . . .*

## 297   To Francesco Leonetti
Bologna

[*In possession of addressee: typewritten with autograph date and signature*]

Rome, 10 February 1953

Dearest Leonetti,

First I got your letter which moved me very much. Overcome by 'the feeling of the years' I almost wept. Then your two little volumes,[1] this very day, finding them on my table when I got back from school; I had barely glanced at them and already knew that I will do a big article, not a nice one, because it is for an unpleasant illustrated magazine (*Il Giovedì*), but a celebratory one.[2] I have a river of things to say, about you, about us, about our time in Bologna which is unforgettable and too full. For years I have been postponing writing a piece to tidy it up so as to deal with it once and for all but I never succeeded; it is still so close and turgid. I would be very happy to see you and Roversi here in Rome and in fact I hope it will be very soon. I am not a great eater and not even a good talker any more, being as demolished as I am, disappointed, full of an internal clarity which serves no good purposes, except to cast light on ruins; but don't be discouraged, we will dine together and talk together just the same. I shall eat an ox.

Many affectionate greetings from your          Pier Paolo

1   See *Antiporta e poemi*, Libreria Palmaverde (Bologna, 1952).
2   See 'Il bolognese Leonetti' ['Leonetti from Bologna'] in *Il Giovedì*, 7 May 1953, and, later, in the collection of articles and essays, *Passione e ideologia* (Einaudi, Turin 1985).

## 298   To Francesco Leonetti
Bologna

[*In possession of addressee: typewritten with autograph date and signature*]

Rome, 22 February 1953

Dear Leonetti,

I received with joy your joyful letter; but now I am afraid of what I have written about you (and which will appear in one of the next numbers of *Giovedì*) because I was cruelly sincere; that is to say I took you seriously as you take life and threw myself on you as you throw yourself on life. All this for an illustrated magazine that does not allow stylistic defences . . . I would advise you to send your book first of all to Giancarlo Vigorelli, the editor of *Giovedì* – then, in my name, to Vittorio Sereni, to Spagnoletti, to Caproni, to Bertolucci; finally (not in my name, because I do not know them personally, but on my advice) to Pampaloni and to Fortini.

Perhaps you have already done so, then so much the better; it means we have some shared opinions. Send it to good old Sciascia in Caltanisetta: he is an admirer of Roversi and will perhaps become one of yours too (you don't care? well you're right, but the provinces . . .). When will you come down to Rome, Galli Boi? I have a great desire to see you.

An embrace from yours,      Pier Paolo Pasolini

## 299   To Eugenio Cirese[1]
Rieti

*In possession of addressee: typewritten with autograph corrections, date and signature]*

Rome, 22 February 1953

Dear Cirese,

I received your volume of *Folksongs*[2] and immediately read it with great interest. I shall talk about it at some length in *Il Giovedì.* Since I shall now have to make an *An Anthology of Italian Folk Poetry* for Guanda your work interests me in a special way. When will the second volume of the *Songs* come out? Should its publication be delayed might I dare to ask you for a typed copy of the unpublished work (provided you have an extra copy). Thanking you very much for the marvellous texts you have introduced me to, I send you my most respectful and warm greetings,

Yours, dev.ly,      Pier Paolo Pasolini

1   Eugenio Cirese, dialect poet from the Molise.
2   See *Canti popolari del Molise con saggi delle colonie e albanesi e slave* ['Folk songs of the Molise with Essays on the Albanian and Slav Colonies'], vol. I., Tipografia Nobile (Rieti, 1953), and reviews by Pasolini in *Il Belli*, May 1953, in *Paragone* No 64 of April 1955 and in *Passione e ideologia*, pp. 269–73.

## 300   To Giacinto Spagnoletti
Milan

*[In possession of addressee: typewritten with autograph correction, date and signature]*

Rome, 22 February 1953

Dear Spagnoletti,

What on earth is this break about? Is something happening to you? Have you had the Lombard flu? Or do you have no opinion of me as a reviewer? Fortunately Ungaretti and Betocchi gave me a present of their volumes; I

*1953*

shall talk about Betocchi some time in March in *Giovedí* [1] and have already done so about Ungaretti. [2] But now there is Bartolini [3] who is more likely to give me a kick in the teeth (as they say in Rome) with some expressions of impatience from his native Marche than his book with a few words of dedication. And here I am, undaunted, stubborn and candid, asking you once again . . .

An affectionate hug from yours,

Pier Paolo Pasolini

1  See Letter 296.
2  See Letter 285.
3  See *Il Giovedí* of 30 July 1953.

## 301   To Luigi Ciceri
Tricesimo

[*In possession of addressee's heirs: typewritten with autograph signature and postscript*]

[Rome, February 1953]

Dear Ciceri,

I see – and do so with much pleasure – that you do not lose time: [1] the typeface seems to me to be fine and the layout of 'Dov'è la mia patria' is also good but perhaps, in terms of taste, it is better to have in mind *I pianti* (of which I am sending you a copy in case you do not have it). As for the name of the publisher it would not seem odd to me if you put LUIGI CICERI PUBLISHER: but if you are not happy about doing so let me tell you that so long as I, my cousin Naldini, Tonuti Spagnol and Riccardo Castellani are alive the Academiuta is not dead: so it is very possible for you to take over the imprint; but to show that there has been a new start, since the whole name is 'Academiuta di Lenga Furlana' [2] you could put EDIZIONI DI LENGA FURLANA, and on the last page spell it out: 'Edizioni di Lenga Furlana edited by Luigi Ciceri'. Now I am waiting for the proofs and your introduction and your advice. Meantime please accept most affectionate greetings from yours,

Pier Paolo Pasolini

PS. The idea of making a collection of texts on poetry and philology seems to me like a good and brave idea.

1  Refers to the publication of *Tal coùr di un frut.*
2  'The Little Academy of the Friulian Language'.

414

## 302   To Luigi Ciceri
Tricesimo
[*In possession of addressee's heirs: typewritten with autograph date and signature*]

Rome, 18 March 1953

Dear Ciceri,

Forgive me if I have taken a long time to reply but big jobs have started again (this time it is an anthology of Italian folk poetry)[1] and always that desperate school . . . So I really do not have time to write a long letter to Brusini:[2] but tell him that I have a rather good impression even if his poetry seems to me to tend too rapidly towards 'mannerism', and that because he avoids difficulties whether of technique or of content: he ought to commit himself more; I don't mean by extending his boundaries (and he is already very conscious of limits), but by concentrating within them, sharpening the images, making the use of adjectives more dramatic, etc., etc. His language risks being too transparent, tranquil: a bit boring, in short. All this being said in the most empirical way possible so that it will be the more useful.

Many warm greetings, affectionate greetings from yours,

Pier Paolo Pasolini

1   *Canzoniere italiano: Antologia della poesia popolare italiano*, Guanda (Parma, 1955).
2   Alan Brusini, Friulian dialect poet.

## 303   To Leonardo Sciascia
Palermo
[*In possession of addressee: typewritten with autograph date and signature*]

Rome, 19 March 1953

Dear Sciascia,

Although two or three lines by Betocchi – quoted in parenthesis – are missing I am sending you the little note on Naldini written in record time.[1] The two or three missing lines will reach you in a couple of days. I got the 3000 lire for the story – many thanks, dear Sciascia. Many warm greetings from yours,

Pier Paolo Pasolini

1   See 'Nota per Naldini' by Pasolini in *Galleria*, August 1953.

## 304  To Enrico Falqui
[*Falqui Foundation, National Library, Rome: autograph*]

Rome, 27 March 1953

Dear Falqui,

I am sorry your letter reached me because it now seems that my letter lacks at least that initial courage to which you incite me. But I assure you that I had been meaning to write to you since the 17th (and, to be precise, courageously) about your article, confronted with which, as you say, I found my breath taken away. Not that I do not think that many of your worries, many of your negative observations, are fair, etc.; I have always been the first to warn anyone who had illusions about 'the secret treasure' that this treasure is not after all so precious, and to understand that the chapter on dialect is only a secondary chapter in the history of twentieth-century literature. What is dominant here is perhaps the theoretical aspect, the interest in the *phenomenon* in the field of culture and customs; the results are what they are (it does not seem to me, however, that they ought to be discarded or that they are such as to leave worries about their somewhat modest contribution to poetry: but some of the products are very fine – Di Giacomo, Russo, Giotti, etc. – and these had sooner or later to be given a place in a history . . .). I am repeating things to you which you know very well, I am confronting you with virtues which you recognize *a priori*; what *took my breath away* is the disproportion between what is not said in your article, or is said under your breath, and what is said with a wealth of detail; it seems to me, that is, that your disappointment has the upper hand in too spectacular a manner. On the other hand you know very well that we are ourselves to blame for any disappointments . . . But it is not so much this that wounded me. Speaking generally I might say that the 'negative element' in your article lies not so much in the *disappointment* in the dialect poets as in your own wider *disappointment* with everything that is going on in the world. Do you think I am exaggerating? It may be my impression but I see in you, in your way of speaking, of writing, of feeling, a kind of resentment, of boredom or disgust with what is happening around you; and you are perfectly right in a certain sense and up to a certain point. We are living in an atrocious world, a world that is wicked because it is stupid, and every day we have to record an infinite number of acts of weakness on the part of the wolves who surround us. But is a criticism – even if carried out in a place that is not pure, like a newspaper – possible without love? All cold and shut away in a defensive position and ready for a polemic which is too bitter and basically contemptuous to be constructive? There you have it – I feel my work being demolished by your words, taken apart; the prey to a kind of dismay, of black lack of confidence, I thought that my work had been one entire mistake. I did not think even for an instant that you would be able to discuss things further or to restate the problem. You gave me the impression of a catastrophe made all the more searing and painful by a certain ambiguous irony which you are perhaps by now so used to employing on the world that you have in part lost consciousness of it; always because of your position as a man wounded once and for all, and therefore hardened in bitterness which (certainly along with excessive harshness) I read in you. In short, it does not seem to me that it was very generous on your part to make me pay for your feelings of resentment because of someone called Russo, for example (the *judgement* on the *realism* of the great figures of the nineteenth century was Russo's; but mine was merely an adoption of it and it was right to make this clear), or your dislike of certain little poets of the Left (but was it right to make so much of Vivaldi?; did devoting to him those four or five lines not amount implicitly to a misinterpretation of my critical work and my choice?); and then why that stabbing thrust concerning the clandestine nature of the dialect poets, from which it emerges that I am the clandestine one, along with a few others who are more conceited than necessary? And in connection with the obscurity of those dialect poets who are presumed to be obscure could you quote *a single obscure poem* from the anthology? These are some of the remonstrances – the ones that affect me most and are perhaps petty – which I can make to you: I cannot enter into a discussion of the general problem precisely because I would come up against the insurmountable wall of your distrust, of your irony, of your (at least apparent) scepticism concerning any form of good faith. With regard to you, I feel some of that exasperation which a person must feel who is suspected of something of which he is not guilty; and exasperation makes me lose my head a little; therefore I am never myself with you.

Now I am working again on the anthology of popular poetry; your thought gnaws at me; will you like it this time? You know very well how much I respect you and how I search in you for that depth of loneliness which lies behind your recalcitrance, which is that of a man broken by his experience of a shameless and glib world.

I greet you warmly, dear Falqui, in fact (and in truth, believe me) with affection.

Yours,     Pier Paolo Pasolini

Posted on 21 March, this letter refers to Falqui's review of the *Poesia dialettale del Novecento* which is to be found in *Novecento letterario*, Vallecchi (Florence, 1957). Falqui had written to Pasolini on 21 March:

*Dear Pasolini,*

*Judging by your silence I have to think it to be certain that you missed my long article*

*1953*

on the 17th on the Anthology. *Unless I displeased you so much as to take your breath away. But I don't think there was any reason for this, all the more since we had already talked about the matter, and if in the meantime things have not got better, my understanding has not become worse either.*

*So take courage and don't hide your opinion from me. If I come asking for it it is because it interests me and because I would not wish to quibble over the intention of my article which took a lot of work and was meant to clarify things.*

*Till soon, cordially,      Falqui*

## 305   To Leonardo Sciascia
Palermo
[*In possession of addressee: typewritten with autograph date and signature*]

Rome, 27 March 1953

Dear Sciascia,

Did you get my note on Naldini?[1] Here in parentheses is the quotation from Betocchi which you needed: ('the life of marvellous adolescents,' as Betocchi writes, 'in which everything is confessed with clarity and the confusion reveals the Mercy which created the world and the Grace which will give it the strength to save itself.')

Very good – the last number of *Galleria.* Congratulations and many warm greetings from yours,

Pier Paolo Pasolini

1   See Letter 303.

## 306   To Eugenio Cirese
Rieti
[*In possession of addressee: typewritten with autograph date, signature and postscript*]

Rome, 29 March 1953

Dear Cirese,

Thank you for the new songs from the Molise:[1] so I shall begin my selection[2] precisely from the Molise and hope that you and your countryside will bring me luck.

The review of your book will appear, I believe, in three or four weeks' time because I still have on my table other books of poetry which had arrived previously. I was thinking of publishing in *Giovedì* along with the review two or three songs as well: you don't have any objection, do you?

Many warm greetings from yours dev.ly,

Pier Paolo Pasolini

418

PS. I was forgetting, do send me *Canti di Rieti* ['Songs from Rieti'] because, yes, they will certainly be very useful. I shall send them back as soon as the work is done, that is to say by the autumn.

1  Molise: a district in Central Italy.
2  Refers to the *Canzioniere italiano.*

## 307  To Enrico Falqui
Rome
[*Falqui Foundation, National Library, Rome: typewritten with autograph signature*]

Rome, 4 April 1953

Dear Falqui,

These things are like avalanches – a little snow that you roll along takes on unforeseen dimensions and it really would be better therefore to be silent, not to provoke that first soft, almost pleasant rolling motion. But I do not resist the temptation to strike back, to enter into a dialectic. I am doing it again by letter because, orally, you frighten me, put me into a state close to aphasia. For the reasons I told you of in my other letter and also because you are that Falqui who was at the high tide of his literary work, desperately fascinating to me when I was still a boy, and in fact, let me tell you (these are things one confesses when one is a little excited) that in the first number of a review[1] which I and my Bolognese friends Leonetti, Roversi and Serra planned with all the sentimental violence and the disproportionate committal of catechumens, the first essays were devoted to Ungaretti, to Carrà[2] and to you. So you see that you have a place in my epic; and I hope you will forgive certain of my reactions which are a little pathological. (In any case in what an arid world one has lived all these years if one is surprised at that 'something which goes too far beyond the literary question' and therefore at 'the consequences to which a poor critic is exposed'. . .) Yes, it is probable that I have the opposite defect to that of aridity; but you are a bit too quick with the bucket of cold water, don't you think? I despair when I see myself considered by you to be a vain person who has 'aims'. But in putting together my anthology I had only one cultural aim – and if I cast light on my Friulian school, which is also that of my friends, I did so entirely openly, it seems to me, and in no way secretly, and I did so for objective reasons while keeping everything in proportion. The Friulian school occupies 25 pages in the anthology, the Neapolitan school 60, Tessa alone 21, Giotti alone 22, Noventa alone (it is his own fault because he did not allow us more) 7, Di Giacomo alone 22. Still calculating things by numbers there is the same proportion in the introduction: the Academiuta finds 4 pages dedicated to it, the

Neapolitan school 18, Tessa alone 4, Giotti alone 4, etc. If you should continue to think that there is a lack of proportion to the other poets chosen (the minor Neapolitans, the Sicilians, the Piedmontese, etc.), please read the texts with the enormous patience the matter demands; but all the texts, the *opera omnia*, and then you will see whether I have been objective or not. Let me tell you that in fact I did myself a disservice from the point of view of vanity; and this too you would discover if you read the entire works of everyone and not the six or seven poems chosen.

I grant that you are right with regard to the Romanesco[3] poetry; but what could I do about it? I have told you already that I raised Trilussa's poems from four or five to the present number and took out three or four of Dell'Arco's. About the latter, I repeat in writing what I have already said to you that we are not *friends*, that ours is a pure case of being together by force of external circumstances and I should not like him to involve me in his factious world. (I have read your piece on 'Trilussa and the Danai'; you have taken the words out of my mouth. And please note too, that – although not brutally – I have let Dell'Arco know that I am on your side.) One last thing: in your letter you defend your good faith as if I had doubted it; but I never dreamt of doubting it. In my disappointment (which you make fun of by calling it 'cosmic', not without making me smile now that it has gone off the boil) I accused you of other very serious, cosmic faults but not of this . . . In any case I shall come and see you soon, dear Falqui, after the ritual telephone call – next week. Meantime many warm greetings and good wishes from yours,

Pier Paolo Pasolini

In a letter to Pasolini written on 31 March Falqui had written:

*In the article you disliked so much there is nothing more than what I had already said to you. So why do you want to deduce from it a sense of disappointment on my part which is cosmic, no less?*

*I am afraid that you tasted the sweetness of praise too early and too continously for you not to have to discover an unbearable bitterness in any criticism. Give me leave to say this.*

*But in your reply there is something that goes too far beyond literary matters for me not to be surprised to see the consequences to which a poor critic finds himself exposed – a critic who in his attempts to understand may – I admit it freely – perhaps make mistakes but always, by heaven, in good faith and fully conscious of having done his duty.*

*Come to see me – we will talk it all over again and you will find that we will part in the end in less disagreement. Because of that anthology I do believe that I have identified its various aims which are contradictory and partly stated, partly secret. And it is not by sitting in judgement on my presumed intentions that their results can be invalidated. Have you given thought, for example, to what place and how much place you granted to yourself and consequently to the Academiuta in a framework which lays claim – reviewing the chronicles of the twentieth century – to such historical importance? These last questions are not intended as the usual final arrows but rather the confirmation that in that article – and a newspaper is more or less pure depending on who writes in it and signs his name there – I*

*was not at all heavy-handed nor did I allow my disappointment to predominate. Nor my
disapproval. Please believe me.*
  *And do come and see me. (Ring me up first.)*
  *I am your friend,      Falqui*

Falqui replies to the letter of 4 April:

*Dear Pasolini,*
  *I am a very bad letter-writer but you should know that when replying to your two missives
I overlooked all the expressions of feeling in which they abounded. And it is not that I did not
appreciate them and enjoy them. 'The bucket of cold water' is emptied over me first. So I go
from one cold to another and will end up with pneumonia.*
  *But who will then console my old age? Books, books, always books.*
  *Meantime come and see me.*
  *I am yours,      Falqui*

1  *Eredi*; see Letter 17.
2  Carlo Carrà (1881–1966), painter, one of the founders of the Futurist movement.
3  Poetry in the Roman dialect.

## 308  To Giacinto Spagnoletti
Milan
[*In possession of addressee: typewritten with autograph signature,
corrections, date and postscript*]

Rome, 4 April 1953

Dear Spagnoletti,

  I have got your book[1] with the fraternal dedication. Many thanks. In spite of
my great curiosity I have not read you yet – I am buried under a heap of verses
and versifying to review; and I should like my reading of you to be calm,
without dribblings from other texts on to yours. What intrigued me was a
note on the cover which talks about 'crepuscularism'; I have just finished my
review of *Linea lombarda* ['The Lombard line'],[2] in which I talk about
persistent crepuscularism, not understood of course in 'a literal but moral
sense', in the six northern poets. But theirs is a biological crepuscularism
(see Lombard folk poetry and dialect poetry) with expressionist effects (see
also 'ethnic' realism and *scapigliatura*) at certain moments of the most
profound desolation. But are you someone from Taranto? Or have you
become a naturalized Lombard? However I foresee that your crepuscularism
is the kind that lies somewhere between the musical and the pictorial
(however little it is sung or painted)* which is Neapolitan in its setting; and
that you are to be put alongside Gatto rather than those people up there. We
shall see . . . I am full of zeal: the more time passes the more we believe in it,
don't we?

I wanted to ask your advice about your unspeakable Schwarz who is asking me for poems to be included in an anthology, etc., etc. (with prior sales of various copies, naturally, but in Italy didn't we have Guanda doing the same thing already?) Let me know what the business looks like. Many affectionate greetings and good wishes from yours,

Pier Paolo Pasolini

*Well, I confess that dipping into your volume I read your very fine 'Via Cavour'.

1  See *A mio padre, d'estate* ['To my father, in summer'], Schwarz (Milan, 1953).
2  See 'I Campi Elisi di Lombardia' ['The Elysian Fields of Lombardy'] in *Il Giovedì*, 28 May 1953: a review of the anthology by Luciano Anceschi, *Linea Lombarda*, Edizioni Magenta (Varese, 1952), now in Pasolini's *Passione e ideologia*.

## 309  To Francesco Leonetti
Bologna
[*In possession of addressee: typewritten with autograph date and signature*]

Rome, 16 April 1953

Dear Leonetti,

Frugiuele[1] will come to *Giovedì*. I had cautiously asked for news from Vigorelli who replied four or five days ago that the article on you had already been typeset, so that I expected it in today's *Giovedì*; instead Bertolucci, as you will have seen, took immediate precedence. So I imagine that in a couple of weeks 'the Bolognese poet' will be camped out among the photographs of parochial high life. Chance so wished it, furthermore, that the day I got your letter I had an appointment with Falqui: naturally I reminded him of the matter. He showed himself to be very well disposed and told me how Cecchi had said to him: 'Have you taken a look at Leonetti?', with the air of having made a little discovery. After which he carefully wrote your address in his notebook (I don't understand why, seeing he has already written to you and so must have known your address . . . I didn't go into the matter. But soon I shall return to the attack with a naïve: 'Have you written your piece on Leonetti then?')

I do not know Sereni's address (but you can write to him at Mondadori) and so too with Fortini (but you can write to him at Communità). For Bertolucci send it to me and I shall give it to him the moment he gets back from Paris. You know twice a week Bertolucci, Bassani, Frassinetti and I dine together in a Bolognese restaurant just because of a regional whim; so if you and Roversi turned up you would be two fellow guests who would fit in very well.

Many affectionate greetings from yours,

Pier Paolo Pasolini

1    News editor of *L'Eco della Stampa*; see Letter 297.

## 310    To Eugenio Cirese
Florence

[*In possession of addressee: typewritten with autograph date and signature*]

Rome, 20 April 1953

Dear Cirese,

Many thanks for your volume of songs from Rieti. It will be very useful to me although you are at pains to stress its lack of perfection . . . The review[1] (more than a review it is a discussion on folk poetry suggested by your book) will appear in *Giovedì* in two or three weeks but not the songs because the editor, deaf and suspicious like all editors, fears that the dialect will be unreadable. We are stuck at the usual point. When shall we ever win our battle?

Many respectful and affectionate greetings from yours,

Pier Paolo Pasolini

1    Not in *Il Giovedì*, but in *Il Belli*, May 1953.

## 311    To Nico Naldini
Casarsa

[*In possession of addressee: typewritten with autograph date, signature and postscript*]

Rome, 23 April 1953

Dear Nico,

I am enclosing the money for the trip. I expect you in Rome on Monday evening (write by express or telegram to tell me the time, which I hope won't be late so that I can come and wait for you at the station). You will stay till 12 May. I hope nothing has turned up to upset things . . . Congratulations on the little piece on Elio[1] (I didn't like the novel much – which is to say not at all, alas; and now it is difficult to write to Elio because I cannot not tell him the truth).*

Give my affectionate greetings to everyone. Till soon,

Pier Paolo

*1953*

*Tell Elio that your review will appear in *Giovedí* or *Letteratura. Bring all your Friulian poems with you* (because I gave the copy you sent me to Betocchi).

1   On Elio Bartolini's novel *Due ponti a Caracas* ['Two bridges at Caracas'], Mondadori (Milan, 1953).

## 312   To Gino Montesanto
Rome
[*In possession of addressee: typewritten with autograph date and signature*]

Rome, 25 April 1953

Dear Montesanto,

Thank you for your novel[1] – apart from a certain naïvety which here and there reveals the handiwork of a diligent, aprioristic narrator (indeed it seems to me that your principal theoretical error – which like all errors is important up to a certain point, like all theoretical errors – is that of being convinced that in man there is a need to *narrate* while the only need, I believe, is that to *express oneself*; also, of course, through narrative modes. Narration in itself can produce only minor products, short stories even if very decent ones on the lines of Bandello[2] but not of Boccaccio)[3] and apart from a certain lack of linguistic imagination because of which you fall into repetitions or give us psychological figures too hastily (superfluously), and apart, finally, from what one might call a few populist notes which here and there make the common people a little mawkish because of the way in which their simplicity is surrounded by myth . . . your book is definitely one of the strongest I have read by the latest generation of authors. You have a manly and calm sense of how far one can go, of measure; morally you are entirely as you should be (and that is very important in the internal mechanics of the novel, in the organization of authentic objectivity) and linguistically in the grey tones, which are a little crepuscular and a little neo-realist (the seed of the Panzinis[4] and Morettis[5] has not withered), you achieve a continual effect of delicacy, of authenticity. Let me say that from your novel there comes a strong feeling of sympathy: something very rare indeed.

A warm greeting from yours,          Pier Paolo Pasolini

1   *Sta in noi la giustizia* ['Justice is within us'], Rizzoli (Milan, 1952).
2   Matteo Bandello (1485-1561), sixteenth-century writer of short stories.
3   Giovanni Boccaccio (1313-1375), poet and prose-writer. His chief narrative work is the *Decameron,* a collection of short stories.
4   Alfredo Panzini (1863-1939), professor of Italian literature, novelist and essayist.
5   Mario Moretti (1885-1979), poet and novelist.

## 313   To Piero Chiara
Varese

[*In possession of addressee: typewritten with autograph date and signature*]

Rome, 25 April 1952

Dear Chiara,

A little late, because I was late in reading it, thank you for your piece in the *Anthology*. It is one of the closest and most intelligent and I am really very grateful to you. And our collection of 'young poets', when will it appear? Will it appear?[1]

Many warm greetings from yours,

Pier Paolo Pasolini

1   See Letter 246.

## 314   To Luigi Ciceri
Tricesimo

[*In possession of addressee: typewritten with autograph corrections, date and signature*]

Rome, 5 May 1953

Dear Ciceri,

I am sorry about your troubles with the printing[1] – you really did not deserve them but it all doubles my gratitude and friendship for you. As for the errors I would prefer corrections by pen (perhaps done by that specialist you speak of) to the 'errata corrige' which usually no one consults. It seems to me too that that dog of a printer asked you for too much.

Try confronting him with all his stupidities to make him bring down the price . . .

As for the Friulian reviews see to them yourself; I do not wish to have anything to do with these people and these papers. As for the critics outside Friuli, I shall take care of them with the copies you send me.

Many affectionate greetings from yours

Pier Paolo Pasolini

1   Refers to the printing of *Tal còur di un frut.*

*1953*

## 315   To Oreste Macrí
Arezzo

[*In possession of addressee: typewritten with autograph corrections, date and signature*]

Rome, 11 May 1953

Dear Macrí,

I am sending a little book of mine[1] which a friend in Udine decided to print, braving the horrors of artisanal typography; and here is the fine result… But I am taking advantage of the accompanying letter to shake off some of the dust of silence surrounding our discussion at *Giovedì* – a discussion as discreet and fragmentary outwardly as it was passionate and vehement within: I understood very well what you wanted to say to me although it remained unexpressed within me, encapsulated in another terminological world, so close to my own, so full of internal *sympathia*, but naturally also so different. My intuition is very rapid but my perception not equally so; therefore before replying to you in a way that is somewhat exhaustive I was waiting until our 'terms' found neutral ground: instead Penna came and the dinner at 'Otello's', things very nice in their way but which left in my gullet the pleasure of a discussion that was at last fruitful and one in which there was a common interest along with the greatest purity and passion. The 'theoretical' question with its great fascination – which is so intense as to go beyond the poetical history of a race (you see what words jump out when one discusses these topics), and to polarize interest at the historical-linguistic origins (which are also ideal) – naturally also interested me greatly and continues to interest me (and in fact I am dealing with it in a more direct way now, in that I am preparing a new anthology of Italian folk poetry for Guanda): for the dialect poets of the twentieth century that problem in a practical sense, a *parte obiecti*, not a *parte subiecti*,[2] had less reason to exist, if those poets were for the most part backward compared to the contemporary production in Italian, and had a conception that was as obstinately faithful as it was superficial of the regional (that is to say profoundly Italian) ethnos. But how much one could still say … Will you come back to Rome occasionally? In that case telephone Bertolucci, in that way we can arrange to meet with a little peace and calm – something that would give me great pleasure because, perhaps you do not think so, but my loyalty to you goes back to when I was at the *liceo* in Bologna in the 'Esemplari' years.

Cordial greetings and good wishes from yours,

Pier Paolo Pasolini

426

1   *Tal còur di un frut.*
2   'from the objective point of view' and 'from the subjective point of view'.

## 316   To Leonardo Sciascia
Palermo
*In possession of addressee: typewritten with autograph date and signature]*

Rome, 11 May 1953

Dear Sciascia,

I had already written as a review a piece on you, G.C. Contini and Guido Cavani,[1] intending to give it to Ulivi for *Letteratura.*

But Ulivi has suggested something better, which is to adapt the piece as a 'presentation' and to publish some of the poems of those presented. So please send me a little group of unpublished things (some of the ones I already saw a few months ago, do you remember?)

Many affectionate greetings from yours,

Pier Paolo Pasolini

1   Guido Cavani (1897–1967), autodidact, poet and novelist.

## 317   To Cesare Padovani
Nogara (Verona)
*[In possession of addressee: typewritten with autograph date and signature]*

Rome, 16 May 1953

Dear Cesarino,

Forgive me if, unknown to you and without being requested, I intervene like this in your life, let us say in your literary life. I have this moment finished reading (by chance because I never read this stuff) an article about you in *Oggi*[1] – rather moving, to tell the truth, and a little humiliating for you. You must try to be resistant to the sickness of those people who, in order to boost the circulation of a paper, would be capable of anything, even of making (as in your case) an extremely indelicate excursus into someone's inner life, taking advantage of the fact that it is the inner life of a boy . . . Do see that your situation is very dangerous – there is nothing worse than suddenly becoming a 'property'. If you paint and write poetry seriously for a profound reason and not just to find consolation for your physical misfortunes (or even, as they say, for therapeutic reasons), watch jealously over what you do, be absolutely discreet about it; also because you are only a boy and your drawings, your poems can only be the products of a boy. With the exceptions, so far as I know, of Rimbaud and Mozart, all boy prodigies have had mediocre success and I think, to be precise, that the only way to keep hold of things is to shut yourself up in yourself and to work – but really work.

It was not to say these things to you that I wrote however; I wanted to get into contact with you only because I saw in the famous article that you write poetry in dialect. That interests me tremendously. You must know that at eighteen I too began to write poems in dialect (Friulano) (but I too had begun to write verses very early, at seven: my illness was not physical but psychological); then I kept on working, trying as well as expressing myself to understand myself. A dozen years have passed and now, with a degree in literature and teaching (I teach boys like you), I am in the full flood of my literary work. I am sending some documents about it; I cannot send you the big *Anthology of Dialect Poetry of the Twentieth Century* which appeared from the publishing house of Guanda in Parma this year because I have only one copy left for myself.

I am writing all these things to you so that you have an idea of me and will reply to me honestly: why do you write in dialect? Or if you really do not know (to know why is a difficult critical act), why do you love dialect? I should be very grateful if you were to answer and perhaps send me some samples of your dialect poems on which I could give you an opinion which would be absolutely lacking in those cloying journalistic sentiments I spoke about, and perhaps give you some advice on technique or on reading.

A handshake from yours,        Pier Paolo Pasolini

This letter was sent after reading an article in *Oggi* of 21 May 1953. Cesare Padovani was fifteen. A brain lesion caused at birth had paralysed his mouth, his right arm and his legs; with great efforts he has succeeded in partly overcoming his paralysis and had learnt to use his left hand to write and draw.

1    *Oggi*: a popular illustrated weekly.

## 318   To Francesco Leonetti
Bologna
[*In possession of addressee: typewritten with autograph date and signature*]

Rome, 20 May 1953

Dear Leonetti,

I wrote a piece[1] about you immediately, I had hardly finished reading you than I had already interpreted you. Therein lies the good and the bad of my critical piece. But sooner or later I shall come back to my review (I have in mind to write a study on *L'ultima generazione* ['The last generation']), smoothing it out and making it clearer by that kind of philological examination which the nature of *Giovedì* excludes. Meantime forgive me if I fell so ravenously on your 'psychology', and if my portrait of you was a bit crude. When will you come to Rome?

I shall not miss an opportunity to spur on Falqui (and I shall get my cousin Nico Naldini to do a review of you in the little Sicilian review *Galleria*, which you will know).

An affectionate hug from yours,

Pier Paolo Pasolini

1   See Letter 297.

## 319   To Giacinto Spagnoletti
Milan
[*In possession of addressee: typewritten with autograph corrections, date and signature*]

Rome, 29 May 1953

Dear Spagnoletti,

What a joy to get your letter! I know that I am accustomed to know an infinite number of things about my poetry,[1] thousands of details, of reasons, of relationships; in short I have a competence which has a quality of wholeness that is my own wholeness, the comprehensiveness of which is my comprehensiveness. But precisely for this reason I perhaps do not know what my poetry is like: I mean as an object, as a poor finished object (because how can we keep it unfinished?) You, in your letter, overwhelmed me with the picture of what my poetry is like when interpreted by one who sees it along with thousands of others: as if all I have given and that I can give has in fact been 'finished'. And truly that joy in singing which you see in it – or rather that irrational need to sing – gave me a childish happiness: a little as if I saw myself depicted in history, well established in a square millimetre of time which is not simply human (stupendous but destined simply to pass, to pass agonizingly) but historical; where your words as a critic bear witness to me – a critic who makes of the critical apparatuses a means of being able to grant himself legitimately the pure happiness of direct speech.

I shall talk (but immersed in the critical apparatus, as a defence, out of modesty) about your book in *Giovedì*;[2] it was Vigorelli, to my relief – for on my own I would not have made up my mind because of the obvious difficulties – who proposed it to me. And I am working something out about your 'southern crepuscularism', about your thirst for the ability to communicate, which is to be attained at the cost of any sacrifice of the formal values in which you have been formed . . .

Well done to have left the odious Scharz (the w is lacking: a lapsus? a reaction to the excess of electoral 'vivas' or a secret desire to insert an upside down w?)³

Yours,     Pier Paolo Pasolini

This letter was written in reply to a letter of 16 May 1953, where Spagnoletti writes:

*I have spent three days savouring your book; where I did not understand you helped me with the translation at the foot of the page. It has been one of the finest presents of poetry of this year ... Your poems – especially these ones – make me live peacefully in a universe without intelligence, of pure density of feeling; even the most painful and full of suffering... Marvellous Pasolini! You never cease to enchant me.*

1    A reference to the volume of poems in Friulian dialect *Tal còur di un frut.*
2    The review of Spagnoletti's collected poems appeared in *Giovedì* on 17 September 1953.
3    The Italian conventional sign for Viva is W (which can be seen as two linked Vs); the upside down W becomes M for Morte (death).

## 320   To Nico Naldini
Casarsa
[*In possession of addressee: typewritten with autograph date and signature*]

Rome, 12 June 1953

Dear Nico,

I'm sorry to know that you are sunk in the disgusting sloth of Casarsa, which means of course the impotent inability to overcome it, which is your fault. The only way to overcome it is to work. This is not to play the moralist but I have really come to the conviction that the most intense and certain pleasure is that which one feels after working; the whole day and therefore one's whole life is filled by it. I experience that sense of disgust on the days when I am incapable of putting together something 'done' and sometimes it is not my fault but perhaps that of circumstances. You have the whole calendar to fill with 'tasks done', why don't you do it? After all it is only a question of overcoming a slight initial nausea, the rottenness of discomfort. When you really can't do anything else write a horrible, desperate poem, a clumsy piece in a diary: something worthwhile emerges in the end. Nothing from Guicciardi and not even the shadow of the other two reviews. It is shameful. Then Dell'Arco and I are waiting for you to tell us to write to Maier and you are sailing along abjectly, forgetful of your thesis. Did you see that a piece on Colombi Guidotti by Bartolini appeared in *Giovedì* so yours will be in *Letteratura*. Many greetings to Bart.¹ and tell him it is not out of the question that I too will write about him somewhere or other before the end of the year. I am more and more desperately engulfed in work, so much so that I am getting one of those 'states of exhaustion' which, looking down from the height of my health, I have always despised in others. There is the anthology, there are the articles for *Giovedì*; new things I have taken on for *Paragone*, two or three pieces for the radio (among them a story which is driving me mad), and now something else is taking shape (marvellous at other times), that is to say writing a script in collaboration with Gadda of Bandello's stories . . . Well. To all this I would also add the story for Pordenone[2] (not a bit of *Ferrobedò*, no; if anything, a 'Lied'[3] set in Friuli, which I have been working away at, Penelope-like, for *Botteghe Oscure*),[4] only if you were to assure me of a more than 95 per cent chance. I hug you affectionately and all the others with you.

Pier Paolo

1   Elio Bartolini.
2   To compete in the 'Premio Pordenone' for narrative.
3   Published in *L'approdo letterario*, April–June 1954; it subsequently appeared with variants in *Il sogno di una cosa*.
4   *Botteghe Oscure*, an important Roman literary journal.

## 321   To Nico Naldini

Casarsa
[*In possession of addressee: typewritten with autograph date and signature*]

Rome, 22 June 1953

Dear Nico,

Only today did I get your express letter; so I won't have time to write to Maier along with Dell'Arco by Wednesday. But I shall write within the week so that by the beginning of June, when you go back to Trieste, the matter will be dealt with. About the Pordenone prize, it doesn't seem to me that there is much time and I am telling you again that I intend to take part only if victory is almost certain: the reason is that I have very little time – just think that in the next fortnight (almost the length of time before the entry for the prize has to be in) I have to do two talks for the Third Programme, a story (a haunting one), also for the Third Programme, two radio scripts on tremendous archaeological conferences, not to mention the usual reviews (I am supposed to have Gadda for *Paragone* and Bartolini (Luigi) for *Giovedì*; and then *Ferrobedò* to finish because Banti[1] has written explicitly saying that she would like to publish it before the end of the year in the *Paragone* series . . . So you see I must think twice about setting to to finish and then copy out the 20–30 pages of 'Lied'. But the 100,000 lire would come in handy (for you too, given your immediate descent on Rome from Pordenone) . . .

Kisses to everyone, a hug from your,         Pier Paolo

*1953*

1   Anna Banti (1895–1978), novelist and publisher, wife of Longhi, Pasolini's professor of History of Art at Bologna.

## 322   To Nico Naldini
Casarsa
[*In possession of addressee: typewritten with autograph signature*]

[Rome, July 1953]

Dear Nico,

Today I am sending off the short story LIED to the Pordenone prize. It is a somewhat marginal piece but I think not bad (less so for you who know all the backgrounds in all their unrivalled reality which for others have a whiff of exoticism).

Let's hope, for God's sake. There were no precise titles for your thesis: one subject was: 'A contribution to the study of *scapigliatura*: a linguistic comparison of the texts of Faldella and Cagna' (it would consist of a critical bibliography on the subject, in the comparison and in some final aesthetic comments) (Bompiani has recently published the anthology of scap. piem. edited by Contini).[1] Other subjects were 'the history and anthologies of dialect literatures' (you could suggest the 'Venetian' for the North and the 'Calabrian and Sicilian' for the South; they are the ones that offer the greatest possibilities for work; the others have already been studied or do not exist). Write at once about the letter to Mayer. I am buried in work; but there are always those three or four hours a day (and then it is wonderful weather).

   A kiss,      Pier Paolo

1   Piedmontese *scapigliatura.* See *Racconti della Scapigliatura piemontese,* Bompiani (Milan, 1953).

## 323   To Leonardo Sciascia
Palermo
[*In possession of addressee: typewritten with autograph date and signature*]

Rome, 4 July 1953

Dear Sciascia,

The translations from the Catalan in *Quaderno romanzo* were by Carles Cardó, an *émigré* priest (and a good poet himself and indeed author of a very fine history of Spain) with whom Contini had put me in contact, seeing that Cardó was in exile in Fribourg. I have heard nothing more of him and have lost the old address. Perhaps Contini has not lost sight of him but how can one ask Contini now that he seems to be having a bad time because of the move and of a mountain of accumulated work? Cardó's translations were a bit clumsy here and there however, and so I had to 'look them over' myself. I do not know Foix. I have not yet had the payment for Naldini nor the invitation you tell me about for the 'Congress on narrative'. Well, in future it will be 1000 lire a page . . .

Praise be to God now!

Affectionate greetings from yours,

Pier Paolo Pasolini

## 324   To Leonardo Sciascia
Palermo
[*In possession of addressee: typewritten with autograph date and signature*]

Rome, 14 July 1953

Dear Sciascia,

I am pleased about your project: what energy![1] I spoke yesterday evening to Caproni (has he written to you?) who is very much in favour of the affair but says he does not have twenty-four poems ready; but he is always undecided and pessimistic where he himself is concerned and I shall take steps to shake him up and convince him (as is true) that he is full of good 'rejected' poems. But when were you thinking of publishing? This does not seem to me to be the right time; I would advise you to put it off until the beginning of autumn. As far as I am concerned 'L'Appennino' is at your disposal in *Paragone*,[2] which published it without even the most ethereal printing error. Many warm greetings from yours,

Pier Paolo Pasolini

1 The reply to a letter in which Sciascia had announced his intention to publish a series of small volumes of 24 poems each in a limited edition of 300 copies. Pasolini would be in the first three. Sciascia was keen to include 'L'Appennino'.
2 See *Paragone*, December 1952.

## 325   To Sergio Maldini
Bologna
[*In possession of addressee: typewritten with autograph date and signature*]

Rome, 14 July 1953

Dear Sergio,

What will you think of me . . . but you are wrong: ever since I got it I have had your novel on the top of the pile of 'books received' in order to read it; but *I cannot manage to do so*. I have a frightening mass of work on my shoulders with deadlines which are quite simply contractual. Forgive me but I shall read you at the first breathing space and will write to you again. Many affectionate greetings from your affectionate butterfly hunter, that is to say,

P.P.P.

1   See Letter 288.

## 326   To Luciano Erba
Milan
[ *In possession of addressee: typewritten with autograph date and signature*]

Rome, 15 July 1953

Dear Erba,

Many thanks for your letter[1] and the pre-friendship which is thus inaugurated under the patronage of Anceschi . . . Good about Chiara's anthology[2] which, from what I hear, seems very interesting and in which I am very happy to be included. I would be very happy to contribute to *Itinerari* (although I am killed with work) but you would have to tell me with what literary 'genre' and in short to give me a kind of prescription (meantime I shall see the review, something which so far I have not had the chance to do; I live shamelessly in a periphery which is not only topographical).

Many warm greetings from yours,      Pier Paolo Pasolini

1   Erba had invited Pasolini to contribute to the Genoese review *Itinerari*.
2   *Quarta generazione* ('Fourth Generation'), Edizioni Magenta (Varese, 1954).

## 327   To Francesco Leonetti
Bologna
[ *In possession of addressee: typewritten with autograph date and signature*]

Rome, 15 July 1953

Dear Leonetti,

I ought to have thanked you ages ago for the Fanfani[1] – all the more since it is a book which has interested me very much; just as the 'laments' will interest me.[2] You will have noticed that our interests are very parallel: ah philology, *refugium peccatorum.*[3]

I embrace you affectionately,
Yours,      Pier Paolo Pasolini

1 Pietro Fanfari (1815–79), philologist, student of Italian dialects.
2 *gridi*: laments (dialect poems).
3 A refuge for sinners.

## 328   To Luigi Russo
Marina di Pietrasanta

[*In the Belfagor Archive, Florence: typewritten with autograph date and signature*]

Rome, 21 July 1953

Dear Professor,[1]

Perhaps I should not do so, but knowing the confusion that reigns in these matters I wish to draw your attention to the fact that Guanda has decided, at the last moment and perhaps too late, to make me take part in the Viareggio–Savinio prize with my introductory essay to the dialect *Anthology*. Guanda's business reasons are to some extent mine: I therefore beg you not to take this somewhat ingenuous and mild letter of mine as proof of presumptuous ambition if what I aim at, along with the publisher, is that the book should be talked about a little in the jury's discussions . . . Forgive me and accept my most respectful and warm greetings from yours dev.ly,

Pier Paolo Pasolini

1 He uses the very formal form: *Egregio professore.*

## 329   To Biagio Marin
Trieste

[*In possession of addressee: typed with autograph date and signature*]

Rome, 31 July 1953

Dear Marin,

Forgive the delay but to be able to tell you something I had to wait for Dell'Arco to come back from Sicily because it is he who is in contact with the printing presses and the printers. He is back at last and I at once sent him figures for the estimate. To avoid going round and round, Dell'Arco himself will write to you about it in a few days. As for the glossary I would be of the opinion not to do one; the common reader and even the uncommon one does not have the patience, in my view, to go and consult it and were he to do so, certain immediate, warm impressions from his reading would be lost. Better to have little notes at the foot of the page beneath the poem. Now tell me – is it my impression or has a certain hardness of tone entered into your letters to me? I very much fear that I was discourteous in asking you for that dedication.¹ I hoped that the affectionate confidence which had been established between us permitted me to take a few liberties within the limits of weaknesses which were still permissible. Forgive me and meanwhile I swear to you that I no longer think about it – that it is a matter of no importance. If I come up to Friuli it will be at the beginning of September and I shall not fail to come and shake your hand.

Affectionate greetings from yours,

Pier Paolo Pasolini

1   In a lost letter Pasolini had asked Marin to dedicate to him his new volume of poems.

## 330   To Cesare Padovani
Nogara (Verona)
[*In possession of addressee: typed with autograph date, signature and postscript*]

Rome, 31 July 1953

Dear Cesare,

Thank you for your intelligent letter and forgive the delay with which I reply: I am drowned in work and envy your holiday (all the more since I too, at your age, used to go to spend the summer holidays in those parts, at Riccione: we are travelling along the same road . . .)

But pay no attention to my delays and always, if you wish, reply to me as if these delays did not exist – you have time, lucky you! The two little answers to the 'why' which I had suddenly confronted you with,¹ although agnostic – which is natural – are very fine and intelligent in their simplicity. To ask a boy like you why he writes verse is like asking the rain why it rains or a flower why it has a scent. We are dealing with an irrational fact and before one can define it rationally . . . I like the prose of your letter much more than your dialect verses which, apart from a certain clumsiness and infantile naïvety (which in itself could be all right), reveal the presence of influences – let us call them literary ones – which are not good. There is implicitly, behind your words, the mistaken opinion that dialect has to be at the service of conventional emotional transports which lack bite and are served up with an obligatory comic tone. Something which will have been enthused over by the new Veronese poets of *Musa triveneta*.² They are amateurs and superficial people – maybe nice as human beings but very unprepared and slick as literary persons. You probably have the gifts to put you on a more serious road. And in this connection I certainly advise the *ginnasio* and the *liceo*; you will overcome the difficulties, never fear.

There are very few boys who write like you – I know it from bitter and discouraging experience. But remember that there is nothing better than to fight with 'difficulties' and that facility is, in general, the worst enemy of poetry and also of good literature (if these are things you really have at heart).

Affectionate greetings* from yours,

Pier Paolo Pasolini

*Also to your mother.
PS. I would be very happy to go and visit your exhibition³ this September. It is incredible; I too began to paint at your age and if I don't any more it is because I don't have time . . . I forgot to tell you that about now there will probably be in Cervia the deputy, Aldo Spallicci, who is a good dialect poet from Romagna; you could try to see him and speak to him, perhaps introducing yourself in my name.

1  See Letter 317.
2  'The Muse of the Three Venetos': a literary periodical.
3  'Competition for the best drawing by Italian children': an exhibition in Verona.

## 331  To Luciano Erba
Milan

[*In possession of addressee: typed with autograph date and signature*]

Rome, 6 August 1953

Dear Erba,

Here they are right away with dazzling rapidity (copying by machine due to a vacant morning or rather one thrown away) 'the not too deep bottom of my drawer' – two of them so that you can choose, since I am pathologically hesitant and lacking in confidence in choosing . . . Thank you very much also for the good wishes for the holidays (which I am passing with Penna among great views of the Tiber) which I return with all my heart if I can contrive to catch your fleeting image between 'the two Lombard trains'.

Warm greetings from yours,      Pier Paolo Pasolini

This letter was written in reply to a letter of 3 August 1953, in which Erba writes:

*I am writing to you between two trains to thank you for your courteous reply and to confirm to you my request for your collaboration on* Itinerari [. . .] *I think there is no point in asking you for a critical piece on demand, particularly since there would be no time* [. . .] *So I am betting on the – not too deep – bottom of your drawer.*

*1953*

## 332  To Nico Naldini
Casarsa

[*In possession of addressee: typewritten with autograph date and signature*]

Rome, 21 August 1953

Dear Nico,

I needn't tell you my anger and displeasure with Bartolini. Pass on to him that I know very well that 'Lied' is one of my lesser things, one begun a year ago and now (now that I would no longer write like that), perforce finished a little mechanically simply because I knew that he was among the judges. If not it would be a fragment left at the bottom of my drawer. That after all if he doesn't want to give a prize to 'Lied' let him give a prize through 'Lied' to something else by me which is necessary and resolved; because it is not right for him to assume rigid and (pseudo) honest attitudes for the 'Pordenone' prize when he would end up by giving a type like the Ceroni woman a prize . . . He should be ashamed, in short. Meanwhile please write a letter to Betocchi (because I cannot do so out of modesty), taking on the responsibility for having made me take part . . . We shall write to Maier as soon as the August holiday is over – but it would be a good idea if you were once and for all to state the exact date which would coincide with your journey to Trieste. Will you be teaching at the famous Village then? If not, I think that for about a month from the middle of October you ought to come and teach instead of me (I have to finish the tremendous anthology and then take part in a congress in Sicily). The three little poems you sent me are very good. Keep on working and studying: I assure you that it is the only compensation and consolation; choose a branch of knowledge and specialize; it is a magnificent psychological pedestal on which you can place any little statue you like. I am working like mad but I am also having a good deal of fun at certain magnificent after-dinner sessions by the Tiber.

A hug,      Pier Paolo

1   See Letter 320.

## 333  To Leonardo Sciascia
Palermo
[*In possession of addressee: typewritten with autograph date and signature*]

Rome, 21 August 1953

Dear Sciascia,

As you see from the crossing out I was writing to someone else, that is to say to the director of public education; I have changed my mind because I do not know how to head the letter and then what terminology to use. In short I am asking you to act as intermediary, to communicate to them that I am very happy to accept the invitation, that it is an honour for me, etc., and that I am waiting for them to announce the topic on which I should intervene. Many heartfelt thanks to you – one of my most passionate desires is to set foot in Sicily. The article for *Letteratura* has been ready for a long time; tomorrow I shall take it to Ulivi (if Ulivi is in Rome). Affectionate greetings from yours,

Pier Paolo Pasolini

## 334  To Gianfranco D'Aronco
Udine
[*In possession of addressee: typewritten with autograph date and signature*]

Rome, 31 August 1953

Dear D'Aronco.

I know that you have a huge corpus of *villotte*[1] and Friulian folk poetry. I am now compiling an anthology of Italian folk poetry for Guanda,[2] and would like to make use of the best collections for the various regions; there is nothing better in Friuli than your unpublished material. Can I count on your help? At the beginning of September I am probably coming up to Friuli; would you please write and tell me whether I can have the Friulian texts at my disposal; I shall come specially to Udine to consult them anywhere and at any time. Can I hope for an immediate reply from you? (And a favourable one?) I would also naturally count on some advice from you, because I am by no means a specialist in the subject, about the informational and philological apparatus; for this I shall naturally thank you publicly, along with Toschi and De Martino who have promised me some help in Rome. Hoping to see you soon therefore and many warm greetings from your rival and friend,

Pier Paolo Pasolini

1  Friulian folksong.
2  The *Canzoniere italiano.*

## 335   To Carlo Pasolini
Rome
[*In possession of Pasolini's heirs: autograph*]

Casarsa, 2 September 1953

Have won a slice (30,000) of the Pordenone prize. Better than nothing.

You will have seen that I left a letter for Falqui and certainly you will already have posted it.

In my haste I left the article on Cavani[1] with the relevant poems in a folder on which Caproni's telephone number was written. You ought to phone Caproni to ask him for Ulivi's address (which I have forgotten) and to send the package to Ulivi; but first you should type out the three poems by Cavani marked with a little circle.

Many kisses to you and mother,      Pier Paolo

1   It appeared in *Paragone* No 72, December 1955.

## 336   To Luigi Ciceri
Tricesimo
[*In possession of addressee's heirs: typewritten with autograph signature and postscript*]

[Rome, September 1953]

Dear Ciceri,

I have been wanting to write to you for ages: I still have to thank you and to express by the light of a note, however skimpy, the pleasure it gave me to see you and get to know you again. There is no need for us to stand on ceremony with each other; we understand each other, don't we? I shall do all I can to take part in the Philological Prize and in fact have the idea for a 'triptych' (to be called 'Il veciu testamint' ['The Old Testament'][1] which is very attractive to me; but shall I have the time to write it? I am overwhelmed by work. Another little favour I have to ask you for: to thank Comelli[2] for his review; it is one of the pieces which has given me most pleasure, it is so refined, calm, concrete. The moment I have the time I shall send you the delicious little poems of the adolescent boy, Spagnol.

Affectionate greetings from yours,

Pier Paolo Pasolini

PS. Next month – I don't know the date – if I can shall let you know – there will be a review of *Tal cùor* on the radio by Spagnoletti.

1  See *La nuova gioventú.*
2  See the review of *Tal còur di un frut* by Giovanni Comelli in *Sot la nape* ['Under the chimney'], vol. 3, May–June 1953.

## 337  To Adriano Seroni
Florence

[*In the Archive of 'Approdo letterario', Rai, Florence: typewritten with autograph date and signature*]

Rome, 14 September 1953

Dear Seroni,

I shall certainly do a piece on Gadda[1] by the deadline; I think I shall deal with a comparison between Gadda and Verga, which reminds me that we shall see each other in Sicily at the beginning of November, and many warm greetings.

Yours,      Pier Paolo Pasolini

1  A review for radio of Gadda's *Novelle dal Ducato in fiamme.*

## 338  To Adriano Seroni
Florence

[*In Rai Archive, Florence: typewritten with autograph date and signature*]

Rome, 20 September 1953

Dear Seroni,

Here just in time is the piece on Gadda – written in all haste as perhaps shows . . . Cordial greetings from yours,

Pier Paolo Pasolini

## 339  To Cesare Padovani
Nogara (Verona)

[*In possession of addressee: typewritten with autograph date and signature*]

[Rome,] 24 September 1953

Dear Cesarino,

Two painful lines (amid the sea of old books and the horrible index-cards in which I am drowning) to justify myself. The day we should have met (I think it was the 2nd) I was in Friuli and Trieste (in pursuit of books as usual). I had instructed an aunt of mine (who is a guest of ours) to go to the appointment but that day she was not very well. A real piece of bad luck. I was very sorry. But perhaps before Christmas I shall be back in Friuli in which case I shall stop in Padua between trains (it is so long, apart from anything else, that I have been meaning to see the Giottos there; it would be very nice to go there together).

Affectionate greetings from yours,

Pier Paolo Pasolini

## 340   To Luigi Ciceri
Tricesimo

[*In possession of addressee's heirs: typewritten with autograph date and signature*]

Rome, 25 September 1953

Dear Ciceri,

I keep at you with a constant trickle of favours; forgive me. I am going mad with my work[1] (you know too that the National Library in Rome is crumbling besides being in a state of disorder; so much so that it is entirely shut for two weeks). I had asked Cantarutti (as you know) to lend me a book in his possession (Chiurlo) and one from the library in Udine (Ive A., *Canti popolari istriani* ['Istrian folksongs'], Rome, 1877); yesterday only Chiurlo arrived. Now you should go to the library and take out the volume by Ive in your own name and send it to me at once. You will have it back in three or four days at the most. Can you do this? Again I ask your forgiveness and grasp your hand affectionately,

Yours,      Pier Paolo Pasolini

1   Refers to the preparation of the anthology of Italian popular poetry.

## 341   To Francesco Leonetti
Bologna

[*In possession of addressee: typewritten with autograph date and signature*]

[Rome,] 25 September 1953

Dear Leonetti,

Here your nobility of character will show itself. Today I had the *coup de grâce* in the library; for a fortnight the National Library is shut *for all purposes*.

I have to hand over N. Italy[1] to Guanda on 10 October; so I am in despair. I clutch at you: could you not ask for the books I gave you a list of for yourself or pretend to ask for them for Roversi and send them to me privately? Some employees in the library at Udine (Cantarutti who is a friend of mine) and in Venice (Sguerzi, whom I know through my cousin) have already done this: why could you not do it? Note that in a very few days you would have the books back intact with the greatest punctuality and precision. I am truly distressed at throwing this damnable shadow over our friendship which is being reborn; but I am sure that our 'reborn friendship' will survive it. You have been extremely nice to me – you and all your little family. You could not have a greater success in terms of feelings.

This was Bassani's impression too – he has confirmed to me in full that you are invited to contribute to *Botteghe Oscure*: send him a little group of poems. Or better, take them with you when we go to Sicily. I embrace you affectionately (really and not as an epistolary formula). Ah, I was forgetting – send me the data (I was about to say the bibliographical data) about your marvellous shaving soap.

Yours,　　　Pier Paolo

1　Refers to the first part of the *Canzoniere italiano*.

## 342　To Giacinto Spagnoletti
Milan
[*In possession of addressee: typewritten with autograph date and signature*]

Rome, 29 September 1953

Dearest Spagnoletti,

It is fate – I always have to begin my letters by apologizing for the delay. But you know very well how this letter was already formed – very long, very affectionate – within me even before becoming concrete in this one which is inevitably incomplete as well as being tardy (but believe me I am passing through days of anguish to be able to send the new anthology[1] to Guanda in time; and it is a tremendous task – in two days, for example, I have had to read three thousand *villotte* and select them. What you say about my criticism is very just (not the words of praise which I anxiously fear I do not merit, but the psychological attitude of me as writer). There would be a long, inner story to be told about this. Simplifying things to the point of banality: I would be an introvert, clinically 'fixed' in a narcissistic phase, not endowed, that is, with cognitive capabilities, with the ability to objectify, with historical conscious-ness, in short. So much biologically speaking; but naturally I have never meant to give in to nature and have ended thus after going through a dramatic situation, internal and not internal, by becoming (as they keep telling me) 'intelligent' from the purely 'sensitive' being I was. Naturally my critical work bears traces of that Calvary – thus for example I make up for depth with sharpness, etc., etc. But for me it is a victory of which I am proud; I feel a real 'interest' in the world, for my surroundings, and especially for the books I pass judgement on.

I am really sorry that your coming to Rome keeps being put off. I think we really like each other and that that liking demands to be cemented by habit and idiosyncrasies . . . But you work a lot and I follow your work – which is a sure way of being close. Many good wishes for the reworking of the novel[2] and above all, for the new son (a good wish that frightens me and almost make me burst with cosmic weeping). I would be very happy to prepare a small book for Sereni's collection,[3] especially if you were to help me with the selection which is a hell of a job . . . If you can also let me know beforehand about the note for *Approdo*,[4] since I should like, in my turn, to let good old Ciceri know.

An affectionate embrace from yours,

Pier Paolo Pasolini

1   *Canzoniere italiano.*
2   *Le orecchie del diavolo* ['The devil's ears'], Sansoni (Florence, 1953).
3   A reply to Spagnoletti's invitation to contribute to a collection by Sereni. Pasolini chose 'Il canto popolare' ['Folksong'].
4   A review on radio by Spagnoletti of *Tal còur di un frut* for the literary programme *Approdo letterario.*

## 343   To Tonuti Spagnol
Monte San Primo di Magreglio (Como)
[*In possession of addressee: typewritten*]

[Rome, autumn 1953]

Dearest Tonuti,

For months I have owed you a reply; but guilty in principle I am subsequently justified by not having known your address any longer. Your letters always give me very great pleasure and I have to tell you that no review flattered me more than the one you write so nicely in your letter on *Tal còur*. Now I have, I think, a good piece of news for you: Ciceri, the man who published my little book, would like to publish one of yours. So you must send me as quickly as possible everything you have recently written in Friulano. Remember that I have here, well looked after, your old notebook and also a few more recent poems; but I should like to have as many as possible to be able to make a good choice. Reply right away then because Ciceri would like to publish you before Christmas.

A most affectionate hug from yours,

Pier Paolo

This letter was written in reply to a letter from Spagnol in which he says that after completing his military service he had spent a couple of months in Versuta, which was very sad because the best of the young people had emigrated. He had found a copy of *Tal còur di un frut* in a bookshop. He says of it: '*Reading your poetry word by word, things present themselves with simple vivacity, poetry is one with nature, one is aware of feelings which leave something joyful in the heart.*'

## 344  To Giacinto Spagnoletti
Milan
[*In possession of addressee: typewritten with autograph corrections and signature*]

[Rome, October 1953]

Dear Spagnoletti,

An exceedingly laconic letter to say that I have received your postcard (the points in which I shall comply with), and above all, to thank you for your very pleasant words in *Approdo*. I have reimmersed myself in the fossil gardens of Alcina of my old Friulian diaries to get something passable out of them for Sereni's collection . . . But I think I shall leave the choice to you.

An affectionate hug from yours,

Pier Paolo Pasolini

## 345  To Francesco Leonetti
Bologna
[*In possession of addressee: typewritten with autograph date, signature and postscript*]

Rome, 5 October 1953

Dearest Leonetti,

It was simply the desperation of ten days ago that made me write that letter which I later so atrociously regretted above all for the blackmail which I really could have spared [you]. But you come out of it triumphant – with all your 'nobility' more than in evidence, exploding. I am saying it jokingly but I am not joking. I fully accept your lesson about the patience one has to exercise in terms of libraries; this time it was a frontal attack, in Garibaldi's style. The next time I shall be Fabius Maximus.[1] Meantime I am not suffering; the books have arrived[2] and partly been used, in a few days they will go back to Bologna and their adventure will have had a happy conclusion.

But apart from all this, which is beginning to unblock, I am happy, I repeat, to have found you again; when I think about you I feel a real surge of liking.

*1953*

Till soon and a big hug from yours,

Pier Paolo

PS. Affectionate greetings to your family.

1   Quintus Fabius Maximus, the Roman consul whose policy of caution in fighting
Hannibal won him the nickname of Cunctator, 'the one who delays'.
2   See Letter 341.

## 346   To Leonardo Sciascia
Palermo
[*In possession of addressee: typewritten with autograph date and signature*]

Rome, 5 October 1953

Dear Sciascia,

I should like to take advantage of your collection[1] to 'free myself' of some things which hang heavy in my past... 'L'Appennino' is fairly recent, has been read, and moreover will come out in America, very well translated by Weaver.[2] Could it be left out? My whole book, which has been lying there in Mondadori for three years (after a favourable reception and indeed the certainty of publication), is made up of four sections: *L'usignolo della Chiesa Cattolica*, *Diarii* (I, '43–'47), *Diarii* (II, '48–'49) and *Lingua*. Almost all the poems, especially the 'diaries' have come out rather chaotically in reviews and I should therefore like to give your collection one of these 'sections' according to your choice.[3] If this is all right with you, write and tell me at once so that I can prepare and send you the manuscripts. I shall also send the book to Mazza and many thanks. Affectionate greetings from yours,

Pier Paolo Pasolini

1   See Letter 324.
2   See the translation by William Weaver in the American review *Folder*, vol. II, no. 1
(1954–5).
3   Sciascia replies to this letter saying he cannot make the choice and asking Pasolini to do
so because Pasolini knows the tone of the collection.

446

## 347   To Eugenio Cirese
Bari

[*In possession of addressee: typewritten with autograph date and signature*]

Rome, 18 October 1953

Dear Cirese,

Many congratulations on your review,¹ which has started off well, with elegance together with a real regional culture. I hope it will above all go on developing the theme proposed by De Martino² – one which you at once took up in its full scope. Agree with you too on your comments on the little referendum by *Il Belli* (why does it not send its questions to the eighteen so as to complete it?) Forgive the telegraphic nature of this letter. But I shall probably write to you in the next ten days or so since I shall perhaps have to carry out for Rai a little piece of research into popular literature.³ Warm, or rather affectionate greetings from yours,

Pier Paolo Pasolini

1   *La Lapa* – *Topics concerning history and folk literature*, published in Rieti.
2   Ernesto De Martino (1908–65), ethnologist, author of *Il mondo magico*
['The magic world'].
3   This appeared in *Radiocorriere*, Rai's weekly journal, on 28 December 1953.

## 348   To Francesco Leonetti
Bologna

[*In possession of addressee: typewritten with autograph date and signature*]

Rome, 29 October 1953

Dear Leonetti,

A very hasty note, among the complicated workings of my day in which I live only on my nerves; I am at last sending you the parcel later than foreseen. I shall keep Visconti for two or three days.

I read in *Galleria* a very good short story by you. Since the invitation from *Botteghe Oscure* still stands, along with the poems you could therefore send me one or two stories – even long ones – if you have any. In any case we shall see each other in a fortnight on our holidays in Sicily.

A strong and affectionate hug from yours,

Pier Paolo

## 349   To Francesco Leonetti
Bologna
[*In possession of addressee: typewritten with autograph date and signature*]

Rome, 6 November 1953

Dearest Leonetti,

So we shall certainly see each other on Sunday but rather than at my place (it is difficult to get there by oneself) it is better for us to meet at 4 o'clock at the Caffè Greco in via Condotti.[1] Forgive the haste of this note which I am writing while the bus is already there in the mud waiting for me.

An affectionate hug, yours,      Pier Paolo

1   A well-known meeting-place for writers and artists.

## 350   To Mario Boselli
Genoa
[*In possession of addressee: typewritten with autograph signature*]

Rome, 21 November 1953

Dear Boselli,

Look – I would say one should do this: entrust to me the 'panorama' of poetry on which I am well up and sure of myself (I am a little behind with the criticism; I should read at least half-a-dozen volumes and there is not much time, very little in fact) – and entrust to someone else – I would suggest Romano, or a student of Contini's, Dante Isella, who is very good – the survey of the critical work. If that is all right with you reply by return of post. To me it seems the best solution.

An affectionate hug from yours,

Pier Paolo Pasolini

PS. The headings of my 'panorama' would be in general: 1) around Montale; 2) around Ungaretti; 3) outsiders; 4) the last generation and future perspectives. The central thread: the progress beyond the taste of *La Ronda*[1] and hermeticism by a revival of a history of poetic language which has roots in *La Voce*[2] and in the last great realist tradition of the nineteenth century. (Take these words *cum grano salis*[3] and don't attribute to them the rather fetid taste which their most recent use has attributed to them.)

This letter was written in a reply to an invitation to contribute to the Genoese review *Nuova Corrente* ['New Current'].

1   *La Ronda* (1919–22), avant-garde literary review.

2   *La Voce* (1908–16), neo-idealistic literary review.
3   *cum grano salis*: with a pinch of salt.

## 351   To Vittorio Sereni
Milan
[*In possession of addressee: typewritten with autograph corrections, date and signature*]

Rome, 21 November 1953

Dear Sereni,

I am replying with a slight delay to a letter[1] which I not only should have replied to at once but immediately accompanied the reply with the package of poems which you ask me for, and which I willingly give you. I am atrociously busy with overdue deadlines; you know how it happens; all at once, after months of having no work. But certainly in ten days or a fortnight I shall send you three little collections of verses – not anthologized: sections of the unpublished and unfinished book – so that you can choose. A piece of the diary (from '48), a little group entitled *Lingua* (written between '47 and '49) and a composition in the form of a ballad which I have called 'Folksong', begun last year and finished in these days. With much gratitude I greet you affectionately,

Yours,      Pier Paolo Pasolini

1   In reply to a letter from Sereni asking for contributions from Pasolini to the series discussed in Letter 342.

## 352   To Gianfranco Contini
Florence
[*In possession of addressee: typewritten with autograph date and signature*]

Rome, 22 November 1953

Dear Contini,

Your letters have always a magical power; inoculated by joy for a week I have not noticed the old drudgery of the railway and school: Ciampino is close at hand, my pupils are geniuses, the suburban peas are flowers. My ill-feeling has at last subsided over the cracks in the National Library which held up my work – an orgy and an orgasm on folk poetry for a new anthology by Guanda . . . the light is so rosy that the 'poetical stuff of *Tal còur* is projected into my future. Perhaps you do not realize how much my wager with myself has turned into a wager with you, so that your 'enforced silence' sometimes makes me feel not resentment but fear, a tremendous panic over failing . . . But now I hope that sometimes you will come to Rome. In the meantime I clasp your hand affectionately,

Yours,      Pier Paolo Pasolini

This is a reply to the following letter from Contini:

*Domodossola, 10 xi 1953*

*Dearest P.P.P.,*

*Tomorrow I go back to Florence (via del Cantone 9) and realize that the holidays have run their course and that although I had all the leisure to write you a long letter I did not find one privileged minute distinct from the others by some particular necessity in order to turn that possibility into action. I wanted to tell you, but properly, but with all due consideration, that* Tal còur di un frut *seemed to me to be the object, simply the most pure, invented, vital and consoling poetical material (as one says, painterly material), which for long (very long years) has come into my sphere of perception. I am saying this to you crudely and apodictically but you must approve of my intent. Since your* trobar *is heuristic and linguistic, I mean physically linguistic, it occurred to me to quote your* félibrige *as an examplary symptom in an austerely and professionally glottological lecture last September. But the vessels were not communicating, and if I do not write to you it is only by an act of faith (which in this case would arrive at the truth) that you can think of my feeling for you which cannot be broken off. From you my enforced silence demands much, I know. Forgive me and believe me yours,*

*Gianfranco Contini*

## 353   To Adriano Seroni
### Florence
[*In Rai Archive, Florence: typewritten with autograph date and signature*]

Rome, 25 November 1953

Dear Seroni,

For months I ought to have written to you – it is about Gadda[1] who did not hear my piece in *Approdo* and would like to read it; I do not have a copy because when I was retyping it I put the carbon-paper in the wrong way round . . . Could you provide? And I should like to ask you a favour as well – one that is a little, no very, indiscreet, because I know you look after the narrative section of *Approdo*; but if it is not possible naturally tell me so without beating about the bush. I would like to follow Gadda with a piece on Banti's *Bastardo*. . . Do forgive me and accept the most warm greetings from yours,

Pier Paolo Pasolini

1   See Letter 337.

## 354   To Leonardo Sciascia
Palermo
[*In possession of addressee: typewritten with autograph date and signature*]

Rome, 30 November 1953

Dearest Sciascia,

Romanò has decided to call the book *Un giorno d'estate* ['A summer day'],¹ and would like to preface it, textually, with this dedication: 'to m'.

He will send you as soon as possible – if he has not already sent it yesterday – the piece on Bertolucci's thriller.²

I too could send a piece for *Galleria* which I did for the radio: an enquiry into 'popular poetry as mass culture' with replies from Cirese, Vann' Antò, De Martino, Sàntoli and Vidossi, and with particular regard to Sicily (Puppet Theatre and with a semi-popular little poem on the bandit Giuliano).³ Is it any use to you? I shall also send you my poems and those of Naldini (as far as I am concerned I think they are the last ones in Friulano).

I never wrote to Councillor Castiglia to thank him – and I am ashamed but I have not had time, and then letters like that are such a trouble. If you were able somehow or other to convey to the organizers my feelings of gratitude you would be doing me a great favour.

When will my little volume come out?⁴ Please note that I too would like to correct the proofs so as to become the butt of my own anger should any typographical atrocities remain there.

I embrace you affectionately,

Yours,      Pier Paolo Pasolini

1   See Letter 324.
2   See Letter 291.
3   See 'Poesia popolare e cultura di massa' in *Radiocorriere* of 28 December 1953.
4   See *Dal diario*.

## 355   To Adriano Seroni
Florence
[*In possession of addressee: typewritten with autograph date and signature*]

Rome, 4 December 1953

Dear Seroni,¹

Here is the piece on Banti, I simply could not keep rigidly within the limit of seventy lines. I hope it will still be all right. Warm and affectionate greetings, yours,

Pier Paolo Pasolini

1   He uses the formal mode of address: *Gentile.*

## 356   To Vittorio Sereni
Milan
[*In possession of addressee: typewritten with autograph signature*]

Rome, 5 December 1953

Dear Sereni,

I am sending you these two 'pamphlets' – not anthologized (which is what you wanted) but 'sections of the book' representing a single period which is the same in both of them: the immediate postwar years spent in not so much the province of Friuli as in its countryside. You cannot know what a sea of nausea I have been swimming in in these days when making the selection: these years and that poetry are merely garbage but for me – not for others who do not know my history – it is truly stuff that belongs to the past. I was very surprised when Contini at that time wrote to me about my decadentism, pulled my leg a little about my 'maudit' attitudes: just think – I wasn't aware of it. I was so blinded by my psychological abnormality, by the continuity of my most private and incommunicable life as a boy, by the lack of culture of the small-town background that surrounded me, in which, instead of being a provincial (but there was a certain provincialism in my dandyism), I was a mystic. To this unreligious mysticism my case – I am speaking clinically – of narcissisitic fixation contributed; this made me continually live linked to what an ancient religion calls 'the Double'; and then – to make this double existence more difficult – there was my extremely acute, desperate and naïve morality – that of a boy who was not a Catholic but without Croce coming into it naturally, and how he would have called me a bourgeois 'idealist'; I therefore lived in a manic almost superstitious dialogue with my conscience along the lines of an almost Jesuistic casuistry. As happens in adolescence I alternated between extreme gaiety – and in me there was the poetic-religious 'joy' of the provincials – and extreme discomfort. No objective-realistic capacity therefore: the world was unknowable except in its legendary and poetic form. Hence, perhaps, a certain greater validity for my Friulian poetry in which the setting was purely poetical but there was . . .

My God, how I am rambling on – But forgive me – I have, I don't know why, a tremendous need to justify myself, to wash away all that sinful irrationality and all the tender feeling which still exists in me for those my heroic days of youthful adventures. Of which I have not entirely freed myself, indeed in this letter there are still some traces . . .

Now I do not know how far this experience of mine is documentary and can therefore be of use to you for your series. Perhaps 'Il canto popolare' ['The popular song'] will fit better (but I nourish infinite doubts which here are of a different kind); and if you prefer my latest things why could one not put together 'L'Appennino' (which came out in *Paragone* two or three numbers ago) and 'Picasso' (which came out in the last number of *Botteghe Oscure*)? have you read them? If you think that a more interesting little volume might emerge, tell me. And that would console me because we are talking about poetry already published and tested . . . Forgive the extremely long, suffocating letter and accept my most affectionate greetings,

Yours,      Pier Paolo Pasolini

1  See Letter 351.
2  See *Paragone* of December 1952 and *Botteghe Oscure*, XII, 1953.

## 357   To Tonuti Spagnol
Monte San Primo di Magreglio (Como)
[*In possession of addressee: typewritten with autograph date and signature*]

Rome, 6 December 1953

Dearest Tonuti,

Four hasty lines with the headache of a whole Sunday spent writing. I am waiting for your poems,[1] all the poems you have written since those I have here in the little pink notebook. It doesn't matter if they have aready been published. People always do that – first they are published in reviews and then they are collected in a volume. So hurry up and accept my most affectionate greetings and a brotherly hug from yours,

Pier Paolo

1  See Letter 343.

*1953*

## 358  To Tonuti Spagnol
Monte San Primo di Magreglio (Como)
[*In possession of addressee: typewritten with autograph date and signature*]

Rome, 11 December 1953

Dear Tonuti,

The usual couple of hasty lines written acrobatically in an odd moment. Thank you for your poems which I shall select and recopy in the Christmas holidays. I should like to ask you a favour which asked of anyone else would be indiscreet but not for you, I think – would you like to dedicate the book to me?[1] I would be very happy; besides I feel that in this way I am expressing a genuine desire on your part of which you simply have not thought. You will certainly get reviews, among them – in a special tone – one by me. A big hug,

Yours,      Pier Paolo

1   The project to publish the poetry of Tonuti Spagnol was realized only many years later in 1985: *La Cresima e Timp piardut* ['Confirmation and lost time'], edited by A. Giacomini, Edizioni Concordia Sette (Pordenone).

## 359  To Francesco Leonetti
[*In possession of addressee: typewritten with autograph date, signature and postscript*]

Rome, 31 December 1953

Dearest Leonetti,

Forgive me if you can, if it is at all possible, for this very long, terrible delay. The reasons are the usual ones which you know, and unfortunately they are still good ones: I am always at this damned typewriter. But apart from that I wanted to give you some positive news, which I did not have till now. Only yesterday, at dinner, raising his arms to heaven, Bassani said: 'I have read Leonetti! Very good! He is the best one up there in Bologna!' etc. So as far as *Botteghe Oscure* goes we have arrived. As for *Paragone*, I assure you you will get there – to use your terminology – but two things are needed: that you should send more poems, because both the editors and the publisher very much want to make a 'selection', and that you should have a little patience because Bassani is editor of both *Botteghe Oscure* and *Paragone,* and one can't ask him for two such similar things at one and the same time. I'd like to write a long letter to you now – to chat a little about us but I am obsessed by datelines and am breaking off. I send you one of those hugs which suffice to express without comment all the affection and warm feelings of your,

Pier Paolo

PS. I was forgetting the good wishes. So let them be handwritten! For you and your lovely family and I am not forgetting Roversi.

# 1954

## 360   To Vittorio Sereni

Milan

[*In possession of addressee: typewritten with autograph date and signature*]

Rome, 2 January 1954

Dear Sereni,

At last I am sending you 'Popular song' – I have been so long partly because I wanted to have the final corrections put in and to see if they worked, but above all because I wanted to quote some popular verse – Piedmontese and Sicilian – from books which are only to be found in the National Library and the National was shut; now that it is open these books are out on loan . . . But I did not want to delay longer and am sending you the typescript with a half-line missing and with a few changes to be made here and there. In consequence the 'note' is also incomplete as you see (besides having been dashed off somewhat hastily this morning). But you can get an idea of the whole even without these minimal details and judge whether it is all right or not. I am sorry about the delay and the scruples and along with the condolences – they are inevitably a little formal – for your father's death accept the most affectionate greetings and good wishes from yours,

Pier Paolo Pasolini

## 361   To Mario Boselli

Genoa

[*In possession of addressee: typewritten with autograph date and signature*]

Rome, 6 January 1954

Dear Boselli,

Forgive me if I have taken long to reply – the reasons are the usual ones, alas! So I shall do the 'panorama' for you[1] but I cannot promise to let you have it before the end of January. It is not that I am lazy or slow in doing things; but I have a mass of things to do; if only you knew what a tragic affair the anthology of popular poetry I am preparing for Guanda is . . . Affectionate greetings with many good wishes,

Yours,      Pier Paolo Pasolini

1   See Letter 350. This 'panorama' was never written.

## 362   To Adriano Seroni
Florence

[*In the Rai Archive, Florence: typewritten with autograph date and signature*]

Rome, 12 January 1954

Dear Seroni,

Many thanks for your letter – very well then, agreed – I shall add some quotations and will orchestrate it for two voices. There is not much hurry, I think. But I shall do it as soon as possible. If you have not sent my talk to Gadda yet so much the better; send it directly to me if you have a moment since I should like to re-read it.

Many warm greetings from yours,

Pier Paolo Pasolini

## 363   To Luigi Ciceri
Tricesimo

[*In possession of addressee's heirs: typewritten with autograph date and signature*]

Rome, 12 January 1954

Dearest Ciceri,

Do please forgive this damnable brevity of mine; but I am crushed by Guanda's anthology, by a heap of reviews, and, fortunately, by work for Rai. When I finally tear myself away from the typewriter I have it up to here. I am very happy that you liked my short story[1] (it comes from *Il Ferrabedò*, the novel I hope to publish in the course of this year; and – I don't know whether my father told you – in a few months' time my Friulian *Romancero* from '41 to today will appear in the *Paragone* collection).[2] I got your letter only the day before yesterday and so I could not get in touch with your wife.

I think that studies on Nievo might interest various reviews; but certainly it depends a little on their length and other external circumstances. If you want me to help you you should let me have them; I shall put you in contact with two or three editorial boards and they are sure to appear in one or other of our best reviews. I am typing out Spagnol's poems – a work I would have finished by now if time . . . I have no news about Bartolini's 'idiocy' – will you send me the exact information? (unless it is a case of a piece in an old number of *Giovedí*).

An affectionate hug from yours,

Pier Paolo Pasolini

1   The first chapter of what was to become *Ragazzi di vita.*
2   *La meglio gioventú.*

## 364   To Giacinto Spagnoletti
Milan
[*In possession of addressee: typewritten with autograph date and signature*]

Rome, 14 January 1954

Dear Spagnoletti,

Forgive this absurd card but I would have to go down into the mud of Rebibbia to buy a decent one; meanwhile I must take advantage of a brief moment. Here I am thanking you for your note yesterday on 'Picasso'[1] – a note which filled the air and our little kitchen with the joy of my parents and myself like an explosion. The bet with myself has been a little like a bet with you as well, ever since you included me in your anthology, and I am very happy indeed when I hear that you may have things confirmed. These days I am a bit unhappy because I sent Sereni a companion poem to 'Picasso'[2] and have heard nothing – I am afraid Sereni did not like it very much and he doesn't like to tell me. Given the greater closeness between the two of us could you act as intermediary?

I embrace you with great affection,      Pier Paolo

1   A review on the radio of the poem which had appeared in *Botteghe Oscure.*
2   *Il canto popolare.*

## 365   To Nico Naldini
Gradisca d'Isonzo
[*In possession of addressee: typewritten with autograph date and signature*]

Rome, 14 January 1954

Dear Nico,

Since your defection at Christmas nothing more. The most profound silence. Why? This is to beg for your answer to the questionnaire from *Lapa.*[1] I have enough problems without you giving me them as well. Basically all that is needed is two monosyllables to reply to the two short questions. Along with this begging request, two exhortations – first, to work at your thesis, secondly, to write poetry. Now I am sending three of your poems to *Galleria*, which is doing a fine special number devoted to the dialect poets. Other three I shall send to *Montaggio* ['Montage'] which will devote an equally fine number to the dialect poets. Then there is nothing else unpublished by you. But you do have stuff there. It is pure, shameful laziness, criminal confusion. Forgive this rather passionate letter – but don't you deserve it?

An affectionate hug,        Pier Paolo

1   A literary review dealing with popular literature.

## 366   To Leonardo Sciascia
Palermo
[*In possession of addressee: typewritten with autograph date and signature*]

Rome, 19 January 1954

Dear Sciascia,

I am not sure if I am late – if I am forgive me not only because of the usual burden of work but for not knowing the deadline.

I am sending you the radio inquiry[1] – naturally in terms of typography all the 'voices' have to be removed. If it is all right (I fear it may be a little long) let me know so that I do a very short 'Appendix for *Galleria*' for you to add at the end.

I am also sending you a little group of poems by myself and Naldini.[2] They are some of my latest (unpublished) ones; in a few months' time my complete collection in Friulano will come out in the *Paragone* series.[3] What about the little book by Romanò, Roversi and me? Romanò asks me for news with impatience and emotion and I don't know how to answer him.

An affectionate greeting from yours,

Pier Paolo Pasolini

1   See Letter 354.
2   See 'Piccola antologia di poeti dialettali', in *Galleria*, May 1954.
3   See *La meglio gioventú*.

*1954*

## 367   To Vittorio Sereni
Milan
[*In possession of addressee: typewritten with autograph corrections, date and signature*]

Rome, 1 February 1954

Dear Sereni,

I am happy with your choice – I too am for *Il canto popolare* although it is too recent for me to able to judge it from my point of view as well. In general if there is a risk of its being all prose, that is to say that I fall out – discovered and put to shame – I prefer that this should happen *à propos* the confession of my relationship to the external world rather than of my *autobiography*. You attribute courage to me – perhaps, I should be happy because of it – but I feel I have been *forced* to make certain choices, forced by an excess, by a constant violence in my psychology: either when I was interested above all in my internal experiences or now when I have been ejected – to try to know as well as I can this *not I* who is so dear to me, in relation to whose circumstances I am so full of gratitude and love (which are unjustifiable, given my adventures and difficulties).

I am aware now that, although I managed in time to form myself at the same age as you, I did not in fact go in search of 'poetry' even if I was impregnated by the anxiety of that search and up to my neck in consciousness of the autonomy of art. I repeat: at that time the violence of my psychological 'case' (sensual and moral) was too great, now the violence of my relationship, which has been more or less normally re-established with the historical world, is too strong. I could not (although I thought I was doing so) think of poetry, where in similar circumstances I used to take (or now take) pen in hand. If only you knew how I envy your control, your calm, the complete accord between your emotional state (which is always so much in harmony with the psychological background) and your verses... However in connection with *Canto popolare* I hope that if it has a certain validity it is not valid because of certain emotional provincialisms in so far as it is sensual and nostalgic about 'L'Italia', but because of a different kind of pathos which I would not be able to define for you but which I would say is no longer sensual and nostalgic (at least in that sense). As for the painter, I don't know who to think of. Would Zigaina suit you?

Thanks and affectionate greetings from yours,

Pier Paolo Pasolini

This letter was written in reply to a letter from Sereni, in which the latter writes:

*Over and above your usual courage there is also that – I do not know how rare in you but very rare above a certain level – of running the risk of writing ugly verses in order to say something important to you and which, were it not said, would take away a good part of the meaning from the more beautiful verses.*

He promises to send a contract and a small advance as soon as things are settled, and asks Pasolini to recommend an artist for a drawing to be placed in the volume.

## 368   To Leonardo Sciascia
Palermo
*[In possession of addressee: typewritten with autograph signature]*

Rome, 1 February 1954

Dear Sciascia,

I am pleased that the little volumes are progressing and perhaps more for Romanò than for myself.

The number of *Galleria* which you outline to me seems very good, so much so that I should prefer to publish in it, instead of the inquiry[1] which for various reasons has not been as successful as I wished, two paragraphs from my introduction to the *Anthology of Popular Poetry* – paragraphs which deal with the style of popular poetry and the 'relationship' between popular poetry and dialect poetry.[2] So do not have the inquiry set up in type and within a week at the most you will have my new and more engaged text. Listen, why don't you turn to Cocchiara for a piece? He might give you something interesting especially if it is about the relationship between popular and folk poetry ... I shall also send you some other verses by me and by Naldini (if that lazy creature has any more unpublished ones).[3] How is your work going? Have you written any new poems? An affectionate hug from yours,

Pier Paolo Pasolini

1  See Letter 354.
2  *Un paragrafo sulla poesie popolare*, in *Galleria*, May 1954.
3  Replies to a letter from Sciascia saying that since the other poets have 50–70 poems each he would like the same number from Pasolini and Naldini.

1954

## 369   To Carlo Betocchi
Florence
[*In possession of addressee: autograph*]

[Postmark: Rome, 10 February 1954]

Dear Betocchi,

Caproni asks me to send you Penna's address[1] and I am doing so with the usual shameful delay of some days. Forgive me. Am very pleased to have the opportunity of sending you my greetings which, given their object, are some of my most affectionate. And many greetings too to your wife and the little girl.

Yours,      Pier Paolo Pasolini

1   Vallecchi, the publisher for whom Betocchi worked, intended to produce a poetry series 'of middle age'. Penna did not in the end participate.

## 370   To Vittorio Sereni
Milan
[*In possession of addressee: typewritten with autograph date, signature and postscript*]

Rome, 24 February 1954

Dear Sereni,

Thanks for your long and affectionately detailed letter – and forgive me if I reply instead so briefly and drily. The fact is that I am dying with sleep and fatigue and I am forcing myself to reply this evening because I have before me days which are even more ferociously burdened. As to the date of publication, arrange things as you think best, I really have no preference and no haste.

As for the choice, I would rather be for one thing or the other: either *Lingua* or *Il canto popolare* (with a predilection, naturally, for the latter). I would not opt for placing them together[1] ... I shall write as soon as possible to Zigaina[2] (if some other opportunity does not present itself – Zigaina is too much, is too officially of the Left for an ex-Communist like me).

Affectionate greetings,

Yours,      Pier Paolo Pasolini

PS. If you see him, say hello to Spagnoletti from me.

1   Sereni had suggested a volume including *Il canto popolare* and *Lingua*, perhaps with a poem linking them and with a title like 'Two Moments'.

**2** Giuseppe Zigaina (b. 1924), painter of Friulian people and landscapes.

## 371   To Francesco Leonetti
Bologna

[*In possession of addressee: typewritten with autograph date, signature and postscript*]

Rome, 24 February 1954

Dearest Leonetti,

I ought to have written to you long ago to thank you for two (or three) very nice letters. I did not do so because of absolute, continuous, obsessive lack of time but this time also because I had a piece of news for you that isn't good. And although I am only the ambassador, I am the bearer – in the sense that I feel it – of something very painful. The Princess[1] of *Botteghe Oscure* found your poems 'unpleasant'; you will understand that this is, if correctly interpreted, a compliment, but certainly publication was preferable. Bassani feels very bad about it and so do I. I hope to write you a more cheerful letter in a few days. Apart from this there would be so much to say – and I have to refrain (it is after supper, gloomily dark, in Rebibbia the dogs are barking, I am dead tired after a day which was totally embedded in my brain!).

I embrace you with much affection,

Yours,      Pier Paolo

PS. Going by what you say I expect to see you soon in Rome. Then I shall be in the new house. But perhaps I shall be in Bologna (with Bassani) and that very soon, I believe.

1   Marguerite Caetani (1880–1965), Duchess of Sermonetta, American literary *grande dame* in Paris and Rome, founded influential literary magazine *Botteghe Oscure* (1948–60).

## 372   To Giacinto Spagnoletti
Milan

[*In possession of addressee: typewritten with autograph date and signature*]

Rome, 1 March 1954

Dearest Giacinto,

In the last few days you will have had a little volume of verses by Marin, *Ceneri calde* ['Warm ashes']; it was I who had it sent to you and this is an accompanying letter – or rather, one to commend it to you and to hope you have a good read.

1954

You will see that there are some very fine things among others which are mediocre and a little conventional – but on the whole it seems more than worthy of a mention in *Approdo*. I am taking the opportunity to give a sign of life and to send you my most affectionate greetings,

Yours,     Pier Paolo Pasolini

## 373  To Nico Naldini
Gradisca d'Isonzo
[*In possession of addressee: typewritten with autograph date and signature*]

Rome, 8 March 1954

Dear Nico,

I was really becoming cross at your silence when you finally made up your mind. But now there is a new reason to be cross: Marin invited you to dinner in Trieste (following a letter from me in which I said that you would get his book reviewed – something I am counting on) and you not only did not go but did not even reply. Call it laziness but for me this is rudeness and also (forgive me) presumption. Try to do better . . .

The thesis on Justinian looks to me as if it might do very well – like a hundred other theses; I hope you aren't going to consider them all and that you won't lazily take three months on each one. Decide on Justinian and let it be a final decision.

Write verses, good or bad; for the reasons I have told you so often.

Send me Marangoni's address because I want to send him back the Friulian books; please don't make me wait a year.

Forgive this sharp and impatient letter – but lay your hand on your heart and see whether I am right or wrong.

An affectionate hug,

Yours,     Pier Paolo

## 374  To Leonardo Sciascia
Palermo
[*In possession of addressee: typewritten with autograph date, signature and postscript*]

Rome, 12 March 1954

Dear Sciascia,

Dragged along by the cinematographic events in Comacchio,[1] I have to delay the dispatch a little. But don't be discouraged. Next Friday I shall send you the 'three paragraphs on popular poetry'[2] without any doubt; you can count on that unreservedly. Do forgive me and accept my most affectionate greetings from yours,

Pier Paolo Pasolini

PS. A little appendix and something annoying for you – instead of 'Europa' I should like to publish in my little book[3] the two lyrics which I am enclosing: 'Lingua' ['Speech'] and 'La croce fissione' ['The crucifixion']. If there are any small printing costs set them off against the fee for contributing to *Galleria*.

1  For research for the film *La donna del fiume* ['The woman of the river'] by Mario Soldati, on the script for which Pasolini collaborated with Giorgio Bassani.
2  See Letter 368.
3  *Dal Diario* ['From the diary'].

## 375  To Biagio Marin
Trieste
[*In possession of addressee: typewritten with autograph addition, date and signature*]

Rome, 14 March 1954

Dear Marin,

I ought to have written to you for ages but first I had to make a little trip to Ferrara and Comacchio[1] and I have come back to Rome with a heavy cold and the accompanying fever; then as you see from the changed address I have moved house and these have been days of chaos; finally the undertow of work broken off has caught me again. Forgive me therefore, and don't be upset by my atrociously erratic correspondence. I read with much pleasure the article by Prezzolini[2] – as for Spagnoletti, I have no news but I shall ask for it and am sure he will talk about your work. On my cousin's part[3] a profound, disgusting silence all along the line. Has he shown you any sign of life? Meanwhile I shall consult with Dell'Arco about who could review you for *Galleria*.

On Saturday 27 March a piece by me about Giotti[4] was broadcast on the Third Programme and some of his poems were read. These were the days when I was wandering about in the valleys of Comacchio and unfortunately I could not catch it. If you get the chance, tell him. Will you be coming down to Rome again? Meantime accept my most affectionate greetings,

Yours,      Pier Paolo Pasolini

New address: V. Fonteiana 84–26, Rome.

1   See Letter 374.
2   A review of *Sénere colde* (*Ceneri calde*) in *Il Tempo*, 4 March 1954.
3   Nico Naldini.
4   Virgilio Giotti; see 'Omaggio a Giotti', in *Il Belli*, December 1954.

## 376   To Mario Boselli
Genoa

[*In possession of addressee: typewritten with autograph date and signature*]

Rome, 18 March 1954

Dear Boselli,

I am writing to you really sick at heart – I am really not used to shortcomings, I feel as uncomfortable and full of remorse as a little schoolboy.[1] But I swear to you that I simply could not manage: you know very well that I teach in a school very far from here (an hour and a half to two hours by tram or bus) and that I am deep in other tasks – but I could have not broken my promise had not an unexpected piece of work come my way – for the cinema, something I had been dreaming about for four years (for lucre), and for it I dropped everything.[2] It is bread, do you understand, Boselli – it is a breathing space in my family's hard life. Try to understand and forgive me. The most I can do is to send you for the first number a kind of introductory foreword – a kind of summary of a future essay. If that is sufficient, write and tell me at once.

Once again I beg you to forgive me and send my most warm greetings,

Yours,      Pier Paolo Pasolini

1   See Letter 350.
2   His collaboration on a film script for Mario Soldati marks the beginning of his association with the cinema; up to now he had found employment only as an extra.

## 377   To Vittorio Sereni
Milan

[*In possession of addressee: typewritten with autograph addition, date and signature*]

Rome, 29 March 1954

Zigaina has sent me the drawing and here it is.[1] As a drawing it looks very fine to me and also suitable for use as an illustration; I am not sure if it is very suitable for a block but I don't know much about that . . . Is there any news? So what time of year has been decided on for my book to appear?[2] Forgive these dry questions and the skimpiness of the letter; but we are moving house and I am writing to you amid unspeakable confusion and am ill into the bargain. Accept most affectionate greetings from yours,

Pier Paolo Pasolini

New address: V. Fonteiana 84

1   See Letter 370.
2   *Il canto popolare.*

## 378   To Leonardo Sciascia
Palermo
[*In possession of addressee: typewritten with autograph date and signature*]

Rome, 29 March 1954

Dearest Sciascia,

We really are in Someone's hands: during the trip to Comacchio I caught a terrible cold with a temperature up to 40 and a terrifying return journey cheered only by the hospitality at the Longhis. What with injections, pills and suppositories I am almost cured, but I am still behind schedule with you; I have here only one of the three 'paragraphs' from my Introduction;[1] maybe that will be enough, I think (although I am annoyed not to include a piece on Calabria in which I examined the relationship between popular poetry and dialect poetry). Because just in these very days we are moving house and you know what it means to pack and unpack books, bookcases. Write to me at once if what I am sending you is enough and if you can wait another week at least for the little paragraph on Calabria.

Disappointed as I am in *Letteratura*, given the previous matters you know about, I had sent you the other two poems a little heedlessly. Well, don't let us bother about it; leave 'Europa' in.[2] But remember that I should like to correct the proofs of the two *diaries* which were not included and of the note which I shall probably re-do almost entirely at least in the first half.

I am pleased to be coming to Sicily. But send me details, that is to say: when should the trip take place, who would the 'we' be who will be my hosts (I would not like to be a burden on your shoulders!), if it is possible to line up another University or Institute in which to give the same lecture (for example, in Messina, through Vann'Antò.)

Molino's[3] poem is very nice; but everything is already set up for *Fiera*. And as I have explained to you I do not have the time to undo it and put it together

467

again. However, I shall see; maybe it will come in useful for *Il Belli*; and as for Molino, I would present him willingly.

Many affectionate greetings,

Pier Paolo Pasolini

1   See Letter 368.
2   Replies to a letter from Sciascia in which the latter says he would rather not substitute two other poems by Pasolini and would prefer instead to keep in 'Europa', 'which I like very much'.
3   Carmelo Molino, Sicilian dialect poet.

## 379   To Alan Brusini
Tricesimo
[*In possession of addressee: typewritten with autograph date and signature*]

Rome, 31 March 1954

Dear Brusini,

I have been in Trieste and have been back for a while, and to tell the truth it was I who was waiting for an indication from you, telling me that I was expected in Udine.

Is that not what we agreed at Dreher's Beerhouse? Your collection seemed very good to me; the best current work in Friuli. Certainly here and there it needs to be pruned and retouched. As for its publication, for now I do not have very cheerful news: Sciascia has big problems (a trial for slandering a damned fascist), and for the time being his collection has a fixed timetable.

In short it is a case of being patient and postponing things. Give Ciceri my affectionate greetings.

A handshake from yours,       Pier Paolo Pasolini

## 380   To Leonardo Sciascia
Palermo
[*In possession of addressee: typewritten with autograph date and signature*]

Rome, 12 April 1954

Dear Sciascia,

Here are the proofs of the poems, with a new – shorter – note. Under the title *Dal Diario* ['From the diary'] I have added, as you see, a little epigraph by Pascal. I have left out two poems without regret. There are one or two rather delicate corrections to be made (especially in the second verse of 'Europa'): I rely on you.

I also include the notes to the 'Paragraph':[1] I hope to have put the little numbers in the text – in any case it is very easy to find the places for them.

So I am putting Molino in *Fiera*,[2] but a little hastily; I hope he will be pleased just the same.

Many affectionate greetings,

Yours,      Pier Paolo Pasolini

1   See Letter 368.
2   Sciascia had asked Pasolini to insert a group of poems by Molino in *La Fiera letteraria*.

## 381   To Francesco Leonetti
## Bologna

[*In possession of addressee: typewritten with autograph addition, date and signature*]

Rome, 16 April 1954

Dearest Leonetti,

I passed through Bologna twice towards the end of March, but going we were behind with our travel programme and we did not stop, on the way back I had a temperature of 40 with a chill that shook my coenaesthesis to its foundations. I left your book with Bassani's brother who will by now have let you have it back, perhaps with a report on my state of health which, at that time, was terrible. Now I am fairly well in spite of the ferocious way school has started up again and the undertow of work deferred; but I have moved house and these have been new days of turmoil externally and in depth. The princess,[1] that bloody woman living among her millions, is unfortunately not even 'old and ugly' to comfort us – yes, she is old, but very clean, very perfect, which goes with her Anglo-Saxon birth, and with her life which has been passed practically in an eternal boring and exciting holiday.[2] However, your publication in *Paragone* is certain. But remember that the *Botteghe Oscure* are not definitely shut;[3] there is always the possibility that you have some things less 'unpleasant' to the princess's palate, and then there is your prose, which I exhort you to carry on with.

I embrace you with much affection,

Yours,      Pier Paolo

New address: V. Fonteiana 84–26, Rome.

1   See Letter 371.

2  *Botteghe Oscure*: literally 'the dark shops' – hence the pun.
3  Leonetti had written saying he was disappointed but not in tears at being refused by the princess and asking Pasolini to say whether she is old and ugly or young and beautiful, '*in which case to be rejected would . . . gravely hurt my* amour propre'.

## 382   To Tonuti Spagnol
Como
[*In possession of addressee: typewritten with autograph addition, date and signature*]

Rome, 16 April 1954

Dear Tonuti,

If you get this letter forgive its brevity and dry tone. I am writing with no faith that it will reach you; in your last letter you tell me that you have moved but don't tell me the new address!

As far as distractions go things aren't bad . . . The publication of your poems has been put back to September, a better time of year than summer. In fact in these last months I simply did not have time to get them ready for publication. If you write any more in the meantime, send them to me. I wish you all the very best for your new set-up and embrace you fraternally,

Yours,     Pier Paolo

## 383   To Franco Farolfi
Sondalo
[*In possession of addressee: typewritten with autograph signature*]

[Rome, 1954]

Dearest Franco,

I got your very nice letter – a Dostoyevskian one. It reminds me of Ippolito's 'Message'¹ as an attachment to the pole of attraction (this time the exact situation of your flat just like the wall of Steiner's house, I think, in Ippolito's message. Except that your letter is basically very optimistic. You have a future before you, a hope (which I for example do not have). And so I was greatly cheered when reading you – not only because of the optimism but also for your – and therefore my – incorrigibility. We have remained the two adolescents who used to talk for hours about *The Idiot*, with a whole world superimposed, thousands of scars and calluses (I more than you), for you illness has been a bit of a bell-glass which has protected you and kept you more intact, while I have been turned inside out on the world like a glove.

And in fact, your defect is that of being a little ungenerous towards other sick people (including me and Modigliani . . .) because of nostalgia for Health (flashy, undifferentiated Health), my defect is that of being empty, without nostalgia, disqualified (if the qualities owe their value to emotion).

However, like the libido, purity is also inexhaustible; it renews itself internally on its own. It is never lost, corruption is impossible. I hope you understand this and so will forgive me for the disappointment I gave you by destroying that old friend of yours by the superimposition of this new person for whom the world is in fragments. Just as I forgive in you a certain moving coarseness of fibre. By forgiving we dust down and polish up a little our 'heroic' images. Send me your poems. I shall send you mine in due course, I am too tired and busy to embark on a new piece of work however small. But do send them to me at once. I embrace you with much affection (I forgot to tell you that now for me your presence here in Rome is taking shape, even if it is somewhat distant, a neo-friendship and a neo-youth together).

Yours,      Pier Paolo

1   Ippolito Nievo.

## 384   To Franco Farolfi
Sondalo
[*In possession of addressee: typewrittten with autograph date, signature and postscript*]

Rome, 26 April 1954
Via Fonteiana 84, 26

Dearest Franco,

I received your letter, your biographical document, with very great pleasure. The advice I give you is naturally that which is on the side of courage – the advice to try things, to do things. Advice the value of which is general, nor ought you to expect anything else from me, without reserves or accusations if, in the event, that advice should turn out to be negative. Then there is a little selfishness on my part – that is the pleasure of having you here in Rome.

As for the house, I can't give you precise information off the top of my head – I should have to do some research and I have less time than usual . . . Zambianchi will join me (he is coming in two or three months to live opposite my house – so opposite that we will be able to speak from the window without shouting, so that, if you come to Rome, you can at any time kill two birds with one stone). Meantime I can tell you this: that if you have liquid cash of about four million you can get yourself a nice big flat (let us say seven million), paying the rest in monthly instalments like a rent.

As you see I am expressing myself in very general terms; but keep it in mind. To go and shut oneself up in a wretched flat in the extreme outskirts is never convenient. So I would say that should you really bring to fruition the decision to come to Rome; you should come here, on the spot, for a few days; it is the only way to see how things really are by trying them out and discussing them.

An affectionate hug,

Yours,      Pier Paolo

PS. As you see I have moved house to a very nice and dignified place (a place, in short, worthy of Zambianchi).

## 385   To Leonardo Sciascia
Palermo
[*In possession of addressee: typewritten with autograph date and signature*]

Rome, 10 May 1954

Dear Sciascia,

What has happened to you? I knew nothing about it – I don't think even Dell'Arco knew . . . My fears for you, which are now belated, are no use any longer, because I hope that your convalescence will be happy and very rapid. If you can, write to me soon and reassure me completely. Please accept a particularly affectionate embrace from your friend,

Pier Paolo

## 386   To Franco Farolfi
Sondalo
[*In possession of addressee: typewritten with autograph signature and postscript*]

[Rome, 1954]

Dearest Franco,

Forgive me, forgive me for the long silence, but, dear God, have you really no idea what my day is like? – I am doing a film,[1] I am putting together a very difficult anthology,[2] I continually have new articles to do (and then now I am not well – I have some little thing wrong with my kidneys, I believe, and don't even have the time to see a doctor). Then today I am leaving for Bari where they have invited me to give a lecture and I could not get out of it. So I am writing to you in great haste. I do not have the peace of mind to be able to advise you – in any case you know that I am always in favour of a move by you to Rome.

Houses can be found – here near to mine there are at least three going from 700,000 to 900,000 lire the room – very joyous and comfortable houses. But I do not know what to do: you would have to come and go into things; basically one or two days would be enough. As for work, this is a new district and you could think of setting up a clinic on your own. If you have time I can get you literary work; but *carmina non dant panem*,[3] let that be very clear. Write soon and accept the most affectionate greetings from yours,

Pier Paolo

PS. No sign of Zambianchi with the poems.

1 Refers to the script for *La donna del fiume* by Mario Soldati (see Letter 376).
2 *Canzioniere italiano*
3 *carmina non dant panem:* songs do not give bread.

## 387 To Vittorio Bodini
Lecce
[*In possession of addressee: typewritten with autograph addition, date and signature*]

Rome, 30 May 1954

Dear Bodini,

Thank you for the number of *L'Esperienza* ['Experience'][1] and for the invitation to contribute to it.

Then today I saw Caproni with the poems in his pocket to be sent to you – which incited me too to do the same at once. I went through my drawers and this poem[2] I am enclosing seemed less boring than the rest; if you don't like it I won't be offended. Many cordial greetings and good wishes,

Yours,    Pier Paolo Pasolini

1 The quarterly review of poetry and criticism *L'Esperienza Poetica* ['The poetic experience'], edited by Vittorio Bodini.
2 'Il Rubicone' ['The Rubicon'] in *L'Esperienza Poetica* No 2, April–June 1954.

1954

## 388   To Leonardo Sciascia
Palermo

[*In possession of addressee: typewritten with autograph date and signature*]

Rome, 30 May 1954

Dearest Sciascia,

The little volumes are lovely! I am really very grateful to you. I saw
Romanò; he too is very happy. Now I am waiting for the thirty copies to send
to friends and to the critics . . . Up to now only Bassani, with whom I am
working, has seen the volume, and was struck by the dignity and taste of the
little edition. So much so that the idea at once came to me: why not publish in
the next group of three writers that very fine short story by Bassani 'The last
years of Clelia Trotti', which appeared in *Paragone* in 1952? Write and tell me
what you think. I hope you are entirely back to normal and that I may see you
soon in Rome. Now that I have changed address it will be easier to spend a
little time together.

An affectionate embrace,

Yours,      Pier Paolo Pasolini

## 389   To Luigi Ciceri
Tricesimo

[*In possession of addressee's heirs: typewritten with autograph date and
signature*]

Rome, 15 June 1954

Dear Ciceri,

Many thanks for your letter which I found really moving. Your affection and
sympathy carry much more weight with me than the rancour of those
imbeciles you know of[1] – and it makes up for a great deal. Concerning the
prize, you should know that they are lying: I sent three poems[2] (the notice
said precisely that it had to be a question of a group of poems, specifying that
the minimum was three), among them *no* translation: only that in one poem
'Il veciu testamint' ['The Old Testament'], which speaks of the last war in
Friuli, the final verses are freely adapted from two passages from the Bible
(which I explained meticulously in a note, because these hypocrites would
certainly not even have noticed). I shall soon send you Spagnol's poems but
you must do the note, perhaps using the little piece which I dedicated to him
in *Fiera*: really to talk of those years in Versuta, of the experiences of the
Academiuta, both mine and those of my young friends, is something which
grieves me too much, I cannot do it. As for Brusin's poems, please send them

474

back to me – at first glance they didn't seem bad to me, then there was the move to a new house, and now I have looked for them in vain in the confusion of the cupboards. I have none of my own poems (apart from a few rejects to be put right) – in fact in a few days *La meglio gioventú* will come out – that is to say, the entire corpus of my Friulian poems – in the *Paragone* series (Sansoni).

So it is a moment of exceptional importance for me. The idea of a *Stroligut* I like very much; I shall think about it (as far as material goes, etc.), and I shall write to you again about it. Someda de Marco³ writes to me asking me for permission to publish one of my poems in *Strolic*, 'Biel zuvinin' ['Beautiful youth']; I don't know how he read it, and in any case, it will appear shortly in a review which my father will soon let you have. I don't know what to reply to Someda; certainly these days I am rather angry with those circles . . .

You would do me a great favour if you spoke to him and, after explaining how matters stand (that is to say the insult from the Philological Society and my feelings), give him carte blanche to publish. Very fine, what you published in *Nuova antologia*, which is always one of our most serious reviews.

I embrace you affectionately,

Yours,     Pier Paolo Pasolini

This letter was written in reply to a letter in which Ciceri expressed his anger with the Philological Society for not having awarded Pasolini the prize on the pretext that he had submitted only two poems, of which, according to them, one was a translation. He had resigned from the Society.

1   The members of the jury for the poetry prize of the Philogical Society: see Letter 336.
2   The Friulian triptych 'Il vecchio testamento'.
3   Pietro Someda De Marco, a Friulian poet.

## 390   To Biagio Marin
Trieste
[*In possession of addressee: typewritten with autograph date and signature*]

Rome, 15 June 1954
Dear Marin,

How sorry I am at having to make you wait for an answer . . . Caught in the usual pile-up and, into the bargain, in poor health because of an obstinate and inexplicable cold, I have put it off from day to day. And to think that your last letters have given me so much joy.

As for our affairs, Falqui I have not seen again, but Caproni sent a review to

*Il Giornale* and shortly one by me should come out in *Paragone* in the autumn. You want to read some of my things . . . but the few things which have come out in book form are all secondary, and besides, the little volumes are out of print. I am sending you my latest small book of poems,[1] which I now consider to be old. But now *La meglio gioventú* is about to come out from Sansoni – and this is the one which I consider my first published work. Naturally I shall let you have it as one of my dearest friends.

An affectionate hug from yours,

Pier Paolo Pasolini

1   *Tal còur di un frut.*

## 391   To Silvana Mauri
Milan

[*In possession of addressee: typewritten with autograph date and signature*]

Rome, 22 June 1954

Dearest Silvana,

Thank you for your very nice letter which reached me, however, at a bad time of examinations when the parenthesis of freedom between them and school was already over. I finish tomorrow but fear it is already too late to come and see you to my great disappointment because I had looked forward with great enthusiasm to the trip to you. If there is still time write to me but write to me quickly. I shall come alone because Bassani is in Amsterdam for ten days or so. Tell Ottiero that I wrote the review of his book[1] punctually and gave it to *Contemporaneo*, but that idiot (forgive me) Salinari refused it because it was too 'refined' and not in the style of his paper. I shall publish it somewhere else (perhaps in *Lo Spettatore* ['The Spectator']). So perhaps – or in any case – till soon, and forgive this horrible little letter.

Affectionate greetings,          Pier Paolo

1   *Memorie dell'incoscienza*, Einaudi (Turin, 1954). The review did not appear.

## 392   To Leonardo Sciascia
Palermo
[*In possession of addressee: typewritten with autograph date and signature*]

Rome, 22 June 1954

Dear Sciascia,

Thank you for the fine number of *Galleria*[1] which gave me so much pleasure and caused my parents so much joy.

Roversi's poems I like very much and I think that some time this year I shall speak about them – probably in *Paragone.*

Bassani is very happy that you have accepted my idea to publish 'Clelia' – as for his companions in the trio we thought of two short stories which appeared in *Botteghe Oscure* by Morante[3] and Ginzburg.[4] Would that suit you? As for the poet about whom you ask for my advice I have no doubts: Leonetti. Accept the most affectionate greetings from yours,

Pier Paolo Pasolini

1   Refers to the number of May 1954.
2   See Letter 388.
3   Elsa Morante (1912–85), novelist, author of *L'isola di Arturo* [*Arthur's Island*].
4   Natalia Ginzburg (1916–91), novelist, author of *Lessico familiare* ['Family dictionary'].

## 393   To Vittorio Sereni
Milan
[*In possession of addressee: typewritten with autograph date, signature and postscript*]

Rome, 10 July 1954

Dear Sereni,

I got your No 1. I like the edition very much. It has a feeling of actuality without rhetoric . . . (I will say the opposite about the text by Arpino[1] which seems to me rather vulgar: actual and rhetorical). I see that my little book is announced with the title *Canto popolare* ['Popular song'] whereas it is absolutely necessary (given that it means something else) that it should be *Il canto popolare* ['The popular song']. Forgive me those dry statements which sound like a legal document but I am writing under the eyes of Bassani who is waiting for me to go out . . . I wanted to recommend some names to you, if you are interested: first of all two poets from Bologna – Roversi and Leonetti who seem very interesting to me, really. Then a certain Pagliarani a notable book of verses by whom has just come out in what is now that horrible collection by Schwarz.

I greet you affectionately,

Yours,        Pier Paolo Pasolini

Leonetti: via Oriani 33, Bologna (an address used also by Roversi who has published a book of poems in the *Galleria* editions, among them a fine one, 'Rachele', which appeared here in *Botteghe Oscure*).

1   Giovanni Arpino (1927–87), novelist and journalist.

## 394   To Roberto Roversi
Bologna
[*In possession of addressee: typewritten with autograph date and signature*]

Rome, 23 July 1954

Dear Roversi,

I have been meaning to write to you for a while for two similar reasons in that it is once more a question of congratulations; first, for the appearance of your book[1] containing, among other really fine things, that little masterpiece 'Rachele'; second, for your intention to publish 'the best of' Nettore Neri. Also a fortnight ago Leonetti wrote to me more on your behalf than his own – he was worried that I showed signs of intending to review you more out of friendship than conviction; I assure you (and him) that friendship does not come into it . . . As for Guglielmi I remember having read some poems by him six or seven years ago in a little Bolognese review; they impressed me and I thought, in fact was convinced for a while, that Guglielmi was a postwar pseudonym of Leonetti's. The verses you send me now also seem very interesting to me and I shall certainly show them to Bassani. I mentioned your name, that of Leonetti and now also that of Guglielmi to Sereni for those rather interesting editions which he edits for *Meridiana* (the first volume by Arpino came out recently). Will you be coming down to Rome – you and Leonetti? I shall probably pass through Bologna in the autumn in which case we shall embrace again this time I hope. Many affectionate greetings from yours,

Pier Paolo Pasolini

1   *Poesie per l'amatore di stampe* ['Poems for the print-lover'].

## 395   To Vittorio Sereni
Milan

[*In possession of addressee's heirs: typewritten with autograph correction, date and signature*]

Rome, 24 July 1954

Dear Sereni,

You are right to be a little angry at my last letter: I can very well understand how it can have been a little irritating and you don't know how sorry I am, and think I am an idiot. But I beg you to bear in mind that, as I told you, I was writing in great haste under the eyes of Bassani so I had to invent unspeakable little formulae like 'vulgar but not actual', 'actual but not vulgar', etc., to turn into a telegram a letter which was intended to be long and exhaustive. Since I know how committed you are when you produce your things and in what an absolute way you work . . . I should like only, to make up for the harm done, to make a point about one thing; to tell you, that is to say, that Arpino will fit very well into the collection – by writing to you that I did not like him I did not by any means intend to tell you that it would be better to exclude him . . . If he does not stand up to a letter written on an absolute scale he stands up very well – and is very interesting – to a documentary letter. Perhaps – for other reasons – a little like my 'popular song'. This I am very aware of.

*Il canto popolare* can go to press as it is – I shall make some corrections in proof; to look it over I have an identical copy in my drawer. Many good wishes for your work and an affectionate embrace from yours,

Pier Paolo Pasolini

1   This letter was written in reply to a letter of 3 August in which Sereni writes: '*Don't think that I was angry. Sorry, yes, but at that time particularly, a trifle sufficed. At any rate we shall see better when the profile of the collection is clearer.*'

## 396   To Vittorio Sereni
Milan

[*In possession of addressee: typewritten with autograph signature*]

Rome, 7 August 1954

Dear Sereni,

The new little error in the title does not worry me: a capital C or a small one does not change the meaning. In fact let me tell you that the little alteration in meaning which derives from the capital letter does not displease me in so far as *Il canto popolare* is more the title of an essay than *Il Canto popolare*. So I would end up by opting for this second variant which is due to dark typographical *anangke*.[1] As for the Carducci prize that Bo spoke to you about, it was not a very pleasant affair, and one which I accepted only for the money – the distasteful need of the 150 thousand lire; I say this not so much because I shared the prize with Volponi, who is modest and nice, but for the third person, a certain Tedeschi (an ex-follower of Marinetti,[2] as Pea pointed out later), who had been discovered because of some idiotic epigrams enthused over by that prick Bocelli. Bo and Piccioni evidently were only weakly on my side. I have never understood why Bo is so hostile to me . . . Meantime in this way all my chances – which were in any case not strong – of a second prize at Viareggio are compromised: did you get my Friulian volume in Milan where I sent it to you?[4] As for Mondadori, I don't set much store by his theatrical gesture at Marina di Pietrasanta; but naturally I accepted just as I accepted the formula of the prize, etc. I cannot act in any other way. Accept most affectionate greetings from yours,

Pier Paolo Pasolini

1   *anangke*: the concept of fate derived from Greek classical tragedy.
2   Filippo Marinetti (1876-1944), founder of Futurism, poet, Fascist.
3   *La meglio gioventú.*

## 397   To Leonardo Sciascia
Palermo

[*In possession of addressee: typewritten with autograph date and signature*]

Rome, 7 August 1954

Dear Sciascia,

I am sending the answers to the inquiry.[1] I should have liked to tell you something about Guglielmino but Romanò has been on holiday – we did not see each other for a while and when we did meet I had a *lapsus memoriae* which will not be repeated next time, soon.

Meanwhile I greet you affectionately,

Yours,     Pier Paolo Pasolini

1   Refers to a questionnaire in *Galleria* on American literature in Italy.

## 398 To Biagio Marin
Trieste

[*In possession of addressee: typewritten with autograph date and signature*]

Rome, 1 September 1954

Dear Marin,

This time it is not that I lacked time – I actually have too much of it – but I am lazy in a morbid way, incapable of applying myself to any form of writing because of a kind of anxious impatience, of repugnance. I do not know what it is – perhaps a kind of reaction to the excessive work of recent times. Let's hope it doesn't last; it is terrible. I still have a bad conscience – they have been useless holidays and they didn't even have the effect of resting me well, given the onset of this kind of impotence. And to think that I had made so many calculations – to finish the *Anthology*, to finish the novel[1] . . . And instead nothing – nothing in the most desperate manner. I have a pile of letters to reply to on my table – yours first of all. I was deeply moved by what you said about my cousin,[2] by your brave, vigilant, unrestrainable goodness. I know Nico's situation – but he too knew it and I think he should have been more patient with his headmaster, swallowed everything. Forgive me but I have some right to say this sort of thing because I am to some extent in his circumstances – to go back and forth to Ciampino for 25,000 lire a month, as I do, is something not to be borne. Yet I bear it. So having told Nico off indirectly, now one has to go into the question. Your plan is the best – how can I thank you? I am infinitely grateful to you. I shall take part by bringing Nico to Rome for some time to fill in for me at school, seeing that having done so little in the summer I shall have to get on with my various pieces of work in the autumn. As for my uncle I think that in principle he is willing to help; but I am not the most suitable person to ask him. In fact three years ago when I went through a period much more terrible than what Nico is going through now it was my uncle who helped me, making notable sacrifices. How can I of all people go back and ask him for similar sacrifices? I can support the request for help if it were made by Nico directly or by his mother. Besides, it is certain that my uncle is helping him now.

I have not seen Falqui for a very long time; but in a few days I shall telephone him to ask for news; you have to remember that this is a dead season for letters and everyone is on holiday. As for Gadda, he is very low; he feels himself to be alone and unfortunate. The other evening he said to me with some emotion, in spite of his usual good humour, that he was afraid of dying like De Gasperi[3] . . . I very much fear that he does not feel like coming to Trieste. The first day that I see him in a good humour I shall ask him what he thinks of your invitation. I shall not come up to Friuli. So we shall see each other here in Rome, I hope. Meantime accept warmest greetings from your always affectionate,

Pier Paolo Pasolini

1 *Canzioniere italiano* and *Ragazzi di vita.*
2 Nico Naldini.
3 Alcide De Gasperi: Christian Democrat politician and prime minister.

## 399 To Nico Naldini
Gradisca d'Ionzo

[*In possession of addressee: typewritten with autograph date and signature*]

Rome, 1 September 1954

Dear Nico,

I got your news from our good friend Marin. You will reprove me for not writing to you. And you? For months and months you have not replied to a letter of mine – then at last you decided to write without giving any details. How can you expect me to 'join in' in this way? I have come to this opinion – that your headmaster is a monster but that you are not blameless, and that in any case you ought to have swallowed everything, knowing what awaited you if you lost the post. But now there is no use making recriminations . . . Marin writes to me that he will try to find work for you – until such time as you make up your mind to take your degree this would be ideal. Meanwhile, Marin writes to me, your uncle should help you – but you know how things are and how, in view of the latest business with Aunt Chiarina and Aunt Giannina, our uncle is fed up with his relatives. And, given the grave sacrifices I have already imposed on him, I am the person least suited to go and ask him for fresh ones . . . What I can do for you now is to bring you to Rome for a month or so in the autumn to stand in for me at school while I finish my numerous suspended bits of work. I have passed an unfortunate summer from the point of view of 'creativity', and that depresses me enormously. For the rest, life in Rome is better and better. Many affectionate greetings and cheer up.

Yours,      Pier Paolo

## 400　To Carlo Betocchi
Florence
[*In possession of addressee: typewritten with autograph addition, date and signature*]

Rome, 10 September 1954

Dear Betocchi,

What a long time since I wrote to you! It seems impossible to me, given that for external or internal reasons you are always in my thoughts. Either I talk to Caproni about you or the *Chimera* brings me news, or it is very fine poems (I mean those in *Letteratura*, of which one – I don't remember the title – talks about lines of yellow houses in which our anonymous silence is buried – is a masterpiece) . . . For almost a month (I have spent an arid, really unhappy summer) I have been working on an article for *Chimera*: a contribution to the discussion begun by Luzi and Romanò. I shall send it to you in a few days time – the time it takes to correct and recopy it. If you see them, greet Lisi and Fallacara; and for you (hoping to see you soon, as Caproni says, here in Rome) an affectionate clasp of the hand from

Yours,　　Pier Paolo Pasolini

1　A monthly review to which Betocchi had asked him to contribute.
2　See *Forse a un tramonto* ['Perhaps at a sunset'], in *La Chimera* No 7, October 1954.

## 401　To Biagio Marin
Trieste
[*In possession of addressee: typewritten with autograph date and signature*]

Rome, 10 September 1954

Dear Marin,

This time too I have delayed a little in replying to your letter[1] so full of good news. Let us hope that everything turns out well for Nico and that at last, having found a little calm, he can take his degree. Later he will be able to come to Rome and between myself and my uncle he will find something to do – for example the recognized school where I teach will move to a new district which is more highly populated, and will grow bigger . . .

I delayed answering because Bassani took me with him in his car to make a wonderful trip round central Italy – Florence, Arezzo, Assisi, Perugia, Todi, Spoleto . . . in the footsteps of Giotto and Piero[2] . . . I came back stronger – I hope to be able to get down to work again, I absolutely need to do so; if the impotence of August had continued I would certainly have fallen ill. The only way to retrieve things is to work; otherwise our sinning has no sense – it is hell on earth.

I saw that the Third Programme announces, in the series 'Little Anthology', a broadcast about you. And I have by no means forgotten the piece for *Paragone* and Spagnoletti, who is coming to live in Rome, was very struck by your book and will certainly write about it. Put aside any lack of confidence, then, and try to get down to work yourself too . . .

I send you my best good wishes and the most affectionate greetings,

Yours,      Pier Paolo

1   Replies to a letter from Marin saying that he had had a 'completely sterile summer'. He adds that Nico Naldini has shown him *La meglio gioventú*, 'a magnificent volume full of good things'.
2   Piero della Francesca (1410/20–1492).

## 402  To Antonio Altoviti[1]
London
[*In possession of addressee: typewritten with autograph date and signature*]

Rome, 10 September 1954

Dearest Antonio,

Thank you for your lovely letter. You don't know how much it moved me.

Can it be that our times together are already times long gone? Writing to you I feel like a figure from a poem by Cavafis.[2] And Rome, around me, is always the same – full of wonderful things. You have no idea what white blue-jeans are like . . .

A big hug,      yours, Pier Paolo

1   Antonio Altoviti, a Roman film producer.
2   Cavafis: Constantin Cavafy (1863–1933), Greek poet.

## 403  To Alan Brusini
Tricesmo
[*In possession of addressee: typewritten with autograph date and signature*]

Rome, 10 September 1954

Dear Brusini,

Your poems are really remarkable; a volume really should be made from them; send me the lastest ones you have written (if you have written any) so that I can help you to make a choice for publication. I shall publish three or four in *Il Belli*. Forgive the delay with which I have written and give Ciceri my affectionate greetings. A cordial handshake for you,

   Yours,      Pier Paolo Pasolini

1   See Letter 379.

## 404   To Carlo Betocchi
Florence
[*In possession of addressee: typewritten with autograph date and signature*]

Rome, 24 September 1954

Dear Betocchi,

   Thanks for your card and now forgive the haste of this couple of scanty lines – it is a professional communication. The piece for *Chimera* I have ready, but I need all tomorrow to copy it out and get right some quotations which I had made from memory; so I wanted to warn you that you will get the piece by express letter on Monday and I hope it will still be in time . . . Many affectionate greetings from yours,

   Pier Paolo Pasolini

1   See Letter 400.

## 405   To Biagio Marin
Trieste
[*In possession of addressee: typewritten with autograph date, signature and postscript*]

Rome, 6 October 1954

Dear Marin,

   Forgive the brevity of this letter and its purely practical tone . . .

   The organizers of an Exhibition have invited me to speak in Gorizia on Friulian poetry on the 23rd; it would be useful for me to go if you could combine it with the Trieste lecture planned by you – is that possible? Sunday 24th, for example, or the 21st or 22nd. Write to me at once but don't worry because if it isn't possible it is by no means a disaster . . .

   How are things? Are you working? I had just begun to write with a certain conviction and a certain heat when the new school year 'burst' on me. The torture begins again. It is something the injustice of which torments me, but I shall try not to allow myself to be depressed. Nico has written to me that he is still waiting – and he is not in very good spirits either, poor thing. I hope at least to get an unworried letter from you saying that you are working and have faith. Now you are in Italy and no longer in a Free Territory[1] that should in itself be a cause for comfort even if it is mixed with bitterness at too many years of waiting and at the solution which is still unjust. I embrace you affectionately,

Yours,     Pier Paolo Pasolini

PS. Did you see the article by Vigorelli on my book in the latest number of *Fiera*?

1  Trieste, the subject of dispute between Italy and Yugoslavia at the end of the war, had been declared a Free Territory. It returned to Italy as the result of a plebiscite in 1954.

## 406   To Biagio Marin
Trieste
[*In possession of addressee: typewritten with autograph date and signature*]

Rome, 7 October 1954
Dear Marin,

My letter and your express one crossed. I see that what I proposed in my letter fits almost perfectly with your calculations – so as not to lose too many days of school I should prefer, however, if the Trieste lecture were fixed for the dates I proposed to you – that is the 22nd, 23rd or 24th.

The title could be 'Dialect and its literary problems' if that is all right with you; if not invent a more general one that suits better. We shall chat at our ease in a few days' time . . . An affectionate embrace from yours,

Pier Paolo Pasolini

## 407   To Vittorio Sereni
Milan
[*In possession of addressee: typewritten with autograph date, signature and postscript*]

Rome, 10 October 1954
Dear Sereni,

Here are the proofs, corrected and recorrected, of *Canto popolare*; but I should like to see the second set of proofs as well, in view of the large number of variants I have introduced – is that possible? I also include the little bio-bibliographical note which cost me an atrocious effort. I hope it is all right, if necessary do make some little changes.

I have had the contract which I am sending back today signed; to tell the truth there is no mention in it of copies for the a.,[1] but I hope they are understood.

If you see Fortini[2] give him greetings and thank him for his book;[3] I think I shall say something about it in the review for *Paragone.*

Forgive the dry tone of this letter but here I am limited by a Sunday morning in which I have determined to do a thousand things (school has started, damn it). Many affectionate greetings from yours,

Pier Paolo Pasolini

PS. Could I have Zigaina's drawing back.[4]

1  The author.
2  Fortini (b. 1917), one of the leading modern Italian poets.
3  *Una facile allegoria* ['An easy allegory'], La Meridiana (Milan, 1954).
4  See Letter 377.

## 408  To Biagio Marin
Trieste

[*In possession of addressee: typewritten with autograph date and signature*]

Rome, 13 October 1954

Dearest Marin,

So all set for the 22nd. I shall be at your house on the morning of the 22nd. I have a letter from Fantuzzi and I shall go to Gorizia to repeat the lecture there next day and then to Gradisca. You should tell Nico to alert his friends in Gradisca about this programme; he should tell them, in practical terms, that I shall arrive by car from Gorizia at about eight (and see to it that Nico does it, because in such matters he is usually a little lazy and muddled). I know of course that Nico is in Trieste with you. This fills me with gratitude for your kindness and your generosity to which I really know no parallels in this gloomy world. Till we meet in a few days time, then, and accept most affectionate greetings from yours,

Pier Paolo Pasolini

1954

## 409   To Vittorio Sereni
Milan

[*In possession of addressee: typewritten with autograph date and signature*]

Rome, 16 October 1954

Dear Sereni,

All is well then – I am only waiting for the second proofs. Good – I mean about the change to the bio-biographical note, the copies available, etc. Certainly when I speak about Fortini I shall speak about the series as well. As for the introduction to *Canto popolare* it does not matter; these introductions are always a little false and the 'big names' have compromised themselves too often to be worth anything. Forgive the terrible haste of this letter and accept the most affectionate greetings from yours,

Pier Paolo Pasolini

1   See Letter 407

## 410   To Francesco Leonetti
Bologna

[*In possession of addressee: typewritten with autograph date and signature*]

Rome, 20 October 1954

Dear Leonetti,

You have put yourself in my shoes very well – only you have forgotten that I lose almost the whole day tearing myself apart between the school and the buses for what are the now famous 25,000 lire a month; and on the other hand I am committed up to my eyes (to finish a novel, a long novella, a Pascoli anthology and another about the European Resistance plus the rest...) Nevertheless I am with you and Roversi – ready to work unsparingly with you. Was there ever any doubt?

I embrace you both with much affection,

Pier Paolo

This is the reply to a letter of 18 October in which Leonetti announces his intention to found a new review *Officina* ['Workshop'] and says:

*What is there new for which a letter is not once again inadequate? Nothing other than a proposal for working together which you might also refuse – and indeed would be more reasonable were you to refuse it and more rich and audacious in 'fatality' were you to accept it.*

*Ten years on, and even the time that has passed is, in part, an index of my frightening seriousness (but meantime today I have once again become a 'man of the world'), I say: this is the point where one has to found a review.*

*This project, as you can foresee, is one along with Roversi. Indeed in recent years he has turned up every so often – and I have always said No. We were both immature and indeed things did not always go smoothly between us; my relationship with Roversi was a truly brotherly one but his was not, nor did he manage to be what I felt he could be and vice versa.*

*Last May/June we approached everyone working in Bologna . . . And so, beginning to fondle the idea of a review, we talked about it to various people . . . The group began to form but not fruitfully.*

*But the review was something certain (definite, clear, even if unsure) for me when Roversi . . . emerging from some days of studying and examining anthologies, reviews and books, said to me: 'I won't budge, we can't budge without Pasolini.'*

*It intends to be a review dedicated exclusively to poetry and poetics (and to critical activity concerned with poetry and – exceptionally – other topics); not elegant and 'anthological' but closely argued and tenacious; and a review with principles (which are actually those implicitly contained in your little poems), the review basically of a group, of a tendency; and on the other hand open to all movements, not only those of provincial Italy, and ready to take an interest in them. A review for men in their thirties – not the young men who today find it easy to be destructive – and one which has absolutely no respect for, but is conscious of, recent work (which aims at being by definition anti-traditional and is now part of our tradition, which has to be broken and rediscovered). Men like that have not had their own review. You may smile a little seeing an idea which has perhaps occurred to you in conversation with friends being put forward with commitment – but the difference, if there is one – and there will be one – lies in the commitment; and in the fact that some people perhaps preach reasonably well but rummage around very badly. And bear in mind that I am level-headed and now, having bidden farewell to books and little volumes which will be – or how do I know? – will not be published in the winter, I have actually established a gap of several months given over to thinking about, to looking after this review. Which must be decided on now and put together now or never.*

*I have an exact idea of your situation. So above all there is a question of trust – if it is worth while getting involved with Roversi and me, to produce work in a certain sense in common. It goes without saying that in this connection what must prevail in you is intuition, something instinctive, not reasoned; we offer no solid proofs – but bear in mind that we know that Roversi's old Poems and my Poems, which have already been published, cannot be appreciated or understood if they are not 'reviewed' historically in relation to our most recent work, which is all unpublished (which truly finds much in common with your work and no one else's).*

*Then there are practical reasons. They are important, and if they are it is important to consider and overcome them. The review planned will be able to pay exceptionally and not as a rule. The others to which you contribute pay and are already 'launched'. But that is something quite different. I do not know to what extent your practical life is desperate; in any case naturally one kind of work does not exclude the other; but above all it is a question of realizing that they are two different things – 'to get oneself read' and 'to take a grip on' (or to try to do so) the fate – I won't say of poetry – which at the moment is so ambiguous, ambivalent, confused, indeterminate, that one cannot take a grip on it – but on the fate of poetic taste by imposing a body of poetic work which is absolutely new (which is – and must be – powerful and violent and which is not sufficient on its own and does not achieve much unless one 'takes a grip' on it), and by attempting to contribute directly and vigorously to the elaboration of culture, which is always active and is now passing through a complicated moment.*

*Then there are historical reasons. Sentimental memories will perhaps touch you as they touch us. But in fact you find yourself with so many friends and ones who are bound to you by greater force of habit and are powerful, and so many authoritative people who hold you in esteem while we, if we are anything at all, are a weak spark. This too we wish to take into consideration and forgive me too if I put myself 'in your shoes'. But there will be reasons – which may or may not be valid in this case – why with these people on their side or promoting it the classical review has not succeeded; there may also be reasons which relate to your human concern for your own 'fortunes'. Besides, a review of this kind, which is so immediately useless and so profoundly useful, cannot be put together in Rome where people think more – very properly – about 'getting on' and many interests are created.*

## 411   To Carlo Betocchi
Florence

[*In possession of addressee: typewritten with autograph corrections, date and signature*]

Rome, 26 October 1954

Dear Betocchi,[1]

I hope you did not take me for a crypto-communist. Nor yet for a Marxist (would that I were!). My position is that of someone who is living a drama; I feel that bourgeois arguments have lost meaning for me and that I am reduced to pure irrationality and Christian love. This is a statement, not a thesis. On the other hand nothing replaces these patterns – there is no other, let us call it this crudely, ideal to which I have recourse for the purity of my inner life. Therefore I look with curiosity and trepidation at the Marxist ideal. And this is another statement. I do not know how to choose, I do not wish to, I am unable to do so. But by not choosing I do not live wholly: I give myself over to a pure and simple sensual love for the world, to a piety that is vaguely Christian. On the other hand, how can one not see that the bourgeois world (and I belong there by birth, education, down to my deepest roots) has passed beyond its historical limits, living on pure institutionality, no longer on history? Look at the corruption, the hypocrisy, the conventionality, the cruelty, the selfishness, that reign there, in this Italian province of the bourgeois world. Look how the Christian values are set in a 'Church' in which you believe, but about which you cannot be so blind as not to condemn – no, I don't mean the parish priests – but the Vatican chiefs – and not to feel the horrendous reactionary taste that pervades its whole body from the top of St Peter's to the most humble parish churches in the Appennines. I think that you and I and Luzi are 'for the people', aren't we? Now I see that from the modern people a party has been born and with it an ideology and hence a power, a culture. A culture, as such, necessarily restores the concept of reality. Were you really clear to yourself when in your letter you wrote: 'I do not think that Marxist culture fully interprets reality and we know that this derives from the fact that first we must agree what reality is'? You have not been clear because it is obvious that if you *first* establish what reality is you are carrying out a cultural operation in a cultural setting which is that *previous* to Marxism, that is to say, the bourgeois and Catholic one, and therefore your plea is pure *flatus vocis* in that, to the question 'What is reality?' your bourgeois and Catholic has a reply ready. And on such a basis the possible Marxist interpretation can *only be* refuted. Now I envy you and those of your generation who have the reply ready; and I envy those who believe in the answer of the Marxist philosophy of society – which is still potential. I find myself in the void neither here (although still here because of the violence of memory, because of the compulsion of childhood and of an education) nor there (although ready there in the aspiration, in sympathy with a life that renews itself and proposes a faith, if only by the fact that it is already happening). All this is scandalous, first because it implies a betrayal of my class and therefore of many of those (like you) who are the only ones with whom I have a loving dialogue; second, because it lacks the courage of a definitive, manly choice of the other class and its party. But always a sincere and scandalous position, which is one of the absolute concepts of Christianity, is it not? I do not lack courage, I only feel that at this moment a choice would be a desperate act: an irrational act demanding a form of mysticism should I decide for 'there'; an act of renunciation and a dangerously defective one should I settle down once and for all 'here' – to enjoy ecstasies which are both Catholic and exquisitely bourgeois. Perhaps I did not express myself well in my article – but you will see that all this is said better in a poem which I am correcting and looking over and which will soon appear somewhere.[2] On the other hand I am not at all sorry that my article was an occasion for doubts and discussions – that is precisely what I was looking for, even if not intentionally. Up to now we have agreed with each other so often . . . Now the good times are over. Please accept a very affectionate handshake from yours,

Pier Paolo Pasolini

This is a reply to a letter from Betocchi of 10 October 1954 in which Betocchi says that Pasolini's article – 'as always a very subtle one' – seemed to require a reply and has therefore been sent to Luzi for his comments:

*I confess, as far as I am concerned, it is an article that leaves me doubting; I do not believe that the Marxist doctrine fully interprets reality. Further Luzi's observation that Marxism does not deal with Reality so much as with its dynamics does not seem to me as offhand as it does to you; it seems to me that this observation hits the mark.*

On 14 November Betocchi replies to Pasolini's letter of 26 October:

*1954*

My dear Pasolini,

Yours of 26 October certainly deserved a prompter reply, but nowadays there is no time for anything. God will forgive us if we are overwhelmed by tasks. And we no longer even have the time to distinguish between good and evil. If the prevailing accent in our life fell on the problem of salvation (which is unique to each of us and eternal) and thereby on the problems of the salvation of all, for which each one of us is responsible, be assured that you would not feel yourself bourgeois. Nor will it ever be possible for a culture to interpret the world, not even the Catholic one, if it limits itself to being a culture. Christ alone interprets the world or lives his life in a way that provides an integral solution to the drama of good and evil; if this is lost sight of, or if some other teleology is substituted for it that does not mean to live struggling with Christ's heart in ours, and if we know that we are here to disseminate a justice which is positively none other than justice based on the merits of individual souls (and the merits are only a way of life with the heart of Christ in ours); if we lose sight of the feeling that we live only for this drama, then evidently all the problems are born in which you feel yourself enmeshed.

I have no culture, my dear Pasolini, I am a man. All concepts are culture but with Christ concepts do not exist. There exists only the Gospel and life. Culture is inscribed in the Christian life like a sister, not a wife; one is saved by culture too, but for reasons of brotherhood not for those of right, nor for those of power. Communists and the bourgeoisie are one and the same thing. It helped Christ to talk about Samaritans and pharisees when he wanted to find a way of dealing with the stupidities of the world in its inexact terms.

Your piece appears in the number of La Chimera that is about to appear with a short note by Luzi. I have not read it but I know that it is friendly in tone . . . Be assured that your position has not been confused with a communist one. We made absolutely no mistake. It was not possible.

May God bless you as your good intent deserves. An affectionate embrace from yours – who is always not very clear because the truth is a mystery,

*Betocchi*

1 See Letters 400 and 404.
2 See 'Le ceneri di Gramsci' ['Gramsci's ashes'] in *Nuovi Argomenti*, November 1955–February 1956.

## 412   To Vittorio Sereni
Milan
[*In possession of addressee: typewritten with autograph corrections, signature and postscript*]

[Rome, October 1954]

Dearest Sereni,

Here are the second proofs[1] with a few more little changes. I hope the printer will not be angry. Forgive the curtness of this letter; I have to type out a list of the reviewers . . . and here at my side, hot from the press, are the proofs of the anthology for Guanda, which is making me completely confused.

An affectionate greeting,       Pier Paolo Pasolini

PS. The list is very wide-ranging and probably many of the names will coincide with yours. Those underlined are the ones to whom I should wish books to be sent without fail. And let me know the names on my list to whom you do *not* think it advisable to send it.

1  Of *Il canto popolare.*

## 413  To Vittorio Sereni
Milan
[*In possession of addressee: typewritten with autograph corrections, date and signature*]

Rome, 4 November 1954

Dear Sereni,

The ten copies intended for me will go to Longhi and Banti, Contini, Leonetti, Marin, Ungaretti, Penna, Gadda, Vigorelli, Zigaina. I shall probably buy others. I await the complete list of those sent so that I know where I stand. Did you get in touch with Leonetti and Roversi? It seems that now these two old Bolognese friends of mine want to start a poetry review, taking me on as third editor; I think it will be rather interesting and hope that your contribution will not be lacking. But I shall talk to you again about it. I see that you asked Volponi[1] for poems for your new collection; I am very pleased – he is nice and his poems are good.

Affectionate greetings, yours,      Pier Paolo Pasolini

1  Paolo Volpini (b. 1924), poet and novelist.

## 414  To Livio Garzanti[1]
Milan
[*In possession of addressee: typewritten with autograph date and signature*]

Rome, 6 November 1954

Dear Doctor,

Bertolucci tells me that you are waiting for me to give a sign of life. But how? I feel a little embarrassed for many reasons. I had promised you a long story *Le zoccolette di Mandrione* ['Mandrione's little clogs'] and perhaps, if I managed to overcome my old and naïve scruples, *Il Ferrobedò.*[2] But scruples apart, I simply do not have the time to work it up. Do you know that for a salary of twenty-five thousand lire I go to teach at Ciampino, leaving at seven in the morning and coming back at two, dropping with fatigue? So in order to live I have to turn my attention to contributing to publications; and moreover I now have on my table a pile of proofs – this is an anthology of popular poetry which I am doing for Guanda and which is very complicated and takes a great deal of time and effort. You will understand that in these conditions I cannot for the time being work for myself – which is more important to me. It is the eternal plaint. And forgive my outburst . . . besides I have scruples of another kind – the fear, that is, that in the end you will not like my novel. So I prefer to send you a sample right away – the sixth chapter,[3] which is perhaps the best and which under the title of 'Regazzi di vita' appeared in *Paragone*. Meanwhile I ask you to read these pages . . . Accept the most cordial greetings from yours,

Pier Paolo Pasolini

1   An influential publisher.
2   *Ragazzi di vita.*
3   Published in *Paragone* (October 1953) it became Chapter 4 of *Ragazzi di vita.*

## 415   To Vittorio Sereni
Milan

[*In possession of addressee: typewritten with autograph date and signature*]

Rome, 12 November 1954

Dear Sereni,

I have had your letter and, from the publishers, the advance. Thank you again. Let us hope then that the little book will emerge safely from the printer's impressive Freudian machinery. I should have liked to have a copy of the complete list of persons to whom the books will be sent – so as to avoid duplications – will you let me have it? I wanted to ask you something else – you remember I referred to the possibility of doing an article on the Friulian 'houses'? Is that possible? I am beset, as you see, by the need for cash. And forgive me . . . Meantime I warn you that on Sunday my heart will be in Milan along with Volponi's fatty one – both palpitating on the verge of thrombosis.[1] And I am sorry that our joy will be your defeat.

I embrace you,       Pier Paolo Pasolini

1   For the Bologna-Inter football match held in Milan.

## 416   To Livio Garzanti
Milan
[*In possession of addressee: typewritten with autograph corrections and signature*]

[Rome, November 1954]

Dear Garzanti,

I have received compliments from many sides for 'Regazzi di vita', but the pleasure you gave me with a publisher's detached and paratactical tone no one else has given me . . . And my worries over future developments grow and build up. In general the novel is ready – it is all very clear in my head (unfortunately so because a mismatch arises between the page in my head and the page in the act of being written). To be exact – the novel consists of 9 chapters of which I, IV (Regazzi di vita), VI are complete; III, V, VII and VIII are written but have to be corrected and finished; II and the last one have to be written almost completely. Knowing myself (who, mark you, am not lazy) and the nature of this work, I think I shall need another five or six months (*melius abundare*),[1] seeing that this month I shall be able to work on it less, having to finish other things.

Do not be afraid (from the commercial point of view) – but it is impossible to summarize the plot decently since there is no plot in the conventional sense of the word. By summarizing one would run the risk of juxtaposing a series of facts and one would have the impression of a tapestry. My narrative 'poetics' (as you would have seen in 'Regazzi di vita') consists in engaging the attention in immediate facts. And that is possible for me because these immediate facts are sited in an ideal structure or narrative arc which then coincides with the moral content of the novel.

That structure might be defined by the general formula: the arc of postwar Rome traced from the chaos of the first days of the Liberation, which were so full of promise, to the reaction of '50–'51. It is a very precise arc which corresponds to the passage of the protagonist and his companions (Ricetto, Alduccio, etc.) from infancy to first youth – or else (and here the match is perfect) from the erotic and amoral age to the age which is already prosaic and immoral. What makes the life of these boys (whom the Fascist war had caused to grow up like savages – illiterate and criminal) 'prosaic and immoral' is society, which once again reacts in an authoritarian manner to their vitality, thus imposing its moral ideology.

Please note that this is 'before' the book – I as narrator do not interfere. Just as I never directly denounce the Fascist responsibility for the construction of those concentration camps – the Roman *borgate*[2] – or the present responsibility of the government, which has not solved the problem. All this is implied in the congeries of facts, which is externally chaotic, internally orderly.

Il Ferrobedò is the distortion in Roman dialect of Società Ferro Beton, which has a big factory between Monteverde Vecchio and Monteverde Nuovo near the Borgata Donna Olympia ('the Skyscrapers'). This is the matrix, the surroundings, that hatch the infancy of Riccetto and the others: at the time of the Liberation it was the symbol of devastation and abandonment – destroyed by the Germans, sacked by the people, filthy, collapsing. We shall see it again at the end of the novel, rebuilt and restored – a symbol of the return to order (only a nearby shed is still full of shit, abandoned). (Please note, I repeat, that this symbolism is perfectly fleshed out in the narrative.)

The second point of reference in terms of symbolism (it is useful only as an outline) is the following: Riccetto, in the first chapter of the novel, boating with some friends on the Tiber – he is a kid but already expert in all forms of baseness, a thief, without scruples, etc. – at a certain point jumps in to save a swallow which is drowning under Ponte Sisto. In the last chapter a little boy – Genesio (one of the most 'rounded' characters in the novel) – drowns in the Aniene, and Riccetto, now almost a youth, does not lift a finger to save him. Between these two moments the whole narrative arc I was telling you of is developed with the mass of facts, of little things that happen, characters, episodes 'in progress';[3] with at the centre the re-education (it is ridiculous and counter-productive) of Riccetto in the Institute for Juveniles at Porta Portese.

Chap. I ('Il Ferrabedò') tells of Riccetto's early infancy, with glimpses of the Germans, the English, postwar low life, corruption; the setting – Donna Olympia and Ciriola.

Chap. II (title to be found) continues the story of the low life of Donna Olympia (Riccetto is one of a group of cardsharps), Riccetto's first sexual experiences at thirteen (whores and perverts) up to 'the collapse of Donna Olympia' – that is to say, the collapse of the elementary school where the families of Riccetto and others are camped.

Chap. III 'Night at Villa Borghese'. After the collapse Riccetto goes to live in a proper housing estate where he has even worse friends. He lives away from home, stealing or worse – now having moments of economic grandeur, now forced to suffer hunger, to go to the friars to eat.

Chap. IV is 'Regazzi di vita'.

Chap. V, 'The hot nights', is the story of two break-ins which are told with more detail and are more important (carried out with a gang of criminals whom he had got to know at the Villa Borghese). Between the first and second break-in he gets to know (in a way that is picaresque in the manner of Boccaccio and too long to summarize) a girl with whom he says he is in love to the point of falling into the 'cliché' of the district tough-guy. He decides –

once again because of exhibitionism – to get things clear in his head and meanwhile, in order to give the girl an engagement ring, he organizes the second break-in in which all his comrades are captured. He escapes but, dead with hunger and fatigue (because of circumstances too long to summarize), is taken and imprisoned at Porta Portese for a crime he has not committed.

Chap. VI ('Bathing in the Aniene') begins a second part of the novel – about a year and a half to two years have passed since the last event. Riccetto is now a somewhat secondary figure and certain of his friends from Tiburtino come into the foreground: Alduccio, Il Begalone, Cacciotta. It is the lowest point of the story: the vulgarity, the immorality of these boys (there are a dozen of them who bathe in the Aniene) seems final and desperate. The youngest ones, after pestering the bigger ones, take Il Piattoletta, a poor rachitic child, 'a victim', 'a subject', playing on Monte Pecoraro and burn him alive, pretending that it is a Red Indian pyre (in fact in the novel it does not follow that he dies and he is left severely burned).

Chap. VII and VIII ('Inside Rome') follow Alduccio and Il Begalone on an immoral trip through the city at night. Both have an atrocious family situation. Alduccio is hated by his mother because he does not work. Given the districts and milieus through which they pass, sexual desire, which is always so unbridled and easy with them, becomes obsessive. At Ponte Garibaldi they find Riccetto and with him have a sinister adventure that takes them to the neighbourhood (deserted building sites) round Donna Olympia near the restored Ferro Beton works. They scrape together a little money – they go down to Campo dei Fiori to a brothel. Alduccio behaves badly here. Returning home, he finds his family quarrelling in an obsessive state of poverty and hatred. He stabs his mother (she is half-undressed like a whore).

Chap. IX ('The Skinny Old Woman', which is Belli's[4] expression for death). We are again on the filthy banks of the Aniene. The usual dozen boys. Alduccio is hiding there among the bushes. But we will learn that his mother is not dead. Some boys from Ponte Mammolo (a slighly more civilized suburb for workers and very petty bourgeoisie) are also hiding there, having been accused by the boys of Tiburtino of having burned Piattoletta. Genesio, the biggest of the young brothers, wants to venture to swim across the river; he drowns in it. Riccetto is now lost among the rest, anonymous – a young man, or almost one, who works as a labourer in Ponte Mammolo, shut off in his selfishness, in the sordidness of a morality which is not his.

As you see the précis does not stand up well because it throws lights on events and neglects an infinite number of things which, in the novel, have the function of 'suspence',[5] which usually in normal stories is entrusted to other ingredients. But you must relate these inadequate stammerings with neither head nor tail to the narrative rhythms of 'Regazzi di vita'.

Forgive the chaotic haste with which I have written – but I am up to the eyes in work. And accept the most warm and grateful greetings from yours,

Pier Paolo Pasolini

1   *melius abundare*: it is better to overflow.
2   *Le borgate*: the slums on the periphery of Rome.
3   In English in the original.
4   Gioacchino Belli (1791–1863), celebrated Roman dialect poet.
5   *sic.* In English in the original.

## 417   To Francesco Leonetti
Bologna

[*In possession of addressee: typewritten with autograph date, signature and postscript*]

Rome, 15 November 1954

Dearest Leonetti,

I am very sorry. It could have been a fine thing, a period in our life. But don't let us give up and let us plan for our not distant future this review for the thirty-year-olds and the second half of the century. Meantime let us write to each other and try to see each other – come to Rome for once! I ought to go to Friuli at the beginning of January – in that case I shall stop off in Bologna for a day. What are you all doing? I am very curious to see your stuff, to learn what is taking shape in you. Tell Roversi that I still intend to do a little note on his book in *Paragone* the moment this period of infernal work is over – that is to say before Christmas, I hope. Accept an affectionate embrace from yours,

Pier Paolo

PS. I have told Sereni, who is editing a poetry series for *Meridiana*, to turn to you and he has replied that he will do so.

This is the reply to a letter from Leonetti saying that the attempt to get funds for the review had been unsuccessful but that he and his collaborators believed that it would come about.

## 418   To Carlo Betocchi
Florence

[*In possession of addressee: typewritten with autograph corrections, date and signature*]

Rome, 17 November 1954

Dearest Betocchi,

There is nothing I believe in more than what you write in your letter:[1] the freedom of the ego in the direction from low to high, which is a meta-historical direction. And it is this that makes me not a communist. But this basically concerns me alone, my personal salvation: do you remember, by chance, what I wrote in my little poem on Picasso[2] (if a society is destined to lose itself it is fated to lose itself; a person, never) . . . Now, we would have to agree (it is always like this) on terms: by 'culture' I meant history in its present manifestation – therefore any act – in the end even the most merely practical one – is a cultural act. If this cultural–historical identification is made, it is clear that on this plane we must externalize love and make it concrete; precisely Christ's meta-historical love. Note that Christ, becoming man, accepted history – not archaeological history but the history which evolves and therefore lives: Christ would not be universal if he were not different for each different historical phase. For me, at this moment, Christ's words 'Love thy neighbour as thyself' mean 'Carry out structural reforms'. And the souls of others are more important than our own. And that is why I am convinced that a drama of choice exists: it is a question of choosing by which road society can become more civilized and economically better organized; and it is the first step, but an essential one. I do not think there is any better way of spending that mite of love we possess. Many thanks, dear Betocchi, and an affectionate greeting (to Luzi as well),

Yours,      Pier Paolo Pasolini

1  Refers to Betocchi's letter of 14 November.
2  See 'Picasso'; in *Botteghe Oscure*, XII, 1953, and, later, in *Le ceneri di Gramsci* ['Gramsci's ashes'], Garzanti (Milan, 1957).

## 419  To Leonardo Sciascia
Palermo
[*In possession of addressee: typewritten with autograph signature*]

Rome, 17 November 1954
Dear Sciascia,

It is a long time since I saw Bassani (he has been travelling and had commitments), but as soon as I see him I shall remind him of the referendum.[1] I have some fears about the story – it seems a publisher wants to print it along with Cecchi's piece about the San Pellegrino meeting as preface. But I shall let you know.

I wanted to ask you – in the number dedicated to American narrative literature would there be room for a (somewhat long) review by me of *The Bastard* by Banti?[2] I had prepared it for Rai but then, because of a series of things and crises (radiophonic ones), it did not come off. Let me know soon and accept most affectionate greetings from yours,

Pier Paolo Pasolini

PS. Do you know about the congress on Dialect Studies in Palermo?

1  See Letter 397.
2  The review was not published.

## 420   To Livio Garzanti
Milan

[*In possession of addressee: typewritten with autograph date and signature*]

Rome, 28 November 1954

Dear Garzanti,

Forgive my delay in replying to you – but I have had a hard week which completely absorbed and lost me [. . .] However, being very acutely conscious that there is nothing in this period more important to me than the relationship which has sprung up with you [. . .] Your advice concerning *Il Ferrobedò*[1] seems very just and sensible to me, especially where the language is concerned; I shall keep that advice in mind now as I write out the story (the dialect words, the slang words, etc. are absolutely necessary to me in order to write – they are, perhaps, the sub-product which must *be born* along with the product; it is they that give me the necessary happiness to understand and describe my characters), but I shall bear it in mind when I correct the book, once it is finished. Then the unnecessary ones will be struck out, the useful ones will remain (even if they are a little obscure – and here style and commercial considerations engage in a polemic . . .)

As for the chapters, I think that there is no danger that they will be self-contained precisely because of the extreme narrative freedom which I jealously preserve through the whole novel, whereby everything finds its place in its rhythm, even the brief flashbacks and the short divagations: the central line is too solid and clear. However we shall talk about this soon, meantime accept my most cordial greetings from

Your most grateful      Pier Paolo Pasolini

1  See Letter 416.

## 421  To Mario Boselli
Genoa
[*In possession of addressee: typewritten with autograph date and signature*]

Rome, 12 December 1954

Dear Boselli,

Thank you for your letter and your new invitation to collaborate addressed to this friend who opts out and does not deliver. But for another month or two I shall not have time to write an article specially – what with school, contributions already promised, a book for Guanda and a film script, I do not have a free half-hour left. So I beg you to forgive me. But I promise that the moment I have a little time I shall certainly give you something (unless you are satisfied with something already there, like some old poem from '49 or '50, because the rest is either published or is on the stocks). Did you get Sansoni's edition of *La meglio gioventù?* There, that is something I would be very keen to have spoken about in your review . . . If you can make a note of it and have not had the book, write to Sansoni to send it to you. Thanks again and I greet you most affectionately,

Yours,      Pier Paolo Pasolini

## 422  To Carl Betocchi
Florence
[*In possession of addressee: typewritten with autograph date and signature*]

Rome, 12 December 1954

Dear Betocchi,

Although overwhelmed by work I would willingly do a note on the book you recommend to me. It fits into a system of study and interests which has for long constituted my cultural centre. I could talk about it in some specialist review like *Folklore* or *La Lapa*, or in some other literary review. Not in the dailies, to which I, in any case, do not contribute and with which I have lost any contact.

In connection with *Chimera* I must say that the comment by Luzi in italics – apart from the presumed lack in me of *pietas rerum*[1] which is absolutely unjust (Luzi perhaps allows himself to be deceived by a certain critical rationality of mine, which is something entirely acquired) – is absolutely acceptable; but I did not like the low blow delivered to me in the leading article 'Dialect', which did not seem in very good faith to me.

If he wished to strike me it would perhaps have been better if he had named and documented his piece. I was very unhappy about it. During these weeks I have no time but if I found a free afternoon to riposte and wrote a piece, 'Polemic with the Florentines', would *Chimera* accept it?

Let me know and, meantime, accept most affectionate greetings from yours,

Pier Paolo Pasolini

Replying on 19 December, Betocchi wrote accepting the article and saying that since Pasolini was the main exponent of certain activities concerning dialect Luzi could not write otherwise. In Betocchi's opinion Luzi's objections might make Pasolini see the possible weak points in his (Pasolini's) thinking.

1  *pietas rerum*: a sense of the sanctity of things.

## 423  To Gianfranco Contini
Florence

[*In possession of addressee: typewritten with autograph date and signature*]

Rome, 17 December 1954

Dear Contini,[1]

I am writing you an absurd letter – expressed not only in terms of its postage[2] [...] Can you phone a 'reference' to Migliorini? If you can and wish to (but quickly, because Migliorini, they tell me, is leaving Florence for Rome, perhaps tomorrow, this is how things stand: being worn down in what was once a heroic physique by three years of teaching at Ciampino (25,000 lire a month and the whole morning and most of the afternoon lost), I am looking for another job and know that a job is coming up among the team on the *Encyclopedia*. I know this from a childhood friend of mine who works there precisely with Migliorini's support. So I got busy out of concern for my family and myself; I received an introduction to the Hon. Ferrabino[3] from an acquaintance of mine from Friuli, Senator Tessitori, who has had (and has shown me) the warmest assurances from Ferrabino. Meantime, a step lower down, Petrocchi spoke about me to the director, Bosco, who in his turn said he was willing to take me on. A drop is needed to make the vessel overflow, a finger to press the button . . . for example, a word with Migliorini who, it seems, is coming to Rome tomorrow precisely to talk to Ferrabino and Bosco.

That is all. I hope you will forgive me and will swallow this message without too much disgust. And think of it, if nothing else, as a pretext to write a couple of lines, a line, a word, for one who is increasingly affectionate towards you,

Pier Paolo Pasolini

Contini replied to this letter saying that Pasolini has been too timid in not talking to him about the matter a few days before, and in not approaching him earlier, and advised Pasolini to go at once to Bosco with a letter from Contini:

*I repeat that I am in default with you but in* amor de lonh *one does not correspond with the episotolary exactness of accountants*... Regazzi di vita *too seemed to me to be a formidable thing*... *Keep me informed, as I think they say, and count me always among your friends – in fact 'first friend' at the top of the list.*

1   Curiously, Pasolini reverts to the formal 'Gentile Contini'.
2   The letter was presumably sent express.
3   A parliamentary deputy.


## 424   To Gianfranco Contini
Florence
[*In possession of addressee: typewritten with autograph date and signature*]

Rome, 28 December 1954

Dearest Contini,[1]

Yes, mine was an excess of discretion. But you will understand... To speak to you about the boring letter which (treacherously) awaited you in Florence, seemed a too unhappy interpolation in our uncertain and very sweet *effata* on an empty stomach and with a full heart, in that room (it seemed very poetic to me), icy in the tepid thin sunlight which shone on our meeting; it was precisely the same weak Italic sun of the cherry orchards above your house in San Quirico. The thought of 'having to speak to you' flashed through my mind every so often as a terrible necessity, but from the secret places where it lay hidden and to which your words about the purple of my tie finally relegated it.

But I am still more grateful for your rebukes. I lived through an evening of pure joy – as always – when I received your letter with the accompanying note. I sent it right away the next day to Bosco who, while remaining vague, gave me some hope. Now in these Christmas days, which are anxious in other areas, I live a little on earnings. I truly hope that in your next Rome there will also be via Fonteiana (by no means to be despised in the inaccessible quarter between the Janiculum and the Villa Pamphili), and accept meantime the most tender greetings from yours affectly

Pier Paolo Pasolini

1   Pasolini uses the very familiar formula 'Carissimo Contini'; he continues however to address him with the formal third person.
2   *effata*: communications.

## 425   To Francesco Leonetti
Bologna

[*In possession of addressee: typewritten with autograph date and signature*]

Rome, 28 December 1954

Dearest Leonetti,

I am writing you a very hasty letter to announce my receipt; your letter caused me immense pleasure and certainly I shall come to Bologna soon. In general I am in agreement with the preparatory programme (a little less with the form of the review, which seems to me a little precious, and less still with the title, which reminds me of 'Il Mulino' ['The mill'] – but these are unimportant matters). I shall write again in three or four days to fix a date for my arrival (you ought to know that I am perhaps going to leave the school, and it is while waiting for this decision that I must send you a more precise letter). I embrace you with much affection along with Roversi,

Yours,      Pier Paolo

This letter was in reply to a letter in which Leonetti mentioned that the new review should appear in February and asked him to send some poems 'unpublished or reworked' for the first number. The review aimed to devote itself to 'principles and texts', would be 'very lively' and would not take its place in the consensus of others. It would be very serious 'but thirty pages on Rilke which no one will read are no use to us – not even free'. It would appear every two months in large format of sixteen pages with double columns. The proposed title was *Il Quartiere* ['The District']. Its aim was to deal with not only what concerns poetry directly but what is interesting from a poetic vantage-point.

# Index of Recipients

(The numbers correspond to those of the letters)

# General Index

84, 88–9, 91, 92, 95–6, 272, 286, 301, 347, 349, 360, 373, 381–2, 440, 480; fractures pelvis, 85, 354; teaches in Ciampino, 89, 365, 406, 449, 493, 502; first film script, 93–4, 465, 466; works for *Il Setaccio*, 187, 188, 190–7, 200, 207, 208; arrested and accused of distributing leaflets, 215–16; *see also individual novels poems, articles, films, etc.*

Pasolini, Susanna (*née* Colussi, PPP's mother): early life and family background, 1, 2; marriage, 1, 4, 5, 17; character, 4; relationship with PPP, 5–6; letter to Carlo, 9; in Second World War, 21, 41, 42; and Guido's death, 51, 54–5, 217; problems with Carlo, 74; and the Ramuscello scandal, 80, 312; in Rome, 81, 87, 321–2, 331, 338, 340; in Montecassiano, 84; PPP's letters to, 224–5, 346–9, 350–1, 352–3; general, 8, 23, 94, 182

*Passione e ideologia*, 92

*Patrie dal Friul*, 292

Paul, St, 324

Pea, 480

Peace Congress, Paris (1949), 77, 305

Pederoba, 359, 360

Pellizzi, 272

'Pena d'amore' ('Pain of love'), 145, 150

Penna, Sandro: friendship with PPP, 82, 83, 346, 350, 437; PPP admires, 305; considers writing about Naldini's poetry, 367; general, 14, 73, 231, 351, 355, 406, 426, 462, 493

People's University of Udine, 266

Peresson, Dino, 74–5, 76

Perugia, 483

Petrarch, 36, 143, 151, 392

Petrocchi, 502

Petroni, Guglielmo, 188, 267, 272; PPP's letters to, 188, 355

Philological Prize, 440

Philological Society *see* Friulian Philological Society

*I pianti* ('The laments'), 64, 265, 269, 272n., 367, 414

*Il pianto della rosa* ('The tears of the rose'), 62

'Picasso', 93, 453, 458, 499

Piccioni, Leone, 91, 381, 480

Piero della Francesca, 96, 244, 256, 483

'La pioggia' ('The rain'), 198

Piovene, Guido, 389

Pirandello, Luigi, 113, 338

Pirona (philologist), 19

Pisa, 34, 212

'Places in the memory', 133

*The Playboy of the Western World* (Synge), 17

*Poesie* (review), 68, 73, 242

*Poesie*, 56, 199n.

*Poesie a Casarsa* ('Poems to Casarsa'), 18, 23, 24–5, 26, 35, 37, 58, 62, 130n., 184, 226, 227, 234, 239, 308, 406

'Un poeta e Dio' ('A poet and God'), 91, 373, 386n.

*Il ponte*, 265, 298

Ponti, Pippo, 254

*Popolo di Friuli*, 175

*Il Popolo di Roma*, 83

Popular Friulian Movement for Regional Autonomy, 67, 75

'The popular song' *see Il canto popolare*

Pordenone, 71, 77, 90, 274, 276, 290